ORDNANCE SURVEY

KU-438-398

STREET ATLAS
Edinburgh
& East Central Scotland

Contents

IV *Key to maps*

VI *Administrative boundaries*

1 *Street maps*

232 *Index explanation and abbreviations*

233 *Index of towns, villages and rural localities*

234 *Index of street names*

PHILIP'S

First edition published 1995 by

Ordnance Survey   and   Philip's
Romsey Road   an imprint of Reed Books
Maybush   Michelin House, 81 Fulham Road, London, SW3 6RB
Southampton SO16 4GU   and Auckland, Melbourne, Singapore and Toronto

ISBN 0-540-06180-8 (Philip's, hardback)
ISBN 0-540-06181-6 (Philip's, softback)
ISBN 0-319-00798-7 (Ordnance Survey, hardback)
ISBN 0-319-00799-5 (Ordnance Survey, softback)

To the best of the Publishers' knowledge, the information in this atlas was correct at
the time of going to press. No responsibility can be accepted for any errors or their
consequences.

The representation in this atlas of a road, track or path is no evidence of the existence
of a right of way.

Printed and bound in Great Britain by
Bath Press, Bath

Key to map symbols

⊕	British Rail station
🚂	Private railway station
●■	Bus or coach station
Ⓗ	Heliport
◆	Police station (may not be open 24 hours)
✚	Hospital with casualty facilities (may not be open 24 hours)
☐	Post office
+	Place of worship
◼	Important building
P	Parking
174	Adjoining page indicator
✕	No adjoining page
▬▬▬	Motorway
▬▬▬	Dual carriageway
▬▬▬	Main or through road
A27	Road numbers (Department of Transport)
┬	Gate or obstruction to traffic (restrictions may not apply at all times or to all vehicles)
- - - -	All paths, bridleways, BOAT's, RUPP's, dismantled railways, etc.
▬▬▬	Track

The representation in this atlas of a road, track or path is no evidence of the existence of a right of way

Abbr	Description	Abbr	Description
Amb Sta	Ambulance Station	LC	Level crossing
Amb Dpo	Ambulance Depot	Liby	Library
Coll	College	Mus	Museum
FB	Footbridge	Acad	Academy
F Sta	Fire Station	Sch	School
Hospl	Hospital	TH	Town Hall or Town House

0	¼	½	¾	1 mile
0	250 m	500 m	250 m	1 Kilometre

The scale of the maps is 3½ inches to 1 mile (1:18103)

The small numbers around the edges of the maps
identify the 1 kilometre National Grid lines

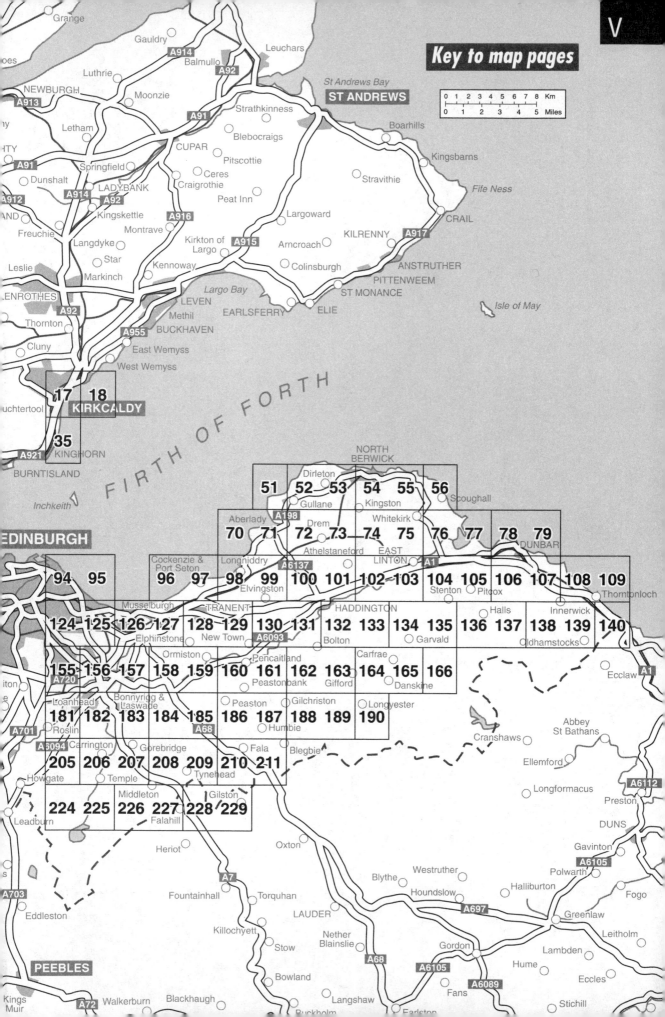

Key to map pages

Km 0 1 2 3 4 5 6 7 8
Miles 0 1 2 3 4 5

Grange
Gauldry
Luthrie
Balmullo
Leuchars
NEWBURGH
Moonzie
St Andrews Bay
ST ANDREWS
A913
Letham
A91
Strathkinness
Boarhills
A912
Springfield
CUPAR
Blebocraigs
Kingsbarns
Dunshalt
Pitscottie
Ceres
Stravithie
Fife Ness
A912
LADYBANK
Craigrothie
Kingskettle
Peat Inn
A916
CRAIL
Freuchie
Montrave
Langdyke
Star
Kirkton of
Largo
Largoward
KILRENNY
A917
Leslie
Markinch
Arncroach
ANSTRUTHER
ENROTHES
Kennoway
Colinsburgh
PITTENWEEM
A92
Largo Bay
ST MONANCE
Thornton
LEVEN
EARLSFERRY
ELIE
Isle of May
Cluny
Methil
A955
BUCKHAVEN
East Wemyss
West Wemyss

FIRTH OF FORTH

17	18
KIRKCALDY
uchtertool
| 35 |
A921 KINGHORN
BURNTISLAND
Inchkeith

NORTH BERWICK
Dirleton
| 51 | 52 | 53 | 54 | 55 | 56 |
Gullane
Kingston
Scoughall
Aberlady
A198
Drem
Whitekirk
| 70 | 71 | 72 | 73 | 74 | 75 | 76 | 77 | 78 | 79 |
Longniddry
Athelstaneford
EAST
DUNBAR
Cockenzie &
Port Seton
LINTON
A1
| 94 | 95 | | 96 | 97 | 98 | 99 | 100 | 101 | 102 | 103 | 104 | 105 | 106 | 107 | 108 | 109 |
Elvingston
Stenton
Pitcox
Thorntonloch
EDINBURGH
Musselburgh
TRANENT
HADDINGTON
Halls
Innerwick
| 124 | 125 | 126 | 127 | 128 | 129 | 130 | 131 | 132 | 133 | 134 | 135 | 136 | 137 | 138 | 139 | 140 |
Elphinstone
New Town
A6093
Bolton
Garvald
Oldhamstocks
Ormiston
Carfrae
| 155 | 156 | 157 | 158 | 159 | 160 | 161 | 162 | 163 | 164 | 165 | 166 |
A720
Pencaitland
Ecclaw
A1
Peastonbank
Gifford
Danskine
Loanhead
Peaston
Gilchriston
Longyester
| 181 | 182 | 183 | 184 | 185 | 186 | 187 | 188 | 189 | 190 |
Roslin
Bonnyrigg &
Lasswade
Humbie
Abbey
St Bathans
A701
A68
Cranshaws
A6094
Carrington
Gorebridge
Fala
Blegbie
Ellemford
| 205 | 206 | 207 | 208 | 209 | 210 | 211 |
Howgate
Temple
Tynehead
Longformacus
A6112
Middleton
Gilston
Preston
| 224 | 225 | 226 | 227 | 228 | 229 |
Leadburn
Falahill
DUNS
Heriot
Oxton
Gavinton
A6105
Polwarth
Eddleston
A7
Blythe
Westruther
Halliburton
Fogo
A703
Houndslow
Fountainhall
Torquhan
LAUDER
A697
Greenlaw
PEEBLES
Killochyett
Nether
Blainslie
Stow
A68
Leitholm
Gordon
A6105
Lambden
Hume
Eccles
Kings
Muir
A72
Walkerburn
Blackhaugh
Bowland
Langshaw
A6089
Fans
Stichill

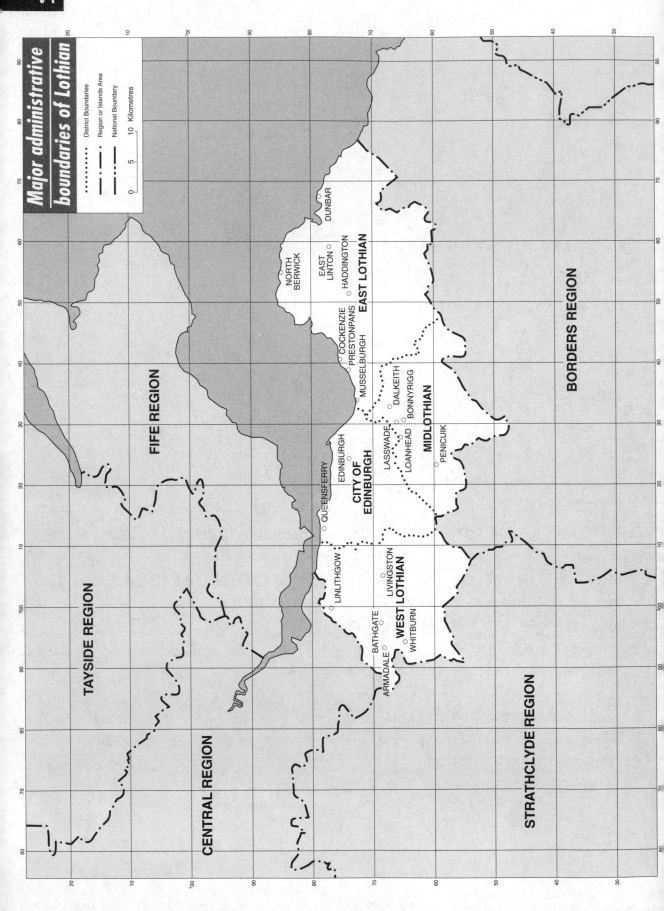

Major administrative boundaries of Lothian

Legend
- District Boundaries
- Region or Islands Area
- National Boundary

Kilometres
0 5 10

FIFE REGION

TAYSIDE REGION

CENTRAL REGION

STRATHCLYDE REGION

BORDERS REGION

CITY OF EDINBURGH

EAST LOTHIAN

MIDLOTHIAN

WEST LOTHIAN

DUNBAR

NORTH BERWICK

EAST LINTON

HADDINGTON

COCKENZIE

PRESTONPANS

MUSSELBURGH

DALKEITH

BONNYRIGG

LASSWADE

LOANHEAD

PENICUIK

EDINBURGH

QUEENSFERRY

LINLITHGOW

LIVINGSTON

BATHGATE

WHITBURN

ARMADALE

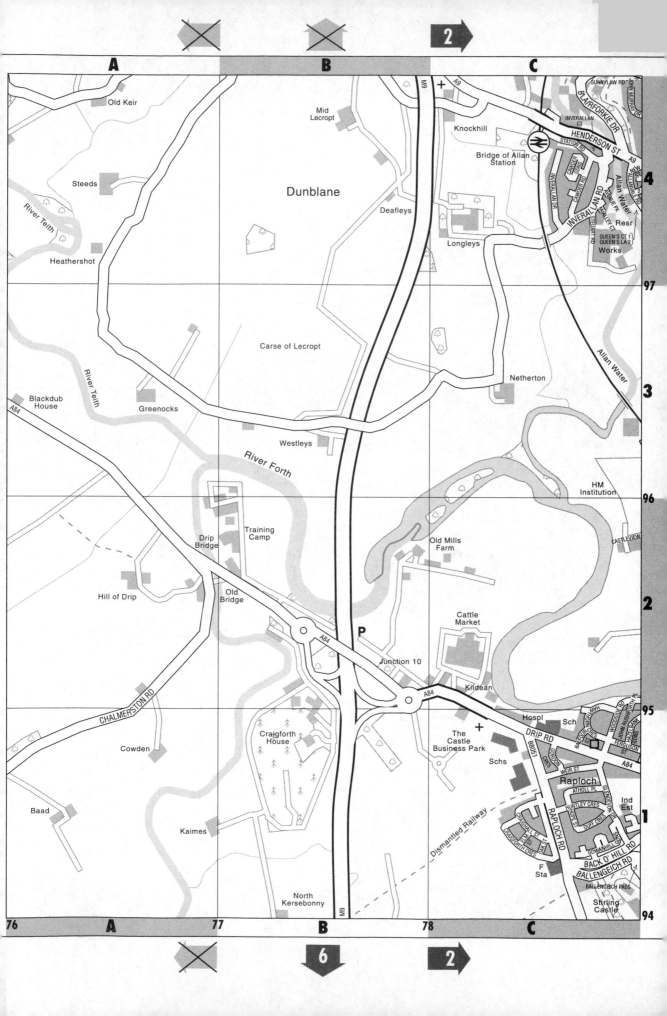

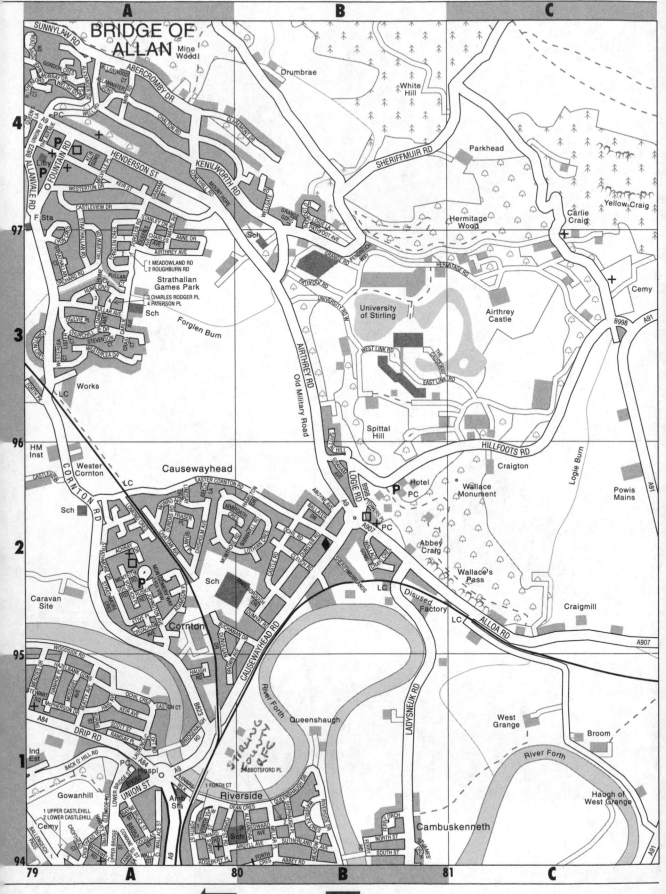

BRIDGE OF ALLAN

Mine Wood

Drumbrae

White Hill

SHERIFFMUIR RD

Parkhead

Yellow Craig

Carlie Craig

Hermitage Wood

Cemy

ABERCROMBY DR

SUNNYLAW RD

HENDERSON ST

KENILWORTH RD

Strathallan Games Park

1 MEADOWLAND RD
2 ROUGHBURN RD

3 CHARLES RODGER PL
4 PATERSON PL

Sch

Forglen Burn

Works

University of Stirling

Airthrey Castle

WEST LINK RD

EAST LINK RD

THE CAUSEWAY

Spittal Hill

HILLFOOTS RD

Craigton

Logie Burn

Powis Mains

HM Inst

Wester Cornton

Causewayhead

CORNTON RD

Sch

Caravan Site

Cornton

Sch

EASTER CORNTON RD

CAUSEWAYHEAD RD

River Forth

Queenshaugh

LADYSNEUK RD

Disused Factory

Wallace Monument

Hotel

Abbey Craig

Wallace's Pass

Craigmill

ALLOA RD

West Grange

Broom

River Forth

Haugh of West Grange

Woodside Rd

Gowanhill

Ind Est

DRIP RD

Hospl

UNION ST

1 UPPER CASTLEHILL
2 LOWER CASTLEHILL

Cemy

Riverside

2 ABBOTSFORD PL

1 FORTH CT

Cambuskenneth

STIRLING COUNTY RFC

A84

A9

B823

A907

A91

B998

B998

A91

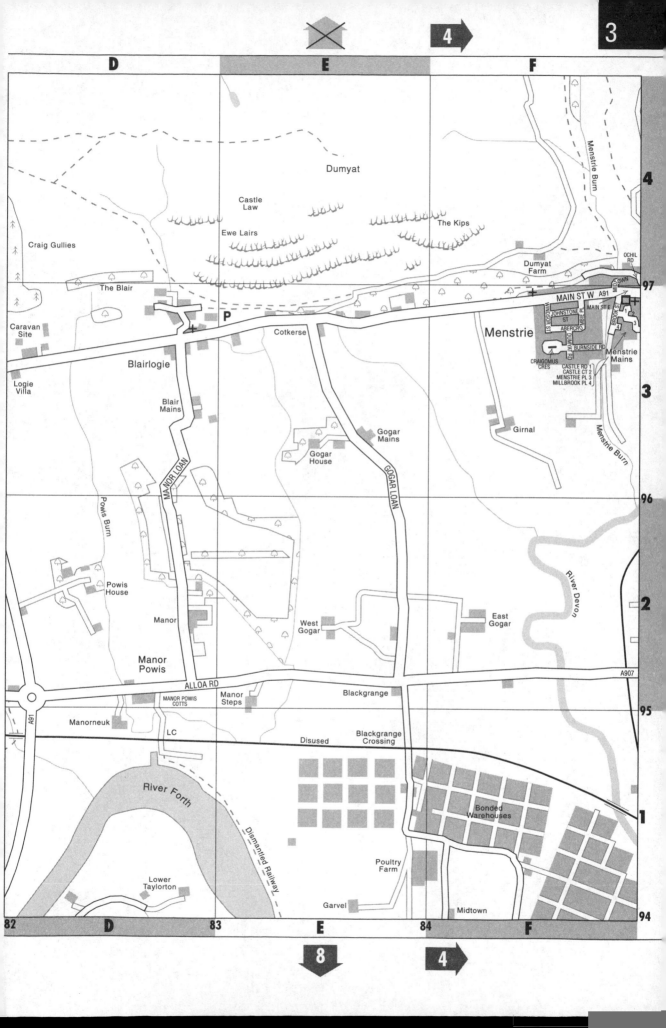

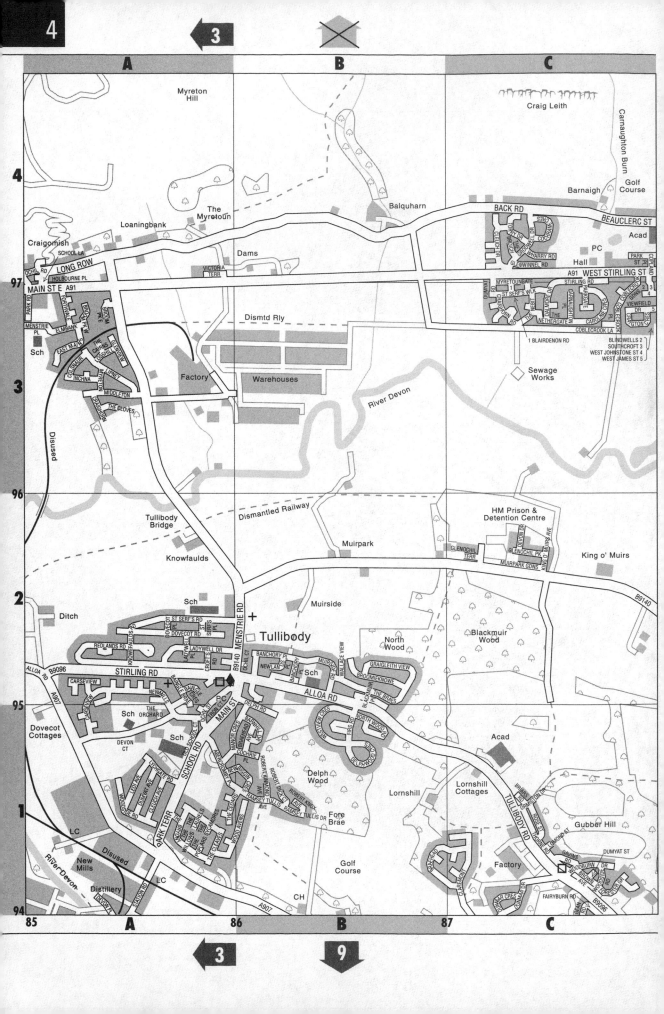

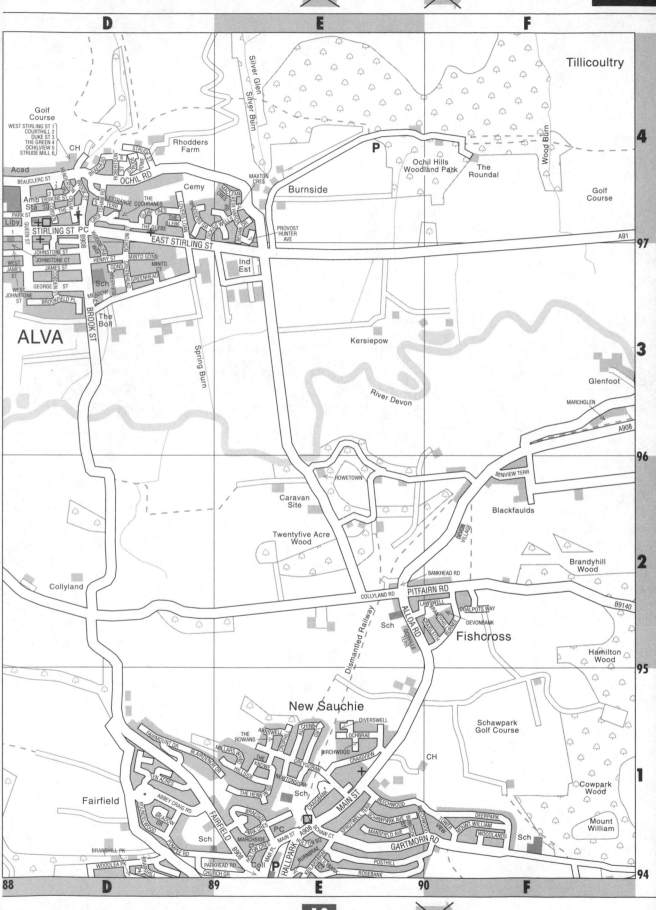

	A	B	C

River Forth

Dismantled Railway

M9

Falleninch

DUMBARTON RD

B8051 RAPLOCH RD

King's Knot

A811

Polrogan Bridge

Bankend

White House

South Kersebonny

KERSEBONNY RD

King's Park Farm

King's Park

CH
BALMORAL PL

QUEEN'S RD

A811

B8051

4

93

Hollandbush

Hayford House

Raploch Burn

St Thomas's Well

ST THOMAS'S

Cemy

THE HOMESTEADS

Broomhill
Douglas Terr

JOHN

Snowdon Place La 1
Snowdon Pl 2

PARK AVE

KING'S PK RD

PC

Johnny's Bridge

Hillhead

KERSEBONNY RD

PARKDYKE

PARK PK

PARK PL

Johnny's Burn

TOUCH RD

Cambusbarron

MILL RD

NORTHEND

STEWART ST

DONALDSON PL

HEYFORD ST

BIRKHILL RD

GRAMPIAN RD

CONEYPARK

DALMORGLEN PK

Batterflatts

Torbrex

LAURELHILL GDNS

SPRINGWOOD AVE

3

MAIN ST

QUARRY RD

FIRPARK TERR

CAULDHAME CRES

THE YETTS

GRIESLY CRES

MILL HILL

THE BRAE

MURRAY PL

Sch

WOODSIDE PL

Liby

UNDERWOOD RD

UNDERWOOD COTTS

ST NINIANS RD

POLMAISE RD

Polmaise Farm

GRAMPIAN RD

Hospl

DERORAN PL

SYCAMORE PL

LABURNUM GR

POLMAISE RD

Old Drove Rd

THOMSON PL

BRUCE TERR

GILLIES HILL

WALLACE PL

KENNINGKNOWES RD

BIRCH AVE

CEDAR

ASH TERR

SYCAMORE PL

Gartur

Cambusbarron Quarry

TORBREX RD

TORBREX FARM RD
ST VALERY DR

TORBREX LA

92

Murray's Wood

Gillies Hill

Touchadam Craig

Polmaise Castle

Bearside

Coxet Hill

WELDPARK CRES

CULTENHOVE CRES

2

Murrayshall Quarry

Fir Park

Haggs Wood

POLMAISE RD

CULTENHOVE PL

GATESIDE RD

GRAYSTALE RD

Castlehill

Murrayshall Farm

91

Graystale

Wallstale

Chartershall House

1

Sauchie Craig

Moor Burn

Bannock Burn

Middlethird Wood

Cultenhove

Chartershall Farm

CHARTERSHALL RD

90

76	A	77	B	78	C

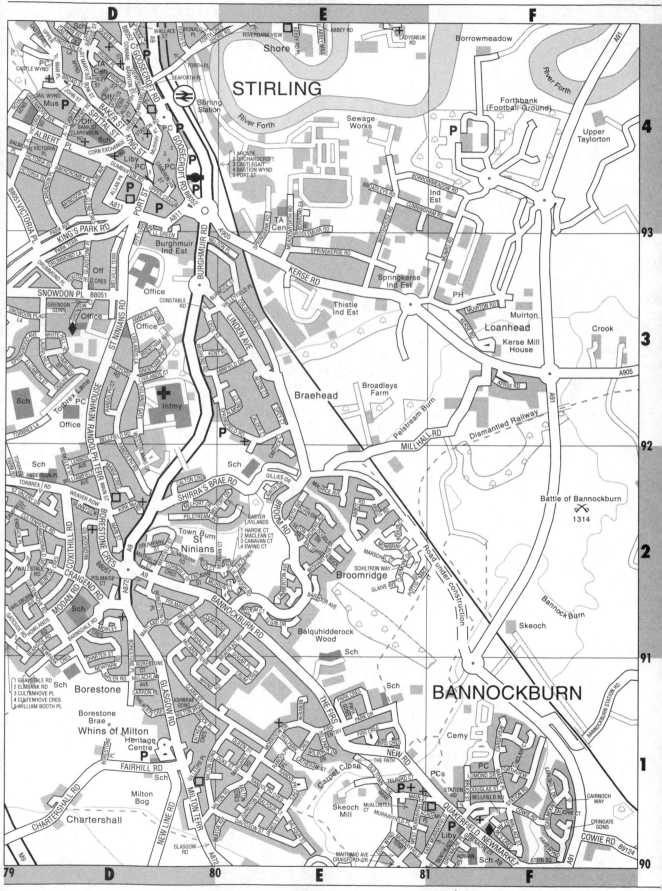

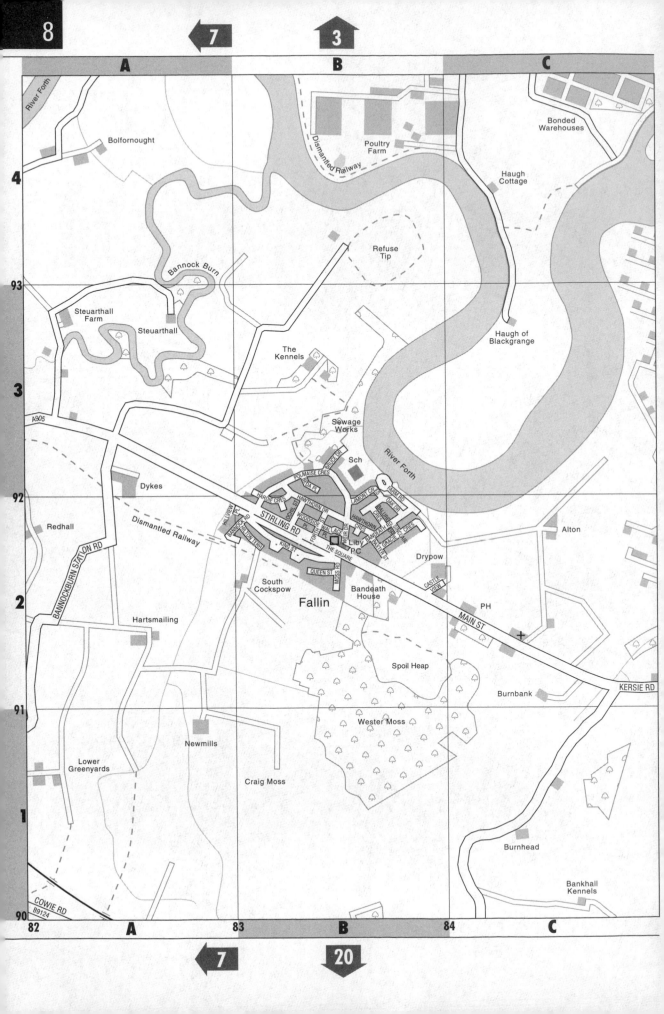

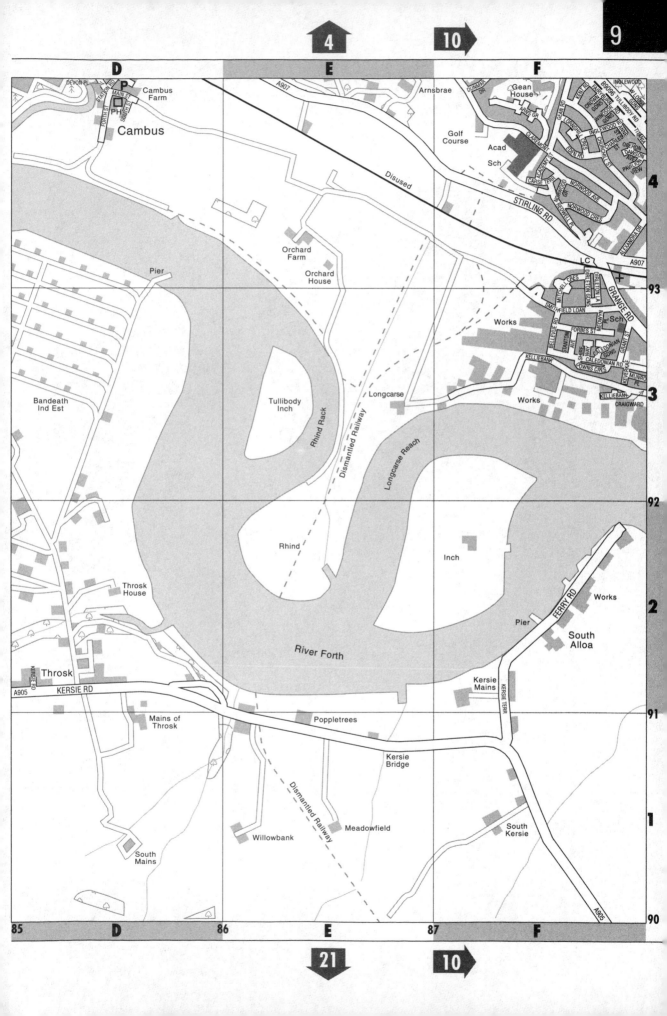

Cambus

Cambus Farm

DEVON PL

STATION RD

FORTH ST

MAIN ST

SOUTH ST

P

PH

Arnsbrae

DUNMAR DR

Gean House

Golf Course

Acad Sch

INGLEWOOD

WOODBURN RD

B9096 TULLIBODY RD

KENT RD

ORCHARD CRES

CRONBERRY

KEIR ST

ARNS GR

INGLEWOOD AVE

OBERON AVE

DAWSON AVE

PAVILION VIEW

CARSE TERR

NORWOOD AVE

ORCHARD

REDWELL PL

NORWOOD CRES

STIRLING RD

A907

MITCHELL CRES

DIRLETON LA

DIRLETON GDNS

GRANGE RD

LC

SMITHFIELD LOAN

BELLEVUE RD

STANTON AVE

SHIRE

NAIRN

CALEDONIAN GDNS

FORBES ST

Sch

GRANT ST

CALEDONIAN RD

OWNS CRES

KELLIEBANK

REVERKAE

MUNRO PL

KELLIEBANK

CRAIGWARD

Works

Works

Disused

Orchard Farm

Orchard House

Pier

Bandeath Ind Est

Tullibody Inch

Rhind Rack

Dismantled Railway

Longcarse

Longcarse Reach

Inch

Rhind

River Forth

Throsk House

Throsk

KERSIE RD

A905

KERSIE RD

Mains of Throsk

Poppletrees

Willowbank

Meadowfield

Dismantled Railway

South Mains

Kersie Bridge

Kersie Mains

KERSIE TERR

South Kersie

FERRY RD

Works

Pier

South Alloa

A905

85 · D · 86 · E · 87 · F · 90

4

10

93

3

92

2

91

1

A   B   C

TITANIA
WOODLEA PK
BRANSHILL PK
Coll
PARKHEAD RD
B908
Coll
HALLPARK
A908
BURNSIDE
KEILARS
Keilarsbrae
Jellyholm
Water Works

BRANSHILL RD
DOVEHILL
Hospl
Cemy
QUARRY PL
Distillery
Jellyholm Rd
Brothy Burn

MARY STEVENSON DR
DOVEHILL
THE LARCHES
ASHLEY TERR
Hospl
GREENFIELD DR
GORDON
SUTHERLAND
WALLACE
CARSEBRIDGE RD

TULLIBODY RD
GARVALLY CRES
HILL ST
NEVIS
QUEEN ST
HILLSIDE TERR
McKINLAY CT
ARGYLL RD
Warehouses

4

VICTORIA ST
PATON ST
KINGS
HILL ST
Sch
ERSKINE ST
KINROSS WELL
SPRINGFIELD DR
ARROL CRES
HILTON CRES
HILTON RD
B909

CLARKMANNAN
PARKWAY
B908
Off
P
SUNNYSIDE RD
SUNNYSIDE
WHINS RD
AMBER TERR
EGBERSTON

A907
STIRLING RD
KELLIE
LUDGATE
MAR PL
Off
PRIMROSE
RING RD
A908
PARK PL
BALFOUR ST
BRUCE ST
LC
F Sta

93
TULLIGARTH PK
A907
TH
B9096
IZATT ST
PRIMROSE
Disused
Hilton

MARSHILL
MAR ST
DRYSDALE
SHILLINGHILL
P
Sch
HAWKHILL RD
CLACKMANNAN RD
P
LC

PC
Ind Est
GLEBE TERR
CHURCH ST
MILL ST
MAPLE CT
HILLVIEW TERR
HILLCREST DR

GRANGE RD
CONINGSBY PL
BEDFORD PL
BANK ST
MILL EAST
BRIDGE
TURRET
PINE GR
TAY CT

BEDFORD PL
BURGH MEWS
KIRKGATE
GREENSIDE CT
DEVON RD
MAREE
ASH GR
Comely Bank

3
Ind Est
Sch
1 STRIPEHEAD
2 UNION ST
3 WEST VENNEL
LEARN
KILNCRAIGS RD
MENTEITH CT
KATRINE CT
Cemy
DEVONWAY
B910

CRAIGWARD
CALEDONIAN
MUNRO AVE
North C
Alloa Tower
EARN
TORRIDON
BURLEIGH WAY
LEVEN CT
ELM GR
Mary Bridge
TOWER PL

Works
CASTLE ST
BROAD ST
SCOTT CRES
EAST
ENGELEN OR
RANNOCH CT
Sch
Back Wood
BACKWOOD CT
B910

EAST CASTLE ST
Sch
LEWIS CT
HARRIS CT
FORTH CRES
ALLOA
KERSE GREEN RD
FRAME PL

Alloa Park
THE WALK
ORKNEY
SHETLAND
ARRAN CT
King's Seat Hill
WOODSIDE TERR
HIGH ST

92
THE SHORE
BOWHOUSE RD
BOWHOUSE GDNS
EARLS CT
RIVERSIDE VIEW
Clackmannan Tower
KIRKBRAE

Sewage Works
Ind Est
Craigrie

2

River Forth

91

1
Park Farm

Refuse Tip

Dunmore Home Farm

90
88   A   89   B   90   C

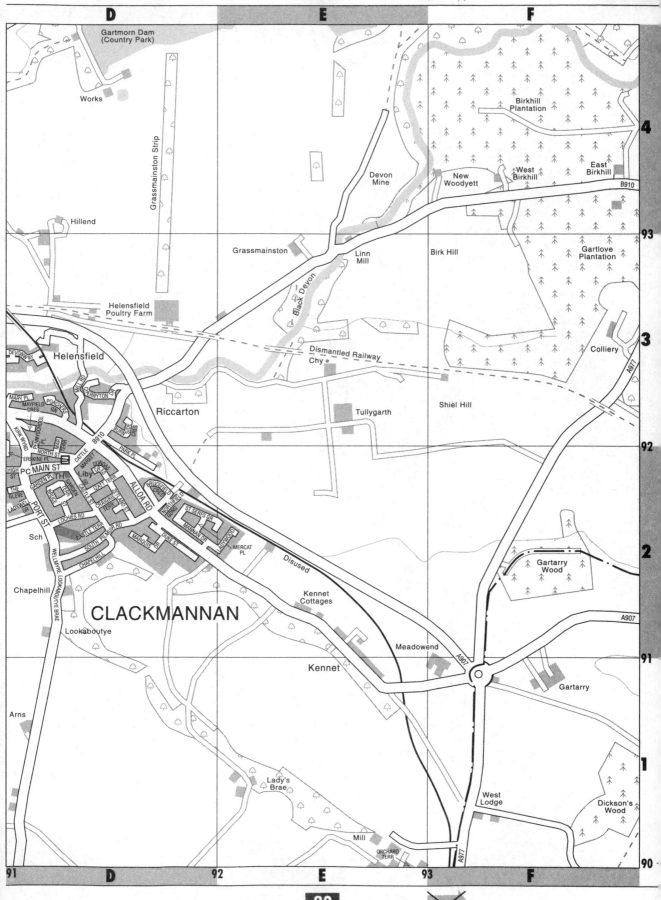

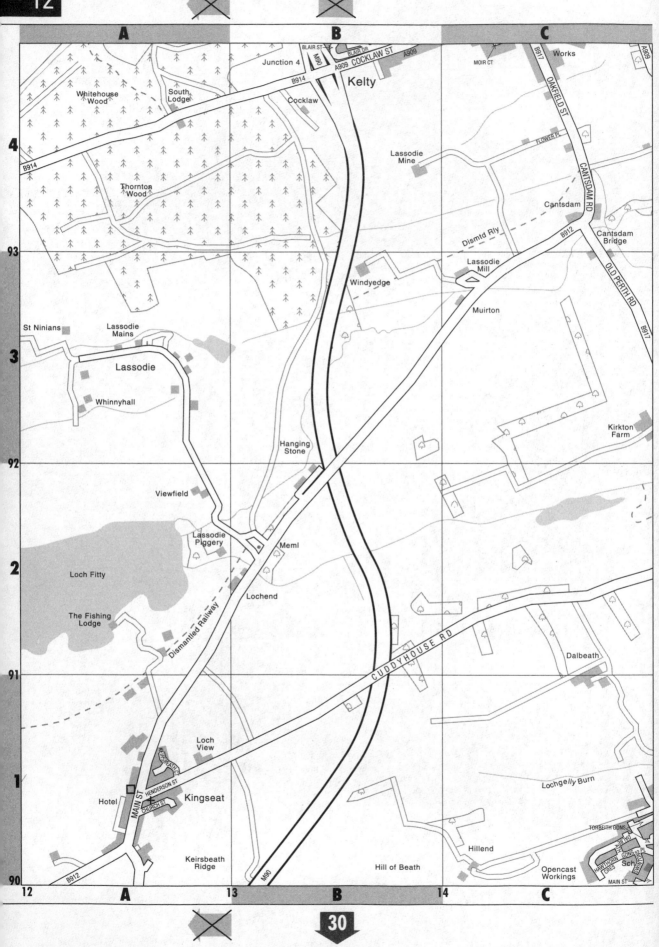

Whitehouse Wood
South Lodge
Junction 4
BLAIR ST
BLAIR DR
M90
COCKLAW ST
A909
A909
Kelty
Cocklaw
B914
MOIR CT
Works
B917
OAKFIELD ST
A909
FLOWER PL
Lassodie Mine
CANTSDAM RD
Thornton Wood
Cantsdam
B912
Cantsdam Bridge
Dismtd Rly
Lassodie Mill
St Ninians
Lassodie Mains
Windyedge
Muirton
OLD PERTH RD
Lassodie
B917
Whinnyhall
Kirkton Farm
Hanging Stone
Viewfield
Lassodie Piggery
Meml
Loch Fitty
Lochend
Dismantled Railway
The Fishing Lodge
CUDDYHOUSE RD
Dalbeath
Lochgelly Burn
Loch View
KIRKFAULD CT
HENDERSON ST
Hotel
MAIN ST
CHURCH ST
Kingseat
TORBEITH GDNS
Hillend
Sch
Keirsbeath Ridge
B912
M90
Hill of Beath
Opencast Workings
MAIN ST

D E F

4

LUMPHINNANS RD

93

B981

Netherton

Netherton Bridge

Lumphinnans Farm

Golf Course

Tollie Hill

Lumphinnans Piggery

Craigbeath Hill

Glenfield Ind Est

GRAY PL
GOLF COURSE RD

PERTH RD
A909

GILMOUR ST
GORDON ST

CEDAR CRES

Amb Dpo

SYCAMORE CRES

HOPE ST

OCHILVIEW PL
HILTON
ELM
GARDEN VIEW

ROBERT SMITH PL

VIEWFIELD TERR

MAIN ST

GALLACHER PL

BRICKFIELD TERR

LEUCHATSBEATH DR
MEADOWFIELD
MORTON
NFIELD
SOUTHFIELD
KIRKTON

GLENFIELD AVE
GLENFIELD GDNS
GLENFIELD CT
GLENFIELD

CR-A/GB-EATH

JOHNSTON PK
JOHNSTON PK

GLENFIELD CRES

STUART PL

LOCHGELLY RD   B981   Sch

VALLEYFIELD PL

Lumphinnans

Foulford Burn

Golf Course

Newton

3

92

Sch

PCs

TULLOCH

Cemy

Sch

Refuse Tip

KIRKFORD

OLD PERTH RD

CUDDYHOUSE RD

Gateside Ind Est

FOULFORD RD

BROOMFIELD RD

PRIMROSE LA

FOULFORD ST

FOULFORD PL

PRETORIA

PROSPECT ST
DRYLIE ST

KEIR ST
GEORGE

RUSSELL ST

ROSEHILL CRES

KING ST

STENHOUSE ST

TAYLOR AVE

AST GR

BOWNLIL GDN

WILSON

SHAMROCK

HIGH ST

Off

BURGH RD
POLWORTH

UNION ST

ELGIN RD

ALEXANDER ST

PC

Liby
TH

CH

COWDENBEATH

P

P

No 7 PIT RD

FACTORY RD

ROSEBANK

New Station

Off
STATION RD

Sewage Works

Thistle Ind Est

A92

2

91

KIRKFORD
CT

PERTH RD

Gateside
CT

BLACKBURN DR

HAMILD

HILLVIEW

YOUNG TERR

MILNE CRES

YOUNG ST

RIVIAN

WOODLANDS ST

CHAPEL ST

PAUL PL

STEIN'S PL

PCs

A909

B981

SCCO PL

PRIMRSY

CHURCH ST

WILKS

RANDOLPH ST

THISTLE ST

MAIN ST

MANSE ST

TERR

Central Park

Sch

MAIN PL

Sch

PATTERSON LA

Moss-Side
RD

PARK RD

SMITH AVE

MOSS-SIDE ST

WALLACE ST

WALKER ST

RAWNEY CRES

HILLCREST

BARCLAY ST

CHERRY PL

WOODSIDE

ROSE ST

SOUTH ST

PILGRAM CT

ARTHUR PL

ARTHUR ST

MARSHALL ST

BRIDGE ST

1

GREENBANK DR
GREENBRAE

MOSSBANK

KING ST

WINSLOW

WESTBURN

BRACKENLINN RD

DA-BEATH CRES

SINCLAIR DR

PC

JAMES CT

JANE S

RAE ST

BROXBURN

CHARLTON PL

CULLALOE VIEW

GARDINER RD

Dismantled Railway

BURNSIDE TERR

MITCHELL CRES

BEATH VIEW RD

ALLAN PK

BRAEMAR DR

MANSEL CRES

KEIR AVE

GARDINER

COPELAND CRES

Woodend Ind Est

Woodend

WOODEND PL

Works

Moss Morran

TORBAIN GDNS
MAIN ST

B917

Hill of Beath

1 TORBEITH GDNS
2 SWINTONS PL

Training Centre

A92

A92

B981

A909

A92

90

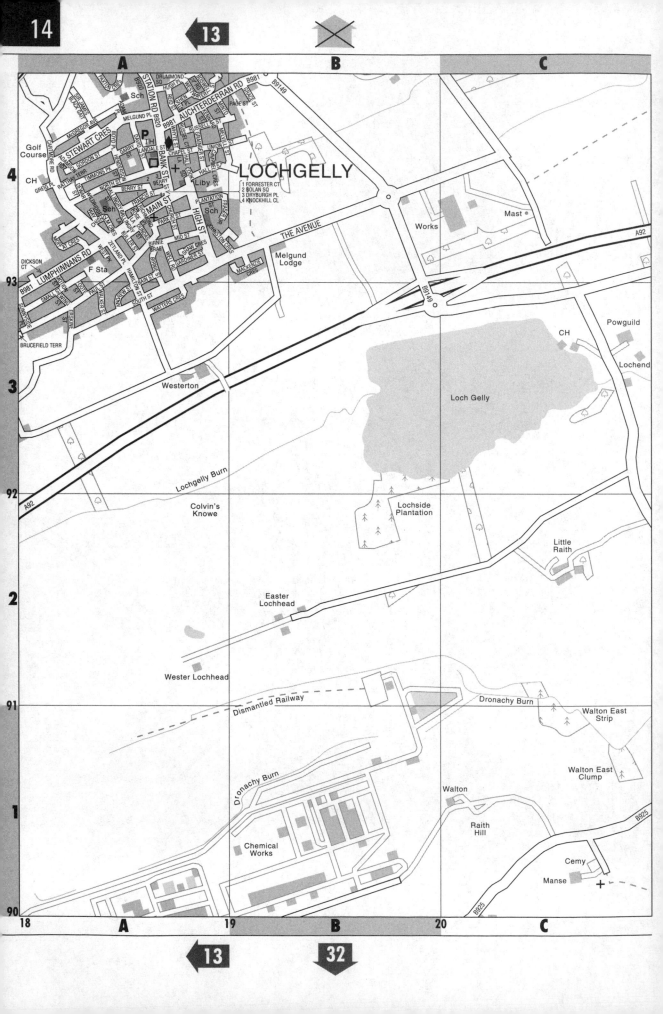

LOCHGELLY

1 FORRESTER CT
2 BOLAN SQ
3 DRYBURGH PL
4 KNOCKHILL CL

Golf
Course

CH

STEWART CRES

STATION RD B920

DRUMMOND
SQ

AUCHTERDERRAN RD

B981

PAGE ST

B9149

Sch

MELGUND PL B920

Sch

P
TH

Liby

BANK ST

MAIN ST

HIGH ST

CHAPEL ST

Sch

PLANTATION

LUMPHINNANS RD

B981

F Sta

DICKSON
CT

BRUCEFIELD TERR

SUNNYSIDE

THE AVENUE

Melgund
Lodge

Works

Mast

A92

B9149

CH

Powguild

Lochend

Westerton

Loch Gelly

Lochgelly Burn

Colvin's
Knowe

Lochside
Plantation

Little
Raith

A92

Easter
Lochhead

Wester Lochhead

Dismantled Railway

Dronachy Burn

Walton East
Strip

Walton East
Clump

Dronachy Burn

Walton

Cemy

Chemical
Works

Raith
Hill

Manse

B9925

B9925

93

92

91

90

4

3

2

1

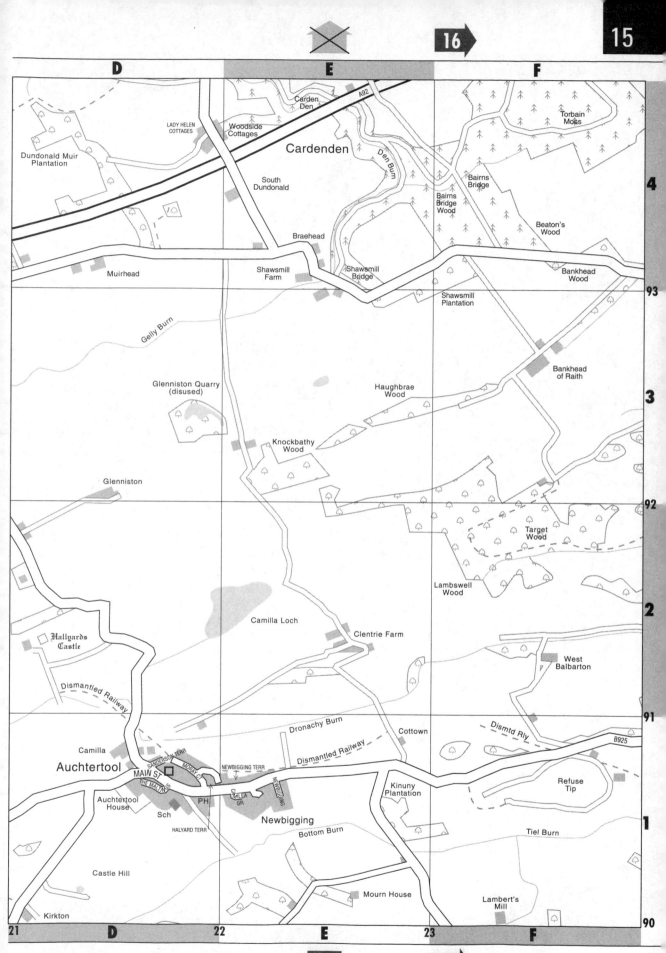

D
E
F

A92

Carden Den

Torbain Moss

LADY HELEN COTTAGES
Woodside Cottages

Dundonald Muir Plantation

Cardenden

Den Burn

Bairns Bridge

4

South Dundonald

Bairns Bridge Wood

Beaton's Wood

Braehead

Bankhead Wood

Muirhead

Shawsmill Farm

Shawsmill Bridge

Shawsmill Plantation

93

Gelly Burn

Bankhead of Raith

Glenniston Quarry (disused)

Haughbrae Wood

3

Knockbathy Wood

Glenniston

92

Target Wood

Lambswell Wood

2

Camilla Loch

Clentrie Farm

Hallyards Castle

West Balbarton

Dismantled Railway

91

Camilla

Dronachy Burn

Cottown

Dismtd Rly

B925

Auchtertool

SANDERSON TERR

Dismantled Railway

MAIN ST
MORAY CT

NEWBIGGING TERR

Refuse Tip

THE MALTINGS

CAMILLA GR

Kinuny Plantation

NEWBIGGING

PH

Auchtertool House

Sch

Newbigging

1

HALYARD TERR

Bottom Burn

Tiel Burn

Castle Hill

Mourn House

Lambert's Mill

Kirkton

90

21
D
22
E
23
F

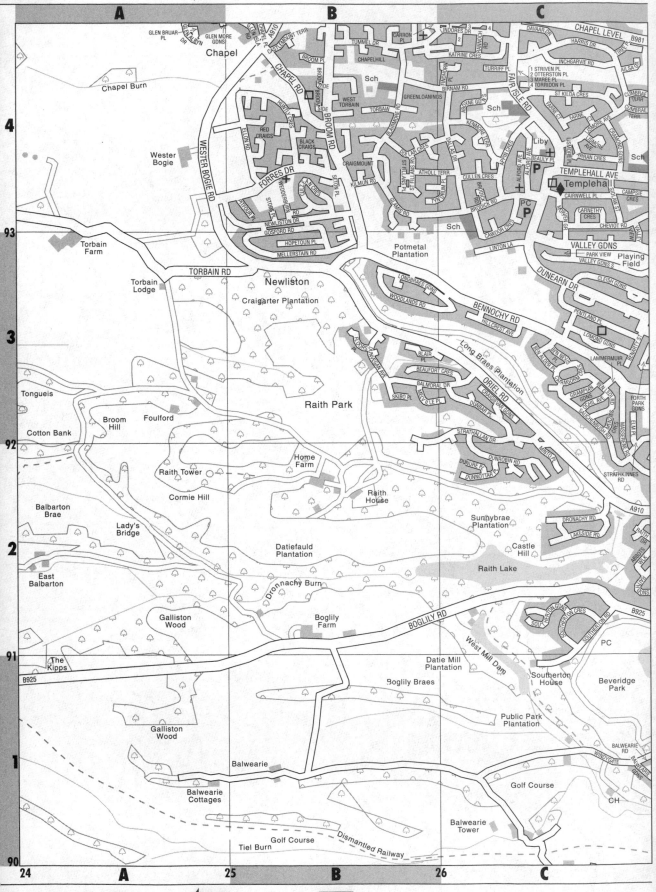

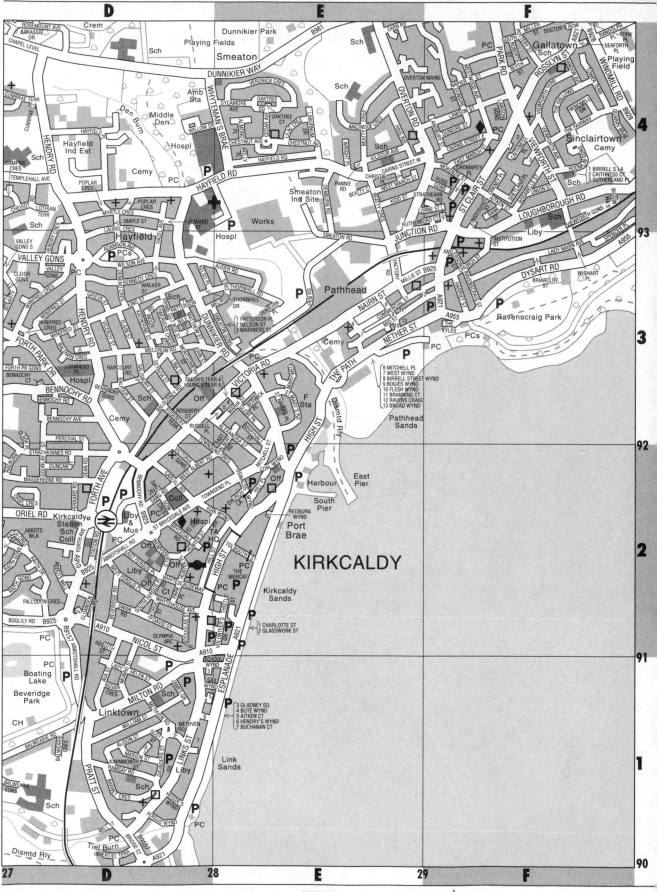

KIRKCALDY

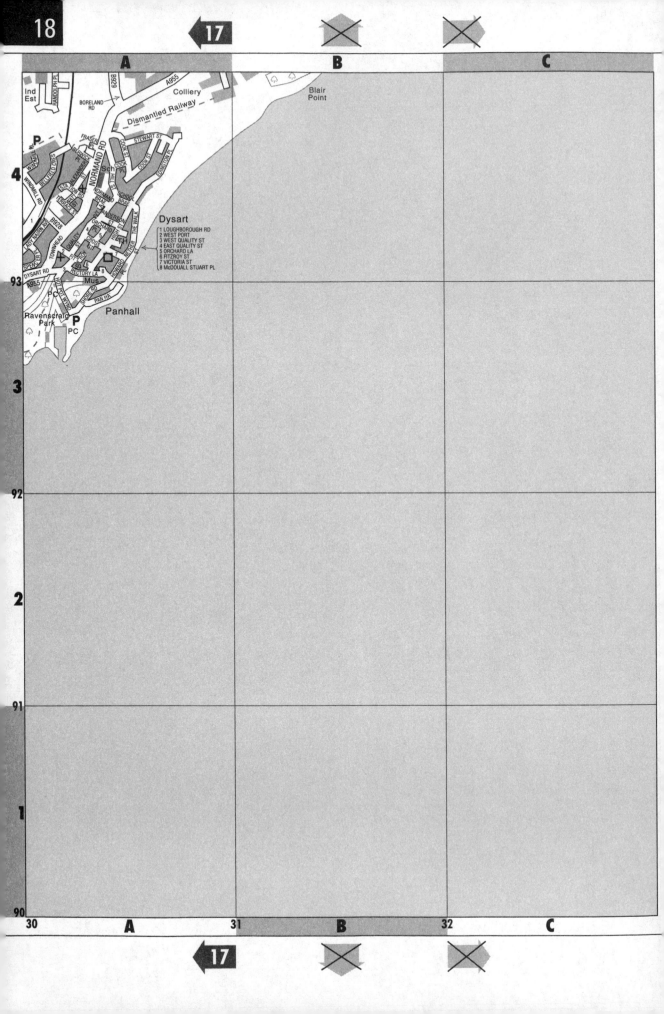

A B C

Ind
Est
P
B929
BORELAND
RD
Colliery
Dismantled Railway
Blair
Point

FRASER
BERWICK
STEWART ST
COOK ST
COOK ST
EDINGTON PL
NORMAND RD
A955
B929
4
WINDMILL RD
Sch
ESTA TON RD
NORMAND
FERNESS ST
SCHOOL
BRAE
ANDERSON
THE WALK
Dysart
1 LOUGHBOROUGH RD
2 WEST PORT
3 WEST QUALITY ST
4 EAST QUALITY ST
5 ORCHARD LA
6 FITZROY ST
7 VICTORIA ST
8 McDOUALL STUART PL

93
A955
DYSART RD
RECTORY LA
Mus
PC
P
PC
SHORE RD
PAN HA
Panhall

Ravenscraig
Park

3

92

2

91

1

90
30 A 31 B 32 C

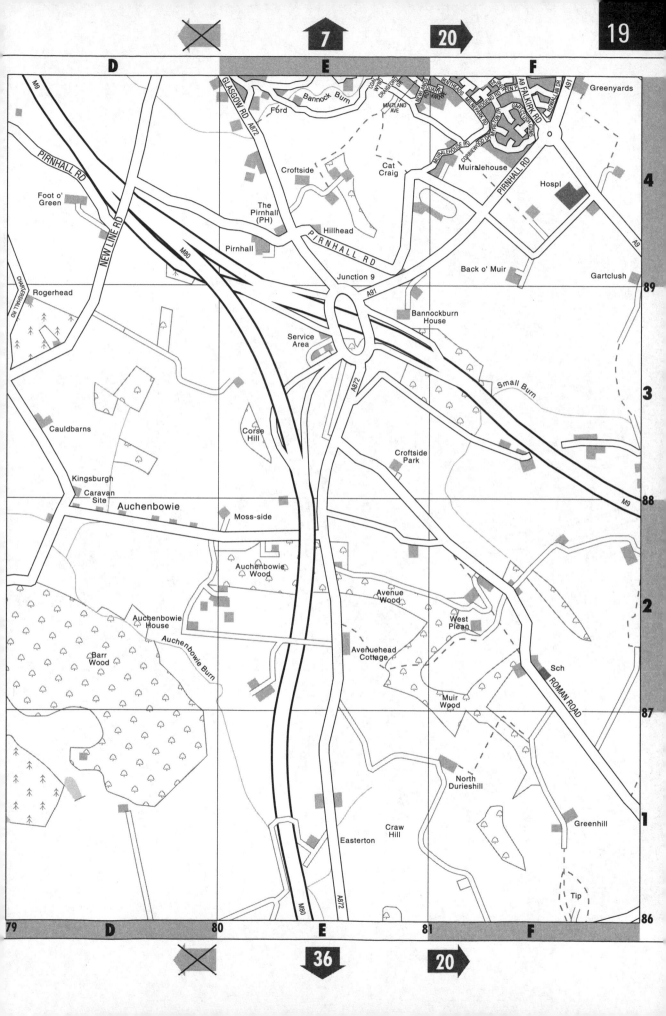

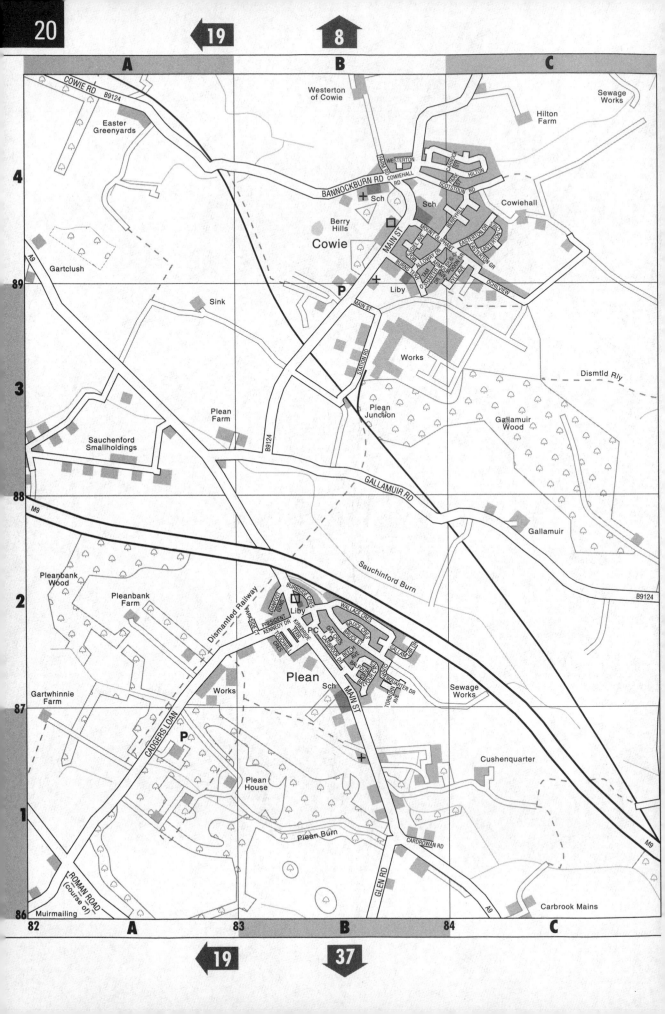

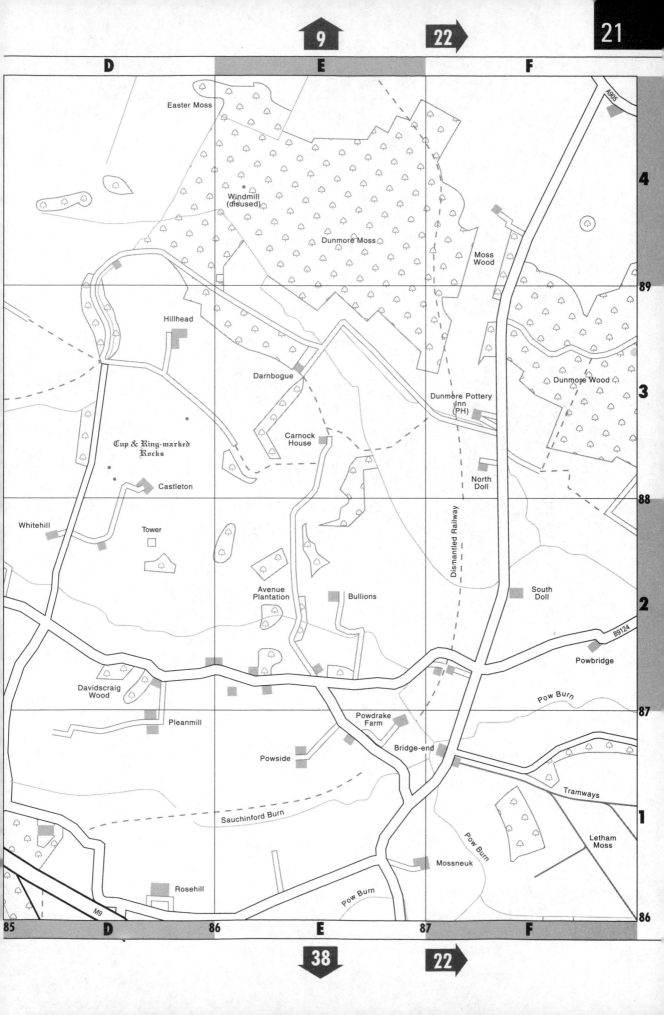

D E F

4

Easter Moss

Windmill
(disused)

Dunmore Moss

Moss
Wood

89

Hillhead

Dunmore Wood

3

Darnbogue

Dunmore Pottery
Inn
(PH)

Cup & Ring-marked
Rocks

Carnock
House

North
Doll

Castleton

88

Whitehill

Tower

Dismantled Railway

Avenue
Plantation

Bullions

South
Doll

2

B9124

Powbridge

Davidscraig
Wood

Pow Burn

87

Pleanmill

Powdrake
Farm

Bridge-end

Powside

Tramways

Sauchinford Burn

Letham
Moss

1

Pow Burn

Mossneuk

Rosehill

M9

Pow Burn

86

85 D 86 E 87 F 86

A905

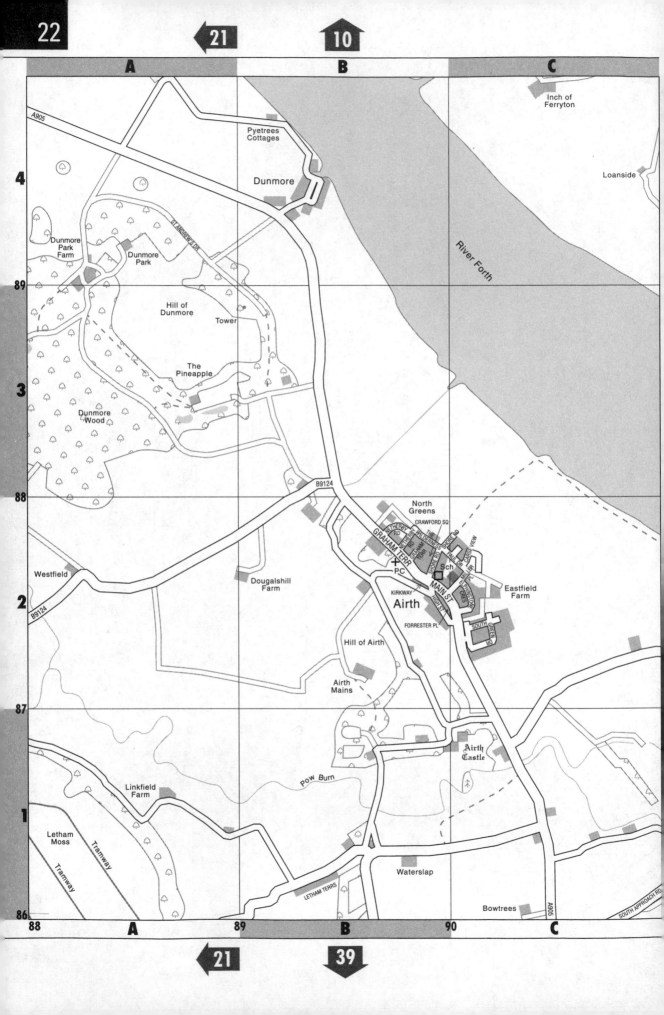

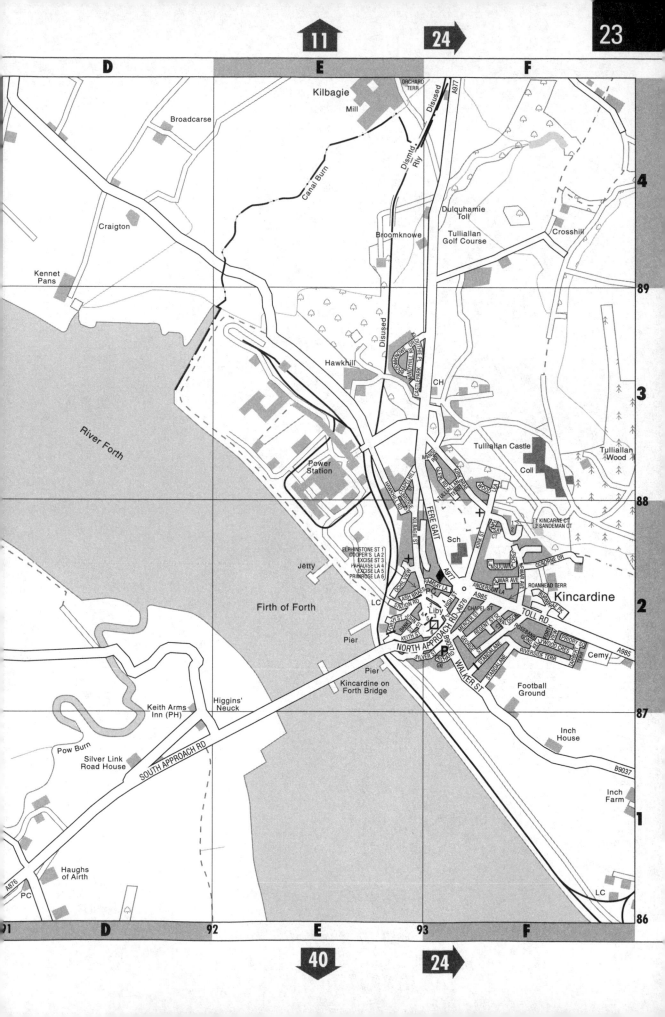

Kilbagie

Broadcarse

Mill

ORCHARD TERR

Craigton

Dulquhamie Toll

Broomknowe

Tulliallan Golf Course

Crosshill

Kennet Pans

Hawkhill

CH

Tulliallan Castle

Coll

River Forth

Tulliallan Wood

Power Station

1 KINCARNE CT
2 SANDEMAN CT

Sch

FERE GAIT

ELPHINSTONE ST 1
COOPER'S LA 2
EXCISE ST 3
PRIMROSE LA 4
EXCISE LA 5
PRIMROSE LA 6

Jetty

RAMSAY LA

Kincardine

LC

PO

WAR AVE

TOLL RD

Firth of Forth

Liby

CHAPEL ST

Pier

NORTH APPROACH RD

MERCER ST

REGENT ST

PRIORY SQ

Cemy

A985

Pier

P

RIVERSIDE TERR

WALKER ST

Kincardine on Forth Bridge

Football Ground

Inch House

Keith Arms Inn (PH)

Higgins' Neuck

87

Pow Burn

Silver Link Road House

SOUTH APPROACH RD

Inch Farm

B9037

Haughs of Airth

A876

PC

LC

91 D 92 E 93 F 86

A   B   C

Peathill Wood

North Wood

4

Mausoleum

Glasgow Moss

Peppermill Dam

89

Windyhill

3

Moor Loch

Keir Plantation

Praybrae Wood

Tulliallan Wood

Devilla Forest

Keir

88

Keir Burn

Keir Dam

2

Culross Moor

Sawmill Plantation

Bordie Moor

Standard Stone

A985

NEW ROW   WESTFIELD

A985

87

Bordie

Lurg

STONY BRAE

B9037

1

Newpans

Mine

Lurg Farm

LONGANNET COTTS

Caverns

B9037

Sands Farm

86

94   A   95   B   96   C

26 ▶

D

Mine

Burrowine

Blinkeerie

Launchout Burn

West Grange

Dismantled Railway

Sight Hill

Overton

Middle Grange

East Grange

89

Balgownie Mains

Oneford Burn

Bluther Burn

Thornyhaw

Righead

Balgownie Wood

3

Park Plantation

Muirhead

88

Shires Mill

B9037

Blairhall

Gallowridge

Kirkton Wood

Blairhall Wood

PC

Couston Wood

2

Keir Burn

Cemy

Kirkton

Blairhall Mains

B9037

Ashes

87

Waas Plantation

GALLOWS LOAN

A985

B9037

WOODHEAD FARM RD

Woodhead

1

Kirkbrae Wood

B9037

Dean Burn

FORTHBANK PL

The Park

KIRK ST

MAIN ST

ERSKINE BRAE

B9037

LOW CSWY

VEERE PK

86

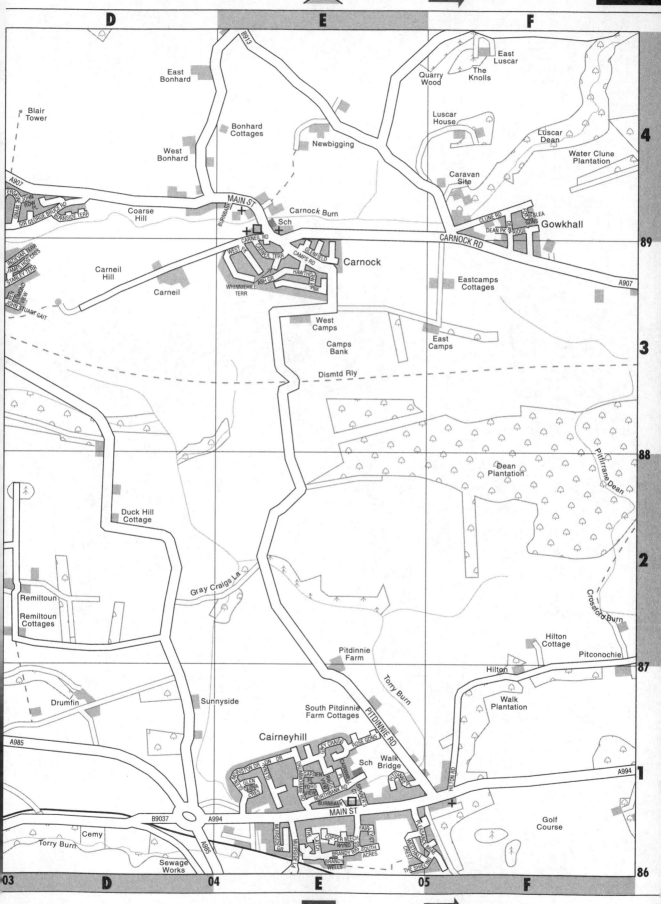

D   E   F

Blair Tower

East Bonhard

Bonhard Cottages

West Bonhard

Newbigging

Quarry Wood

East Luscar

The Knolls

Luscar House

Luscar Dean

Water Clune Plantation

4

A907

INZIEVAR TERR
JOHN ROW PL
SIR GEORGE BRUCE RD
BURNSIDE TERR
CONLAN ROW

Coarse Hill

MAIN ST
BURNBANK

Carnock Burn

Sch

Caravan Site

CLUNE RD
DEAN PK
RIDGE
BESLEA GDNS

Gowkhall

CARNOCK RD

89

CARNEIL RD
WEST PK
CARNEIL TERR
CAMPS RD
GLENFIELD
ASH GR
HAWTHORN PK
WHINNIEHILL TERR

Carnock

Carneil Hill

Carneil

INZIEVAR CRES
JAMES HOG CRES
STANLEY TERR
BEN LOMOND VIEW
JOHN STUART GAIT

Eastcamps Cottages

A907

West Camps

Camps Bank

East Camps

3

Dismtd Rly

Dean Plantation

Pitfirrane Dean

88

Duck Hill Cottage

Crossford Burn

2

Remiltoun

Remiltoun Cottages

Gray Craigs La

Pitdinnie Farm

Hilton Cottage

Pitconochie

Hilton

87

Drumfin

Sunnyside

South Pitdinnie Farm Cottages

Torry Burn

PITDINNIE RD

Walk Plantation

A985

Cairneyhill

EAST CRAIG
ROSE GDNS
THORNTON DR
DRUMGLENMUR
JON DR
GLEN CLOVA CRES
GARDEN PL
FORD
RIGGS
NORTHBANK RD
BURNBANK
CAIRNWELL PK
SPINNERS
PITDINNIE RD
HILTON RD

Sch

Walk Bridge

A994

Golf Course

1

B9037

A994

MAIN ST

A985

MUIRSIDE GR
MUIRSIDE LA
COPPER BEECH WYND
BRANDY RIGS
BRANDY WELLS
LATCH
FAIR
SOUTH ACRES
PLEASANCE BRAE
WESTHALL CRES
THE SHIEL

Cemy

Torry Burn

Sewage Works

86

03   D   04   E   05   F

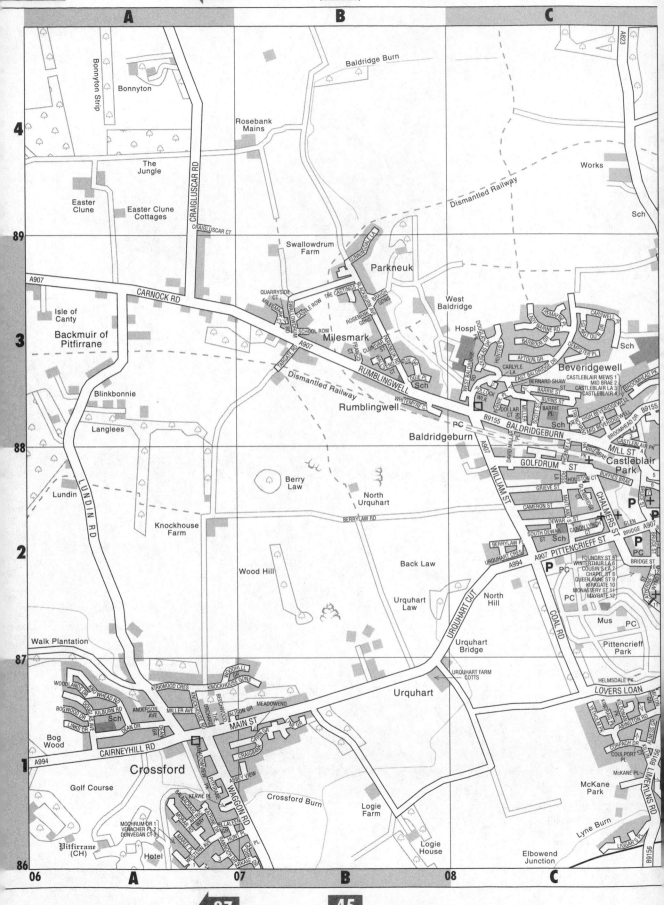

A · B · C

4

Bonnyton Strip
Bonnyton
The Jungle
Rosebank Mains
Baldridge Burn
Works

89

Easter Clune
Easter Clune Cottages
CRAIGLUSCAR RD
CRAIGLUSCAR CT
Swallowdrum Farm
Dismantled Railway
Sch

A907
CARNOCK RD
Isle of Canty
Backmuir of Pitfirrane
QUARRYSIDE CT
MILESMARK ST
CASTLE ROW
SCHOOL ROW
THE CASTINGS
SUNNINGDALE LA
Parkneuk
West Baldridge
Hospl
BLACKBURN AVE
BRAIGH GDNS
ROSEBANK AVE GDNS
PARKNEUK RD
FRANCIS ST
CLUNIVAR ST
CUT GR
LOGIE PL
Milesmark
RUMBLINGWELL
Sch
TREMAYNE PL
LADY HAIRNE RD
CARSWELL PL
BARBOUR GR
AYTOUN GR
DEMSTER PL
Beveridgewell
Sch

3

A907
Dismantled Railway
Rumblingwell
WHITEMYRE CT
CARLYLE LA
BERNARD SHAW
BARRIE ST
BURNS ST
POLLOCK WLK
CASTLEBLAIR MEWS 1
MID BRAE 2
CASTLEBLAIR LA 3
CASTLEBLAIR 4
BROOMHEAD DR
B9155

Blinkbonnie
Langlees
Baldridgeburn
PC
B9155
BALDRIDGEBURN
HIGH BEVERIDGEWELL
MID BEVERIDGEWELL
Sch
CASTLEBLAIR PK

88

Lundin
LUNDIN RD
Berry Law
North Urquhart
PC
GOLFDRUM ST
MILL ST
Castleblair Park
CHRISBRAE
BUFFIES BRAE
5

Knockhouse Farm
BERRYLAW RD
WILLIAM ST
HOUSTON CT
GRIEVE ST
CAMERON ST
DEWAR ST
CANON LYNCH CT
GLENBRIG
MAITLAND ST
ROSS ST
GLEN
BRIDGE
P
A907
P
+

2

Wood Hill
Back Law
SOUTH DEWAR ST
Sch
BERRYLAW PL
URQUHART CRES
A994
A907 PITTENCRIEFF ST
FOUNDRY ST 5
WINTERTHUR LA 6
COUSIN'S LA 7
CHAPEL ST 8
QUEEN ANNE ST 9
KIRKGATE 10
MONASTERY ST 11
MAYGATE 12
PC
P
PC

Urquhart Law
North Hill
URQUHART CUT
COAL RD
Mus
PC
Pittencrieff Park

87

Walk Plantation
Urquhart Bridge
Urquhart Farm Cotts
Urquhart
HELMSDALE PK
LOVERS LOAN

WOODLANDS DR
KNOWHEAD RD
BOGWOOD DR
DOUGLAS AVE
KILBURN RD
Sch
ANDERSON AVE
KIRKWOOD CRES
KNOCKHOUSE GDNS
WOODHILL GR
BEECHWOOD
THE ORCHARD
ALISON GR
MEADOWEND
KELVIN GR
CAIRN GR
VETHOLM ST
KINGHORN PL
ABINGTON RD
COPACH DR
COULPORT DR
LIMEKILNS RD
B9156

Bog Wood
LINKS DR
DEAN DR
MAIN ST
MILLER AVE
CRAIGBANK

1

A994
CAIRNEYHILL RD
THROUGHWAY
PITFIRRANE
ABBEY VIEW
Crossford
Golf Course
WAGGON RD
Crossford Burn
Logie Farm
McKane Park
MCKANE PL

MOCHRUM DR 1
VENACHER PL 2
DUNVEGAN CT 3
KEAVIL PL
BALMACKIE RD
MORAR DR
AFFRIC PL
AVON WAY
KATRINE PL
EILT LA
MAREE PL
HUNT PL
WESTERN AVE
CAIRNGORM DR
RANNOCH PL
OAK LA
PARKAIG
Logie House
Lyne Burn
LIGGAR'S PL
B9156

Pitfirrane (CH)
Hotel
Elbowend Junction

86

06 · A · 07 · B · 08 · C

A **B** **C**

B912

M90

Buckie Burn

Opencast
Workings

Cowdenend
The White House
(PH)

TAVERN
COTTS
Wks

MAIN ST B917

NETHERBEATH RD

A92

4

LONG ROW

PLEASANCE CT

Mains of
Beath

The Hideaway
(PH)

Pleasance

MANSE RD

CHURCH PL
BRANDS
ROW
MOWBRAY

DROVERHALL
PL

PLEASANCE RD

89

ALICE
GR

WESTFIELD
GR

GIBS

HILLVIEW PL

HILLVIEW RD

CRES

MAIN ST

B981

RINGHILL BRAE

B925

LC

Halbeath
Farm

DUNFERMLINE RD

SPRINGHILL BRAE

B925

Dismtd Rly

Townhill
Junction

B925

RED
AVE

PH

Sch

FAIRTA
CRES

DROVERHALL AVE

3

Halbeath
Retail Park

Junction 3

A92

Factory

MUIR
CT

Crossgates

WINDMILL KNOWE

INVERKEITHING RD

North
Knowe

Halbeath

Fod Arms
Hotel (PH)

MAIN ST

A907

Sandybank

LIXEBURN CRES

Prathouse
Cottage

South
Knowe

HALBEATH RD

A907

MACDONALD
SQ

FOD'S

Windmill
Knowe

Coll

Fod
House

Hospl

88

Southfod

Woodlee
Poultry Farm

2

Dry
Arch

The
Den

Prathouse

87

Annfield
Cottages

LINBURN RD

Calais Muir
Wood

Annfield

1

CALAIS
VIEW

Calais

Calais Farm
Cottages

M90

B981

Pitadro
Craigs

86

B916

12 **A** **13** **B** **14** **C**

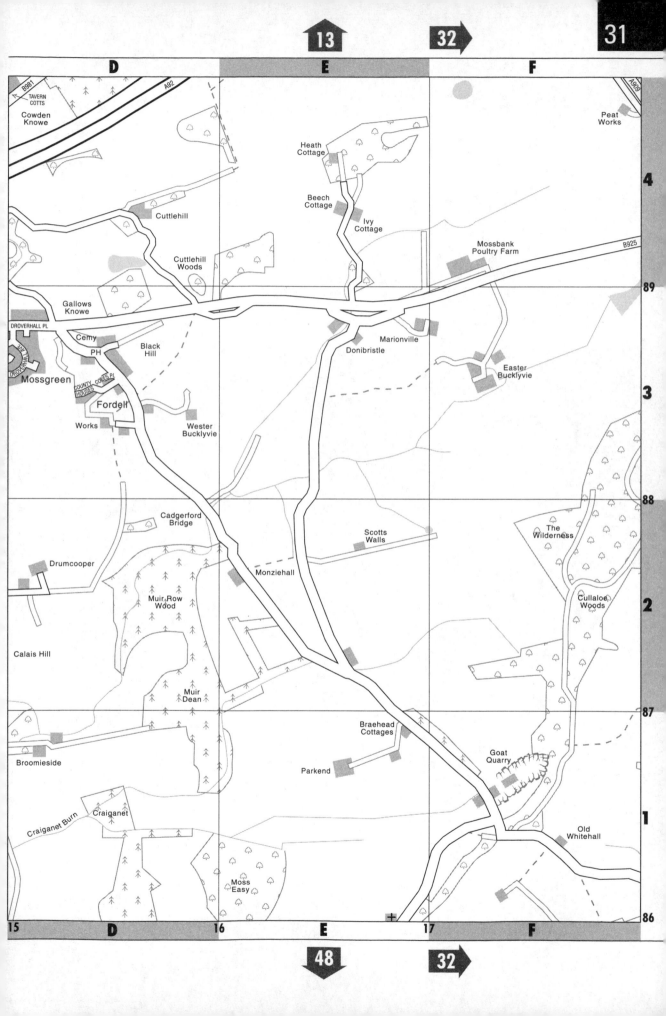

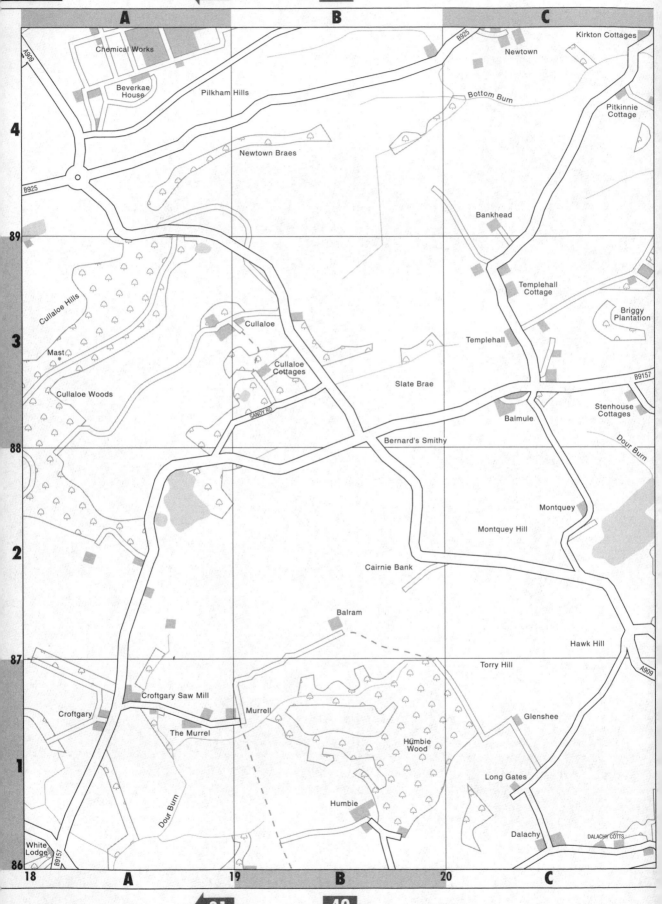

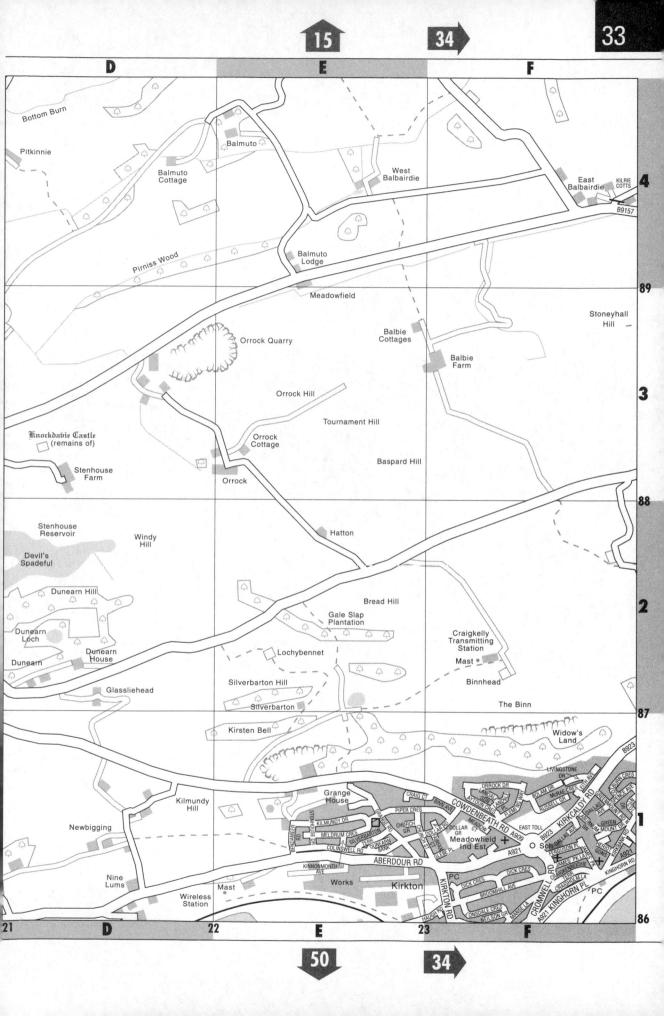

D E F

4

89

3

88

2

87

1

86

Bottom Burn
Pitkinnie
Balmuto
Balmuto Cottage
West Balbairdie
East Balbairdie
KILRIE COTTS
B9157
Pirniss Wood
Balmuto Lodge
Meadowfield
Stoneyhall Hill
Orrock Quarry
Balbie Cottages
Balbie Farm
Orrock Hill
Tournament Hill
Knockdavie Castle (remains of)
Orrock Cottage
Baspard Hill
Stenhouse Farm
Orrock
Stenhouse Reservoir
Windy Hill
Hatton
Devil's Spadeful
Dunearn Hill
Bread Hill
Gale Slap Plantation
Craigkelly Transmitting Station
Dunearn Loch
Dunearn House
Lochybennet
Mast
Dunearn
Binnhead
Glassliehead
Silverbarton Hill
The Binn
Silverbarton
Kirsten Bell
Widow's Land
B923
LIVINGSTONE DR
Kilmundy Hill
Grange House
ORROCK DR
COWDENBEATH RD
KIRKCALDY RD
Newbigging
CRAIG CT
PIPER CRES
BINN AVE
EAST TOLL
B923
A909
Meadowfield Ind Est
Sch
BENDAMEER RD
STENHOUSE DR
KILMUNDY DR
MELDRUM CRES
SILVERBARTON TERR
COLINSWELL RD
CRAIGIEFIELD RD
CHURCH GR
DOLLAR GR
A921
Nine Lums
Mast
KINNONMONTH AVE
DUNEARN BANK
ABERDOUR RD
A921
Works
Kirkton
PC
DICK CRES
DICK CRES
BROOMHILL AVE
KINGHORN PL
PC
Wireless Station
KIRKTON RD
HAUGH RD
LONSDALE CRES
NEILSON ST
MAISIE LA
CROMWELL RD
A921
KINGHORN PL

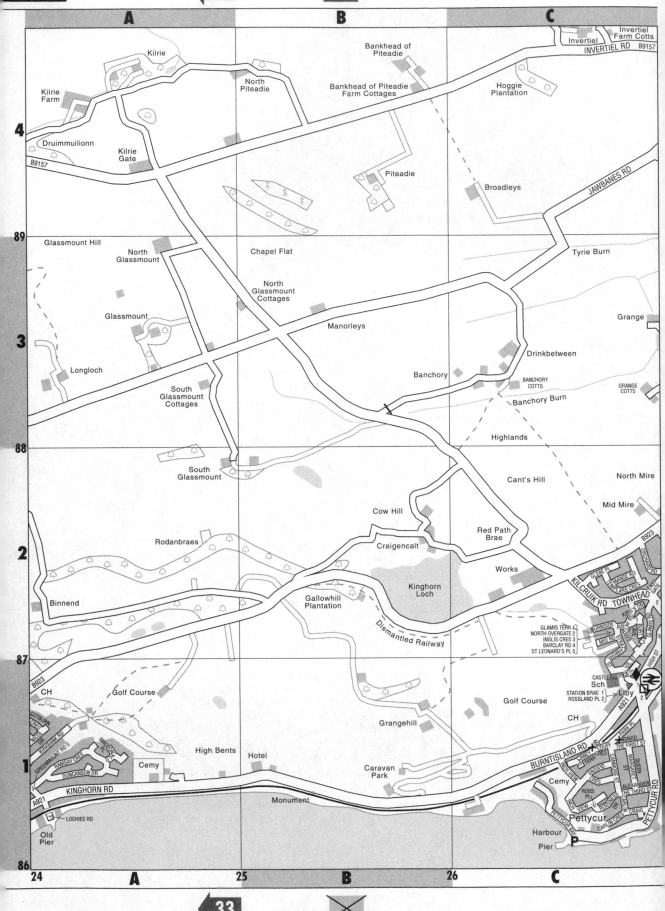

Kilrie

Kilrie Farm

North Piteadie

Bankhead of Piteadie

Bankhead of Piteadie Farm Cottages

Invertiel

Invertiel Farm Cotts

INVERTIEL RD   B9157

Hoggie Plantation

Druimmuilionn

B9157

Kilrie Gate

Piteadie

Broadleys

JAWBANES RD

4

Glassmount Hill

North Glassmount

Chapel Flat

Tyrie Burn

89

Glassmount

North Glassmount Cottages

Manorleys

Grange

Drinkbetween

Banchory

BANCHORY COTTS

GRANGE COTTS

Longloch

South Glassmount Cottages

Banchory Burn

3

Highlands

South Glassmount

88

Cant's Hill

North Mire

Mid Mire

Cow Hill

Red Path Brae

Rodanbraes

Craigencalt

Works

B923

KILCRUIK RD TOWNHEAD

2

Binnend

Gallowhill Plantation

Kinghorn Loch

GLEBE PL
MAISE RD
LAIRS CRES
EAST GATE

GLAMIS TERR 1
NORTH OVERGATE 2
INGLIS CRES 3
BARCLAY RD 4
ST LEONARD'S PL 5

BURNSIDE
KING'S DR
MID RD
BURT

Dismantled Railway

87

B923

CH

Golf Course

Golf Course

CASTLERIG Sch

CH

STATION BRAE 1
ROSSLAND PL 2

Liby

A921

COTBURN CRES
KNOX DR
GREENMOUNT RD S
KIRKBANK RD S
MAGDALENE PL
RAMSAY CRES
DUNCANSON DR

High Bents

Cemy

Hotel

Grangehill

BURNTISLAND RD

PARK PL
DAVID THE FIRST ST
DUFF
ERNIE TERR CRES

1

KINGHORN RD

A921

LOCHIES RD

Caravan Park

Cemy

QUEEN
MARGARET
CRES
ALEXANDER
THE THIRD ST
CRAIG

PETTYCUR RD

Old Pier

Monument

Pettycur

Harbour

Pier

P

86

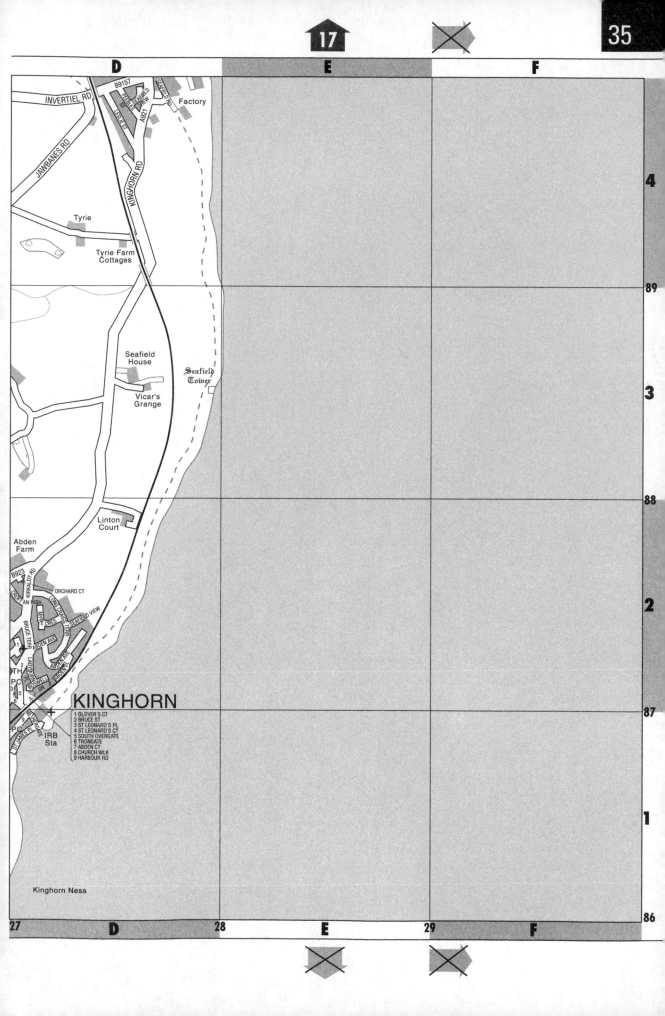

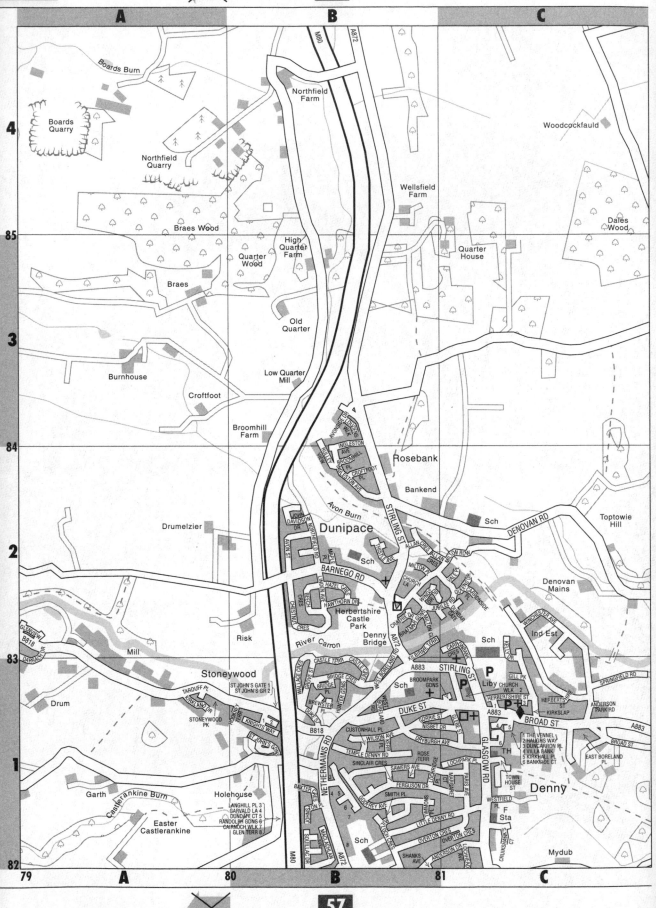

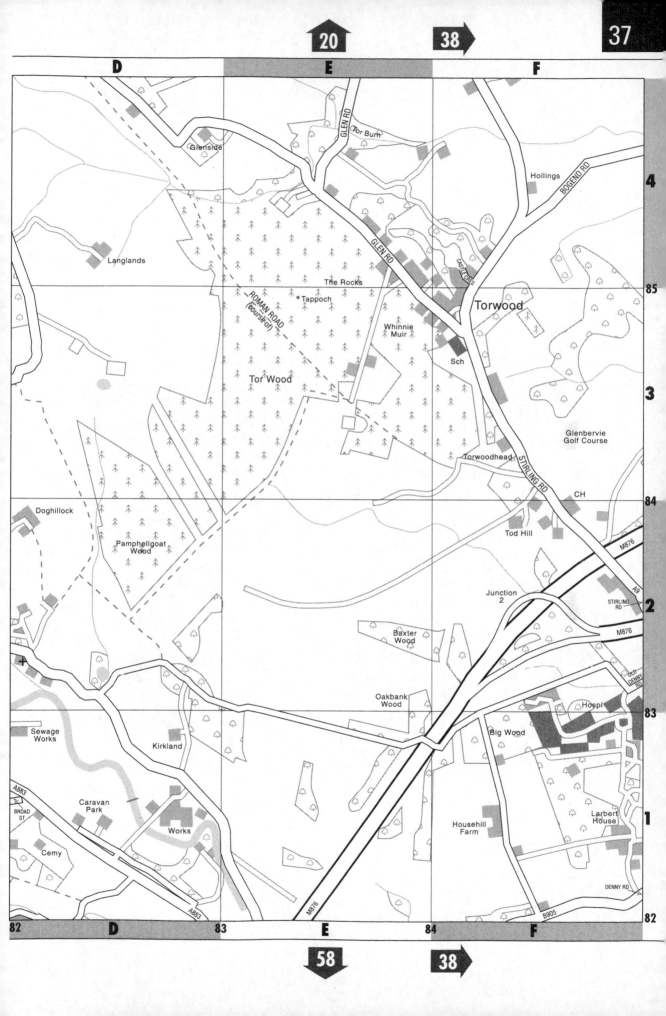

A B C

4

85

3

84

2

83

1

82

85 A 86 B 87 C

Blairs
Bogend
BOGEND RD
M9
Pow Burn
Kersebrock
Drum of Kinnaird
Hill of Kinnaird
M9

North Inches
M876
Junction 8
Titlandhill
HAMILTON RD

Glenbervie Golf Course
Shiels Farm
Bellsdyke Hospital
Inches

M876
Central Park Business Park
North Broomage
BELLSDYKE RD
Antonshill
BLENHEIM PL
FRANCHI DR
B902
MILLAR

STIRLING RD
A9
M876
A88
TAPPOCH
OLD BELLSDYKE RD
GRAHAM AVE
ST MORREN ST
BROOMAGE AVE
Golf Course
Stenhousemuir
TRYST RD
Cemy
PC
KING ST

OLD DENNY RD
GLENBERVIE CRES
CLYDE CRES
FORTH AVE
FALCON DR
EVANS ST
PEMBROKE ST
HILL VIEW RD
Larbert
LADYWELL CT
ROBERT
BRUCE ST
CRAIGIE
TORWOOD AVE
CAMPBELL DR
BALFOUR CRES
ANNBANK RD
QUEEN'S DR
CH
Sch
GLADSTONE RD
SCHOOL
Sch
Sch
STENHOUSE RD

Hospl
STIRLING RD
FOUNDRY LOAN
MUIRHALL RD
HIGH RD
QUEEN'S DR
ELIZABETH AVE
F Sta
LORNE RD
Main St
WAVERLEY RD
JAMES ST
KING ST
TRYST
KIRK AVE
MAIN ST
UNION ST
Sch
Carron Hill
Sch
CASTLE DR

Works
VICTORIA PL
UNION ST
ST GEORGE'S CT
Larbert Station
BROOMAGE PK
SOUTH BROOMAGE AVE
WAVERLEY TERR
McLACHAN ST
VALEVIEW
MUIR ST
CARRON
PARK AVE
BRAEVIEW
PC
Liby
Crownest Park
Carron Dams
Works

Lochside House
PRETORIA RD
RONALD CRES
ST DAVID'S CT
GODFREY CRES
CARRONVALE RD
LAMOND VIEW
SOUTH VIEW
LADESIDE
CEDAR GR
HILLARY RD
River Carron

DENNY RD
B905
A9
River Carron
South Broomage
PINE WLK
FORBES
LIME GR
ELM GR
ACORN
TAYLOR'S RD
BROOMHILL AVE
DOBBIE AVE
Sch
HAWTHORNE PL

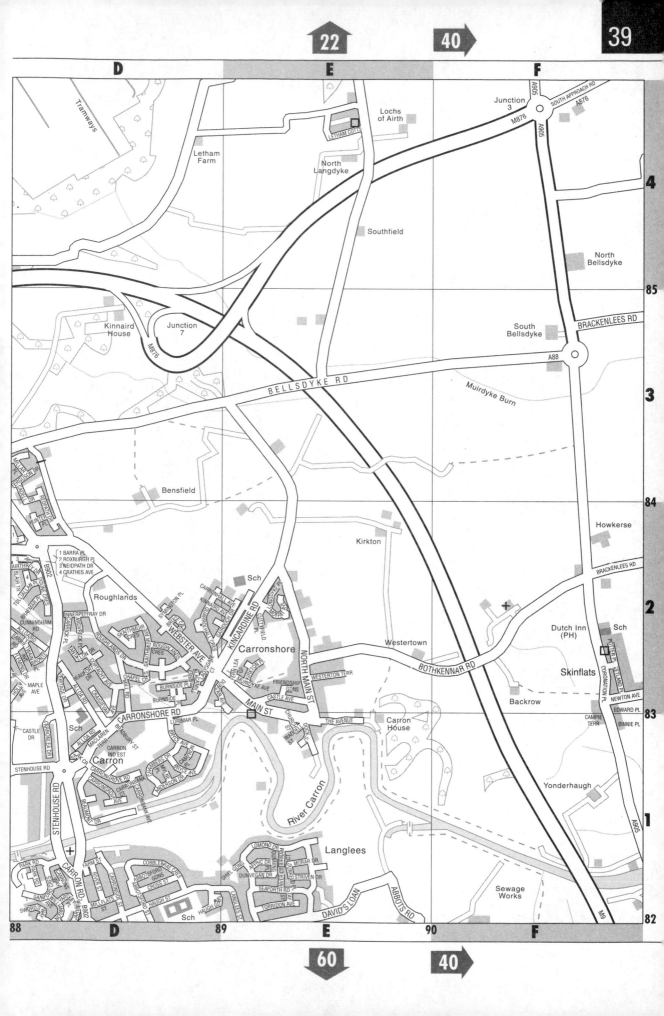

Tramways

Letham Farm

North Langdyke

Lochs of Airth

LETHAM COTTS

Southfield

Junction 3

M876

A905

SOUTH APPROACH RD

A876

A905

North Bellsdyke

Kinnaird House

Junction 7

M876

South Bellsdyke

BRACKENLEES RD

A88

BELLSDYKE RD

Muirdyke Burn

Bensfield

Howkerse

Kirkton

BRACKENLEES RD

MILLER DR
FERGUSON DR
HUNTER PL
TEMPLAR PL
AIRTHREY
BLAIR TR
B902
TULLIALAN DR
PICTURE CRES
CLUNINGHAM RD
ALLOA RD
THANE PL
CRANGIE
EGLINTON PL
FLEMINGTOR
MAPLE AVE
HOLLY AVE
CARRICK PL
ARDVERECK PL
ROUGHLANDS DR
TANTALLON DR
BEAUFORT DR
CHAPEL CRES
CHAPEL RD
ALLOA RD
CRANGIE DR
BEAUMONT DR

1 BARRA PL
2 ROXBURGH PL
3 NEIDPATH DR
4 CRATHES AVE

Roughlands

INNERPEFFRAY DR

SYMINGTON PL
WEBSTER AVE
SKAITHMUIR CRES
ROUGHLANDS
CRES
CHAPEL CT

CARRON HALL AVE
KIMBERLEY AVE
KINNAIRD AVE
CARRONGATE

KINCARDINE RD
CUTTYFIELD PL
DYKE PL

Sch

FERN LEA
HIGH
KIPPEN PL
MUIRDYKE AVE
FRIENDSHIP GDNS

Carronshore

NORTH MAIN ST

Westertown

WESTERTON TERR

BOTHKENNAR RD

Dutch Inn (PH)

Sch

POTTER PL
CORONATION PL
LELAND PL
NEWTON AVE
EDWARD PL
CAMPIE TERR
BINNIE PL

Skinflats

Backrow

Castle Dr

Sch

CARRONLEA AVE

CASTLE DR

CARRONSHORE RD

ALLOA RD
MACLAREN
BRADBURY ST

LORIMAR PL

BURNSIDE PL
BURNSIDE

BRICE AVE
CARRON PL

CASTLE AVE

MAIN ST

CHURCH ST
WADDELL ST
DUCKS

THE AVENUE

Carron House

STENHOUSE RD

Carron

CARRON IND EST

CHAMBERS DR
MYLN LN
BRYCE AVE
ANDERSON DR

Yonderhaugh

CARRONGROVE AVE
CARRONGROVE CT
CARRONBANK AVE
CARRONBANK CT
BEAUMONT DR

River Carron

Langlees

STENHOUSE RD
B902

PARK RD
FARM ST
RIVER ST
CANNONS
SANDFORD
CROSS ST
SWORDS

CARRON RD

COBBLEBRAE CRES

LOMOND DR
SHIEL GDNS
AFFRIC DR
DUNVEGAN DR
MORAR DR
STRIVEN DR

CT BIRNAM
CT BIRNAM

ABBOTSFORD GDNS
SEAFORTH RD
TORRIDON AVE

LANGLEES ST
HAUGH ST
HAUGH RD
MILL FLAT
YARDS LN

DAVID'S LOAN
ABBOTS RD

Sewage Works

M9

A905

M9

4

85

3

84

2

83

1

A **B** **C**

Greendyke

Powfoulis
Manor Hotel

4

Mains of
Powfoulis

Pocknave

Brackenlees

85

Hardlands

Stonehouse
Farm

3

Firth of Forth

BRACKENLEES RD

Orchardhead

84

Newton Mains
Farm

2

Skinflats

NEWTON AVE

NEWTON RD

83

Grangemouth Harbour
& Docks

NORTH SHORE RD

River Carron

Western Channel

1

Sch

Carron Dock

CENTRAL DOCK RD

Off

LC

Glensburgh

A905

WEST CHURCH DR

DALGRAIN RD

SOUTH BRIDGE ST

GRANGE LA

EARL'S RD

STATION RD

CHARING
CROSS

UNION RD

DOCK RD

A904

Iby BO'NESS
RD

1 YORK LA
2 YORK SQ
3 YORK ARC
4 LA PORTE PREC

TH

NELSON
GDNS

LC's

SOUTH SHORE RD

GRANGEBURN RD

POWDRAKE RD

GLENSBURGH RD

DEVON ST

BANK ST

CLYDE DR

AVON ST

TAY ST

KELVIN ST

TWEED ST

DON ST

PO

82

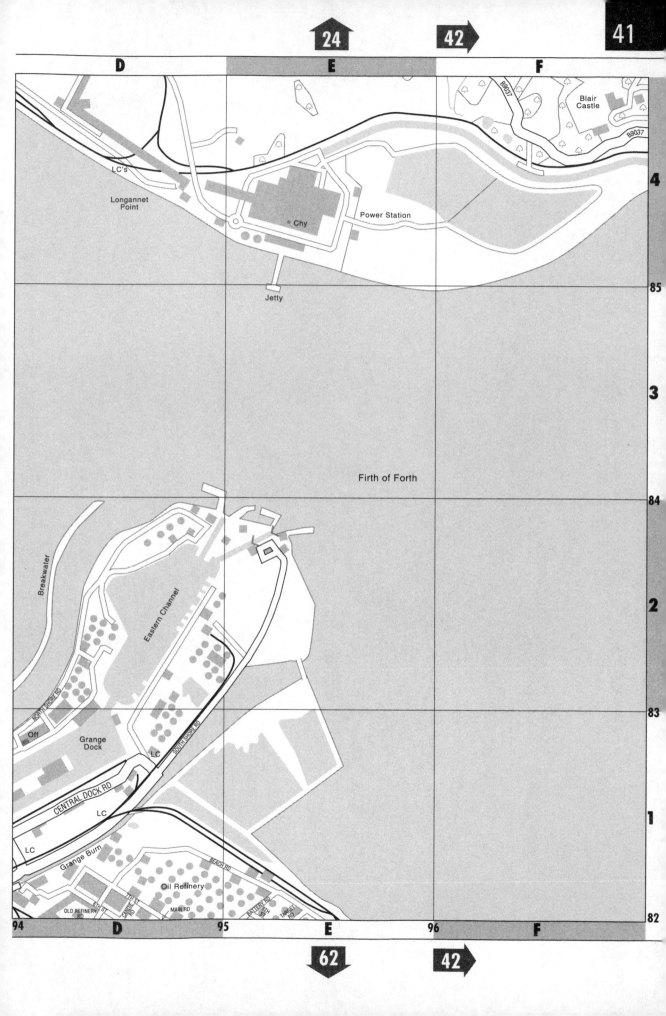

D

E

F

Blair
Castle

B9037

B9037

LC's

Longannet
Point

4

Power Station

Chy

85

Jetty

3

Firth of Forth

84

Breakwater

Eastern Channel

2

NORTH SHORE RD

SOUTH SHORE RD

83

Off

Grange
Dock

LC

CENTRAL DOCK RD

LC

1

LC

Grange Burn

BEACH RD

OLD REFINERY
RD

7TH ST

6TH ST

CARDIE
RD

Oil Refinery

MAIN RD

BATTERY RD

TARGET
RD

82

94

D

95

E

96

F

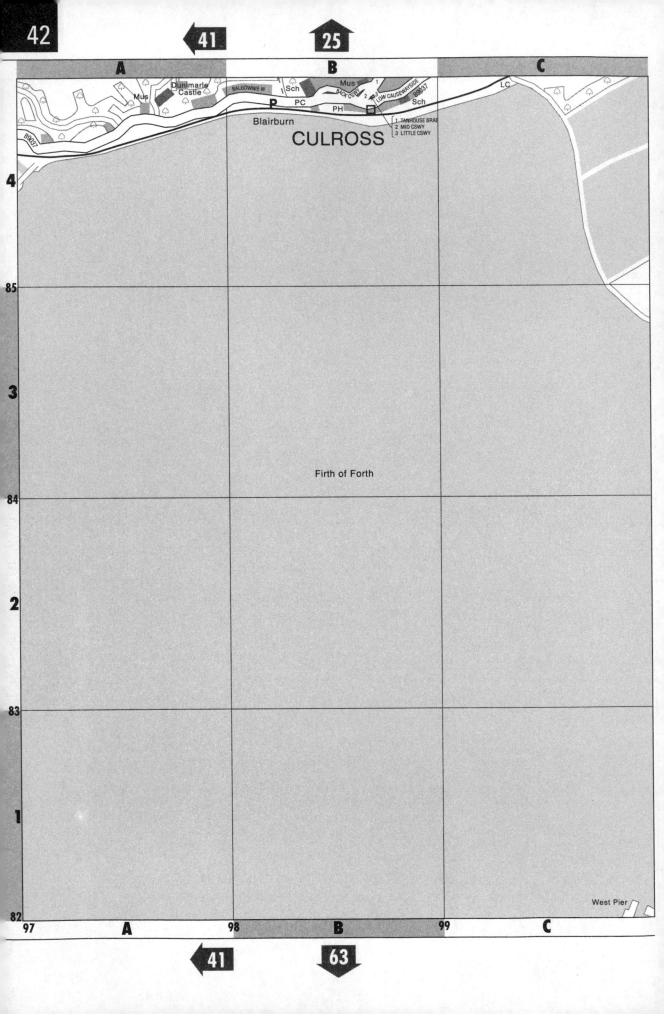

A   B   C

Mus

Dunimarle
Castle

BALGOWNIE W   Sch

Mus

BACK CSWY

LOW CAUSEWAYSIDE

Sch

B9037

LC

B9037

P   PC

PH

Blairburn

CULROSS

1 TANHOUSE BRAE
2 MID CSWY
3 LITTLE CSWY

B9037

4

85

3

Firth of Forth

84

2

83

1

West Pier

82

97   A   98   B   99   C

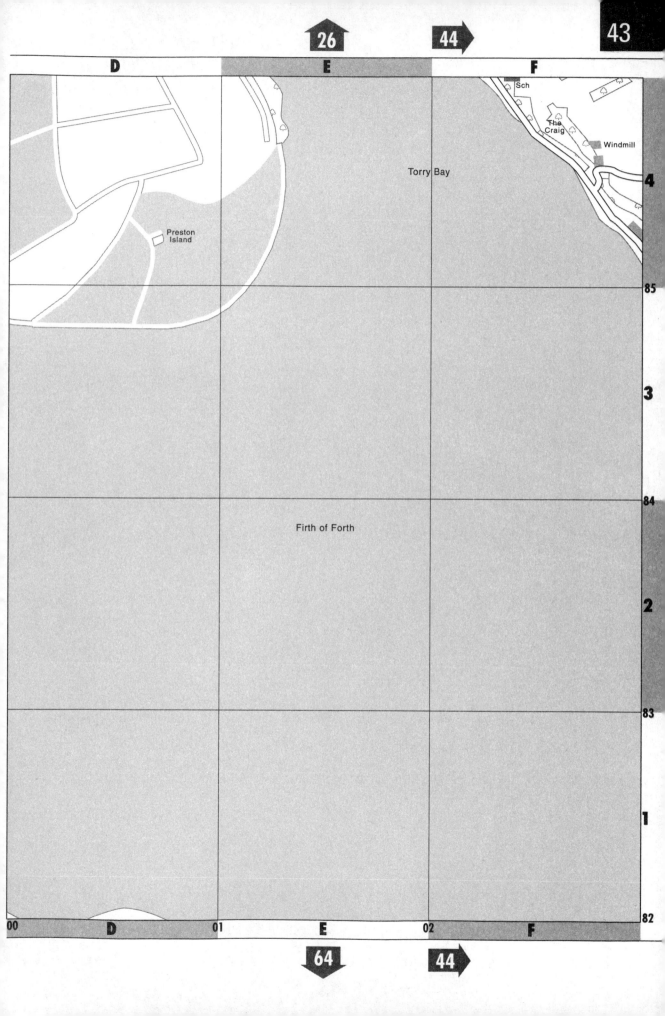

D
E
F

Sch

The
Craig

Windmill

Torry Bay

4

Preston
Island

85

3

84

Firth of Forth

2

83

1

00
D
01
E
02
F
82

43
27

A   B   C

Muirside
Cottage

A985

MUIRSIDE

Muirside

Mire
End

Bankhead

CRAIGWELL

Crombie

4

Sch

CENTRAL RD

MAIN RD

Bullions Farm
Cottages

Shoreside

FARM RD

ORDNANCE RD

85

Waukmill
Cottages

Stripeside

Bullions

Crombie
Farm

A985

Kiln
Hill

Waukmill

Crombie
Point

3

Crombie
Pier

CAMP RD

Kinniny Braes

Ironmill
Bay

84

Crombie
Pier

2

Jetty

Firth of Forth

83

1

82

03   A   04   B   05   C

43
65

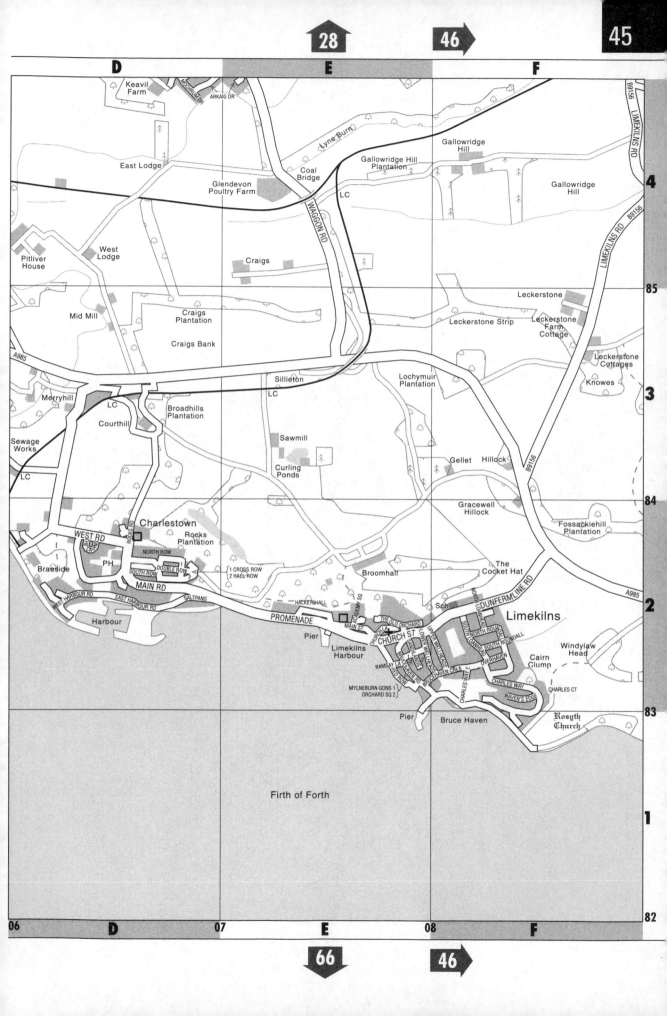

D | E | F

Keavil Farm

MOORFRUIT DR

ARKAIG DR

East Lodge

Lyne Burn

Gallowridge Hill

Gallowridge Hill Plantation

Coal Bridge

WAGGON RD

LC

Gallowridge Hill

4

Glendevon Poultry Farm

B9156

LIMEKILNS RD

West Lodge

Pitliver House

Craigs

Leckerstone

LIMEKILNS RD

85

Mid Mill

Craigs Plantation

Craigs Bank

Leckerstone Strip

Leckerstone Farm Cottage

A985

Sillieton

LC

Lochymuir Plantation

Leckerstone Cottages

Knowes

Merryhill

LC

Courthill

Broadhills Plantation

LC

Sawmill

Curling Ponds

Gellet

Hillock

B9156

3

Sewage Works

LC

Gracewell Hillock

84

Fossackiehill Plantation

Charlestown

ROCKS RD

Rocks Plantation

WEST RD

PH

NORTH ROW

DOUBLE ROW

SOUTH ROW

1 CROSS ROW
2 HAEL ROW

Broomhall

The Cocket Hat

DUNFERMLINE RD

A985

Braeside

MAIN RD

EAST HARBOUR RD

SALTPANS

HALKET'SHALL

Sch

NORTH ROW

Limekilns

2

WEST HARBOUR RD

Harbour

PROMENADE

ACADEMY SQ

MAIN ST

Pier

THE OLD ORCHARD

CHURCH ST

CHURCH LA

LOWER WELLHEADS

UPPER WELLHEADS

NORTH DANIEL RD

SOUTH DANIEL ROW

Windylaw Head

Cairn Clump

Limekilns Harbour

RAMSAY LA

RED ROW

HAEL RD

BRUCEHAVEN CRES

CHARLES WAY

OVERHAVEN

SOUTH ROUNDALL

CHARLES CT

MYLNEBURN GDNS 1
ORCHARD SQ 2

CHARLES WAY

HAVEN'S EDGE

83

Pier

Bruce Haven

Rosyth Church

Firth of Forth

1

82

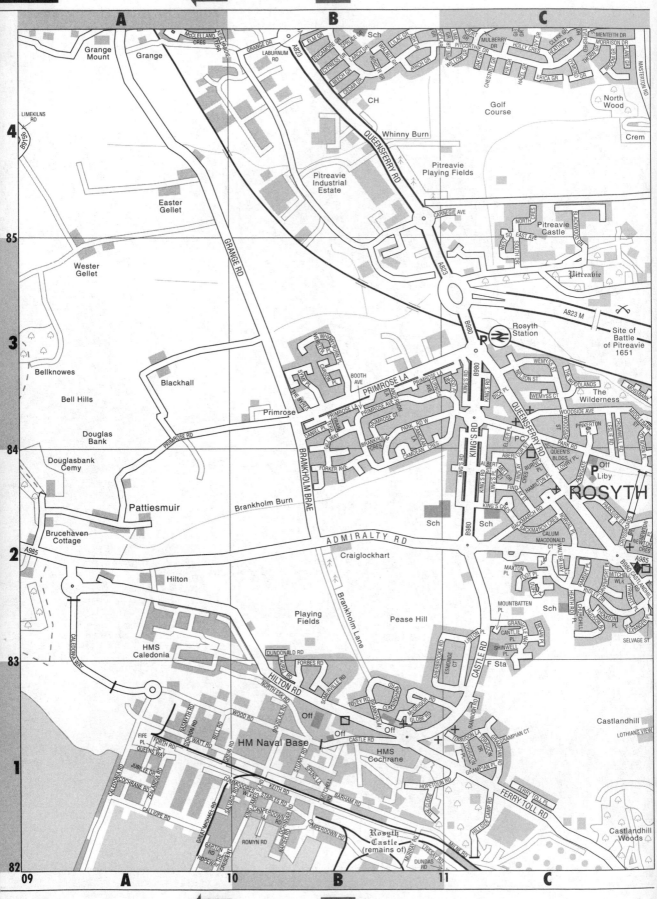

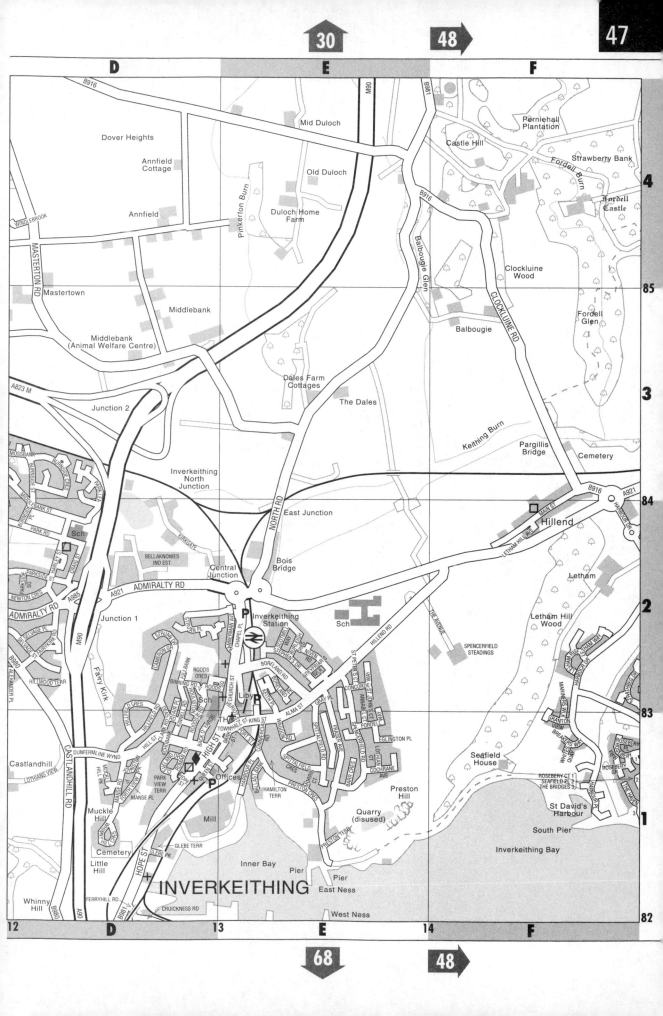

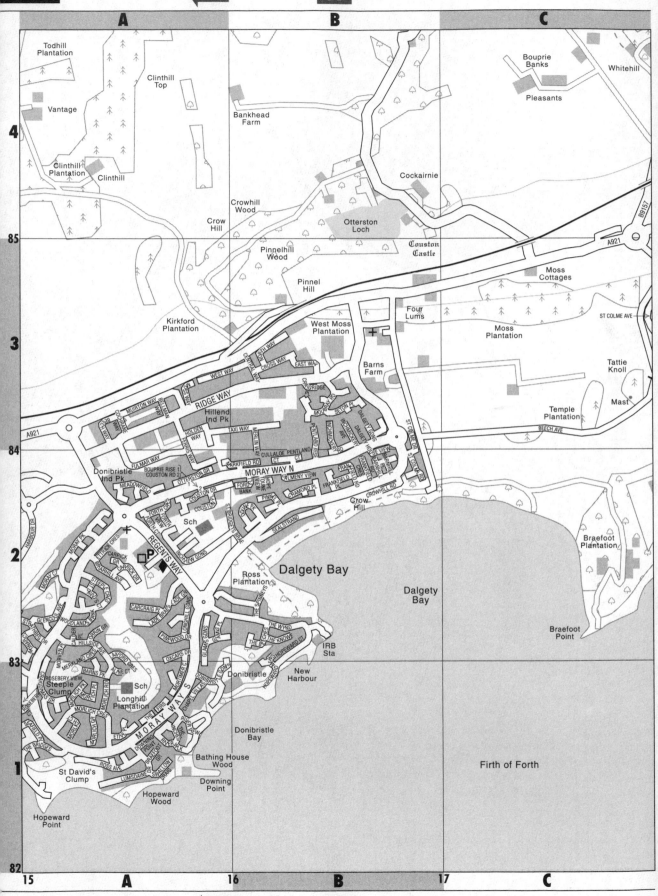

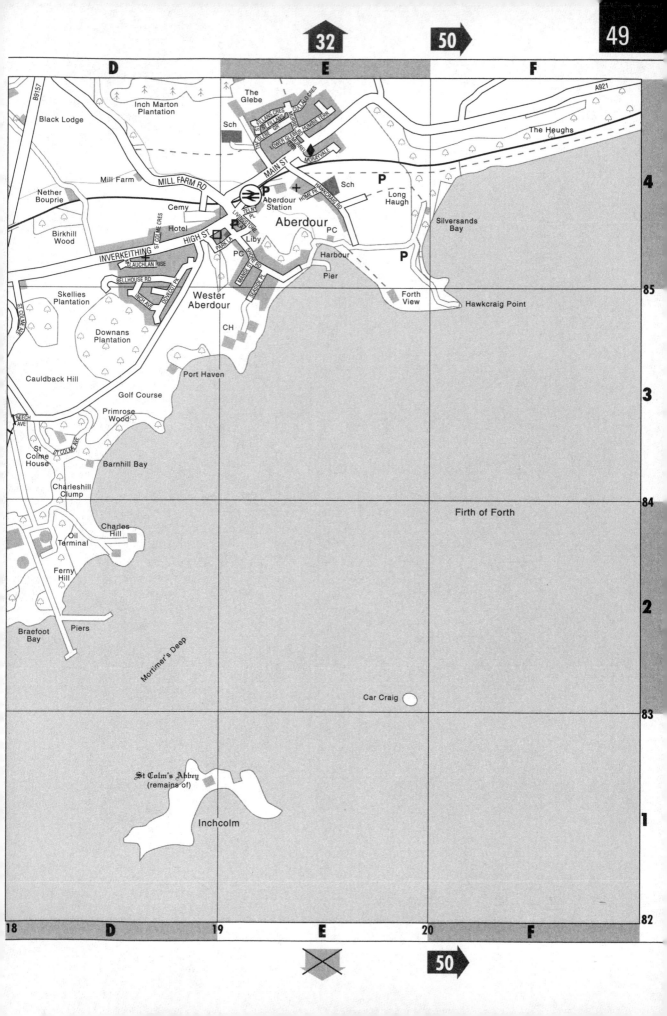

D   E   F

A921

The Glebe

Inch Marton
Plantation

Black Lodge

The Heughs

Sch

Mill Farm

MILL FARM RD

FILLANS CRES
ST FILLANS RD
GLEBE
MORRIS
HUMBIE TERR

MAIN ST

Nether
Bouprie

Cemy

Aberdour
Station

Sch

P

4

Hotel

Aberdour

Long
Haugh

Birkhill
Wood

ST COLME CRES

HIGH ST

Liby

PC

Silversands
Bay

INVERKEITHING

PARK LA

Harbour

P

85

MCLAUCHLAN RISE

BELLHOUSE RD

DOVECOT PK

INCH AVE

MANSE ST
SHORE RD
SEASIDE RD

PC

Pier

Forth
View

Skellies
Plantation

Wester
Aberdour

Hawkcraig Point

Downans
Plantation

CH

Cauldback Hill

Port Haven

Golf Course

3

Primrose
Wood

BEECH AVE

ST COLME AVE

St
Colme
House

Barnhill Bay

Charleshill
Clump

84

Firth of Forth

Oil
Terminal

Charles
Hill

Ferny
Hill

2

Braefoot
Bay

Piers

Mortimer's Deep

Car Craig ○

83

St Colm's Abbey
(remains of)

Inchcolm

1

82

18   D   19   E   20   F

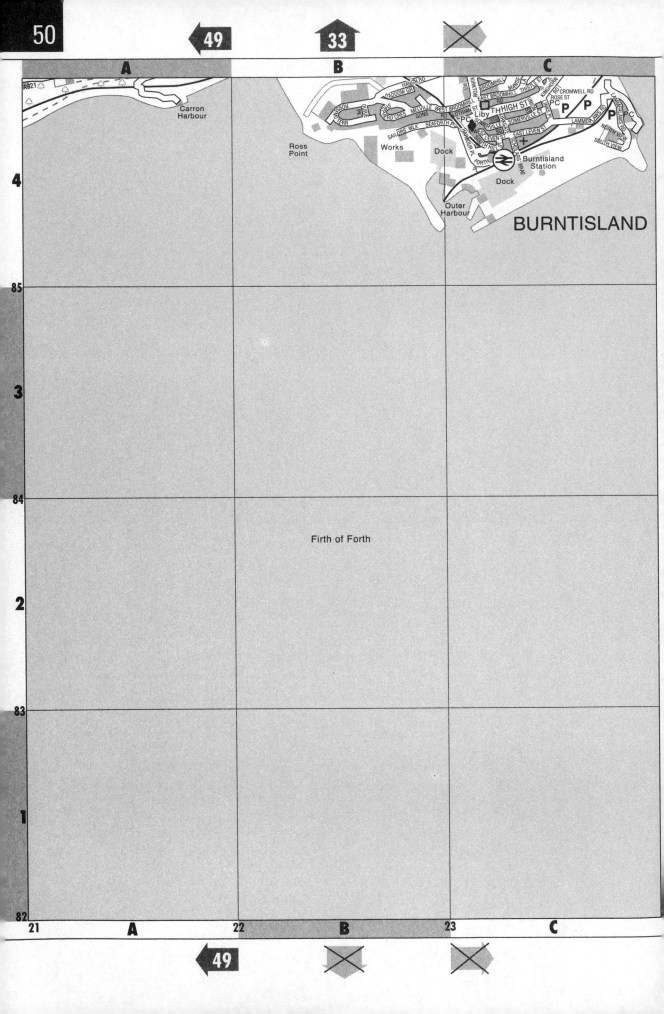

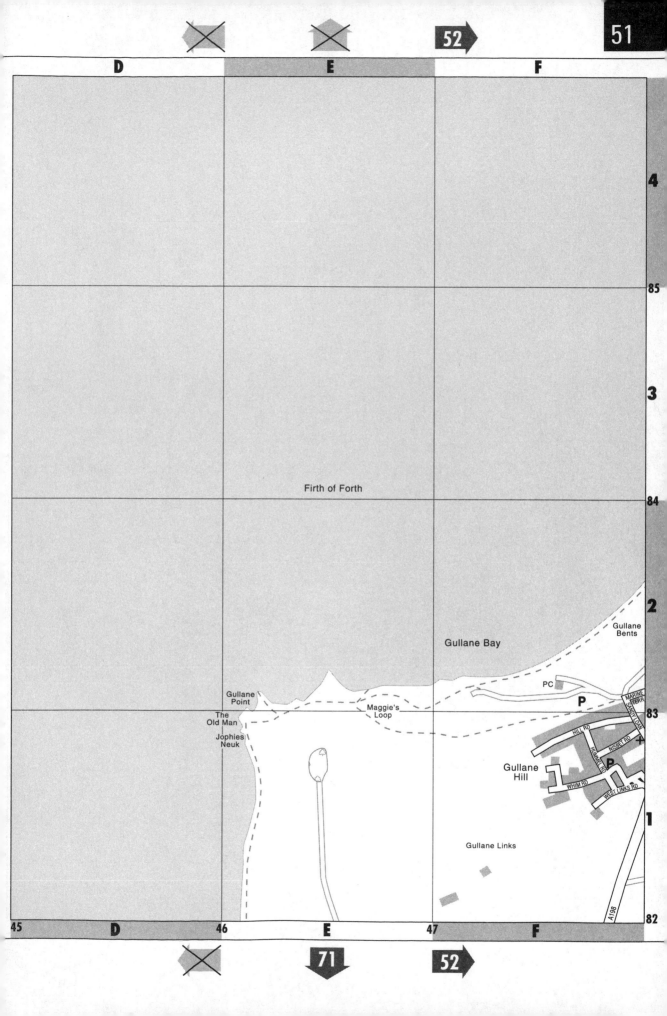

4

85

3

Firth of Forth

84

2

Gullane Bay

Gullane Bents

PC

P

MARINE TERR

Gullane
Point

SANDY LOAN

83

The
Old Man

Maggie's
Loop

HILL RD

+

Jophies
Neuk

NISBET RD

Gullane
Hill

RUNNEL RD

P

WHIM RD

WEST LINKS RD

1

Gullane Links

A198

82

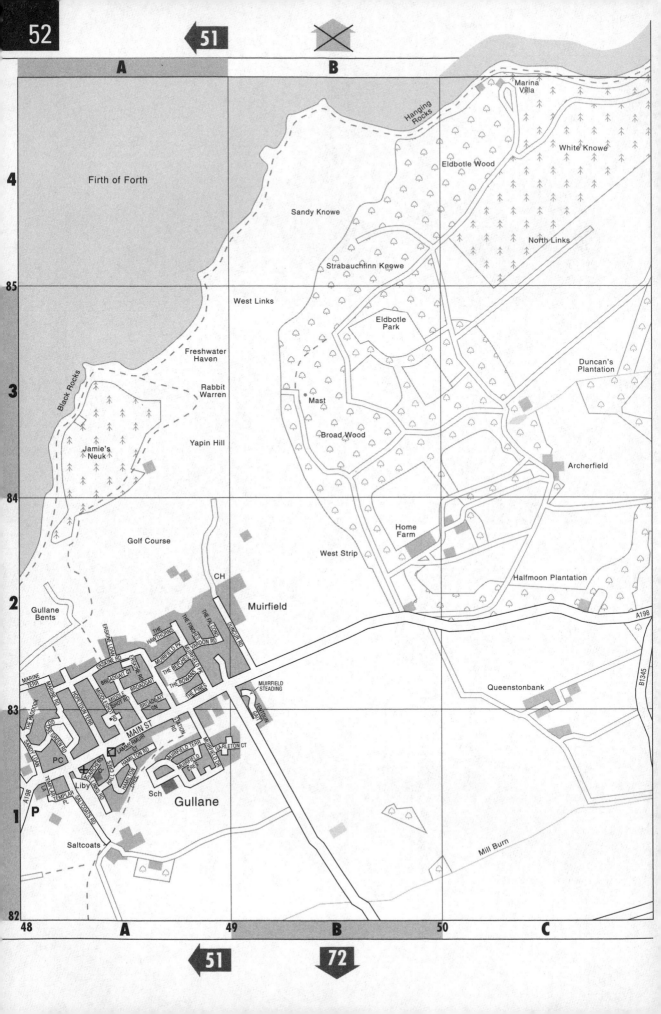

A   B

4

Firth of Forth

Hanging Rocks

Marina Villa

Eldbotle Wood

White Knowe

Sandy Knowe

North Links

85

Strabauchtinn Knowe

West Links

Eldbotle Park

Duncan's Plantation

Freshwater Haven

Black Rocks

Rabbit Warren

3

Mast

Archerfield

Jamie's Neuk

Yapin Hill

Broad Wood

84

Home Farm

Golf Course

West Strip

Halfmoon Plantation

CH

2

Muirfield

A198

Gullane Bents

MARINE TERR

THE HAWTHORNS

THE FINCHES

THE FALCONS

ERSKINE LOAN RD

MUIRFIELD PL

VARDON RD

DUNCUR RD

B1345

MARINE RD

ERSKINE CT

BROADGAIT

MIDDLE SHOT RD

BROADGAIT CT

THE BEECHES

MUIRFIELD PL

THE ROWANS

Queenstonbank

HOPETOUN TERR

RIDDELL RD

BROADGAIT GN

THE PINES

MUIRFIELD STEADING

83

SANDY LOAN

THE GREEN RD

WESTER LOAN

STATION RD

GOOSE GREEN RD

MAIN ST

LAMMERMUIR CT

MUIRFIELD TERR

MUIRFIELD DR

CARLETON CT

PC

HAMILTON RD

MUIRFIELD CRES

THE PADDOCK

A198

EAST LINKS RD

SANDERS RD

Liby

TEMPLAR PK

HAMILTON RD

Sch

STATION RD

Gullane

TEMPLAR PL

SALTCOATS RD

P

1

Saltcoats

Mill Burn

82

48   A   49   B   50   C

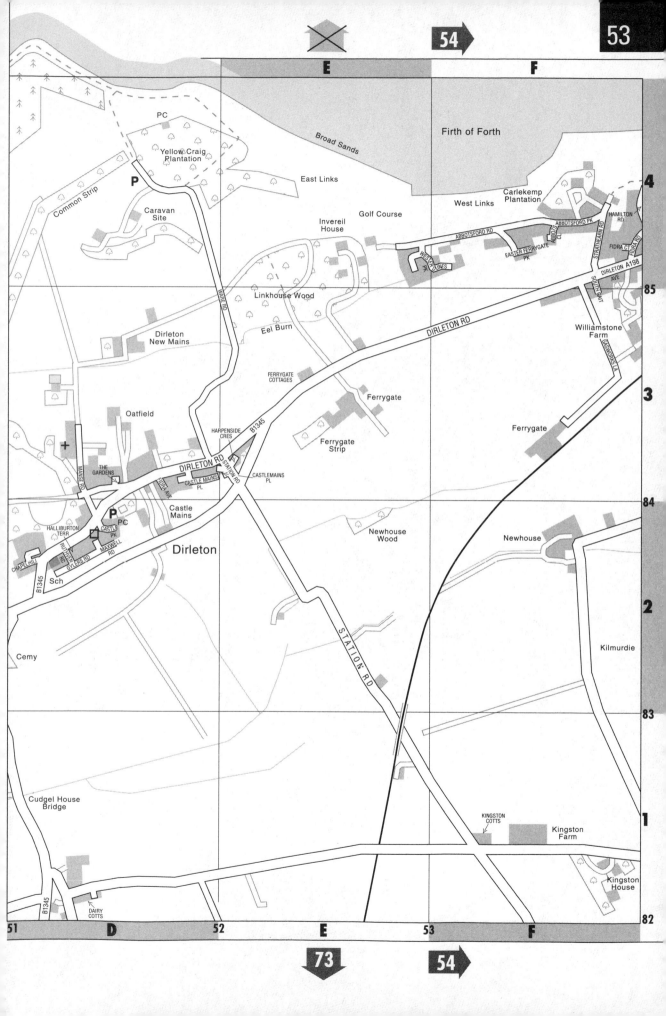

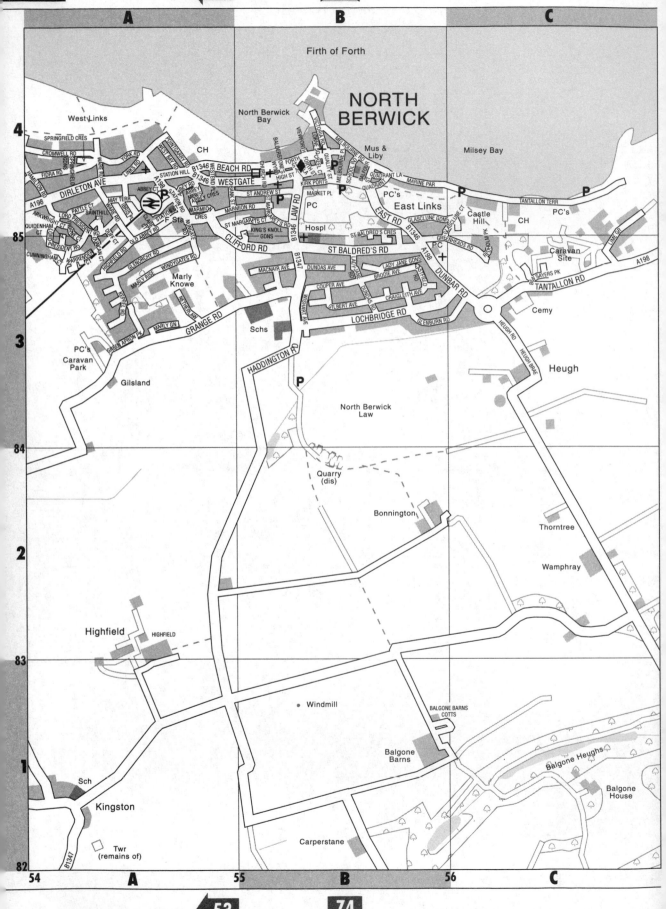

A   B   C

Firth of Forth

NORTH BERWICK

West Links

North Berwick Bay

Milsey Bay

SPRINGFIELD CRES
CROMWELL RD
FIDRA RD
HAMILTON RD
DIRLETON AVE
A198
POINT GARRY RD
YORK RD
LINKS RD
STATION HILL
BEACH RD
B1346
WESTEND
CH
WESTGATE
CHURCH RD
HIGH ST
VICTORIA RD
LORNE SQ
MELBOURNE PL
VIEWFORTH
FORTH
Mus & Liby
SCHOOL RD
BALFOUR
QUADRANT LA
QUADRANT
MARINE PAR
TANTALLON TERR
PC's

MAY TERR
SAINTHILL
ABBEY CT
SPITAL RD
ABBEY RD
ABBEY CRES
MARMION CRES
MARMION RD
ST ANDREW ST
ST MARGARET'S CT RD
KIRK PORTS
MARKET PL
PC
Hospl
East Links
PC's
Castle Hill
CH
PC's

ARKWRIGHT CT
LORD PRESIDENT RD
QUIDENHAM CT
PRESIDENT RD
CUNNINGHAM CT
WARRENDER
F Sta
OLD ABBEY RD
HIGHFIELD RD
GLENORCHY RD
WINDYGATES RD
CLIFFORD RD
B1347
KING'S KNOLL GDNS
ST BALDRED'S CRES
ST BALDRED'S RD
LAW RD
B1346
LADY JANE GDNS
ASHFIELD
GREENHEADS RD
REDCROFT
DUNBAR RD
A198
GLASCLUNE GDNS
GLASCLUNE CT
BEN SAYERS PK
Caravan Site
TANTALLON RD
A198
LIME GR

WARRENDER
MARLY RISE
KEPTIE RD
NETHER BY RD
Marly Knowe
MACNAIR AVE
DUNDAS AVE
COUPER AVE
GILBERT AVE
DUNDAS AVE
BRODIE AVE
CRAIGLEITH AVE
WISHART AVE
Schs
GRANGE RD
HADDINGTON RD
LOCHBRIDGE RD
GLENBURN RD
Cemy
Heugh
HEUGH RD
HEUGH BRAE

PC's Caravan Park
BREE APRON PK
Gilsland
Marly Gn

North Berwick Law

Quarry (dis)

Bonnington

Thorntree

Wamphray

Highfield
HIGHFIELD

Windmill

Balgone Barns Cotts

Balgone Barns

Balgone Heughs

Balgone House

Sch
Kingston
B1347
Twr (remains of)

Carperstane

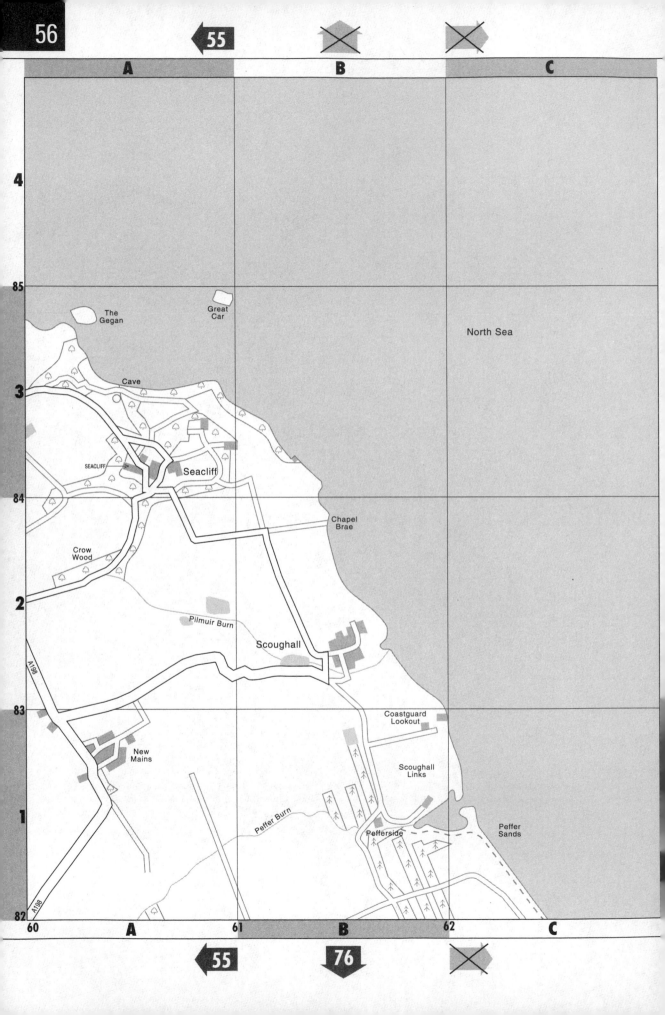

A B C

4

85

The Gegan

Great Car

North Sea

Cave

3

SEACLIFF

Seacliff

84

Chapel Brae

Crow Wood

2

Pilmuir Burn

Scoughall

A198

83

Coastguard Lookout

New Mains

Scoughall Links

1

Peffer Burn

Peffer Sands

Pefferside

A198

82

60 A 61 B 62 C

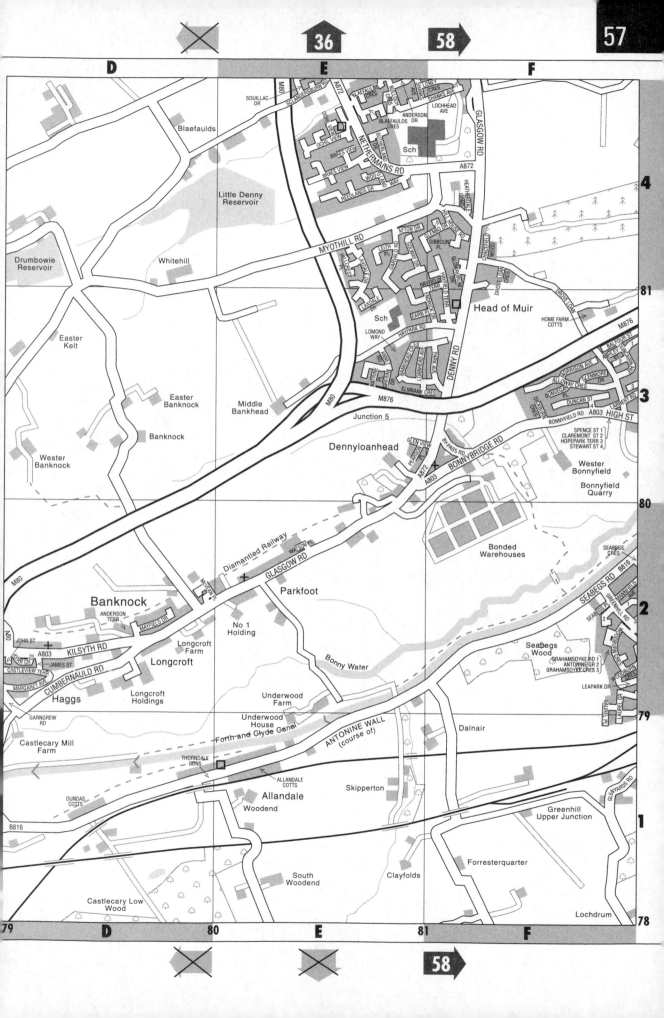

Cuthelton
Chacefield Wood
Junction 1
Nursery
Cemy
Hills of Dunipace
River Carron
Bonnybridge Golf Course
Dismantled Railway
Bogton Farm
Sewage Works
Wester Carmuirs
Works
CH
PRIMROSE ST
FAIRWAYS PL
NORWOOD
BONNYMUIR
ROBERTSON AVE
DRUMMOND PL
FERGUSON GR
ROSE ST
LARBERT RD
CHACEFIELD ST
WHEATLANDS AVE
HIGHLANDS
BONNYVIEW GDNS
DYKES
GATESIDE AVE
GATESIDE AVE
BALFOUR ST
SPENCE ST
URE CRES
SCENE ST
COWAN ST
GREENFIELD ST
Sch
FAIRFIELD AVE
THORNTON
THORNTON AVE
FALKIRK RD
Hospl
Bonny Water
Rowan Tree Burn
A803
WEST CARMUIRS LOAN
PEATHILL RD
MARGARET
WELLPARK TERR
FORD RD
FORD ST
ANDERSON
BARLEYHILL
PRINCESS ST
PATERSON PL
Park
Forth and Clyde Canal
HOMEPARK
DUNURE CRES
DUNURE ST
A803
HIGH ST
PC
Bonnybridge
P P
Liby
Cowden Hill
BRIDGE ST
BONNYSIDE RD
Bonnyside Farm
SEABEGS RD
Sch
Chattan Ind Est
Antonine Wall
Works
B816
Murnin Road Ind Est
SEABEGS CRES
MANNFIELD AVE
BROOMHILL RD
Sch
Works
B816
GRAHAMSDYKE RD
ROMAN RD
Milnquarter
1 GRAHAMSDYKE CRES
2 LEAPARK DR
3 BANTON PL
4 LAURELBANK AVE
WAVERLEY CRES
MILLAR PL
LOCHINVAR PL
PARK ST
PETER ST
CHURCH ST
Works
REILLY RD
HILL
VIEW RD
BONNYHILL RD
LEAPARK DR
GREENHILL RD
LAUREL GR
High Bonnybridge
BROOMSIDE RD
GLENYARDS RD
Greenhill
Margreta
Bonnyhill Farm
Howierig
Wester Drum
Drum Wood
Greenrig

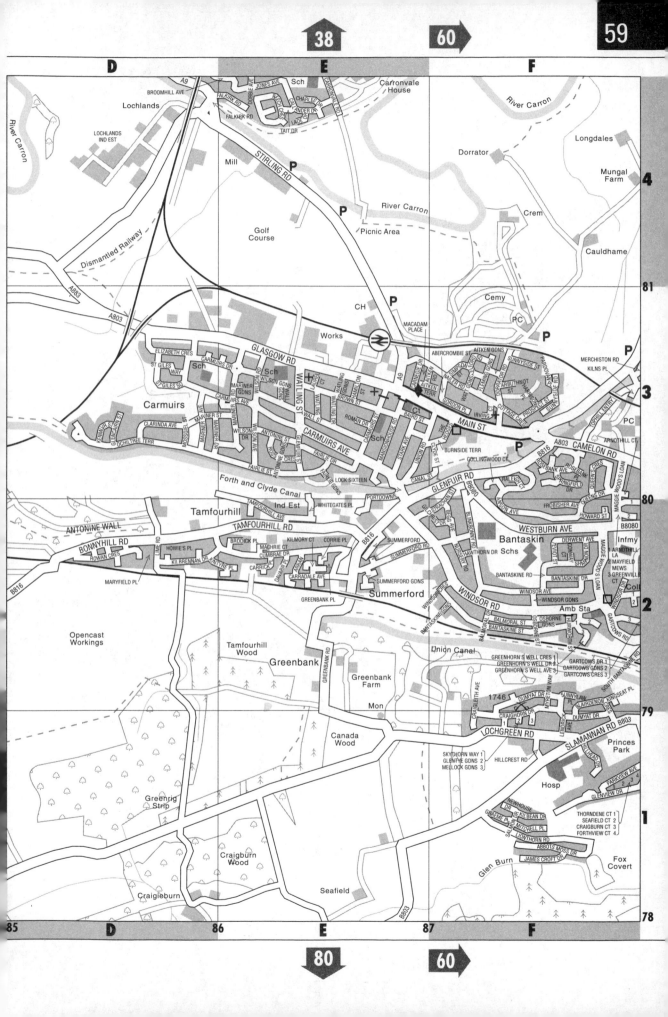

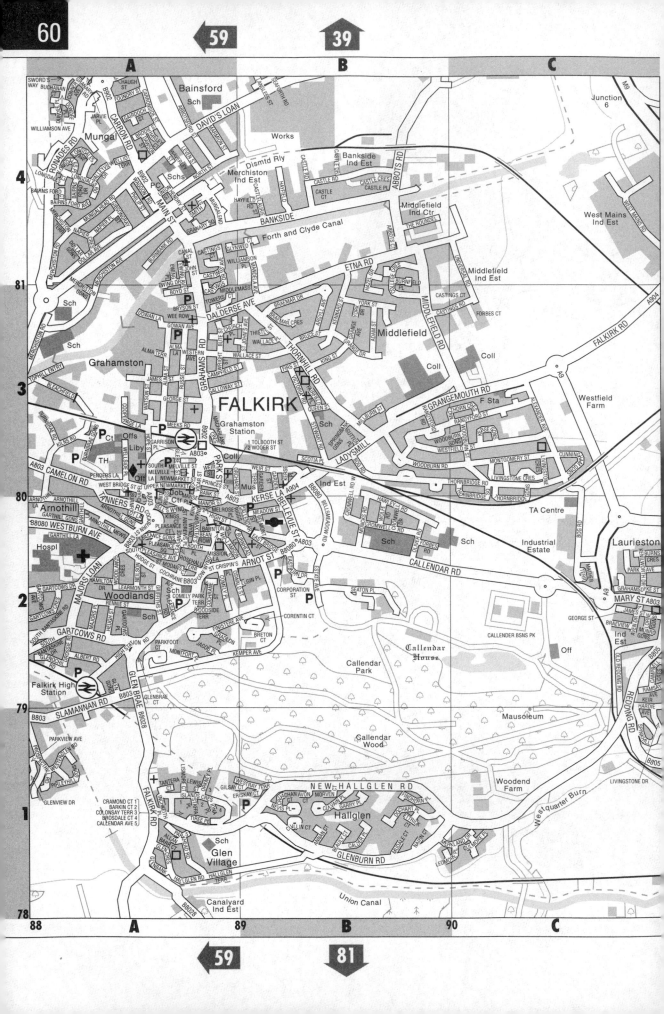

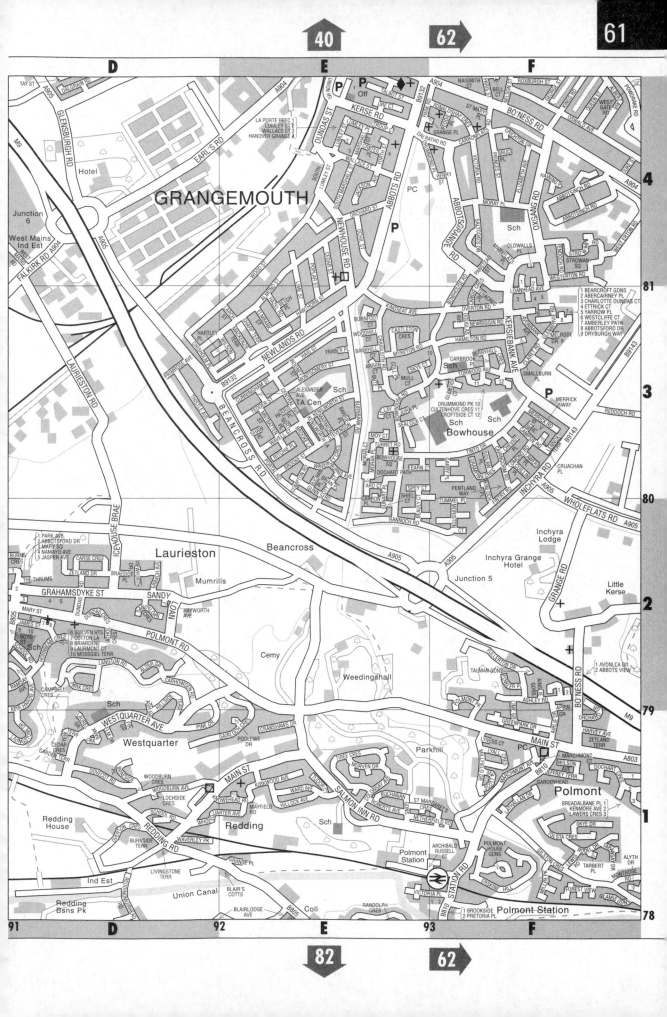

A   **B**   **C**

Firth of Forth

4

WEST GATE RD
OLD REFINERY RD
9TH ST
BATTERY RD
TARGET RD
GUNNER RD
RIFLE RD
BUTT S
PEACE RD
5TH ST
CAROL RD
4TH ST
MAIN RD
3RD ST
ORPINGTON RD
7TH ST
ORCHARD RD
OLDWALLS RD
RANGE RD
BEARCROFT RD
2ND ST
SALTCOATS RD
CLARET RD
AVON RD
POWDRAKE RD
OSWALD AVE
Oil Refinery
WESTERTON RD
TENACRES CRES

BO'NESS RD
A904
1ST ST

River Avon

Sewage Works

81

INCHYRA RD
BO'NESS RD
B9143
ROAD 24
ROAD 25
ROAD 30B
ROAD 28
ROAD 32
ROAD 30C
ROAD 3
ROAD 7
ROAD 11
ROAD 6
ROAD 4A
ROAD 10
ROAD 15
ROAD 4

Chemical Works

Kinneil Kerse

3

REDDOCH RD
Wholeflats
ROAD 33
ARBIE RD
COMPRESSOR HOUSE RD
QUENCH RD
RIVERSIDE RD
EAST RD
SOUTH RD
Works

BUCHAN RD
BRAE RD
2ND ST
3RD ST
MAGNUS RD
FORTIES RD
NINIAN RD
BALMORAL RD
ALPHA ST
BRAVO ST
4TH ST
5TH ST
NELSON RD
7TH ST
BRUCE RD
MILLER RD

A904

East Kerse Mains

80

A905   WHOLEFLATS RD
GRANGEMOUTH RD
A905
INVERAVON ROUNDABOUT
Antonine Wall (course of)
Inveravon

Bo'ness and Kinneil Railway

2

REDDOCH RD
Antonine Wall (course of)
CH
AVONDALE RD
Polmonthill
Sewage Works
Avondale House
River Avon
Avon Banks Wood

79

M9
Golf Course
Millhall Reservoir

Birkhill Clay Mine
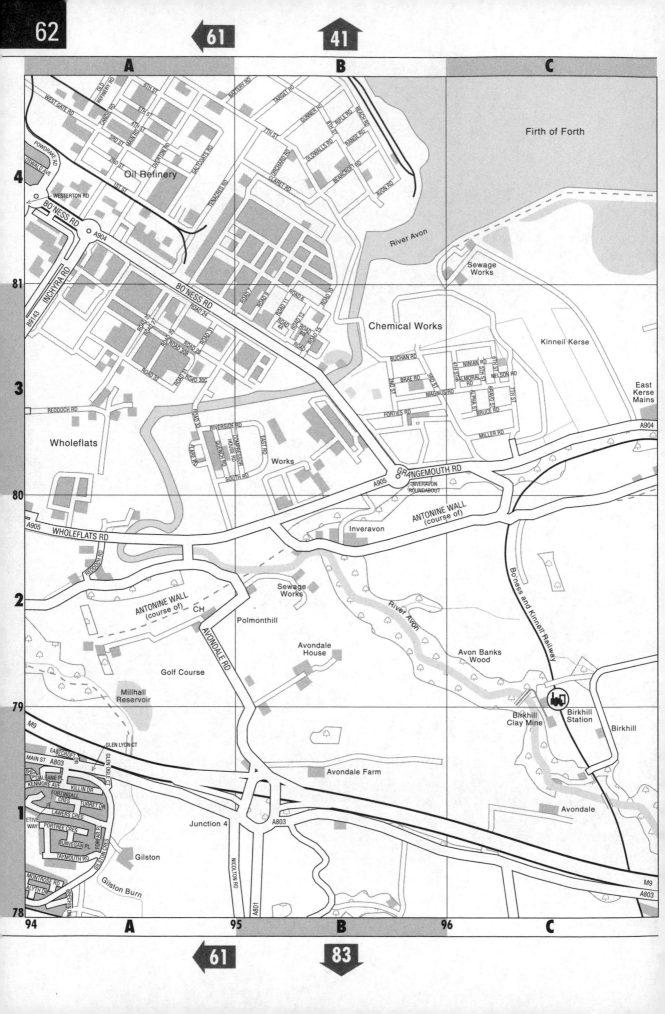
Birkhill Station
Birkhill

1

EASTCROFT RD
GLEN LYON CT
GLEN OGLE CT
MAIN ST   A803
DALBANE PL
KENMORE AVE
KILLIN DR
FORTINGALL CRES
TURRET DR
LAWERS CRES
ETIVE WAY
PORTREE CRES
FORFAR PL
DUNVEGAN PL
GILSTON CRES
TAYMOUTH CRES
MONTROSE RD
ALYTH DR
BRECHIN DR
Gilston

Junction 4
A803
NICOLTON RD
Avondale Farm
Avondale

M9
A803

78

GILSTON BURN
A801

94   **A**   **95**   **B**   **96**   **C**

A B C

Bo'ness & Kinneil Railway
UNION ST
A904
COMMISSIONER'S ST
MAIN ST
DUCK ST
Grangepans
Bo'ness Station
Man o' War Way
THIRLSTANE PL
DOWER CRES
HANEY'S WAY
Bridgeness
Firth of Forth

LINKS RD
THE BOG
HE BRAE
DE-MAR
THIRLSTANE
MAN O' WAR WAY
BOUNDARY
GRANGEPANS
VICTORIA PL
CAIRN'S LA
RATTRAY ST
BRAE
THE RUN
PINGSTONE LA
PHILPINGSTONE RD
FURNACE
TOWER GDNS
BRIDGENESS LA
BRIDGENESS RD
CARRIDEN GLADE

4

STEWART AVE
MARCHLANDS TERR
BRAEHEAD
MARCHLANDS LA
FINGASK RD
JAMES WATT AVE
BENGAL PL
KELTY AVE
MARCH MILL AVE
STEWART AVE
GRANGE TERR
HAMSDYKE
VIEWFORTH
GRAHAMSDYKE TERR
SETON TERR
GRAHAMSDYKE
GRANGE LOAN
DRUMSIDE TERR
FOUNTAINPARK
Sch
SOUTH PINGSTONE
PINGSTONE CRES
HARBOUR RD
Carriden
FORECALE TERR
KNARRES RD
ST JOHN'S
CARRIDEN BRAE

Old Manse Wood

DEAN RD
A993
KINGLASS AVE
Acad
ACADEMY RD
GRAHAM CRES
HADRIAN WAY
DRUMPARK AVE
DRUMPARK AVE
DRUM RD
Kinningars Park

Cat Craig

81

Sch
LOTHIAN CRES
CLYDESDALE ST
LOTHIAN ST
GALZE RD
DRUMACRE RD
MUIREND CT
GRAHAMSDYKE RD
Drum
The Manse of Carriden
Carriden Burn
Carriden House

MUIREPARK QT
MINGLE PL
GALZE PL
Mingle House
1 NORTHBANK PK
2 NORTHBANK DR
Kinglass Farm
Muirhouses
ACRE RD
GLENOAG WAY
HOPE COTTS
LITTLE CARRIDEN
GLEDHILL AVE
MILLER CRES
A903
A904
Willie White's Clump

3

NORTHBANK CT
REDBRAE AVE
RITCHIE PL
BORROWSTOUN RD
BRAEFOOT RD
CATHRINE GR
MINTY ST
HENRY ST
ST JOHN'S WAY
Kinglass Cottage
North Bank
Redbrae Cottages
Bonhard Cottages
Wester Bonhard
Bonhard Place

80

Bonhard House

Bonhard Old Mill
Easter Bonhard
Walton

2

Golf Course
Airngath Farm
CH
Airngath Hill
Hope Monument
Earl o' Moray Hotel
Woolstoun
B903
A904

79

Grange
Champany Inn
Groufoot
A803

Bonnytoun Cottages

1

Bonnytoun Farm
Junction 3
M9

Parkhead Small Holdings
Works
Burgh Muir

78

M9
A803
Burghmuir

00 A 01 B 02 C

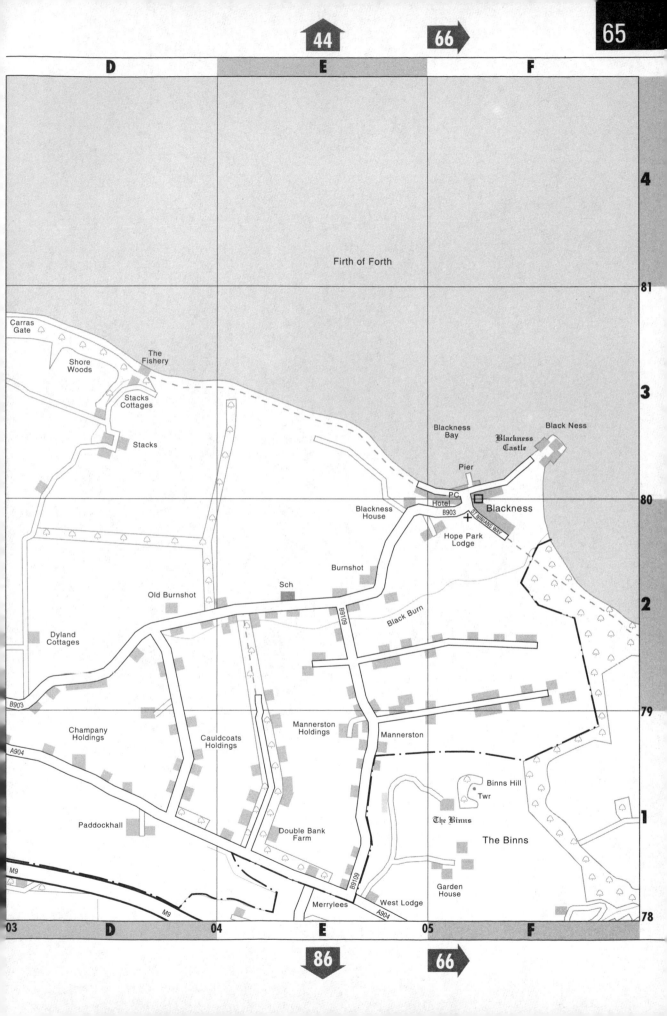

D   E   F

4

Firth of Forth

81

Carras Gate

Shore Woods

The Fishery

3

Stacks Cottages

Stacks

Blackness Bay

Black Ness

Blackness Castle

Pier

PC.

Hotel

Blackness House

B903

ST NINIAN'S WAY

Blackness

80

Hope Park Lodge

Burnshot

Sch

Old Burnshot

Black Burn

B9109

2

Dyland Cottages

79

Champany Holdings

Cauldcoats Holdings

Mannerston Holdings

Mannerston

A904

Binns Hill

Twr

1

The Binns

The Binns

Paddockhall

Double Bank Farm

B9109

M9

M9

Garden House

Merrylees

West Lodge

A904

78

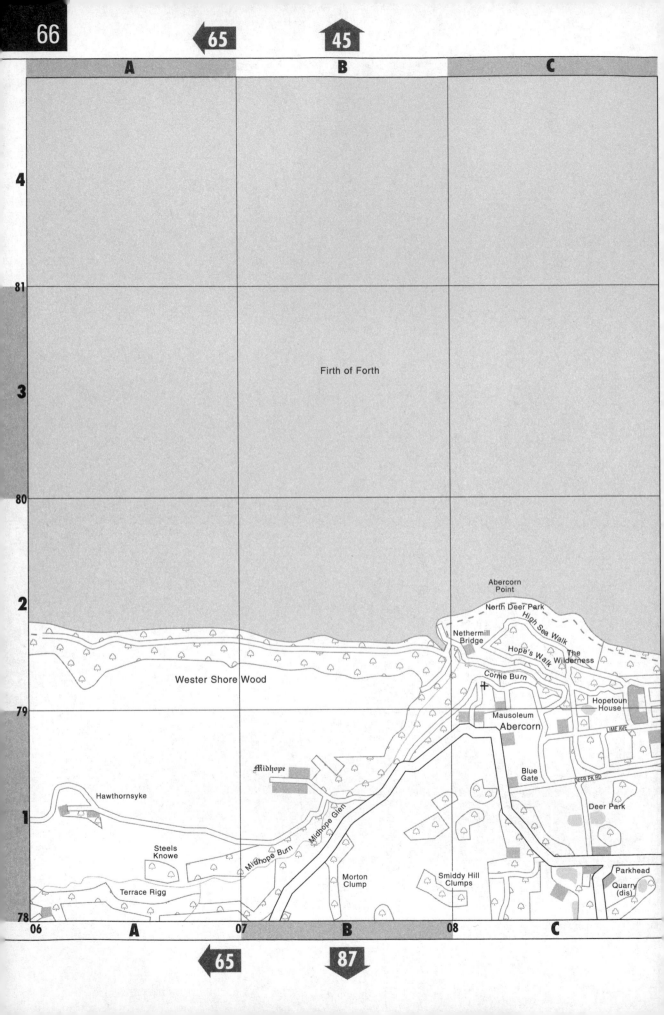

A

B

C

4

81

3

Firth of Forth

80

2

Abercorn
Point

North Deer Park

High Sea Walk

Nethermill
Bridge

Hope's Walk

The
Wilderness

Cornie Burn

Wester Shore Wood

Hopetoun
House

79

Mausoleum

Abercorn

LIME AVE

Midhope

Blue
Gate

DEER PK RD

Hawthornsyke

Midhope Glen

Deer Park

1

Steels
Knowe

Midhope Burn

Parkhead

Morton
Clump

Smiddy Hill
Clumps

Quarry
(dis)

Terrace Rigg

78

06

A

07

B

08

C

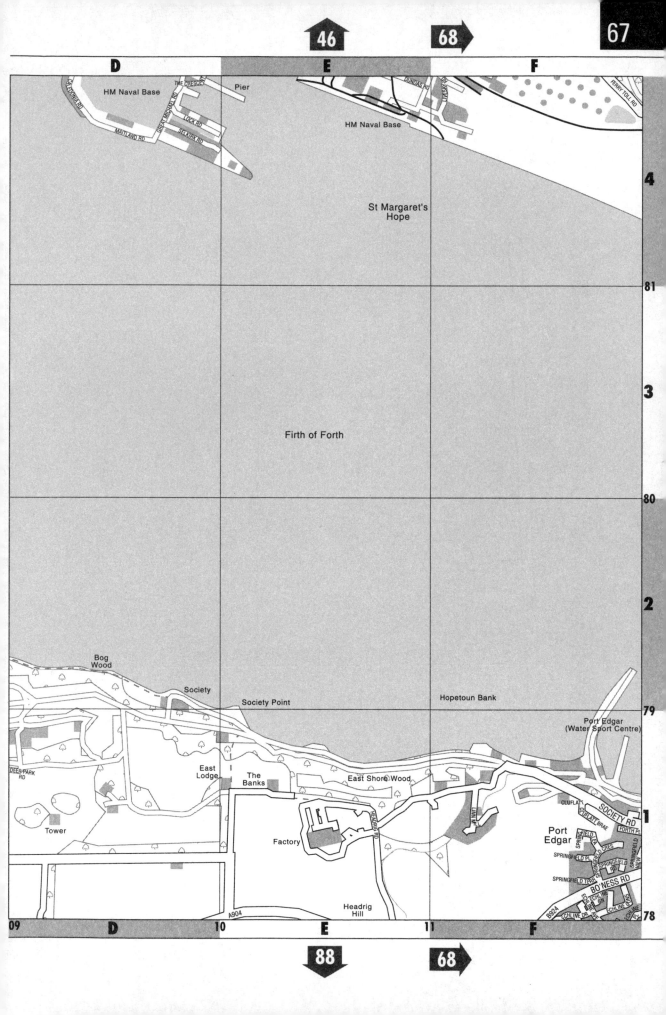

D   E   F

HM Naval Base

CALEDONIA RD

THE CRESCENT

GREAT MICHAEL RD

Pier

MAITLAND RD

LOCK RD

SELKIRK RD

DUNDAS RD

LIVESAY RD

FERRY TOLL RD

HM Naval Base

4

St Margaret's
Hope

81

3

Firth of Forth

80

2

Bog
Wood

Society

Society Point

Hopetoun Bank

79

Port Edgar
(Water Sport Centre)

DEEP PARK RD

East
Lodge

The
Banks

East Shore Wood

CLUFLAT

SOCIETY RD

CLUFLAT BRAE

FORTH PL

Tower

Factory

HEADRIG RD

LINN HF

Port
Edgar

SPRINGFIELD CRES

SPRINGFIELD VIEW

1

SPRINGFIELD PL

SPRINGFIELD LN

SPRINGFIELD TERR

SPRINGFIELD RD

BO'NESS RD

A904

Headrig
Hill

B924

ECHLINE DR

ECHLINE AVE

ECHLINE GDN

ECHLINE PL

78

09   D   10   E   11   F

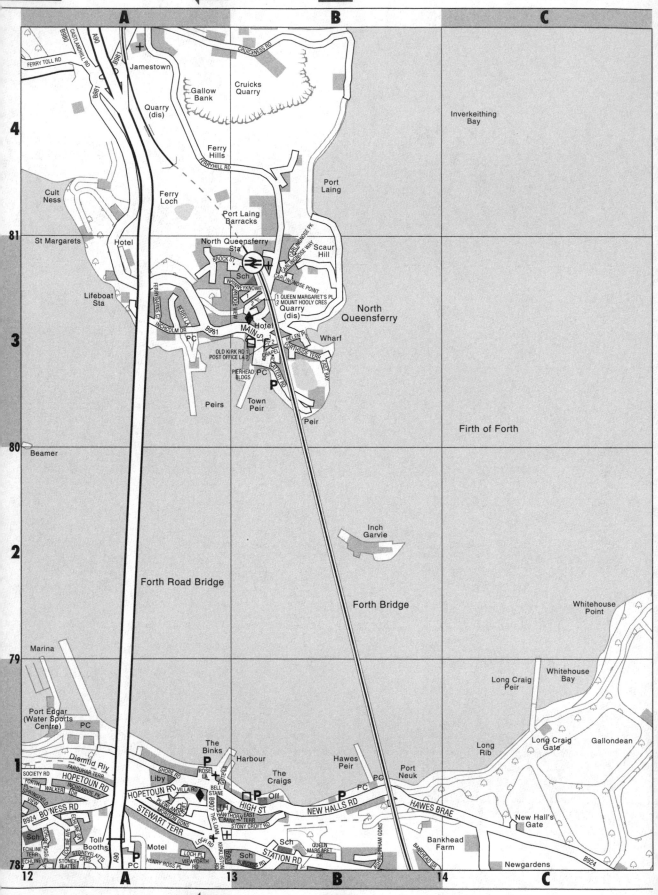

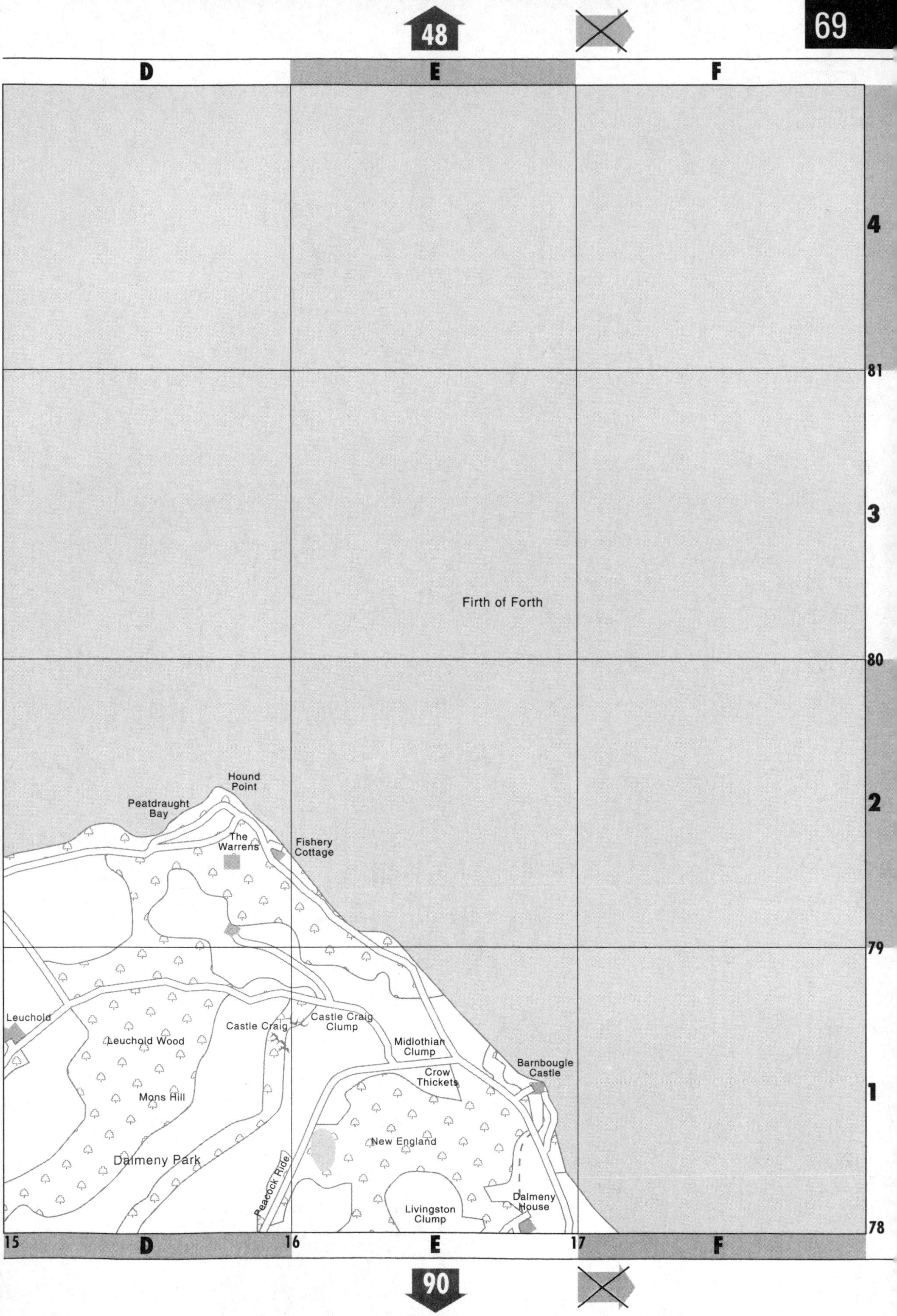

D   E   F

4

81

3

Firth of Forth

80

2

Hound
Point

Peatdraught
Bay

The
Warrens

Fishery
Cottage

79

Leuchold

Castle Craig
Clump

Castle Craig

Midlothian
Clump

Leuchold Wood

Barnbougle
Castle

Crow
Thickets

1

Mons Hill

New England

Dalmeny Park

Peacock Ride

Livingston
Clump

Dalmeny
House

78

15   D   16   E   17   F

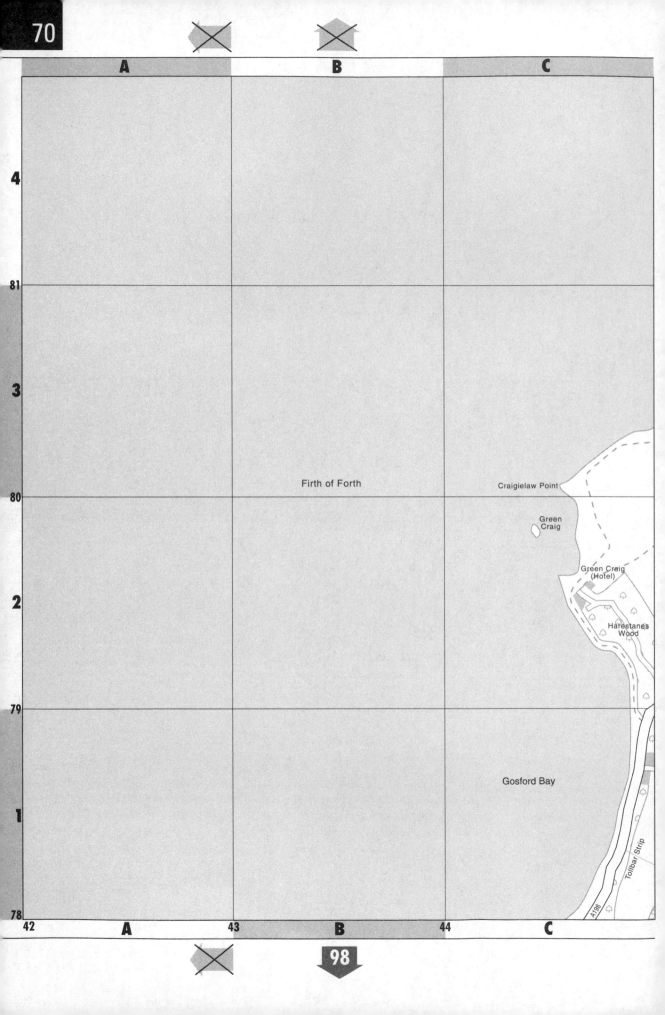

Firth of Forth

Craigielaw Point

Green
Craig

Green Craig
(Hotel)

Harestanes
Wood

Gosford Bay

Tollbar Strip

A198

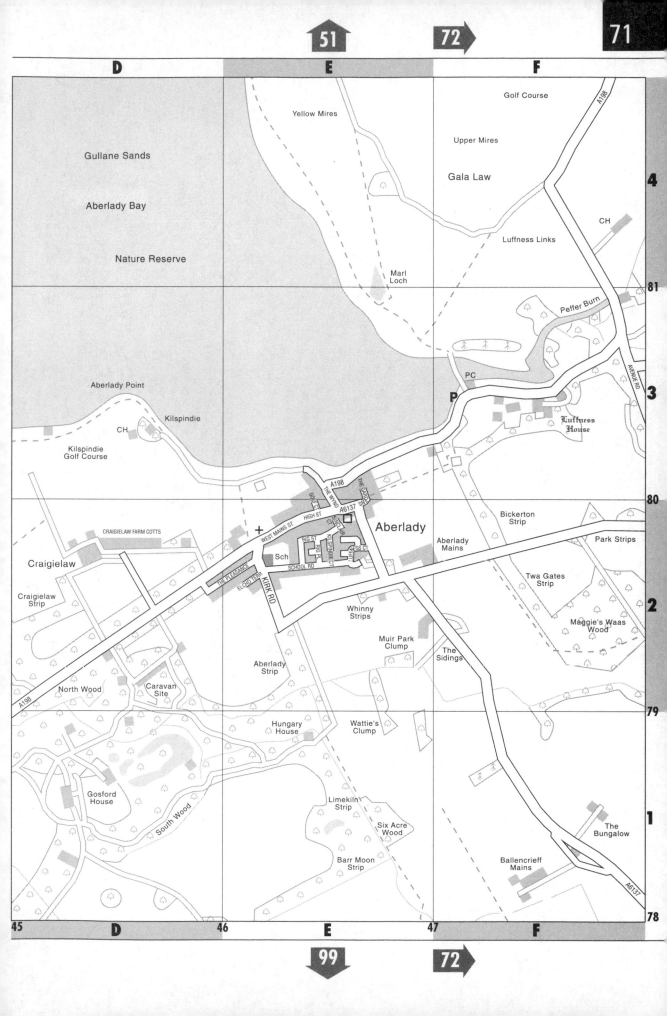

D

E

F

Yellow Mires

Golf Course

Upper Mires

Gullane Sands

Gala Law

4

Aberlady Bay

Luffness Links

CH

Nature Reserve

Marl
Loch

81

Peffer Burn

PC

Aberlady Point

P

Luffness
House

3

Kilspindie

CH

Kilspindie
Golf Course

A198

THE WYND

THE GABLES

AVENUE RD

CRAIGIELAW FARM COTTS

GOLF CT

HIGH ST

A6137

Bickerton
Strip

80

Craigielaw

WEST MAINS ST

+

SINCLAIR CT

Aberlady

Park Strips

Craigielaw
Strip

THE PLEASANCE

Sch

RIG ST

RIG PL

KILSPINDIE CT

LUFFNESS CT

Aberlady
Mains

Twa Gates
Strip

2

ELCHO TERR

SCHOOL RD

KIRK RD

Whinny
Strips

Maggie's Waas
Wood

North Wood

A198

Caravan
Site

Aberlady
Strip

Muir Park
Clump

The
Sidings

79

Hungary
House

Wattie's
Clump

Gosford
House

South Wood

Limekiln
Strip

Six Acre
Wood

1

The
Bungalow

Barr Moon
Strip

Ballencrieff
Mains

A6137

78

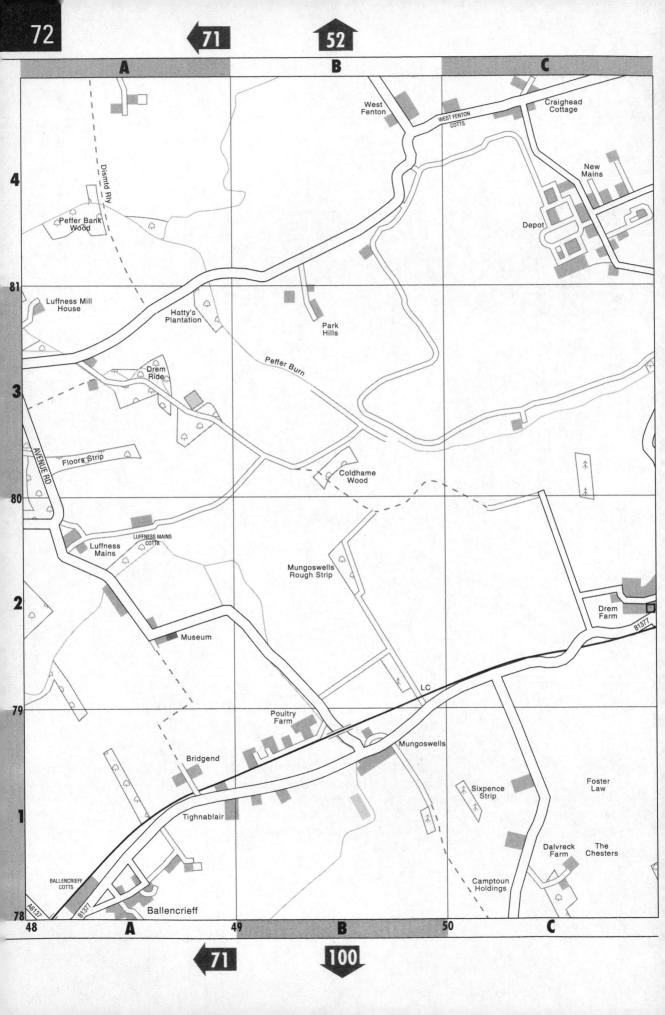

A　　　　　　　　　　B　　　　　　　　　　C

West
Fenton

WEST FENTON
COTTS

Craighead
Cottage

4

New
Mains

Dismtd Rly

Depot

Peffer Bank
Wood

81

Luffness Mill
House

Hatty's
Plantation

Park
Hills

Peffer Burn

Drem
Ride

3

AVENUE RD

Floors Strip

Coldhame
Wood

80

Luffness Mains
Cotts

Luffness
Mains

Mungoswells
Rough Strip

Drem
Farm

2

B1377

Museum

LC

Poultry
Farm

79

Mungoswells

Bridgend

Sixpence
Strip

Foster
Law

1

Tighnablair

Dalvreck
Farm

The
Chesters

Camptoun
Holdings

BALLENCRIEFF
COTTS

A6137

B1377

Ballencrieff

78

48　　　　A　　　　49　　　　B　　　　50　　　　C

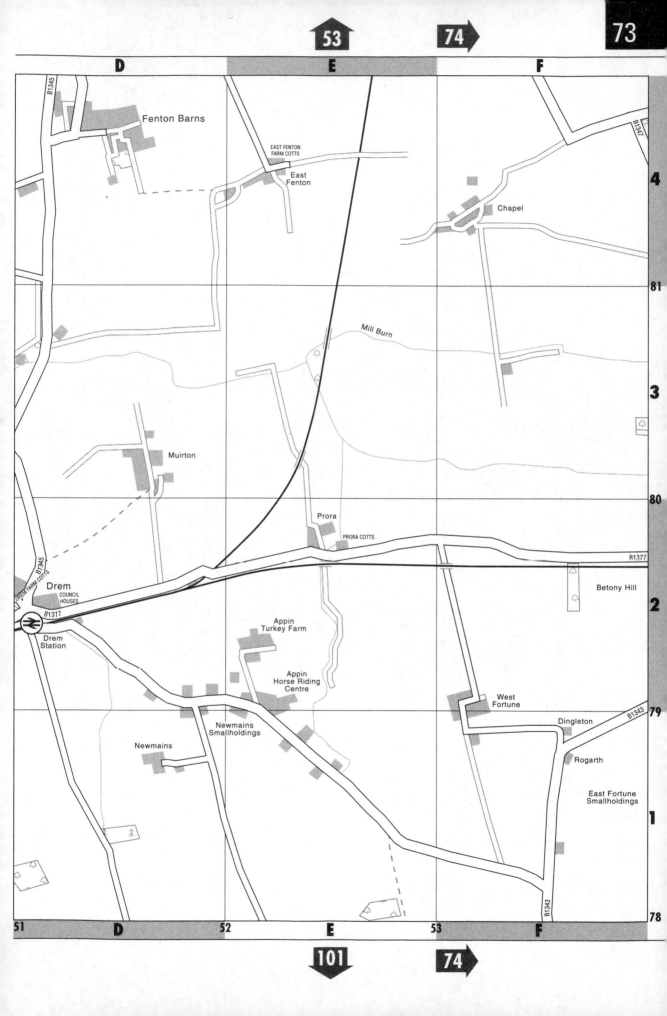

D
E
F

Fenton Barns

EAST FENTON
FARM COTTS

East
Fenton

Chapel

4

81

Mill Burn

3

Muirton

80

Prora

PRORA COTTS

B1377

Drem
COUNCIL
HOUSES

Betony Hill

B1377

2

Drem
Station

Appin
Turkey Farm

Appin
Horse Riding
Centre

West
Fortune

Dingleton

B1343

79

Newmains
Smallholdings

Newmains

Rogarth

East Fortune
Smallholdings

1

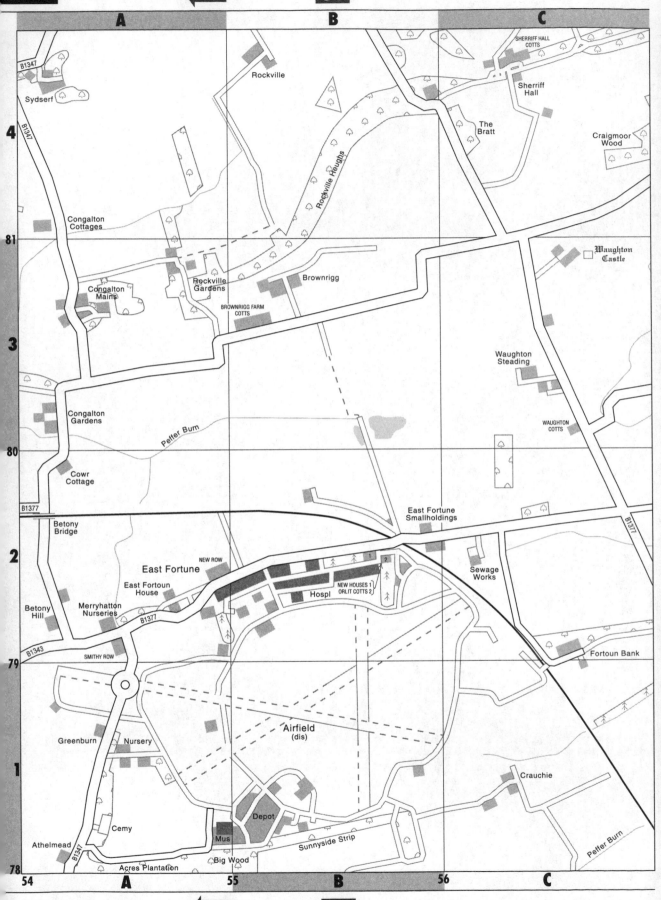

A   B   C

B1347
Sydserf
B1347

Rockville

SHERRIFF HALL COTTS

Sherriff Hall

The Bratt

Craigmoor Wood

4

Rockville Heughs

Congalton Cottages

81

Waughton Castle

Brownrigg

Congalton Mains

Rockville Gardens

BROWNRIGG FARM COTTS

Congalton Gardens

3

Waughton Steading

Peffer Burn

WAUGHTON COTTS

80

Cowr Cottage

East Fortune Smallholdings

B1377

Betony Bridge

2

New Row

East Fortune

1   2

New Houses 1 Orlit Cotts 2

Sewage Works

B1377

East Fortoun House

Merryhatton Nurseries

B1377

Hospl

Betony Hill

B1343

Smithy Row

Fortoun Bank

79

Greenburn

Nursery

Airfield (dis)

1

Crauchie

Cemy

Depot

Mus

Sunnyside Strip

Peffer Burn

Athelmead

B1347

Big Wood

Acres Plantation

78

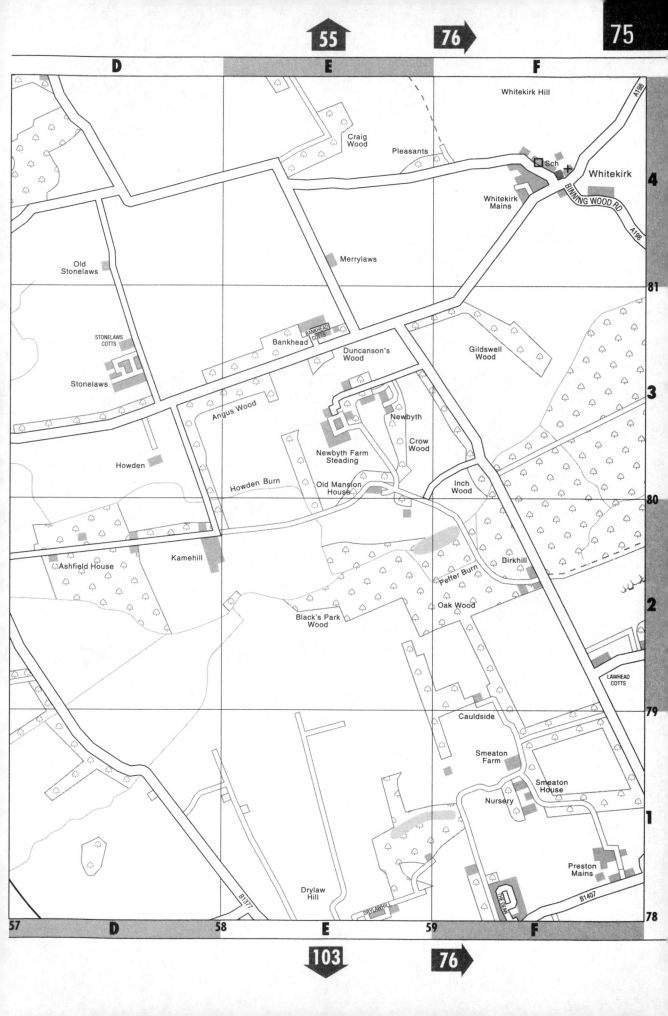

D
E
F

Whitekirk Hill

Craig Wood

Pleasants

Sch

Whitekirk

Whitekirk Mains

4

BINNING WOOD RD

A198

A198

Old Stonelaws

Merrylaws

81

STONELAWS COTTS

BANKHEAD COTTS

Bankhead

Duncanson's Wood

Gildswell Wood

Stonelaws

Angus Wood

Newbyth

3

Crow Wood

Howden

Newbyth Farm Steading

Howden Burn

Old Mansion House

Inch Wood

80

Ashfield House

Kamehill

Birkhill

Peffer Burn

Black's Park Wood

Oak Wood

2

LAWHEAD COTTS

79

Cauldside

Smeaton Farm

Smeaton House

Nursery

1

Preston Mains

Drylaw Hill

DRYLAWHILL

THE DEAN

B1377

B1407

78

A B C

4

Lochhouses Links

Ravensheugh Sands

Peffer Burn

Barebanes Wood

Brownrig Wood

Lochhouses

A198

Whitekirk Bridge

GAUGER'S BUSH

81

Gibb's Hill Wood

Garleton Walk

Tyninghame Links

P

Gauger's Bush

Bruce's Circle

3

Binning Wood

LIMETREE WLK

Old Charcoal Plantation

FIVE GATES

The Avenue

Little Binning Wood

Gardens

80

Lawhead Hill

Tyninghame House

Monument

The Wilderness

Mast Wood

2

St Baldred's Cottage

The Mast

Lawhead

Tyninghame Mains

Buist's Embankment

Mosshouse Point

Tyninghame

B1407

Salt Greens Plantation

79

Dam Bridge

The Jetty

Firth Plantation

1

Acre Plantation

Tyninghame Bridge

Ware Road

B1407

River Tyne

A198

78

60 A 61 B 62 C

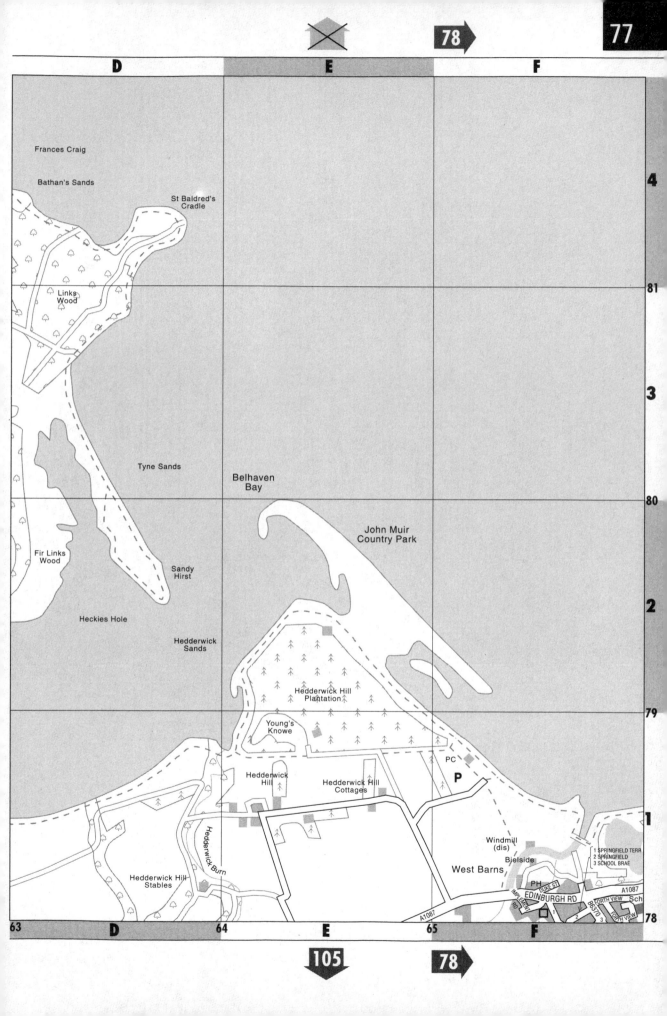

D

E

F

4

81

3

Frances Craig

Bathan's Sands

St Baldred's
Cradle

Links
Wood

Tyne Sands

Belhaven
Bay

80

John Muir
Country Park

Fir Links
Wood

Sandy
Hirst

2

Heckies Hole

Hedderwick
Sands

Hedderwick Hill
Plantation

79

Young's
Knowe

PC

P

Hedderwick
Hill

Hedderwick Hill
Cottages

1

Hedderwick Burn

Windmill
(dis)

1 SPRINGFIELD TERR
2 SPRINGFIELD
3 SCHOOL BRAE

Bielside

West Barns

Hedderwick Hill
Stables

PH

DUKE ST

Sch

A1087

EDINBURGH RD

FORTH VIEW

A1087

B6370

IMPLEMENT RD

FORTH VIEW

78

D

E

A1087

F

A　　　　　　　　B　　　　　　　　C

4

81

3

80

2

Long Craigs

Caravan
Site

The Gripes

Coastguard
Lookout

Meikle
Spiker

Victoria
Harbour

CUSTOM HOUSE
SQ

Old
Harbour

St Margarets

CH

Golf Course

BAYSWELL PK

MARINE RD

GARDENER ST

CASTLE GATE

VICTORIA PL

CASTLE ST

Lifeboat
Sta

BAYSWELL RD

North Rd

MAYVILLE
PK

PC

WESTGATE

LAWSON PL

P

PC

NORTH RD

VIEW FORTH

FLOORS TERR

GARDENER RD

PARSONSPOOL

Liby

1 COLVIN ST
2 THE VENNEL

79

Winterfield
Mains

KNOCKENHAIR RD

YORK PK

POST PK

WINGATE CRES

LAUDERDALE
CRES

LETHA
PK

LETHAM RD

DELISLE

WEST
PORT

A1087

HIGH ST

SILVER ST

CHURCH ST

WOODBUSH

WOODBUSH BRAE

Coastguard Sta

WOODBUSH
CT

BACK RD

PARK AVE

BELHAVEN RD

DOON AVE

BOROUGHDALES

Sch

Sch

PC

TH

COSSARS
WYND

PC

Sch

Sch

GALA GN

LAMMERMUIR CRES

COUNTESS
AVE

EAST LINKS RD

BOWMONT TERR

GOLF HOUSE RD

1

HIGH ST

SOUTH ST

GEORGE ST

SUMMERFIELD RD

ROWAN ST

ELM ST

COUNTESS RD

F Sta

STATION RD

P

QUEEN'S RD

SPOTT RD

ROXBURGHE
TERR

ROXBURGHE PK

Belhaven

DUKE ST

BREWERY
LA

POPLAR ST

PINE ST

BEECH ST

ASH GR

HAZEL
CT

DUNBAR

Dunbar
Station

NEWHOUSE AVE

SPOTT RD

GOLDENSTONES

NEWHOUSE PL

CH

SEAFIELD
CRES

Retreat

Lochend
Gardens

LATCH
RD

BRUNT
CT

ASHFIELD CRES

BEACHMONT
TERR

BEACHMONT
PL

EDINBURGH RD

A1087

Rosebank
House

Hospl

Lochend
Kennels

Hallhill
Cottages

BRUNT RD

LOCHEND RD

LOCHEND
AVE

A1087

78

Sch

66　　　　　　A　　　　　　67　　　　　　B　　　　　　68　　　　　　C

Golf Course

Sports & Social Centre

West Links

Lawrie's Den

The Vaults

Vaults Wood

107

A
B
C

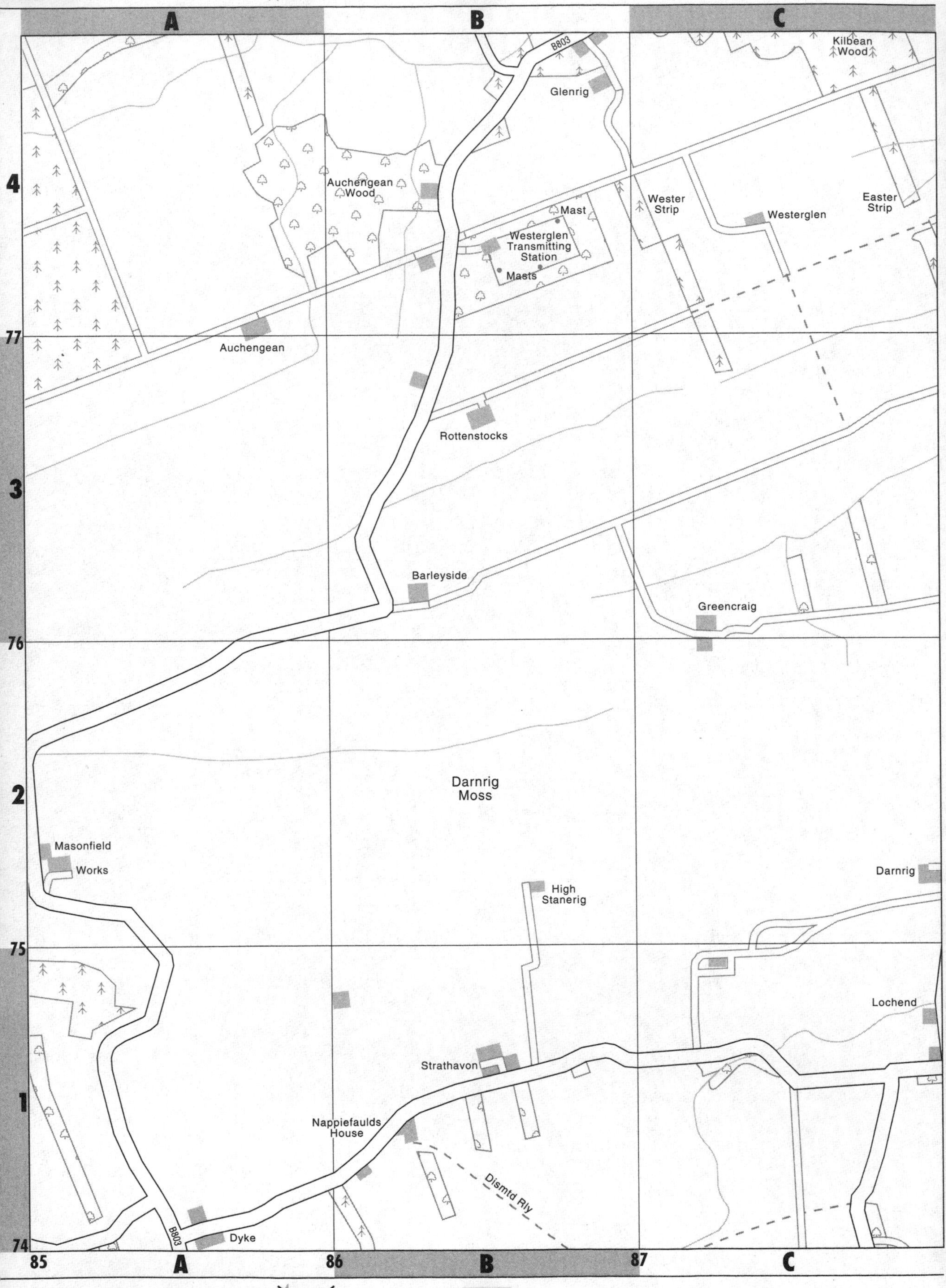

4

Kilbean
Wood

B803

Glenrig

Mast

Westerglen
Transmitting
Station

Masts

Wester
Strip

Westerglen

Easter
Strip

Auchengean
Wood

77

Auchengean

3

Rottenstocks

76

Barleyside

Greencraig

2

Darnrig
Moss

Darnrig

Masonfield
Works

High
Stanerig

75

Lochend

1

Strathavon

Nappiefaulds
House

Dismtd Rly

74

B803

Dyke

A
B
C

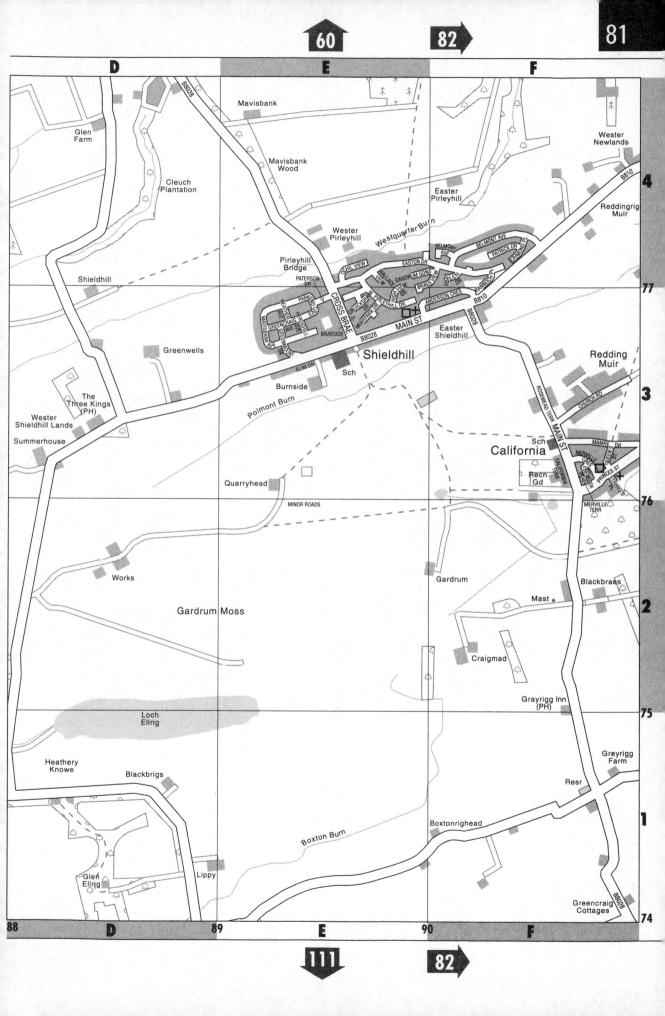

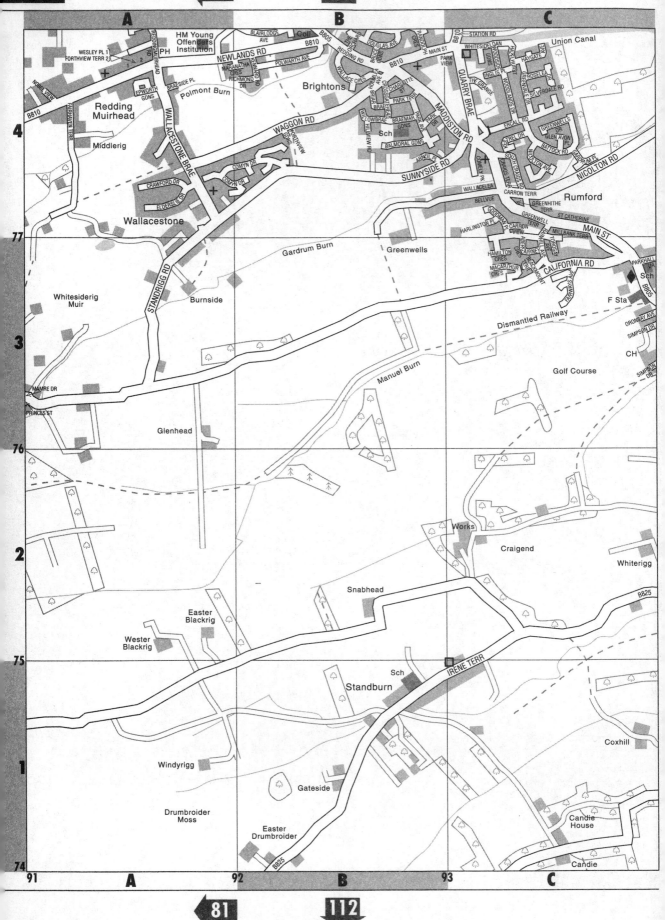

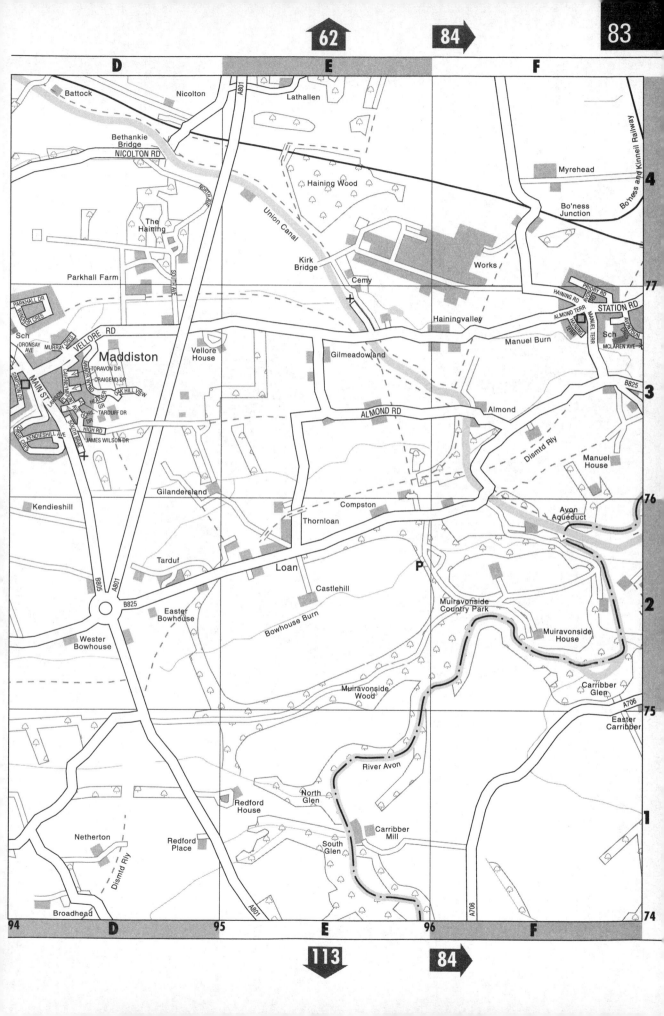

D

Battock
Nicolton
Lathallen

Bethankie
Bridge

NICOLTON RD

NORTH AVE

A801

Union Canal

Haining Wood

Myrehead

Bo'ness
Junction

Bo'ness and Kinneil Railway

4

The
Haining

SOUTH AVE

Kirk
Bridge

Cemy

Works

Parkhall Farm

PARKHALL DR

WINDSOR CRES

Sch

ORONSAY AVE

MURRAY CRES

VELLORE RD

CARRIBER WYND

Vellore
House

Gilmeadowland

Haining RD
PRIORY RD

ALMOND TERR

HAINING

MANUEL TERR

STATION RD

Sch

AVON LOUN

MCLAREN AVE

Manuel Burn

Hainingvalley

77

Maddiston

TORAVON DR

MANOR WYND

CRAIGEND DR

OAK HILL VIEW

HEATHER GR

TARDUFF DR

OCHIL DR

SIMPSON DR

MAIN ST

KENDIESHILL AVE

HIGH RD

SOUTHBRAE

JAMES WILSON DR

ALMOND RD

Almond

B825

Dismtd Rly

Manuel
House

3

Gilandersland

Kendieshill

Compston

Thornloan

Avon
Aqueduct

76

Tarduf

Loan

Castlehill

Bowhouse Burn

P

Muiravonside
Country Park

Muiravonside
House

Carribber
Glen

A706

2

B805

A801

B825

Easter
Bowhouse

Wester
Bowhouse

Muiravonside
Wood

Easter
Carribber

75

Netherton

Redford
House

North
Glen

River Avon

Redford
Place

Carribber
Mill

Dismtd Rly

South
Glen

A706

1

Broadhead

94

D

95

E

96

F

74

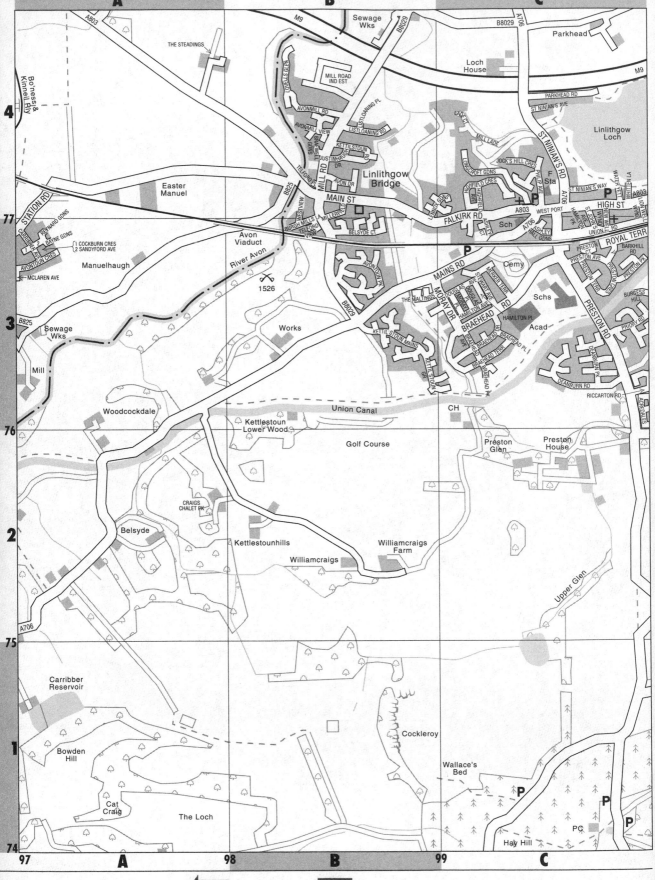

A   B   C

M9

Sewage Wks

B8029

THE STEADINGS

B8029

A706

Parkhead

4

Bo'ness & Kinneil Rly

MILL ROAD IND EST

Loch House

M9

LOVELL'S GLEN

AVONMILL RD

PARKHEAD RD

St NINIAN'S AVE

Linlithgow Loch

AVONMILL VIEW

LISTLOANING PL

LISTLOANING RD

MILL LADE

JOCK'S HILL CRES

F Sta

St NINIAN'S WAY

Easter Manuel

KETTILSTOUN
JUSTIN WAY

LONGCROFT GDNS

PHILIP AVE

WATER YETT

St NINIAN'S RD

RICHFIELD CRES

AVON DR

HIGHFIELD

Linlithgow Bridge

MILL RD

LADE CT

MAIN ST

B825

TELFORD RD

Station Rd

MILLER CT

BELSYDE CT

P

West Port

HIGH ST

LOANHEAD

77

Avon Viaduct

BURGH MILLS

TELFORD VIEW

WESTVIEW

FALKIRK RD

Sch

A803

A706

ROYAL TERR

Reynard Gdns

1 COCKBURN CRES
2 SANDYFORD AVE

River Avon

P

UNION ST

PRESTON CT

BARKHILL RD

BAYNE GDNS

AVONTOUN PK

Cemy

PRESTON AVE

PRESTON PK

CARRIBBER AVE

MAINS RD

MERCER TERR

Burgess Hill

AVONTOUN CRES

1526

B8029

The Maltings

MORAY DR

STEWART AVE

PRIORY RD

McLAREN AVE

Manuelhaugh

DOUGLAS

BRAEHEAD

Schs

HAMILTON PL

Acad

DEANBURN HILL

3

B825

Works

KETTILSTOUN MAINS

HAMILTON AVE

BRAEHEAD TERR

BRAEHEAD PL

PRESTON RD

Sewage Wks

KETTILSTOUN BR

BRAEHEAD PK

Mill

DEANBURN RD

RICCARTON RD

ACREDALES

Woodcockdale

Union Canal

CH

76

Kettlestoun Lower Wood

Preston Glen

Preston House

Golf Course

CRAIGS CHALET PK

2

Belsyde

Kettlestounhills

Williamcraigs Farm

Williamcraigs

Upper Glen

A706

75

Carribber Reservoir

1

Bowden Hill

Cockleroy

Wallace's Bed

P

P

P

Cat Craig

The Loch

PC

Hay Hill

74

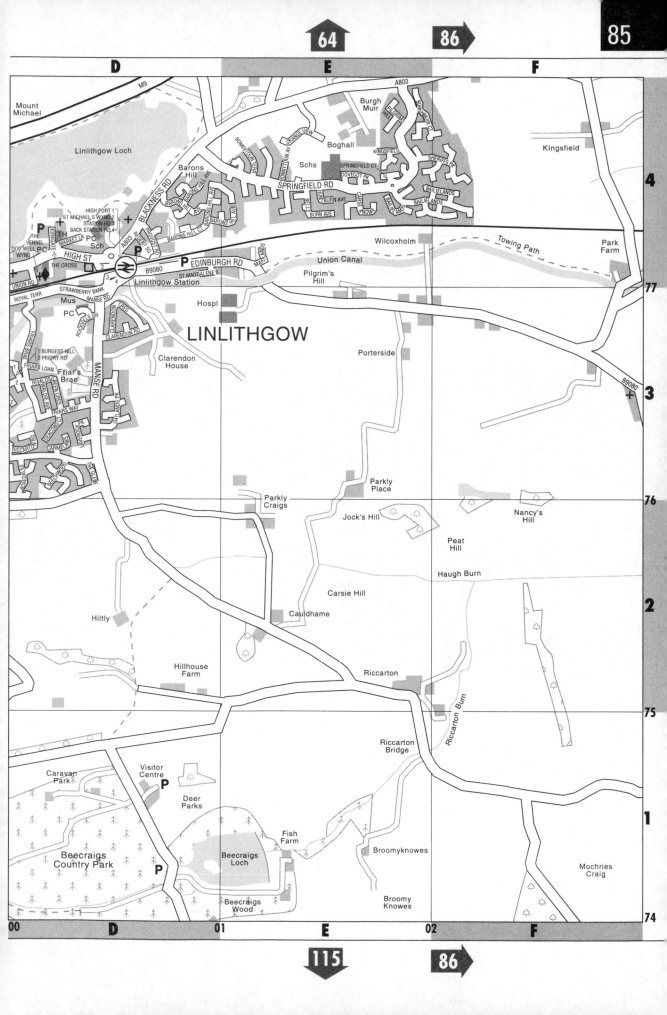

85

65

A   B   C

4

M9

Works

A904

Errick Burn

B9046

M9

Pardovan Burn

Old
Philpstoun

Pardovan
House

Pardovan
Holdings

THE
AVENUE

PARDOVAN
CRES

MAIN ST

CHURCH CT

Philpstoun

77

Union Canal

Champfleurie
House

Fairniehill

Spoil
Heap

B9046

3

B9080

Cameron
Knowe

Bridgend
Farm

Haugh Burn

76

PH

Sch

Threemiletown

Sewage
Works

WILLOWDEAN

AULDHILL
TERR

AULDHILL DR

AULDHILL PL

AULDHILL
COTTS

Gateside

Burnside

THE
COTTS

AULDHILL
ENTRY

AULDHILL RD

WOODSIDE PL

Bridgend

REDHOUSE
COTTS

2

AULDHILL CRES

WOODSIDE
TERR

Waterstone

75

1

Little
Ochiltree

Ecclesmachan Burn

B9046

74

03   A   04   B   05   C

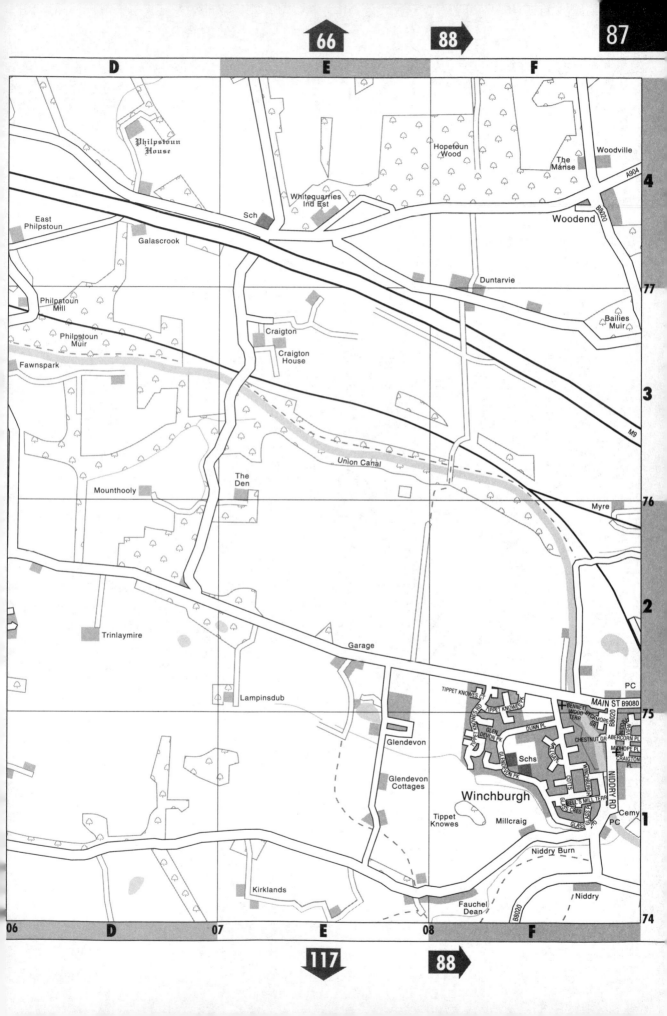

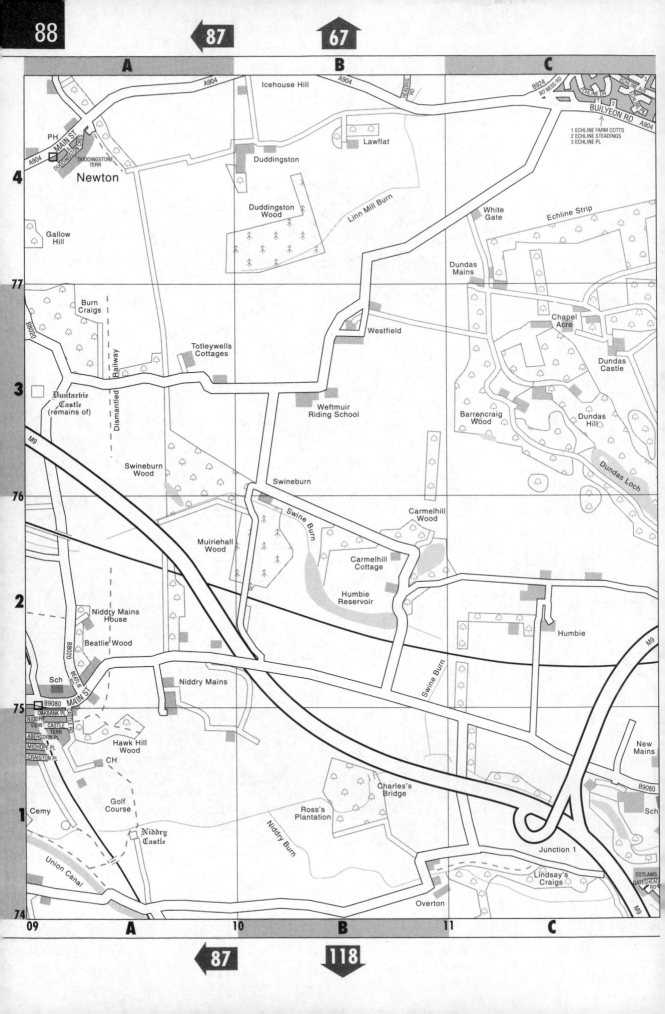

QUEENSFERRY

Newbigging

North Lodge

CH

Golf Course

Milton

Craigend

Dolphington Burn

Craigbrae

Carlowrie Cottages

Easter Carlowrie

Carlowrie Farm

Almondhill Cottages

Almondhill

Newmains Farm La

Wheatlands

Carlowrie

Foxhall

River Almond

Cat Stane

Boathouse Bridge

Kirkliston

Ferry Muir

F Sta

Works

Wester Dalmeny

Dalmeny Station

Bankhead Cottages

Crossall Hill

Easter Dalmeny

Dalmeny

Sch

Main St

Sch

Sewage Works

Oil Storage Depot

Standingstane Rd

BUILYEON RD A904 A8000

A90

Main St

Queensferry Rd

Station Rd

B9080 Main St

Almondside

D E F

4

77

3

76

2

1

75

74

12 13 14
D E F

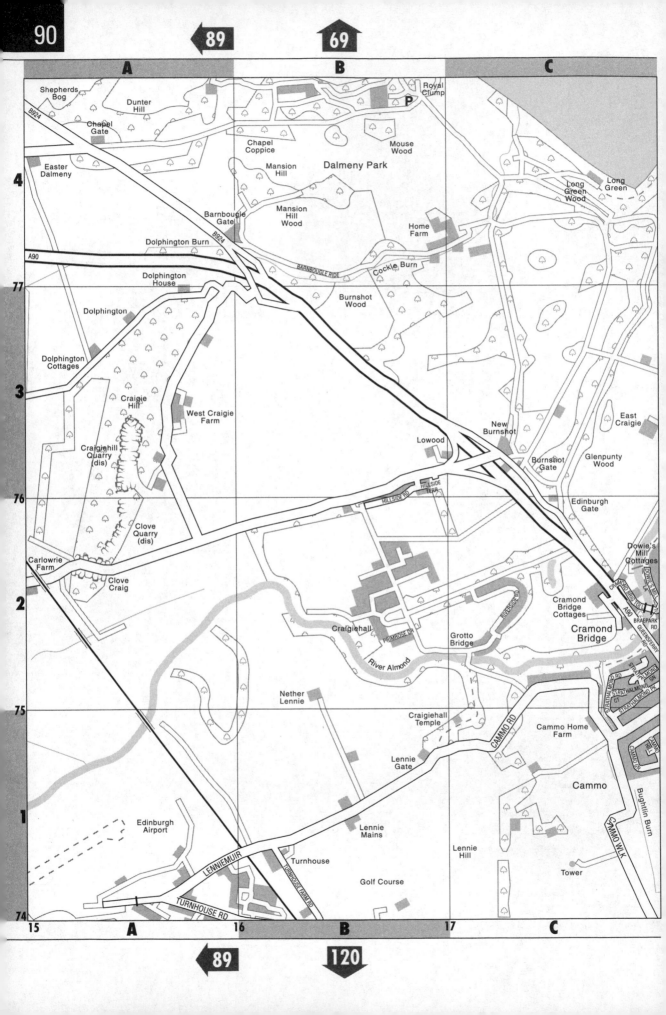

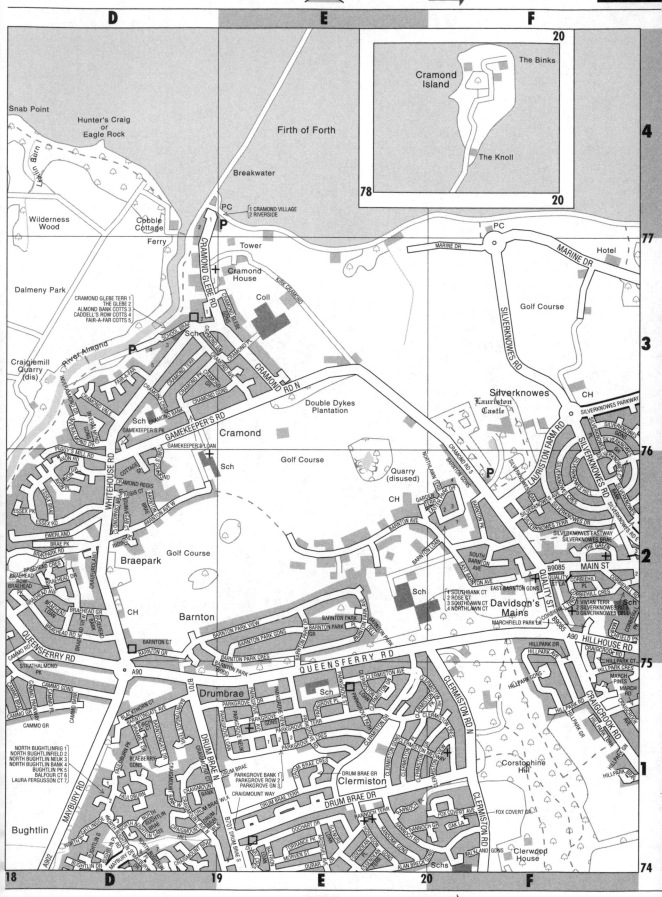

D   **E**   **F**

20

Cramond Island

The Binks

Cramond Island

The Knoll

78   **20**

4

Snab Point

Hunter's Craig or Eagle Rock

Firth of Forth

Breakwater

Wilderness Wood

Cobble Cottage

PC

1 CRAMOND VILLAGE
2 RIVERSIDE

P

PC

77

Ferry

Tower

MARINE DR

MARINE DR

Hotel

Dalmeny Park

Cramond House

KIRK CRAMOND

Coll

SILVERKNOWES RD

Golf Course

CRAMOND GLEBE RD

CRAMOND GLEBE TERR 1
THE GLEBE 2
ALMOND BANK COTTS 3
CADDELL'S ROW COTTS 4
FAIR-A-FAR COTTS 5

Sch

3

Craigiemill Quarry (dis)

River Almond

Silverknowes

Lauriston Castle

CH

FAIR-A-FAR

CRAMOND RD N

GAMEKEEPER'S RD

Cramond

Double Dykes Plantation

SILVERKNOWES PARKWAY

76

WHITEHOUSE RD

GAMEKEEPER'S LOAN

Sch

Golf Course

Quarry (disused)

NORTHLAWN TERR

BARNTON GDNS

CRAMOND RD S

P

CH

GARDEN TERR

EAST PARK GR

SILVERKNOWES TERR

SILVERKNOWES EASTWAY
SILVERKNOWES BRAE
THE GREEN

2

Braepark

Golf Course

BARNTON AVE

BARNTON LOAN

SOUTH BARNTON AVE

EAST BARNTON AVE

B9085

MAIN ST

CORBIEHILL PL

CORBIEHILL CRES

1 SOUTHBANK CT
2 ROSE CT
3 SOUTHLAWN CT
4 NORTHLAWN CT

1 VIVIAN TERR
2 SILVERKNOWES TERR
3 SILVERKNOWES DELL

CH

Barnton

Sch

Davidson's Mains

QUALITY ST LA

Sch

BARNTON PARK VIEW

BARNTON PARK

BARNTON PARK PL

EAST BARNTON GDNS

MARCHFIELD PARK LA

A90

HILLHOUSE RD

BARNTON CT

BARNTON GR

BARNTON PARK CRES

QUEENSFERRY RD

HILLPARK DR

HILLPARK AVE

CRAIGCROOK RD

HILLPARK GDNS

HILLPARK CT

HILLPARK CRES

75

Cammo Rd

QUEENSFERRY RD

STRATHALMOND PK

A90

B701

Drumbrae

PARKGROVE DR

Sch

GROVE PL

CLERMISTON AVE

CLERMISTON HILL

CLERMISTON RD N

HILLPARK GDNS

MARCH PINES

MARCH RD

CAMMO GDNS

PARKGROVE GDNS

PARKGROVE TERR

CLERMISTON MEDWAY

CRAIGCROOK AVE

HILLPARK GR

CAMMO GR

BLACKTHORN CT

PARKGROVE AVE

PARKGROVE VIEW

PARKGROVE CRES

CLERMISTON GDNS

Corstophine Hill

HILLPARK BRAE

1

NORTH BUGHTLINRIG 1
NORTH BUGHTLINFIELD 2
NORTH BUGHTLIN NEUK 3
NORTH BUGHTLIN BANK 4
BUGHTLIN PK 5
BALFOUR CT 6
LAURA FERGUSSON CT 7

MAYBURY RD

BLEABERRY GDNS

DRUM BRAE N

PARKGROVE BANK 1
PARKGROVE ROW 2
PARKGROVE GN 3

DRUM BRAE GR

Clermiston

CRAIGMOUNT WAY

DRUM BRAE TERR

DRUM BRAE DR

RANNOCH TERR

FOX COVERT AVE

FOX COVERT BR

CLERMISTON RD

Clerwood House

Bughtlin

BUGHTLIN DR

MORVEN ST

ALAN BRECK GDNS

Schs

FALKLAND GDNS

74

18   **D**   **19**   **E**   **20**   **F**

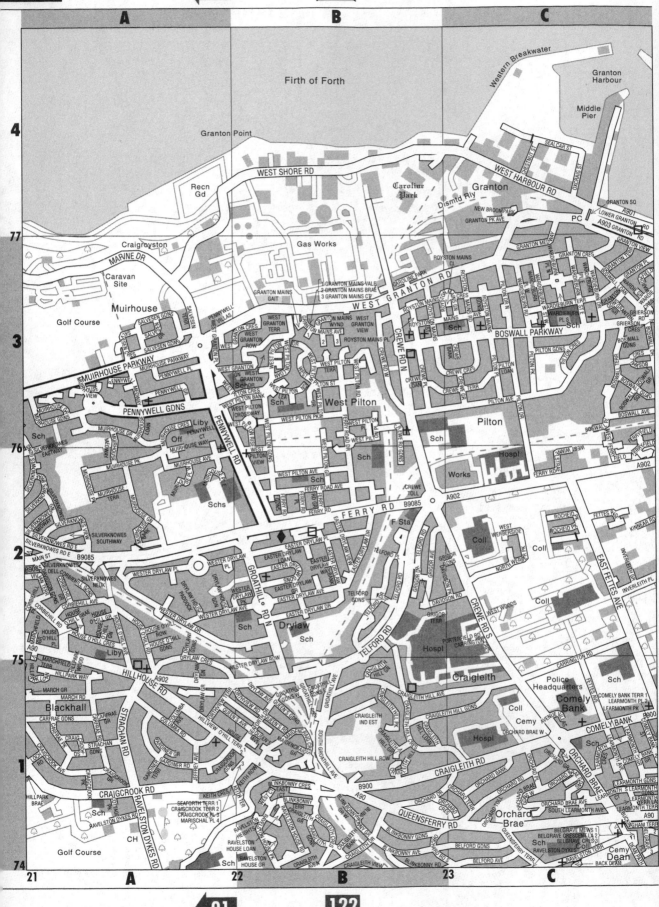

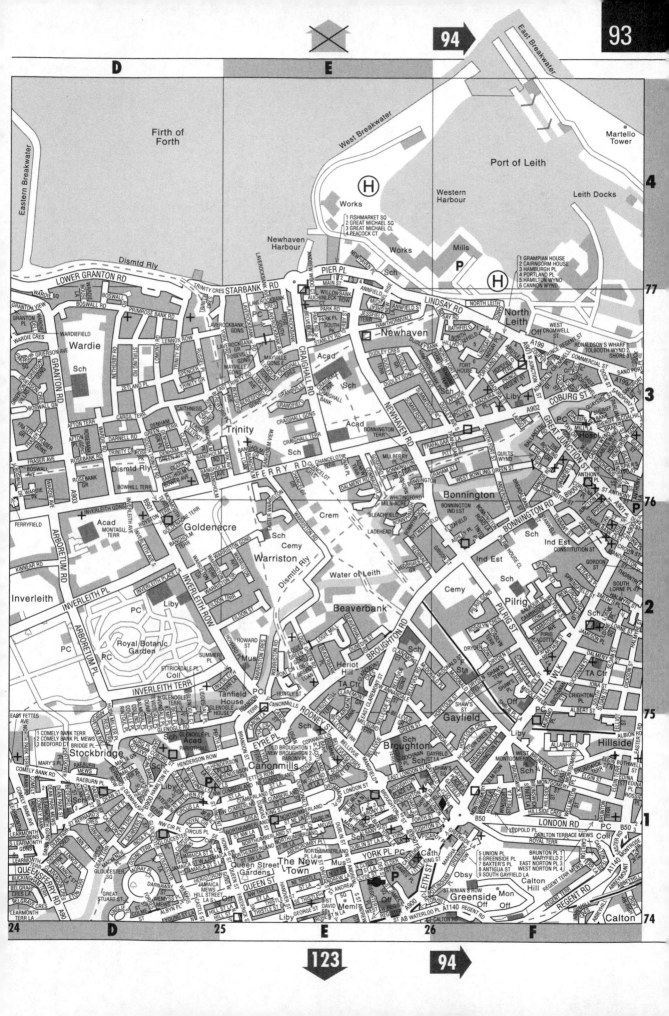

A   B   C

4

Works

Port of Leith

Firth of Forth

77

Docks

East Sands
of Leith

PC

Leith

PC

COMMERCIAL
ST

PC

3

A199

SHORE

Chapel La

Baltic St

A199

Albert Rd

SALAMANDER ST

MARINE ESPL

CONSTITUTION ST

LINKS PL

CARBON PL

76

South Leith

Sch

Sewage
Works

Seafield

LC

Leith
Links

Coll

COCHRANE PL 1
ELM PL 2
FINGZIES PL 3
ROSEVALE PL 4
PARKVALE PL 5
NOBLE PL 6
LINDEAN PL 7

CLAREMONT PK

Cemy

Grem

Claremont
Park

SEAFIELD RD

EAST HERMITAGE PL

RESTALRIG RD

CRAIGENTINNY AVENUE N

2

Acad

Coll

Recn
Gd

Sch

Hermitage

Hospl

Golf Course

CH

FILLYSIDE RD

Quarryholes

Recn
Gds

Cemy

Stadium

Lochend

SLEIGH DR

Restalrig

Craigentinny

SEAFIELD ROAD E

75

Drum

Meadowbank

Sch

CRAIGENTINNY RD

WAKEFIELD AVE

A199

1

Abbeyhill

MARIONVILLE RD

MARIONVILLE AVE

Sch

Tech
Inst
A1140

Sports
Centre

LONDON RD

PORTOBELLO RD

Piershill

Parsons
Green

Hospl

Jock's
Lodge

Piershill
Cemy

Mountcastle

74

27   A   28   B   29   C

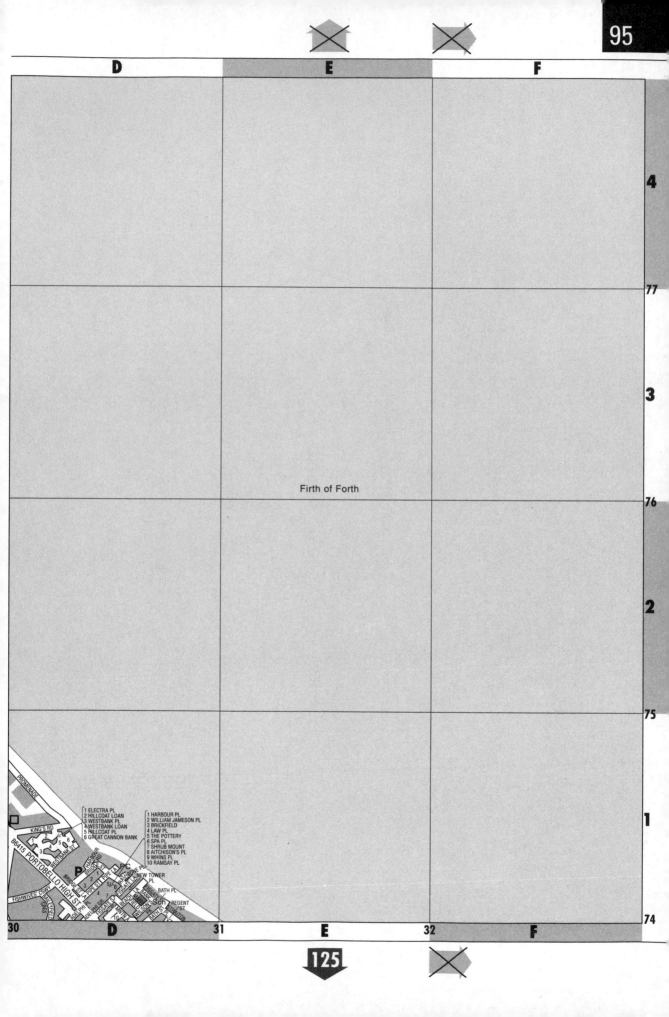

Firth of Forth

1 ELECTRA PL
2 HILLCOAT LOAN
3 WESTBANK PL
4 WESTBANK LOAN
5 HILLCOAT PL
6 GREAT CANNON BANK

1 HARBOUR PL
2 WILLIAM JAMESON PL
3 BRICKFIELD
4 LAW PL
5 THE POTTERY
6 SPA PL
7 SHRUB MOUNT
8 AITCHISON'S PL
9 WHINS PL
10 RAMSAY PL

PROMENADE
KING'S RD
B6415 PORTOBELLO HIGH ST
FISHWIVES CSWY
HARBOUR
BRIDGE ST
PIPE ST
BRIDGE ST
RATHBONE PL
TOWER PL
NEW TOWER PL
BATH PL
REGENT ST
BATH'S PL

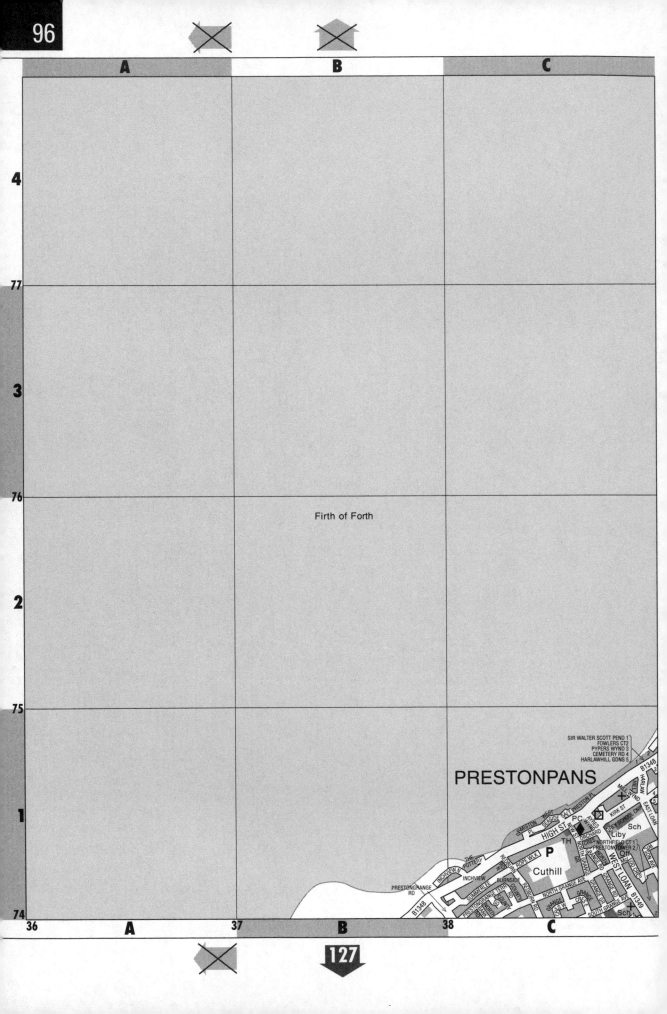

A　　　　B　　　　C

4

77

3

76

Firth of Forth

2

75

SIR WALTER SCOTT PEND 1
FOWLERS CT 2
PYPERS WYND 3
CEMETERY RD 4
HARLAWHILL GDNS 5

PRESTONPANS

1

Cuthill

PRESTONGRANGE
RD

36　　A　　37　　B　　38　　C

74

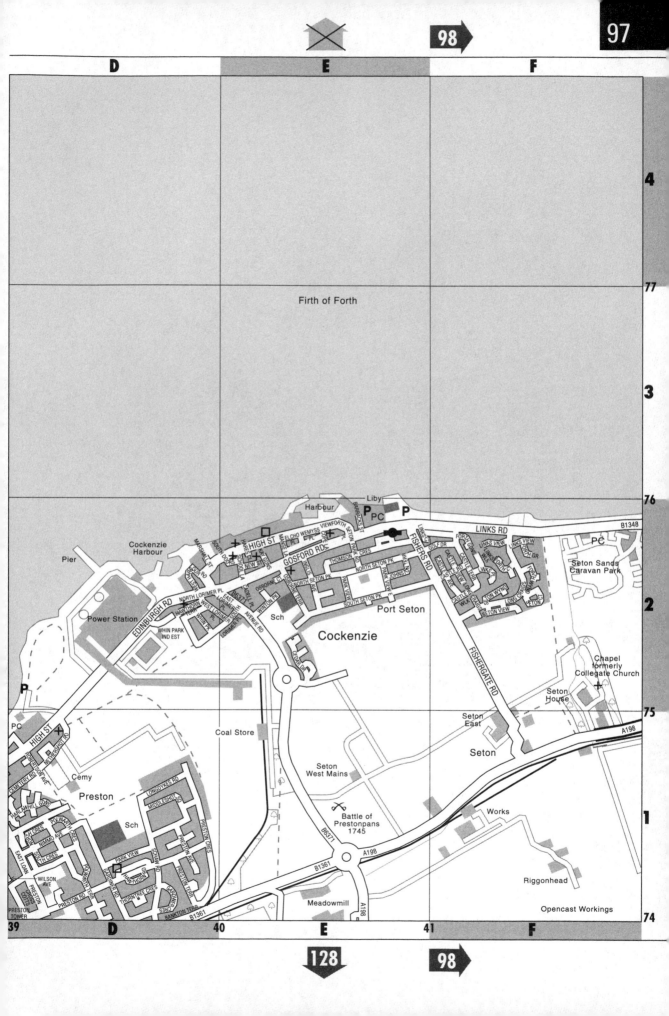

D   E   F

4

77

Firth of Forth

3

76

Liby
Harbour
P PC P
Cockenzie
Harbour
LINKS RD
B1348

Pier
HIGH ST
GOSFORD RD
FISHERS RD
PC
Seton Sands
Caravan Park

Power Station
EDINBURGH RD
WHIN PARK
IND EST
Sch
Port Seton
Chapel
formerly
Collegate Church

Cockenzie

FISHERGATE RD

Seton
House

P

PC
HIGH ST
Coal Store
Seton
East

75

Seton

Cemy
Preston
Seton
West Mains
Works

2

Sch
Battle of
Prestonpans
1745
A198
Riggonhead

1

PRESTON TOWER
B1361
B1361
B1361
A198
Meadowmill
A198
Opencast Workings

74
39   D   40   E   41   F

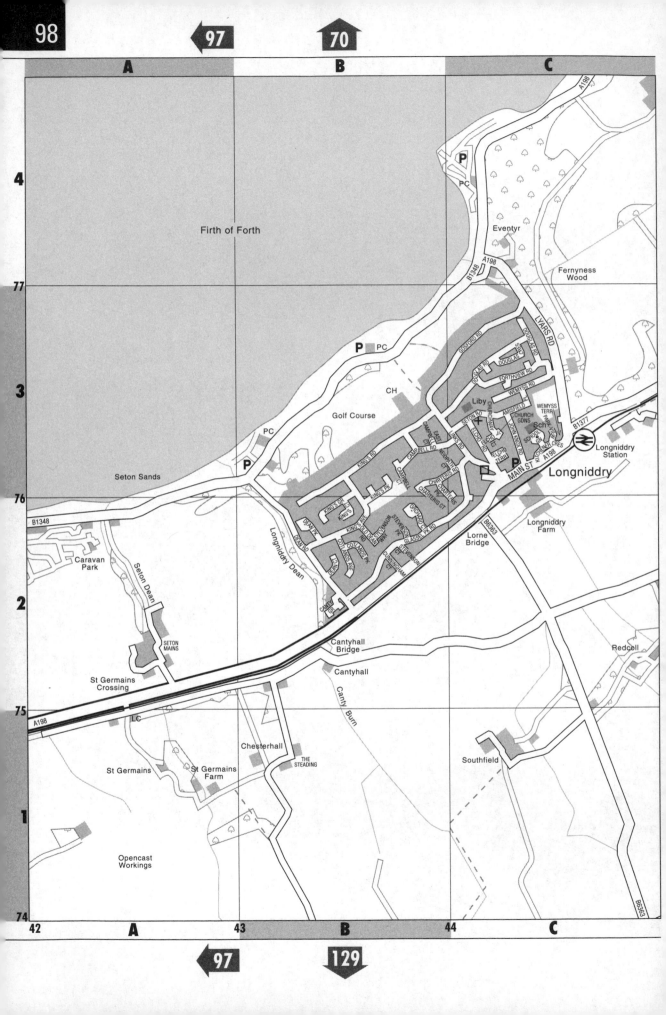

A   **B**   **C**

4

Firth of Forth

P
PC

Eventyr

A198
B1348

Fernyness Wood

77

3

P PC

CH

Golf Course

Liby

CH

PC

P

Seton Sands

P

Gosford Rd
Douglas Rd
Douglas Cr
Forthview Rd
Wemyss Rd

Amisfield
Church Gdns
Wemyss Terr
Park View

Sch
Kitchener Cres
School

Lyars Rd

B1377

Longniddry Station

76

B1348

Seton Dean

Caravan Park

Longniddry Dean

Dean Rd
Dean Pk
King's Gr
King's
King's Pk
King's Ave
King's Gr

Kings Rd
Links Rd
Seton Rd
Campbell Ct
Campbell Rd
East
Campbell
Chapteris Ct
Chapteris Rd
Chapteris
Elcho Rd
Elcho Terr
John Knox Rd
Weir Path
Main St
A198

Stevenson
Stevenson Pk
Orchard Gr Rd
Glassel Pk Rd
Lorne Bridge

B6363

Longniddry

Longniddry Farm

Seton Mains

Canty Gr

Cotlands Ave
Cunningham Ct

Cantyhall Bridge

Cantyhall

Canty Burn

B6363

Redcoll

2

St Germains Crossing

75

A198
LC

Chesterhall
THE STEADING

Southfield

St Germains

St Germains Farm

1

Opencast Workings

74

42   **A**   43   **B**   44   **C**

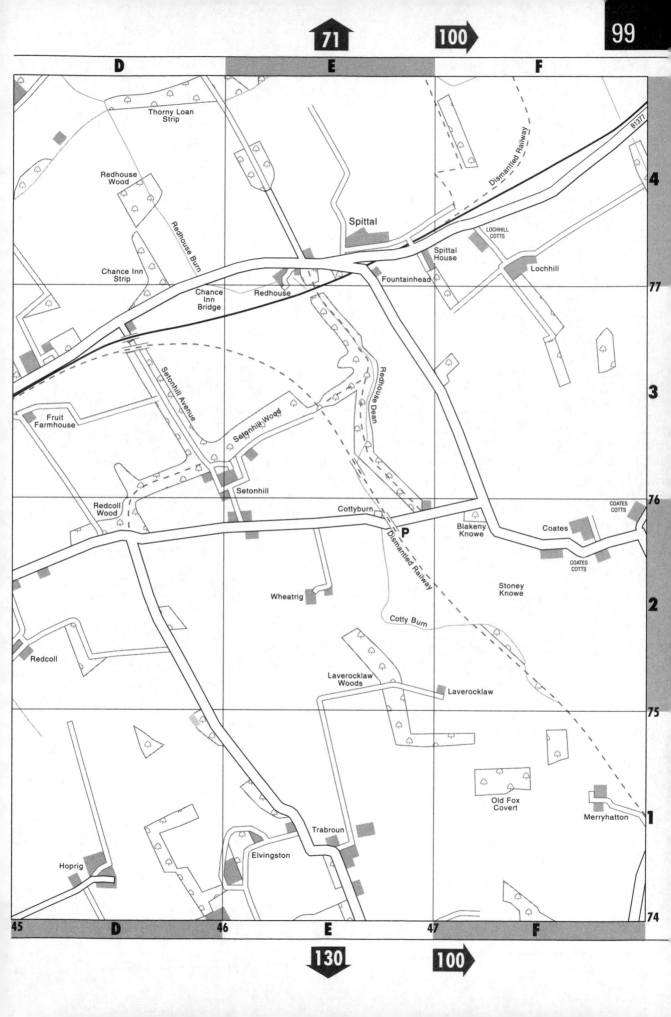

D
E
F

Thorny Loan
Strip

Redhouse
Wood

Redhouse Burn

Chance Inn
Strip

4

Spittal

LOCHHILL
COTTS

Spittal
House

Lochhill

Chance
Inn
Bridge

Redhouse

Fountainhead

77

Setonhill Avenue

Redhouse Dean

3

Fruit
Farmhouse

Setonhill Wood

Setonhill

Redcoll
Wood

76

Cottyburn

Blakeny
Knowe

Coates

COATES
COTTS

P

COATES
COTTS

Dismantled Railway

Stoney
Knowe

Wheatrig

2

Cotty Burn

Redcoll

Laverocklaw
Woods

Laverocklaw

75

Old Fox
Covert

Merryhatton

1

Trabroun

Elvingston

Hoprig

74

Dismantled Railway

B1377

A

B

C

4

Ballencrieff

Corn
Hill

B1377

A6137

Viewmont

Poultry
Farm

Glenarrol

Poultry
Farm

Garleton

Camptoun
House

Camptoun

Gallows
Law

77

Byres

Rye Hill

West Garleton
Farm

Jinging
Hill

Hopetoun
Monument

Byres
Hill

East
Garleton

B1343

EAST GARLETON
COTTS

Garleton Hills

Skid Hill

3

B1343

West Garleton
House

Score Hill

76

West Garleton
Holdings

Phantassie Hill

Bangly Hill

BANGLY BRAE

Blackmains
Toll

Woodlea

2

Bangly
Quarry

Alderston Hill

Alderston
Mains

Huntington

Harperdean

75

UGSTON COTTS

Ugston

Alderston Mains
Dairy

Crow
Wood

Alderston

Industrial
Site

Merryhatton
Cottages

Off

Hospl

1

HARPERDEAN TERR 1
GARLETON DR 2

Hospl

A1

A6137

ABERLADY RD

DUNPENDER DR

South
Lodge

HALDANE AVE

QUEENS AVE

PEFFER

DAVIDSON TERR

BAIRD TERR

HAWTHORNBANK RD

CAPONFLAT
CRES

BEECHWOOD
RD

HOPETOUN DR

LWR ALDERSTON RD

A1

GATESIDE AVE

HOSPITAL RD

ALDERSTON
PL

Hospl

Works

74

48

A

49

B

50

C

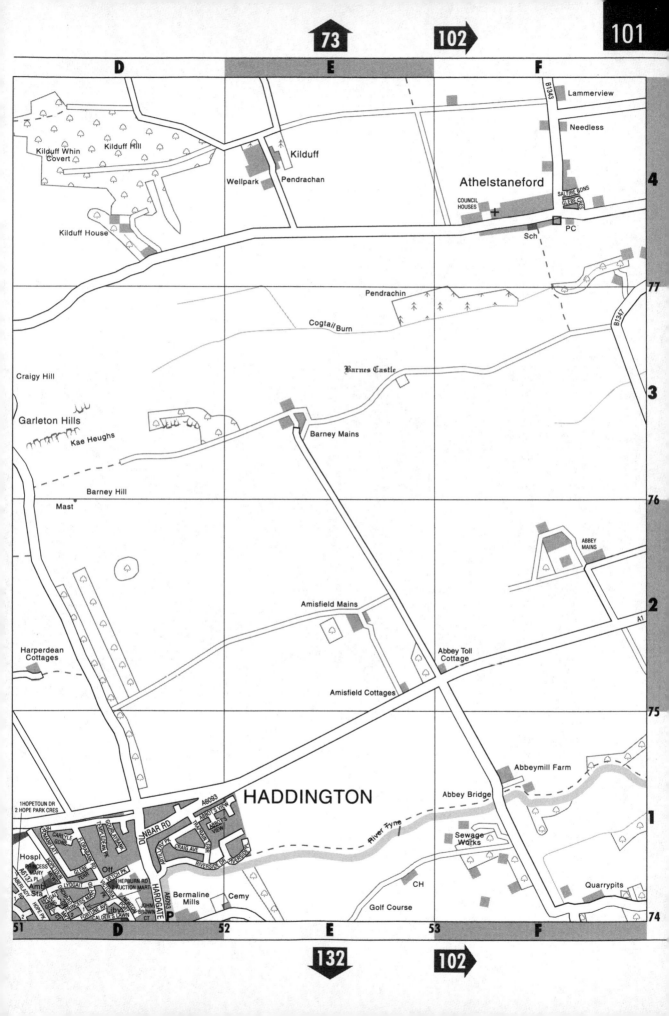

D

Kilduff Whin Covert
Kilduff Hill
Kilduff
Wellpark
Pendrachan
Kilduff House

E

B1343
Lammerview
Needless
Athelstaneford
COUNCIL HOUSES
SALTIRE GDNS
GLEBE
Sch
PC

F

4

77

Pendrachin
Cogtail Burn
B1347

Barnes Castle

Craigy Hill
Garleton Hills
Kae Heughs
Barney Mains

3

Barney Hill
Mast

ABBEY MAINS

76

Harperdean Cottages

Amisfield Mains

Abbey Toll Cottage

A1

2

Amisfield Cottages

75

Abbeymill Farm

HADDINGTON
1 HOPETOUN DR
2 HOPE PARK CRES
ABBOT'S VIEW
ABBOT'S VIEW
Abbey Bridge

River Tyne

Sewage Works

1

Hospl
PRINCESS MARY
A6137 PL
CARLYLE GDNS
FLORABANK RD
DOUR AVENUE
DOUR AVE BANK
GLEBE TERR
CRAIG AVE
CRAIG AVE
RIVERSIDE DR
RIVERSIDE DR
CH
Amb Sta
A6137
HOPE PK
ABERLADY RD
PRINCESS MARY RD
HEPBURN RD
AUCTION MART
VICTORIA
LYDGAIT
Off
VETCH PK
PRINCE
Lib
FORTUNE AV
CALDER'S LAWN
JOHN BROWN CT
HARDGATE
A6093
DUNBAR RD
P
Bermaline Mills
Cemy
Golf Course
Quarrypits

74

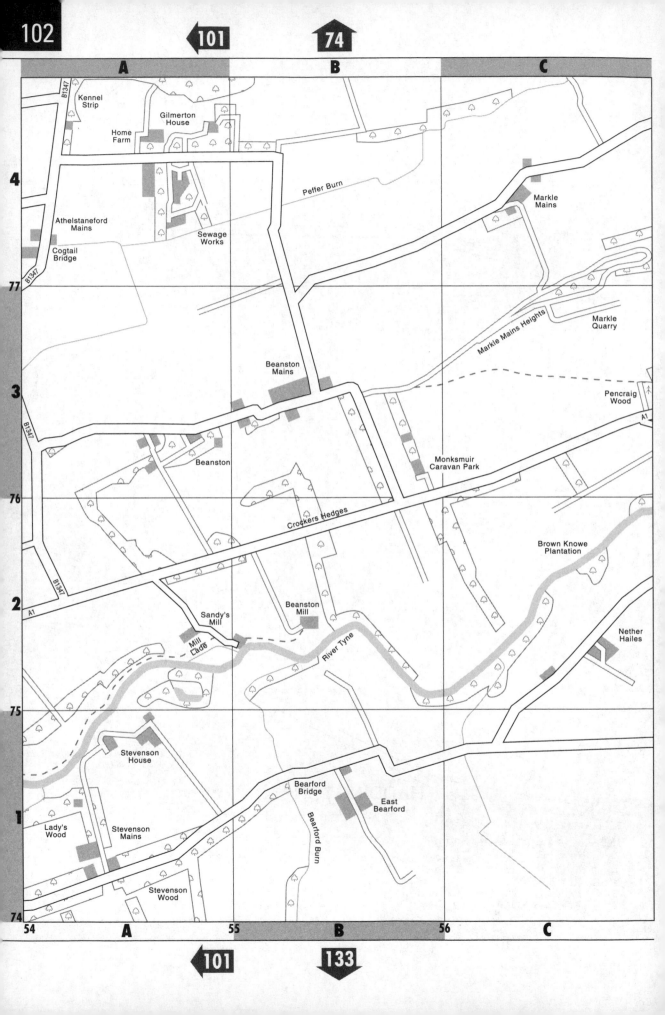

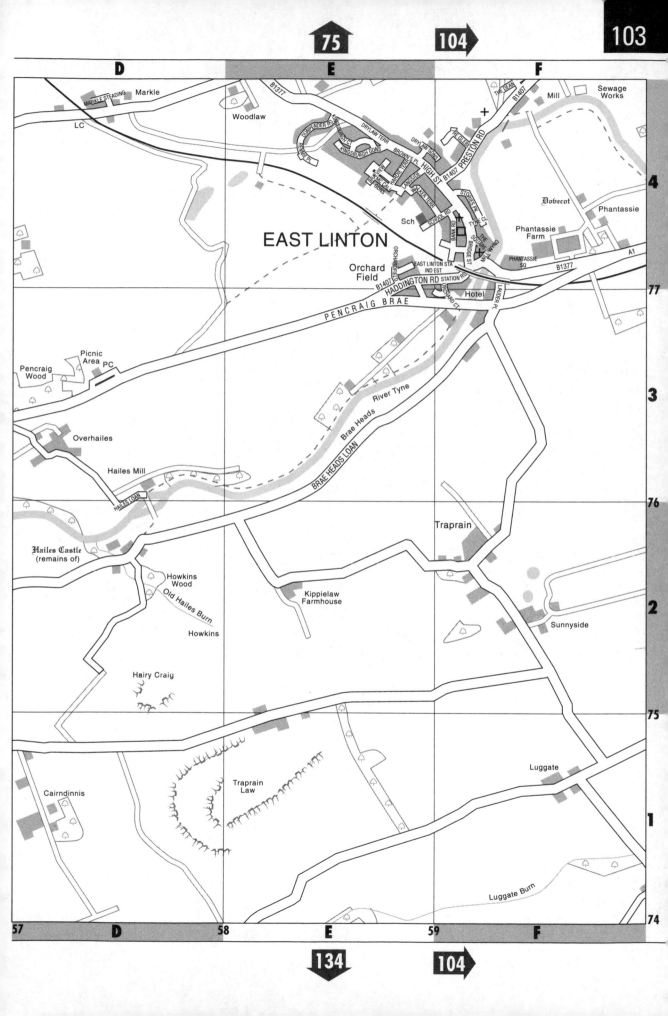

EAST LINTON

Markle Steading
Markle
Woodlaw
LC
Kingsbrgh St.
Kingsbrgh Gdns
Renne Pl.
Dunpender Vs
Drylaw Terr
Drylaw Gdns
Drylaw Gdns
Brown's Pl.
Walker Terr
Markle Terr
Isaac Cal. Gdns
Lansside
The Glebe
Preston Rd
High St
B1407
Stokes Pl.
The Dean
Mill
Sewage Works
Dovecot
Phantassie
Sch
School Rd
Bank Rd
Tyne Cl.
Bridge St
The Square
Mill Wynd
Phantassie Farm
Phantassie Sq
A1
B1377

Orchard Field
East Linton Sta Ind Est
Haddington Rd
Station Rd
Orchard Ct
Orchardfield
Lindèn Pl.
B1407
77
Hotel

Pencraig Brae

Picnic Area
PC
Pencraig Wood
River Tyne
Brae Heads
3
Brae Heads Loan

Overhailes
Hailes Mill
Hailes Loan
76
Traprain

Hailes Castle
(remains of)
Howkins Wood
Old Hailes Burn
Howkins
Kippielaw Farmhouse
2
Sunnyside

Hairy Craig

75
Luggate

Cairndinnis
Traprain Law
1

Luggate Burn
74

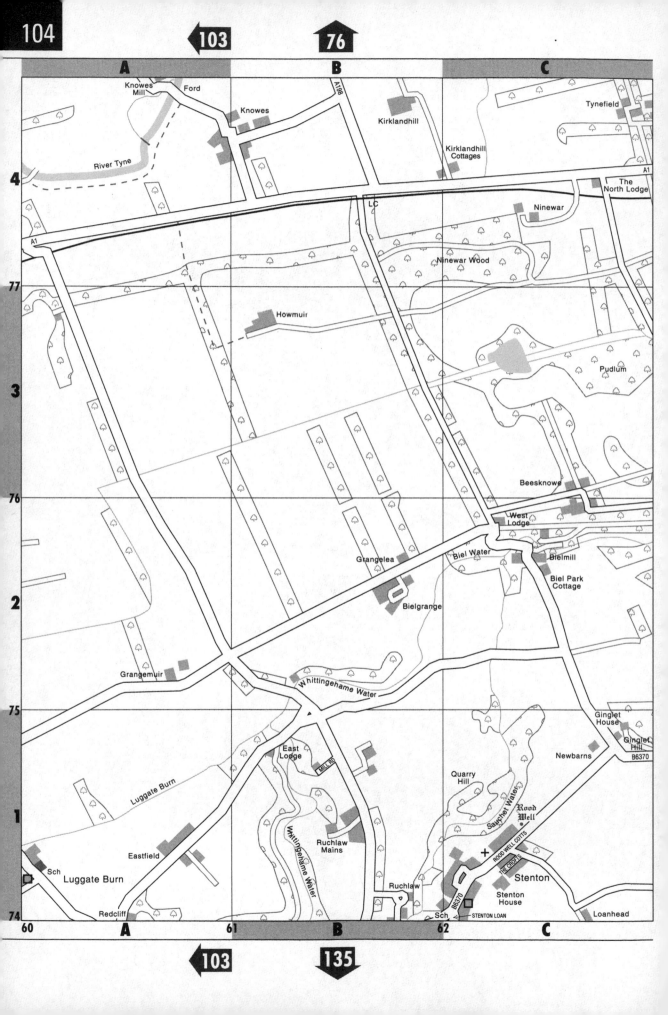

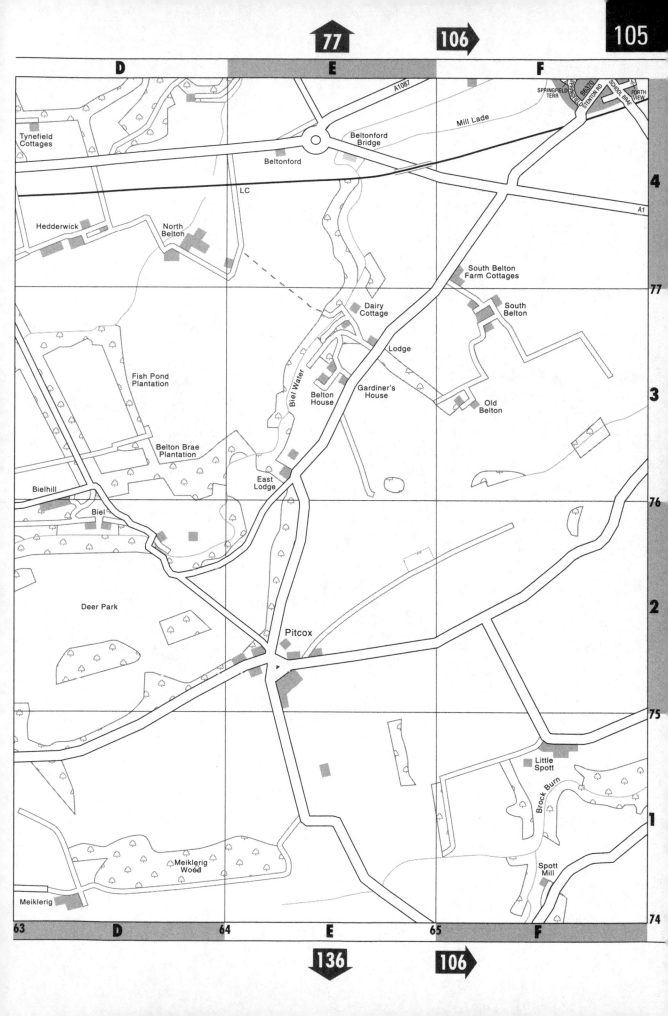

D
E
F

SPRINGFIELD TERR
SPRINGFIELD
B6370
STENTON RD
SCHOOL BRAE
FORTH VIEW

Mill Lade

A1087

Tynefield
Cottages

Beltonford
Bridge

Beltonford

LC

4

A1

Hedderwick

North
Belton

South Belton
Farm Cottages

77

Dairy
Cottage

South
Belton

Fish Pond
Plantation

Biel Water

Lodge

Belton
House

Gardiner's
House

Old
Belton

3

Belton Brae
Plantation

Bielhill

East
Lodge

Biel

76

Deer Park

2

Pitcox

75

Little
Spott

Brock Burn

Meiklerig
Wood

1

Spott
Mill

Meiklerig

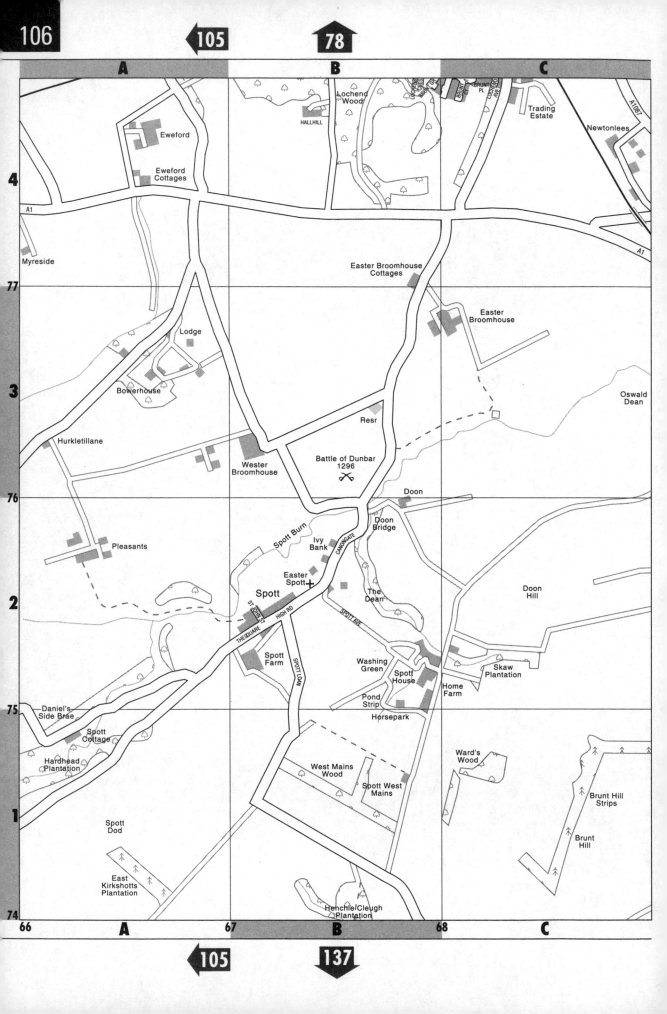

A   B   C

4

77

3

76

2

75

1

74

66   A   67   B   68   C

Eweford

Eweford
Cottages

Myreside

Lodge

Bowerhouse

Hurkletillane

Wester
Broomhouse

Pleasants

Spott Burn

Spott

Easter
Spott

St JOHN'S

THE SQUARE

HIGH RD

SPOTT LOAN

Spott Farm

Daniel's
Side Brae

Spott
Cottage

Hardhead
Plantation

Spott Dod

East
Kirkshotts
Plantation

HALLHILL

Lochend
Wood

Easter Broomhouse
Cottages

Resr

Battle of Dunbar
1296

Ivy
Bank

CANONGATE

Doon

Doon
Bridge

Washing
Green

SPOTT AVE

The
Dean

Spott
House

Pond
Strip

Horsepark

West Mains
Wood

Spott West
Mains

Henchie Cleugh
Plantation

LOCHEND
CRES

BRUNT
CT

BRUNT
PL

LOCHEND
AVE

A1087

Trading
Estate

Newtonlees

A1

Easter
Broomhouse

Oswald
Dean

Doon
Hill

Skaw
Plantation

Home
Farm

Ward's
Wood

Brunt Hill
Strips

Brunt
Hill

A1

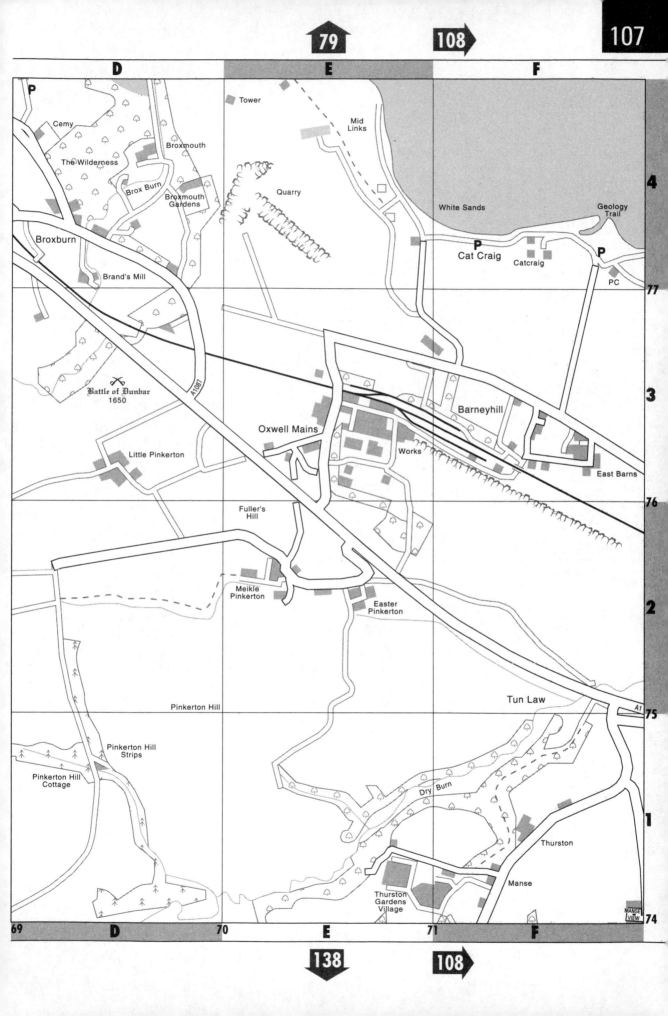

79
108

D
E
F

P

Tower

Mid Links

Cemy

Broxmouth

The Wilderness

Brox Burn

Quarry

White Sands

4

Geology Trail

Broxmouth Gardens

Broxburn

Cat Craig

P

Catcraig

P

PC

Brand's Mill

77

A1087

Battle of Dunbar
1650

Barneyhill

Oxwell Mains

3

Little Pinkerton

Works

East Barns

Fuller's Hill

76

Meikle Pinkerton

Easter Pinkerton

2

Tun Law

A1

Pinkerton Hill

75

Pinkerton Hill Strips

Dry Burn

Pinkerton Hill Cottage

1

Thurston

Manse

Thurston Gardens Village

MANSE VIEW

74

107

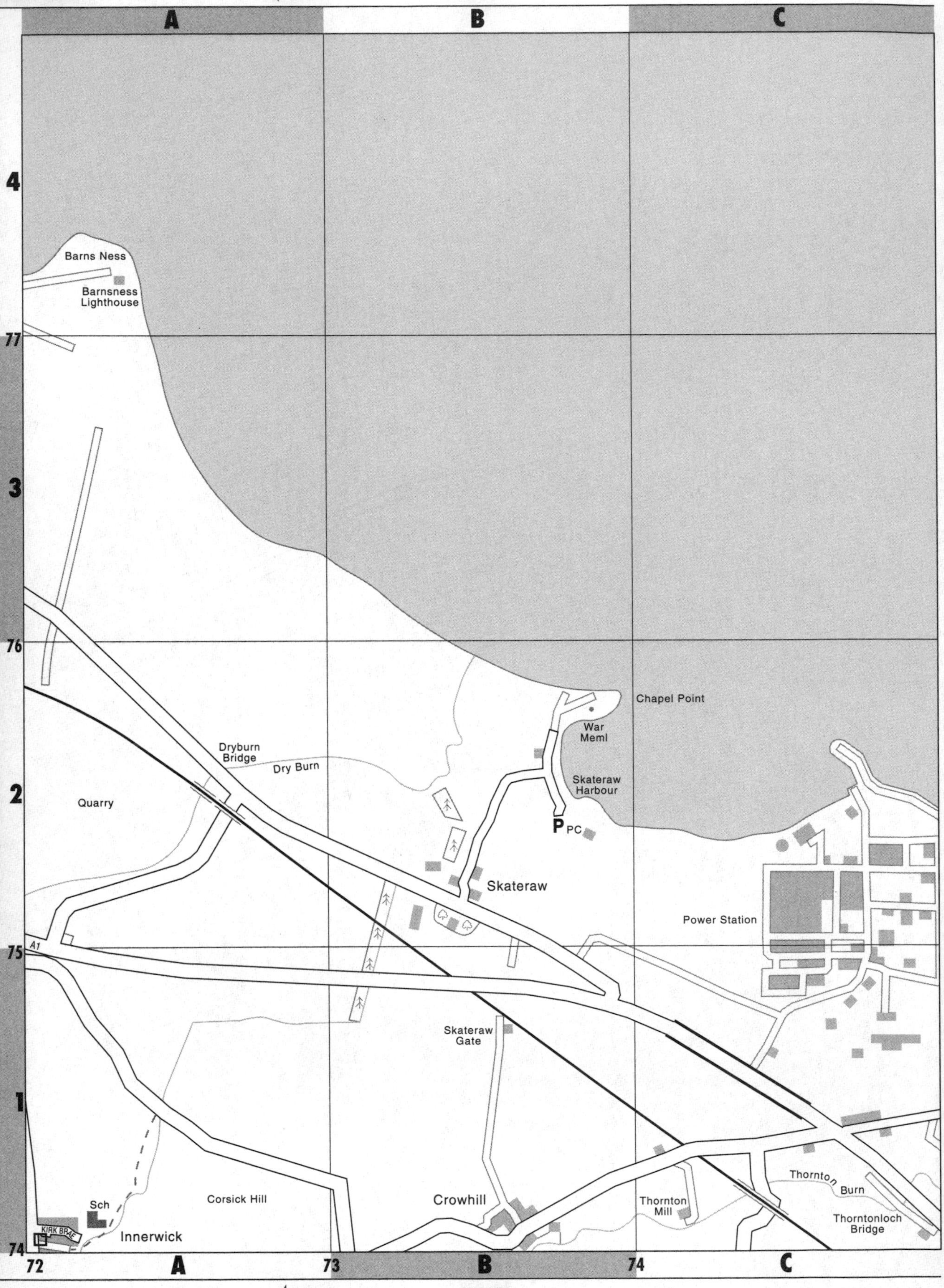

A　　　　　　B　　　　　　C

4

Barns Ness

Barnsness
Lighthouse

77

3

76

Chapel Point

Dryburn
Bridge　　Dry Burn

War
Meml

Skateraw
Harbour

2

Quarry

P PC

Skateraw

Power Station

A1　**75**

Skateraw
Gate

1

Thornton Burn

Sch　　　Corsick Hill

Crowhill

Thornton
Mill

Thorntonloch
Bridge

KIRK BRAE
Innerwick

74

72　　　**A**　　　73　　　**B**　　　74　　　**C**

107　139

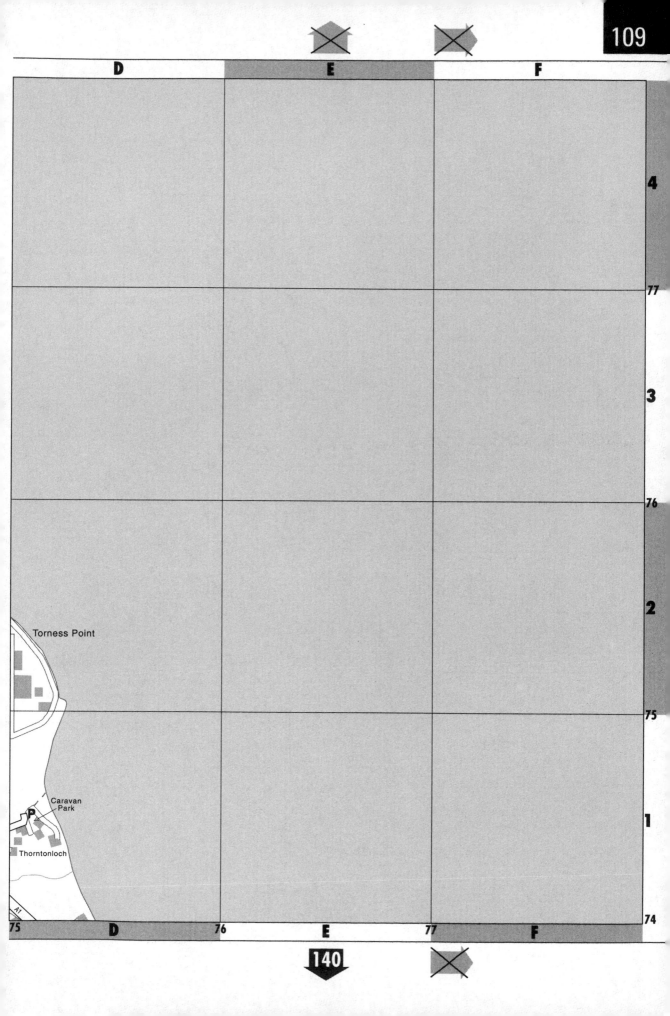

D   E   F

4

77

3

76

2

Torness Point

75

Caravan
Park

P

1

Thorntonloch

A1

74

75   D   76   E   77   F

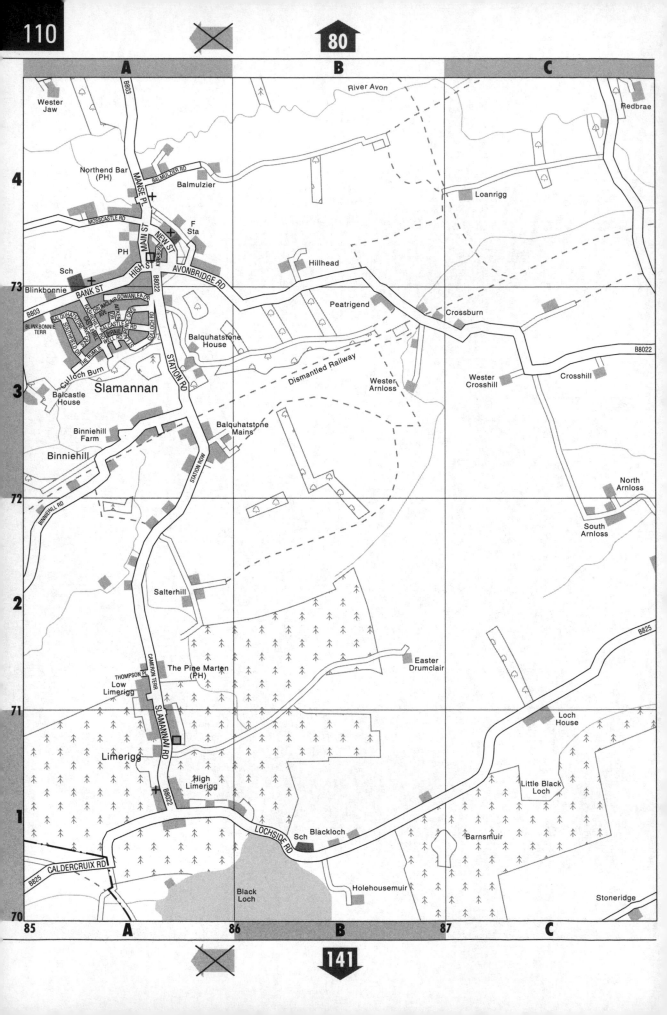

A · B · C

Wester Jaw

River Avon

Redbrae

4

Northend Bar (PH)

Balmulzier

BALMULZIER RD

MANSE PL

Loanrigg

MOSSCASTLE RD

F Sta

NEW ST

MAIN ST

PH

HIGH ST

Hillhead

Sch

AVONBRIDGE RD

73

Blinkbonnie

BANK ST

B8022

Peatrigend

Crossburn

B8803

GOWANLEA DR

DRUMCLAIR

Crosshill

B8022

BLINKBONNIE TERR

BALQUHATSTONE

EAST

THE RUMLIE

WELL RD

Balquhatstone House

Dismantled Railway

Wester Arnloss

Wester Crosshill

Crosshill

3

Culloch Burn

Balcastle House

Slamannan

STATION RD

Binniehill Farm

Balquhatstone Mains

North Arnloss

Binniehill

STATION ROW

South Arnloss

72

BINNIEHILL RD

2

Salterhill

B825

Easter Drumclair

CAMERON TERR

The Pine Marten (PH)

THOMPSON PL

Low Limerigg

SLAMANNAN RD

Loch House

71

Limerigg

Little Black Loch

High Limerigg

B8022

1

LOCHSIDE RD

Blackloch

Sch

Barnsmuir

Holehousemuir

B825

CALDERCRUIX RD

Black Loch

Stoneridge

70

85 · A · 86 · B · 87 · C

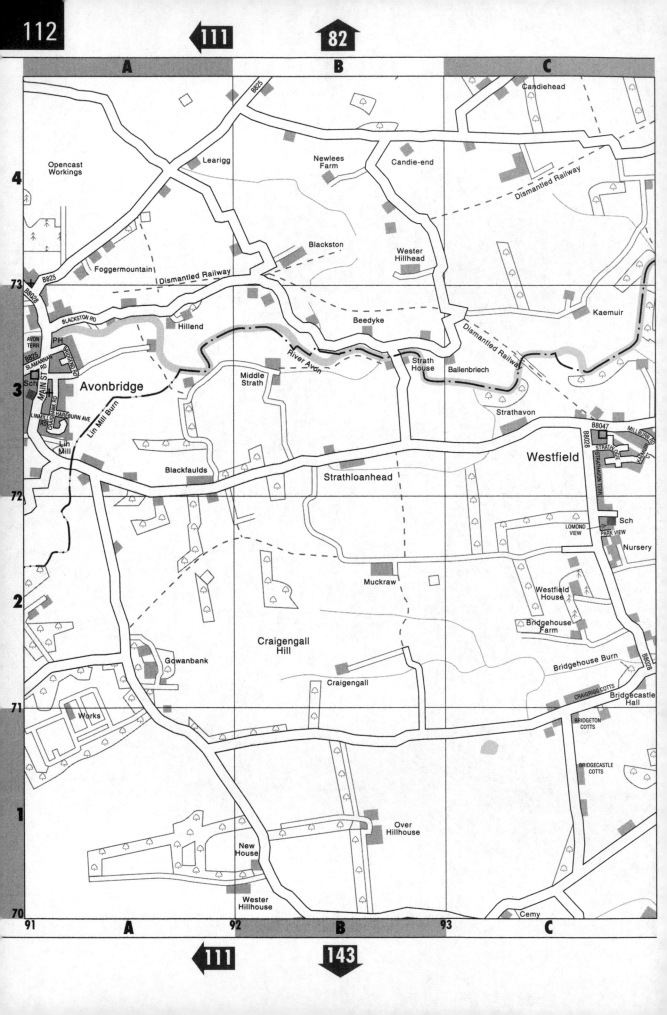

A B C

4

Opencast
Workings

Learigg

Newlees
Farm

Candie-end

Candiehead

Wester
Hillhead

Dismantled Railway

Blackston

B825

Dismantled Railway

73

B825

B8028

BLACKSTOW RD

Hillend

Beedyke

Kaemuir

AVON
TERR

PH

River Avon

Strath
House

Ballenbriech

Dismantled Railway

B825
SLAMANNAN RD

BRIDGEBURN RD

Middle
Strath

Strathavon

3

Sch

MAIN ST

Avonbridge

CRAIGBANK RD

HAREBURN AVE

Lin Mill Burn

LINMILL
RD

Lin
Mill

Blackfaulds

Strathloanhead

Westfield

B8047

B8028

STRATHAVON TERR

STRATHALGIE

MILL BURN RD

KAEMUIR CT

72

Sch

LOMOND
VIEW

PARK VIEW

Nursery

2

Gowanbank

Muckraw

Westfield
House

Bridgehouse
Farm

Craigengall
Hill

Bridgehouse Burn

B8028

Craigengall

CRAIGRIGG COTTS

Bridgecastle
Hall

71

Works

BRIDGETON
COTTS

BRIDGECASTLE
COTTS

1

Over
Hillhouse

New
House

70

Wester
Hillhouse

Cemy

91 A 92 B 93 C

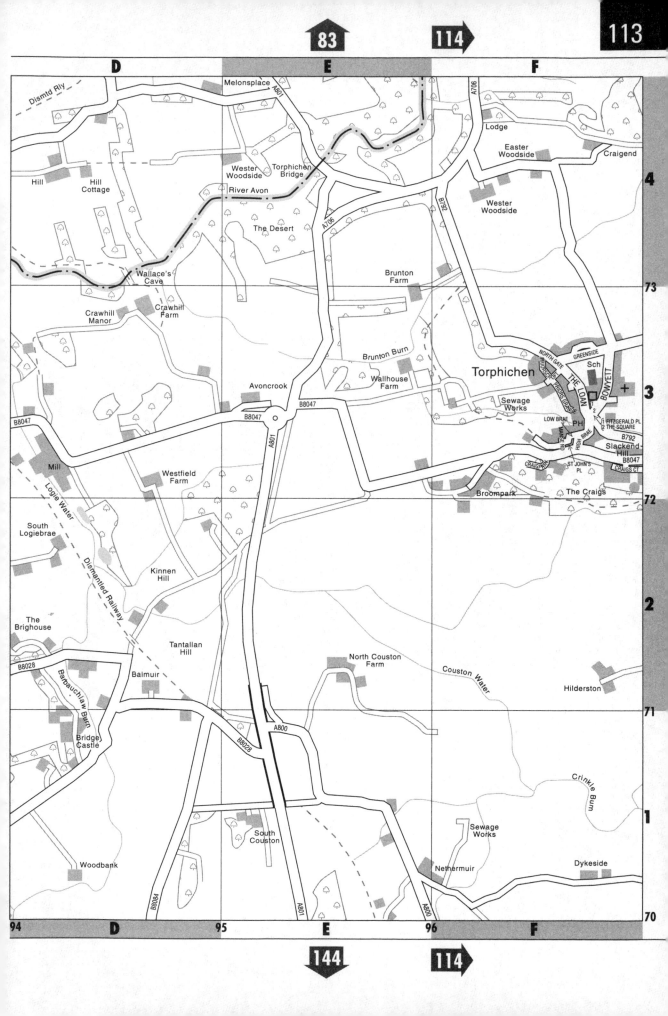

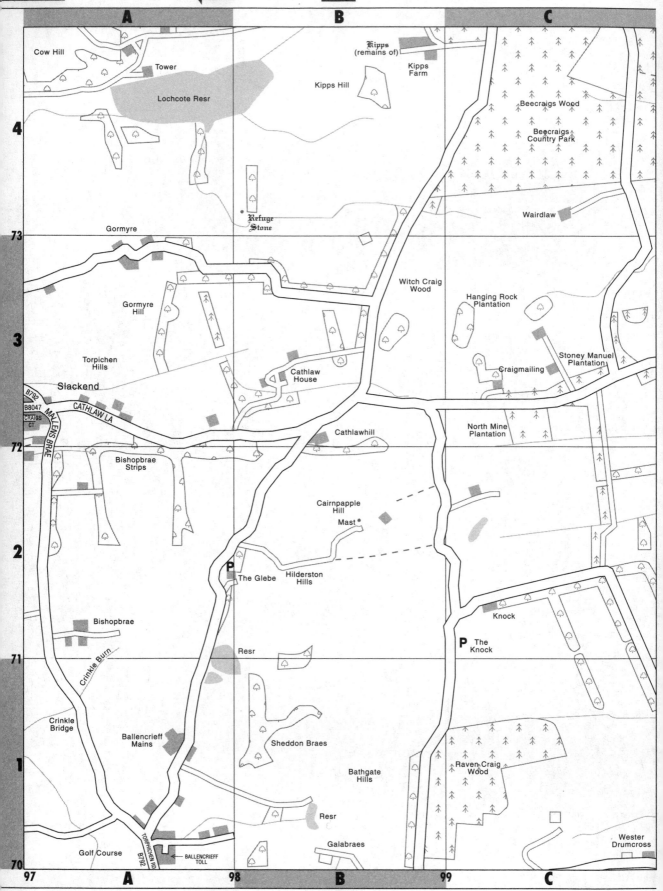

A   B   C

Cow Hill

Tower

Lochcote Resr

Kipps
(remains of)

Kipps Hill

Kipps Farm

Beecraigs Wood

Beecraigs
Country Park

4

Refuge
Stone

Wairdlaw

Gormyre

73

Witch Craig
Wood

Hanging Rock
Plantation

Gormyre
Hill

Craigmailing

Stoney Manuel
Plantation

3

Torpichen
Hills

Cathlaw
House

Slackend

B792

CATHLAW LA

B8047

CRAIGS
CT

MALLEN'S BRAE

Cathlawhill

North Mine
Plantation

72

Bishopbrae
Strips

Cairnpapple
Hill

Mast

2

P

The Glebe

Hilderston
Hills

Knock

Bishopbrae

P The
Knock

71

Resr

Crinkle Burn

Crinkle
Bridge

Ballencrieff
Mains

Sheddon Braes

Raven Craig
Wood

1

Bathgate
Hills

Resr

Wester
Drumcross

Galabraes

Golf Course

TORPHICHEN RD

B792

← BALLENCRIEFF
TOLL

70

97   A   98   B   99   C

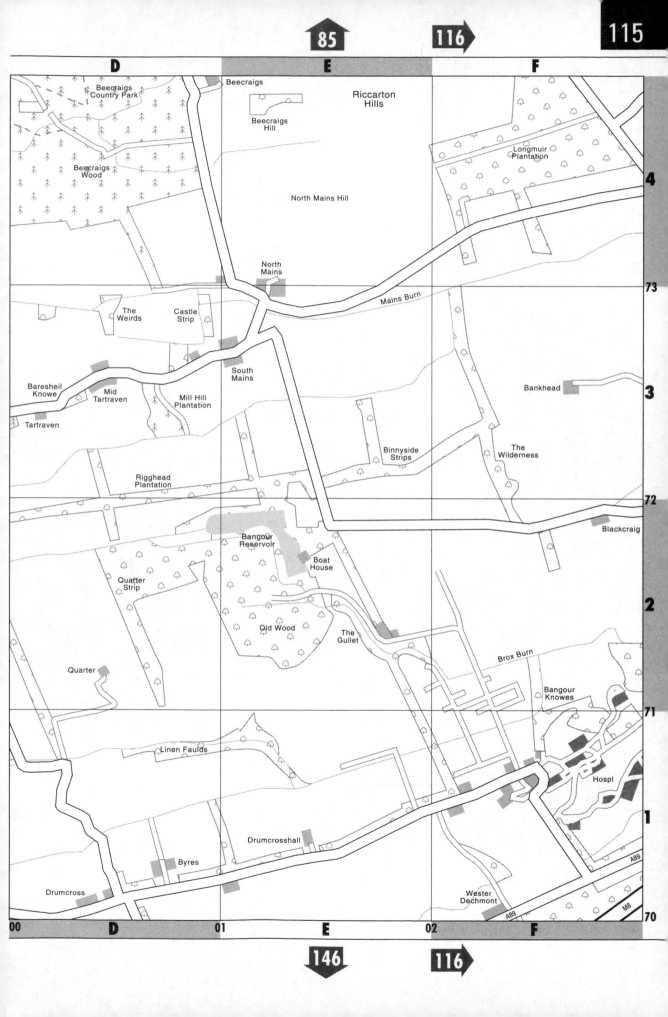

Beecraigs Country Park

Beecraigs

Riccarton Hills

Beecraigs Hill

Longmuir Plantation

Beecraigs Wood

North Mains Hill

4

North Mains

73

Mains Burn

The Weirds

Castle Strip

Baresheil Knowe

South Mains

Bankhead

3

Mid Tartraven

Mill Hill Plantation

Tartraven

Binnyside Strips

The Wilderness

Rigghead Plantation

72

Bangour Reservoir

Blackcraig

Quarter Strip

Boat House

Old Wood

2

The Gullet

Brox Burn

Quarter

Bangour Knowes

71

Linen Faulds

Hospl

1

Drumcrosshall

A89

Byres

Drumcross

Wester Dechmont

A89   M8

70

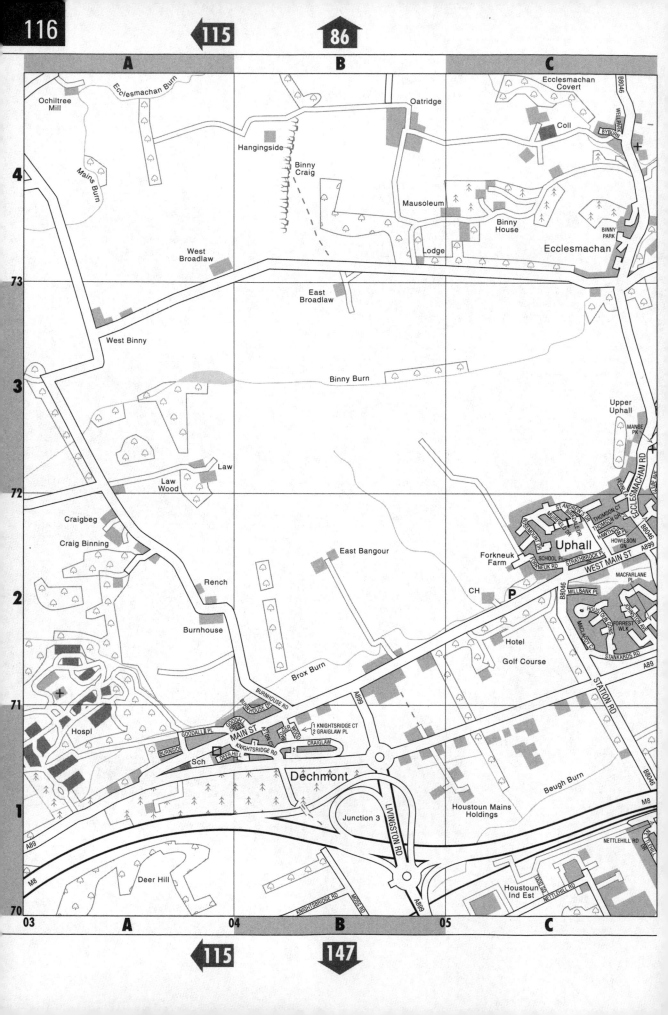

A   B   C

Ochiltree Mill

Ecclesmachan Burn

Mains Burn

Hangingside

Binny Craig

Oatridge

Ecclesmachan Covert

Coll

WELLPARK

BYBURN

B8046

Mausoleum

Binny House

Binny Park

Ecclesmachan

West Broadlaw

East Broadlaw

Lodge

4

73

West Binny

Binny Burn

Upper Uphall

MANSE PK

ECCLESMACHAN RD

GLEN AVE

FERNLEA

3

Law

Law Wood

Craigbeg

Craig Binning

Rench

East Bangour

Forkneuk Farm

CH

P

Uphall

St Andrew's PL

MUIRFIELD DR

THOMSON CT

THOMSON GR

HAWTHORN PL

HOWIESON GN

WEST MAIN ST

MACFARLANE PL

ROSEMOUNT DR

SCHOOL PL

FORKNEUK RD

STRATHBROCK PL

B8046

A89

72

2

Burnhouse

Brox Burn

Hotel

Golf Course

MILLBANK PL

HOUSE O' HILL GDNS

MACKAROY CT

JOHNSTON LANE

FORREST WLK

STANKARDS RD

STATION RD

A89

B8046

71

Hospl

BURNHOUSE RD

BURNHOUSE DR

GOODALL CRES

GOODALL PL

MAIN ST

ACTON PL

KNIGHTSRIDGE RD

BURNSIDE

Sch

DEER HILL

1 KNIGHTSRIDGE CT
2 GRAIGLAW PL

CRAIGLAW

2

Dechmont

Junction 3

LIVINGSTON RD

Beugh Burn

Houstoun Mains Holdings

M8

1

A89

M8

Deer Hill

KNIGHTSBRIDGE RD

MOSS RD

A89

Houstoun Ind Est

NETTLEHILL RD

NETTLEHILL RD

NETTLEHILL DR

70

03   A   04   B   05   C

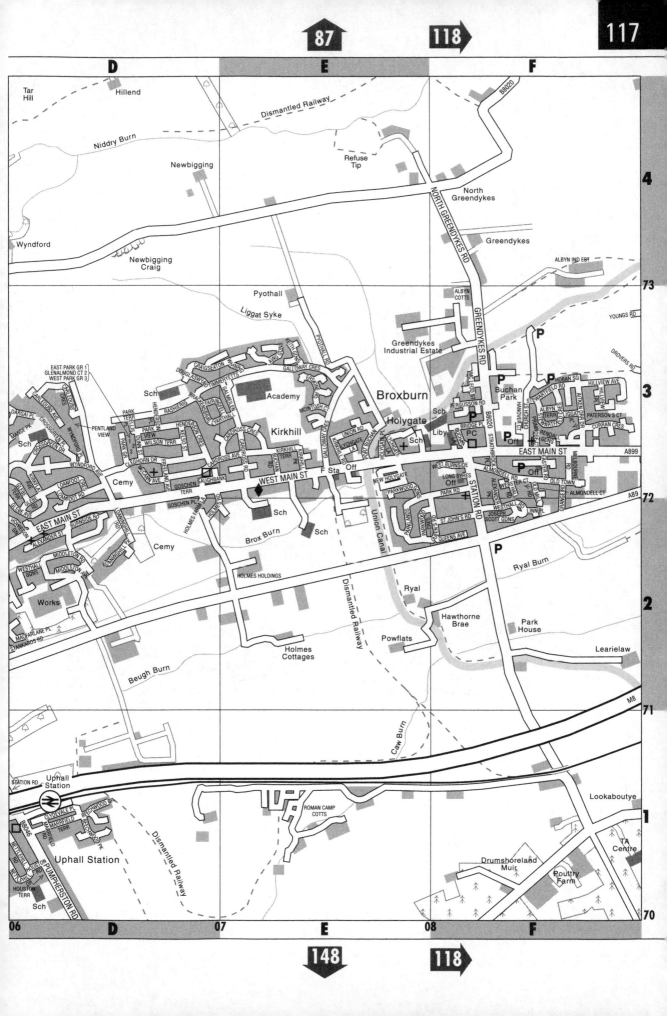

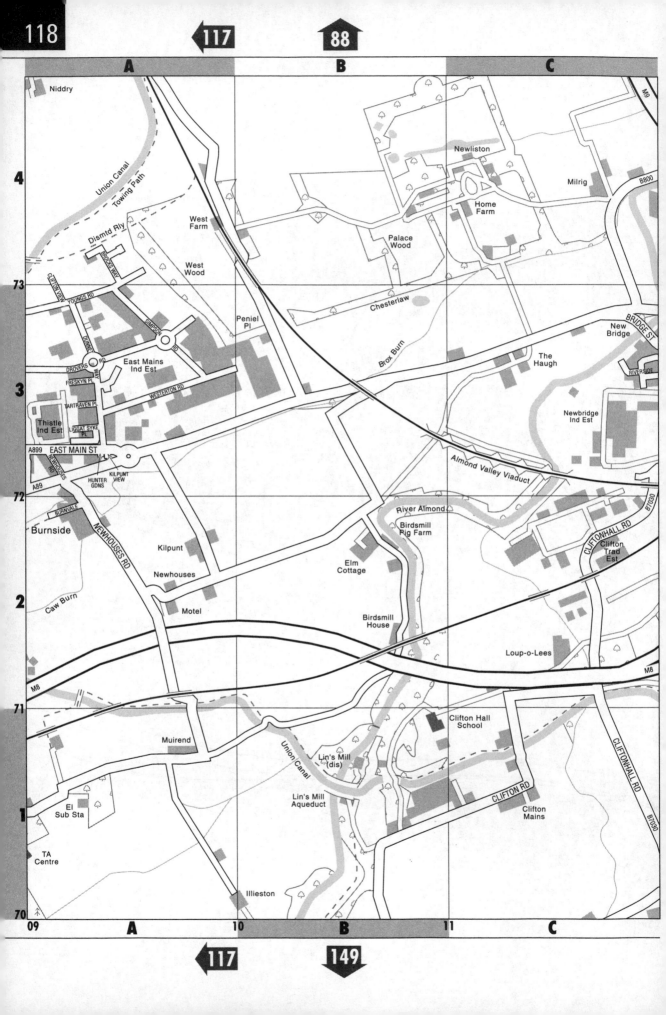

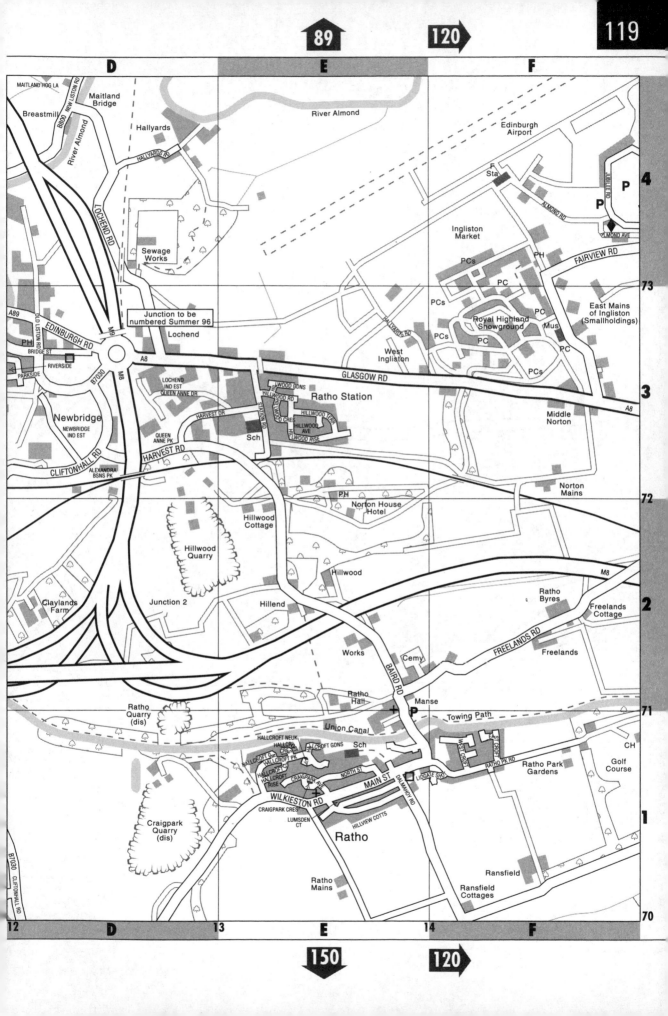

D **E** **F**

MAITLAND HOG LA

Breastmill

Maitland Bridge

River Almond

Hallyards

HALLYARDS RD

NEW LISTON RD

B800

LOCHEND RD

Sewage Works

River Almond

Edinburgh Airport

F Sta

JUBILEE RD

P P

P

ALMOND RD

ALMOND AVE

4

Ingliston Market

FAIRVIEW RD

PCs

PH

73

A89

PH

Edinburgh Rd

EDINBURGH RD

M9

BRIDGE ST

RIVERSIDE

PARKSIDE

B7030

OLD LISTON RD

A8

Junction to be numbered Summer 96

Lochend

PCs

PCs

West Ingliston

Royal Highland Showground

PC

Mus

East Mains of Ingliston (Smallholdings)

PC

PCs

PC

PC

Newbridge

NEWBRIDGE IND EST

M8

LOCHEND IND EST

QUEEN ANNE DR

HARVEST DR

STATION RD

HILLWOOD RD

LWOOD GDNS

HILLWOOD CRES

Ratho Station

HILLWOOD TERR

HILLWOOD AVE

HILLWOOD RISE

GLASGOW RD

HALLYARDS RD

Middle Norton

A8

3

CLIFTONHALL RD

Queen Anne Pk

Sch

HARVEST RD

ALEXANDRA BSNS PK

Hillwood Cottage

Norton House Hotel

PH

Norton Mains

72

Claylands Farm

Hillwood Quarry

Junction 2

Hillend

Hillwood

Works

M8

Ratho Byres

Freelands Cottage

2

FREELANDS RD

Freelands

Ratho Quarry (dis)

Union Canal

Ratho Hall

Cemy

BAIRD RD

Manse

P

Towing Path

71

Craigpark Quarry (dis)

HALLCROFT NEUK

HALLCROFT GDNS

HALLCROFT PK

HALLCROFT RISE

CRAIGPARK AVE

NORTH ST

Sch

WILKIESTON RD

CRAIGPARK CRES

LUMSDEN CT

MAIN ST

DALMAHOY RD

LIDGATE SHOT

WEST CROFT

RATHO PK RD

Ratho Park Gardens

CH

Golf Course

1

HILLVIEW COTTS

Ratho

Ratho Mains

Ransfield

Ransfield Cottages

70

12 **D** **13** **E** **14** **F**

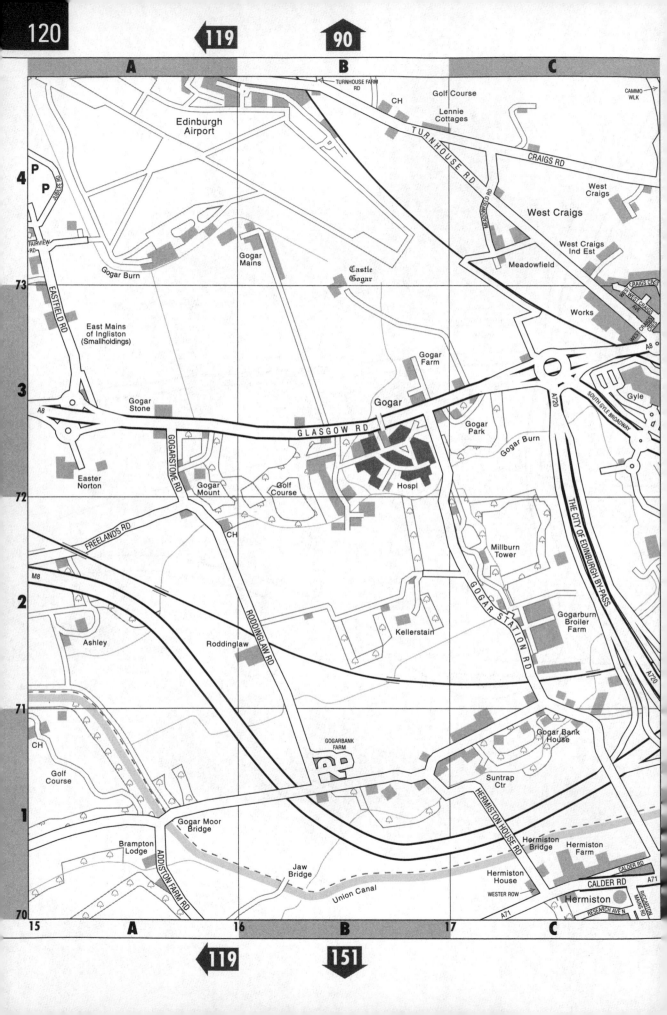

119
90

A   **B**   **C**

TURNHOUSE FARM RD

CH

Golf Course

Lennie Cottages

CAMMO WLK

4   P P

P

Edinburgh Airport

TURNHOUSE RD

CRAIGS RD

West Craigs

West Craigs

FAIRVIEW RD

JUBILEE RD

MEADOWFIELD RD

West Craigs Ind Est

Meadowfield

Gogar Mains

Castle Gogar

WEST CRAIGS CRES

WEST CRAIGS AVE

WEST CRAIGS CRES

73   Gogar Burn

Works

A8

EASTFIELD RD

East Mains of Ingliston (Smallholdings)

Gogar Farm

3   A8

Gogar Stone

Gogar

Glasgow Rd

Gogar Park

Gogar Burn

A720

SOUTH GYLE BROADWAY

Gyle

Easter Norton

GOGARSTONE RD

Gogar Mount

Golf Course

Hospl

72

CH

FREELANDS RD

Millburn Tower

THE CITY OF EDINBURGH BY-PASS

M8

RODDINGLAW RD

Kellerstain

GOGAR STATION RD

Gogarburn Broiler Farm

A720

2   Ashley

Roddinglaw

71

Gogar Bank House

CH

Golf Course

GOGARBANK FARM

Suntrap Ctr

HERMISTON HOUSE RD

Hermiston Bridge

Hermiston Farm

1   Gogar Moor Bridge

Brampton Lodge

ADDISTON FARM RD

Jaw Bridge

Hermiston House

WESTER ROW

Hermiston

CALDER RD

A71

BUCCARTON MAINS RD

Union Canal

A71

CALDER RD

RESEARCH AVE N

70

15   **A**   **16**   **B**   **17**   **C**

119
151

D   E   F

Golf Course

4

MAYBURY RD

BUGHTLIN
GDNS
CAMMO WALK
ALMOND SQ
A9020
A902 SOUTH MAYBURY

MAYBURY DR

BUGHTLIN PK
HATFIELD
KILCHLIN PK
MEARENSIDE
P
BURNBRAE
BURNSIDE
PK
STUART CT
STUART CRES
STUART WYND

CRAIGMOUNT BRAE
Sch
CRAIGMOUNT LOAN
CRAIGMOUNT GRN
CRAIGMOUNT VIEW
CRAIGMOUNT TERR
CRAIGMOUNT GDNS
CRAIGMOUNT PK

DURAR DR
DRUM BRAE NEUK
DRUM BRAE AVE
DRUM BRAE S
DRUM BRAE AG
DRUM BRAE PK APP
DRUM BRAE PL

ROSHIEL ST

ALAN BRECK GDNS   Schs
CLERWOOD WAY
CLERWOOD BANK
CLERWOOD LOAN
Coll
CLERWOOD ROW
CLERWOOD PK
CLERWOOD TERR
CLERWOOD GR

Mast
Twr
Hilliwood
Zoo
PC

AFFLECK CT
FINLAGGAN CT
KILCHURN CT
NEIDPATH CT
TOWARD CT
ROWALLAN CT
KISIMUL CT
DUNOLLIE CT
CAERLAVEROCK CT

CRAIGS RD
East Craigs
Sch

CRAIGMOUNT AVE
PEARCE RD
PEARCE AVE
PEARCE GR

CAROLINE TERR
HILLVIEW RD
HILLVIEW CRES
HILLVIEW TERR
CAROLINE PL

CLERMISTON RD
CAIRNMUIR RD
CORSTORPHINE HILL CRES
CORSTORPHINE HILL AVE
CORSTORPHINE HILL GDNS
OLD KIRK RD

Hospl

73

WEST CRAIGS CRES
MAYBURY RD
A8902

NORTH GYLE LOAN
NORTH GYLE DR
NORTH GYLE AVE
NORTH GYLE TERR
NORTH GYLE GR
GYLE PARK GDNS
DECHMONT RD

CRAIGS GDNS
CRAIGS CRES
CRAIGS BANK
CRAIGS AVE
GLASGOW RD
GYLEMUIR RD

VICTOR PARK TERR
MAYBANK VILLAS
ST NINIAN'S RD
FORRESTER RD
BARONY TERR
TEMPLE
BANK AVE
FEATHERHALL GR

St JOHN'S RD
Corstorphine House Ave
Corstorphine House
GORDON TERR
GORDON LOAN
BELGRAVE RD
BELGRAVE GDNS
GORDON RD

Corstorphine
Hospl
PC
P   A8
DOWNIE GR

The Gyle

CORSTORPHINE BANK TERR
FEATHERHALL CRES N
FEATHERHALL TERR
FEATHERHALL AVE
FEATHERHALL CRES S
FEATHERHALL PL
LADYWELL RD
LADYWELL AVE
LADYWELL GDNS

PC's
MANSE ST
OSWALD TERR
Sch
CORSTORPHINE HIGH ST
Corstorphine High St
KIRK LOAN
GLEBE RD
High St
MANSE RD
Liby

Off   THE PADDOCKHOLM
Off   Off   PINKHILL
TRAQUAIR PK E
TRAQUAIR PK W

CORSTORPHINE RD

The Gyle

MURRAY COTTS
MEADOW PL RD
BROOMPARK RD
LADYWELL RD

SYCAMORE GDNS
CASTLE AVE
DOVECOT RD
Corstorphine Pk Gdns
MEADOWHOUSE RD
TYLER'S ACRE RD
TYLER'S ACRE AVE
TYLER'S ACRE GDNS

Golf Course
CARRICK KNOWE AVE
Sch
CARRICK KNOWE RD
CARRICK KNOWE TERR
CARRICK KNOWE GR
CARRICK KNOWE HILL

3

1 GOGARLOCH MUIR
2 GOGARLOCH HAUGH
GOGARLOCHSYKE
REDHEUGHS RIGG
South Gyle Station
P
GYLE GDNS
SOUTH GYLE GDNS
SOUTH GYLE WYND
SOUTH GYLE PL

BROOMHALL AVE
WESTER BROOM AVE
BROOMHALL RD
BROOMHALL LOAN
BROOMHALL GDNS
BROOMHALL CRES
BROOMHALL DR
BROOMHALL PL
BROOMFIELD CRES
Sch
BROOMBANK TERR
KIRK CRAMOND
BROOMHALL BANK
BROOMHALL PK

CASTLE AVE
ROULL RD
ROULL GR
BROOMHALL TERR
CARRICK KNOWE PARKWAY
CARRICK KNOWE GDNS
CARRICK KNOWE LOAN
CARRICK KNOWE GR

72

SOUTH GYLE BROADWAY
South Gyle
SOUTH GYLE CRES LA
SOUTH GYLE CRES
South Gyle Ind Est
SOUTH GYLE ACCESS

FORRESTER PARK AVE
FORRESTER PARK RD
FORRESTER PARK GR
FORRESTER PARK
FORRESTER LOAN
FORRESTER PARK DR

SAUGHTON MAINS ST
STENHOUSE DR
Saughton
SAUGHTON MAINS PK
SAUGHTON MAINS TERR
SAUGHTON MAINS AVE
SAUGHTON MAINS LOAN

REDHEUGHS AVE
BANKHEAD DR
BANKHEAD CROSSWAY N
BANKHEAD MEDWAY
BANKHEAD
TERR

BROOMHOUSE DR
1 BROOMHOUSE GDNS E
2 BROOMHOUSE GDNS W
BROOMHOUSE PK
BROOMHOUSE TERR
BROOMHOUSE N
Sch
Broomhouse
3 BROOMHOUSE WAY
4 BROOMHOUSE WYND
5 BROOMHOUSE MARKET
6 BROOMHOUSE PATH
7 BROOMHOUSE SQ
LONGSTONE VIEW
Sch

SAUGHTON RD
A71
ST W
ST
STENHOUSE
LONGSTONE TERR
LONGSTONE RD

2

BANKHEAD
IND EST
SIGHTHILL
IND EST
BANKHEAD CROSSWAY S
BANKHEAD WAY
BANKHEAD ST

Sighthill
Public Park
Coll
Sighthill
Coll
SIGHTHILL BANK
P
SIGHTHILL WYND
Liby
F Sta
CALDER RD
Off

BROOMHOUSE RD
B701
CALDER RD
PARKHEAD AVE
PARKHEAD GR
PARKHEAD CRES
PARKHEAD LOAN
PARKHEAD DR

71

THE CITY OF EDINBURGH BY-PASS
M8
A720
Junction 1
MID NEW CULTINS

CALDER RD
SIGHTHILL NEUK
SIGHTHILL ST
SIGHTHILL LOAN
SIGHTHILL PK
SIGHTHILL DR
Sch
MURRAYBURN RD
Parkhead
DUMBRYDEN GDNS
KINGSKNOWE PL
KINGSKNOWE RD

1

CALDER RD
East Hermiston
Union Canal
CALDER VIEW
CALDER PK
CALDER GDNS
CALDER CRES
CALDER GR
Sch
CALDER PL
WESTER HAILES RD
HARBOURFIELD
MURRAYBURN APP

Murray Burn
MURRAYBURN PL
HAILESLAND PL
HAILESLAND GR
HAILESLAND GDNS
WALKERS WYND
MURRAYBURN

HAILESLAND RD
DUMBRYDEN DR
Sch
Golf Course
1 CLOVENSTONE RD
2 WALKERS RIG
3 WALKERS CT

70

121
92

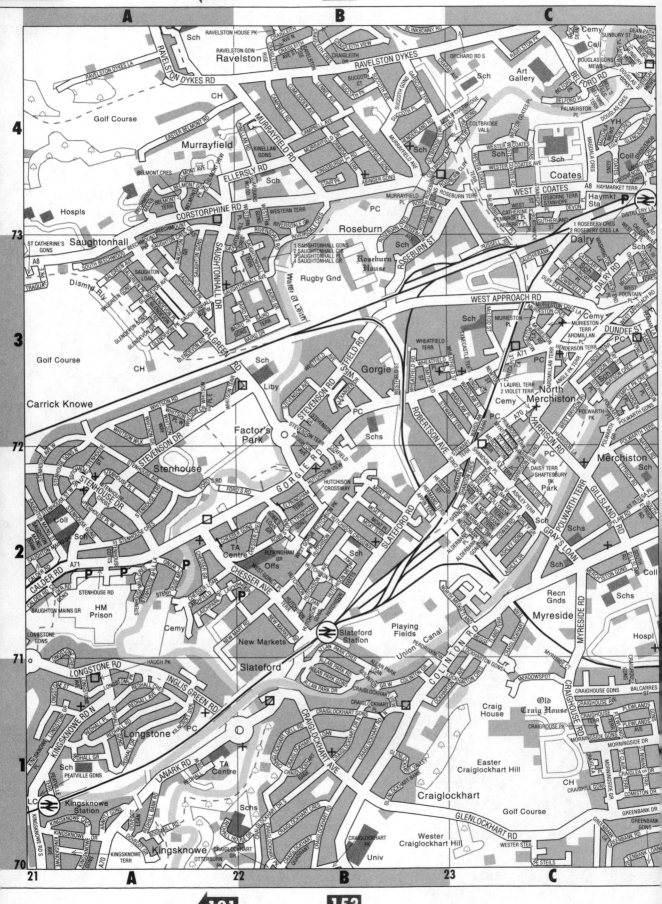

121
153

EDINBURGH

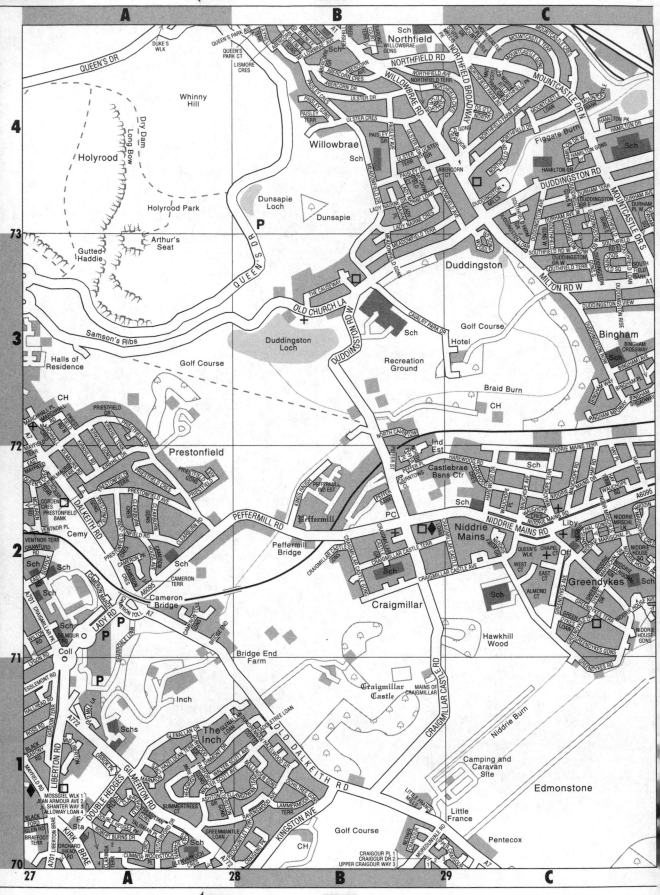

A B C

4

Queen's Dr
Duke's Wlk
Whinny Hill
Queen's Park Ave
Queen's Park Ct
Lismore Cres

Dry Dam
Long Bow

Holyrood

Holyrood Park

Willowbrae

Northfield
Sch
Willowbrae Gdns
Northfield Rd
Northfield Ave
Northfield Broadway
Mountcastle Dr N
Figgate Burn
Hamilton Pk
Sch
Duddingston Rd
Duddingston
Mountcastle Dr S

73

Dunsapie Loch
P
Dunsapie

Queen's Dr

Gutted Haddie

Arthur's Seat

Old Church La
The Causeway
Duddingston Rd W
Cavalry Park Dr
Sch
Golf Course
Hotel
Bingham
Bingham Crossway

3

Samson's Ribs

Halls of Residence

Golf Course

Duddingston Loch

Recreation Ground

Braid Burn
CH
Bingham Way
Bingham Broadway

72

CH
Priestfield Gr
Prestonfield

Mayfield Terr
East Mayfield
Marchall Rd

North Cairntow
Peffer St
Peffer Pl
Peffermill Ind Est
Ind Est
Castlebrae Bsns Ctr
Harewood Rd
Niddrie Mains Terr
Sch
Wauchope Ave
Niddrie Mains Dr
Hay Rd
Sch

Dalkeith Rd
Cobden Cres
Prestonfield Bank
Ventnor Pl
Cemy

Prestonfield Ave
Clearburn Gdns
Priestfield Cres
Priestfield Gdns

Peffermill Rd
Kings Haugh
Peffermill
PC
Niddrie Mains Rd
Niddrie Mains
Liby
Niddrie House

2

Ventnor Terr
Crawford Rd
Sch
Sch
East Suffolk

Cameron Pk
Cameron House Rd
Sch
Cameron Terr

Peffermill Bridge

Craigmillar Castle Gdns
Craigmillar Castle Terr
Sch
Craigmillar Castle Ave
Queen's Wlk
West Ct
East Ct
Almond Ct
Greendykes
Niddrie Marischal
Sch

Cameron Bridge
Cameron Toll

Craigmillar

Hawkhill Wood

Greendykes Terr
Niddrie House Gdns

71

Wilton Rd
Sch
Coll
Lygon Rd
P
P
Lady Rd

Bridge End
Bridge End Farm

Craigmillar Castle Rd

Niddrie Burn

1

Mayfield Rd
Esslemont Rd
Hallhead Rd
Ross Rd
Liberton Rd
Gilmerton Rd

Schs
Inch

The Inch
Old Dalkeith Rd

Craigmillar Castle

Mains of Craigmillar

Camping and Caravan Site
Little France

Edmonstone

70

Double Hedges
Kirk Brae
Liberton Brae

Kingston Ave
Golf Course
CH
Little France Mills
Pentecox

27 A 28 B 29 C

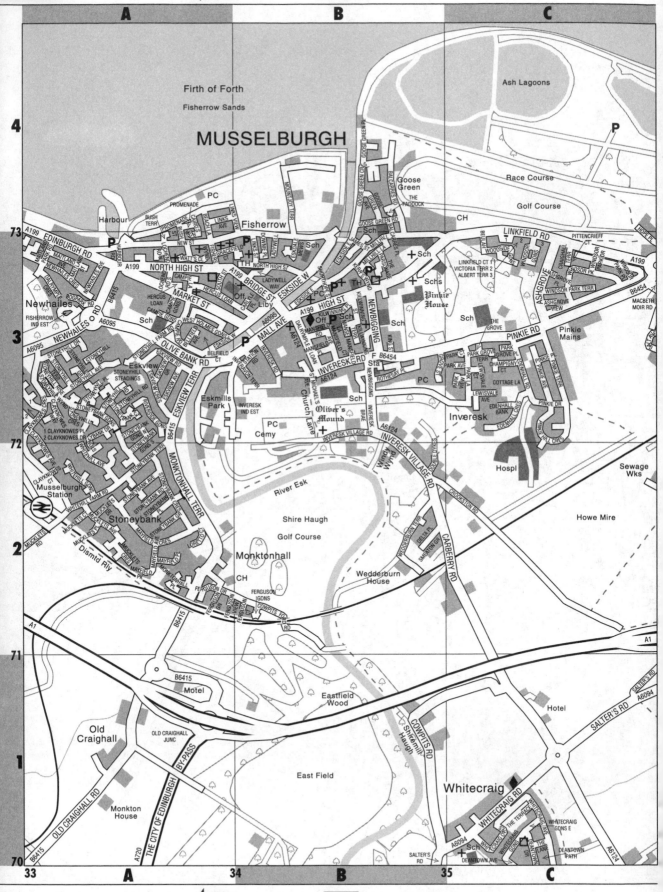

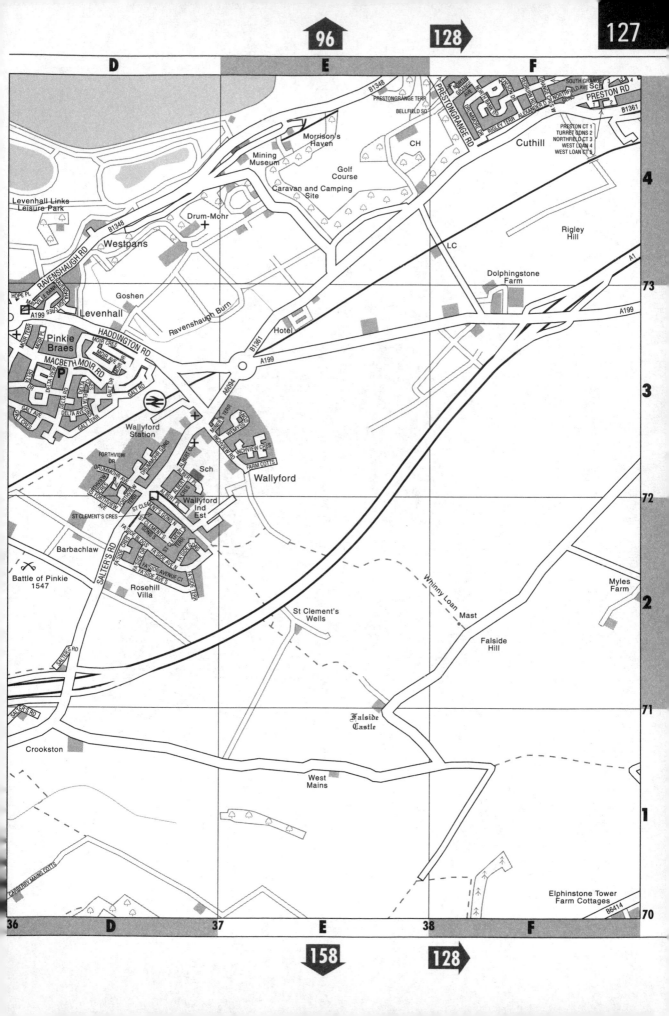

D   E   F

B1348
PRESTONGRANGE TERR
BELLFIELD SQ
PRESTONGRANGE RD

NORTH GRANGE AVE
SOUTH GRANGE 3
REDBURN RD
GRANGE DR
ALEXANDER CRES W
NORTHFIELD AVE
GRANGE GDNS
PRESTON RD
B1361

Morrison's Haven
CH
Cuthill

Mining Museum

PRESTON CT 1
TURRET GDNS 2
NORTHFIELD CT 3
WEST LOAN 4
WEST LOAN CT 5

Golf Course

4

Caravan and Camping Site

Levenhall Links Leisure Park

Drum-Mohr
Rigley Hill

B1348
RAVENSHAUGH RD
Westpans

LC

Dolphingstone Farm

A1

73

HOPE PL
MAYVILLE BANK
RAVENSHAUGH CRES
Goshen
Levenhall

A199

Ravenshaugh Burn

A199

MOIR TERR
Pinkie Braes
HADDINGTON RD
MOIR CRES
MOIR AVE
Hotel

B1361

MACBETH
MOIR RD
P
DELTA VIEW
DELTA RD
DELTA AVE
DELTA TERR
A6094
A199

3

GALT AVE
GALT RD
GALT CRES

Wallyford Station

MILLER'S TERR
WEMYSS
INCHVIEW RD
INCHVIEW CRES
FARM COTTS

FORTHVIEW DR
DRUMMOHR AVE
DRUMMOHR GDNS
ALBERT PL
ALBERT GDNS
Sch
Wallyford

DRUMMOHR CRES
FORTHVIEW TERR
FORTHVIEW AVE
ST FORTHVIEW AVE
ALBERT RD

72

ST CLEMENT'S CRES
ST CLEMENT'S GDNS N
Wallyford Ind Est

Barbachlaw

SALTER'S RD
FA SIDE CRES
FA SIDE GDNS
ST CLEMENT'S GDNS S
FA SIDE DR
FA SIDE AVE N
FA SIDE AVE CT
FA SIDE AVE S
FA SIDE TERR

Myles Farm

Battle of Pinkie 1547

Rosehill Villa

St Clement's Wells

Whinny Loan

Mast
Falside Hill

2

SALTERS RD

71

SALTER'S RD

Falside Castle

Crookston

West Mains

1

CARBERRY MAINS COTTS

Elphinstone Tower Farm Cottages

B6414
70

36   D   37   E   38   F

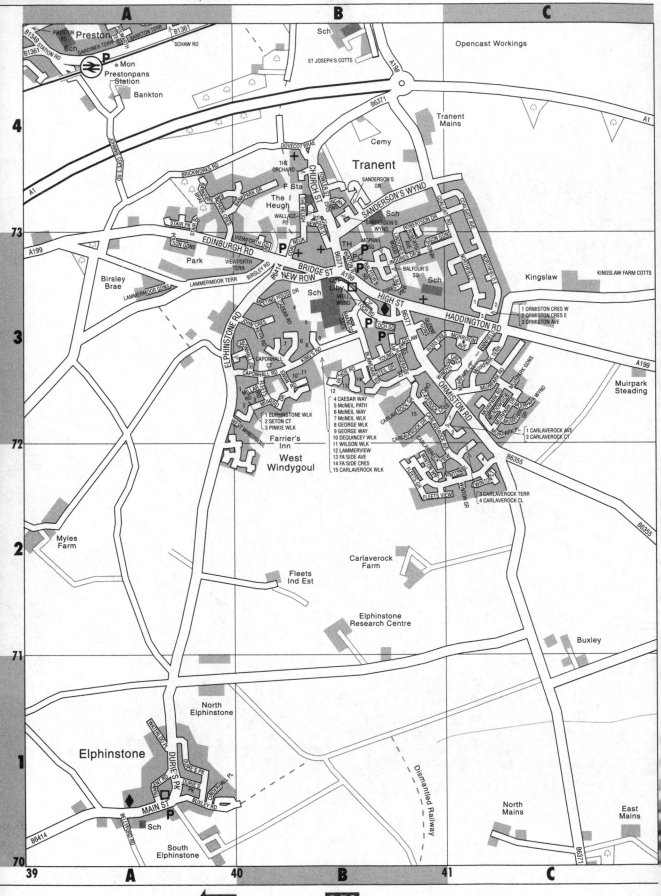

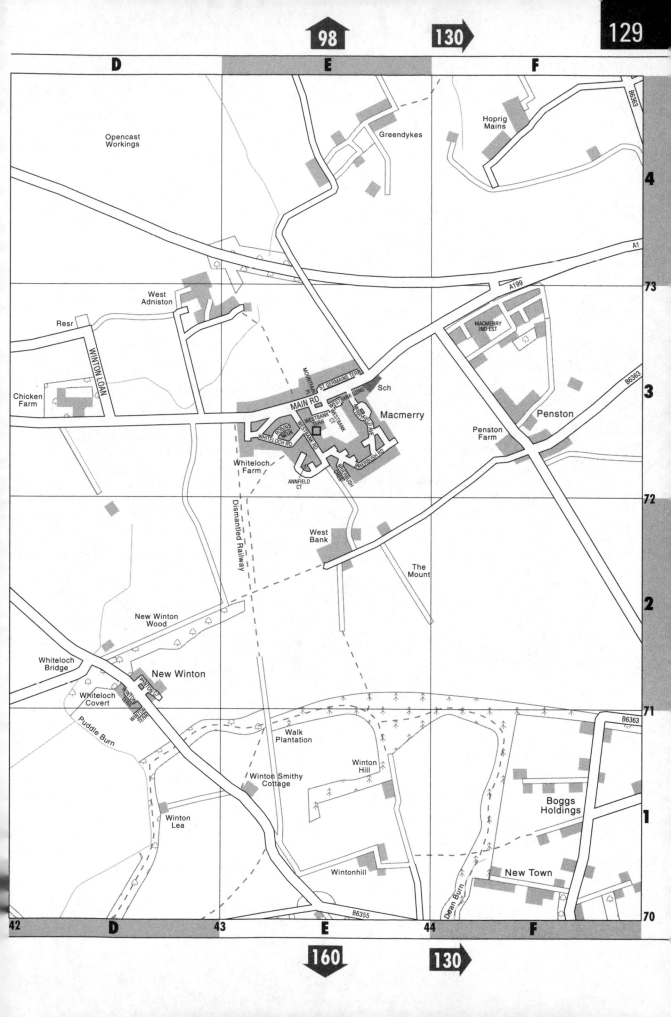

Opencast
Workings

Greendykes

Hoprig
Mains

4

West
Adniston

Resr

WINTON LOAN

Chicken
Farm

A1

A199

MACMERRY
IND EST

73

Sch

St GERMAINS TERR

MOUNTFAIR PL

MAIN RD

WESTBANK GDNS

Macmerry

WESTBANK
TERR

WESTBANK
CT

MERRYFIELD AVE

Penston

B6363

3

Penston
Farm

ROBINS
NEUK

WESTBANK RD

WHITELOCH RD

Whiteloch
Farm

BIRCHBUSH RD

BIRCHBUSH CRES

ANNFIELD
CT

West
Bank

72

Dismantled Railway

The
Mount

New Winton
Wood

2

Whiteloch
Bridge

New Winton

Whiteloch
Covert

WINTON TERR

PENTON ST

Puddle Burn

B6363

71

Walk
Plantation

Winton
Hill

Winton Smithy
Cottage

Boggs
Holdings

Winton
Lea

1

Wintonhill

New Town

Dean Burn

B6355

70

42   43   44

129
99

A **B** **C**

B6363

4 Gladsmuir

Granary

South Lodge

Tangle Muir Wood

Ugstonrigg

A1

Spittalrigg

A1

LAMINGTON

LAMMERVIEW

Brickfield Cottages

Gladsmuir Farmhouse

Woodside

Heathery Wood

BIRK HEDGES

73

Liberty Hall North Wood

Quarry Park

Lamblair Wood

Newbold Revel

Hopefield

Liberty Hall

Green Gates Wood

Haddington Wood

Gladshot

3 Butterdean

Butterdean Plantation

Liberty Hall South Wood

Blinkbonny House

Nairns Mains

B6363

Nairns Mains Farm

72

Samuelston Loanhead

A6093

Nursery Wood

2 Hodges

Cuddie Wood

Jerusalem Croft

B6363

71

B6363

West Mains

Jerusalem Farm

River Tyne

1 Boggs Farm House

Nisbet Loanhead

Boggs Holdings

Herdmanston Mains

70

45 **A** 46 **B** 47 **C**

A6093

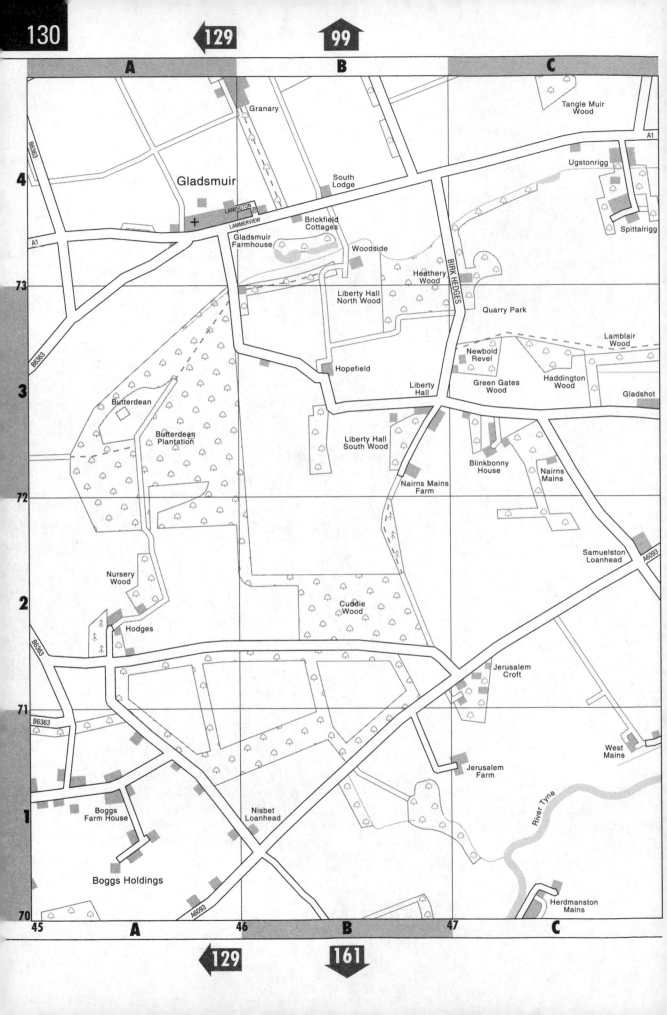

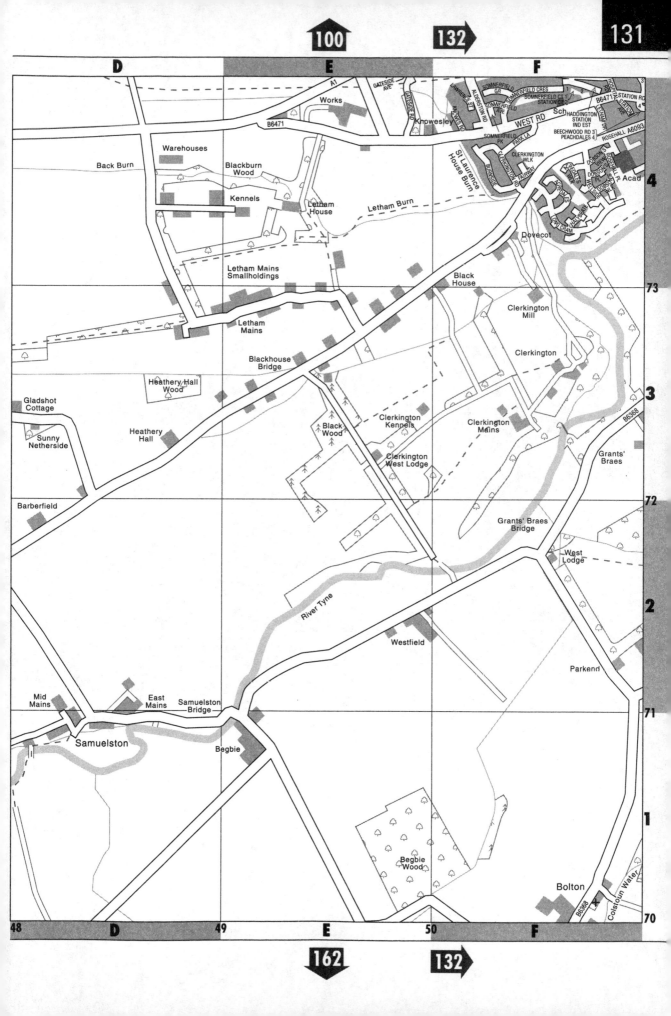

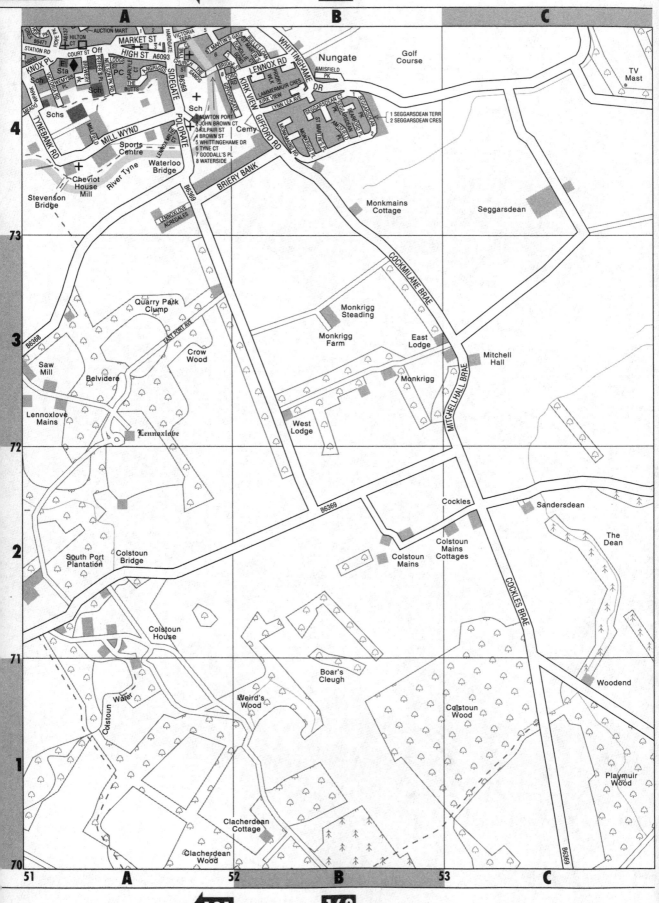

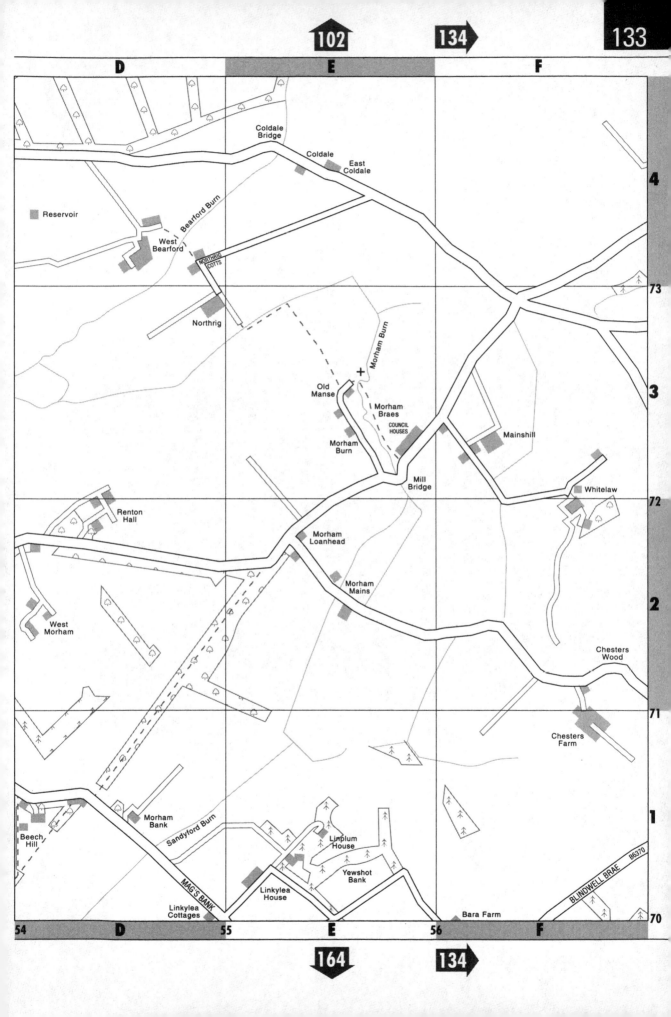

D E F

4

Coldale
Bridge
Coldale
East
Coldale

Reservoir

Bearford Burn

West
Bearford
NORTHRIG
COTTS

73

Northrig

Morham Burn

+

Old
Manse

3

Morham
Braes
COUNCIL
HOUSES
Mainshill

Morham
Burn

Mill
Bridge

Whitelaw

72

Renton
Hall

Morham
Loanhead

West
Morham

Morham
Mains

2

Chesters
Wood

71

Chesters
Farm

Morham
Bank

Beech
Hill

Sandyford Burn

1

Linplum
House

Yewshot
Bank

MAG'S BANK

BLINDWELL BRAE
B6370

Linkylea
House

Bara Farm

Linkylea
Cottages

70

54 D 55 E 56 F

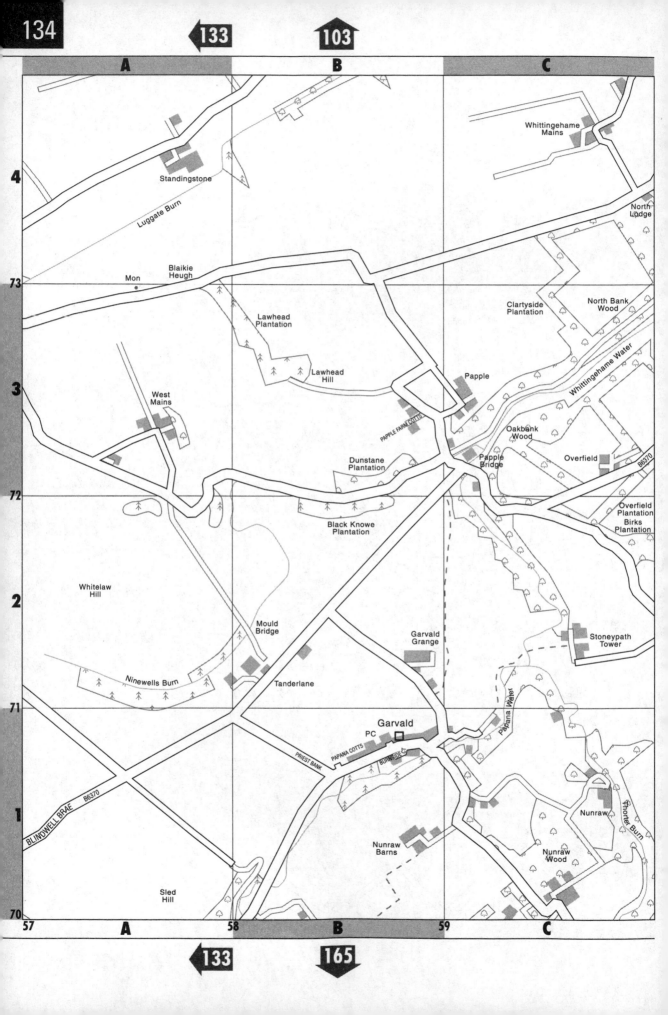

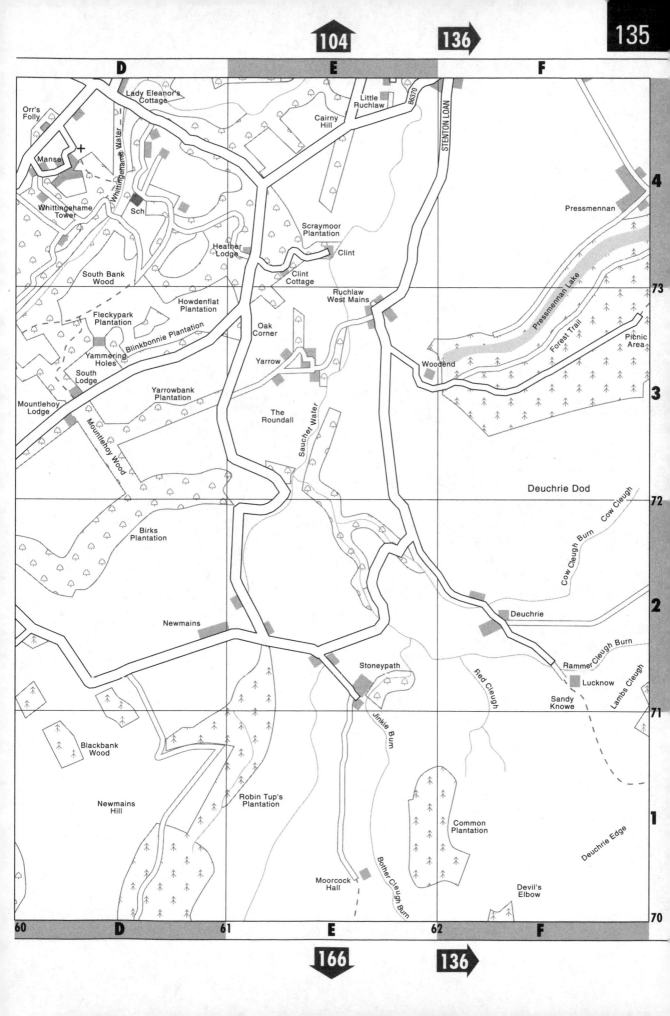

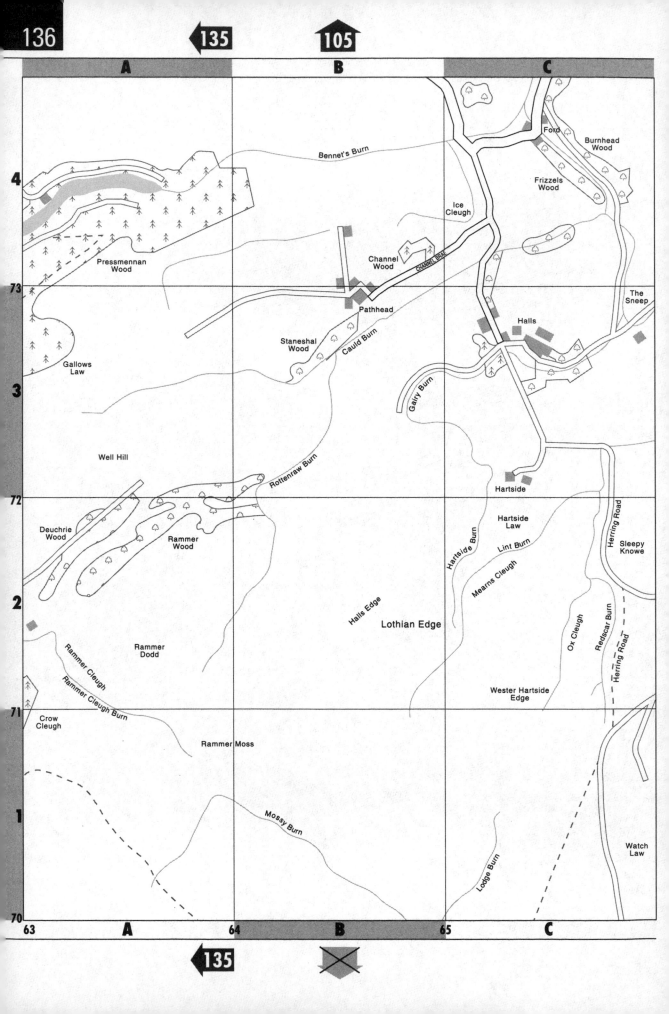

A   B   C

4

Ford
Burnhead
Wood

Bennet's Burn

Frizzels
Wood

Ice
Cleugh

Channel
Wood   CHANNEL BRAE

73   The
                                                     Sneep

Pathhead

Pressmennan
Wood   Staneshal   Halls
                        Wood   Cauld Burn

Gallows
Law

Gairy Burn

3

Well Hill

Hartside

Rottenraw Burn

72   Hartside
                                                     Law

Deuchrie   Hartside   Sleepy
Wood   Rammer   Burn   Lint Burn Knowe
              Wood   Mearns Cleugh
                                                              Herring Road

                                            Halls Edge   Ox Cleugh
2   Redscar Burn
                                      Lothian Edge
              Rammer   Herring Road
              Dodd
Rammer
Cleugh   Wester Hartside
Rammer Cleugh Burn   Edge

71 Crow
    Cleugh

              Rammer Moss

                                                              Watch
1   Law
              Mossy Burn
                                            Lodge Burn

70
63   A   64   B   65   C

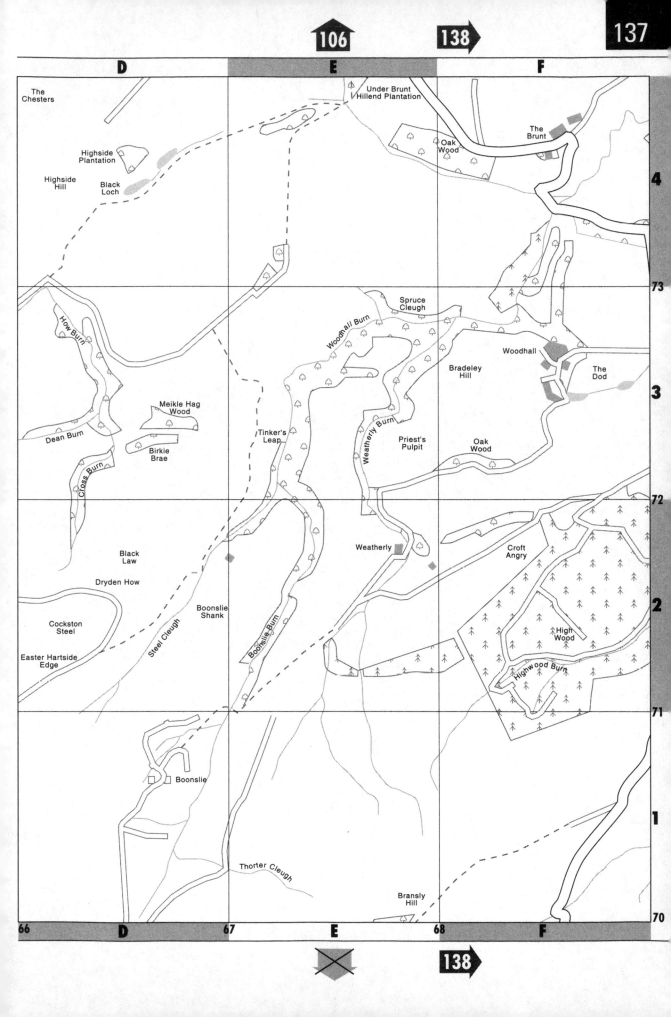

106
138 →

D E F

The Chesters

Highside Plantation

Highside Hill

Black Loch

Under Brunt
Hillend Plantation

Oak Wood

The Brunt

4

73

How Burn

Spruce Cleugh

Woodhall Burn

Woodhall

Bradeley Hill

The Dod

3

Meikle Hag Wood

Dean Burn

Birkie Brae

Tinker's Leap

Weatherly Burn

Priest's Pulpit

Oak Wood

Cross Burn

72

Black Law

Dryden How

Weatherly

Croft Angry

High Wood

Highwood Burn

2

Cockston Steel

Steel Cleugh

Boonslie Shank

Boonslie Burn

Easter Hartside Edge

71

Boonslie

1

Thorter Cleugh

Bransly Hill

70

A   B   C

4

Aikendean
Wood

Birky Bog
Plantation

Whittly
Strip

73

Windford Dub
Plantation

Thurston
Mains

Thurston Mains Burn

Cemy

East
Lodge

Meml

Temple
Mains

Grey's
Acre

Woodhall
Farm

Tripslaw
Strip

3

Tripslaw Hill
Plantation

Falsely
Cottage

Finley
How

Elmscleugh Water

Mast

72

Falsely
Hill

Swallow
Brae

Elmscleugh

Bonnetty
Knowe

Blackcastle Hill

Elms Cleugh

Elmscleugh
Wood

Needle Cleugh

2

Cocklaw Hill

Berry Hill

Needle Hill

71

Weather Law

Needle
Wood

Wester
Aikengall

Sheeppath
Hill

Sheeppath
Glen

Aikengall Water

Cockit Hat
Wood

Main
Wood

Aller Bog

1

Top Fold
Wood

Aikengall

Oldhamestocks Burn

70

69   70   71

A   B   C

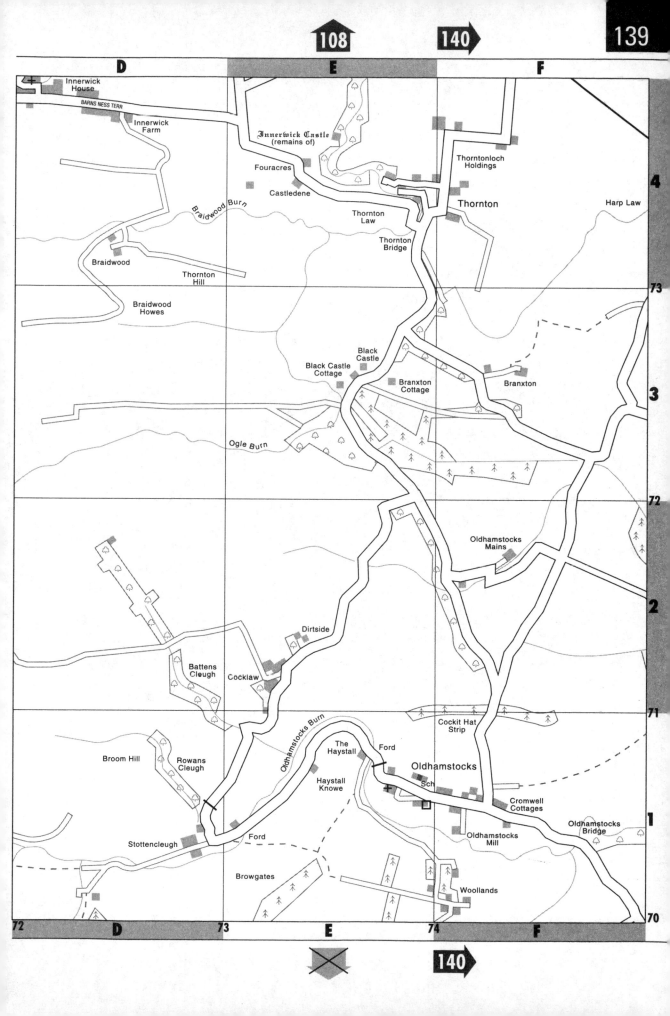

A   B   C

A1

4

Lawfield

73

Bilsdean
Creek

The Linn

Birnieknowes

Bilsdean

Gutcher's
Hole

3

Clay
Knowe

PC

Dunglass
Old Bridge

Broomward

Bilsdean
Bridge

Dunglass
Bridge

Rams
Heugh

Braid Law

Gallows Law
Plantation

Dunglass
New Bridge

Dunglass
Viaduct

Castle Dyke
Cottage

Dunglass
Mains

Deanberry
Hole

72

Gallows
Law

Dunglass
Church

Dunglass

Killflat
Wood

CG
Sta

Cove

Bilsdean
Banks

Bilsdean Burn

Forth Brae

Cats Hole
Plantation

Rules
Law

Dunglass Burn

Pathhead

2

Closehead

Gowdies
Well

Belvidere
Wood

Eildbalks
Wood

Cockburnspath

Cati
Heugh

PC
Sch

TOLLVIEW

Hotel

Springfield

Dean Mill
Bog

CALLANDER PL

HOPRIG RD

THE SQUARE

71

Braeside
Cottage

Chapelhill
Cotts

HOPRIG RD

HOPRIG PK

CROFTS RD

CROFTS RD

Dovecot
Hall

Cockburnspath Burn

Kirklands

Sand
Pit

Chapelhill

1

Berwick Burn

A1

Hazeldean Burn

Neuk
Farm

Kinegar
Strip

70

75   A   76   B   77   C

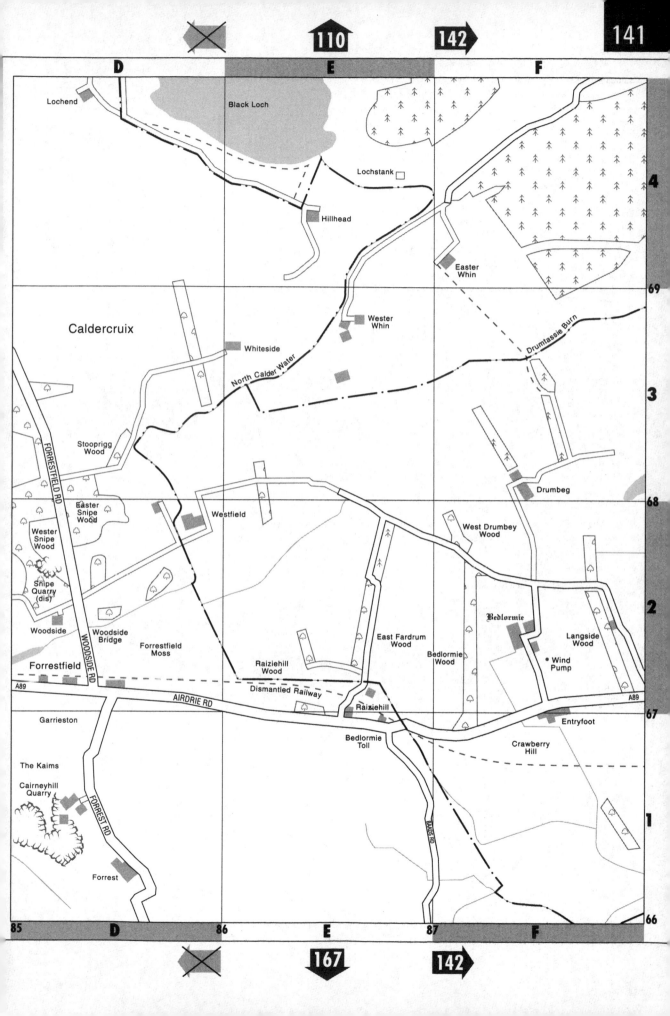

Lochend

Black Loch

Lochstank

4

Hillhead

69

Easter
Whin

Caldercruix

Wester
Whin

Whiteside

Drumtassie Burn

North Calder Water

3

Stooprigg
Wood

Drumbeg

68

FORRESTFIELD RD

Easter
Snipe
Wood

Westfield

West Drumbey
Wood

Wester
Snipe
Wood

Snipe
Quarry
(dis)

Bedlormie

2

Langside
Wood

East Fardrum
Wood

Wind
Pump

Woodside

WOODSIDE RD

Woodside
Bridge

Forrestfield
Moss

Raiziehill
Wood

Bedlormie
Wood

Forrestfield

A89

Dismantled Railway

A89

AIRDRIE RD

67

Raiziehill

Garrieston

Entryfoot

Bedlormie
Toll

Crawberry
Hill

The Kaims

Cairneyhill
Quarry

BAUDS RD

FORREST RD

1

Forrest

85   86   87   66

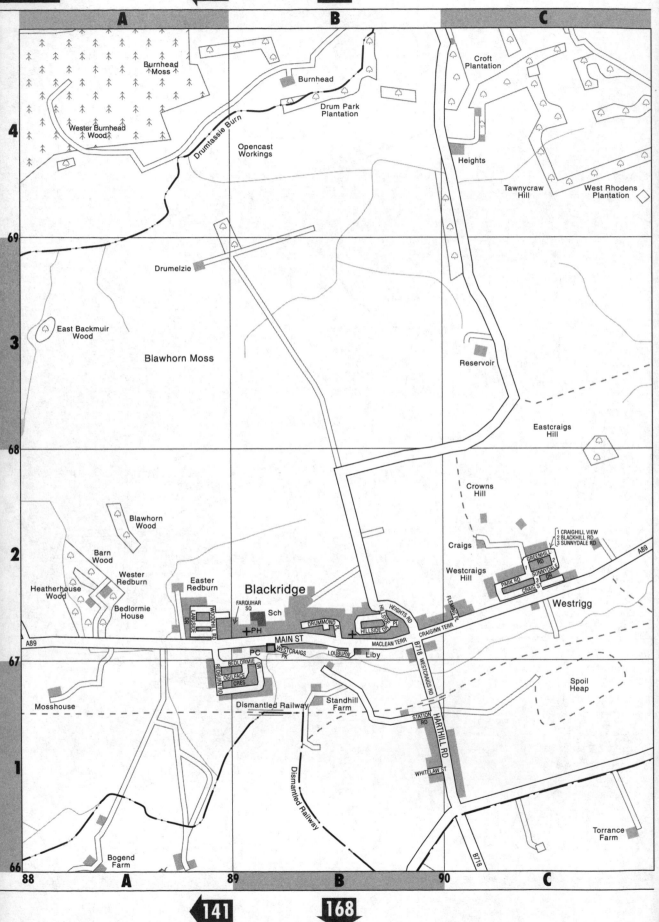

A　　　　　B　　　　　C

Burnhead
Moss

Wester Burnhead
Wood

Burnhead

Drum Park
Plantation

Croft
Plantation

Drumtassie Burn

Opencast
Workings

Heights

Tawnycraw
Hill

West Rhodens
Plantation

4

69

Drumelzie

East Backmuir
Wood

Blawhorn Moss

Reservoir

Eastcraigs
Hill

3

68

Crowns
Hill

Blawhorn
Wood

Barn
Wood

Wester
Redburn

Heatherhouse
Wood

Bedlormie
House

Easter
Redburn

FARQUHAR
SQ

Sch

Blackridge

Craigs

Westcraigs
Hill

1 CRAIGHILL VIEW
2 BLACKHILL RD
3 SUNNYDALE RD

GREENHILL
RD

SUNNYDALE
DR

PARK RD

CRAIG ST

Westrigg

A89

2

LAWSIDE DR

WOODHILL RD

PH

DRUMMOND
PL

HILLSIDE DR

HEIGHTS RD

HILLSIDE PL

MACLEAN TERR

CRAIGINN TERR

FLEMING PL

MAIN ST

A89

PC

WESTCRAIGS
PK

LOUBURN

Liby

B718 WESTCRAIGS RD

67

BEDLORMIE
DR

REDBURN RD

OGILFACE
CRES

Mosshouse

Dismantled Railway

Standhill
Farm

STATION
RD

HARTHILL RD

Spoil
Heap

Dismantled Railway

WHITELAW ST

1

Torrance
Farm

B718

Bogend
Farm

66

88　　　　　89　　　　　90

A　　　　　B　　　　　C

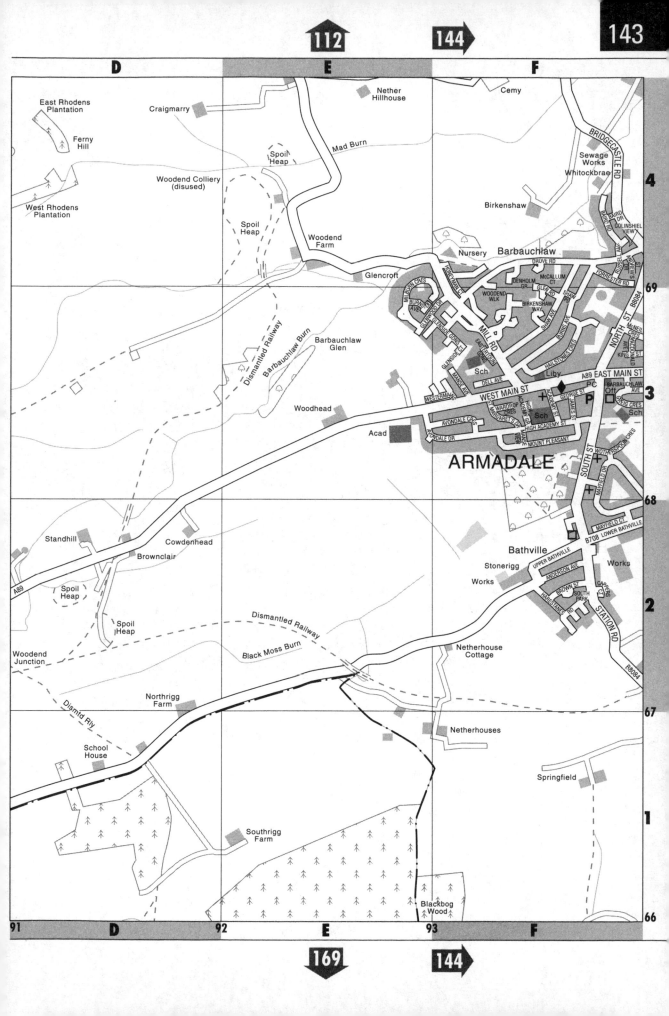

D   E   F

East Rhodens Plantation
Ferny Hill
Craigmarry
Nether Hillhouse
Cemy
BRIDGECASTLE RD
Spoil Heap
Mad Burn
Sewage Works
Whitockbrae
4
Woodend Colliery (disused)
Birkenshaw
BAIRD RD
BAIRD DR
COLINSHIEL VIEW
West Rhodens Plantation
Spoil Heap
Woodend Farm
Nursery
Barbauchlaw
ANDREW'S ST
FORRESTER RD
JOHNSTONE ST
DROVE RD
McCALLUM CT
DENHOLM GR
GLEN RD
NORTH ST
B8084
69
HONEYMAN LN
MILBURN CRES
Glencroft
Woodend WLK
Birkenshaw Way
McNEIL CRES
MACDONALD AVE
KING ST
Dismantled Railway
BURNS AVE
GLENWORD DR
GLENSIDE GDNS
GLENSIDE CT
SHAW AVE
SHAW AVE
BURNS CRES
Barbauchlaw Glen
Barbauchlaw Burn
MILL RD
EASTBURN GDNS
HAILSTONES CRES
Woodhead
GLENSIDE RD
MANSE AVE
DELL AVE
Sch
Liby
A89 EAST MAIN ST
PC
BARBAUCHLAW AVE
3
WESTERMAINS
WEST MAIN ST
ACADEMY ST
HIGH ST
GEORGE ST
JAMES ST
P
CRAIG CRES
Sch
Acad
AVONDALE CRES
AVONDALE DR
ST MARGARET'S LN
WARDROP CRES
MANSE VIEW
HIGH ACADEMY ST
MOUNT PLEASANT
Off
SOUTH ST
WOTHERSPOON CRES
ARMADALE
MAYFIELD DR
68
Standhill
Cowdenhead
MAYFIELD CT
B708 LOWER BATHVILLE
Brownclair
Bathville
Stonerigg
UPPER BATHVILLE
ANDERSON AVE
Works
CAPERS CT
A89
Spoil Heap
Works
BROWN ST
SOUTH PARK
HARESTANES RD
STATION RD
2
Spoil Heap
Dismantled Railway
Netherhouse Cottage
B8084
Woodend Junction
Black Moss Burn
Dismtd Rly
Northrigg Farm
67
School House
Netherhouses
Springfield
1
Southrigg Farm
Blackbog Wood
66

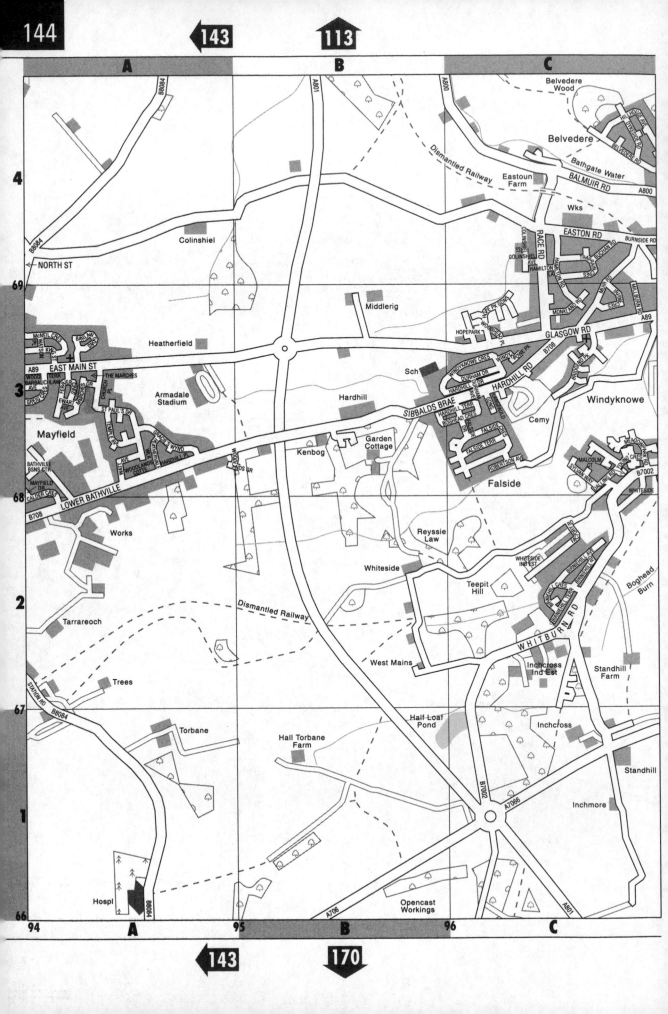

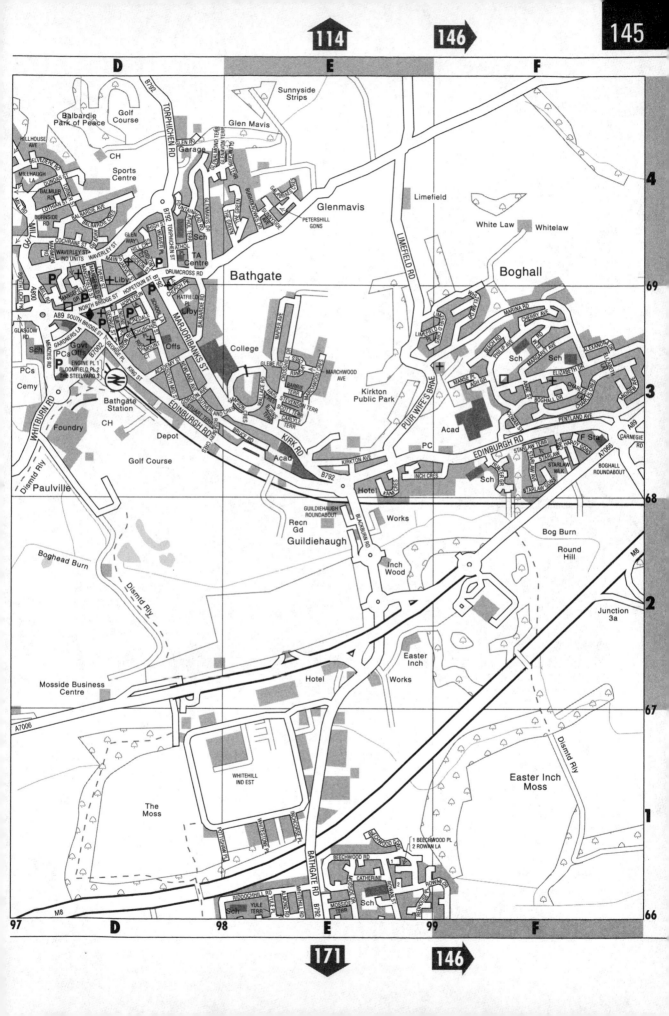

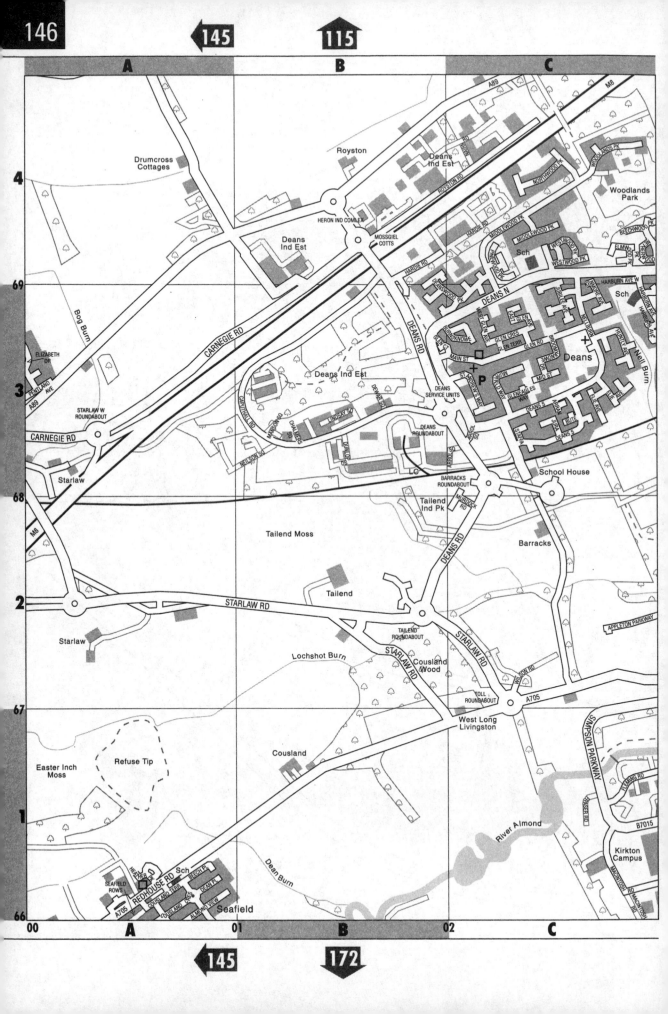

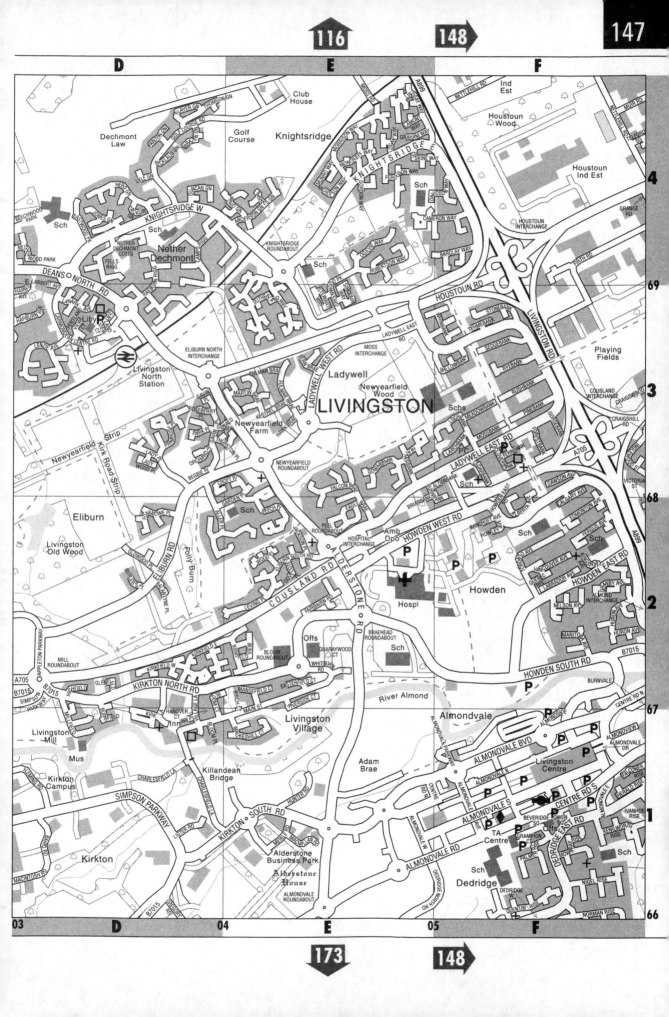

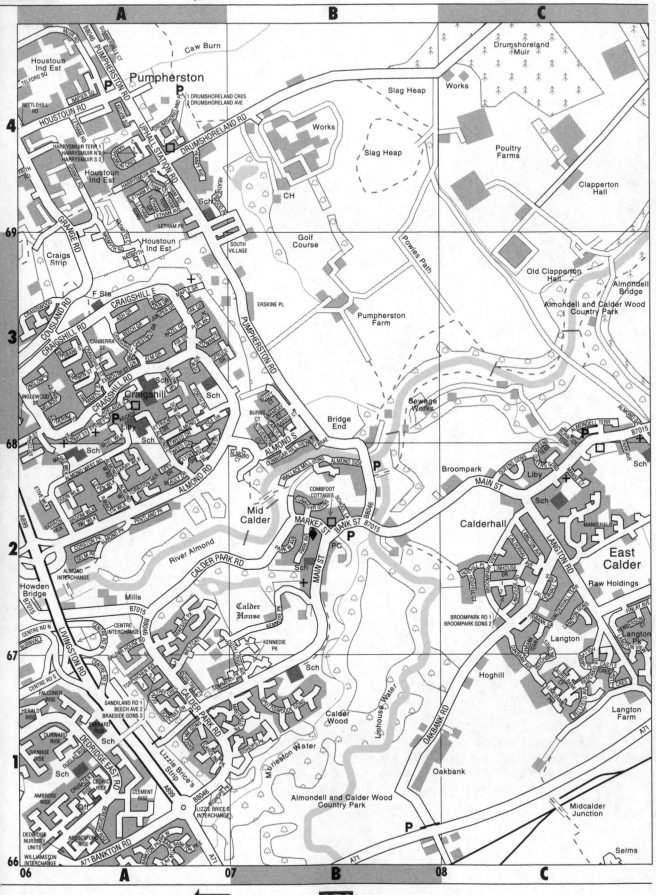

D E F

4

69

3

68

2

67

1

66

Strathbrock and Kirkhill Woodlands

P

River Almond

Shiel Mill

PC

Almondell Plantations

Nethershiel

Almondell and Calder Wood Country Park

Illieston

West Clifton

WEST CLIFTON FARM COTTS

West Clifton Cottages

North Lodge

West Bonnington

Bonnington House

BONNINGTON

Overshiel

Elmbank

LINDEAN TERR

A71

Coxydene

B7015

Whitehill

Raw Holdings

P

Camps

Works

Poultry Farm

Works

MAIN ST

Sch

B7031

Raw Farm

Dismantled Railway

Burnhouse

Gogar Burn

Humbie

Humbie Smallholdings

Raw Holdings

Milrig Smallholdings

Milrig

Kirknewton Mains

Dismtd Rly

LIMEKILNS

GR

FINLAY AVE

ORMISTON CRES

ORMISTON DR

Ormiston Mains

B7031

LANGTON VIEW

Kirknewton Station

Highfield

LC

STATION RD

Sch

BRIDGEND LANE

KAIMES AVE KAIMES KAIMES GDNS

KAIMES CRES

ROOSEVELT RD

FORTH VIEW

HILLHOUSE TERR

HILLHOUSE CRES

MEADOWBANK VIEW

PARK TERR

CHURCHILL WAY

Hill House

MAIN ST

Graveyard

Kirknewton

ST DAVIDS RD

SMITHY BRAE

Greenloan Cottage

Ormiston

Ormiston Farm

Ormiston Plantation

Overton Farm

THE LOW DOORS

Kirknewton House

Betty's Fauld

Lawheads

Cockmylane

Wester Strip

Middle Strip

Jubilee Wood

B7031

09 D 10 E 11 F

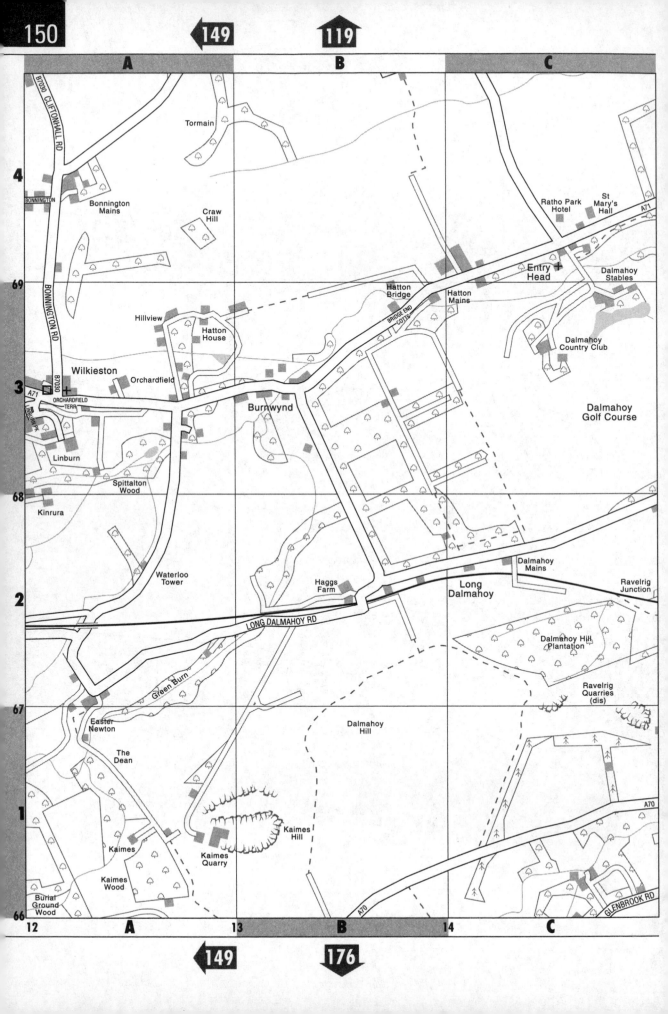

D   E   F

Addiston Mains
Addiston Bridge
ADDISTON FARM RD
A71

Lodge
Crow Wood
Addistoun
Gogar Burn

Heriot-Watt University
RESEARCH AVE
BOUNDARY RD N
FIRST GAIT
SECOND GAIT
HUGH GAIT
FOURTH GAIT
RESEARCH PK RD
RESEARCH PK AVE
MEDIOCK RD
THE AVENUE
Riccarton
Liby
CAMERON SMAILL RD

Lover's Loan

4

Ellswood Cottage

69

Warriston

South Strip

3

Weaver's Knowe

Muir o' Dean

Malcomstone

Cocklaw

Currievale
Curriehill Station
CURRIEHILL RD
RICCARTON DR
RICCARTON MAINS RD

Gowanhill
Murray Burn

68

Newhouse

LC
NEWMILLS RD
CURRIEVALE DR
CURRIEVALE PARK
CURRIEVALE GR
Sch
FORTH VIEW CRES
PALMER RD
PENTLAND AVE
Sch
PALMER PL
PENTLAND VIEW
FORTH VIEW RD
DOLPHIN GDNS W
DOLPHIN GDNS E
DOLPHIN RD
PENTLAND VIEW
A70

2

Dismantled Railway
RAVELRIG RD
ADDISTON GR
ADDISTON PK
ADDISTON CORS
HORSBURGH BANK
HORSBURGH GDNS
HORSBURGH
DALMAHOY CRES
TURNER PK
TURNER AVE
STATION LOAN
NEWMILLS RD
OLD
NEWMILLS CRES
NEWMILLS RD
CURRIEHILL CASTLE DR
WYVIS GR
WYVIS PK
CHERRY TREE PK
CHERRY TREE AVE
CHERRY TREE LOAN
CHERRY TREE GDNS
CHERRY TREE CRES
CHERRY TREE PL
CHERRY TREE
RONAN TREE AVE
RONAN TREE
STEWART CRES
STEWART AVE
STEWART PL
STEWART CRES
WAULKMILL LOAN
Water of Leith Walkway
Lennox Tower
Duncan's Belt

Ravelrig Hill
Pilmuir Farm
LANARK RD W
Water of Leith
Lymphoy

67

Hannah Field
LANARK RD W
RAVELRIG HILL
RAVELRIG
RAVELRIG BRAE
Ravelrig
BRIDGE RD
Sch
LARCHFIELD
LARCHFIELD NEUK
BURDIEHOUSE
JOHNSBURN RD
Sch
LADYCROFT
LADYCROFT
Malleny House
BAVELAW RD
BAVELAW GDNS
Sawpit Wood
Black Wood

1

Larch Grove
Bankhead
Bankhead House
GLENBROOK RD
JOHNSBURN RD
JOHNSBURN GR
DAPHNE
JOHNSBURN PK
LOVEDALE RD
LOVEDALE GDNS
LOVEDALE CRES
LOVEDALE AVE
DEANPARK CT
DEANPARK PL
DEANPARK BANK
DEANPARK VIEW
DEANPARK CRES
DEANPARK AVE
BAVELAW GR
Balerno
MANSFIELD AVE
MALLENY AVE
HARLAW RD
1 QUARRY HOWE
2 SLAESIDE

66

15   D   16   E   17   F

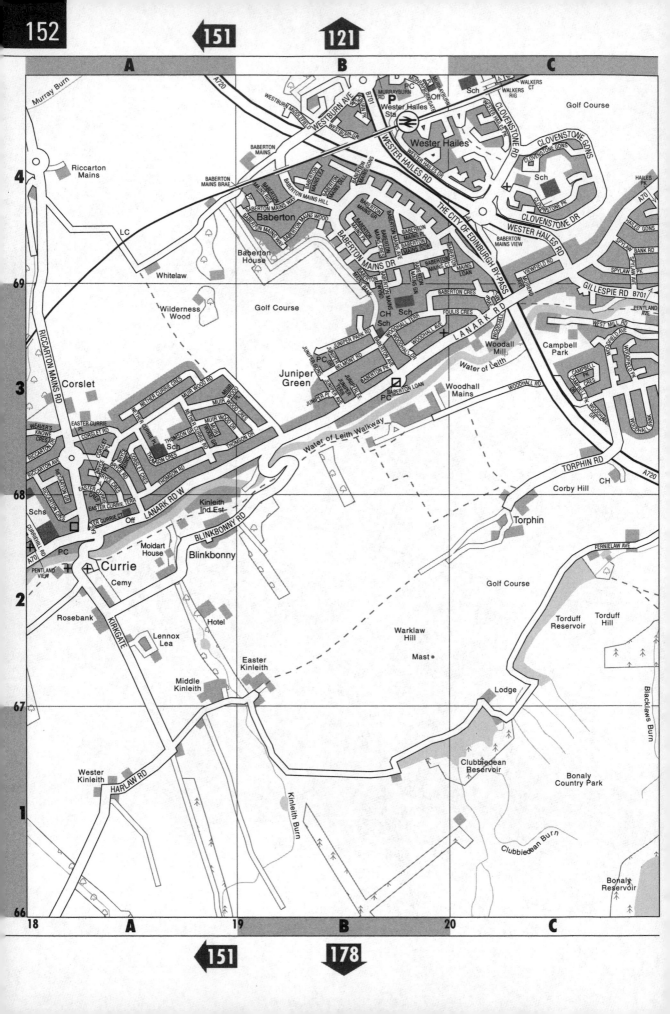

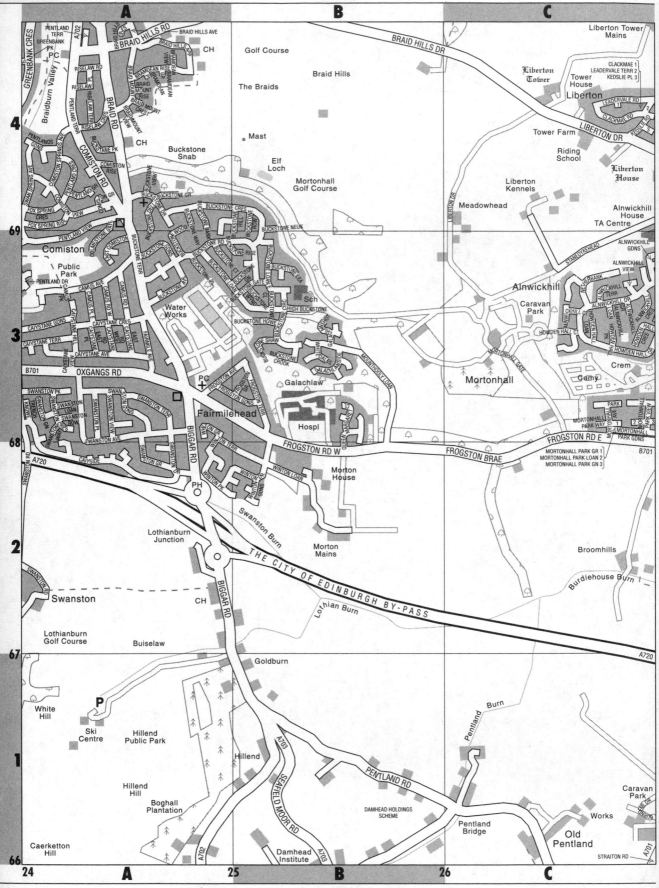

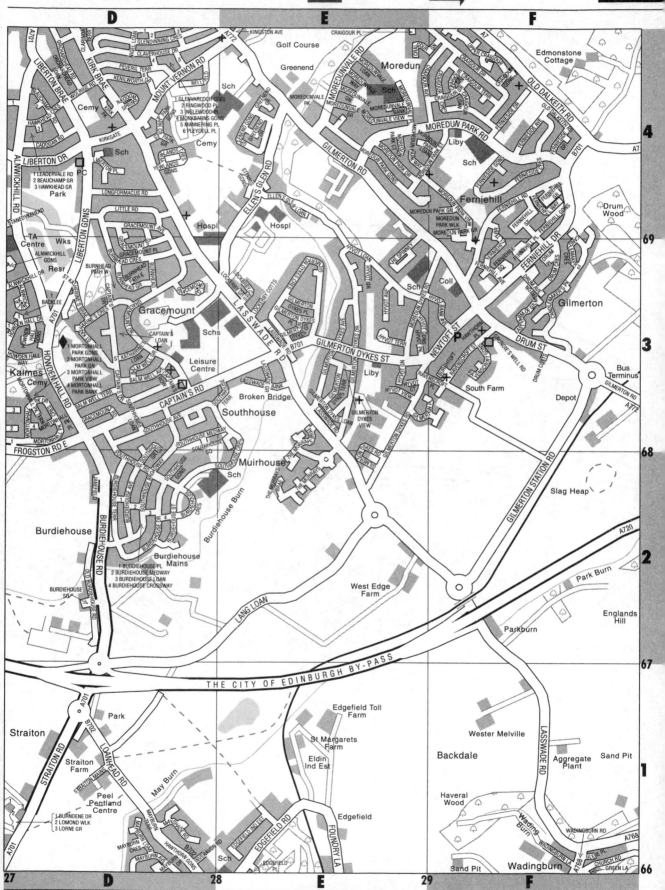

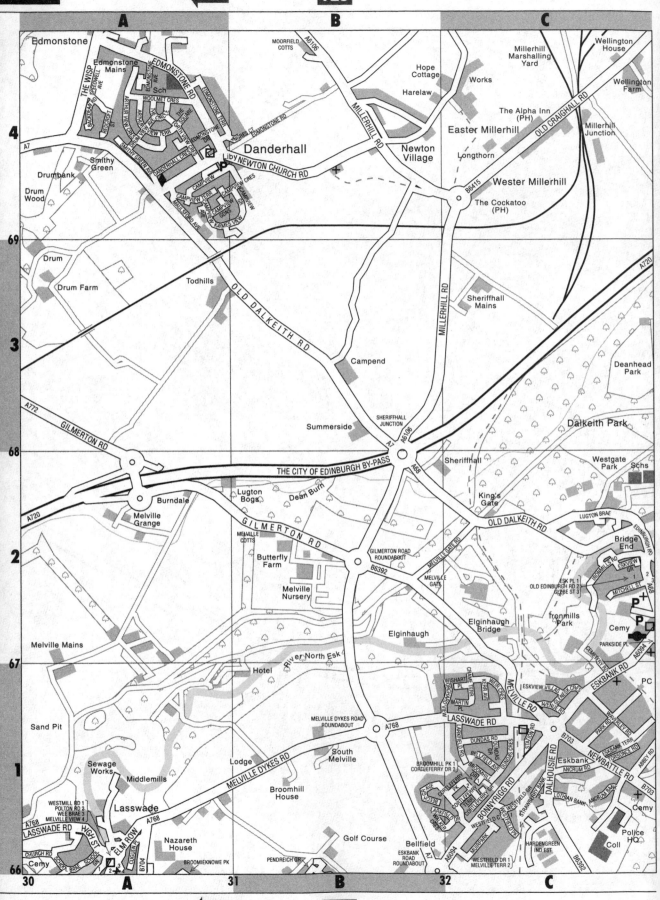

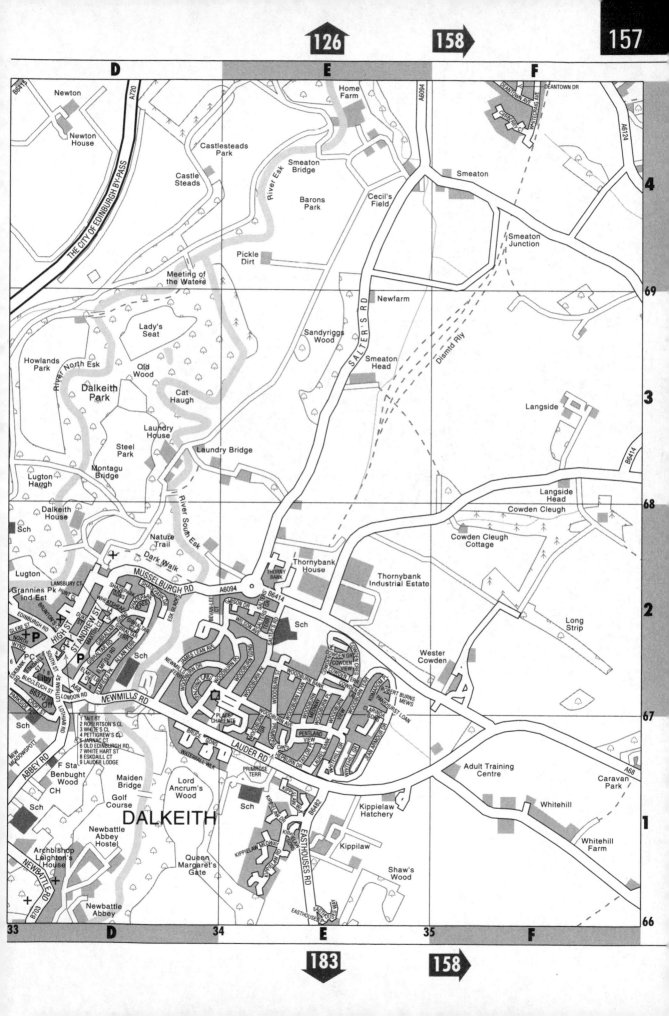

D · **E** · **F**

Newton

Newton House

Castlesteads Park

Castle Steads

THE CITY OF EDINBURGH BY-PASS

Smeaton Bridge

River Esk

Barons Park

Home Farm

Cecil's Field

Smeaton

4

DEANTOWN DR

Pickle Dirt

Meeting of the Waters

SALTER'S RD

Newfarm

Smeaton Junction

69

Lady's Seat

Howlands Park

River North Esk

Old Wood

Dalkeith Park

Cat Haugh

Sandyriggs Wood

Smeaton Head

Dismtd Rly

Langside

3

Laundry House

Steel Park

Montagu Bridge

Laundry Bridge

Langside Head

Lugton Haugh

Cowden Cleugh

68

Dalkeith House

Sch

River South Esk

Nature Trail

Dark Walk

THORNY BANK

Thornybank House

Cowden Cleugh Cottage

Lugton

MUSSELBURGH RD

A6094

B6414

Thornybank Industrial Estate

Grannies Pk Ind Est

EDINBURGH RD

HIGH ST

ST ANDREW ST

Sch

James Lean Ave

NEWMILLS RD

Sch

Cowden View

Wester Cowden

Long Strip

2

GLEBE ST

P

PC

P

Lib

LONDON RD

A68

Robert Burns Mews

Adult Training Centre

Caravan Park

1

ABBEY RD

F Sta

Benbught Wood

CH

Sch

Maiden Bridge

Golf Course

LAUDER RD

1 TAIT ST
2 ROBERTSON'S CL
3 WHITE'S CL
4 PETTIGREW'S CL
5 JARNAC CT
6 OLD EDINBURGH RD
7 WHITE HART ST
8 ESKDAILL CT
9 LAUDER LODGE

PRIMROSE TERR

WATERFALL WALK

Lord Ancrum's Wood

Sch

Kippielaw Hatchery

Whitehill

DALKEITH

Newbattle Abbey Hostel

Queen Margaret's Gate

KIPPIELAW MEDWAY

EASTHOUSES RD

Kippilaw

Shaw's Wood

Whitehill Farm

Archbishop Leighton's House

NEWBATTLE RD

Newbattle Abbey

EASTHOUSES

66

A **B** **C**

St John's
Hospice

Sch

Carberry Hill

Hillhead

B6414

Carberry Tower

Queen Mary's
Mount

4

A6124

Backhill

Bellyford Burn

69

Smeaton
Shaw

Crossgatehall

Works

Hadfast

Chalkieside

B6414

Airybank
House

HADFAST RD

3

CHAPEL BANK

STEWART PK

DALRYMPLE LOAN

SOUTHFIELD RD

CRANSTON DR

Sch

Cousland

68

Bartholomew's
Firlot

Southfield

Airfield

2

Easter
Cowden

Fordel
Park

67

Cowden Bog
Wood

A6124

Fordel
Inn

A68

Fordel
Dean

Fordel
Mains

A6093

1

Fordel Bank
Plantation

Fordel Dean
Bridge

Cotty Burn

Fuffet
Wood

A6093

North
Lodge

A68

66

36 **A** **37** **B** **38** **C**

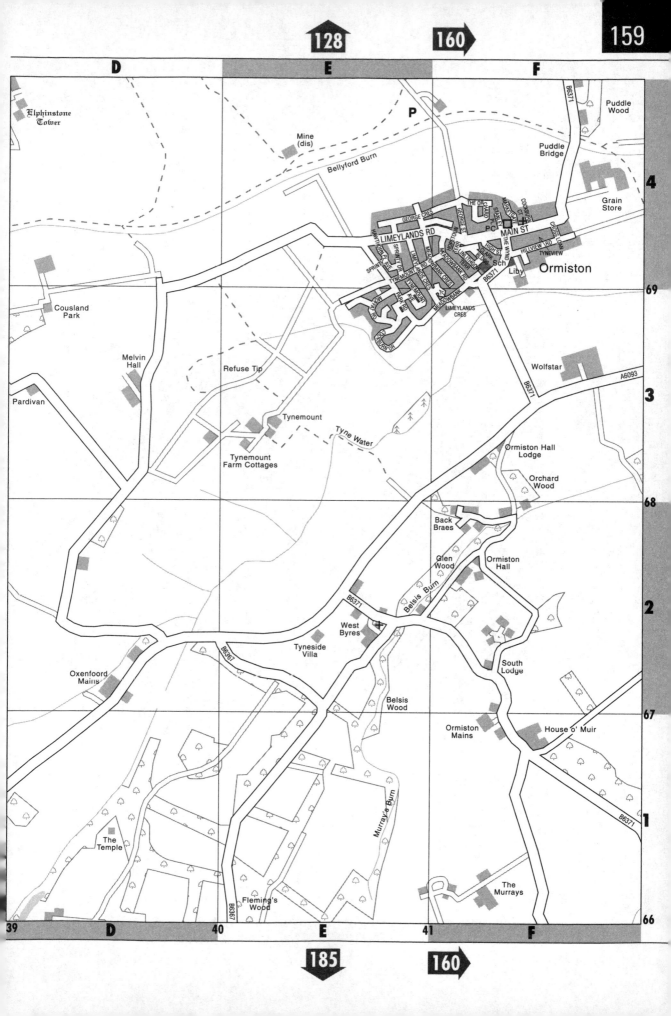

D E F

4

Elphinstone
Tower

Mine
(dis)

P

Bellyford Burn

Puddle
Wood

Puddle
Bridge

Grain
Store

69

GEORGE CRES
LIMEYLANDS RD
HAWTHORN AVE
SPRING DR
TYNEMOUNT AVE
TYNEMOUNT RD
THE ORCHARD CT
STANLEY PL
MARKET ST
GEORGE ST
HIGH ST
THE WYND
CLARK PL
MEADOWBANK RD
LIMEYLANDS RD
KEIR HARDIE RD
MEADOWBANK CRES
HILLVIEW RD
TYNEVIEW
CROSS LOAN
COCKBURN
PO
Sch
Liby

Ormiston

LIMEYLANDS
CRES

Cousland
Park

Melvin
Hall

Refuse Tip

Wolfstar

A6093

3

Pardivan

Tynemount

Tyne Water

Ormiston Hall
Lodge

Orchard
Wood

B6371

68

Tynemount
Farm Cottages

Back
Braes

Glen
Wood

Ormiston
Hall

2

B6371

West
Byres

Belsis Burn

South
Lodge

Oxenfoord
Mains

B6367

Tyneside
Villa

Belsis
Wood

67

Ormiston
Mains

House o' Muir

B6371

The
Temple

Murray's Burn

1

Fleming's
Wood

The
Murrays

B6367

66

39 D 40 E 41 F

A   B   C

Mill

Winton West
Mains

Walk Plantation

Tyne Water

Winton
House

B6355

Dean Bridge
(New)

Dean Bridge
(Old)

Winton
Cottage

Red Mains

B6363

Holding
No. 31

A6093

B6355

Park View

4

Puddle Burn

Pirnie
Braes

Pencaitland

Vinefields

Sewage
Works

Rabbit
Knowe

DOVECOT WAY

THE GLEBE

THE GREEN

69

Beech Terr

Farm Cotts

DOVECOT PK

Sch

Easter
Pencaitland

Broomrigg

CASTLE
VIEW

LEMPOCKWELLS RD

MILLWAY

Kiloran

WOODHALL

Wester
Pencaitland

WOODHALL
RD

A6093

Roselea

P

QUEEN'S DR

PERCIVAL
PL

Tyneholm

Picnic
Site

Blackford Burn

TREVELYAN CRES

HUNTLAW RD

LAMBERTON
CT

3

Black
Wood

BRUCE
GR

Woodhall

68

Burnt Wood

Big Wood

Fountainhall

Huntlaw

Lempockwells

2

67

Glenkinchie
Distillery

1

Kinchie Burn

Peastonbank

Temple Hall

B6371

66

42   A   43   B   44   C

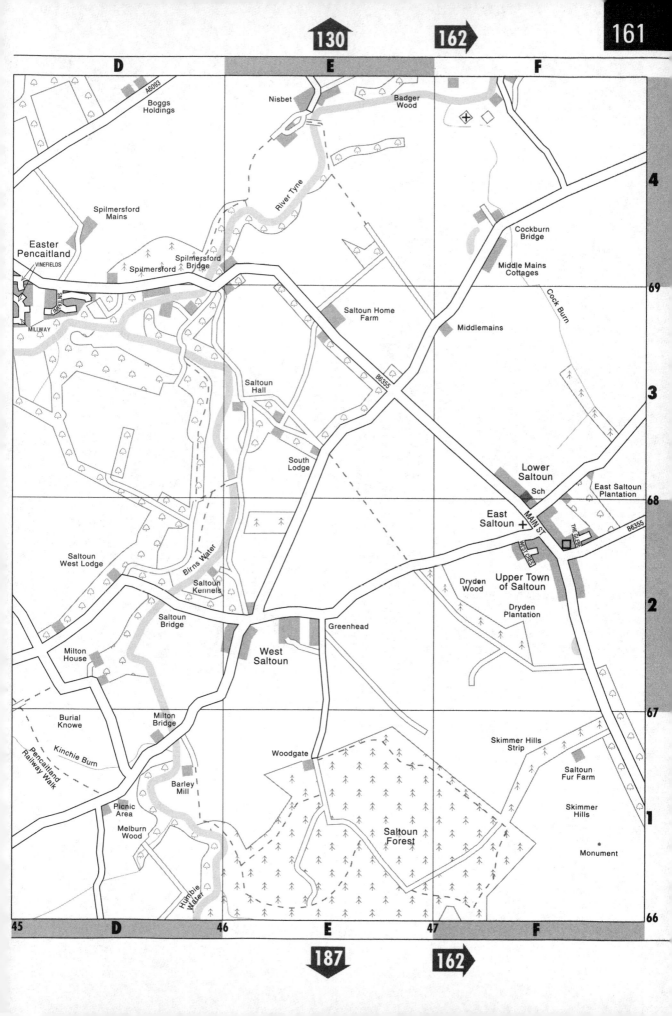

D

Boggs
Holdings

A6093

Nisbet

Badger
Wood

River Tyne

4

Spilmersford
Mains

Cockburn
Bridge

Easter
Pencaitland

VINEFIELDS

Spilmersford
Bridge

Spilmersford

Middle Mains
Cottages

69

LIME KILNS

Saltoun Home
Farm

Middlemains

Cock Burn

MILLWAY

B6355

Saltoun
Hall

3

South
Lodge

Lower
Saltoun

Sch

East Saltoun
Plantation

Saltoun
West Lodge

Birns Water

East
Saltoun

MAIN ST

THE GLEBE

B6355

68

WEST CREST

Saltoun
Kennels

Dryden
Wood

Upper Town
of Saltoun

Milton
House

Saltoun
Bridge

Greenhead

Dryden
Plantation

2

West
Saltoun

Burial
Knowe

Milton
Bridge

67

Kinchie Burn

Skimmer Hills
Strip

Pencaitland
Railway Walk

Woodgate

Saltoun
Fur Farm

Barley
Mill

Picnic
Area

Skimmer
Hills

Melburn
Wood

Saltoun
Forest

Monument

1

Humbie Water

66

45

D

46

E

47

F

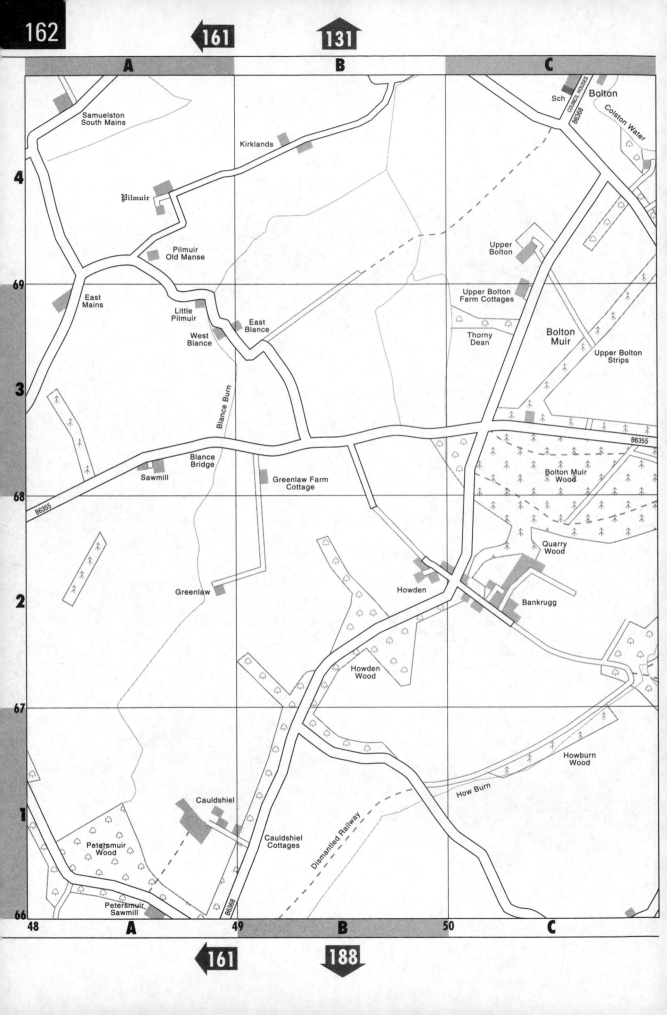

A B C

4

Samuelston
South Mains

Kirklands

Pilmuir

Sch
Bolton

Colston Water

COUNCIL HOUSES
B6368

Upper
Bolton

Pilmuir
Old Manse

69

East
Mains

Little
Pilmuir

East
Blance

West
Blance

Upper Bolton
Farm Cottages

Thorny
Dean

Bolton
Muir

Upper Bolton
Strips

3

Blance Burn

B6355

Blance
Bridge

Sawmill

Greenlaw Farm
Cottage

Bolton Muir
Wood

68

B6355

Greenlaw

Howden

Quarry
Wood

Bankrugg

2

Howden
Wood

67

Howburn
Wood

How Burn

1

Cauldshiel

Petersmuir
Wood

Cauldshiel
Cottages

Dismantled Railway

B6368

66
48 49 50

Petersmuir
Sawmill

A B C

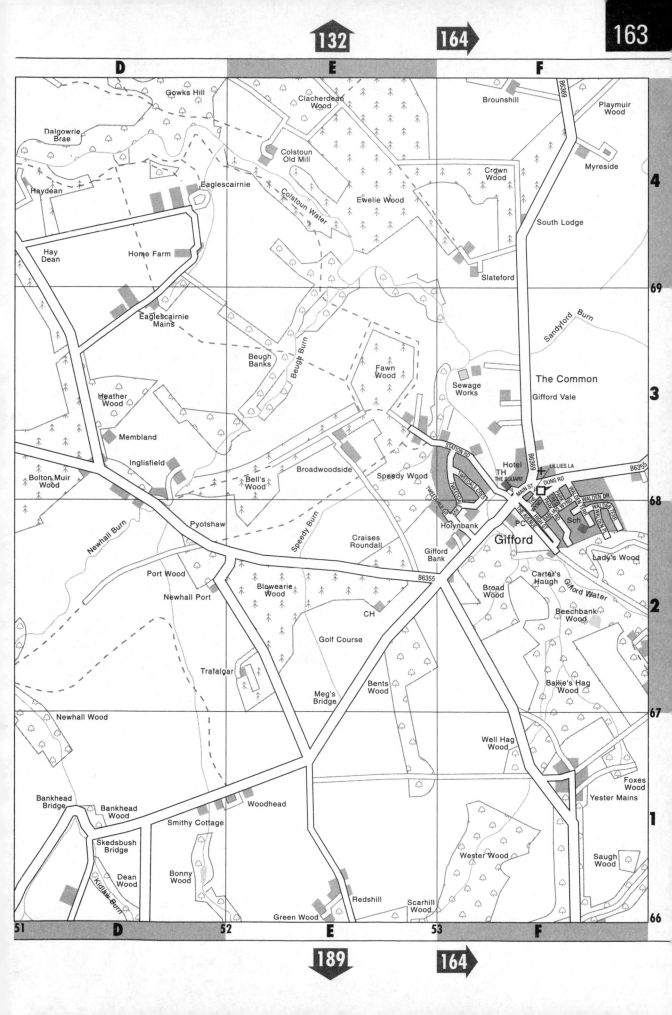

D   E   F

Gowks Hill

Dalgowrie
Brae

Clacherdean
Wood

Brounshill

Playmuir
Wood

Colstoun
Old Mill

Haydean

Eaglescairnie

Colstoun Water

Ewelie Wood

Crown
Wood

Myreside

4

South Lodge

Hay
Dean

Home Farm

Slateford

69

Eaglescairnie
Mains

Beugh Burn

Sandyford Burn

Beugh
Banks

Fawn
Wood

The Common

Sewage
Works

Gifford Vale

3

Heather
Wood

Membland

Inglisfield

Bell's
Wood

Broadwoodside

Speedy Wood

STATION RD

Hotel
TH
THE SQUARE

B6369

LILLIES LA

B6355

Bolton Muir
Wood

Newhall Burn

Pyotshaw

Speedy Burn

Craises
Roundall

Holynbank

MAIN ST.
DUNS RD

PC

Sch

68

Gifford

TWEEDALE CRES
TWEEDALE GR.

THE WYND
HADDINS WYND
HIGH ST.
PARK CRES
WALDEN TERR
WALDEN DR
WALDEN PL

Port Wood

Newhall Port

Blawearie
Wood

Gifford
Bank

Gifford Bank

B6355

Carter's
Haugh

Lady's Wood

Gifford Water

CH

Broad
Wood

Beechbank
Wood

2

Trafalgar

Meg's
Bridge

Bents
Wood

Bailie's Hag
Wood

Golf Course

Newhall Wood

Well Hag
Wood

67

Bankhead
Bridge

Bankhead
Wood

Woodhead

Foxes
Wood

Yester Mains

Smithy Cottage

Skedsbush
Bridge

Dean
Wood

Bonny
Wood

Wester Wood

Saugh
Wood

1

Kidlaw Burn

Redshill

Scarhill
Wood

Green Wood

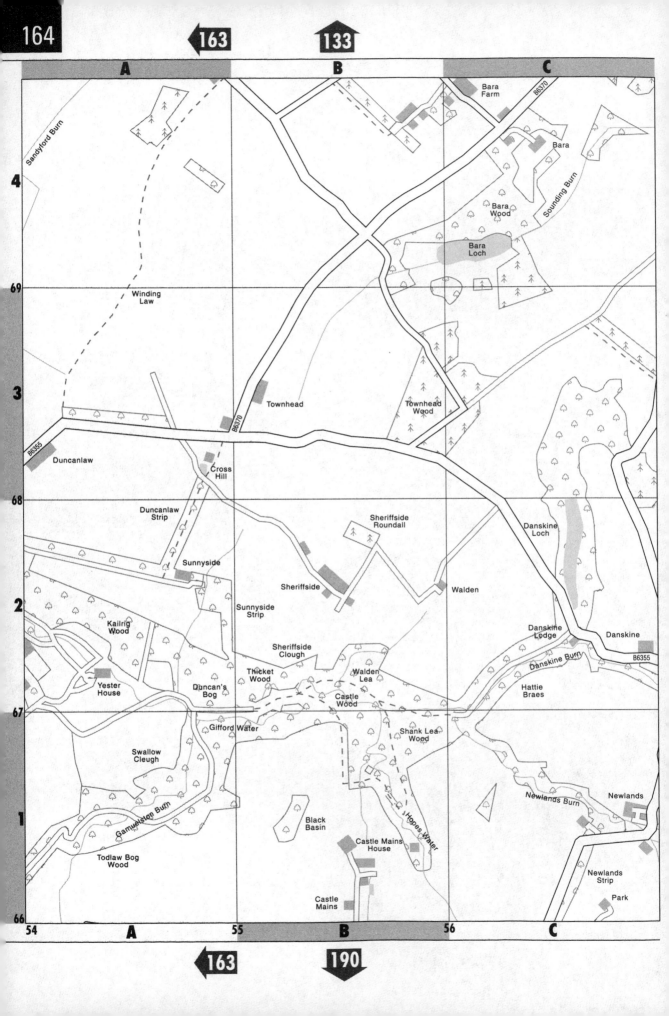

163
133

A
B
C

Bara Farm

B6370

Bara

Sandyford Burn

4

Bara Wood

Sounding Burn

Bara Loch

69

Winding Law

3

Townhead

Townhead Wood

B6370

B6355

Duncanlaw

Cross Hill

68

Duncanlaw Strip

Sheriffside Roundall

Danskine Loch

Sunnyside

Sheriffside

Walden

2

Kailrig Wood

Sunnyside Strip

Danskine Lodge

Danskine

Sheriffside Clough

B6355

Thicket Wood

Walden Lea

Danskine Burn

Yester House

Duncan's Bog

Castle Wood

Hattie Braes

67

Gifford Water

Shank Lea Wood

Swallow Cleugh

Newlands Burn

Newlands

Black Basin

Hopes Water

1

Gamuelston Burn

Castle Mains House

Newlands Strip

Todlaw Bog Wood

Park

66

Castle Mains

54
A
55
B
56
C

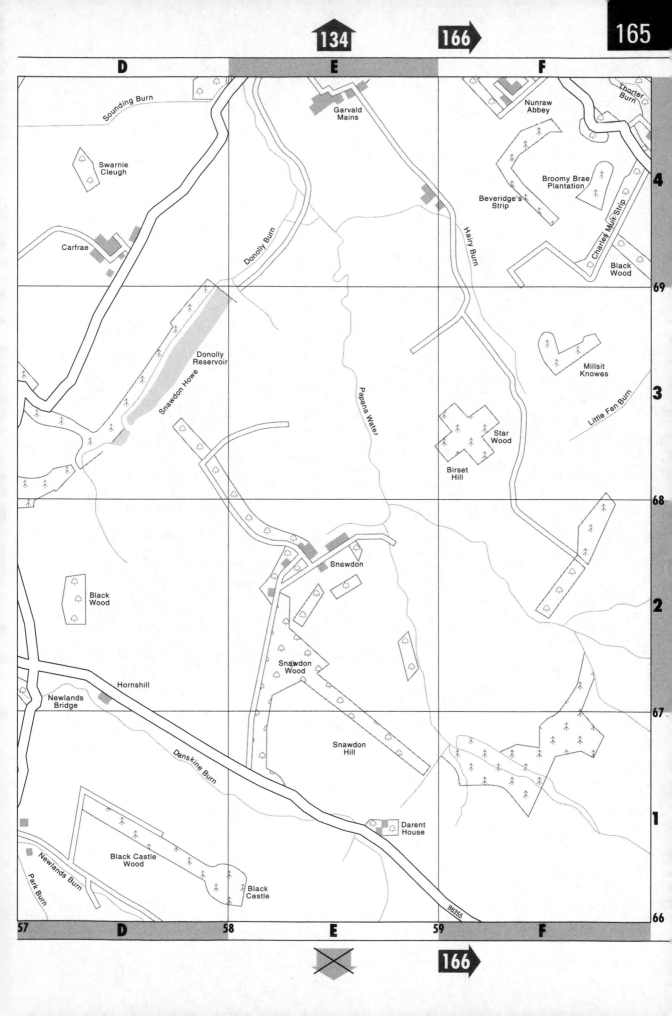

Sounding Burn

Swarnie Cleugh

Carfrae

D

Donolly Burn

Garvald Mains

Hairy Burn

Nunraw Abbey

Thorter Burn

Broomy Brae Plantation

Beveridge's Strip

Charles Muir Strip

Black Wood

4

69

Donolly Reservoir

Snawdon Howe

Papana Water

Millsit Knowes

Little Fen Burn

Star Wood

Birset Hill

3

68

Black Wood

Snawdon

2

Snawdon Wood

Hornshill

Newlands Bridge

Danskine Burn

Snawdon Hill

67

Darent House

1

Black Castle Wood

Newlands Burn

Park Burn

Black Castle

B6355

66

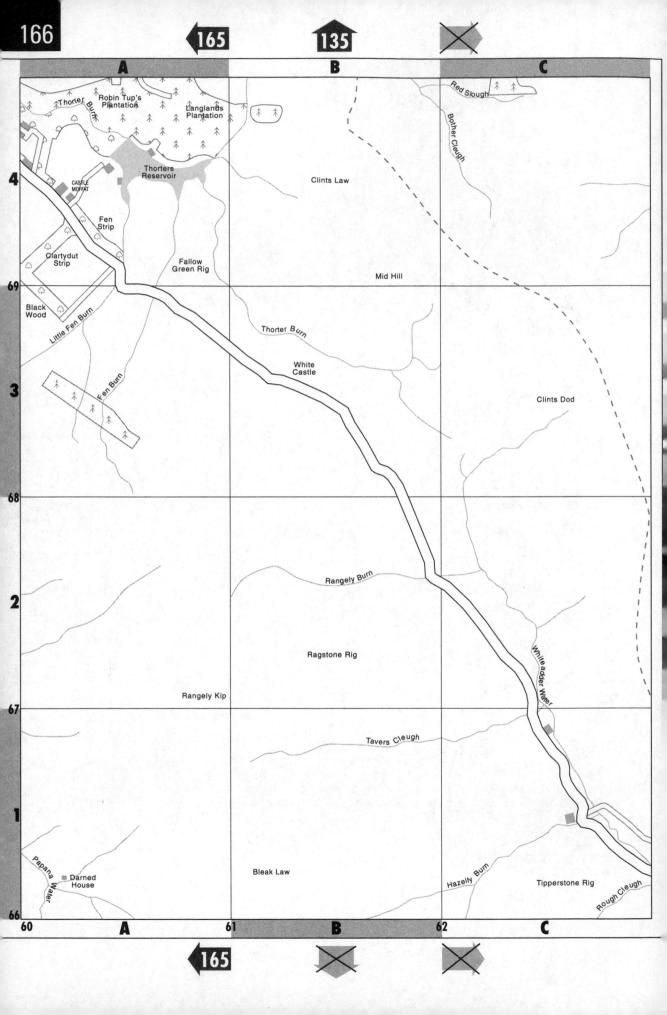

A B C

Thorter Burn
Robin Tup's Plantation
Langlands Plantation
Red Slough

Thorters Reservoir

Bother Cleugh

Clints Law

4

CASTLE MOFFAT

Fen Strip

Mid Hill

Clartydut Strip

Fallow Green Rig

69

Black Wood

Little Fen Burn

Thorter Burn

White Castle

Clints Dod

3

Fen Burn

68

Rangely Burn

2

Ragstone Rig

White adder Water

Rangely Kip

67

Tavers Cleugh

1

Papana Water

Darned House

Bleak Law

Hazelly Burn

Tipperstone Rig

Rough Cleugh

66

60 A 61 B 62 C

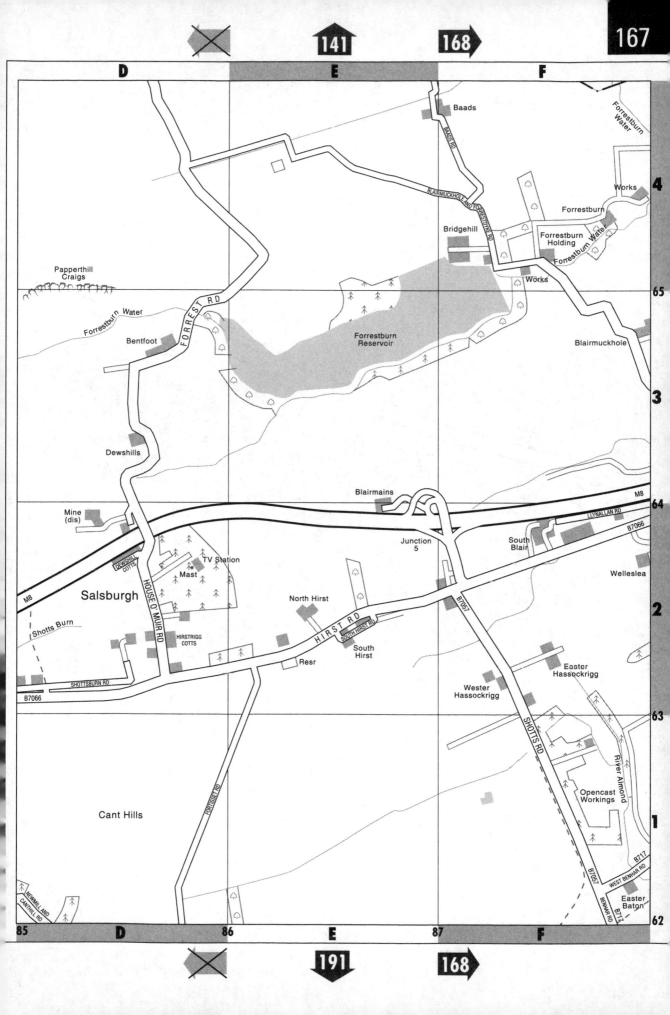

D   E   F

Baads

Forrestburn Water

BAADS RD

4

Works

BLAIRMUCKHOLE AND FORRESTDYKE RD

Forrestburn

Bridgehill

Forrestburn Holding

Forrestburn Water

Papperthill Craigs

Works

65

Forrestburn Water

FORREST RD

Bentfoot

Forrestburn Reservoir

Blairmuckhole

Dewshills

3

Blairmains

M8

Mine (dis)

64

LLYNALLAN RD

B7066

DEWSHILL COTTS

TV Station

Junction 5

South Blair

Welleslea

Mast

Salsburgh

HOUSE O' MUIR RD

North Hirst

HIRST RD

B7057

2

M8

Shotts Burn

HIRSTRIGG COTTS

SOUTH HIRST RD

South Hirst

Easter Hassockrigg

SHOTTSBURN RD

Resr

Wester Hassockrigg

SHOTTS RD

B7066

63

River Almond

Cant Hills

FORTISSET RD

Opencast Workings

1

B7057

BENHAR RD

B717

NEWMILL AND CANTHILL RD

WEST BENHAR RD

Easter Baton

62

85   D   86   E   87   F

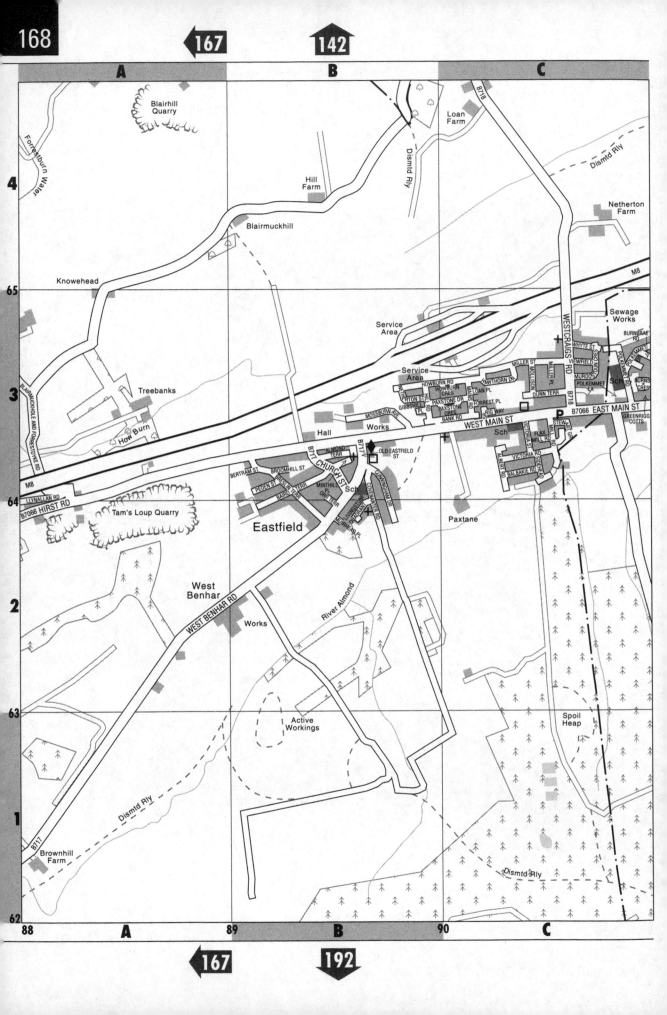

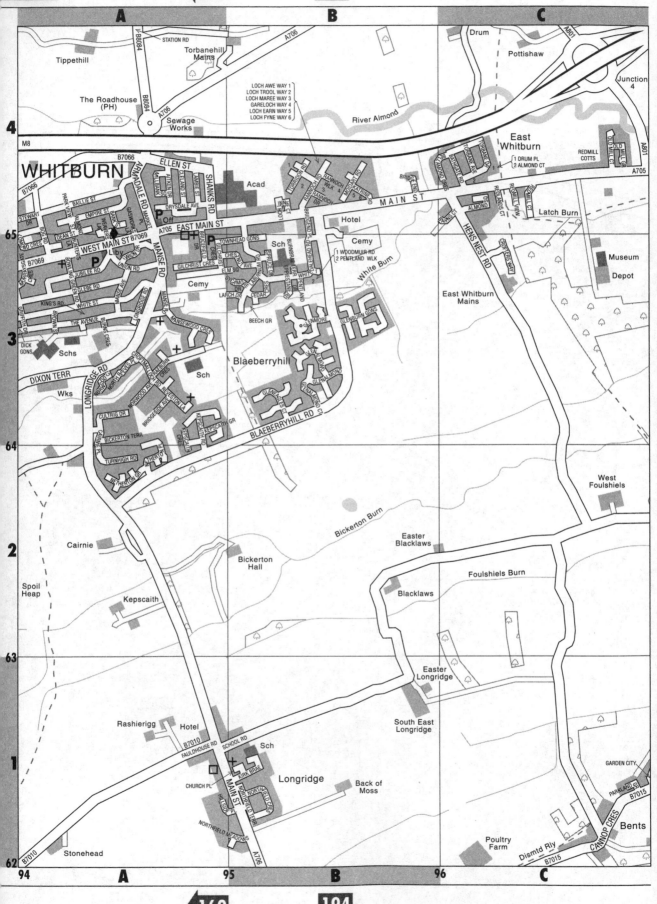

LOCH AWE WAY 1
LOCH TROOL WAY 2
LOCH MAREE WAY 3
GARELOCH WAY 4
LOCH EARN WAY 5
LOCH FYNE WAY 6

WHITBURN

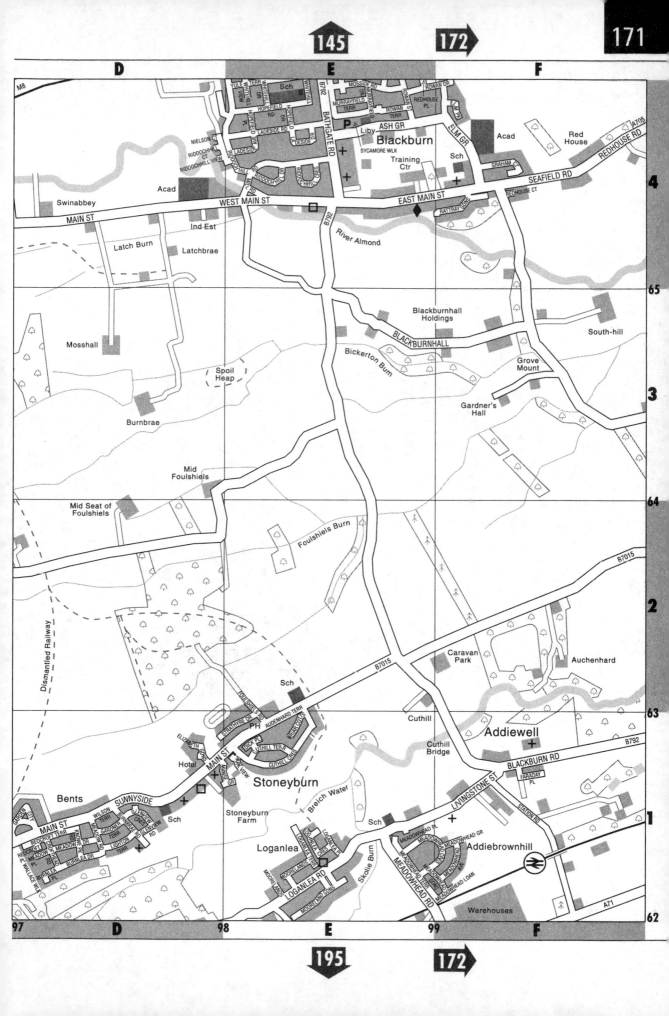

M8

WHITEHILL TERR
YULE VIEW
WHITEHILL RD
HOPEFIELD PL
HOPEFIELD DR
HOPEFIELD RD
LADESIDE RD

Sch

MOSSIDE RD
MURRAYFIELD DR
MURRAYFIELD TERR

ROWAN S
ROWAN DR

REDHOUSE PL

ELM PK

Liby ASH GR
Blackburn
SYCAMORE WLK

Acad

Red House

REDHOUSE RD

A705

NIELSON CT
RIDDOCHHILL CT
RIDDOCHHILL VIEW

DESIDE

Training Ctr

Sch

GRAHAM CT

Acad

Swinabbey

Acad

DESIDE

RIDDOCHHILL
RIDDOCHHILL RD
RIDDO

P

SYCAMORE WLK

REDHOUSE CT

SEAFIELD RD

4

Latch Burn

Latchbrae

MAIN ST

WEST MAIN ST

Ind Est

B792

EAST MAIN ST

RATTRAY GDNS

River Almond

65

Mosshall

Blackburnhall Holdings

BLACKBURNHALL

South-hill

Spoil Heap

Bickerton Burn

Grove Mount

3

Burnbrae

Gardner's Hall

Mid Foulshiels

Mid Seat of Foulshiels

64

Foulshiels Burn

Dismantled Railway

B7015

2

Caravan Park

Auchenhard

Sch

B7015

Cuthill

63

Sch

FOULSHIELS RD
STRATHYRE DR
PH
AUDENHARD TERR
BRAE LOAN

Addiewell

ELIZABETH GDNS
MAIN ST
DIXON RD
CUTHILL TER
MAIN ST
CUTHILL CRES

Cuthill Bridge

BLACKBURN RD

B792

Hotel

PARK VIEW
MAINS GR

Stoneyburn

Breich Water

FARADAY PL

LIVINGSTONE ST

STATION RD

Bents

SUNNYSIDE

Sch

Stoneyburn Farm

Sch

1

GARDEN CT
MAIN ST
WILSON TERR
GLENVIEW TERR
GARDNER TERR
KNOWE DR
MEADOW PK
GLENVIEW RD
LIGHTON TERR
REDCROFT TERR
MEADOW RD
REDCROFT PL
BURNLEA DR
BURNLEA PL
WALLACE WLK

Loganlea

MOORELANDS
LOGANLEA CRES
LOGANLEA TERR
LOGANLEA RD
MOORELANDS
MOORELAND GDNS

Skolie Burn

MEADOWHEAD PL
MEADOWHEAD GR
MEADOWHEAD CRES
MEADOWHEAD
MEADOWHEAD RD
MEADOWHEAD AVE
MEADOWHEAD LOAN

Addiebrownhill

Warehouses

A71

62

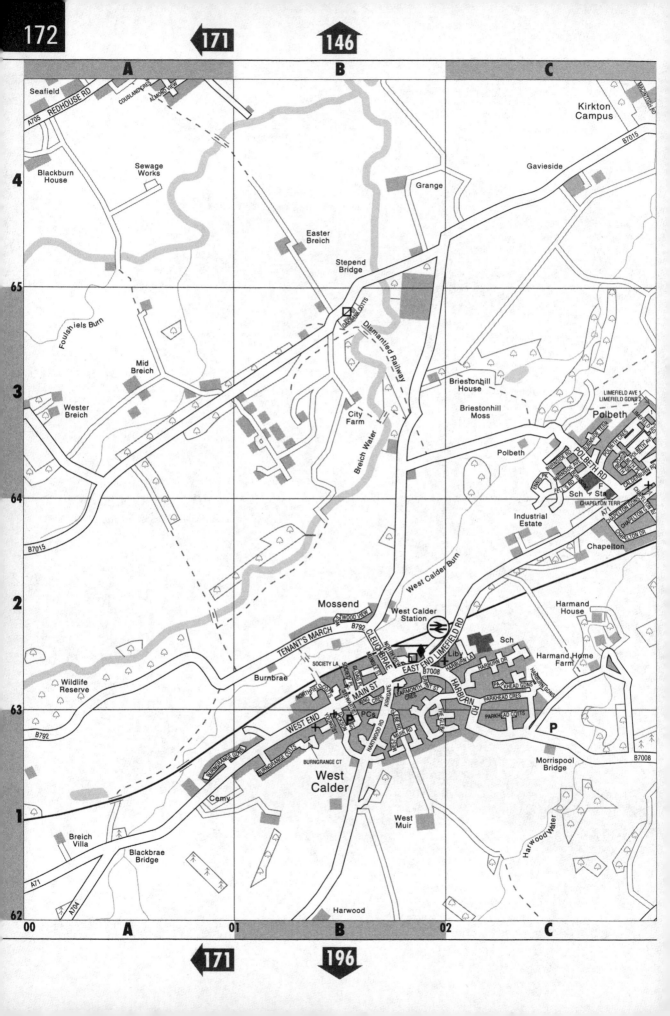

A   B   C

Seafield
REDHOUSE RD
A705
COUSLAND CRES
ALMOND VIEW

Blackburn
House

Sewage
Works

4

Kirkton
Campus
B7015

Gavieside

Easter
Breich

Stepend
Bridge

Foulshiels Burn

65

OAKBANK COTTS

Dismantled Railway

Briestonhill
House

Mid
Breich

Briestonhill
Moss

3

Wester
Breich

City
Farm

Polbeth

LIMEFIELD AVE 1
LIMEFIELD GDNS 2

Polbeth

POLBETH RD
BURNSIDE TERR
POLBETH CRES

Breich Water

BURNSIDE RD
BURNSIDE AVE
ENNIS PK
FELL'S RD
Sch   F
Sta
CHAPELTON TERR
A71

B7015

Industrial
Estate

64

CHAPELTON GDNS
CHAPELTON DR
Chapelton

West Calder Burn

Harmand
House

2

Mossend
WOOD VIEW
B792
West Calder
Station

CLEUCH BRAE

LIMEFIELD RD

Sch

Harmand Home
Farm

Wildlife
Reserve

TENANT'S MARCH

SOCIETY LA

EAST END
B7008

Liby

HARBURN LA

HARBURN DR

HARBURN GDNS

Burnbrae
B792

Burnbrae

NORTHFIELD COTTS
MAIN ST
KING CRES
KIRKGATE
LEARMONTH CRES
GRANT ST
PA
KHEAD GDNS
PARKHEAD CRES

HARBURN RD

THE GLEBE

PARKHEAD COTTS

63

WEST END
YOUNG ST
HARWOOD RD
MUIR RD
PCs

P

P

B7008

B792

BURNGRANGE GDNS
BURNGRANGE COTTS
BURNGRANGE CT

West
Calder

Morrispool
Bridge

1

Cemy

West Muir

Harwood Water

Breich
Villa

Blackbrae
Bridge

West
Muir

A71
A704

62

Harwood

00   A   01   B   02   C

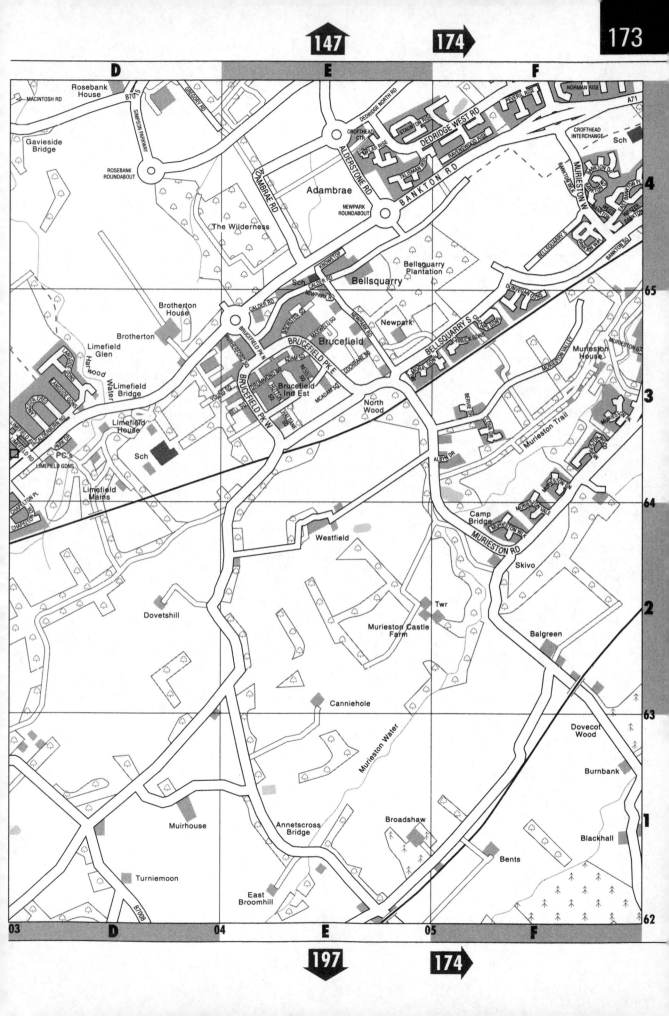

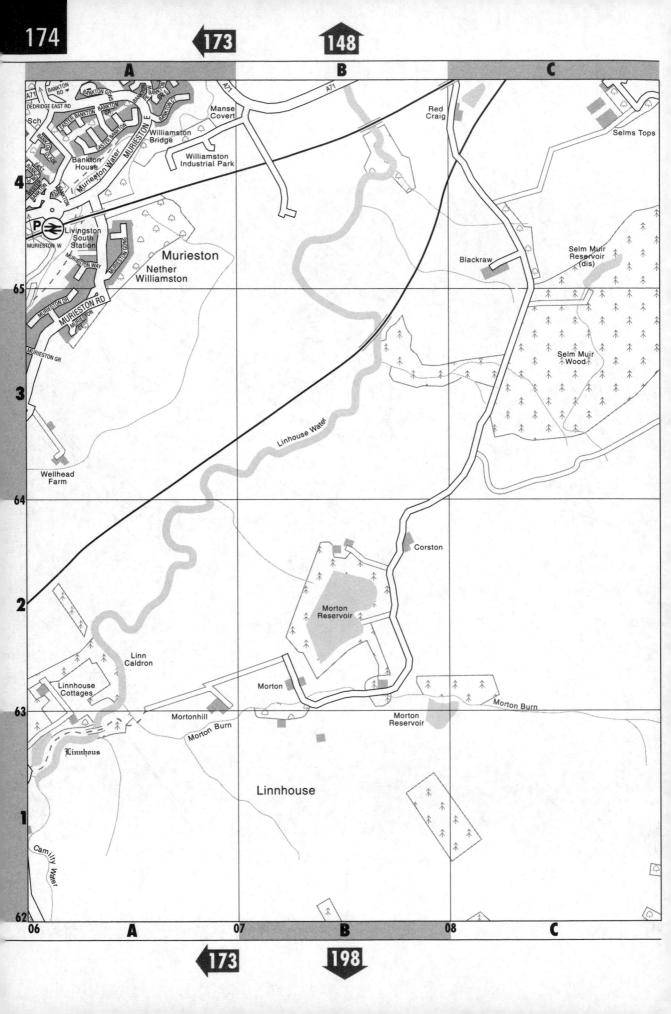

173
148

A   B   C

BANKTON
RD
A71
DEDRIDGE EAST RD
Sch
EASTER BANKTON
BANKTON
GDNS
BANKTON
GR
BANKTON
BANKTON BRAW
BANKTON CT
Manse
Covert
A71
Red
Craig
Selms Tops

Williamston
Bridge
Williamston
Industrial Park

Bankton
House
EASTER BANKTON

MURIESTON E
MURIESTON WATER

4

Blackraw
Selm Muir
Reservoir
(dis)

P
Livingston
South
Station
MURIESTON W
MURIESTON WAY
MURIESTON GDNS

Murieston
Nether
Williamston

65

Selm Muir
Wood

MURIESTON DR
MURIESTON RD
MURIESTON CT

3

MURIESTON GR

Linhouse Water

Wellhead
Farm

64

Corston

2

Morton
Reservoir

Linn
Caldron

Linnhouse
Cottages

Morton

Morton Burn

63

Mortonhill
Morton Burn

Morton
Reservoir

Linnhous

Linnhouse

1

Camilty Water

62

06   A   07   B   08   C

173
198

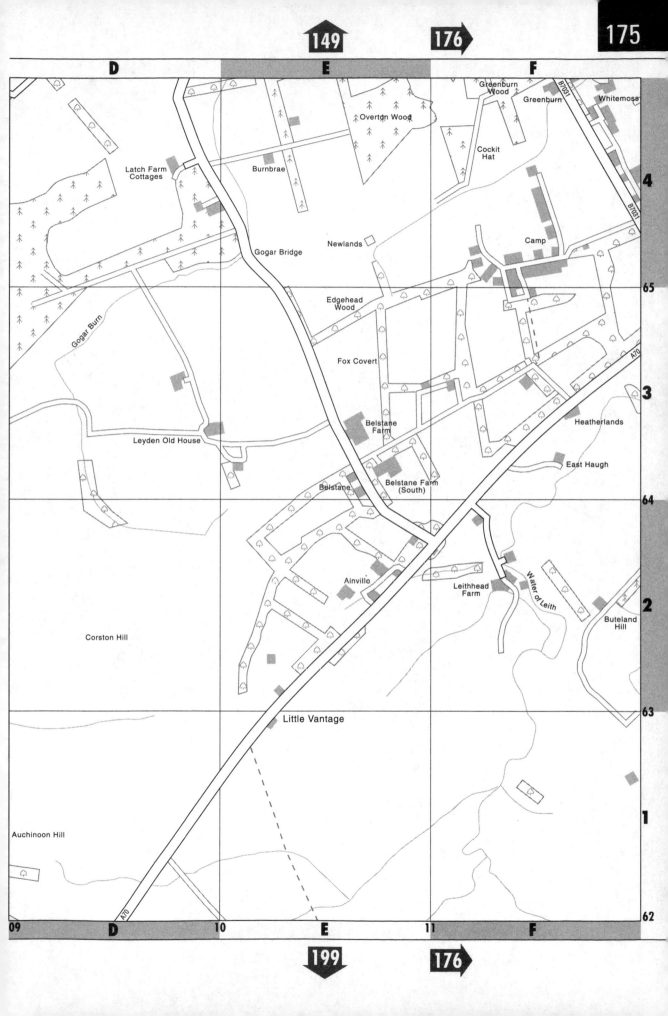

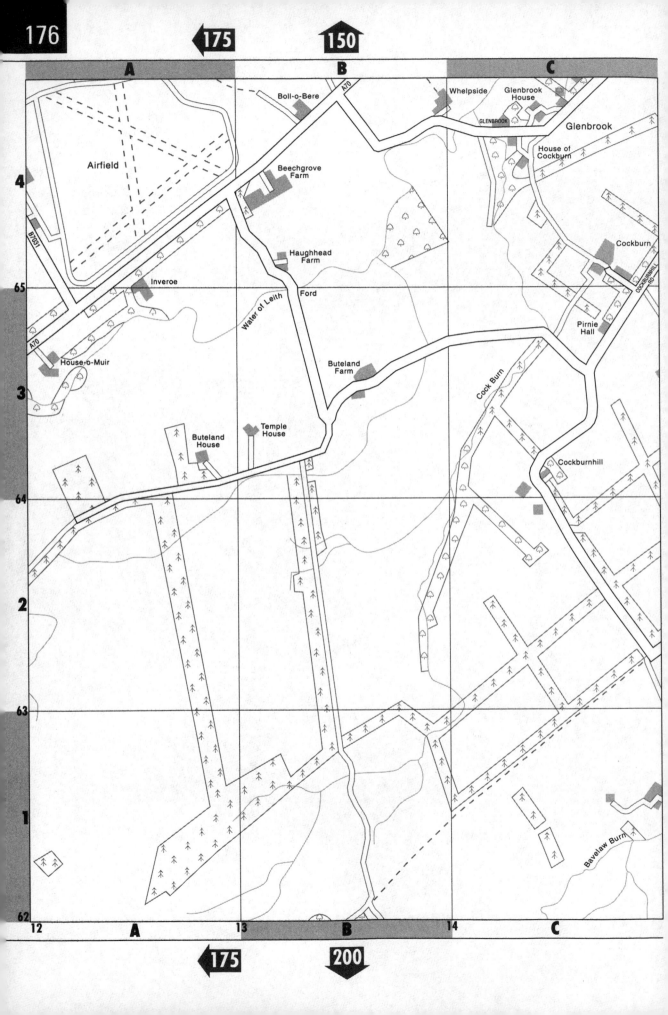

A   B   C

Airfield

Boll-o-Bere

B7031

Beechgrove
Farm

Whelpside   Glenbrook
House

GLENBROOK   Glenbrook

House of
Cockburn

4

Haughhead
Farm

Cockburn

Inveroe

A70

Water of Leith   Ford

COCKBURNHILL RD

65

Pirnie
Hall

House-o-Muir

Buteland Farm

Cock Burn

3

Buteland
House

Temple
House

Cockburnhill

64

2

63

1

Bavelaw Burn

62

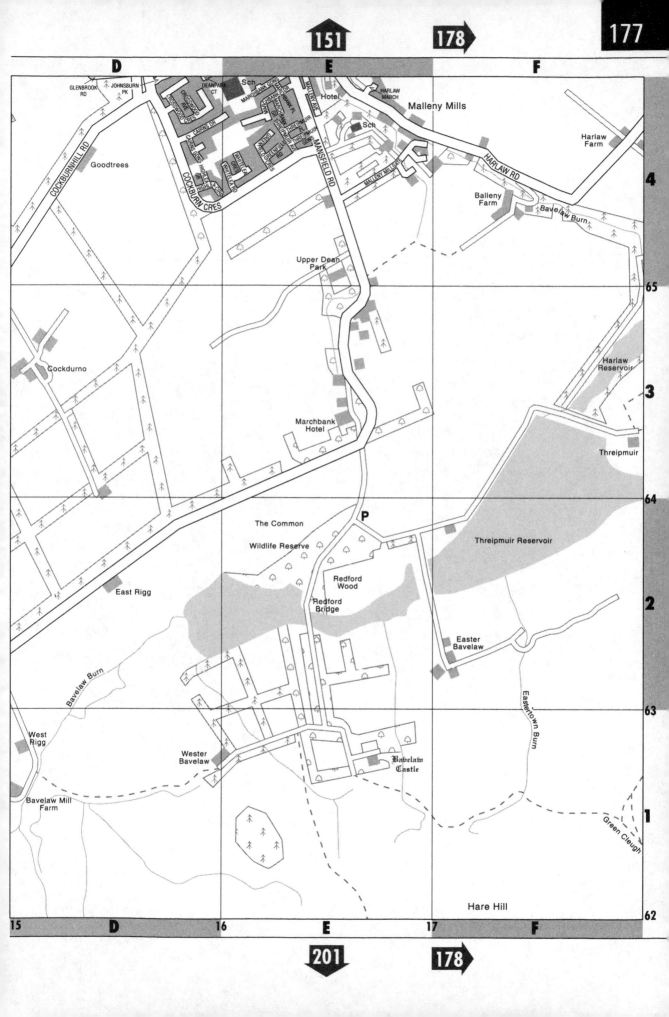

151
178 →

D   **E**   **F**

GLENBROOK
RD

JOHNSBURN
PK

DEANPARK
CT

Sch

Hotel

HARLAW
MARCH

Malleny Mills

Harlaw
Farm

4

CROSSWOOD
CRES

CROSSWOOD
AVE

CAIRNS DR

CAIRNS GDNS

HIGHFIELD RD

WHITELEA
RD

MARCHBANK GDNS

MARCHBANK RD

MARCHBANK PL

THREIPMUIR
GDNS

GREENFIELD
RD

MALLENY AVE

MANSFIELD RD

MALLENY MILL GATE

HARLAW RD

Balleny
Farm

Bavelaw Burn

COCKBURNHILL RD

Goodtrees

COCKBURN CRES

Upper Dean
Park

65

Cockdurno

Harlaw
Reservoir

3

Marchbank
Hotel

Threipmuir

64

The Common

Wildlife Reserve

P

Threipmuir Reservoir

East Rigg

Redford
Wood

Redford
Bridge

Easter
Bavelaw

2

Bavelaw Burn

63

Eastertown Burn

West
Rigg

Wester
Bavelaw

Bavelaw
Castle

Bavelaw Mill
Farm

1

Green Cleugh

Hare Hill

62

15   **D**   **16**   **E**   **17**   **F**

201
178 →

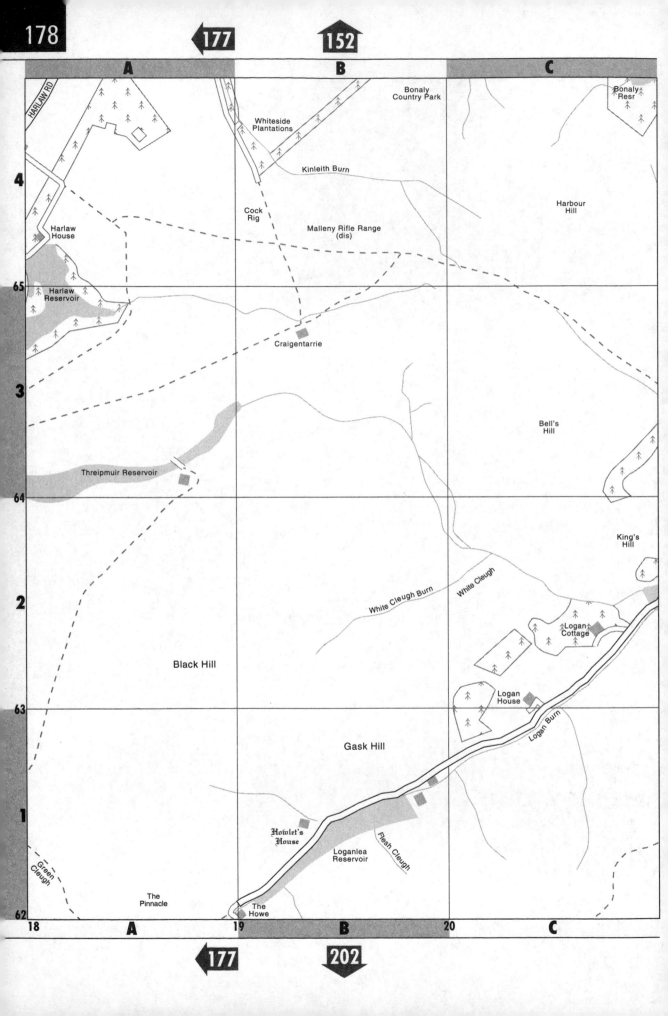

A **B** **C**

HARLAW RD

Bonaly
Country Park

Bonaly
Resr

Whiteside
Plantations

Kinleith Burn

4

Harbour
Hill

Cock
Rig

Malleny Rifle Range
(dis)

Harlaw
House

65

Harlaw
Reservoir

Craigentarrie

3

Bell's
Hill

Threipmuir Reservoir

64

King's
Hill

White Cleugh

White Cleugh Burn

2

Logan
Cottage

Black Hill

Logan
House

63

Logan Burn

Gask Hill

1

Howlet's
House

Flesh Cleugh

Green
Cleugh

Loganlea
Reservoir

The
Pinnacle

The
Howe

62

18   **A**   19   **B**   20   **C**

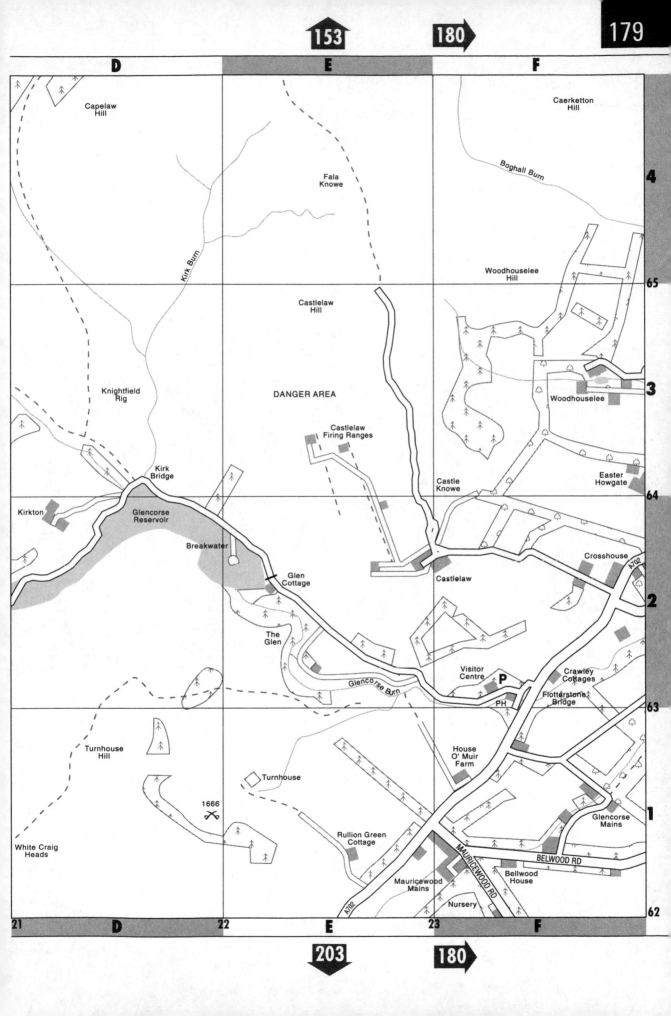

Capelaw
Hill

Caerketton
Hill

Boghall Burn

Fala
Knowe

Woodhouselee
Hill

4

Kirk Burn

65

Castlelaw
Hill

Knightfield
Rig

DANGER AREA

Woodhouselee

3

Castlelaw
Firing Ranges

Easter
Howgate

Kirk
Bridge

Castle
Knowe

64

Kirkton

Glencorse
Reservoir

Crosshouse

A702

Breakwater

Castlelaw

2

Glen
Cottage

The
Glen

Visitor
Centre

Crawley
Cottages

P

Flotterstone
Bridge

Glencorse Burn

PH

63

Turnhouse
Hill

House
O' Muir
Farm

Turnhouse

1666

Glencorse
Mains

1

White Craig
Heads

Rullion Green
Cottage

MAURICEWOOD RD

BELWOOD RD

Bellwood
House

Mauricewood
Mains

A702

Nursery

62

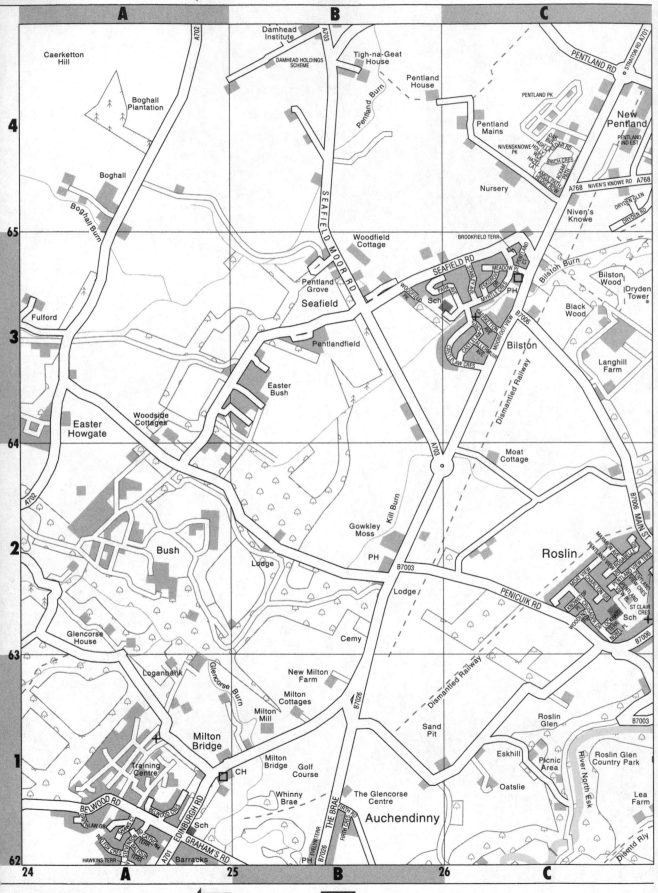

A B C

Caerketton Hill

Boghall Plantation

Boghall

Boghall Burn

Fulford

Easter Howgate

Woodside Cottages

Bush

Glencorse House

Loganbank

Milton Bridge

Training Centre

BELWOOD RD

GREENLAW GR
SPANS RD
RED ROY CRES
STEVENSON TERR
CATRION TERR
BELWOOD CRES
ST FOUR TERR
HAWKINS TERR

EDINBURGH RD

A701

GRAHAM'S RD

Sch

Barracks

Damhead Institute

DAMHEAD HOLDINGS SCHEME

A703

Tigh-na-Geat House

Pentland Burn

Pentland House

SEAFIELD MOOR RD

Woodfield Cottage

Pentland Grove

Seafield

Pentlandfield

Easter Bush

Lodge

New Milton Farm

Milton Cottages

Milton Mill

Glencorse Burn

Milton Bridge

CH

Golf Course

Whinny Brae

The Glencorse Centre

Auchendinny

EVELYN TERR

THE BRAE

B7026

FIRTH CRES

FIRTH TERR

PH

Cemy

Lodge

Gowkley Moss

PH

B7003

Lodge

Kill Burn

A703

Sand Pit

Dismantled Railway

B7026

PENTLAND RD

STRATTON RD

A701

New Pentland

PENTLAND PK

PENTLAND IND EST

OAK AVE
ASH
ASAR RD
HOLLY
WILL
BIRCH CRES
HAZEL
SIMOS PATH
ACKAM
PAVIE
HEDGE ROW

Pentland Mains

NIVENSKNOWE PK

A768

NIVEN'S KNOWE RD

A768

Nursery

Niven's Knowe

DRYDEN GLEN

DRYDEN RD

BROOKFIELD TERR

Bilston Burn

Bilston Wood

Dryden Tower

SEAFIELD RD

MEADOW PL

PENTLAND CT

STANLEY AVE

PEEBROVE
MYRTLE CRES

PARK AVE

Sch

PH

B7006

GLEBE
SEGTON AVE
MOORFOOT VIEW

CASTLE LAW
CASTLELAW TERR
CASTLE LAW AVE
CASTLE LAW CRES

Bilston

Black Wood

Langhill Farm

Dismantled Railway

Moat Cottage

Roslin

B7006

MAIN ST

MARMION AVE
PENTLAND VIEW TERR
PENTLAND VIEW CRES

MOAT VIEW

HARELON CRB

KNOWE TOP
WOODSIDE
CROSKERY PL
LOCK HART
NOBEL PL

PENTLAND VIEW

ST CLAIR CRES

Sch

B7006

PENICUIK RD

Roslin Glen

B7003

Eskhill

Picnic Area

Oatslie

Roslin Glen Country Park

River North Esk

Lea Farm

Dismtd Rly

Dismantled Railway

24 25 26

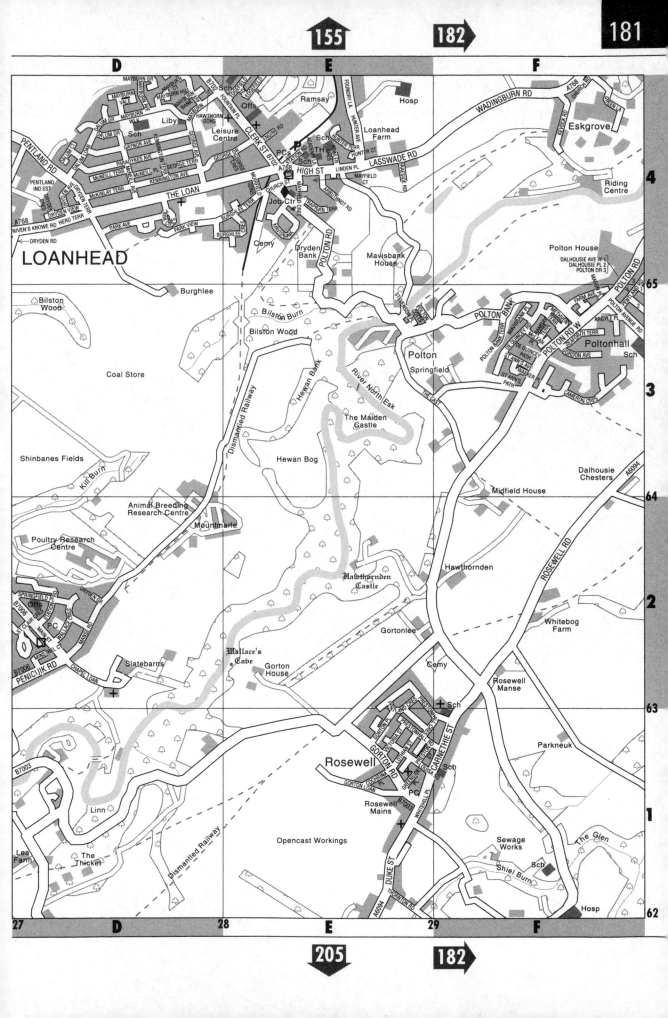

D

E

F

4

65

3

64

2

63

1

62

WADINGBURN RD

A768

GREEN LA

KEVOCK RD

CHURCH RD

POLTON RD

Eskgrove

Riding
Centre

Hosp

Loanhead
Farm

LASSWADE RD

Polton House

DALHOUSIE AVE W 1
DALHOUSIE PL 2
POLTON DR 3

POLTON AVENUE RD

FARM AVE

Ramsay

Offs

Sch

Sch

Hunter Terr

Hunter Ave

Hunter Ct

FOUNDRY LA

HUNTER TERR

PARKSIDE RD

LINDEN PL

MAYFIELD
CT

MAYFIELD RD

ARBUTHNOT RD

TRAPRAIN TERR

POLTON RD

STEVENSON RD

POLTON CT

POLTON BANK

POLTON RD W

METHVEN TERR

MCLEAN PL

BASNEY CT

SEAFORTH TERR

ARGYLE PL

Poltonhall

Sch

GORDON AVE

CAMERON CRES

ST ANN'S AVE

WALKER ST

ST ANN'S
PATH

DE QUINCEY RD

DE QUINCEY
PATH

POLTON PARK TERR

Polton

Springfield

THE CA??

River North Esk

The Maiden
Castle

Mavisbank
House

Dryden
Bank

Cemy

VANDBANK

Job Ctr

CHURCH ST

HIGH ST

A768

STATION RD

CLERK ST B702

FOUNTAIN RD

ENGINE RD

B702

MIDFIELD GDNS

MUIRFIELD GDNS

GEORGE DR

GEORGE CRES

George Terr

GEORGE AVE

GAYNOR AVE

KENNINGTON AVE

McNEILL PL

McNEILL TERR

McKINLAY TERR

PARADYKES AVE

THE LOAN

PARK AVE

PARK VIEW

BURGHLEE TERR

BURGHLEE CRES

BURGHLEE

PENTLAND RD

DALUM GR

DALUM DR

DALUM LOAN

DRYDEN DRES

DRYDEN VIEW

WHITEHILL RD

HERD TERR

NIVEN'S KNOWE RD

← DRYDEN RD

A768

PENTLAND
IND EST

LOANHEAD

MAYBURN GR

MAYBURN HILL

MAYBURN AVE

MAYBURN VALE

MAYBURN BANK

MAYBURN WLK

HAWTHORN GDNS

Sch

Sch

PCs

P

Leisure
Centre

Liby

+

Burghlee

Bilston
Wood

Bilston Burn

Bilston Wood

Hewan Bank

Hewan Bog

Dismantled Railway

Coal Store

Shinbanes Fields

Kilf Burn

Animal Breeding
Research Centre

Mountmarle

Poultry Research
Centre

SPRINGFIELD PL

DRYDEN GR

B7006

STATION RD

MAINS RD

WALLACE CRES

CLAIR CRES

MINS?? CT

B7006

PENICUIK RD

CHAPEL LOAN

MAIN ST

PC

Offs

+

Slatebarns

Wallace's
Cave

Gorton
House

Linn

Lea
Farm

The
Thicket

Dismantled Railway

Opencast Workings

Hawthornden
Castle

Gortonlee

Cemy

Rosewell
Manse

Midfield House

Hawthornden

ROSEWELL RD

A6094

Dalhousie
Chesters

Whitebog
Farm

Parkneuk

GORTON RD

GORTON LOAN

PRESTON RD

PRESTON CRES

PRESTONHOLM

COCHRANE PL

GREEN??

WHITEHILL PL

CARNETHIE ST

B7003

Rosewell

PC

+

Sch

Sch

Rosewell
Mains

DUKE ST

THORNTON RD

A6094

Sewage
Works

Shiel Burn

Sch

The Glen

Hosp

+

27

28

29

D

E

F

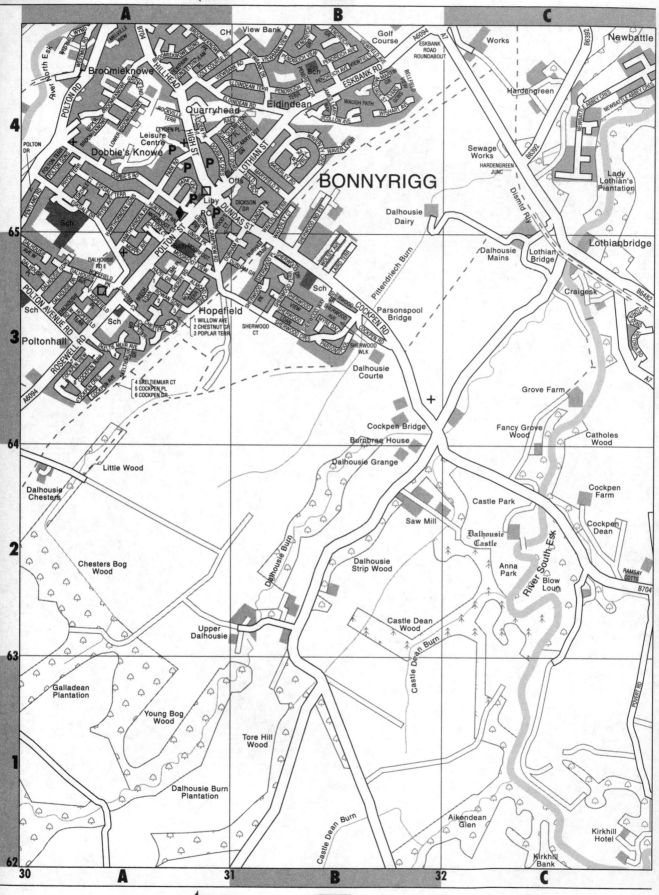

BONNYRIGG

Newbattle

Broomieknowe

Quarryhead

Eldindean

Dobbie's Knowe

Hopefield

Poltonhall

1 WILLOW AVE
2 CHESTNUT GR
3 POPLAR TERR

4 SKELTIEMUIR CT
5 COCKPEN PL
6 COCKPEN DR

Hardengreen

Lady Lothian's Plantation

Sewage Works

Dalhousie Dairy

Dalhousie Mains

Lothianbridge

Lothian Bridge

Craigesk

Dalhousie Courte

Grove Farm

Parsonspool Bridge

Sherwood WLK

Cockpen Bridge

Fancy Grove Wood

Catholes Wood

Cockpen Farm

Burnbrae House

Dalhousie Grange

Cockpen Dean

Little Wood

Castle Park

Saw Mill

Dalhousie Chesters

Dalhousie Castle

Ramsay Cotts

Chesters Bog Wood

Dalhousie Strip Wood

Anna Park

Blow Loun

Galladean Plantation

Upper Dalhousie

Castle Dean Wood

Young Bog Wood

Tore Hill Wood

Aikendean Glen

Kirkhill Hotel

Dalhousie Burn Plantation

Castle Dean Burn

Kirkhill Bank

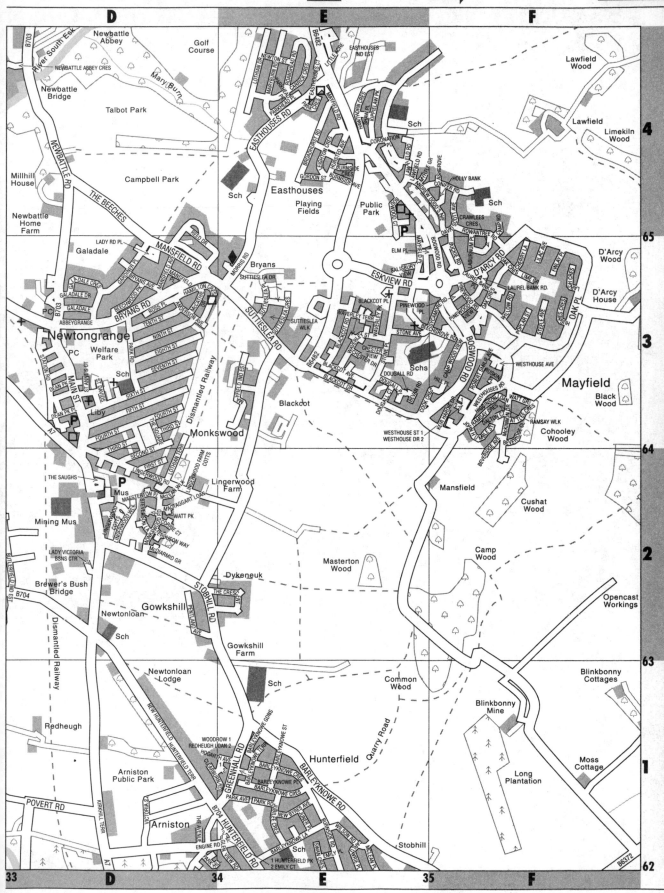

D E F

4

65

3

64

2

63

1

62

33 D 34 E 35 F

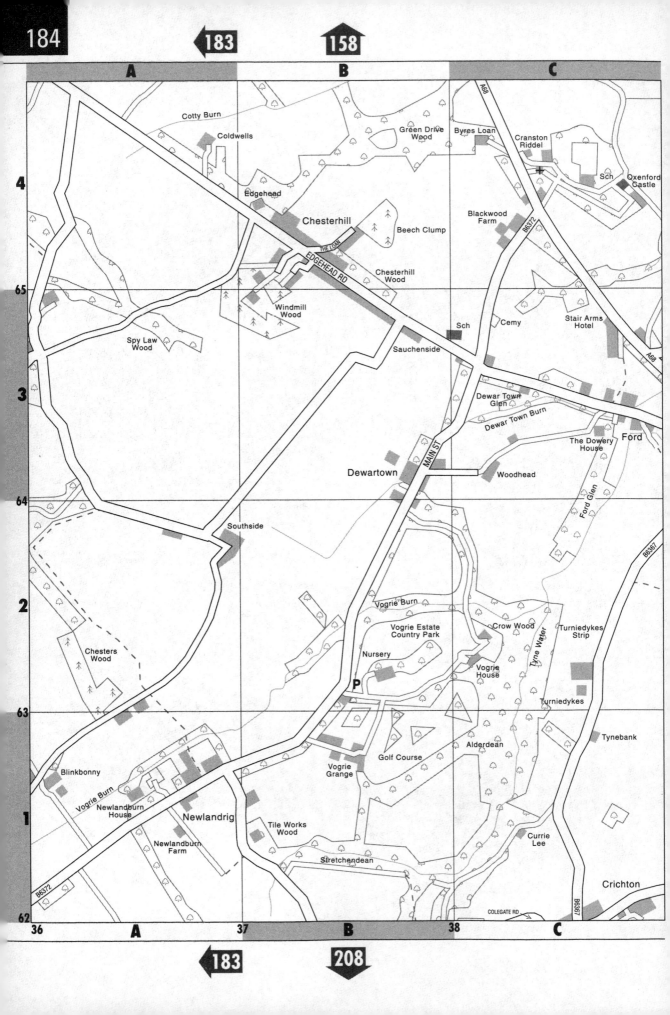

A   B   C

Cotty Burn

Coldwells

Green Drive Wood

Byres Loan

Cranston Riddel

A68

Sch

Oxenford Castle

Edgehead

Chesterhill

Beech Clump

Blackwood Farm

B6372

THE LOAN

EDGEHEAD RD

Chesterhill Wood

Sch

Cemy

Stair Arms Hotel

4

Windmill Wood

Sauchenside

Spy Law Wood

Dewar Town Glen

Dewar Town Burn

Ford

65

MAIN ST

The Dowery House

3

Dewartown

Woodhead

Ford Glen

Vogrie Burn

Crow Wood

Turniedykes Strip

Southside

64

Chesters Wood

Vogrie Estate Country Park

Nursery

Vogrie House

Tyne Water

B6367

2

P

Turniedykes

Blinkbonny

Vogrie Grange

Golf Course

Alderdean

Tynebank

63

Vogrie Burn

Newlandburn House

Newlandrig

Tile Works Wood

Currie Lee

1

Newlandburn Farm

Stretchendean

Crichton

B6372

COLEGATE RD

B6367

62

36   A   37   B   38   C

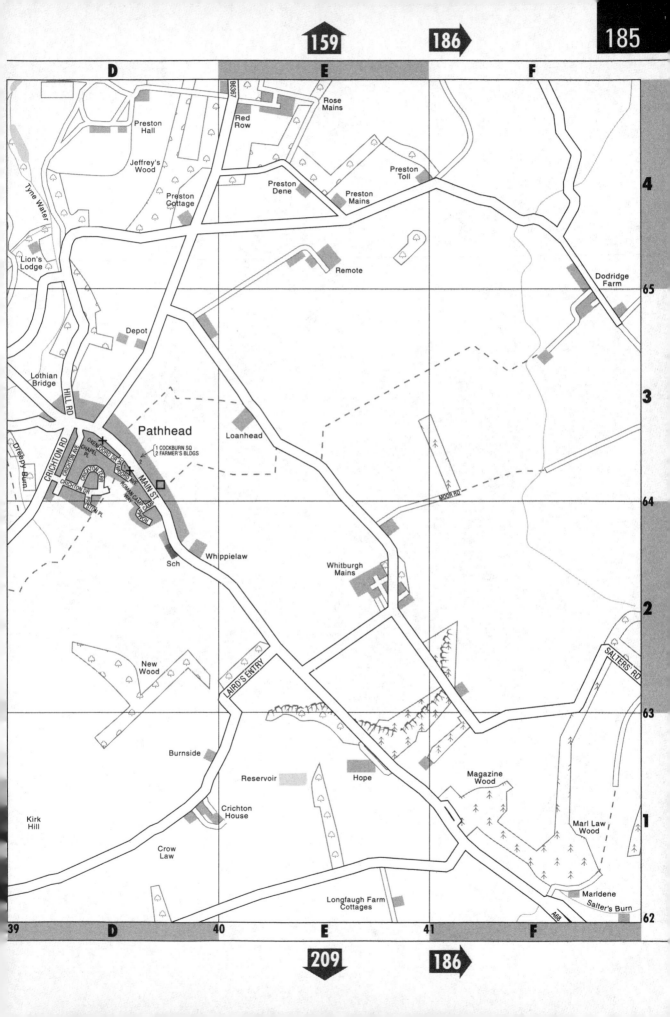

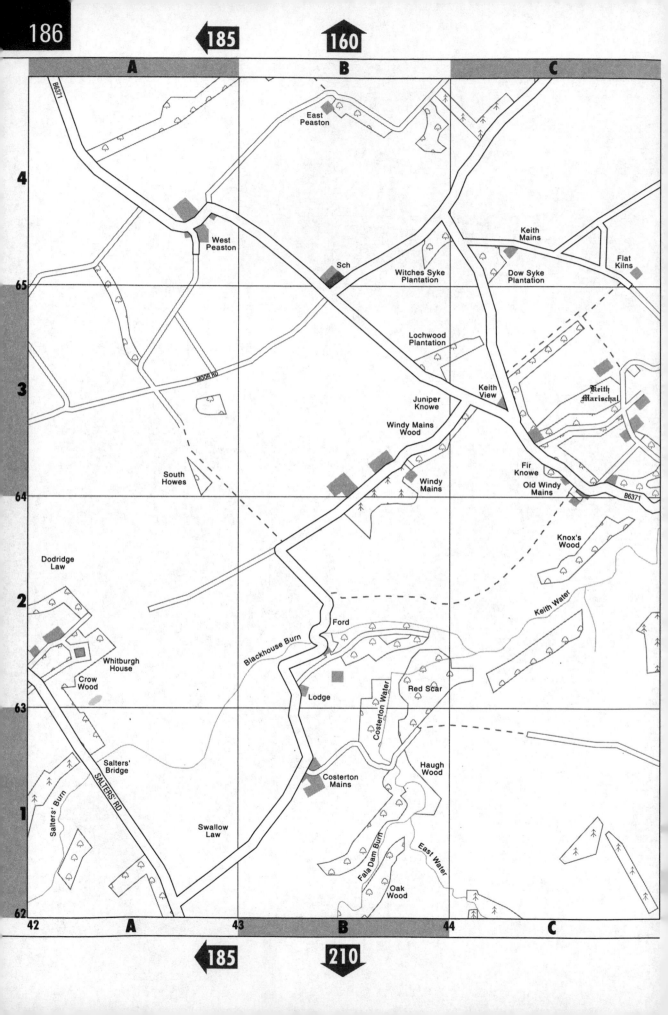

185
160

A   **B**   **C**

B6371

East
Peaston

4

West
Peaston

Sch

Keith
Mains

Flat
Kilns

Witches Syke
Plantation

Dow Syke
Plantation

65

MOOR RD

Lochwood
Plantation

Keith
View

Keith
Marischal

3

Juniper
Knowe

Windy Mains
Wood

South
Howes

Fir
Knowe

Windy
Mains

Old Windy
Mains

B6371

64

Knox's
Wood

Dodridge
Law

Keith Water

2

Ford

Whitburgh
House

Blackhouse Burn

Crow
Wood

Costerton Water

Red Scar

Lodge

63

Salters'
Bridge

Haugh
Wood

Salters' Burn

SALTERS' RD

1

Costerton
Mains

Swallow
Law

Fala Dam Burn

East Water

Oak
Wood

62

42   **A**   43   **B**   44   **C**

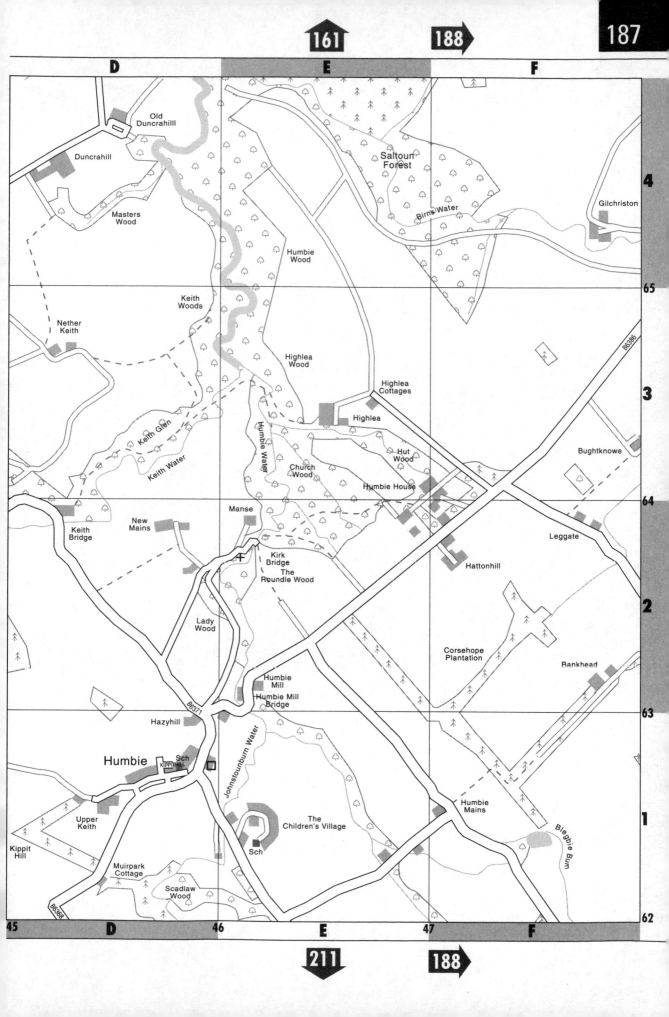

Old Duncrahilll

Duncrahill

Saltoun Forest

Birns Water

Gilchriston

4

Masters Wood

Humbie Wood

Keith Woods

65

Nether Keith

Highlea Wood

Highlea Cottages

B6386

Keith Glen

Humble Water

Highlea

3

Hut Wood

Bughtknowe

Keith Water

Church Wood

Humbie House

Keith Bridge

New Mains

Manse

64

Leggate

Keith Bridge

Kirk Bridge

The Roundle Wood

Hattonhill

2

Lady Wood

Corsehope Plantation

Bankhead

B6371

Humbie Mill

Humbie Mill Bridge

Hazyhill

63

Humbie

Sch
KIPPITHILL

Johnstounburn Water

Humbie Mains

Blegbie Burn

1

Upper Keith

The Children's Village

Kippit Hill

Sch

Muirpark Cottage

Scadlaw Wood

B6368

45   D   46   E   47   F   62

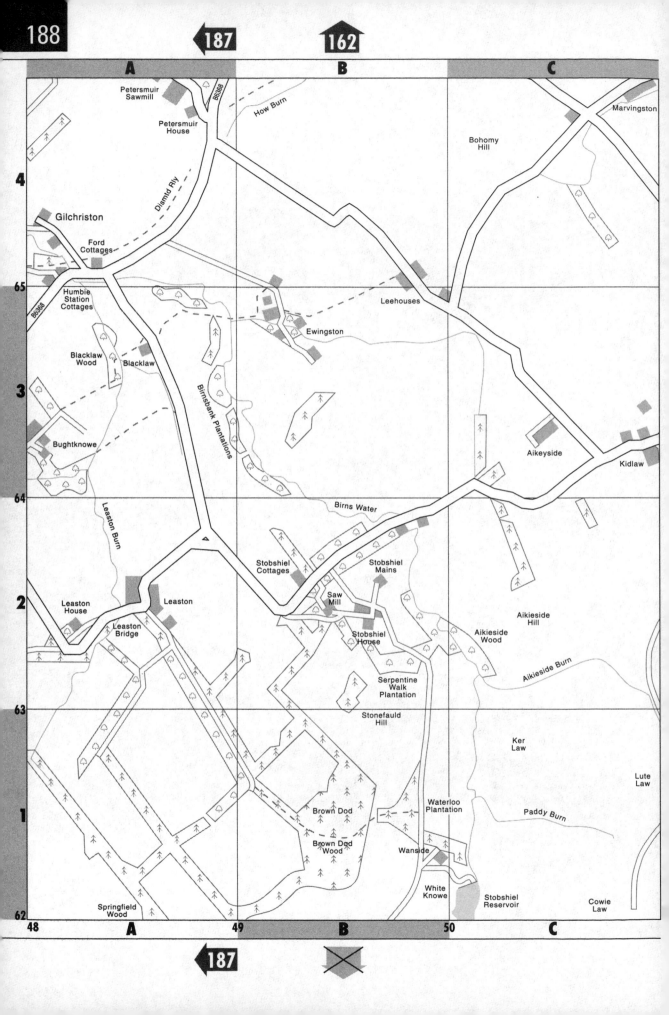

A B C

Petersmuir
Sawmill

How Burn

Marvingston

Petersmuir
House

Bohomy
Hill

4

Dismtd Rly

B6368

Gilchriston

Ford
Cottages

65

Humbie
Station
Cottages

Leehouses

B6368

Blacklaw
Wood

Blacklaw

Ewingston

3

Birnsbank Plantations

Bughtknowe

Aikeyside

Kidlaw

64

Birns Water

Leaston Burn

Stobshiel
Cottages

Stobshiel
Mains

Aikieside
Hill

2

Leaston
House

Leaston

Saw
Mill

Stobshiel
House

Aikieside
Wood

Aikieside Burn

Leaston
Bridge

Serpentine
Walk
Plantation

63

Stonefauld
Hill

Ker
Law

Lute
Law

1

Brown Dod

Waterloo
Plantation

Paddy Burn

Brown Dod
Wood

Wanside

White
Knowe

Stobshiel
Reservoir

Cowie
Law

62

Springfield
Wood

48 **A** 49 **B** 50 **C**

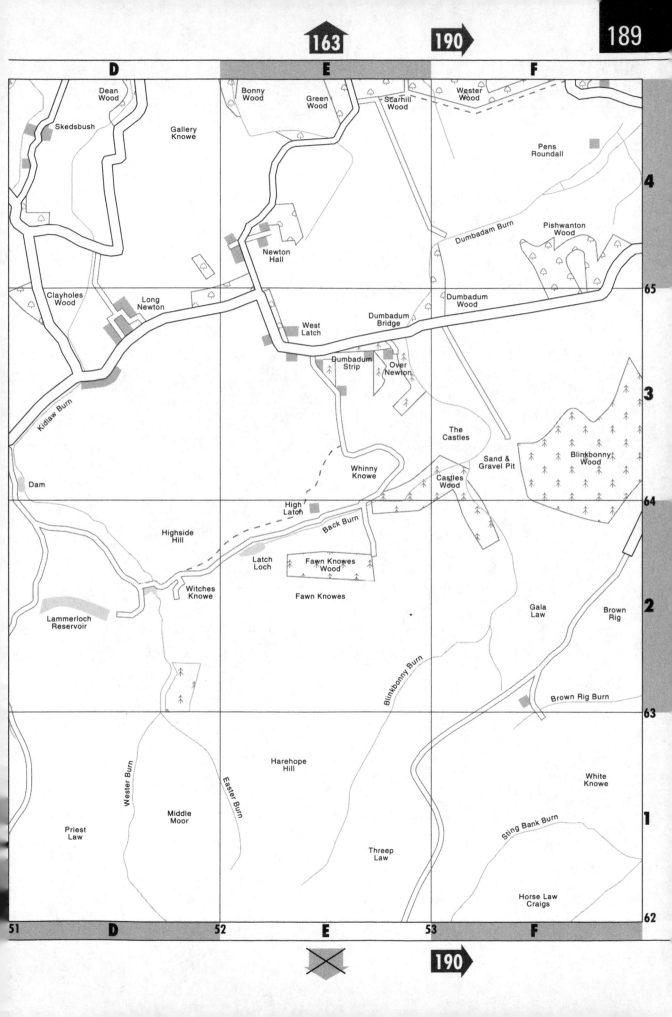

Dean
Wood

Skedsbush

Gallery
Knowe

Bonny
Wood

Green
Wood

Scarhill
Wood

Wester
Wood

Pens
Roundall

Newton
Hall

Dumbadam Burn

Pishwanton
Wood

Clayholes
Wood

Long
Newton

West
Latch

Dumbadum
Bridge

Dumbadum
Wood

Kidlaw Burn

Dumbadum
Strip

Over
Newton

The
Castles

Sand &
Gravel Pit

Blinkbonny
Wood

Dam

Whinny
Knowe

Castles
Wood

High
Latch

Back Burn

Highside
Hill

Latch
Loch

Fawn Knowes
Wood

Witches
Knowe

Fawn Knowes

Gala
Law

Brown
Rig

Lammerloch
Reservoir

Blinkbonny Burn

Brown Rig Burn

Harehope
Hill

White
Knowe

Wester Burn

Easter Burn

Middle
Moor

Sting Bank Burn

Priest
Law

Threep
Law

Horse Law
Craigs

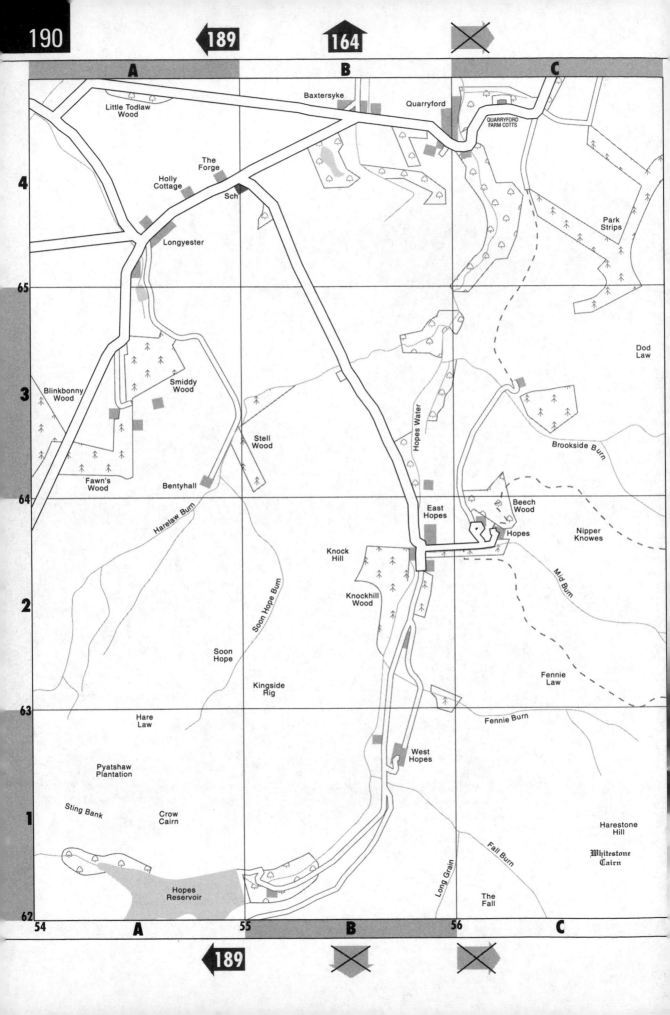

A B C

Little Todlaw Wood

Baxtersyke

Quarryford

QUARRYFORD FARM COTTS

The Forge

Holly Cottage

Sch

4

Longyester

Park Strips

65

Dod Law

Blinkbonny Wood

Smiddy Wood

Hopes Water

3

Stell Wood

Brookside Burn

Fawn's Wood

Bentyhall

Harelaw Burn

Beech Wood

64

East Hopes

Hopes

Nipper Knowes

Knock Hill

Mid Burn

Soon Hope Burn

Knockhill Wood

2

Soon Hope

Fennie Law

Kingside Rig

63

Hare Law

Fennie Burn

Pyatshaw Plantation

West Hopes

Sting Bank

Crow Cairn

1

Harestone Hill

Long Grain

Fall Burn

Whitestone Cairn

Hopes Reservoir

The Fall

62

54 A 55 B 56 C

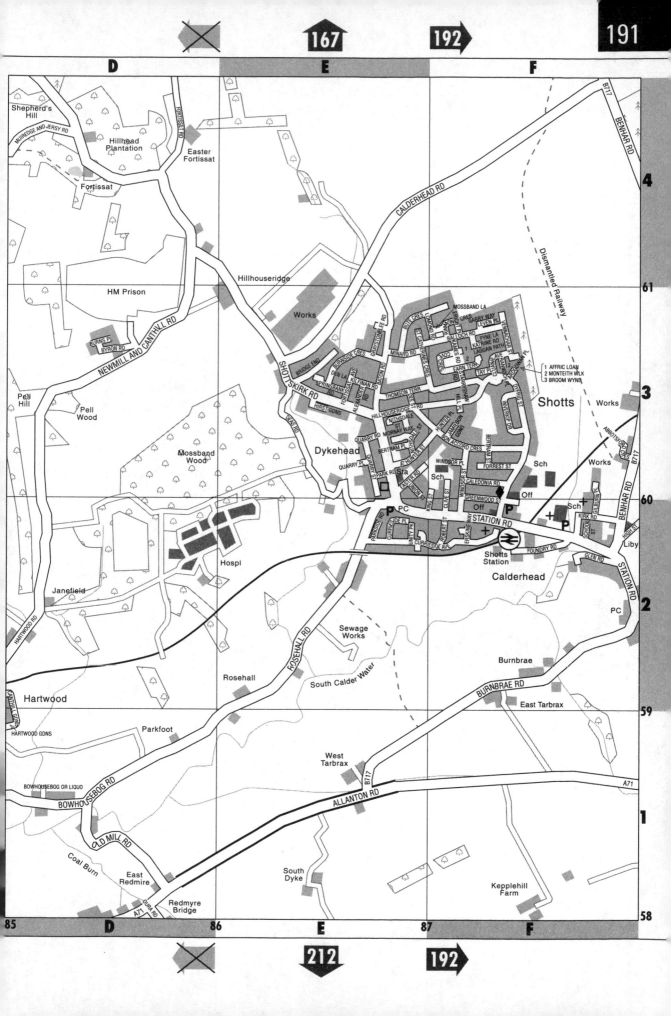

A B C

4

B717

61

BENHAR RD

CH

Amb Sta

Golf Course

Starryshaw Farm

3

B717

South Calder Water

Spoil Heap

Stanebent

Cairneyhead

Torbothie

Stane

STABLE RD

60

GRAY ST

HIGH ST

ULG WAY
GAIR WYND

CHARLES ST

TORBOTHIE RD

SOUTHFIELD RD

CLYDE DR

KEVIN DR

CALDER DR

HAWTHORN DR

SOUTHFIELD CRES

Torbothie

PC

Sch

CEMETERY RD

2

MANSE RD

CHARLOTTE ST

NEVIS PL

Cemy

1 ETIVE WAY
2 ULG WAY
3 GAIR WYND
4 BOWMORE WLK
5 TORRIN LOAN
6 DORNIE WYND
7 MORAR WAY
8 COIRE LOAN
9 SUNA PATH
10 SALEN LOAN

B7010

MAIN ST

SANDYHILL RD

AUCHVILLE RD

1 GARTEN
2

LOCHASE CRES

SHIEL GDNS

TULLOCH RD

APPIN TERR

MELDRID AVE

WYVIS PL

ONICH PL

LAGGAN AVE

SANDYVALE PL

Stane

BLINNY CT 1
TARBRAX PATH 2

BRIDGE PL

KNOLL CROFT

WAVANY GDNS

LANSDOWNE CRES

HURLY TERR

SPRINGHILL RD

Springhill

B7010

STANE RD

59

BLACKHALL

BELMONT DR

MULLROA

BROWN ST

BERRYHILL PL

BEECHMOUNT CT

LARCHFIELD LA

NORTHFIELD AVE

ELMWOOD RD

Works

Springhill

SPRINGHILL AND LEADLOCH RD

Knowton Farm

B7010

B715 HEADLESSCROSS RD B715

Dismantled Railway

A71

Works

Lingore Linn

A71

1

Dismtld Rly

58

88 A 89 B 90 C

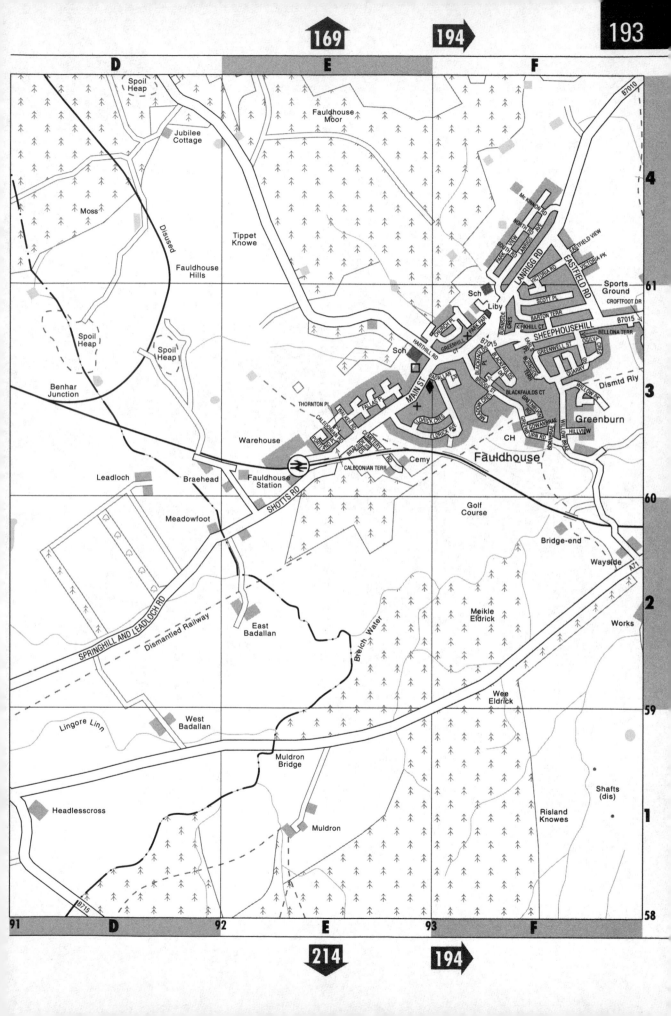

193
170

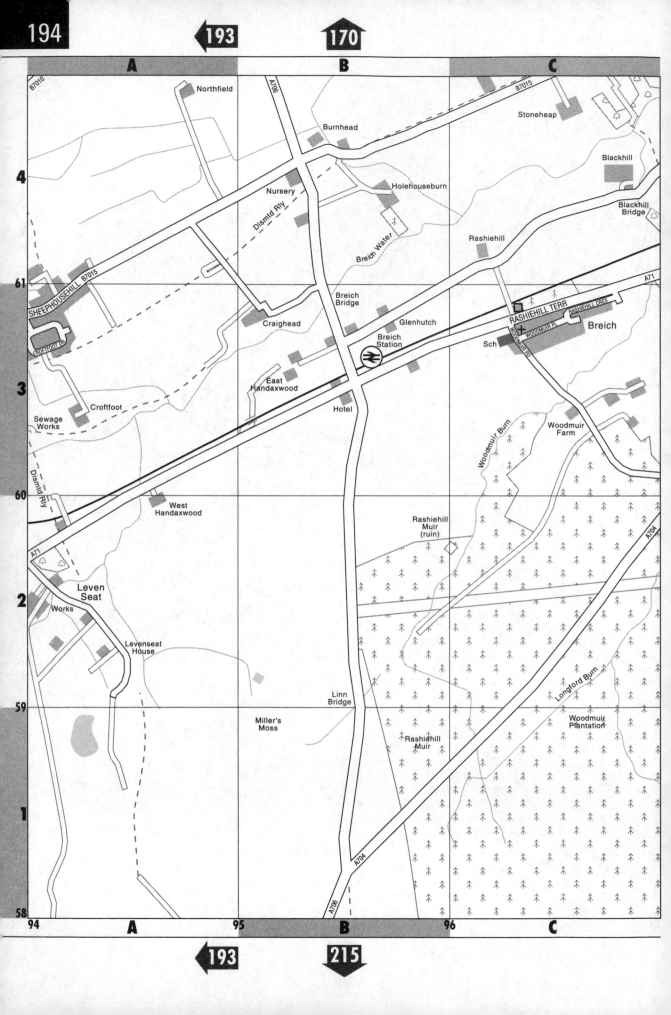

193
215

195
172

A704

Cairnview
Mains

West
Mains

Cow
Hill

Little
Harwood

Hartwood

Hartwood
Bridge

Harwood Water

Hartwood
Mains

Mossend

Mid
Hartwood

West
Harwood

Bog Burn

Baadsmill

Baad's Mill
Bridge

Vein Syke

Adie's Syke

Coal Burn

Pearie
Law

Cobbinshaw
Reservoir

Benry
Bog

Benry
Bridge

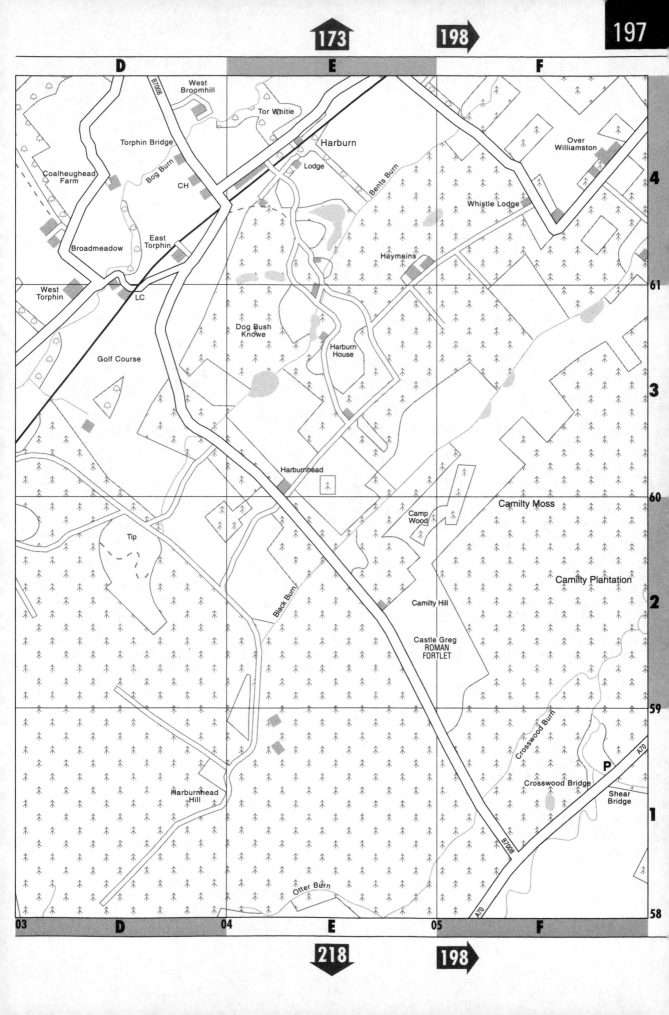

D
E
F

West Broomhill
B7008
Tor Whitie
Harburn
Torphin Bridge
Lodge
Coalheughead Farm
Bog Burn
CH
Bents Burn
Whistle Lodge
4
Broadmeadow
East Torphin
Haymains
West Torphin
LC
61
Dog Bush Knowe
Golf Course
Harburn House
3
Harburnhead
Camp Wood
Camilty Moss
60
Tip
Camilty Plantation
Black Burn
Camilty Hill
2
Castle Greg ROMAN FORTLET
59
Crosswood Burn
A70
P
Crosswood Bridge
Harburnhead Hill
Shear Bridge
1
B7008
Otter Burn
A70
58

03
D
04
E
05
F

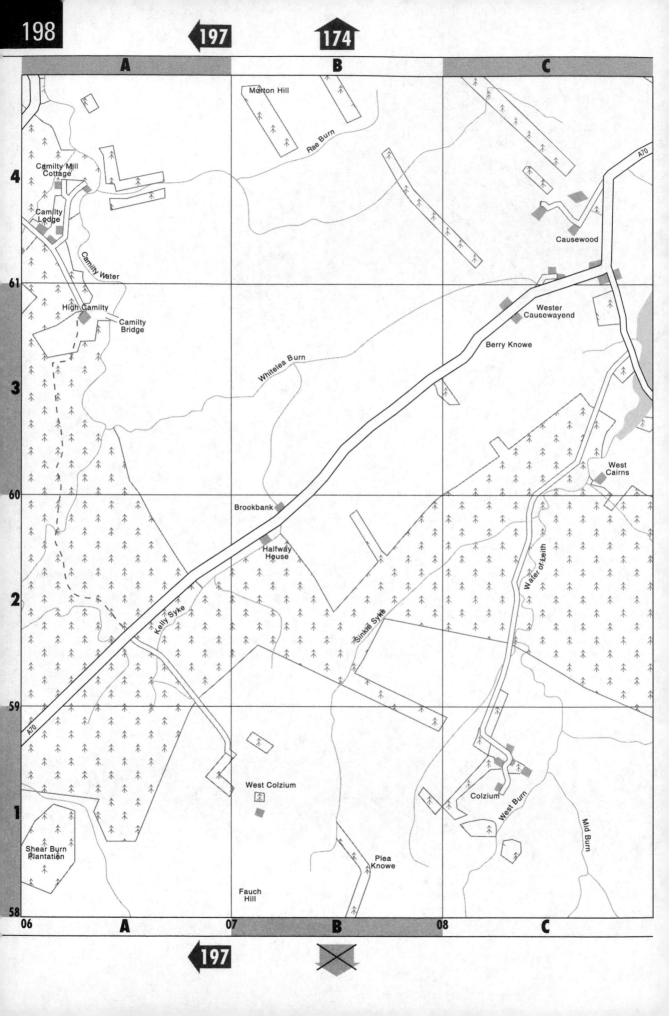

Morton Hill

Rae Burn

Camilty Mill
Cottage

Camilty
Lodge

A70

Causewood

Camilty Water

61

4

High Camilty

Camilty
Bridge

Wester
Causewayend

Berry Knowe

Whitelea Burn

3

West
Cairns

60

Brookbank

Halfway
House

Water of Leith

Kelly Syke

2

Sinkie Syke

59

A70

West Colzium

Colzium

West Burn

Mid Burn

1

Shear Burn
Plantation

Plea
Knowe

Fauch
Hill

58

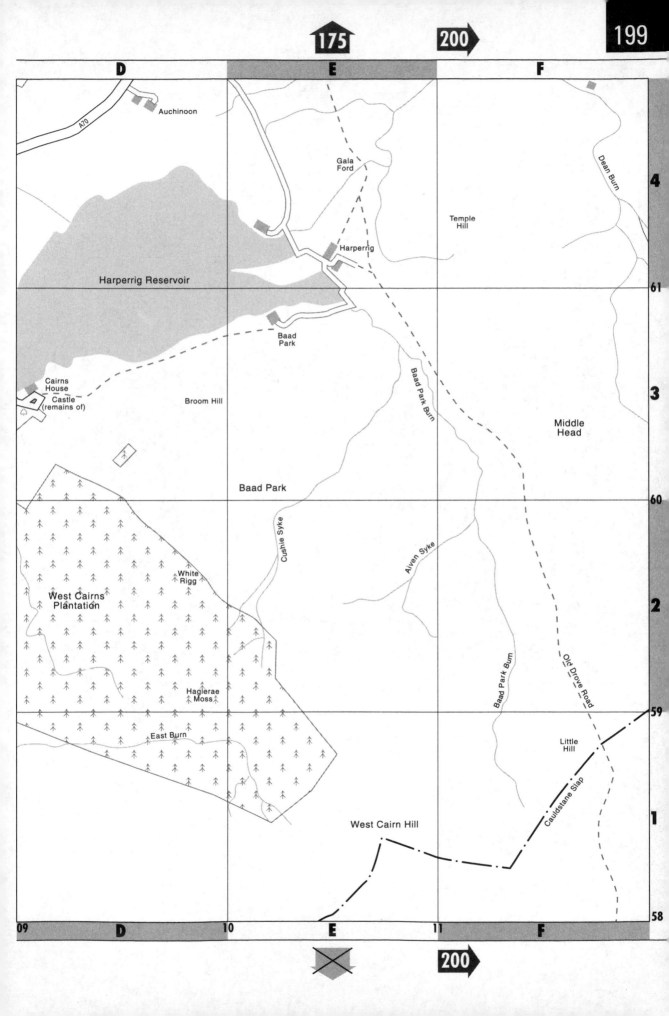

D · E · F

4

61

3

60

2

59

1

58

Auchinoon

A70

Gala
Ford

Temple
Hill

Dean Burn

Harperrig

Harperrig Reservoir

Baad
Park

Cairns
House
Castle
(remains of)

Broom Hill

Baad Park Burn

Middle
Head

Baad Park

Cushie Syke

Aiven Syke

West Cairns
Plantation

White
Rigg

Haglerae
Moss

Baad Park Burn

Old Drove Road

East Burn

Little
Hill

Cauldstane Slap

West Cairn Hill

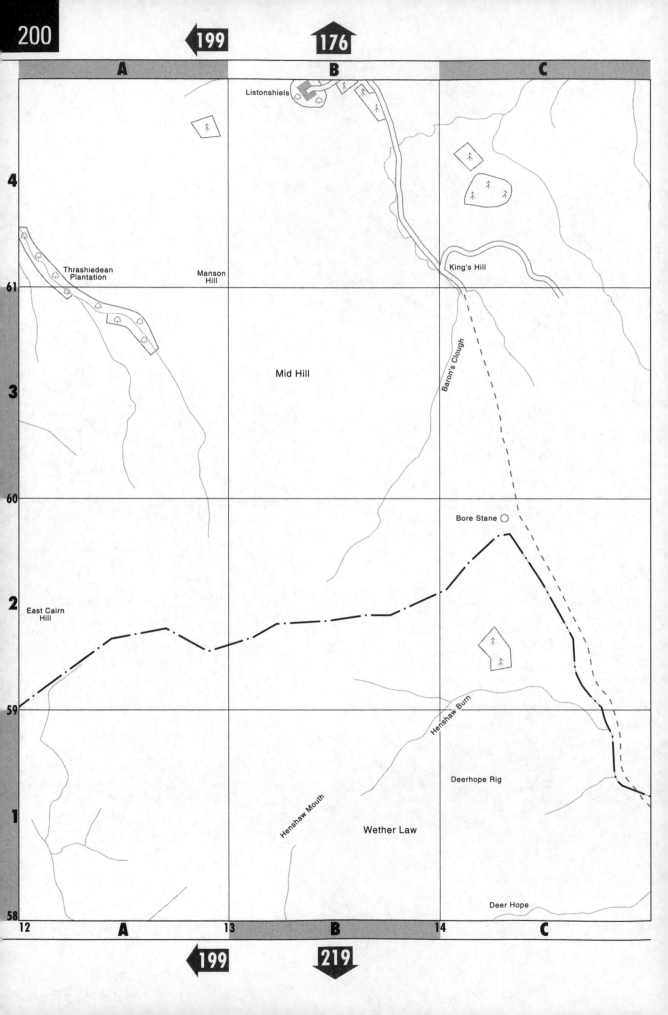

A
B
C

Listonshiels

4

Thrashiedean
Plantation

Manson
Hill

King's Hill

61

Mid Hill

Baron's Clough

3

60

Bore Stane

2

East Cairn
Hill

59

Henshaw Burn

Deerhope Rig

1

Henshaw Mouth

Wether Law

Deer Hope

58

12
A
13
B
14
C

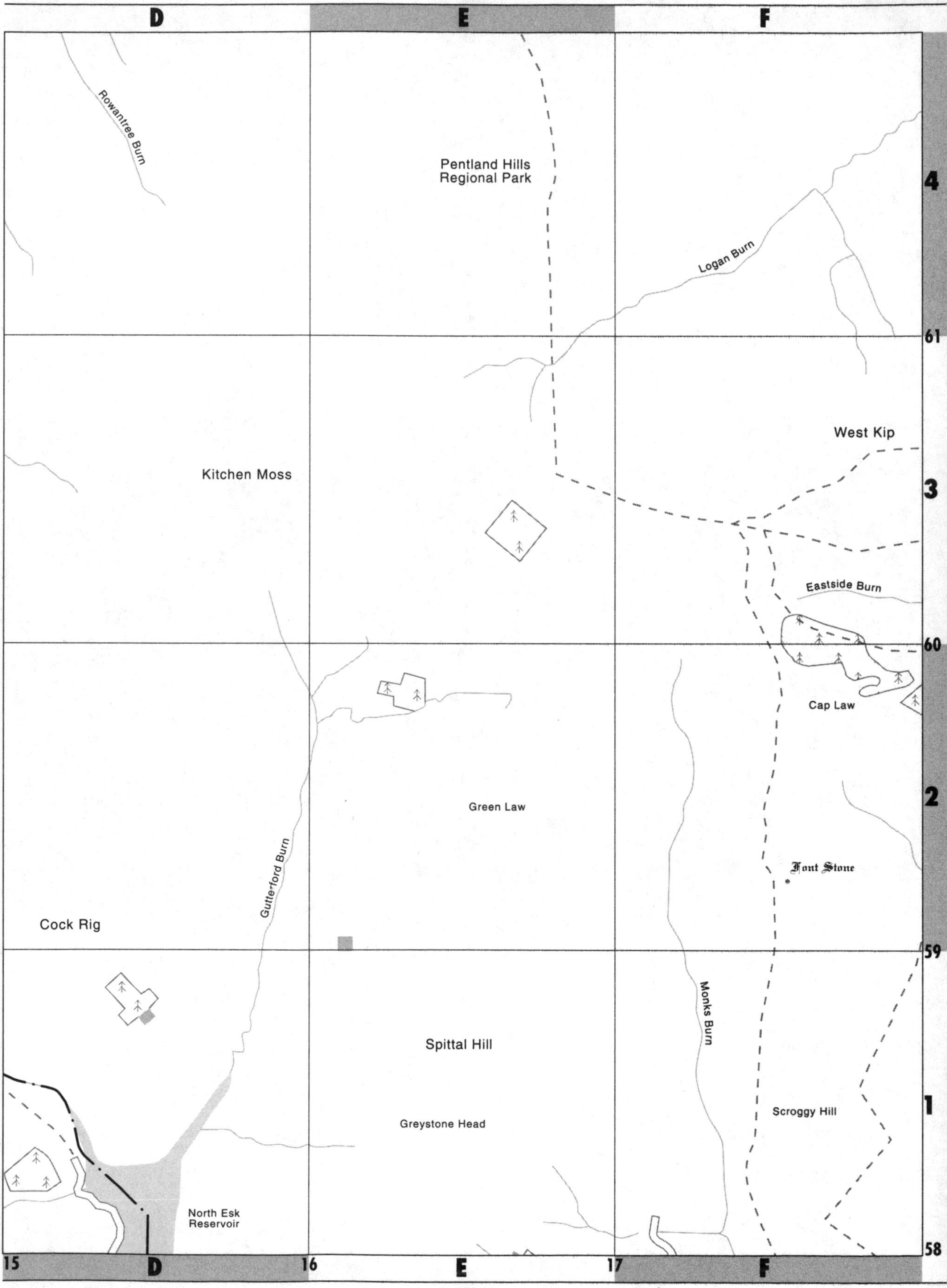

D   E   F

Rowantree Burn

Pentland Hills
Regional Park

Logan Burn

4

61

West Kip

Kitchen Moss

3

Eastside Burn

60

Cap Law

Green Law

2

Font Stone

Cock Rig

Gutterford Burn

59

Spittal Hill

Monks Burn

Greystone Head

Scroggy Hill

1

North Esk
Reservoir

58

15   D   16   E   17   F

201
178

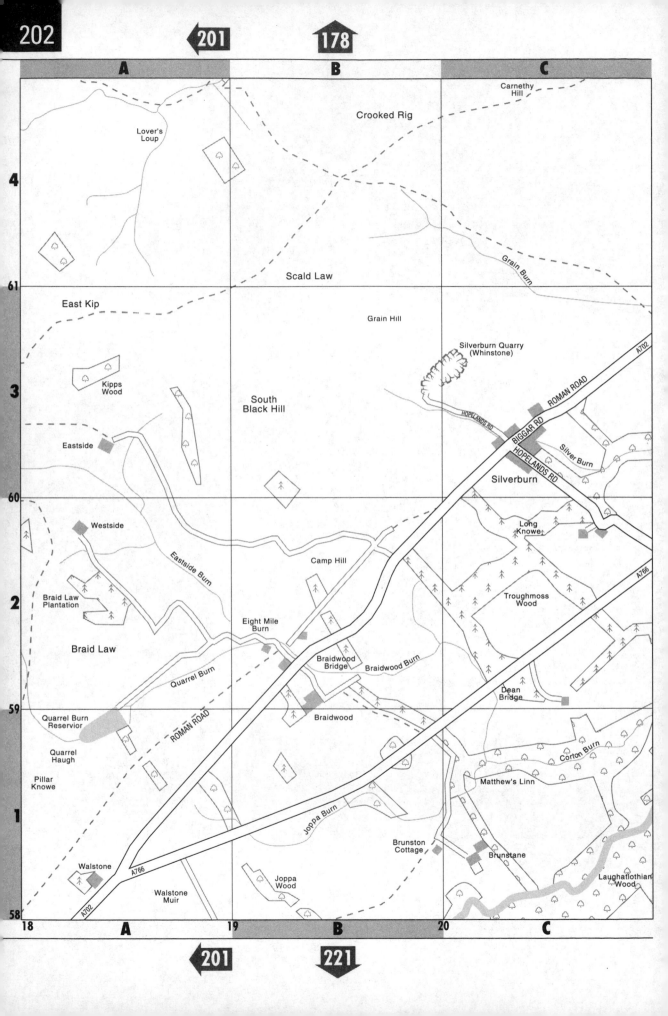

A   **B**   **C**

Crooked Rig

Carnethy Hill

Lover's Loup

4

Scald Law

Grain Burn

61

East Kip

Grain Hill

Silverburn Quarry (Whinstone)

3

Kipps Wood

South Black Hill

ROMAN ROAD

HOPELANDS RD

BIGGAR RD

Eastside

HOPELANDS RD

Silver Burn

Silverburn

60

Westside

Long Knowe

Eastside Burn

Camp Hill

Braid Law Plantation

Troughmoss Wood

2

Eight Mile Burn

Braid Law

Braidwood Bridge

Braidwood Burn

Quarrel Burn

Dean Bridge

59

Quarrel Burn Reservoir

Braidwood

Quarrel Haugh

ROMAN ROAD

Corton Burn

Pillar Knowe

Matthew's Linn

Joppa Burn

1

Brunston Cottage

Brunstane

Walstone

A766

Joppa Wood

Laughatlothian Wood

A702

Walstone Muir

58

18   **A**   **19**   **B**   **20**   **C**

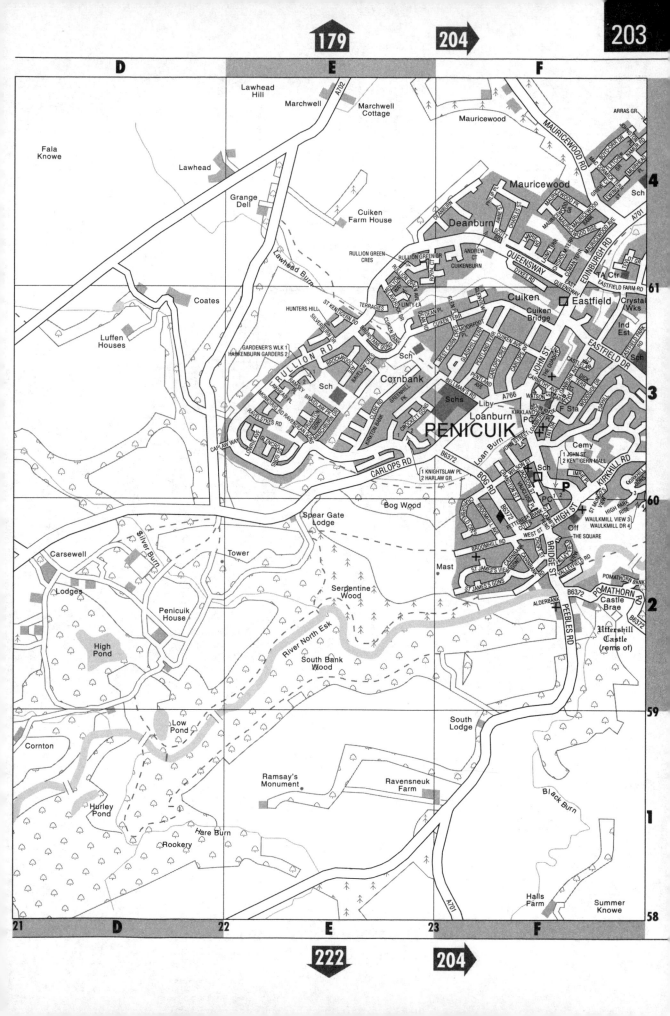

D E F

Lawhead
Hill
Marchwell
Marchwell
Cottage
Mauricewood
ARRAS GR

Fala
Knowe
Lawhead
Grange
Dell
Cuiken
Farm House
Mauricewood
Sch 4

Deanburn
QUEENSWAY
Cuiken
Eastfield
Crystal
Wks
61

Coates
Lawhead Burn
RULLION GREEN
CRES
RULLION GREEN GR
CUIKENBURN
ANDREW
CT
Cuiken
Bridge
Ind
Est
EASTFIELD DR
Sch

Luffen
Houses
HUNTERS HILL
Cornbank
Sch
PENICUIK
Loanburn
Liby
F Sta
Cemy
KIRKHILL RD
3

CARLOPS RD
Bog Wood
BOG RD
HIGH ST
P
60
THE SQUARE

Carsewell
Silver Burn
Spear Gate
Lodge
Tower
Serpentine
Wood
Mast
St JAMES'S VIEW
POMATHORN
Castle
Brae
PEEBLES RD
Uttershill
Castle
(rems of)
2

Lodges
Penicuik
House
High
Pond
River North Esk
South Bank
Wood
South
Lodge
59

Cornton
Low
Pond
Ramsay's
Monument
Ravensneuk
Farm
Black
Burn
1

Hurley
Pond
Rookery
Hare Burn
Halls
Farm
Summer
Knowe
58

21 D 22 E 23 F

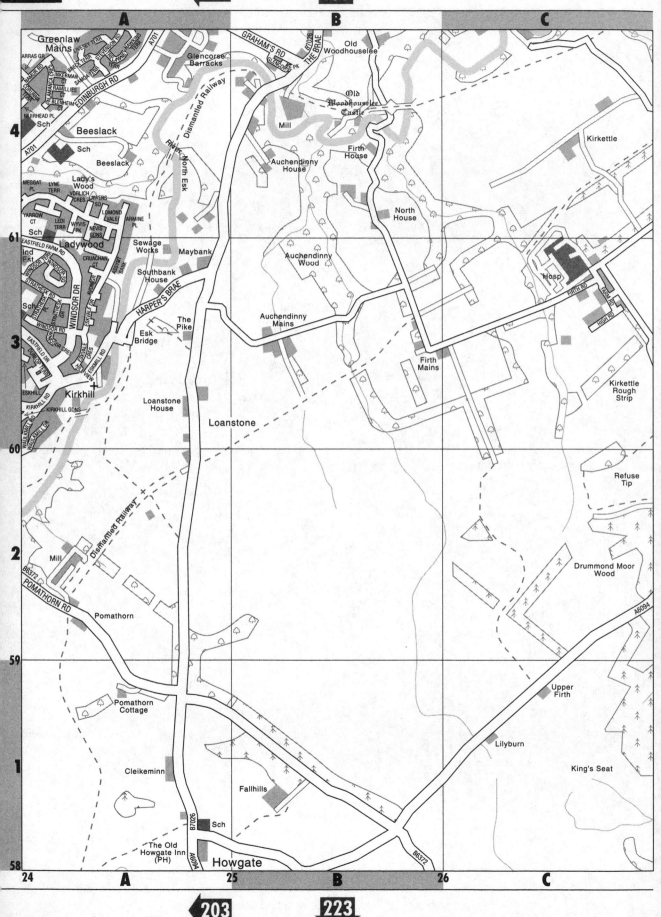

A   B   C

Greenlaw Mains

VESEY TERR
ARRAS GR
HAWKINS TERR
STEVENSON TERR
GRECE TERR
SOBRAON TERR
INKERMAN CT
JAMAICA ST
BLENHEIM CT
RAMILLIES CT
CORUNNA CT
MANURA RD
CURZON ST
MUIRHEAD PL
Sch

Glencorse Barracks

GRAHAM'S RD
GLENCORSE PK
THE BRAE
B7026

Old Woodhouselee

Dismantled Railway

River North Esk

Old Woodhouselee Castle

A701
EDINBURGH RD

4

Beeslack
Sch
Beeslack

Kirkettle

Mill

Auchendinny House

Firth House

MEGGAT PL
LYNE TERR
VORLICH CRES
LAWERS SQ
Lady's Wood
LEDI TERR
VALE/
LOMOND
NEVIS GDNS
WYVIS PK
ARMINE PL

YARROW CT
Sch

61

EASTFIELD FARM RD
Ind Est
Ladywood
WINDSOR TERR
CRUACHAN CT
ASSYNT BANK
WINDSOR US

Sewage Works
Maybank

North House

Auchendinny Wood

Hosp
FIRTH RD

Southbank House

HARPER'S BRAE

STRATHESK RD
STRATHESK PL
WINDSOR DR
Sch
EASTFIELD DR
WINDSOR RD
MANACH CRES
ESKVALE FH
ESKVALE CRES
ESKMILL RD

The Pike

Auchendinny Mains

FARM RD
HIGH RD

3

QUARRY FERRY
ESKHILL
HILL VIEW
Kirkhill
KIRKHILL RD
KIRKHILL GDNS
WAULKMILL RD
WAULKMILL DR

Esk Bridge

Firth Mains

Kirkettle Rough Strip

Loanstone House

Loanstone

60

Dismantled Railway

Refuse Tip

Mill
B6372

2

POMATHORN RD

Pomathorn

Drummond Moor Wood

A6094

59

Pomathorn Cottage

Upper Firth

Cleikeminn

Lilyburn

1

Fallhills
Sch

King's Seat

B6207
A6094
The Old Howgate Inn (PH)

Howgate
B6372

58

24   A   25   B   26   C

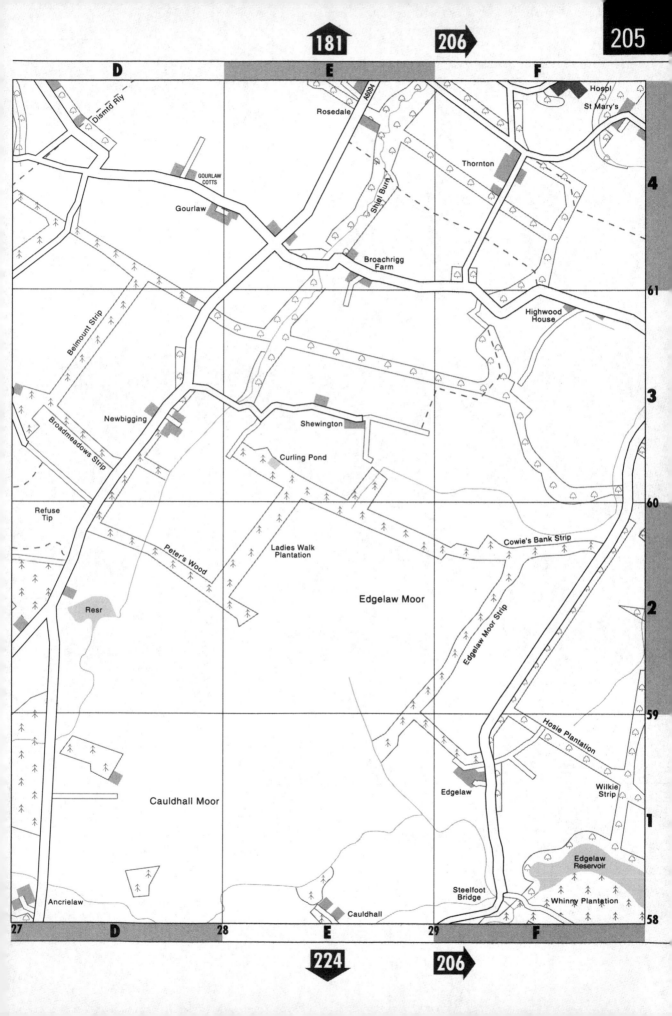

D E F

Dismtd Rly
Rosedale
Hospl
St Mary's
A6094
Thornton
GOURLAW COTTS
Gourlaw
Shiel Burn
4
Broachrigg Farm
Highwood House
61
Belmount Strip
3
Newbigging
Shewington
Broadmeadows Strip
Curling Pond
Refuse Tip
60
Peter's Wood
Ladies Walk Plantation
Cowie's Bank Strip
Edgelaw Moor
Resr
Edgelaw Moor Strip
2
Hosie Plantation
59
Cauldhall Moor
Edgelaw
Wilkie Strip
1
Edgelaw Reservoir
Ancrielaw
Steelfoot Bridge
Whinny Plantation
Caudhall
58

27 D 28 E 29 F

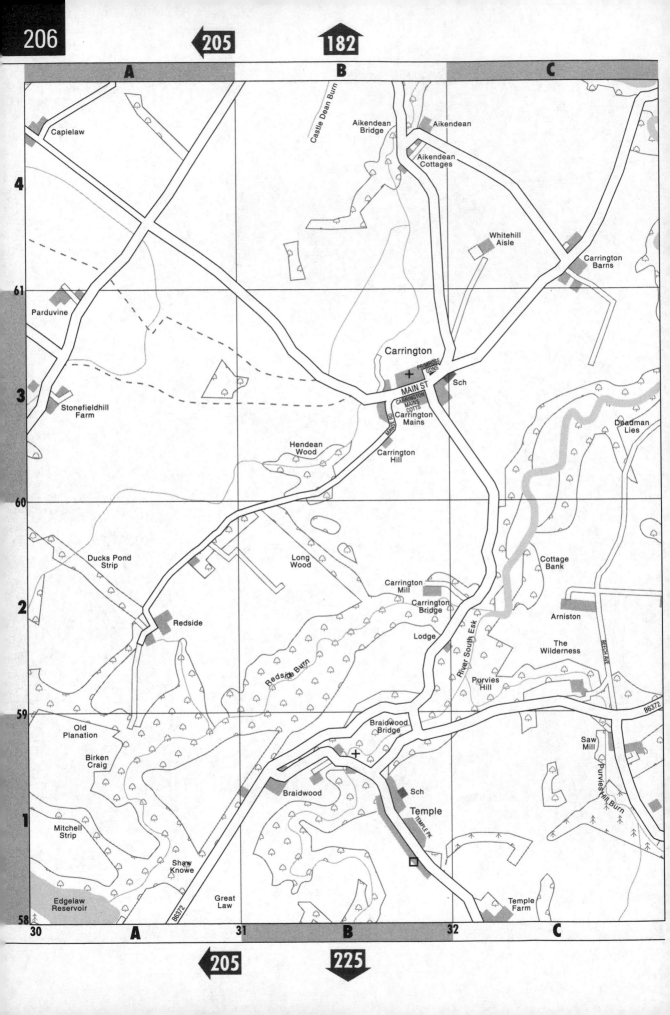

A   B   C

Castle Dean Burn

Capielaw

Aikendean
Bridge

Aikendean

Aikendean
Cottages

4

Whitehill
Aisle

Carrington
Barns

61

Parduvine

Carrington

PRIMROSE
GDNS

Sch

MAIN ST

3

Stonefieldhill
Farm

CARRINGTON
MAINS
COTTS

Carrington
Mains

Deadman
Lies

Hendean
Wood

Carrington
Hill

60

Ducks Pond
Strip

Long
Wood

Cottage
Bank

Carrington
Mill

Arniston

2

Redside

Carrington
Bridge

Lodge

The
Wilderness

River South Esk

Redside Burn

Purvies
Hill

BEECH AVE

59

Old
Planation

Braidwood
Bridge

Saw
Mill

B6372

Birken
Craig

Braidwood

Sch

Purvies Hill Burn

1

Mitchell
Strip

Temple

TEMPLE PK

Shaw
Knowe

B6372

Edgelaw
Reservoir

Great
Law

Temple
Farm

58

30   A   31   B   32   C

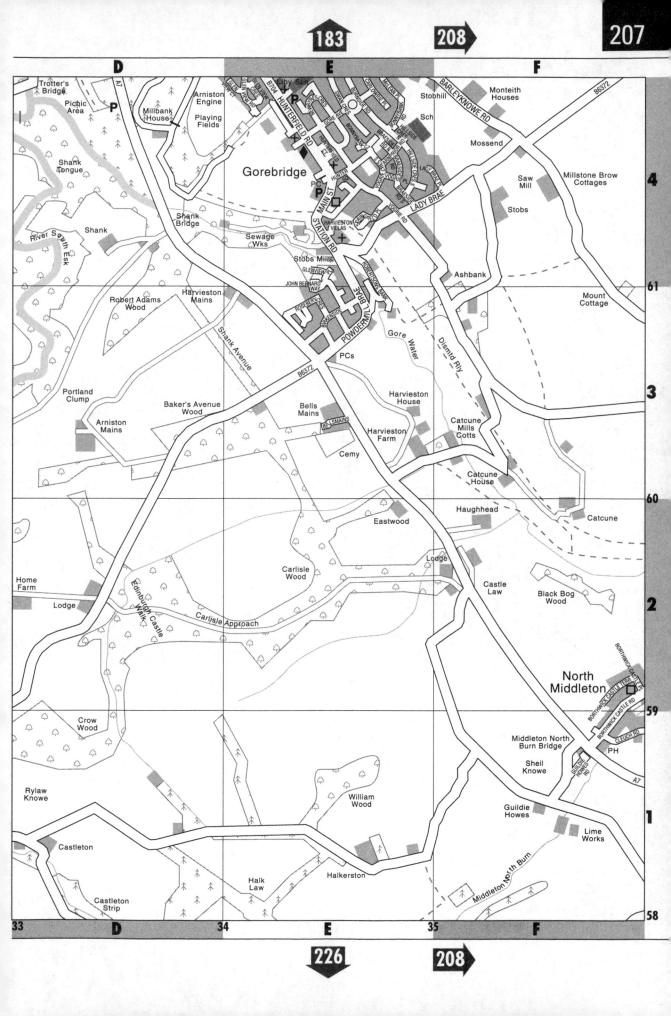

Gorebridge

North Middleton

207
184

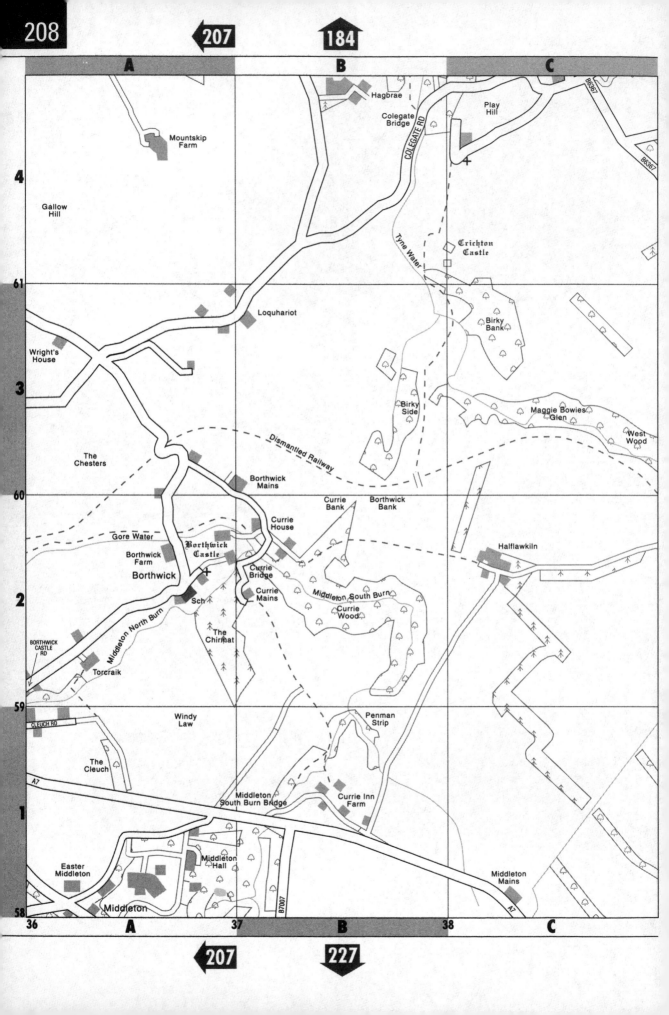

A   B   C

Hagbrae

Colegate Bridge

COLEGATE RD

Play Hill

Mountskip Farm

4

Gallow Hill

Crichton Castle

Tyne Water

61

Loquhariot

Birky Bank

Wright's House

3

Birky Side

Maggie Bowies Glen

West Wood

The Chesters

Dismantled Railway

Borthwick Mains

60

Currie Bank

Borthwick Bank

Gore Water

Currie House

Borthwick Farm

Borthwick Castle

Halflawkiln

Borthwick

Currie Bridge

Middleton South Burn

2

Sch

Currie Mains

Currie Wood

BORTHWICK CASTLE RD

The Chirmat

Middleton North Burn

Torcraik

59

CLEUCH RD

Windy Law

Penman Strip

The Cleuch

A7

Middleton South Burn Bridge

Currie Inn Farm

1

Easter Middleton

Middleton Hall

B7007

Middleton Mains

A7

58

Middleton

36   A   37   B   38   C

207
227

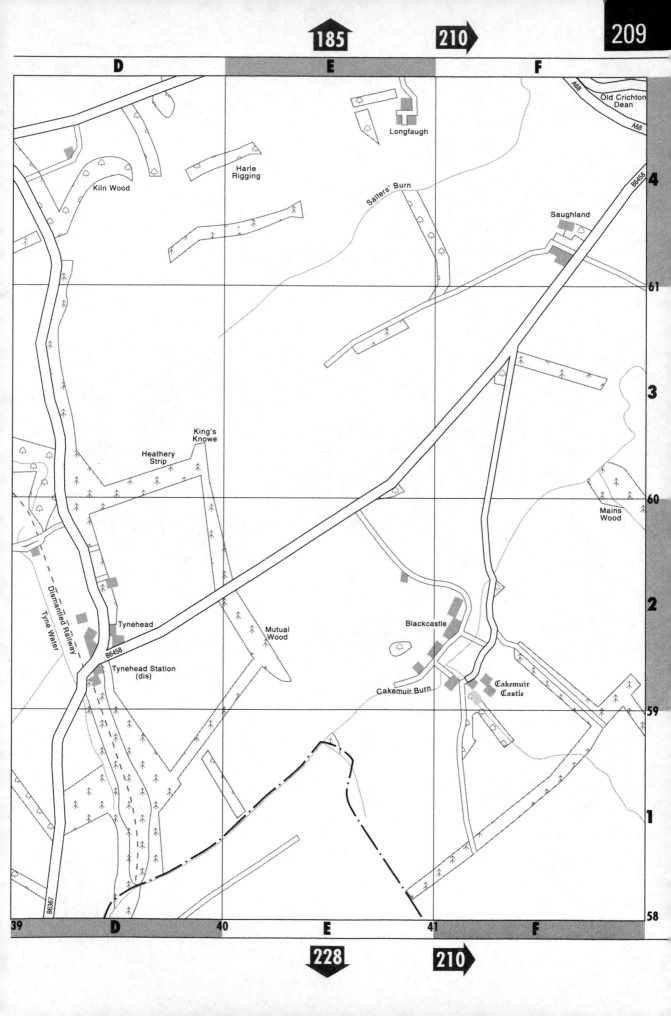

D

Longfaugh

Harle
Rigging

Kiln Wood

Salters' Burn

A68

Old Crichton
Dean

A68

B6458

4

Saughland

61

3

King's
Knowe

Heathery
Strip

60

Mains
Wood

Dismantled Railway

Tyne Water

Tynehead

B6458

Mutual
Wood

Blackcastle

2

Tynehead Station
(dis)

Cakemuir Burn

Cakemuir
Castle

59

1

B6367

58

A
B
C

Hough Head
House

Gardiner's
Hall Wood
SALTERS RD
Fala Dam
Wood
Fala
Mill
Fala Dam Burn

Fala Dam Burn

East Water

Fala
Hall

A68

B6458

Routhenhill

4

Bleak
Law

Fala
Dam

Fala Brae
Dam

Routing
Burn

Routing
Glen

Watergate
Toll

B6457

Fala

Sch

61

Cakemuir Burn

Blackshiels

B6457

3

Frostineb

Fala Mains
Wood

Fala Mains
Wood

Woodcote
Bridge

Juniperlea
Hotel

Fala
Mains

60

Black Burn

Partridge Burn

New
Salvandi

Deanburn
House

A68

2

Mains
Wood

North
Wood

High
Wood

Salvandi

59

Fala
Luggie

Dean Burn

1

Fala Flow
Loch

Fala Moor

Fala
Flow

58

42
A
43
B
44
C

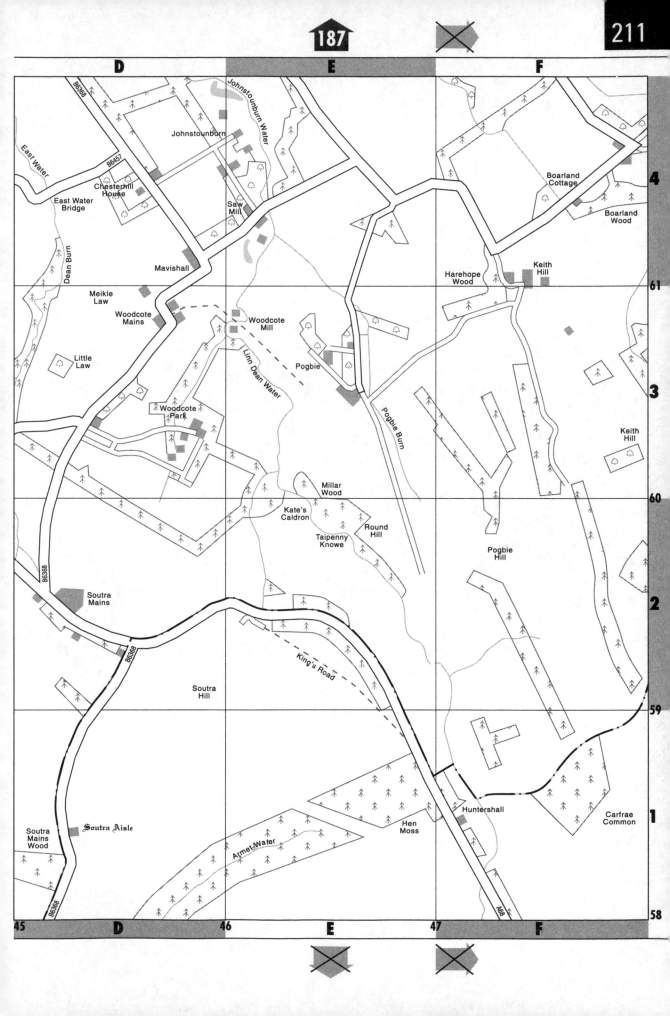

D

E

F

4

61

3

60

2

59

1

58

East Water

B6368

Johnstounburn

Johnstounburn Water

B6457

Chesterhill House

East Water Bridge

Saw Mill

Boarland Cottage

Boarland Wood

Keith Hill

Mavishall

Harehope Wood

Dean Burn

Meikle Law

Woodcote Mains

Woodcote Mill

Little Law

Linn Dean Water

Pogbie

Pogbie Burn

Keith Hill

Woodcote Park

Millar Wood

Kate's Caldron

Round Hill

Taipenny Knowe

Pogbie Hill

B6368

Soutra Mains

King's Road

Soutra Hill

Huntershall

Carfrae Common

Soutra Mains Wood

Soutra Aisle

Hen Moss

Armet Water

A68

B6368

45

46

47

D

E

F

A | **B** | **C**

KIRK PATH

ALLANTON RD A71

A71

COLTNESS

Sch

SCHOOL LA

Damside (PH)

REDMIRE CRES

OAKFIELD

HARTFIELD TERR

KINGSHILL RD

HOUSTONFIELD CRES

AVE

SPRINGHILL RD

WILSON RD

Allanton

HAWTHORN PL

Hartfield

Coal Burn

Netherhall

Dismantled Railway

Opencast Workings

57

4

Newark Plantation

3

Upper Daviesdykes

DURA RD

56

Kirkhall

Dismtd Rly

Lower Daviesdykes

Dismtd Rly

Lodge Hill

Winterhill

Dura

Brow Farm

2

Mountpleasant

Sunnyside

Auchterhead

55

Summerside

Kingshill

Auchter Water

1

54

85 | **A** | 86 | **B** | 87 | **C**

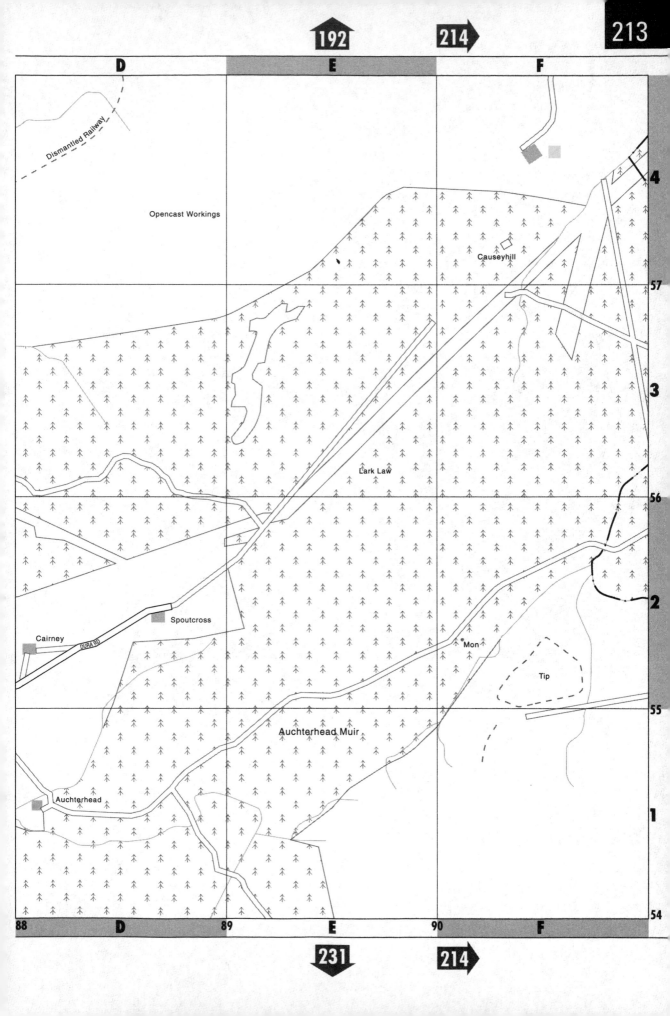

D

Dismantled Railway

Opencast Workings

Causeyhill

4

57

3

Lark Law

56

Cairney

Spoutcross

DURA RD

Mon

Tip

2

55

Auchterhead Muir

Auchterhead

1

54

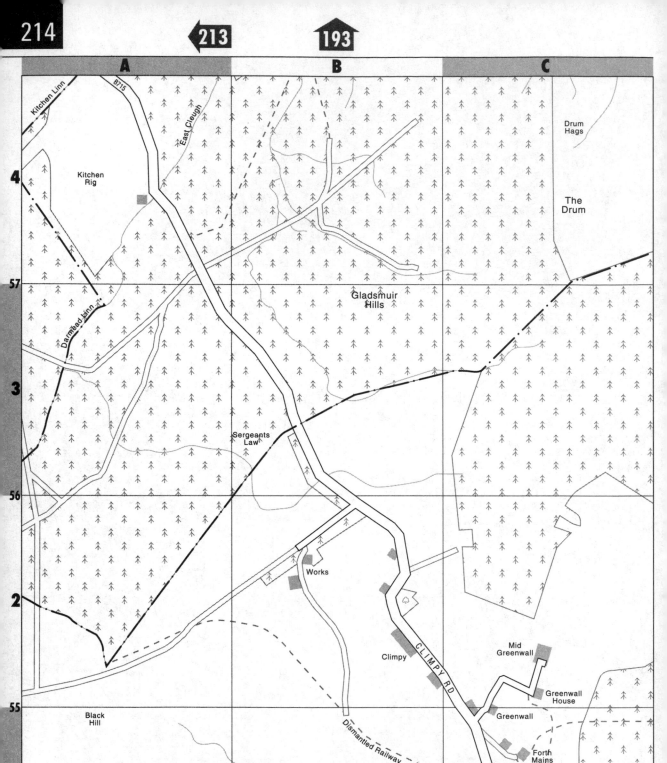

Kitchen Linn

B715

East Cleugh

Kitchen
Rig

Drum
Hags

4

57

The
Drum

Darmead Linn

Gladsmuir
Hills

3

Sergeants
Law

56

Works

2

Climpy

CLIMPY RD

Mid
Greenwall

Greenwall
House

55

Black
Hill

Dismantled Railway

Greenwall

Forth
Mains

Whaup
Knowe

Abbet Burn

Wester
Greenwall

1

B715

54

91   A   92   B   93   C

D E F

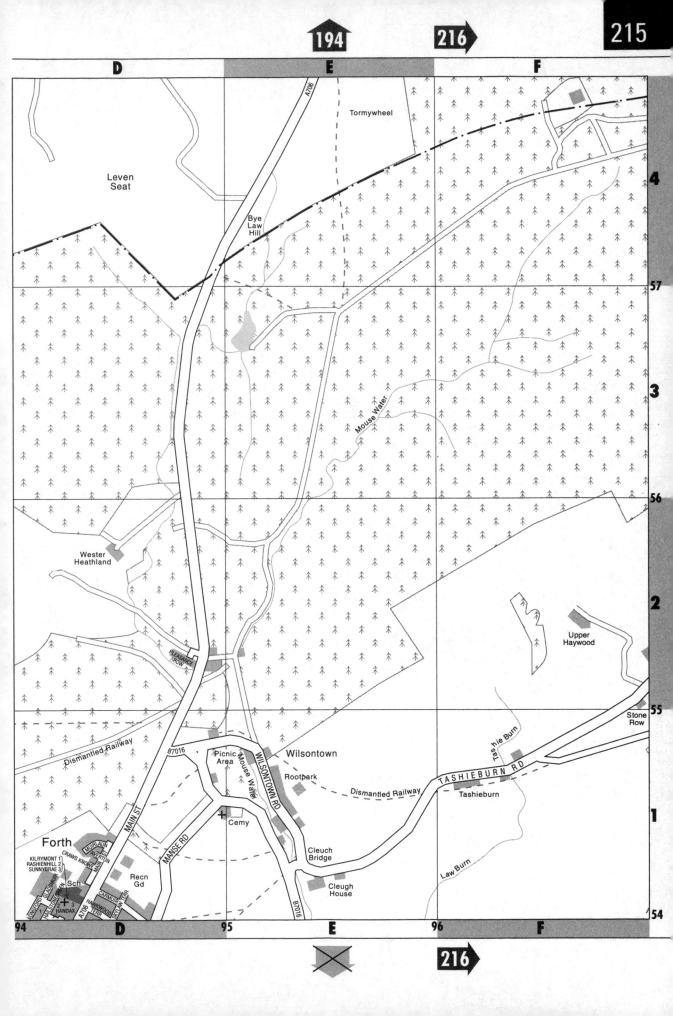

Leven Seat

Tormywheel

A-706

Bye Law Hill

4

57

Mouse Water

3

56

Wester Heathland

2

Upper Haywood

PLEASANCE ROW

55

Stone Row

Dismantled Railway

B7016

Picnic Area

Mouse Water

WILSONTOWN RD

Wilsontown

Rootpark

Tashie Burn

TASHIEBURN RD

Tashieburn

Dismantled Railway

1

MAIN ST

Cemy

MANSE RD

Cleuch Bridge

Cleuch House

Law Burn

Forth

KILRYMONT 1
RASHIENHILL 2
SUNNYBRAE 3

CRAWS KNOWE
MUIRLAUN
AVERTON

Recn Gd

Sch

CARMUIR
HAWWOOD TERR
SKYLAW TERR

A706

LONGFORD
TAIT STONE BREN
HANDAX
GLASSMUIR

54

215
195

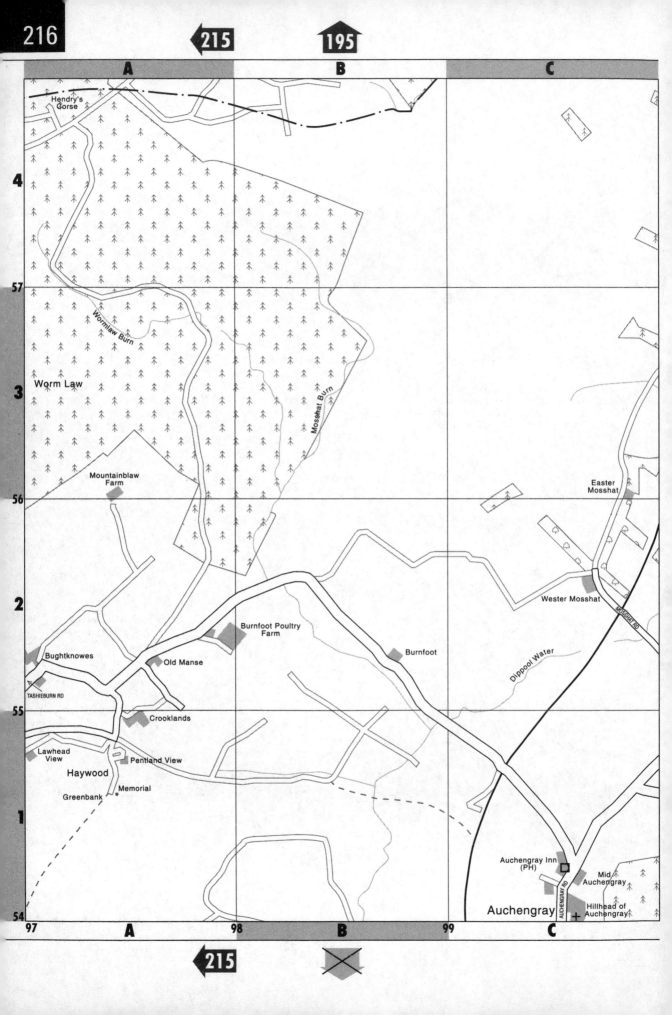

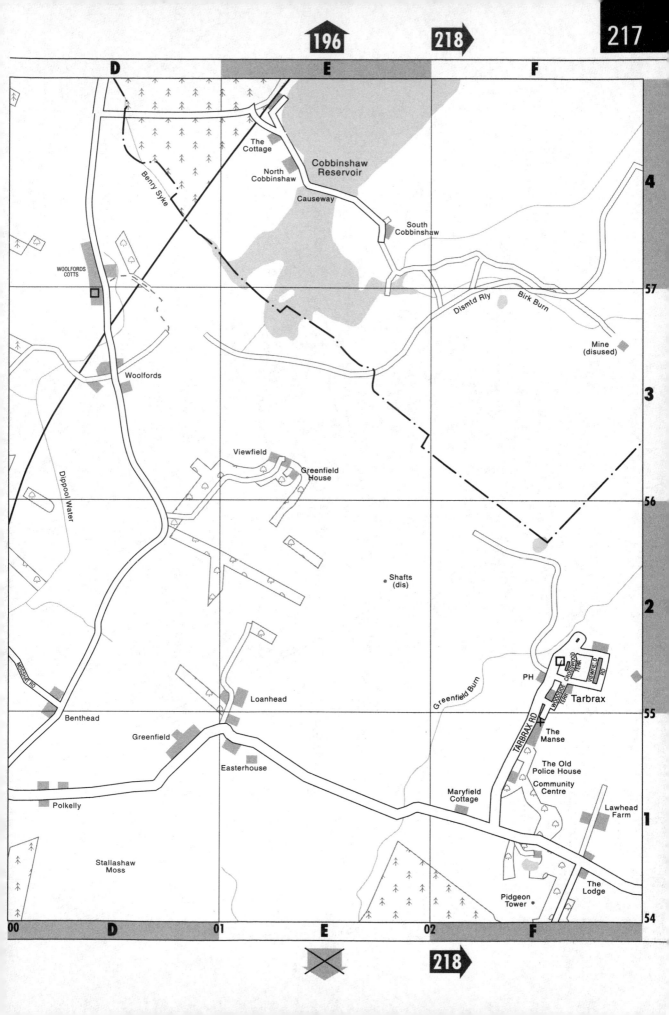

D E F

The Cottage
North Cobbinshaw
Cobbinshaw Reservoir
Causeway
South Cobbinshaw

Benty Syke

WOOLFORDS COTTS

Dismtd Rly
Birk Burn
Mine (disused)

Woolfords

Dippool Water

Viewfield
Greenfield House

Shafts (dis)

Greenfield Burn

MOSSAT RD

Loanhead

WOODSIDE TERR
CROSSWOOD TERR
VIEWFIELD RD
PH
Tarbrax

Benthead

Greenfield

Easterhouse

TARBRAX RD

The Manse

The Old Police House
Community Centre

Maryfield Cottage

Polkelly

Lawhead Farm

Stallashaw Moss

Pidgeon Tower

The Lodge

00 D 01 E 02 F

4

57

3

56

2

55

1

54

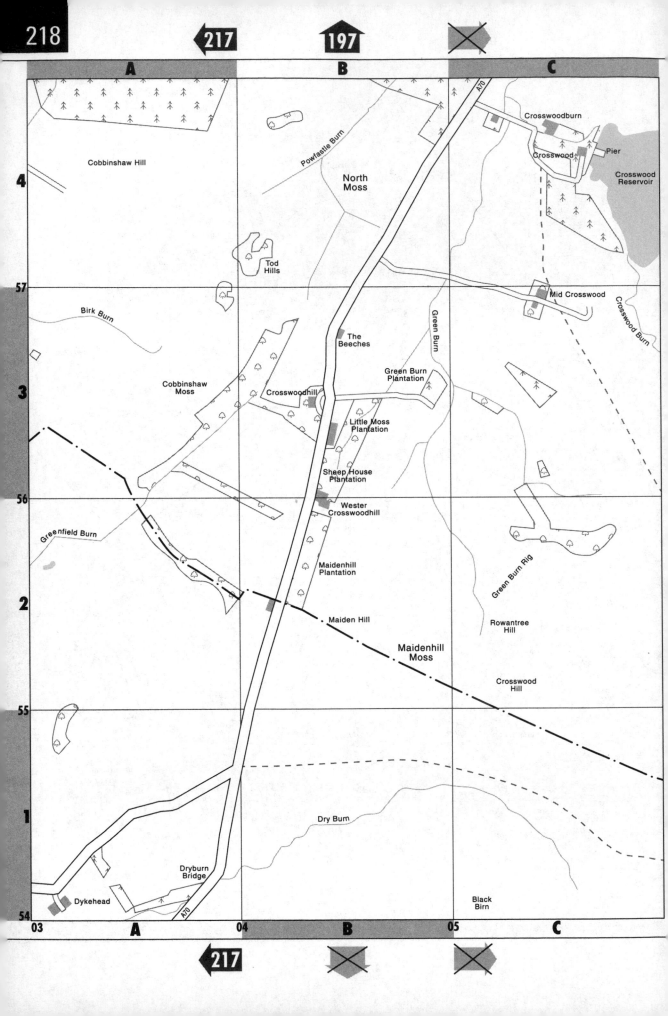

200 220

D E F

4

The Mount

Ravendean Burn

Lyne Water

Lynslie Burn

Cairn Muir

Little
Hill

Grain Heads

Fairliehope Burn

57

3

Hareshaw Sike

Petrifying
Spring

Glenmade Burn

56

Baddinsgill
Reservoir

Black Pots

Mount Maw

Little
Knock

2

Kennels

Colin's Rig

OLD DROVE RD

Baddinsgill Burn

55

Baddinsgill
House

Baddinsgill
Farm

Dipper
Wood

Lower Glen Ely
Wood

Glen Ely

1

Upper Glen Ely
Wood

Windy Gowl

Lyne Water

Faw Mount

ROMAN ROAD
(course of)

Cock
Rig

Wakefield

54

220

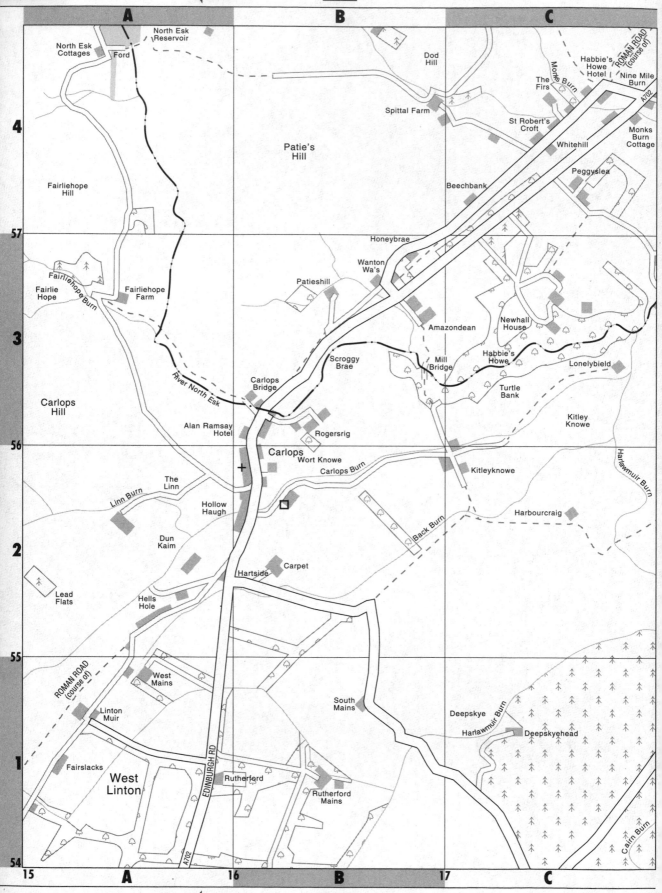

North Esk
Reservoir
North Esk
Cottages
Ford
Dod
Hill
Habbie's
Howe Hotel
Nine Mile
Burn
The
Firs
St Robert's
Croft
Spittal Farm
Whitehill
Monks
Burn
Cottage
Patie's
Hill
Beechbank
Peggyslea
Fairliehope
Hill
Honeybrae
Wanton
Wa's
Fairliehope Burn
Fairlie
Hope
Fairliehope
Farm
Patieshill
Amazondean
Newhall
House
Habbie's
Howe
Lonelybield
River North Esk
Scroggy
Brae
Mill
Bridge
Turtle
Bank
Carlops
Hill
Carlops
Bridge
Kitley
Knowe
Alan Ramsay
Hotel
Rogersrig
Carlops
Wort Knowe
Carlops Burn
Kitleyknowe
Harlawmuir Burn
The
Linn
Linn Burn
Hollow
Haugh
Back Burn
Harbourcraig
Dun
Kaim
Hartside
Carpet
Lead
Flats
Hells
Hole
ROMAN ROAD
(course of)
West
Mains
South
Mains
Deepskye
Harlawmuir Burn
Linton
Muir
EDINBURGH RD
Deepskyehead
Fairslacks
West
Linton
Rutherford
Rutherford
Mains
Cairn Burn
A702
ROMAN ROAD
(course of)
A702

Walstone Moss

Saw
Mill

A702

Walstone Muir

Monks Burn

River North Esk

Auchencorth

The Gawk Stone

Marfield

The
Steele

Marfield
Loch

Pillars

Hare Moss

The
Steele

Auchencorth Moss

Harlawmuir

Harlawmuir Burn

Harlaw Muir

Cairn Burn

Deepsyke Forest

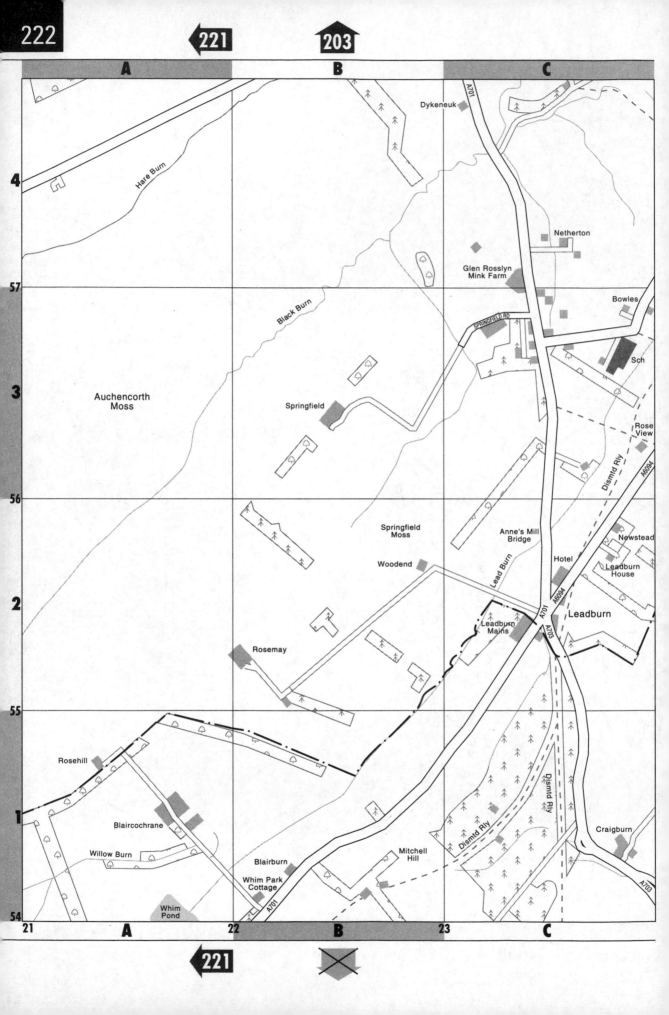

A   B   C

4

Dykeneuk

Hare Burn

Netherton

Glen Rosslyn
Mink Farm

Bowles

57

Black Burn

SPRINGFIELD RD

Sch

3

Auchencorth
Moss

Springfield

Rose
View

A6094

Dismtd Rly

56

Springfield
Moss

Anne's Mill
Bridge

Newstead

Woodend

Hotel

Leadburn
House

Lead Burn

A6094

2

Leadburn

Leadburn
Mains

A701

A703

Rosemay

55

Rosehill

Dismtd Rly

1

Blaircochrane

Dismtd Rly

Craigburn

Willow Burn

Mitchell
Hill

Blairburn

Whim Park
Cottage

A701

A703

Whim
Pond

54

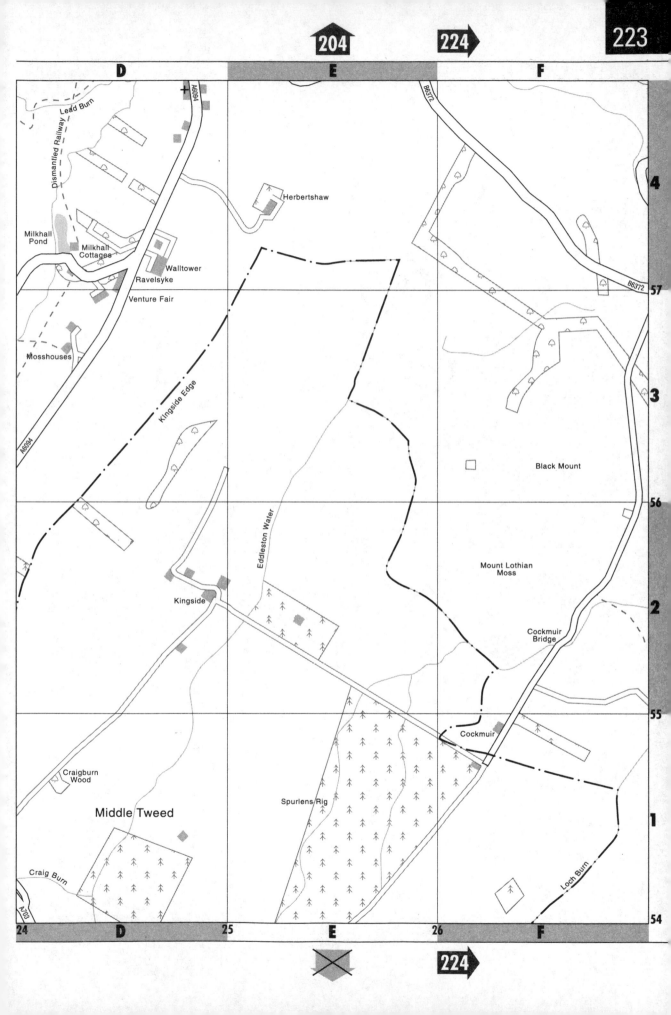

D   E   F

A6094

Lead Burn

Dismantled Railway

Herbertshaw

Milkhall Pond

Milkhall Cottages

Walltower

Ravelsyke

Venture Fair

Mosshouses

Kingside Edge

B6372

B6372

57

Black Mount

3

Eddleston Water

56

Mount Lothian Moss

Kingside

2

Cockmuir Bridge

55

Cockmuir

Craigburn Wood

Spurlens Rig

Middle Tweed

1

Craig Burn

A703

Loch Burn

54

24   D   25   E   26   F

223
205

A   B   C

4

Cauldhall Glen
Plantation

Steelfoot
Strip

Peter's
Plantation

Pond
Wood

Smithy
Strip

Fullarton

57

B6372

Fullarton Water

Mount
Lothian

Gillygub
Dean

Fountainside

Easter
Wood

B6372

3

Side
Plantation

56

B6372

Upper
Side

Allan
Clump

2

Loch Burn

Upper
Side

55

Toxsidehill
Wood

Tweedale Burn

1

Stell
Plantation

The
Old Wood

Toxsidehill

Gladhouse
Plantation

Toxside

54

27   A   28   B   29   C

223

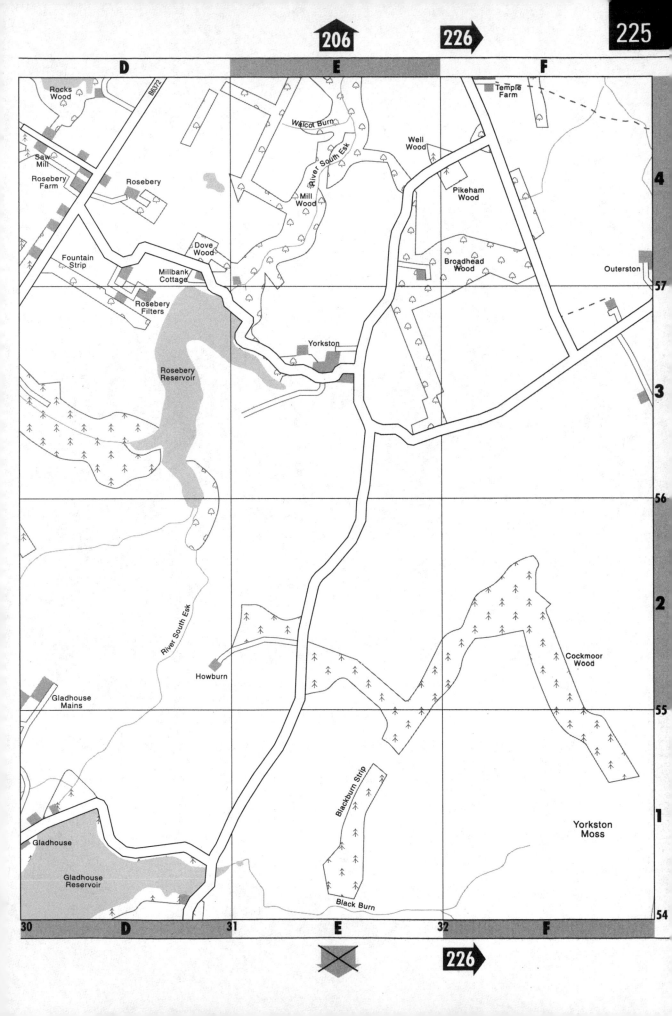

D

Rocks
Wood

B6372

Temple
Farm

E

F

4

Saw
Mill

Rosebery
Farm

Rosebery

Walcot Burn

River South Esk

Well
Wood

Pikeham
Wood

Fountain
Strip

Dove
Wood

Mill
Wood

Broadhead
Wood

Outerston

Millbank
Cottage

57

Rosebery
Filters

Yorkston

Rosebery
Reservoir

3

56

River South Esk

2

Howburn

Cockmoor
Wood

Gladhouse
Mains

55

Blackburn Strip

Yorkston
Moss

1

Gladhouse

Gladhouse
Reservoir

Black Burn

54

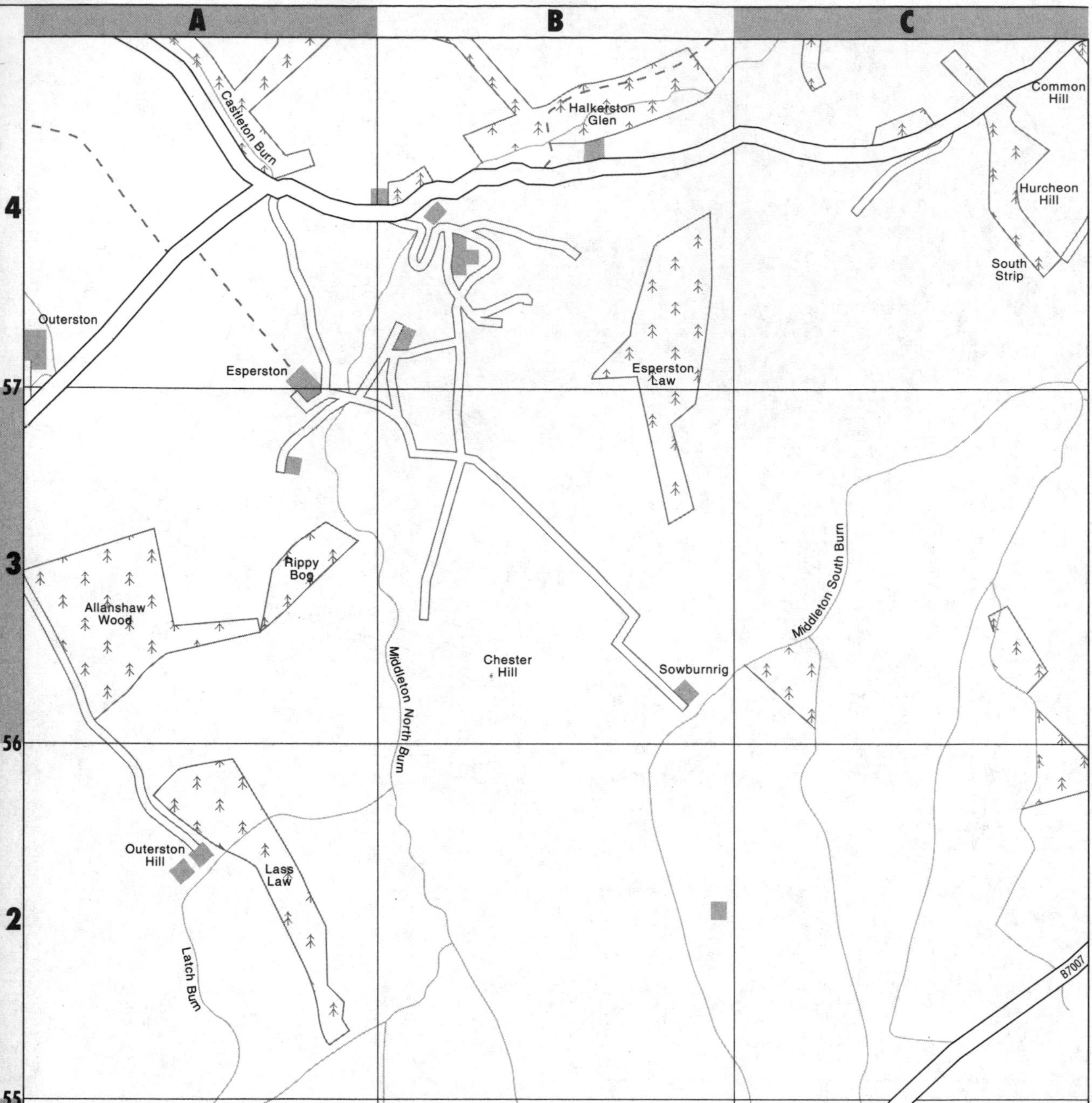

A **B** **C**

Castleton Burn

Halkerston Glen

Common Hill

Hurcheon Hill

South Strip

4

Outerston

Esperston

Esperston Law

57

Rippy Bog

3

Allanshaw Wood

Middleton North Burn

Chester
· Hill

Sowburnrig

Middleton South Burn

56

Outerston Hill

Lass Law

Latch Burn

2

B7007

55

1

Wull Muir

B7007

54

33 **A** **34** **B** **35** **C**

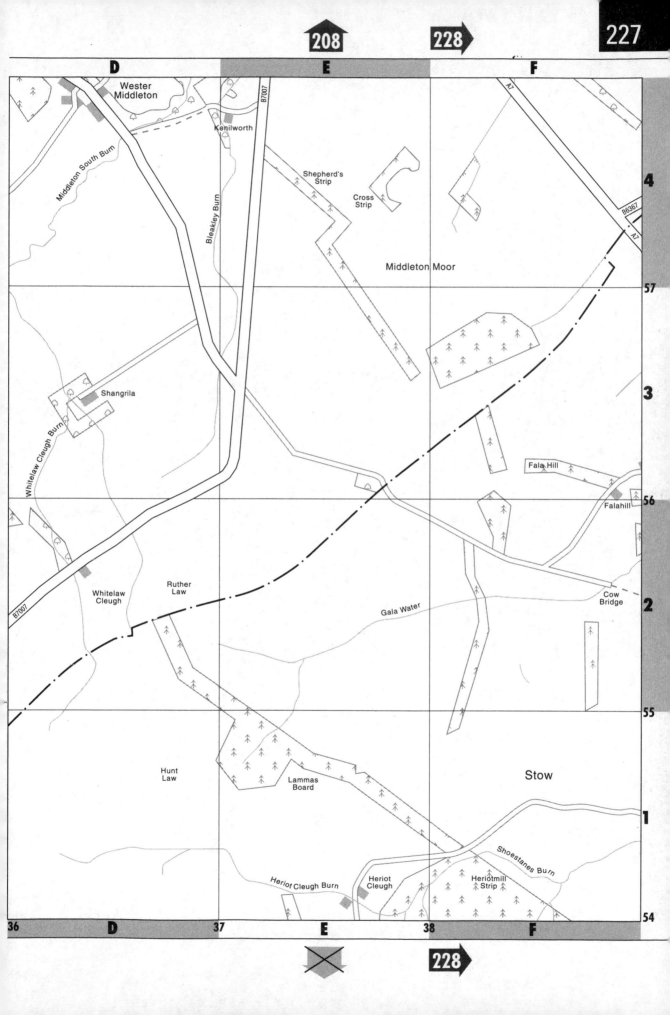

D

E

F

Wester
Middleton

Kenilworth

Shepherd's
Strip

Cross
Strip

Middleton Moor

Middleton South Burn

Bleakley Burn

B7007

A7

B6367

A7

4

57

Shangrila

Fala Hill

3

Whitelaw Cleugh Burn

Falahill

56

Whitelaw
Cleugh

Ruther
Law

Gala Water

Cow
Bridge

2

B7007

Hunt
Law

Lammas
Board

Stow

55

Heriot Cleugh Burn

Heriot
Cleugh

Heriotmill
Strip

Shoestanes Burn

1

A   B   C

Cowbraehill

Cakemuir
Hill

Cakemuir
Edge

B6367

Dismtd Rly

A7

Cakemuir Burn

57

Sandy
Knowe

3

Falahill

56

FALAHILL
COTTS

Nettlingflat

2

55

Gaia Water

Dismtd Rly

Robertston

Hangingshaw
Hill

Heriot

SHOESTANES RD

SHOESTANES
TERR

HERIOT WAY B709

SHOESTANE

1

Shoestanes

Shoestanes Burn

Heriot
House

B709

A7

Sandyknowe

Hangingshaw
Quarry

Crookston North
Mains Hill

54
39   A   40   B   41   C

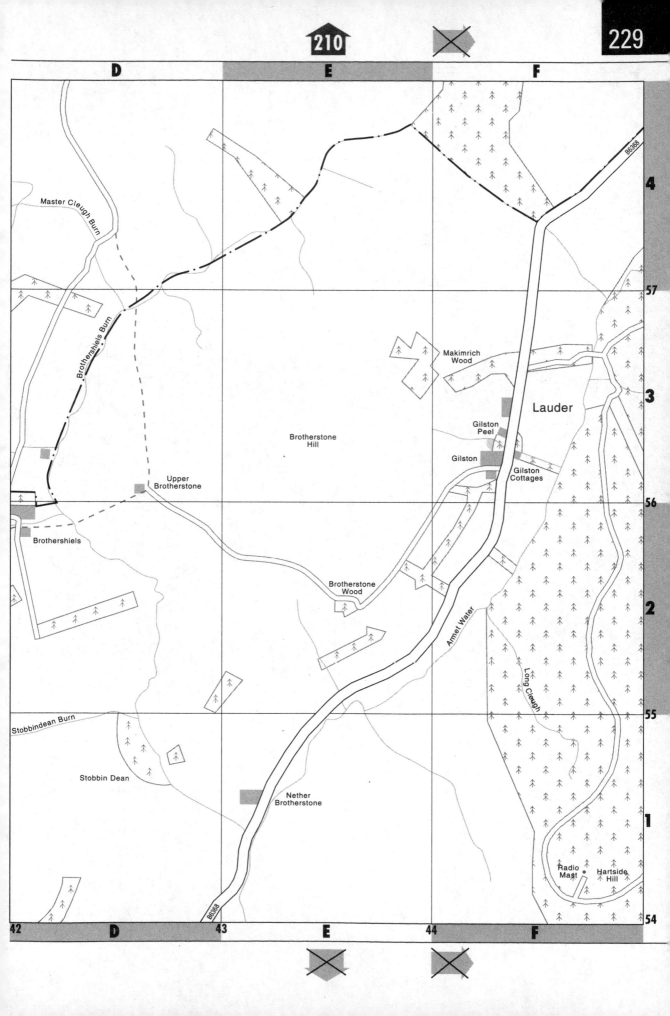

D E F

4

57

Master Cleugh Burn

Brothershiels Burn

Makimrich
Wood

3

Lauder

Brotherstone
Hill

Gilston
Peel

Gilston

Upper
Brotherstone

Gilston
Cottages

56

Brothershiels

Brotherstone
Wood

Armet Water

2

Long Cleugh

Stobbindean Burn

55

Stobbin Dean

Nether
Brotherstone

1

Radio
Mast

Hartside
Hill

B6368

54

42 D 43 E 44 F

212

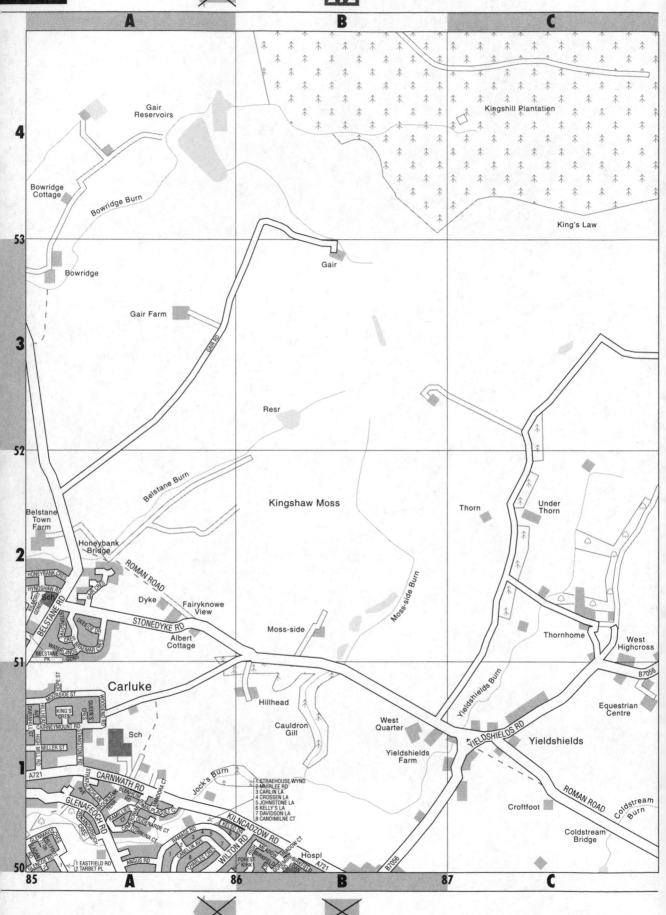

A   B   C

Kingshill Plantation

4

Gair
Reservoirs

Bowridge
Cottage

Bowridge Burn

King's Law

53

Bowridge

Gair

Gair Farm

GAIR RD

3

Resr

52

Belstane Burn

Kingshaw Moss

Thorn

Under
Thorn

Belstane
Town
Farm

Honeybank
Bridge

Moss-side Burn

2

HONEYBANK CRES

ROMAN ROAD

HYNDSHAW RD

GAIT CRES

Sch

Dyke

Fairyknowe
View

BELSTANE RD

DEESIDE DR

STONEDYKE RD

Moss-side

Thornhome

West
Highcross

BRAEMAR CRES
WATERLANDS CRES

Albert
Cottage

BELSTANE
PK
GDNS

51

Yieldshields Burn

B7056

Carluke

MOORSIDE ST

WOODEND RD

Hillhead

West
Quarter

Equestrian
Centre

KING'S
CRES

QUEEN'S
CRES

Cauldron
Gill

YIELDSHIELDS RD

Yieldshields

CAIRNEYMOUNT RD

Sch

Yieldshields
Farm

HILLHEAD AVE
CAIRNHILL PL

MILLER ST

STANISTONE RD

HIGH
MILL RD

1

A721

CARNWATH RD

Jock's Burn

1 STRAEHOUSE WYND
2 MUIRLEE RD
3 CARLIN LA
4 CROSSEN LA
5 JOHNSTONE LA
6 KELLY'S LA
7 DAVIDSON LA
8 CANDIMILNE CT

ROMAN ROAD

Croftfoot

Coldstream Burn

GLENAFEOCH RD

KILNCADZOW RD

RAMAGE RD

KELSO DR

Coldstream
Bridge

CORRUNA CT

WILTON RD

CAMELUK AVE

FOREST
KIRK

MEADOW

B7056

CHARLES CRES

ANGUS RD

Hospl

A721

1 EASTFIELD RD
2 TARBET PL

50

85   A   86   B   87   C

Black Law

Birniehall

Netherton Burn

Springfield
Reservoir

Thornmuir

Hill of
Westerhouse

Middlehope
Farm

Easterseat

Springfield

Knowehead

Middlehouse

YIELDSHIELDS RD

Netherton Burn

Westerhouse

Damhead

East
Highcross

Coldstream Burn

Candymill Burn

Roman
Road

Mid
Coldstream

Craigend

EXPLANATION OF THE STREET INDEX REFERENCE SYSTEM

Street names are listed alphabetically and show the locality, the page number and a reference to the square in which the name falls on the map page.

Example:	Melville Dr. Edin..123 E3

Melville Dr	This is the full street name, which may have been abbreviated on the map.
Edin	This is the abbreviation for the town, village or locality in which the street falls.
123	This is the page number of the map on which the street name appears.
E3	The letter and figure indicate the square on the map in which the centre of the street falls..The square can be found at the junction of the vertical column carrying the appropriate letter and the horizontal row carrying the appropriate figure.

ABBREVIATIONS USED IN THE INDEX
Road Names

Approach	App	Green	Gn
Arcade	Arc	Grove	Gr
Avenue	Ave	Heights	Hts
Boulevard	Bvd	Industrial Estate	Ind Est
Buildings	Bldgs	Junction	Junc
Business Park	Bsns Pk	Lane	La
Business Centre	Bsns Ctr	North	N
Broadway	Bwy	Orchard	Orch
Causeway	Cswy	Parade	Par
Centre	Ctr	Park	Pk
Circle	Circ	Passage	Pas
Circus	Cir	Place	Pl
Close	Cl	Precinct	Prec
Common	Comm	Promenade	Prom
Corner	Cnr	Retail Park	Ret Pk
Cottages	Cotts	Road	Rd
Court	Ct	South	S
Courtyard	Ctyd	Square	Sq
Crescent	Cres	Stairs	Strs
Drive	Dr	Steps	Stps
Drove	Dro	Street,Saint	St
East	E	Terrace	Terr
Embankment	Emb	Trading Estate	Trad Est
Esplanade	Espl	Walk	Wlk
Estate	Est	West	W
Gardens	Gdns	Yard	Yd

Key to abbreviations of Town, Village and Rural locality names used in the index of street names.

Aberdour	Abe	49	E4	Cockburnspath	Cock	140	C2	Halbeath	Hal	30	A3	Ormiston	Orm	159	F4
Aberlady	Aber	71	E2	Cockenzie	Cocke	97	E2	Harthill	Hart	169	D3	Pathhead	Path	185	D3
Addiewell	Add	171	F1	Cowdenbeath	Cow	13	F2	High Valleyfield	H Val	26	A1	Pencaitland	Pen	160	B4
Airth	Air	22	B2	Cowie	Cowie	20	B4	Howgate	How	204	A1	Penicuik	Peni	203	F3
Allanton	Alla	212	A4	Crossford	Crossf	28	A1	Humbie	Hum	187	D1	Plean	Plea	20	B2
Alloa	All	10	B3	Crossgates	Cross	30	C3	Inverkeithing	Inver	47	E1	Polmont	Pol	61	F1
Alva	Alva	5	D3	Culross	Cul	42	B4	Kelty	Kel	12	B4	Prestonpans	Pres	96	C1
Armadale	Arm	143	F3	Currie	Curr	152	A2	Kincardine	Kin	23	F2	Pumpherston	Pump	148	A4
Athelstaneford	Ath	101	F4	Dalgety Bay	D Bay	48	B2	Kinghorn	King	35	D2	Queensferry	Que	89	D4
Auchendinny	Auch	180	B1	Dalkeith	Dalk	157	D1	Kirkcaldy	Kirk	17	E2	Ratho	Rat	119	E1
Auchengray	Auc	216	C1	Dalmeny	Dal	89	F4	Kirkliston	Kirkl	89	D1	Rosewell	Rose	181	E1
Auchtertool	Aucht	15	D1	Danderhall	Dan	156	B4	Kirknewton	Kir	149	F1	Roslin	Rosl	180	C2
Avonbridge	Avon	112	A3	Dechmont	Dech	116	B1	Larbert	Lar	38	A2	Rosyth	Ros	46	C2
Balerno	Bale	151	E1	Denny	Den	36	C1	Lauder	Lau	229	F3	Salsburgh	Sals	167	D2
Banknock	Bank	57	D2	Dirleton	Dir	53	D2	Laurieston	Laur	61	D2	Shieldhill	Shi	81	E3
Bannockburn	Bann	7	F1	Dunbar	Dunb	78	B1	Limekilns	Lime	45	F2	Shotts	Shot	191	F3
Bathgate	Bath	145	E4	Dunblane	Dun	1	B4	Linlithgow	Lin	85	D3	Slamannan	Slam	110	A3
Blackburn	Black	171	E4	Dunfermline	Dunf	29	E2	Linnhouse	Linn	174	B1	Stenhousemuir	Sten	38	B2
Blackridge	Blac	142	B2	Dunipace	Duni	36	B2	Livingston	Liv	147	E3	Stirling	Stir	7	E4
Blairhall	Bla	26	A4	East Calder	E Cal	148	C2	Loanhead	Loan	181	D4	Stoneyburn	Ston	171	E1
Bo'ness	B'ness	63	F4	East Linton	E Lin	103	E4	Lochgelly	Loch	14	B4	Stow	Stow	227	F1
Boghall	Bog	145	F4	Eastfield	East	168	B2	Lochgelly	Long	98	C3	Tillicoultry	Till	5	F4
Bonnybridge	Bon	58	A3	Edinburgh	Edin	123	E3	Longniddry	Long	98	C3	Torphichen	Torp	113	F3
Bonnyrigg	Bonn	182	B4	Elphinestone	Elph	128	A1	Maddiston	Madd	83	D3	Torryburn	Torr	26	C1
Bridge of Allan	B of A	2	A4	Falkirk	Falk	60	B3	Mayfield	May	183	F3	Torwood	Tor	37	F3
Bridgend	Brid	86	B2	Fallin	Fall	8	B2	Menstrie	Men	3	F3	Tranent	Tran	128	B4
Broxburn	Brox	117	E3	Fauldhouse	Fau	193	F3	Middle Tweed	M Twee	223	D1	Tullibody	Tull	4	B2
Burntisland	Burn	50	C4	Fishcross	Fish	5	F2	Muirhouses	Muir	64	B3	Uphall	Uph	116	C2
Caldercruix	Cald	141	D3	Forth	For	215	D1	Murieston	Muri	174	A4	West Calder	W Cal	172	B1
California	Cali	81	F3	Gifford	Giff	163	F2	Musselburgh	Muss	126	B4	West Linton	W Lin	220	A1
Cambus	Camb	9	D4	Gladsmuir	Glad	130	A4	New Sauchie	N Sau	5	E1	Westfield	West	112	C3
Cambusbarron	Cam	6	B3	Gorebridge	Gore	207	E4	Newton	New	88	A4	Whitburn	Whit	170	A4
Cardenden	Card	15	E4	Grangemouth	Gran	61	E4	Newtongrange	Newt	183	D3	Whitecraig	White	126	C1
Carluke	Car	230	A1	Gullane	Gull	52	A1	North Berwick	N Ber	54	B4	Winchburgh	Winch	87	F1
Clackmannan	Clack	11	D2	Haddington	Hadd	101	E1	North Middleton	N Mid	207	F2				
								Oakley	Oak	26	C4				

1st St. Gran

1st St. Gran 62 A4
2nd St. B'ness 62 B3
2nd St. Gran 62 A4
3rd St. B'ness 62 B3
3rd St. Gran 62 A4
4th St. B'ness 62 C3
4th St. Gran 62 A4
5th St. B'ness 62 C3
5th St. Gran 62 A4
6th St. Gran 41 D1
6th St. B'ness 62 C3
7th St. B'ness 62 C3
7th St. Gran 62 B4
8th St. Gran 62 B4
Abbey Craig Rd. N Sau 5 D1
Abbey Cres. N Ber 54 A4
Abbey Ct. N Ber 54 A4
Abbey La. Edin 94 A1
Abbey Mains. Hadd 101 F2
Abbey Mews. N Ber 54 A4
Abbey Mill. Stir 7 E4
Abbey Park Pl. Dunf 29 D2
Abbey Rd. Dalk 157 D1
Abbey Rd. Dunb 78 B1
Abbey Rd. N Ber 54 A4
Abbey Rd Pl. Stir 7 E4
Abbey Rd. Stir 2 B1
Abbey St. Edin 94 A1
Abbey St. H Val 26 A1
Abbey Strand. Edin 123 F4
Abbey View. Crossf 28 B1
Abbey View. Dunf 29 F1
Abbeygrange. Newt 183 D3
Abbeyhill Cres. Edin 93 F1
Abbeyhill. Edin 93 F1
Abbeymount. Edin 93 F1
Abbot Rd. Bann 7 E2
Abbot St. Dunf 29 D2
Abbot's View. Hadd 101 F1
Abbots Cl. N Ber 53 F4
Abbots Ct. Falk 60 B4
Abbots Moss Dr. Falk 59 F1
Abbots Rd. Falk 60 B4
Abbots Rd. Gran 61 E4
Abbots View. Pol 61 F2
Abbots Wlk. Kirk 16 C2
Abbotsford Cres. Edin 123 D2
Abbotsford Cres. Shot 191 F3
Abbotsford Ct. Edin 123 D2
Abbotsford Dr. Gran 61 F3
Abbotsford Dr. Laur 61 D2
Abbotsford Gdns. Falk 39 D1
Abbotsford Pk. Edin 123 D2
Abbotsford Pk. N Ber 53 F4
Abbotsford Pl. Stir 2 B1
Abbotsford Rd. N Ber 53 F4
Abbotsford Rise. Muri 148 A1
Abbotsford St. Falk 60 A4
Abbotsgrange Rd. Gran 61 F4
Abbotshall Rd. Kirk 17 D1
Abbotsinch Rd. Gran 61 F4
Abden Ave. King 35 D2
Abden Ct. King 35 D2
Abden Pl. King 35 D2
Abel Pl. Dunf 29 F2
Abercairney Cres. Madd 82 C3
Abercairney Pl. Gran 61 F4
Abercorn Ave. Edin 124 B4
Abercorn Cres. Edin 124 B4
Abercorn Ct. Edin 124 B4
Abercorn Dr. Edin 124 B4
Abercorn Gr. Edin 124 B4
Abercorn Pl. Winch 87 F1
Abercorn Rd. Edin 124 B4
Abercorn Terr. Edin 125 E4
Abercrombie Pl. Men 3 F3
Abercrombie St. Falk 59 F3
Abercromby Dr. B of A 2 A4
Abercromby Pl. Edin 93 E1
Abercromby Pl. Stir 7 D4
Abercromby Pl. Tull 4 A1
Aberdour Cres. Dunf 29 E1
Aberdour Pl. Dunf 29 E1
Aberdour Rd. Burn 33 E1
Aberdour Rd. Dunf 29 F1
Aberlady Rd. Hadd 100 C1
Aberlour St. Ros 46 C2
Abinger Gdns. Edin 122 B4
Abington Rd. Dunf 28 C1
Aboyne Ave. Stir 2 B2
Aboyne Gdns. Kirk 16 C4
Academy La. Loan 181 D4
Academy Pk. Edin 94 A2
Academy Pl. Bann 7 F1
Academy Rd. B'ness 64 A4
Academy Rd. Stir 7 D4
Academy Sq. Lime 45 E2
Academy St. All 9 F4
Academy St. Arm 143 F3
Academy St. Bath 145 D3
Academy St. Edin 94 A2
Acheson Dr. Pres 127 F4
Achray Ct. All 10 B3
Achray Dr. Stir 2 A2
Ackam Path. Loan 180 C4
Acorn Cres. Lar 38 B1
Acre Rd. Muir 64 B3

Acredale. Bath 145 D3
Acredale. Lin 85 D3
Acredales. Hadd 131 F4
Acredales Wlk. Hadd 131 F4
Adam Cres. Sten 38 C1
Adam Pl. Loch 14 A4
Adam Sq. Muri 173 E3
Adam St. Falk 60 B3
Adambrae Rd. Muri 173 E4
Adamson Ave. Kirk 17 D3
Adamson Cres. Dunf 29 E3
Adamson Pl. Stir 2 A2
Adamson Rd. Loch 14 A4
Addiston Cres. Bale 151 E2
Addiston Farm Rd. Rat 120 A1
Addiston Gr. Bale 151 E2
Addiston Pk. Bale 151 E2
Adelaide St. Liv 148 A3
Adelphi Gr. Edin 125 D4
Adelphi Pl. Edin 125 D4
Admiral Terr. Edin 123 D3
Admiralty Rd. Inver 47 E2
Admiralty Rd. Lime 46 B2
Admiralty Rd. Ros 46 B2
Admiralty St. Edin 93 F3
Affleck Ct. Edin 121 D4
Affric Dr. Falk 39 E1
Affric Loan. Shot 191 F3
Affric Way. Crossf 28 A1
Afton Ct. Dech 116 B1
Afton Ct. Stir 7 E3
Afton Dr. Bank 57 E4
Afton Gr. Dunf 29 F3
Afton Pl. Edin 93 D3
Afton Terr. Edin 93 D3
Agnew Terr. Edin 93 E3
Ailsa Gr. Kirk 16 C4
Ainslie Gdns. Pol 61 F2
Ainslie Pl. Edin 93 D1
Aird's Cl. Edin 123 E4
Airdrie Rd. Cald 141 D2
Airlie Dr. Pol 61 F1
Airth Dr. Stir 7 E2
Airthrey Ave. B of A 2 A3
Airthrey Dr. Sten 39 D2
Airthrey Rd. B of A 2 A3
Airthrey Rd. Stir 2 B2
Aitchison Dr. Lar 38 A2
Aitchison's Pl. Edin 95 D1
Aitken Cres. Stir 7 D1
Aitken Ct. Kirk 17 D1
Aitken Dr. Slam 110 A3
Aitken Dr. Whit 170 A4
Aitken Gdns. Falk 59 F3
Aitken Orr Dr. Brox 117 F3
Aitken Rd. Falk 59 E3
Aitken St. Kirk 17 F4
Aitken Terr. Falk 59 E3
Akarit Rd. Sten 38 C1
Alan Breck Gdns. Edin 91 E1
Albany La. Edin 93 E1
Albany St. Dunf 29 D2
Albany St. Edin 93 E1
Albert Ave. Gran 61 F4
Albert Cl. Muss 127 D3
Albert Cres. Muss 127 D3
Albert Pl. Muss 127 D3
Albert Pl. Stir 7 D4
Albert Rd. East 168 C3
Albert Rd. Edin 94 A3
Albert Rd. Falk 60 A2
Albert St. Edin 93 F2
Albert St. Ros 46 C2
Albert Terr. Edin 123 D2
Albert Terr. Muss 126 C2
Alberta Ave. Liv 147 F2
Albion Pl. Edin 94 A1
Albion Rd. Edin 94 A1
Albion Terr. Edin 94 A1
Albyn Cotts. Brox 117 F3
Albyn Dr. Muri 173 F3
Albyn Ind Est. Brox 117 F4
Albyn Pl. Edin 93 D1
Albyn Terr. Brox 117 F3
Alder Gr. Dunf 29 E1
Alder Gr. Laur 61 D2
Alderbank Gdns. Edin 122 C2
Alderbank. Liv 147 F3
Alderbank. Peni 203 F2
Alderbank Pl. Edin 122 C2
Alderbank Terr. Edin 122 C2
Alderston Dr. Dunf 29 E3
Alderston Pl. Hadd 100 C1
Alderston Rd. Hadd 131 F4
Alderstone Rd. Muri 173 E4
Alexander Ave. Gran 61 E3
Alexander Dr. B of A 2 A4
Alexander Dr. Edin 122 B3
Alexander Dr. Pres 127 F4
Alexander Pk. Brox 117 F2
Alexander Pl. Ros 46 C2
Alexander Rd. Shot 191 F3
Alexander St. Cow 13 D3
Alexander St. Kirk 18 A4
Alexander St. Uph 117 D2
Alexander The Third St.

King 34 C1
Alexandra Bsns Pk. Kirkl .. 119 D3
Alexandra Dr. All 9 F4
Alexandra Dr. Bog 145 F3
Alexandra Pl. Stir 2 B1
Alexandra St. Dunf 29 D3
Alexandra St. Kirk 17 E3
Alford Ave. Kirk 16 C4
Alfred Pl. Edin 123 F2
Alice Cox Wlk. Dunf 29 E1
Alice Gr. Cross 30 C3
Aline Ct. D Bay 48 A1
Alison Gr. Crossf 28 A1
Alison St. Kirk 17 D1
Allan Barr Ct. Falk 60 A1
Allan Cres. Dunf 29 F1
Allan Cres. Duni 36 B2
Allan Ct. Gran 40 C1
Allan Park Cres. Edin 122 B2
Allan Park Dr. Edin 122 B1
Allan Park Gdns. Edin 122 B1
Allan Park Loan. Edin 122 B1
Allan Park Rd. Edin 122 B1
Allan Pk. Cow 13 D1
Allan Pk. Kirkl 89 D1
Allan Pk. Stir 7 D4
Allan Rd. Whit 169 F3
Allan St. Edin 93 D1
Allan Terr. Dalk 157 D2
Allanbank Rd. Lar 38 B1
Allandale Cotts. Bon 57 E1
Allanfield. Edin 93 F1
Allanton Rd. Shot 191 E1
Allanvale Rd. B of A 1 C4
Allanwater Gdns. B of A 2 A4
Allanwood Ct. B of A 2 A4
Allen Gr. Bla 26 C4
Aller Pl. Liv 147 D2
Allermuir Ave. Rosl 180 C3
Allermuir Rd. Edin 153 D3
Allison Pl. Kirkl 89 D1
Alloa Rd. B of A 3 D2
Alloa Rd. Clack 11 D2
Alloa Rd. N Sau 5 E2
Alloa Rd. Sten 39 D2
Alloa Rd. Tull 4 B2
Alloway Cres. Bon 57 F3
Alloway Dr. Cowie 20 B4
Alma La. Falk 60 A3
Alma St. Falk 60 A3
Alma St. Inver 47 E2
Alma Terr. Falk 60 A3
Almond Ave. Kirkl 119 F4
Almond Bank Cotts. Edin ... 91 D3
Almond Cres. Bonn 182 A3
Almond Ct. Edin 124 C2
Almond Ct. Liv 148 B2
Almond Ct. Stir 7 E3
Almond Ct. Whit 170 C4
Almond E. Liv 148 A3
Almond Gn. Edin 121 D4
Almond Gr. E Cal 148 C3
Almond Gr. Que 89 E4
Almond Interchange. Liv .. 148 A2
Almond Pk. Liv 148 A2
Almond Pl. Kirk 17 E4
Almond Rd. Black 145 E1
Almond Rd. Dunf 29 F1
Almond Rd. Kirkl 119 F4
Almond Rd. Liv 148 A2
Almond Rd. Madd 83 E3
Almond S. Liv 148 B3
Almond Side. E Cal 148 B2
Almond Sq. Edin 121 D4
Almond Sq. Whit 170 C4
Almond St. Gran 61 E3
Almond St. Whit 170 A4
Almond Terr. East 168 B3
Almond Terr. Madd 83 F3
Almond View. Black 146 A1
Almond W. Liv 148 A2
Almond West Rd. Liv 148 A2
Almondbank Terr. Edin 122 C2
Almondell Ct. Brox 117 F3
Almondell Rd. Brox 117 F3
Almondell Terr. E Cal 148 C3
Almondhill Rd. Kirkl 89 D1
Almondside. Kirkl 89 D1
Almondside. Muri 147 F1
Almondvale Ave. Muri 147 F1
Almondvale Bvd. Muri 147 F1
Almondvale Dr. Muri 147 F1
Almondvale E. Muri 147 F1
Almondvale N. Muri 147 F1
Almondvale Parkway. Muri 147 F1
Almondvale Rd. Liv 147 E1
Almondvale Roundabout.
  Muri 147 F1
Almondvale S. Liv 147 F1
Almondvale W. Muri 147 E1
Almondview. Muri 147 F1
Alness Gr. Dunf 28 C1
Alnwickhill Cres. Edin 154 C3
Alnwickhill Ct. Edin 154 C3
Alnwickhill Dr. Edin 154 C3
Alnwickhill Gdns. Edin 154 C3
Alnwickhill Gr. Edin 154 C3
Alnwickhill Loan. Edin 154 C3

Alnwickhill Pk. Edin 155 D3
Alnwickhill Rd. Edin 155 D4
Alnwickhill Terr. Edin 154 C3
Alnwickhill View. Edin 154 C3
Alpha St. B'ness 62 C3
Alva Pl. Edin 94 A1
Alva St. Edin 123 D4
Alyth Dr. Pol 62 A1
Amberley Path. Gran 61 F3
Ambrose Rise. Muri 148 A1
Amisfield Pk. Hadd 132 B4
Amisfield Pl. Hadd 132 B4
Amisfield Pl. Long 98 C3
Amos Path. Loan 180 C4
Amulree Pl. B' ness 63 E4
Ancrum Bank. Dalk 156 C1
Ancrum Rd. Dalk 156 C1
Anderson Ave. Arm 143 F2
Anderson Ave. Crossf 28 A1
Anderson Ave. Newt 183 D3
Anderson Cres. Cali 81 F3
Anderson Dr. Cow 13 D1
Anderson Dr. Den 36 C1
Anderson Dr. Sten 39 D1
Anderson Gn. Liv 147 E4
Anderson La. Ros 46 B3
Anderson Park Rd. Den 36 C1
Anderson Pl. Edin 93 F3
Anderson Pl. Stir 7 D2
Anderson St. Bon 58 A3
Anderson St. Kirk 17 F3
Anderson St. Kirk 18 A4
Anderson Terr. Bank 57 D2
Andrew Ave. Bog 145 F3
Andrew Cres. Sten 38 B2
Andrew Dodd's Ave. May .. 183 F4
Andrew St. Loch 14 A3
Andrew Wood Ct. Edin 93 E3
Angle Park Terr. Edin 122 C3
Angres Ct. Dan 156 B4
Angus Rd. Car 230 A1
Angus St. B' ness 63 E3
Ann St. Edin 93 D1
Annabel Ct. Inver 47 E1
Annan Ct. Falk 60 B1
Annandale St. Edin 93 F1
Annandale Street La. Edin .. 93 F1
Anne Dr. B of A 2 A3
Anne Dr. Sten 38 C2
Anne St. All 9 F4
Anne St. Bog 145 F3
Anne St. Peni 203 F4
Annet Rd. Bank 57 E3
Annfield Ct. Glad 129 E3
Annfield Dr. Stir 7 E3
Annfield. Edin 93 E3
Annfield Gdns. Stir 7 D3
Annfield St. Edin 93 E3
Annfield. Tran 128 C3
Anson Ave. Falk 59 F2
Antigua St. Edin 93 F1
Antonine Ct. B'ness 63 E3
Antonine Gdns. Falk 59 E3
Antonine Gr. Bon 57 F2
Antonine St. Falk 59 E3
Appin Cres. Dunf 29 D2
Appin Cres. Kirk 16 C4
Appin Gr. Pol 61 F2
Appin Terr. Edin 122 B2
Appin Terr. Shot 192 A2
Appleton Parkway. Liv 146 C2
Arboretum Ave. Edin 93 D1
Arboretum Pl. Edin 93 D2
Arboretum Rd. Edin 93 D2
Arbroath Cres. Stir 2 A2
Arbuthnot Rd. Loan 181 E4
Arbuthnot St. Falk 59 F3
Arcade. Liv 148 A3
Arcade. Stir 7 D4
Archers Ave. Stir 7 E2
Archers Cl. Gull 52 A1
Archibald Pl. Edin 123 E4
Archibald Russell Ct. Pol ... 61 F1
Ard Ct. Gran 61 E3
Ardeer Pl. Dunf 29 E1
Arden St. Edin 123 E3
Ardgowan Pl. Shot 191 F4
Ardmillan Pl. Edin 122 C3
Ardmillan Terr. Edin 122 C3
Ardshiel Ave. Edin 91 E1
Ardvreck Pl. Sten 39 D2
Argyle Cres. Edin 125 E4
Argyle Park Terr. Edin 123 E3
Argyle Pl. Bonn 181 F3
Argyle Pl. Edin 123 E3
Argyle St. Edin 93 F3
Argyll Ave. Falk 60 B3
Argyll Ave. Stir 2 B1
Argyll Pl. All 10 B4
Argyll St. All 10 B4
Arkaig Dr. Crossf 28 B1
Arkwright Ct. N Ber 54 A4
Armadale Rd. Whit 170 A4
Armine Pl. Peni 204 A4
Armour Ave. Cowie 20 B4
Arneil Pl. Pol 82 B4

Arnot St. Falk 60 B2
Arnothill Ct. Falk 59 F3
Arnothill. Falk 60 A2
Arnothill Gdns. Falk 60 A2
Arnothill La. Falk 59 F2
Arnothill Mews. Falk 60 A2
Arnott Gdns. Edin 122 A1
Arnprior Rd. Gore 207 E4
Arns Gr. All 9 F4
Arran Cres. Kirk 16 C4
Arran Ct. All 10 A3
Arran Ct. Gran 61 E3
Arran. Liv 146 C3
Arran Pl. Edin 125 E4
Arran Terr. Falk 59 E2
Arras Gr. Auch 204 A4
Arrol Cres. All 10 B4
Arrol Pl. Que 89 E4
Arrol Sq. Liv 146 C3
Arthur Pl. Cow 13 E2
Arthur St. Cow 13 E2
Arthur St. Dunf 29 D3
Arthur St. Edin 93 F2
Arthur Street La. Edin 93 F2
Arthur View Cres. Dan 156 A4
Arthur View Terr. Dan 156 A4
Arthur's Dr. Sten 38 C1
Artillery Pk. Hadd 101 D1
Ash Braes. Kin 23 E2
Ash Gr. All 10 B3
Ash Gr. Black 171 E4
Ash Gr. Bog 145 F3
Ash Gr. Cow 13 D2
Ash Gr. Dunb 78 A1
Ash Gr. Dunf 46 B4
Ash Gr. Laur 61 D1
Ash Gr. Liv 148 A3
Ash Gr. Oak 27 E3
Ash Gr. Sten 38 C1
Ash La. Loan 180 C4
Ash Terr. Stir 6 C3
Ashbank Terr. E Cal 148 C3
Ashbrae Gdns. Stir 7 D1
Ashburnham Gdns. Que 68 B1
Ashburnham Rd. Que 89 E4
Ashfield Ct. Dunb 78 C1
Ashfield Pl. Dunb 78 C1
Ashgrove. May 183 F4
Ashgrove. Muss 126 C3
Ashgrove Pl. Muss 126 C3
Ashgrove View. Muss 126 C3
Ashley Ct. Lin 84 C3
Ashley Dr. Edin 122 C2
Ashley Gdns. Edin 122 C2
Ashley Gr. Edin 122 C2
Ashley Hall Gdns. Lin 84 C3
Ashley Pl. Edin 93 F2
Ashley Rd. Pol 61 F2
Ashley St. Bon 57 F3
Ashley Terr. All 10 A4
Ashley Terr. Edin 122 C2
Ashton Gr. Edin 124 A1
Ashville Terr. Edin 94 A2
Asquith St. Kirk 17 D2
Assembly St. Edin 94 A3
Assynt Bank. Peni 204 A3
Atheling Gr. Que 89 E4
Athol Cres. Laur 61 D2
Athol Pl. Bath 145 D4
Athol Pl. Dunf 29 E2
Athol Terr. Bath 145 D4
Atholl Cres. Edin 123 D4
Atholl Crescent La. Edin ... 123 D4
Atholl Pl. Stir 1 C1
Atholl Terr. Kirk 16 B4
Attlee Cres. May 183 F3
Auchengray Rd. Auc 216 C1
Auchinbaird. N Sau 5 E1
Auchingane. Edin 153 F3
Auchinleck Ct. Edin 93 E3
Auchterderran Rd. Loch 14 A4
Auction Mart. Hadd 101 D1
Audenhard Terr. Ston 171 E1
Auld Orch. Bonn 182 B4
Auldgate. Kirkl 89 D1
Auldhame Cotts. E Lin 55 F3
Auldhill Ave. Brid 86 B2
Auldhill Cotts. Brid 86 B2
Auldhill Cres. Brid 86 B2
Auldhill Dr. Brid 86 B2
Auldhill Entry. Brid 86 B2
Auldhill Pl. Brid 86 B2
Auldhill Rd. Brid 86 B2
Auldhill Terr. Brid 86 B2
Ava St. Kirk 17 D1
Aven Dr. Laur 60 C2
Avenue Pk. B of A 1 C4
Avenue Pk. E Cal 148 B2
Avenue Pk W. E Cal 148 B2
Avenue Rd. Cocke 97 E2
Avenue Rd. Dalk 156 C1
Avenue The. B of A 2 A4
Avenue The. Brid 86 B4
Avenue The. Giff 163 F2
Avenue The. Gore 183 D1
Avenue The. Inver 47 F2
Avenue The. Loch 14 B4

235

Avenue The. Rat — Bendameer Rd. Burn

Avenue The. Rat 151 F4
Avenue The. Sten 39 E1
Avenue The. Whit 170 A3
Avenue Villas. Edin 92 C1
Averton. For 215 D1
Avon Ct. Falk 60 B1
Avon Dr. Lin 84 B4
Avon Gr. Edin 91 D2
Avon Gr. Peni 204 A3
Avon Pk. Avon 111 F3
Avon Pl. B' ness 63 F4
Avon Pl. Edin 91 D2
Avon Rd. Bath 145 D4
Avon Rd. Edin 91 D2
Avon Rd. Gran 62 B4
Avon Rd. Madd 83 F3
Avon St. Duni 36 B2
Avon St. Gran 40 A1
Avon Terr. Avon 112 A3
Avonbank Ave. Gran 61 F3
Avonbridge Rd. Slam 110 A4
Avondale Cres. Arm 143 F3
Avondale Dr. Arm 143 F3
Avondale Pl. Edin 93 D1
Avondale Rd. Pol 62 A2
Avonlea Dr. Pol 61 F2
Avonmill Rd. Lin 84 B4
Avonmill View. Lin 84 B4
Avonside Dr. Duni 36 B3
Avontoun Cres. Madd 84 A3
Avontoun Pk. Lin 84 B3
Ayres Wynd. Pres 96 C1
Aytoun Cres. Burn 33 F1
Aytoun Gr. Dunf 28 C3

Baads Rd. Cald 141 E1
Baberton Ave. Curr 152 B3
Baberton Cres. Curr 152 C3
Baberton Loan. Curr 152 B3
Baberton Mains Ave. Curr 152 B4
Baberton Mains Bank. Curr 152 B4
Baberton Mains Brae. Curr 152 B4
Baberton Mains Cres. Curr 152 B4
Baberton Mains Ct. Curr 152 B4
Baberton Mains Dell. Curr 152 B4
Baberton Mains Dr. Curr 152 B4
Baberton Mains. Edin 152 B4
Baberton Mains Gdns. Curr 152 B4
Baberton Mains Gn. Curr 152 B4
Baberton Mains Gr. Curr 152 B4
Baberton Mains Hill. Curr 152 B4
Baberton Mains Lea. Curr 152 B4
Baberton Mains Loan. Curr 152 C4
Baberton Mains Pk. Curr 152 B4
Baberton Mains Pl. Curr 152 B4
Baberton Mains Rise. Curr 152 B4
Baberton Mains Row. Curr 152 B4
Baberton Mains View. Curr 152 C4
Baberton Mains View. Edin 152 C4
Baberton Mains Way. Curr 152 B4
Baberton Mains Wood. Curr 152 B4
Baberton Mains Wynd. Curr 152 B4
Baberton Pk. Curr 152 B3
Bablins Wynd. Giff 163 F2
Back Cswy. Cul 42 B4
Back Dean. Edin 122 C4
Back O' Hill Rd. Stir 2 A1
Back O' Yards. Inver 47 D1
Back Rd. Alva 4 C4
Back Rd. Dunb 78 A1
Back Station Rd. Lin 85 D4
Backdean Rd. Dan 156 A4
Backlee. Edin 155 D3
Backmarch Cres. Ros 46 C2
Backmarch Rd. Ros 46 C2
Backwood Ct. Clack 10 C3
Badallan Pl. Fau 193 F3
Badger Wood. Dech 116 B1
Baileyfield Cres. Edin 125 D4
Baileyfield Rd. Edin 94 C1
Baileyfield Rd. Edin 125 D4
Bailie Gr. Edin 125 D3
Bailie Path. Edin 125 D3
Bailie Pl. Edin 125 D3
Bailie Terr. Edin 125 D3
Bailielands. Lin 85 E4
Baillie St. Whit 170 A4
Baillie Waugh Rd. Stir 7 E2
Bain St. Loch 14 A4
Baingle Brae. Tull 4 A2
Baingle Cres. Tull 4 A2
Baird Ave. Edin 122 B3
Baird Dr. Arm 143 F4
Baird Dr. Edin 122 B3
Baird Gdns. Edin 122 B3
Baird Gr. Edin 122 B3
Baird Rd. Arm 143 F4
Baird Rd. Liv 147 D1
Baird Rd. Rat 119 E2
Baird St. Falk 59 E3
Baird Terr. East 168 B3
Baird Terr. Edin 122 B3
Baird Terr. Hadd 100 C1
Bairns Ford Ave. Falk 60 A4
Bairns Ford Ct. Falk 60 A4
Bairns Ford Dr. Falk 60 A4
Bakehouse Cl. Edin 123 F4
Baker St. B' ness 63 F3
Baker St. Stir 7 D4
Balantyne Pl. Liv 147 D2
Balbakie Rd. East 168 C3
Balbardie Ave. Bath 145 D4
Balbardie Cres. Bath 145 D4
Balbardie Rd. Bath 145 D3
Balbirnie Pl. Edin 122 C4
Balcarres Ct. Edin 123 D1
Balcarres Pl. Muss 126 B4
Balcarres Rd. Muss 126 B4
Balcarres St. Edin 123 D1
Balcastle Rd. Slam 110 A3
Balderston Gdns. Edin 124 A1
Balderstone's Wynd. N Ber 54 B4
Baldridgeburn. Dunf 28 C3
Baldwin Cres. Kirk 17 D3
Balfour Cres. Lar 38 B1
Balfour Cres. Plea 20 B2
Balfour Ct. Dunf 29 E3
Balfour Ct. Edin 91 D1
Balfour Pl. Edin 93 F2
Balfour St. All 10 B4
Balfour St. Bann 7 E1
Balfour St. Bon 57 F3
Balfour St. Edin 93 F2
Balfour St. Kirk 17 D3
Balfour St. N Ber 54 B4
Balfour St. Stir 1 C1
Balfour Terr. Auch 180 A1
Balfour's Sq. Tran 128 B3
Balfron Loan. Edin 91 E1
Balgone Barns Cotts. E Lin 54 B1
Balgreen Ave. Edin 122 A3
Balgreen Gdns. Edin 122 A3
Balgreen Pk. Edin 122 A3
Balgreen Rd. Edin 122 A3
Balgreen Rd. Edin 122 B2
Baliol St. King 34 C1
Ballantyne Rd. Edin 93 F3
Ballast Bank. Inver 47 E1
Ballater Dr. Stir 2 B2
Ballencrieff Toll. Bath 114 A1
Ballengeich Pass. Stir 2 A1
Ballengeich Rd. Stir 1 C1
Ballingry La. Loch 14 A4
Ballingry St. Loch 14 A4
Balloch Rd. Shot 191 F3
Balm Well Ave. Edin 155 D3
Balm Well Gr. Edin 155 D3
Balm Well Terr. Edin 155 D3
Balmoral Dr. Falk 59 F2
Balmoral Dr. Kirk 16 B3
Balmoral Gdns. Muri 173 E3
Balmoral Gdns. Pol 82 B4
Balmoral Pl. Edin 93 D1
Balmoral Pl. Sten 38 C2
Balmoral Pl. Stir 7 D4
Balmoral Rd. B'ness 62 C3
Balmoral St. Falk 59 F2
Balmuir Rd. Bath 144 C4
Balmulzier Rd. Slam 110 A4
Balnacraig. Crossf 28 A1
Balquhatstone Cres. Slam 110 A3
Balquhidderock. Stir 7 E2
Balsusney Rd. Kirk 17 D3
Baltic St. Edin 94 A3
Balure Cres. Fall 8 B2
Balvaird Pl. Dunf 29 E3
Balwearie Cres. Kirk 17 D1
Balwearie Gdns. Kirk 16 C1
Balwearie Rd. Kirk 17 D1
Banchory Cotts. King 34 C3
Banchory Pl. Tull 4 B2
Bancroft Ave. Liv 147 F2
Bandeath Rd. Fall 8 B2
Bandon Ave. Kirk 17 F4
Bangholm Ave. Edin 93 D3
Bangholm Bower Ave. Edin 93 D3
Bangholm Gr. Edin 93 E3
Bangholm Loan. Edin 93 E3
Bangholm Pk. Edin 93 D3
Bangholm Pl. Edin 93 D3
Bangholm Rd. Edin 93 D3
Bangholm Terr. Edin 93 D2
Bangholm View. Edin 93 E3
Bangly Brae. Ath 100 A2
Bangor Rd. Edin 93 F3
Bank Rd. E Lin 103 F4
Bank Rd. East 168 C3
Bank St. All 10 A3
Bank St. E Cal 148 B2
Bank St. Edin 123 E4
Bank St. Falk 60 A3
Bank St. Gran 40 A1
Bank St. Inver 47 E1
Bank St. Kin 23 E2
Bank St. Kirk 17 F4
Bank St. Loch 14 A4
Bank St. N Ber 54 A4
Bank St. Peni 203 F2
Bank St. Slam 110 A3
Bank St. Stir 7 D4
Bank St. Whit 170 A4
Bankhead Ave. Edin 121 E2
Bankhead Broadway. Edin 121 D2
Bankhead Cotts. E Lin 75 E3
Bankhead Cres. Bank 57 E3
Bankhead Crossway N. Edin 121 D2
Bankhead Crossway S. Edin 121 E1
Bankhead Dr. Edin 121 D2
Bankhead Gr. Dal 68 B1
Bankhead Ind Est. Edin 121 E2
Bankhead Medway. Edin 121 E2
Bankhead Pl. Edin 121 E1
Bankhead Rd. N Sau 5 E2
Bankhead St. Edin 121 E1
Bankhead Terr. Edin 121 D1
Bankhead Way. Edin 121 D1
Bankhill Ct. Gran 61 E3
Bankpark Brae. Tran 128 A4
Bankpark Cres. Tran 128 A4
Bankpark Gr. Tran 128 B4
Bankside Ct. Den 36 C1
Bankside. Falk 60 B4
Bankton Ct. Muri 174 A4
Bankton Dr. Muri 173 F4
Bankton Gdns. Muri 174 A4
Bankton Glade. Muri 174 A4
Bankton Gn. Muri 173 F4
Bankton Gr. Muri 174 A4
Bankton Park E. Muri 148 A1
Bankton Pk W. Muri 148 A1
Bankton Rd. Muri 173 E4
Bankton Sq. Muri 173 F4
Bankton Terr. Pres 128 A4
Bankton Way. Muri 173 F4
Bankton Wlk. Muri 173 F4
Bannerman Ave. Inver 47 E2
Bannerman St. Dunf 29 D3
Bannoch Brae. Dunf 29 E2
Bannock Rd. Fall 8 B2
Bannockburn Rd. Cowie 20 B4
Bannockburn Rd. Stir 7 E2
Bannockburn Station Rd. Fall 8 A2
Bantaskine Dr. Falk 59 F2
Bantaskine Gdns. Falk 59 F2
Bantaskine Rd. Falk 59 F2
Bantaskine St. Falk 59 F2
Banton Pl. Bon 58 A2
Baptie Pl. B' ness 63 F3
Barassie Dr. Kirk 17 D4
Barbauchlaw Ave. Arm 143 F3
Barbour Ave. Stir 7 E2
Barbour Gr. Dunf 28 C3
Barclay Pl. Edin 123 D3
Barclay Rd. King 34 C2
Barclay St. Cow 13 D2
Barclay Terr. Edin 123 D3
Barclay Way. Liv 147 F4
Barham Rd. Ros 46 B1
Barkhill Rd. Lin 84 C3
Barkin Ct. Falk 60 A1
Barlaw Gdns. Arm 144 A3
Barleyhill. Bon 58 A3
Barleyknowe Cres. Gore 183 E1
Barleyknowe Gdns. Gore 183 E1
Barleyknowe La. Gore 183 E1
Barleyknowe Pl. Gore 183 E1
Barleyknowe Rd. Gore 183 E1
Barleyknowe St. Gore 183 E1
Barleyknowe Terr. Gore 183 E1
Barn Rd. Stir 7 D4
Barnbougle Ride. Dal 90 B4
Barnego Rd. Duni 36 B2
Barnes Gn. Liv 147 F4
Barnet Cres. Kirk 17 D1
Barnhill Dr. Tull 4 B1
Barnhill Pl. D Bay 48 B2
Barnhill Rd. D Bay 48 B2
Barns Ct. Whit 170 C4
Barns Ness Terr. E Lin 139 D4
Barns Pk. D Bay 48 A1
Barnsdale Rd. Stir 7 D2
Barnshot Rd. Edin 153 D3
Barnton Ave. Edin 91 E2
Barnton Ave W. Edin 91 D2
Barnton Brae. Edin 91 D2
Barnton Ct. Edin 91 D2
Barnton Gdns. Edin 91 F2
Barnton Gr. Edin 91 D2
Barnton La. Falk 60 A2
Barnton Loan. Edin 91 F2
Barnton Park Ave. Edin 91 E2
Barnton Park Cres. Edin 91 E2
Barnton Park Dell. Edin 91 E2
Barnton Park Dr. Edin 91 E2
Barnton Park Gdns. Edin 91 E2
Barnton Park Gr. Edin 91 E2
Barnton Park Pl. Edin 91 E2
Barnton Park View. Edin 91 E2
Barnton Park Wood. Edin 91 D1
Barnton Pk. Edin 91 F2
Barnton St. Stir 7 D4
Barntongate Ave. Edin 91 D1
Barntongate Dr. Edin 91 D1
Barntongate Terr. Edin 91 D1
Barnwell Rd. Stir 2 B2
Barons Hill Ave. Lin 85 D4
Barons Hill Ct. Lin 85 D4
Baronscourt Rd. Edin 94 B1
Baronscourt Terr. Edin 124 B4
Barony Ct. B' ness 63 F3
Barony Pl. Edin 93 E1
Barony St. Edin 93 E1
Barony Terr. Edin 121 E4
Barr Cres. Inver 47 E1
Barra Pl. Sten 39 D2
Barracks Roundabout. Liv 146 C3
Barracks St. Cocke 97 E2
Barrie Ct. Liv 148 B3
Barrie Pl. Dunf 28 C3
Barrie Pl. Gran 61 E3
Barrie Rd. Sten 38 C2
Barrie St. Dunf 28 C3
Barrie Terr. Bath 145 E3
Barton Rd. Ros 46 A1
Barton Terr. Fau 193 F3
Bass Rock View. N Ber 55 D4
Bastion Wynd. Stir 7 D4
Bath Pl. Edin 95 D1
Bath Rd. Edin 94 A3
Bath St. Edin 125 D4
Bath St La. Edin 125 D4
Bathfield. Edin 93 F3
Bathgate Rd. Black 171 E4
Bathgate Rd. Whit 170 C4
Bathville Bsns Ctr. Arm 144 A3
Baton Rd. Shot 191 E3
Battery Rd. Gran 62 B4
Battery Rd. Inver 68 B3
Battock Rd. Madd 82 C4
Bavelaw Cres. Peni 203 E3
Bavelaw Gdns. Bale 151 E1
Bavelaw Rd. Bale 151 E1
Baxter Cres. Den 36 B1
Baxter St. Fall 8 B2
Baxter's Pl. Edin 93 F1
Baxter's Wynd. Falk 60 A2
Bayne Gdns. Madd 84 A3
Bayne St. Stir 2 A1
Bayswell Pk. Dunb 78 B2
Bayswell Rd. Dunb 78 B2
Beach La. Edin 95 D1
Beach La. Muss 126 A4
Beach Rd. Gran 41 D1
Beach Rd. N Ber 54 A4
Beachmont Ct. Dunb 78 C1
Beachmont Pl. Dunb 78 C1
Bean Row. Falk 60 A2
Beancross Rd. Gran 61 E3
Bearcroft Gdns. Gran 61 F4
Bearcroft Rd. Gran 62 B4
Bearford Pl. Hadd 132 B4
Bearside Rd. Stir 7 D2
Beath View. Dunf 29 F2
Beath View Rd. Cow 13 D1
Beatlie Rd. Winch 88 A2
Beaton Ave. Bann 7 E1
Beatty Ave. Stir 2 A1
Beatty Cres. Kirk 17 E4
Beatty Ct. Kirk 17 E4
Beatty Pl. Dunf 29 E3
Beauchamp Gr. Edin 155 D4
Beauchamp Rd. Edin 155 D4
Beauclerc St. Alva 5 D4
Beaufort Cres. Kirk 16 B3
Beaufort Dr. Sten 39 D2
Beaufort Rd. Edin 123 E2
Beauly Ct. Falk 60 B1
Beauly Ct. Gran 61 E2
Beauly Dr. Liv 148 A2
Beauly Pl. Kirk 16 C4
Beaumont Dr. Sten 39 D1
Beaverbank Pl. Edin 93 E2
Beaverhall Rd. Edin 93 E2
Beck Cres. Dunf 29 E3
Beda Pl. Fall 8 B3
Bedford Ct. All 10 A3
Bedford Ct. Edin 93 D1
Bedford Pl. All 10 A3
Bedford St. Edin 93 D1
Bedford Terr. Edin 125 E4
Bedlormie Dr. Blac 142 B1
Beech Ave. Abe 48 C3
Beech Ave. D Bay 48 C3
Beech Ave. E Cal 148 A1
Beech Ave. N Mid 206 C2
Beech Ave. Plea 20 B2
Beech Cres. Duni 36 B2
Beech Cres. Lar 59 E4
Beech Gr Ave. Dalk 156 B1
Beech Gr. Dunf 46 B4
Beech Gr. Liv 148 A3
Beech Gr. Whit 170 B3
Beech La. Stir 2 A2
Beech Loan. Bonn 182 A3
Beech Pl. Black 146 A1
Beech Pl. Gran 61 E3
Beech Pl. Liv 147 E2
Beech Rd. Bog 145 F3
Beech St. Dunb 78 A1
Beech Terr. Pen 160 B3
Beech Way. D Bay 48 A3
Beechbank Cres. E Cal 148 C1
Beeches The. D Bay 48 B2
Beeches The. Gull 52 A2
Beeches The. Newt 183 D4
Beechgrove Rd. May 183 F3
Beechmount Cres. Edin 122 A4
Beechmount Ct. Shot 192 A1
Beechmount Pk. Edin 122 A3
Beechwood. Crossf 28 A1
Beechwood Gdns. Black 145 E1
Beechwood Gr. Pump 117 D1
Beechwood. Lin 85 D3
Beechwood Mains. Edin 122 A4
Beechwood. N Sau 5 E1
Beechwood Pk. Liv 146 C4
Beechwood Pk. Newt 183 D3
Beechwood Pk. Pump 117 D1
Beechwood Pl. Black 145 E1
Beechwood Rd. Black 145 E1
Beechwood Rd. Hadd 131 F4
Beechwood Terr. Edin 94 A2
Begbie Pl. Liv 147 D3
Begg Ave. Falk 59 F2
Beldorney Pl. Dunf 29 E3
Belfield Ct. Muss 126 A3
Belford Ave. Edin 92 C1
Belford Gdns. Edin 92 C1
Belford Pk. Edin 122 C4
Belford Pl. Edin 122 C4
Belford Rd. Edin 122 C4
Belford Terr. Edin 122 C4
Belgrave Cres. Edin 93 D1
Belgrave Crescent La. Edin 93 D1
Belgrave Gdns. Edin 121 F4
Belgrave Mews. Edin 92 C1
Belgrave Pl. Edin 92 C1
Belgrave Rd. Edin 121 F3
Belhaven Pl. Edin 123 D1
Belhaven Rd. Dunb 78 B1
Belhaven Terr. Edin 123 D1
Bell Ct. Gran 40 C1
Bell Pl. Edin 93 D1
Bell Rd. Ros 46 A1
Bell Sq. Muri 173 E3
Bell Stane. Que 68 A1
Bell's Mill Terr. Winch 87 F1
Bell's Mills. Edin 122 C4
Bell's Wynd. Falk 60 A2
Bellaknowes Ind Est. Inver 47 D2
Bellamond Cres. Whit 170 B4
Bellenden Gdns. Edin 124 B1
Bellevue Ave. Dunb 78 C1
Bellevue Cres. Edin 93 E1
Bellevue. Edin 93 E1
Bellevue Gdns. Edin 93 E2
Bellevue Gr. Edin 93 E1
Bellevue. Madd 82 C4
Bellevue Pl. Edin 93 E1
Bellevue Rd. All 9 F3
Bellevue Rd. Edin 93 E2
Bellevue St. Edin 93 E1
Bellevue St. Falk 60 B2
Bellevue Terr. Edin 93 E1
Bellfield Ave. Dalk 156 C1
Bellfield Ave. E Cal 148 C1
Bellfield Ave. Muss 126 A3
Bellfield Cres. Kirk 18 A4
Bellfield La. Edin 125 D4
Bellfield Rd. Bann 7 F1
Bellfield Rd. Stir 7 D3
Bellfield Sq. Pres 127 F4
Bellfield St. Edin 125 D4
Bellfield Terr. Edin 125 D4
Bellfield View. Bonn 182 B4
Bellhouse Rd. Abe 49 D4
Bellman Way. D Bay 48 A3
Bellman's Rd. Peni 203 F3
Bellona Terr. Fau 193 F3
Bells Brae. Edin 123 D4
Bells Burn Ave. Lin 85 E4
Bellsdyke Rd. Air 39 E3
Bellsdyke Rd. Lar 38 B2
Bellsdyke Rd. Sten 38 B2
Bellsmains. N Mid 207 E3
Bellsmeadow Rd. Falk 60 B2
Bellsquarry S. Muri 173 F3
Bellyeoman La. Dunf 29 E3
Bellyeoman Rd. Dunf 29 E3
Bellyford Rd. Elph 128 A1
Belmont Ave. Edin 122 A4
Belmont Ave. Shi 81 F4
Belmont Cres. Edin 122 A4
Belmont Dr. Shot 192 A1
Belmont Gdns. Edin 122 A4
Belmont Pk. Edin 122 A4
Belmont Rd. Curr 152 B3
Belmont St. Falk 60 B2
Belmont Terr. Edin 122 A4
Belmont View. Edin 122 A4
Belstane Pk. Car 230 A2
Belstane Rd. Car 230 A2
Belsyde Ct. Lin 84 B3
Belvedere Pk. Edin 93 E3
Belvedere Rd. Bath 144 C4
Belwood Cres. Auch 180 A1
Belwood Rd. Auch 179 F1
Ben Alder Pl. Kirk 16 C3
Ben Ledi Rd. Kirk 16 C3
Ben Lomond View. Oak 27 D3
Ben Nevis Pl. Kirk 16 C3
Ben Sayers Pk. N Ber 54 C3
Benarty St. Kirk 16 C3
Bendachin Dr. Dunf 29 F3
Bendameer Rd. Burn 33 E1

Benhar Rd. East ... 167 F1
Benhar Rd. Shot ... 192 A3
Benjamin Dr. B'ness ... 63 F3
Bennett Wood Terr. Winch .. 87 F2
Bennochy Ave. Kirk ... 17 D3
Bennochy Ct. Kirk ... 17 D3
Bennochy Gdns. Kirk ... 17 D3
Bennochy Rd. Kirk ... 16 C3
Bentheads. Bann ... 19 F4
Benview. Bann ... 7 E1
Benview Terr. Fish ... 5 F2
Beresford Ave. Edin ... 93 E3
Beresford Gdns. Edin ... 93 E3
Beresford Pl. Edin ... 93 D3
Beresford Rise. Muri ... 148 A1
Berkeley St. Edin ... 7 D2
Bernard Shaw St. Dunf ... 28 C3
Bernard St. Edin ... 94 A3
Bernard Terr. Edin ... 123 F3
Berry St. Loch ... 14 A4
Berryhill. Cowie ... 20 C4
Berryhill Cres. Gran ... 61 F3
Berryhill Pl. Shot ... 192 A1
Berrylaw Pl. Dunf ... 28 C2
Berrylaw Rd. Crossf ... 28 B2
Bertram Pl. Shot ... 191 E3
Bertram St. East ... 168 B3
Bertram St. Shot ... 191 F3
Bervie Dr. Muri ... 173 F3
Berwick Pl. Kirk ... 17 E3
Berwick Pl. Kirk ... 18 A4
Beulah. Muss ... 126 C3
Bevan Dr. Alva ... 5 E4
Bevan Pl. Ros ... 46 C2
Bevan Rd. May ... 183 E3
Bevan-lee Ct. Dalk ... 157 D2
Beveridge Ave. May ... 183 F3
Beveridge Cl. May ... 183 F3
Beveridge Rd. Kirk ... 17 D2
Beveridge Sq. Muri ... 147 F1
Beveridge St. Dunf ... 29 E1
Bickerton Pl. Whit ... 170 A3
Bickram Cres. Bla ... 26 B4
Biggar Rd. Edin ... 154 A2
Biggar Rd. Peni ... 202 C3
Biggin Wa's. Kirk ... 17 F4
Bingham Ave. Edin ... 124 C3
Bingham Broadway. Edin .. 125 D3
Bingham Cres. Edin ... 125 D3
Bingham Crossway. Edin .. 124 C3
Bingham Dr. Edin ... 125 D3
Bingham Medway. Edin ... 124 C3
Bingham Pl. Edin ... 124 C3
Bingham Way. Edin ... 124 C3
Binn Ave. Burn ... 33 F1
Binnie Pl. Gran ... 39 F1
Binniehill Rd. Slam ... 110 A3
Binning Rd. Inver ... 47 D2
Binning Wood Rd. E Lin ... 75 F4
Binny Park. Brid ... 116 C4
Birch Ave. Stir ... 6 C3
Birch Cres. Loan ... 180 C4
Birch Ct. Edin ... 91 D1
Birch Ct. Liv ... 147 E1
Birch Gr. Dunf ... 46 B4
Birchbank. Cow ... 13 D1
Birchwood. N Sau ... 5 E1
Birk Hedges. Hadd ... 130 C3
Birkdale Dr. Uph ... 116 C2
Birkenshaw Way. Arm ... 143 F3
Birkenside. Gore ... 207 E3
Birkfield Loan. Car ... 230 B1
Birkfield Pl. Car ... 230 B1
Birkhill Cres. B'ness ... 63 F3
Birkhill Rd. Cam ... 6 C3
Birkhill Rd. Stir ... 6 C3
Birkhill St. B'ness ... 63 F3
Birnam Ct. Falk ... 39 E1
Birnam Rd. Kirk ... 16 C4
Birnie Brae. Loch ... 14 A4
Birnie St. Loch ... 14 A4
Birniehill Ave. Bath ... 144 C2
Birniehill Cres. Bath ... 144 C2
Birniehill Rd. Bath ... 144 C2
Birniehill Terr. Bath ... 144 C2
Birniewell Rd. Slam ... 110 A3
Birrell Dr. Dunf ... 29 E1
Birrell Street Wynd. Kirk ... 17 E3
Birrell's La. Kirk ... 17 F4
Birsley Rd. Tran ... 128 B3
Bishops Pk. E Cal ... 148 A1
Bishops Pk. E Cal ... 148 B1
Black Craigs. Kirk ... 16 B4
Blackbarony Rd. Edin ... 124 A1
Blackburn Ave. Dunf ... 28 B3
Blackburn Dr. Cow ... 13 D2
Blackburn Rd. Add ... 171 F1
Blackburn Rd. Bog ... 145 E2
Blackburnhall. Ston ... 171 E3
Blackchapel Cl. Edin ... 125 D2
Blackchapel Rd. Edin ... 125 D2
Blackcot Ave. May ... 183 E3
Blackcot Dr. May ... 183 E3
Blackcot Pl. May ... 183 E3
Blackcot Rd. May ... 183 E3
Blacket Ave. Edin ... 123 F3
Blacket Pl. Edin ... 123 F3
Blackfaulds Ct. Fau ... 193 F3

Blackfaulds Dr. Fau ... 193 F3
Blackfaulds Pl. Fau ... 193 F3
Blackford Ave. Edin ... 123 E2
Blackford Bank. Edin ... 123 E2
Blackford Gate. Edin ... 123 E2
Blackford Glen Rd. Edin ... 123 F1
Blackford Hill Gr. Edin ... 123 E1
Blackford Hill Rise. Edin ... 123 E1
Blackford Hill View. Edin ... 123 E1
Blackford Rd. Edin ... 123 E2
Blackfriars St. Edin ... 123 F4
Blackhall St. Shot ... 192 A2
Blackhill Rd. Blac ... 142 C2
Blackie Rd. Edin ... 94 A2
Blacklaw Rd. Dunf ... 29 E1
Blackmill Cres. Sten ... 39 D2
Blackmount Terr. Madd ... 82 C3
Blackmuir Pl. Tull ... 4 B2
Blackness Rd. Lin ... 85 D4
Blackston Rd. Avon ... 112 A3
Blackthorn Ct. Edin ... 91 D1
Blackwood Cres. Edin ... 123 F3
Blackwood Gn. Dunf ... 46 C4
Blaeberry Gdns. Edin ... 91 D1
Blaeberryhill Rd. Whit ... 170 B3
Blaefaulds Cres. Den ... 57 E4
Blair Ave. B'ness ... 63 F3
Blair Dr. Dunf ... 29 D3
Blair Dr. Kel ... 12 B4
Blair Pl. Kirk ... 16 B3
Blair St. Edin ... 123 E4
Blair St. Kel ... 12 B4
Blair Terr. Sten ... 39 D2
Blair's Cotts. Laur ... 61 E1
Blairdenon Cres. Falk ... 59 F2
Blairdenon Dr. N Sau ... 5 D1
Blairdenon Rd. Alva ... 4 C3
Blairforkie Dr. B of A ... 1 C4
Blairlodge Ave. Laur ... 82 B4
Blairlodge Ave. Pol ... 82 B4
Blairmore Rd. Kirk ... 16 B4
Blairmuckhole And Forrestdyke Rd.
   Sals ... 167 F4
Blairwood Wlk. Oak ... 26 C4
Blake St. Dunf ... 29 E1
Blamey Cres. Cow ... 13 D1
Blantyre Terr. Edin ... 123 D2
Blawearie Rd. Tran ... 128 B3
Bleachfield. Edin ... 93 E2
Bleachfield. Falk ... 60 A3
Blenheim St. Auch ... 204 A4
Blenheim Pl. Sten ... 38 C3
Blenheim Rd. Car ... 230 A1
Blindwell Brae. Giff ... 133 F1
Blindwells. Alva ... 4 B2
Blinkbonnie Terr. Slam ... 110 A3
Blinkbonny Ave. Edin ... 92 B1
Blinkbonny Cres. Edin ... 92 B1
Blinkbonny Gdns. Edin ... 92 B1
Blinkbonny Gr. Edin ... 92 B1
Blinkbonny Gr W. Edin ... 92 B1
Blinkbonny Rd. Curr ... 152 A2
Blinkbonny Rd. Falk ... 59 F2
Blinkbonny Terr. Edin ... 92 B1
Blinny Ct. Shot ... 192 A2
Bloom Ct. Liv ... 147 D2
Bloom Pl. Liv ... 147 D2
Bloom Roundabout. Liv ... 147 E2
Bloomfield Pl. Bath ... 145 D3
Blyth St. Kirk ... 17 F4
Bo'mains Rd. B'ness ... 63 F3
Bo'ness Rd. Gran ... 62 A3
Bo'ness Rd. Pol ... 61 F2
Bo'ness Rd. Que ... 67 F1
Boat Gn. Edin ... 93 E2
Bog Rd. Falk ... 60 B3
Bog Rd. Falk ... 60 C2
Bog Rd. Peni ... 203 F3
Bog Rd. Whit ... 170 A3
Bog The. B'ness ... 64 A4
Bogend Rd. Bann ... 19 F4
Bogend Rd. Lar ... 38 A4
Bogend Rd. Tor ... 37 F4
Boghall Dr. Bog ... 145 F3
Boghall Roundabout. Bog . 145 F3
Boghead Cres. Bath ... 144 C3
Bogies Wynd. Kirk ... 17 E3
Boglily Rd. Kirk ... 16 C2
Bogpark Rd. Muss ... 126 A3
Bogsmill Rd. Edin ... 122 A1
Bogwood Ct. May ... 183 A4
Bogwood Dr. Crossf ... 28 A1
Bogwood Rd. May ... 183 A4
Bohun Ct. Bann ... 7 E2
Bolam Dr. Burn ... 33 F1
Bolan Sq. Loch ... 14 A4
Bomar Ave. B'ness ... 64 A4
Bon Accord Cres. Shot ... 191 F3
Bonaly Ave. Edin ... 153 D3
Bonaly Brae. Edin ... 153 D3
Bonaly Cres. Edin ... 153 D3
Bonaly Dr. Edin ... 153 D3
Bonaly Gdns. Edin ... 153 D3
Bonaly Gr. Edin ... 153 D3
Bonaly Rd. Edin ... 153 D3
Bonaly Rise. Edin ... 153 D3
Bonaly Steading. Edin ... 153 D3
Bonaly Terr. Edin ... 153 D3

Bonaly Wester. Edin ... 153 D3
Bonar Pl. Edin ... 93 E3
Bonnar St. Dunf ... 29 D2
Bonnington Ave. Edin ... 93 E3
Bonnington Gr. Edin ... 93 E3
Bonnington Ind Est. Edin ... 93 F2
Bonnington. Rat ... 150 A4
Bonnington Rd. E Cal ... 150 A3
Bonnington Rd. Edin ... 93 F2
Bonnington Rd. Rat ... 150 A3
Bonnington Road La. Edin .. 93 F2
Bonnington Terr. Edin ... 93 E3
Bonnybank Ct. Gore ... 207 E4
Bonnybank Rd. Gore ... 207 E4
Bonnybridge Rd. Bank ... 57 F3
Bonnybridge Rd. Bon ... 57 F3
Bonnyfield Rd. Bon ... 57 F3
Bonnyhaugh. Edin ... 93 E2
Bonnyhaugh La. Edin ... 93 E2
Bonnyhill Rd. Bon ... 58 A2
Bonnyhill Rd. Falk ... 59 D2
Bonnyrigg Rd. Dalk ... 156 C1
Bonnyside Rd. Bon ... 58 A3
Bonnyton Pl. Dunf ... 29 E2
Bonnytoun Ave. Lin ... 85 E4
Bonnytoun Terr. Lin ... 85 E4
Bonnyview Gdns. Bon ... 58 A3
Bonnywood Ave. Bon ... 58 A4
Booth Ave. Ros ... 46 B3
Booth Pl. Falk ... 60 A2
Boothacre La. Edin ... 94 B2
Boreland Pk. Inver ... 47 E2
Boreland Rd. Inver ... 47 E2
Boreland Rd. Kirk ... 18 A4
Borestone Cres. Stir ... 7 D1
Borestone Ct. Stir ... 7 D1
Borestone Pl. Stir ... 7 D1
Boroughdales. Dunb ... 78 B4
Boroughloch La. Edin ... 123 F3
Boroughloch Sq. Edin ... 123 F3
Borrowlea Rd. Stir ... 7 E4
Borrowmeadow Rd. Stir ... 7 F4
Borrowstoun Cres. B'ness .. 63 F3
Borrowstoun Pl. B'ness ... 63 F3
Borrowstoun Rd. B'ness ... 64 A3
Borthwick Castle Pl.
   N Mid ... 207 F2
Borthwick Castle Rd.
   N Mid ... 207 F1
Borthwick Castle Terr.
   N Mid ... 207 F2
Borthwick Pl. Edin ... 122 C4
Boswall Ave. Edin ... 92 C3
Boswall Cres. Edin ... 92 C3
Boswall Dr. Edin ... 93 D3
Boswall Gdns. Edin ... 92 C3
Boswall Gn. Edin ... 93 D3
Boswall Gr. Edin ... 93 D3
Boswall Loan. Edin ... 92 C3
Boswall Parkway. Edin ... 92 C3
Boswall Pl. Edin ... 92 C3
Boswall Quadrant. Edin ... 92 C3
Boswall Rd. Edin ... 93 D3
Boswall Sq. Edin ... 92 C3
Boswall Terr. Edin ... 92 C3
Boswell Dr. King ... 35 D2
Boswell Rd. Oak ... 26 C3
Boswell Rd. Loch ... 14 A4
Bothkennar Rd. Air ... 39 F2
Bothkennar Rd. Sten ... 39 F2
Bothwell St. Dunf ... 29 D1
Bothwell St. Edin ... 94 A1
Boundary Rd E. Rat ... 151 F4
Boundary Rd N. Rat ... 151 F4
Boundary St. B'ness ... 64 A4
Bouprie Rise. D Bay ... 48 A2
Bourtree Gr. Bla ... 26 B4
Bow St. Stir ... 7 D4
Bowhill Terr. Edin ... 93 D3
Bowhouse Gdns. All ... 10 A3
Bowhouse Rd. All ... 10 A3
Bowhouse Rd. Gran ... 61 F3
Bowhouse Sq. Gran ... 61 E3
Bowhousebog Or Liquo.
   Shot ... 191 D1
Bowhousebog Rd. Shot ... 191 D1
Bowling Green Rd. Kirkl ... 89 D1
Bowling Green Rd. Whit ... 170 A3
Bowling Green St. Cow ... 13 E2
Bowling Green The. Edin ... 93 F3
Bowmont Pl. Edin ... 123 F3
Bowmont Terr. Dunb ... 78 C1
Bowmore Wlk. Shot ... 192 A2
Bowyett. Torp ... 113 F3
Boyd Pl. Loch ... 14 A4
Boyd St. Falk ... 60 A3
Boyd St. Laur ... 61 D2
Boyd's Entry. Edin ... 123 F4
Boyd-Orr Dr. Auch ... 203 F4
Brackenlees Rd. Air ... 40 A3
Brackensbrae. Uph ... 117 D3
Bradbury St. Sten ... 39 D1
Brae Heads Loan. E Lin ... 103 E3
Brae Pk. Edin ... 91 D2
Brae Rd. B'ness ... 62 B3
Brae The. Auch ... 180 B1
Brae The. Bann ... 7 E1
Brae The. Cam ... 6 B3

Braefoot Gr. D Bay ... 48 A1
Braefoot Rd. B'ness ... 64 A3
Braefoot Terr. Edin ... 124 A1
Braehead. All ... 4 B1
Braehead. Alva ... 5 D4
Braehead Ave. Edin ... 91 D2
Braehead Ave. Lin ... 84 C3
Braehead Ave. Tull ... 4 B1
Braehead. B'ness ... 63 F4
Braehead Bank. Edin ... 91 D2
Braehead Cres. Edin ... 91 D2
Braehead Dr. Edin ... 91 D2
Braehead Dr. Lin ... 84 C3
Braehead Gr. B'ness ... 63 F4
Braehead Gr. Edin ... 91 D2
Braehead Loan. Edin ... 91 D2
Braehead Pk. Edin ... 91 D2
Braehead Pk. Lin ... 84 C3
Braehead Pl. Lin ... 84 C3
Braehead Rd. Edin ... 91 D2
Braehead Rd. Lin ... 84 C3
Braehead Rd. Stir ... 7 E2
Braehead Roundabout. Liv 147 E2
Braehead Row. Edin ... 91 D2
Braehead Terr. Lin ... 84 C3
Braehead View. Edin ... 91 D2
Braekirk Ave. Kir ... 149 E1
Braemar Cres. Car ... 230 A2
Braemar Cres. Falk ... 60 B3
Braemar Dr. Falk ... 60 B3
Braemar Gdns. Duni ... 36 B2
Braemar Gdns. Pol ... 82 B4
Braemar Pl. Sten ... 39 D2
Braemount. Cow ... 13 D1
Braepark Rd. Edin ... 91 D2
Braes The. Tull ... 4 B2
Braes View. Den ... 57 E4
Braes View. Shi ... 81 F4
Braeside Gdns. E Cal ... 148 A1
Braeside. N Sau ... 5 E1
Braeside Pk. E Cal ... 148 A2
Braeside Pl. Laur ... 61 D1
Braeside Pl. Laur ... 61 D2
Braeside Pl. Shi ... 82 A4
Braeside Rd. Gore ... 207 E4
Braeside Rd. Loan ... 181 E4
Braeside Rd N. Gore ... 207 E4
Braeside Rd S. Gore ... 207 E4
Braeside. Shi ... 81 E3
Braeview. E Lin ... 103 E4
Braeview. Lar ... 38 B1
Braeview. Lar ... 60 C2
Braewell Gdns. Lin ... 84 B4
Braid Ave. Edin ... 123 D1
Braid Cres. Edin ... 123 D1
Braid Farm Rd. Edin ... 123 D1
Braid Gn. Liv ... 147 E4
Braid Hills App. Edin ... 154 A4
Braid Hills Ave. Edin ... 123 D1
Braid Hills Cres. Edin ... 154 A4
Braid Hills Dr. Edin ... 154 A4
Braid Hills Rd. Edin ... 154 A4
Braid Mount. Edin ... 154 A4
Braid Mount Crest. Edin ... 154 A4
Braid Mount Rise. Edin ... 154 A4
Braid Mount View. Edin ... 154 A4
Braidburn Cres. Edin ... 123 D1
Braidburn Terr. Edin ... 123 D1
Braidlaw Pk. Peni ... 203 E3
Braigh Gdns. Dunf ... 28 B3
Bramble Dr. Edin ... 91 D1
Bramdean Gr. Edin ... 154 A4
Bramdean Pl. Edin ... 154 A4
Bramdean Rise. Edin ... 154 A4
Bramdean View. Edin ... 154 A4
Brand Dr. Edin ... 125 D4
Brand Gdns. Edin ... 125 E4
Brandfield St. Edin ... 123 D3
Brandon St. Edin ... 93 E1
Brandon Terr. Edin ... 93 E2
Brands Row. Cross ... 30 C4
Brandy Riggs. Crossf ... 27 E1
Brandy Wells. Crossf ... 27 E1
Brandyhill. Fish ... 5 F2
Brankholm Brae. Ros ... 46 B2
Brankholm Cres. Ros ... 46 B3
Brankholm La. Ros ... 46 B3
Branning Ct. Kirk ... 17 E3
Branshill Rd. N Sau ... 10 A4
Bravo St. B'ness ... 62 C3
Bread St. Edin ... 123 D4
Bread Street La. Edin ... 123 D4
Breadalbane Pl. Pol ... 61 F1
Breadalbane St. Edin ... 93 F2
Breakers Way. D Bay ... 47 F1
Brechin Dr. Pol ... 62 A1
Breck Terr. Auch ... 204 A4
Brentham Ave. Stir ... 7 D3
Brentham Cres. Stir ... 7 D3
Breslin Terr. East ... 168 B3
Breton Ct. Falk ... 60 B2
Brewery La. Dunb ... 78 A1
Brewery Pk. Hadd ... 132 A4
Brewlands Ave. B'ness ... 63 E3
Brewster Pl. Den ... 36 B1
Brewster Sq. Muri ... 173 E3
Briar Brae. Pol ... 82 B4

Briar Cotts. Ston ... 171 E1
Briar Pl. Dunf ... 29 E2
Briar Rd. Dunf ... 29 E2
Briarbank. Liv ... 147 E3
Briarbank Terr. Edin ... 122 C2
Briarcliff St. Kirk ... 17 F3
Briardene. Laur ... 61 D2
Briarhill Ave. D Bay ... 48 A2
Briars Rd. All ... 4 C1
Brickfield. Edin ... 95 D1
Brickworks Rd. Tran ... 128 A4
Bridge Cres. Den ... 36 B1
Bridge End Cotts. Rat ... 150 B3
Bridge End. Edin ... 124 A2
Bridge End. Shot ... 191 E3
Bridge End. Whit ... 170 B4
Bridge Pl. Brox ... 117 F3
Bridge Pl. Den ... 36 B1
Bridge Pl. Edin ... 93 D1
Bridge Pl. Shot ... 192 A2
Bridge Rd. Bale ... 151 E1
Bridge Rd. Edin ... 153 D3
Bridge St. Bon ... 58 A3
Bridge St. Cow ... 13 E2
Bridge St. Dunf ... 28 C2
Bridge St. E Lin ... 103 F4
Bridge St. Edin ... 95 D1
Bridge St. Fau ... 193 F3
Bridge St. Hadd ... 132 B4
Bridge St. Kin ... 23 E2
Bridge St. Kirk ... 17 D1
Bridge St. Kirkl ... 119 D3
Bridge St La. Edin ... 95 D1
Bridge St. Muss ... 126 B3
Bridge St. Peni ... 203 F2
Bridge St. Tran ... 128 B3
Bridge View. Inver ... 68 B3
Bridgecastle Cotts. West ... 112 C1
Bridgecastle Rd. Arm ... 143 F4
Bridgehaugh Rd. Stir ... 2 A1
Bridgend Pk. Bath ... 144 C3
Bridgend Pl. Whit ... 170 B4
Bridgend Rd. Avon ... 112 A3
Bridgeness Cres. B'ness ... 64 B4
Bridgeness La. B'ness ... 64 B4
Bridgeness Rd. B'ness ... 64 B4
Bridges The. D Bay ... 48 A1
Bridgeside Ave. Whit ... 170 A3
Bridgeton Cotts. West ... 112 C1
Brierbush Cres. Glad ... 129 E3
Brierbush Rd. Glad ... 129 E3
Briery Bank. Hadd ... 132 B4
Briery Bauks. Edin ... 123 F4
Brig-O-Doon Gr. Cowie ... 20 C4
Bright's Cres. Edin ... 123 F2
Brighton Pl. Edin ... 125 D4
Brighton St. Edin ... 123 F4
Brisbane St. Liv ... 148 A3
Bristo Pl. Edin ... 123 E4
Bristo Port. Edin ... 123 E4
Britwell Cres. Edin ... 94 B1
Broad St. All ... 10 A3
Broad St. Cow ... 13 E1
Broad St. Den ... 36 C1
Broad St. Stir ... 7 D4
Broad Wynd. Edin ... 94 A3
Broad Wynd. Kirk ... 17 E3
Broadgait Ct. Gull ... 52 A2
Broadgait Gn. Gull ... 52 A2
Broadgait. Gull ... 52 A2
Broadhurst Rd. May ... 183 E4
Broadleys Rd. Stir ... 7 E4
Brock Pl. Stir ... 7 D1
Brock St. Inver ... 68 A3
Brocks Way. Brox ... 118 A4
Brockwood Ave. Peni ... 203 E3
Brodick Pl. Falk ... 59 E4
Brodick Rd. Kirk ... 16 C4
Brodie Ave. N Ber ... 54 B3
Brodie St. Falk ... 60 A4
Broich The. Alva ... 4 C4
Bronte Pl. Sten ... 39 D2
Brook St. Alva ... 5 D3
Brook St. Men ... 3 F3
Brookbank Terr. Car ... 230 A1
Brooke La. Gran ... 61 E3
Brooke St. Gran ... 61 E3
Brookfield Pl. Alva ... 5 D3
Brookfield Terr. Rosl ... 180 C3
Brookside. Pol ... 61 F1
Broom Ct. Stir ... 7 E2
Broom Gr. Dunf ... 46 C4
Broom Pk E. Men ... 4 A3
Broom Pk W. Men ... 4 A3
Broom Pl. Kirk ... 16 B4
Broom Rd. Kirk ... 16 B4
Broom Rd. Stir ... 7 E2
Broom Wlk. Liv ... 148 A2
Broom Wynd. Shot ... 191 F3
Broomage Ave. Lar ... 38 A2
Broomage Cres. Lar ... 38 A2
Broomage Dr. Lar ... 38 A2
Broomage Pk. Lar ... 38 B1
Broombank Terr. Edin ... 121 E2
Broomburn Gr. Edin ... 121 F2
Broomfield Cres. Edin ... 121 F2
Broomfield Dr. Dunf ... 29 D3
Broomfield Rd. Cow ... 13 E3
Broomfield Terr. Edin ... 121 F3

237

Broomhall Ave. Edin — Candlemaker Row. Edin

Broomhall Ave. Edin 121 F2
Broomhall Bank. Edin 121 E3
Broomhall Cres. Edin 121 E3
Broomhall Dr. Edin 121 E3
Broomhall Gdns. Edin 121 E3
Broomhall Loan. Edin 121 E3
Broomhall Pk. Edin 121 E3
Broomhall Pl. Edin 121 E3
Broomhall Rd. Edin 121 E3
Broomhall Terr. Edin 121 E3
Broomhead Dr. Dunf 28 C3
Broomhead Pk. Dunf 28 C3
Broomhill Ave. Burn 33 F1
Broomhill Ave. Lar 38 A1
Broomhill Ave. Peni 203 F2
Broomhill. Burn 50 C4
Broomhill Dr. Dalk 156 C1
Broomhill Pk. Dalk 156 C1
Broomhill Pl. Duni 36 B2
Broomhill Pl. Stir 6 C3
Broomhill Rd. Bon 58 A2
Broomhill Rd. Peni 203 F2
Broomhill St. East 168 B3
Broomhouse Ave. Edin 121 E2
Broomhouse Bank. Edin 121 F2
Broomhouse Cres. Edin 121 F2
Broomhouse Ct. Edin 121 F2
Broomhouse Dr. Edin 121 F2
Broomhouse Gdns E. Edin 121 F2
Broomhouse Gdns W. Edin 121 E2
Broomhouse Gr. Edin 121 F2
Broomhouse Loan. Edin 121 F2
Broomhouse Market. Edin 121 F2
Broomhouse Medway. Edin 121 F2
Broomhouse Path. Edin 121 F2
Broomhouse Pk. Edin 121 F2
Broomhouse Pl N. Edin 121 F2
Broomhouse Pl S. Edin 121 F2
Broomhouse Rd. Edin 121 E2
Broomhouse Row. Edin 121 F2
Broomhouse Sq. Edin 121 F2
Broomhouse St N. Edin 121 F2
Broomhouse St S. Edin 121 F1
Broomhouse Terr. Edin 121 F2
Broomhouse Way. Edin 121 F2
Broomhouse Wlk. Edin 121 F2
Broomhouse Wynd. Edin 121 F2
Broomieknowe. Bonn 182 A4
Broomieknowe. Dunf 29 E2
Broomieknowe Gdns. Bonn 182 A4
Broomieknowe Pk. Bonn 182 A4
Broomieknowe. Tull 4 B2
Broomknowe Dr. Kin 23 E3
Broomlea Cres. Edin 121 E3
Broompark Gdns. Den 36 C1
Broompark Gdns. E Cal 148 C2
Broompark Rd. E Cal 148 C2
Broompark Rd. Edin 121 F3
Broompark View. E Cal 148 C2
Broomridge Rd. Stir 7 E2
Broomside. Kirk 16 B4
Broomside Pl. Lar 38 B1
Broomside Rd. Bon 58 A2
Broomside Terr. Edin 121 F2
Broomyknowe Dr. Liv 146 C3
Broomyknowe. Edin 153 D4
Brora Pl. Crossf 28 B1
Brosdale Ct. Falk 60 A1
Brougham Pl. Edin 123 E3
Brougham St. Edin 123 D3
Broughton Market. Edin 93 E1
Broughton Pl. Edin 93 E1
Broughton Place La. Edin 93 E1
Broughton Rd. Edin 93 E2
Broughton St. Edin 93 E1
Broughton Street La. Edin 93 E1
Brown Ave. All 4 C1
Brown Ave. Stir 2 A1
Brown St. Arm 143 F2
Brown St. Edin 123 F4
Brown St. Falk 59 E3
Brown St. Hadd 132 A4
Brown St. Shot 192 A2
Brown St. Whit 170 A3
Brown's Cl. Edin 123 F4
Brown's Pl. E Lin 103 E4
Brownrigg Farm Cotts. E Lin 74 B3
Bruart Ave. Sten 38 C2
Bruce Cres. Plea 20 B2
Bruce Cres. Sten 39 D2
Bruce Dr. Fall 8 B3
Bruce Dr. Sten 38 C2
Bruce Gdns. Dalk 157 D1
Bruce Gdns. Pol 82 B4
Bruce Gr. Pen 160 C3
Bruce Pl. Gran 61 F4
Bruce Rd. B'ness 62 C3
Bruce Rd. Bath 145 E3
Bruce St. All 10 B4
Bruce St. Bann 7 F1
Bruce St. Clack 11 D2
Bruce St. Dunf 28 C2
Bruce St. Edin 123 D1
Bruce St. Falk 60 B3
Bruce St. King 35 D2
Bruce St. Plea 20 B2
Bruce St. Stir 2 A1
Bruce Terr. Cam 6 B3
Bruce Terr. King 35 D2
Brucefield Ave. Dunf 29 D1
Brucefield Cres. Clack 11 D2
Brucefield Dr. Whit 170 A3
Brucefield Feus. Dunf 29 E2
Brucefield Pk E. Muri 173 E3
Brucefield Pk N. Muri 173 E3
Brucefield Pk W. Muri 173 E3
Brucefield Terr. Loch 13 F3
Brucehaven Cres. Lime 45 F2
Brucehaven Rd. Lime 45 E2
Brunstane Bank. Edin 125 E3
Brunstane Cres. Edin 125 E3
Brunstane Dr. Edin 125 E3
Brunstane Gardens Mews. Edin 125 E4
Brunstane Gdns. Edin 125 E4
Brunstane Gdns. Peni 203 E3
Brunstane Rd. Edin 125 E4
Brunstane Rd N. Edin 125 E4
Brunstane Rd S. Edin 125 E3
Brunswick Rd. Edin 93 F1
Brunswick St. Edin 93 F1
Brunswick Street La. Edin 93 F1
Brunswick Terr. Edin 93 F1
Brunt Gr. Dunb 106 B4
Brunt La. Dunb 78 B1
Brunt Pl. Dunb 106 C4
Brunton Pl. Edin 93 F1
Brunton Terr. Edin 93 F1
Brunton's Cl. Dalk 157 D2
Bruntsfield Ave. Edin 123 D3
Bruntsfield Cres. Edin 123 D3
Bruntsfield Gdns. Edin 123 D3
Bruntsfield Pl. Edin 123 D3
Bruntsfield Terr. Edin 123 D3
Bryans Ave. Newt 183 D3
Bryans Rd. Newt 183 D3
Bryce Ave. Edin 94 C1
Bryce Ave. Sten 39 D1
Bryce Cres. Curr 152 A3
Bryce Gdns. Curr 152 A3
Bryce Gr. Edin 94 C1
Bryce Pl. Curr 152 A3
Bryce Rd. Curr 152 A3
Bryony The. Tull 4 A1
Bryson Rd. Edin 122 C3
Bryson St. Falk 60 A3
Buccleuch Pl. Edin 123 E3
Buccleuch St. Dalk 157 D2
Buccleuch St. Edin 123 F3
Buccleuch Terr. Edin 123 F3
Buchan La. Brox 117 F3
Buchan Pl. Gran 61 E3
Buchan Rd. B'ness 62 B3
Buchan Rd. Bath 144 C4
Buchan Rd. Brox 117 E3
Buchanan Ct. B' ness 63 F3
Buchanan Ct. Falk 60 A4
Buchanan Ct. Kirk 17 D1
Buchanan Dr. Stir 2 A2
Buchanan Gdns. Pol 61 E1
Buchanan St. Dunf 29 D2
Buchanan St. Edin 93 F2
Buckie Rd. May 183 F3
Buckingham Terr. Edin 93 D1
Buckstane Pk. Edin 154 A4
Buckstone Ave. Edin 154 A3
Buckstone Bank. Edin 154 A4
Buckstone Circ. Edin 154 B3
Buckstone Cl. Edin 154 B3
Buckstone Cres. Edin 154 A4
Buckstone Crook. Edin 154 B3
Buckstone Ct. Edin 154 A3
Buckstone Dell. Edin 154 A4
Buckstone Dr. Edin 154 A4
Buckstone Gate. Edin 154 B3
Buckstone Gdns. Edin 154 A3
Buckstone Gn. Edin 154 B3
Buckstone Gr. Edin 154 A4
Buckstone Hill. Edin 154 B4
Buckstone Howe. Edin 154 B3
Buckstone Lea. Edin 154 B3
Buckstone Loan E. Edin 154 B3
Buckstone Loan. Edin 154 B3
Buckstone Neuk. Edin 154 B4
Buckstone Pl. Edin 154 A3
Buckstone Rd. Edin 154 A3
Buckstone Rise. Edin 154 B3
Buckstone Row. Edin 154 B4
Buckstone Shaw. Edin 154 B3
Buckstone Terr. Edin 154 A3
Buckstone View. Edin 154 A4
Buckstone Way. Edin 154 A4
Buckstone Wood. Edin 154 A3
Buckstone Wynd. Edin 154 B3
Buffies Brae. Dunf 28 C2
Bughtknowes Dr. Bath 145 E4
Bughtlin Dr. Edin 91 D1
Bughtlin Gdns. Edin 121 D4
Bughtlin Gn. Edin 91 D1
Bughtlin Loan. Edin 121 D4
Bughtlin Pk. Edin 121 D4
Bughtlin Pl. Edin 91 D1
Builyeon Rd. Que 89 D4
Buller St. Loch 14 A4
Bullet Loan. Hadd 132 B4
Bulloch Cres. Den 36 B1
Buntine Cres. Stir 7 D2
Burdiehouse Ave. Edin 155 D2
Burdiehouse Cres. Edin 155 D2
Burdiehouse Crossway. Edin 155 D2
Burdiehouse Dr. Edin 155 D2
Burdiehouse Loan. Edin 155 D2
Burdiehouse Medway. Edin 155 D2
Burdiehouse Pl. Edin 155 D2
Burdiehouse Rd. Edin 155 D2
Burdiehouse Sq. Edin 155 D2
Burdiehouse St. Edin 155 D2
Burdiehouse Terr. Edin 155 D2
Burgess Hill. Lin 85 D3
Burgess Rd. Que 89 E4
Burgess St. Edin 94 A3
Burgess Terr. Edin 124 A2
Burgh Mews. All 10 A3
Burgh Mills La. Lin 84 B3
Burgh Rd. Cow 13 E2
Burghlee Cres. Loan 181 D4
Burghlee Cres. Loan 181 E4
Burghlee Terr. Loan 181 E4
Burghmuir Ct. Lin 85 E4
Burghmuir Rd. Stir 7 D3
Burghtoft. Edin 155 F3
Burleigh Cres. Inver 47 E2
Burleigh Way. All 10 B3
Burlington St. Edin 93 F3
Burn Dr. Stir 7 E2
Burnbank. Liv 147 E3
Burnbank. Oak 27 E4
Burnbank Rd. Falk 60 A4
Burnbank Rd. Gran 61 E3
Burnbrae. Edin 121 D4
Burnbrae. Fau 193 F3
Burnbrae Gdns. Alva 5 D3
Burnbrae Gdns. Falk 60 A3
Burnbrae. N Sau 10 B4
Burnbrae Pk. Kin 23 F2
Burnbrae Rd. Falk 60 A3
Burnbrae Rd. Hart 169 D3
Burnbrae Rd. Shot 191 F2
Burnbrae Rd. Ston 171 D1
Burnbrae Terr. Whit 170 B3
Burndene Dr. Edin 155 D1
Burnee. Fish 5 F2
Burney Pl. Ros 46 C2
Burnfield. Liv 147 D1
Burnfield Pl. Falk 60 B4
Burnfoot Ct. Gran 61 E3
Burnfoot La. Falk 60 A2
Burngrange Cotts. W Cal 172 B1
Burngrange Ct. W Cal 172 B1
Burngrange Gdns. W Cal 172 A1
Burnhead Cres. Edin 155 D3
Burnhead Gr. Edin 155 D3
Burnhead La. Falk 60 B2
Burnhead Loan. Edin 155 D3
Burnhead Path E. Edin 155 D3
Burnhead Path W. Edin 155 D3
Burnhead Rd. Lar 38 B2
Burnhouse Dr. Dech 116 B1
Burnhouse Dr. Whit 169 F3
Burnhouse Ind Est. Whit 169 F3
Burnhouse Rd. Dech 116 B2
Burnlea Dr. Ston 171 D1
Burnlea Pl. Ston 171 D1
Burns Ave. Arm 143 F3
Burns Ave. Gran 61 E3
Burns Cres. Hart 168 C3
Burns Cres. Laur 60 C2
Burns Cres. Whit 170 A3
Burns Ct. Liv 148 B3
Burns Pl. Shot 191 D3
Burns St. Dunf 28 C3
Burns St. Edin 94 A2
Burns St. H Val 26 A1
Burns St. Stir 2 A1
Burns Terr. Bath 145 E3
Burns Terr. Cowie 20 B4
Burnside Ave. Arm 143 E3
Burnside Ave. King 34 C2
Burnside Ave. May 183 E4
Burnside Ave. W Cal 172 C3
Burnside Cres. Clack 11 D3
Burnside Cres. Fau 193 F3
Burnside Cres. May 183 E4
Burnside Cres. Plea 20 B2
Burnside Cres. Ros 47 D3
Burnside Cres. Shot 191 E3
Burnside Ct. Giff 134 B1
Burnside. Dech 116 A1
Burnside. Edin 121 D4
Burnside. Hadd 131 F4
Burnside La. W Cal 172 C3
Burnside Pk. Bale 151 E1
Burnside Pl. Ros 47 D2
Burnside Pl. Sten 39 D2
Burnside. Pres 96 C1
Burnside Rd. Bath 144 C4
Burnside Rd. Gore 183 E1
Burnside Rd. Men 3 F3
Burnside Rd. Uph 117 D2
Burnside Rd. W Cal 172 C3
Burnside St. N Sau 5 E1
Burnside St. Ros 47 D3
Burnside St. Stir 7 E3
Burnside Terr. Cow 13 D1
Burnside Terr. E Cal 148 C3
Burnside Terr. Falk 59 F3
Burnside Terr. Fau 193 F3
Burnside Terr. Laur 61 D1
Burnside Terr. Oak 27 D4
Burnside Terr. W Cal 172 C3
Burnsknowe. Liv 146 C3
Burntisland Rd. King 34 C1
Burnvale. Brox 118 A2
Burnvale. Muri 147 F2
Burt Ave. King 34 C2
Burt Gr. Dunf 29 F1
Burt St. Dunf 29 D3
Bush St. Muss 126 A3
Bush Terr. Muss 126 A3
Bute Cres. Dunf 29 F2
Bute Cres. Shot 191 E3
Bute. Liv 146 C3
Bute Pl. Gran 61 E3
Bute St. Falk 60 A3
Bute Wynd. Kirk 17 D1
Butler's Pl. Liv 147 D2
Butlerfield Ind Est. Newt 183 D2
Butts The. Hadd 132 A4
Buxley Rd. Elph 128 A1
By-Pass Rd. Bank 57 F3
Byburn. Brid 116 C4
Byres The. Ros 46 B3
Byron Rd. Shot 191 D3

Cables Wynd. Edin 93 F3
Caddell's Row Cotts. Edin 91 D3
Cadell Dr. Sten 39 D3
Cadell Pl. Cocke 97 E2
Cadgers Loan. Plea 20 A1
Cadiz St. Edin 94 A3
Cadogan Rd. Edin 155 D4
Cadzow Ave. B' ness 63 F3
Cadzow Cres. B' ness 63 F4
Cadzow La. B' ness 63 F4
Cadzow Pl. Edin 94 A1
Caerketton Ave. Rosl 180 C3
Caerlaverock Ct. Edin 121 D4
Caesar Rd. Tran 128 B3
Caesar Way. Tran 128 B3
Caird's Row. Muss 126 A4
Cairn Gr. Crossf 28 B1
Cairn's La. B'ness 64 A4
Cairnbank Gdns. Peni 203 F2
Cairnbank Rd. Peni 203 F2
Cairncubie Rd. Dunf 29 E4
Cairneyhill Rd. Crossf 28 A1
Cairneymount Ave. Madd 83 D3
Cairneymount Rd. Car 230 A1
Cairngorm Cres. Kirk 16 C3
Cairngorm House. Edin 93 F3
Cairngorm Rd. Gran 61 F3
Cairnhill Ct. Car 230 A1
Cairnie Pl. Whit 170 A3
Cairnmuir Rd. Edin 121 F4
Cairnoch Way. Bann 7 F1
Cairnoch Wlk. Den 36 B1
Cairns Dr. Bale 177 D4
Cairns Gdns. Bale 177 D4
Cairns Street E. Kirk 17 F4
Cairns Street W. Kirk 17 E4
Cairns The. Lime 45 D2
Cairns The. Men 4 A3
Cairntows Cl. Edin 124 B2
Cairnwell Pl. Crossf 27 E1
Cairnwell Pl. Kirk 16 C4
Caithness Ct. Kirk 17 F4
Caithness Pl. Edin 93 D3
Caithness Pl. Kirk 17 F4
Caiyside. Edin 154 A2
Caiystane Ave. Edin 154 A3
Caiystane Cres. Edin 154 A3
Caiystane Dr. Edin 153 F3
Caiystane Gdns. Edin 154 A3
Caiystane Hill. Edin 154 A3
Caiystane Terr. Edin 154 A3
Caiystane View. Edin 154 A3
Calais View. Dunf 29 F1
Calaisburn Pl. Dunf 29 F1
Calder Cres. Arm 144 A3
Calder Cres. Edin 121 D1
Calder Ct. Edin 121 E1
Calder Ct. Stir 7 E3
Calder Dr. Edin 121 E1
Calder Dr. Shot 192 A2
Calder Gdns. Edin 121 E1
Calder Gr. Edin 121 E1
Calder House Rd. E Cal 148 A2
Calder Park Rd. E Cal 148 A1
Calder Pk. Edin 121 E1
Calder Pl. D Bay 48 A2
Calder Pl. Edin 121 E1
Calder Pl. Falk 60 B1
Calder Rd. Edin 121 E1
Calder Rd Gdns. Edin 122 A2
Calder Rd. Muri 173 E3
Calder Rd. Rat 121 D1
Calder View. Edin 121 D1
Calder's Lawn. Hadd 101 D1
Calderburn Rd. W Cal 173 D3
Caldercruix Rd. Cald 110 A1
Calderhall Ave. E Cal 148 C2
Calderhall Cres. E Cal 148 C2
Calderhall Terr. E Cal 148 C2
Calderhead Rd. Shot 191 E4
Caledonia Rd. Ros 46 A1
Caledonia Rd. Shot 191 F3
Caledonia Way. Ros 46 A2
Caledonian Cres. Edin 123 D3
Caledonian Gdns. All 9 F3
Caledonian Pl. Edin 123 D3
Caledonian Rd. All 9 F3
Caledonian Rd. Edin 123 D3
Caledonian Rd. Fau 193 E3
Caledonian Terr. Fau 193 E3
Calgary Ave. Liv 147 F2
California Rd. Madd 82 C3
California Terr. Cali 81 F3
Callander Dr. Lar 59 E4
Callander Pl. Cock 140 C2
Callendar Ave. Falk 60 A1
Callendar Rd. Falk 60 B2
Callendar Riggs. Falk 60 B2
Callender Bns Pk. Falk 60 C2
Calliope Rd. Ros 46 A1
Calton Cres. Stir 7 D2
Calton Hill. Edin 93 F1
Calton Rd. Edin 123 F4
Calum Macdonald Ct. Ros 46 C2
Cambridge Ave. Edin 93 F2
Cambridge Gdns. Edin 93 F2
Cambridge St. Edin 123 D4
Cambusnethan St. Edin 94 A1
Camdean Cres. Ros 46 B3
Camdean La. Ros 46 B3
Camelon Rd. Falk 59 F3
Cameron Cres. Bonn 181 F3
Cameron Cres. Edin 124 A2
Cameron Gr. Inver 47 D2
Cameron House Ave. Edin 124 A2
Cameron March. Edin 124 A2
Cameron Pk. Edin 124 A2
Cameron Pl. Sten 39 D1
Cameron Smaill Rd. Rat 151 F4
Cameron St. Dunf 28 C2
Cameron Terr. Edin 124 A2
Cameron Terr. Slam 110 A2
Cameron Toll. Edin 124 A2
Cameron Toll Gdns. Edin 124 A2
Cameron Way. Liv 147 F4
Cameronian Dr. Car 230 A1
Cameronian St. Stir 7 D4
Camilla Gr. Aucht 15 E1
Cammo Bank. Edin 91 D1
Cammo Brae. Edin 91 D1
Cammo Gdns. Edin 91 D1
Cammo Hill. Edin 90 C1
Cammo Parkway. Edin 91 D1
Cammo Pl. Edin 91 D1
Cammo Rd. Edin 90 C1
Cammo Wlk. Edin 90 C1
Camp Rd. Lime 44 B3
Camp Rd. May 183 F4
Camp Wood View. May 183 F3
Campbell Ave. Edin 122 B4
Campbell Cres. Laur 60 C2
Campbell Cres. Loch 14 A4
Campbell Ct. Long 98 B3
Campbell Ct. Stir 6 C2
Campbell Dr. Lar 38 A1
Campbell Pk Cres. Edin 152 C3
Campbell Pk Dr. Edin 152 C3
Campbell Rd. Edin 122 B4
Campbell Rd. Long 98 B3
Campbell St. Dunf 29 D2
Campbell's Cl. Edin 123 F4
Camperdown Rd. Ros 46 B1
Campfield St. Falk 60 A3
Campie Gdns. Muss 126 A3
Campie La. Muss 126 A3
Campie Rd. Muss 126 A3
Campie Terr. Gran 39 F1
Camps Rd. Oak 27 E3
Camps Rigg. Liv 147 D4
Campsie Cres. Kirk 16 C4
Campsie Rd. Gran 61 F3
Campus Roundabout. Muri 147 E1
Campview Ave. Dan 156 A4
Campview Cres. Dan 156 B4
Campview. Dan 156 A4
Campview Gdns. Dan 156 A4
Campview Gr. Dan 156 B4
Campview Rd. Bonn 182 A3
Campview Terr. Dan 156 A4
Camus Ave. Edin 154 A3
Camus Pk. Edin 154 A3
Camus Pl E. Edin 154 A3
Camus Rd E. Edin 154 A3
Camus Rd W. Edin 154 A3
Canaan La. Edin 123 D2
Canal St. Falk 59 E3
Canal St. Falk 60 A4
Canavan Ct. Stir 7 E2
Canberra St. Liv 148 A3
Candie Cres. Gran 61 F3
Candie Rd. Gran 62 A4
Candimilne Ct. Car 230 A1
Candlemaker Row. Edin 123 E4

Candlemaker's Cres. Edin 155 F3
Candlemaker's Pk. Edin 155 F3
Candleriggs. All 10 A3
Caneluk Ave. Car 230 A1
Canmore Dr. Sten 38 C2
Canmore Gr. Dunf 29 D3
Canmore St. Dunf 29 D2
Canmore St. King 34 C1
Canmore St. Que 89 D4
Canmore Terr. Dunf 29 D4
Canning St. Edin 123 D4
Canning Street La. Edin 123 D4
Cannon Wynd. Edin 93 F3
Cannons Way. Falk 39 D1
Cannop Cres. Ston 170 C1
Canon La. Edin 93 E1
Canon Lynch Ct. Dunf 28 C2
Canon St. Edin 93 E1
Canongate. Edin 123 F4
Canonmills. Edin 93 E2
Canthill Gdns. Shot 191 D2
Cantlie Pl. Ros 46 C2
Cantsdam Rd. Kel 12 C4
Canty Gr. Long 98 B2
Capelaw Rd. Edin 153 D3
Caplaw Way. Peni 203 E3
Caponflat Cres. Hadd 100 C1
Caponhall Ct. Tran 128 B3
Caponhall Dr. Tran 128 B3
Caponhall Rd. Tran 128 B3
Cappers Ct. Arm 143 F2
Captain's Dr. Edin 155 D3
Captain's Loan. Edin 155 D3
Captain's Rd. Edin 155 D3
Captain's Row. Edin 155 D3
Caputhall Rd. Liv 146 B3
Carberry Ct. White 157 F4
Carberry Mains Cotts.
  White 127 D1
Carberry Pl. Edin 122 C4
Carberry Rd. Muss 126 C2
Carbrook Dr. Plea 20 B2
Carbrook Pl. Gran 61 F3
Carcraig Pl. D Bay 48 A2
Cardross Ave. Uph 117 D3
Cardross Cres. Brox 117 E3
Cardross Rd. Brox 117 E3
Cardrowan Rd. Plea 20 B1
Carfrae Gdns. Edin 92 A1
Carfrae Gr. Edin 92 A1
Carfrae Pk. Edin 92 A1
Carfrae Rd. Edin 92 A1
Cargil Terr. Edin 93 D3
Carhowden Rd. Laur 61 D2
Carlaverock Ave. Tran 128 B3
Carlaverock Cres. Tran 128 B3
Carlaverock Ct. Tran 128 C3
Carlaverock Dr. Tran 128 B3
Carlaverock Gr. Tran 128 B3
Carlaverock Terr. Tran 128 C2
Carlaverock View. Tran 128 B2
Carlaverock Wlk. Tran 128 B3
Carledubs Ave. Uph 117 D3
Carledubs Cres. Uph 117 D3
Carlie Ave. B of A 2 A3
Carlin Craig. King 34 C1
Carlin Cres. King 34 C1
Carlin La. Car 230 A1
Carlingnose Pk. Inver 68 B3
Carlingnose Point. Inver 68 B3
Carlingnose Way. Inver 68 B3
Carlops Ave. Peni 203 F3
Carlops Cres. Peni 203 F3
Carlops Rd. Peni 203 E3
Carlowrie Ave. Dal 89 F4
Carlowrie Cres. Dal 89 F4
Carlowrie Pl. Gore 207 E4
Carlton St. Edin 93 D1
Carlton Terr. Edin 93 F1
Carlton Terrace La. Edin 93 F1
Carlton Terrace Mews. Edin 93 F1
Carlyle Ct. Hadd 132 A4
Carlyle Ct. Liv 148 B3
Carlyle Gdns. Hadd 101 D3
Carlyle La. Dunf 28 C3
Carlyle Pl. Edin 94 A1
Carlyle Pl. Muss 126 B3
Carlyle Rd. Kirk 17 D2
Carlyle St. H Val 26 A1
Carlyle Terr. Bath 145 E3
Carmel Ave. Kirkl 89 D1
Carmel Rd. Kirkl 89 D1
Carmelaws. Lin 85 D3
Carmelite Rd. Que 89 D4
Carmondean Centre Rd.
  Liv 147 D3
Carmuir. For 215 D1
Carmuirs Ave. Falk 59 E3
Carmuirs Dr. Falk 59 E3
Carmuirs St. Falk 59 E3
Carnaughton Pl. Alva 4 C3
Carnbee Pl. Dunf 29 E2
Carnegie Ave. Dunf 46 C4
Carnegie Dr. Dunf 29 D2
Carnegie Dr. Falk 59 E3
Carnegie Rd. Bog 146 A3
Carnegie St. Edin 123 F4
Carneil Rd. Oak 27 E4

Carneil Terr. Oak 27 E3
Carnethie St. Rose 181 F1
Carnethy Ave. Edin 153 D3
Carnethy Ave. Peni 203 F3
Carnethy Cres. Kirk 16 C4
Carnethy Ct. Peni 203 F3
Carnock Rd. Dunf 28 A3
Carnock Rd. Oak 27 F3
Carnock St. Cowie 20 C4
Carnwath Rd. Car 230 A1
Caroline Cres. Alva 4 C3
Caroline Gdns. E Cal 148 A1
Caroline Gdns. Edin 121 F4
Caroline Park Gr. Edin 92 B3
Caroline Pk. E Cal 148 A1
Caroline Pl. Edin 121 F4
Caroline Terr. Edin 121 E4
Carpet La. Edin 94 A3
Carradale Ave. Falk 59 E2
Carribber Ave. Madd 84 A3
Carrick Cres. May 183 E4
Carrick Ct. Stir 7 E3
Carrick Dr. D Bay 48 A2
Carrick Gdns. Muri 173 F3
Carrick Gr. D Bay 48 A2
Carrick Knowe Ave. Edin 121 F3
Carrick Knowe Dr. Edin 121 F3
Carrick Knowe Gdns. Edin 121 F3
Carrick Knowe Gr. Edin 121 F3
Carrick Knowe Hill. Edin ... 121 F3
Carrick Knowe Loan. Edin . 121 F3
Carrick Knowe Parkway.
  Edin 121 F3
Carrick Knowe Pl. Edin 121 F3
Carrick Knowe Rd. Edin 121 F2
Carrick Knowe Terr. Edin .. 121 F3
Carrick Pl. Falk 59 E2
Carrick Pl. Sten 39 D2
Carriden Brae. Muir 64 B3
Carriden Glade. B'ness 64 B4
Carrington Cres. Edin 92 C2
Carrington Mains Cotts.
  Newt 206 B3
Carrington Rd. Edin 92 C1
Carron La. Dunf 29 F2
Carron Pl. Edin 94 A3
Carron Pl. Gran 61 E2
Carron Pl. Kirk 16 C4
Carron Pl. Stir 7 D1
Carron Rd. Falk 60 A4
Carron Terr. Madd 82 C4
Carron View. Madd 82 C4
Carron Wlk. Liv 148 A2
Carronbank Ave. Sten 39 D1
Carronbank Cres. Den 36 C2
Carronbank Ct. Sten 39 D1
Carronflats Rd. Gran 61 F4
Carrongrove Ave. Sten 39 D1
Carrongrove Rd. Sten 39 D1
Carronhall Ave. Sten 39 E2
Carronlea Dr. Sten 39 D1
Carronshore Rd. Sten 39 D1
Carronside Pl. Duni 36 C2
Carronside St. Falk 60 A4
Carronvale Ave. Lar .... 38 ·B1
Carronvale Rd. Lar 38 B1
Carronview. Lar 38 B1
Carse Cres. Laur 61 D2
Carse Knowe. Lin 85 E4
Carse Terr. All 9 F4
Carse View. Air 22 C2
Carse View. B' ness 63 E3
Carsebridge Rd. N Sau 10 B4
Carseview. Bann 7 F1
Carseview. Tull 4 A1
Carson Pl. Ros 46 B3
Carswell Pl. Dunf 28 C3
Cartmore Rd. Loch 14 A4
Cassel's La. Edin 93 F2
Casselbank St. Edin 93 F2
Cast The. Rose 181 E3
Castings Ave. Falk 60 A4
Castings Ct. Falk 60 A4
Castings Ct. Falk 60 C3
Castings Dr. Falk 60 A3
Castings Rd. Falk 60 C3
Castings The. Dunf 28 B3
Castlandhill Rd. Ros 47 D1
Castle Ave. Cocke 97 F2
Castle Ave. Edin 121 E3
Castle Ave. Sten 39 E2
Castle Cres. Den 36 B1
Castle Cres. E Cal 148 C1
Castle Cres. Falk 60 B4
Castle Cres. Tor 37 F4
Castle Ct. Falk 60 B4
Castle Ct. Men 3 D4
Castle Ct. Stir 7 D4
Castle Dr. Falk 60 B4
Castle Dr. Sten 38 C1
Castle Gate. Dunb 78 B2
Castle Mains Pl. Dir 53 D2
Castle Moffat. Giff 166 A4
Castle Pk. Dir 53 D2
Castle Pl. Dunb 78 B2
Castle Pl. Falk 60 B4
Castle Rd. Cocke 97 F2

Castle Rd. Falk 60 B4
Castle Rd. Men 3 F3
Castle Rd. Ros 46 C1
Castle Rd. Stir 2 B2
Castle Rd. Winch 88 A1
Castle Row. Dunf 28 B3
Castle St. All 10 A3
Castle St. Clack 11 D2
Castle St. Dunb 78 B2
Castle St. Edin 123 D4
Castle Terr. Clack 11 D2
Castle Terr. Cocke 97 F2
Castle Terr. Den 36 B1
Castle Terr. Edin 123 E4
Castle Terr. Winch 88 A1
Castle View. Cocke 97 F2
Castle View. Fall 8 B2
Castle View. Pen 160 B3
Castle Wlk. Cocke 97 F2
Castle Wynd. Stir 7 D4
Castleblair. Dunf 28 C2
Castleblair La. Dunf 28 C3
Castleblair Mews. Dunf 28 C3
Castleblair Pk. Dunf 28 C3
Castlegait. Stir 7 D4
Castlehill Ave. Slam 110 A3
Castlehill. B'ness 63 E4
Castlehill. Edin 123 E4
Castlelaurie St. Falk 60 B4
Castlelaw Cres. Rosl 180 C3
Castlelaw Ct. Peni 203 F3
Castlelaw Rd. Edin 153 D3
Castlemains Pl. Dir 53 E3
Castlemount Terr. Kirk 16 B4
Castlepark. Kin 23 E3
Castlerig. King 34 C1
Castleton Cres. Gran 61 E3
Castleview. B of A 2 A2
Castleview Dr. B of A 2 A4
Castleview Terr. Bank 57 D2
Cathcart Pl. Edin 122 C3
Cathedral La. Edin 93 E1
Catherine St. Bann 7 E1
Catherine Terr. Black 145 E1
Cathlaw La. Torp 114 A3
Cathrine Gr. B'ness 64 A3
Catriona Terr. Auch 180 A1
Cattle Market. Clack 11 D3
Cauldhame Cres. Cam 6 B3
Causeway The. B of A 2 B3
Causeway The. Edin 124 B3
Causewayhead Rd. Stir 2 B1
Causewayside. Edin 123 F3
Cavalry Park Dr. Edin 124 B3
Cawder Gdns. B of A 1 C4
Cawder Rd. B of A 1 C4
Cawdor Cres. Kirk 16 C3
Cecil St. Stir 7 D3
Cedar Ave. Kirk 17 E4
Cedar Ave. Stir 6 C3
Cedar Cres. Laur 61 D1
Cedar Cres. Loch 13 E3
Cedar Cres. Whit 170 B3
Cedar Dr. Cocke 97 E2
Cedar Gr. Dunf 46 B4
Cedar Gr. Stir 38 B1
Cedar Rd. Loan 180 C4
Cedar St. Dunb 78 A1
Cedar St. Gran 61 E4
Cedarbank. Liv 147 F3
Cedars The. Tull 4 A1
Cedric Rise. Muri 148 A1
Cemetery Rd. Dalk 156 C1
Cemetery Rd. Fau 193 E3
Cemetery Rd. Pres 96 C1
Cemetery Rd. Shot 192 A2
Central Ave. Gran 61 E3
Central Dock Rd. Gran 40 C1
Central Dr. Sten 38 C2
Central Rd. Lime 44 B4
Central Way. D Bay 48 B3
Centre Interchange. E Cal . 148 A1
Centre Rd N. Liv 147 F1
Centre Rd S. Muri 147 E1
Chacefield St. Bon 58 A3
Chacefield Wood. Bank 57 F4
Chalmers Cres. Edin 123 E3
Chalmers Sq. Liv 146 B3
Chalmers St. Dunf 28 C2
Chalmers St. Edin 123 E3
Chalmerston Rd. Cam 1 A2
Chalton Rd. B of A 2 A4
Chalybeate. Hadd 131 F4
Chamberfield Rd. Dunf 29 E3
Chamberlain Rd. Edin 123 D2
Chambers Dr. Sten 39 D1
Chambers St. Edin 123 E4
Champigny Ct. Muss 126 C3
Chancelot Cres. Edin 93 E3
Chancelot Gr. Edin 93 E3
Chancelot Terr. Edin 93 E3
Channel Brae. E Lin 136 B4
Chapel Bank. Path 158 B3
Chapel Cres. Sten 39 D2
Chapel Ct. Edin 124 C2
Chapel Ct. Sten 38 C2
Chapel La. Edin 94 A3
Chapel La. Falk 60 A3

Chapel Level. Kirk 16 C4
Chapel Loan. Rosl 181 D2
Chapel Pl. H Val 26 A1
Chapel Pl. Inver 47 E2
Chapel Pl. Inver 68 B3
Chapel Pl. Kirk 16 B4
Chapel Pl. Path 185 D3
Chapel Rd. Kirk 16 B4
Chapel St. Cow 13 E2
Chapel St. Dunf 28 C2
Chapel St. Edin 123 F3
Chapel St. H Val 26 A1
Chapel St. Kin 23 F2
Chapel St. Loch 14 A4
Chapel Villas. D Bay 48 A1
Chapelfauld Gn. Dunf 29 F2
Chapelhill. Clack 11 D2
Chapelhill. Dir 53 D2
Chapelhill. Kirk 16 B4
Chapelhill St. Kin 23 E3
Chapelton Ave. W Cal 172 C2
Chapelton Dr. W Cal 172 C2
Chapelton Gdns. W Cal 172 C2
Chapelton Gr. W Cal 172 C2
Chapelton Pl. W Cal 173 D2
Chapelton Terr. W Cal 172 C2
Chapelwell Pl. Dunf 29 F2
Charing Cross. Gran 40 B1
Charles Ave. B of A 2 A3
Charles Cres. Bog 145 E3
Charles Cres. Car 230 A1
Charles Ct. Lime 45 F2
Charles Dr. Lar 59 E4
Charles La. Bog 145 E3
Charles Rodger Pl. B of A 2 A3
Charles St. All 9 F4
Charles St. Dunf 29 D1
Charles St. Edin 123 E4
Charles St. Peni 203 F4
Charles St. Shot 192 A2
Charles St. Stir 7 D3
Charles Street La. Edin 123 E4
Charles Way. Lime 45 F2
Charles Way S. Lime 45 F2
Charlesfield La. Liv 147 D1
Charlotte Dundas Ct. Gran 61 F3
Charlotte La. Edin 123 D4
Charlotte Sq. Edin 123 D4
Charlotte St. Kirk 17 D2
Charlotte St. Pol 82 B4
Charlotte St. Shot 192 A2
Charlton Gr. Rosl 180 C2
Charter St. Stir 7 D2
Charterhall Gr. Edin 123 E2
Charterhall Rd. Edin 123 E1
Charteris Ct. Long 98 B3
Charteris Pk. Long 98 B3
Charteris Rd. Long 98 B3
Chartershall Rd. Bann 7 D1
Chartershall Rd. Bann 19 D3
Chattan Ave. Stir 2 A2
Cherry Ave. Bog 145 F3
Cherry La. May 183 E3
Cherry Pl. Cow 13 E2
Cherry Rd. Bon 182 A3
Cherry Tree Ave. Curr 151 F2
Cherry Tree Cres. Curr 151 F2
Cherry Tree Gdns. Curr 151 F2
Cherry Tree Gr. Curr 151 E2
Cherry Tree Loan. Curr 151 F2
Cherry Tree Pk. Curr 151 E2
Cherry Tree Pl. Curr 151 F2
Cherry Tree View. Curr 151 F2
Cherrybank. Dunf 29 E3
Cherryton Dr. Clack 11 D3
Chesser Ave. Edin 122 B2
Chesser Cres. Edin 122 B2
Chesser Gdns. Edin 122 A2
Chesser Gr. Edin 122 A2
Chesser Loan. Edin 122 A2
Chester Ct. Bonn 182 A3
Chester Dr. May 183 E3
Chester Gr. Bonn 182 A3
Chester Gr. Edin 123 D4
Chester View. May 183 E3
Chesters View. Bonn 182 A3
Chestnut Ave. Kirk 17 E4
Chestnut Ave. Whit 170 B3
Chestnut Cres. Duni 36 B2
Chestnut Gr. Bonn 182 A3
Chestnut Gr. Dunf 46 C4
Chestnut Gr. Liv 148 A3
Chestnut Gr. Sten 38 C2
Chestnut Gr. Winch 87 F1
Chestnut St. Edin 92 C4
Cheviot Pl. Gran 61 F3
Cheviot Rd. Kirk 16 C4
Cheyne St. Edin 93 D1
Chisholm Ave. Stir 2 A2
Chisholm Cres. Loch 14 A4
Chisholm Pl. Gran 61 D3
Chisholm St. Dunf 29 E4
Chisholm Terr. Peni 203 F3
Christian Cres. Edin 125 E4
Christian Gr. Edin 125 D3
Christie Pl. Kirk 17 E4
Christie St. Dunf 29 D3

Christiemiller Ave. Edin 94 C1
Christiemiller Gr. Edin 94 C1
Christiemiller Pl. Edin 94 C1
Church Ct. Brid 86 B3
Church Gdns. Long 98 C3
Church Gr. Burn 33 E1
Church Gr. N Sau 5 E1
Church Hill. Edin 123 D2
Church Hill Pl. Edin 123 D2
Church La. Duni 36 B2
Church La. Kirk 17 E2
Church Pk. Bath 145 D3
Church Pl. Arm 144 A3
Church Pl. Bath 145 D3
Church Pl. Cross 30 C4
Church Pl. Falk 60 A3
Church Pl. Fau 170 B1
Church Pl. Fau 193 F3
Church Rd. B' ness 63 F4
Church Rd. Bonn 155 F1
Church Rd. Cali 81 F3
Church Rd. N Ber 54 B4
Church St. All 10 A3
Church St. Bon 58 B2
Church St. Brox 117 F3
Church St. Cow 13 E2
Church St. Dunb 78 C1
Church St. East 168 B3
Church St. Hadd 132 A4
Church St. Hal 12 A1
Church St. Inver 47 E2
Church St. Kirk 17 F3
Church St. Lime 45 E2
Church St. Loan 181 E4
Church St. Loch 14 A4
Church St. Sten 38 C2
Church St. Tran 128 B4
Church Wlk. Den 36 C1
Church Wlk. King 35 D2
Church Wynd. B' ness 63 F4
Churchhill Dr. Edin 123 D2
Churchill Dr. B of A 2 A3
Churchill Pl. Ros 46 C2
Churchill St. All 9 F4
Churchill Way. Kir 149 F2
Churchway. Long 98 C3
Cinderhall Pl. Elph 128 A1
Circle The. Dan 156 A4
Circus Gdns. Edin 93 D1
Circus La. Edin 93 D1
Circus Pl. Edin 93 D1
Citadel Pl. Edin 93 F3
Citadel St. Edin 93 F3
City Of Edinburgh By-Pass The.
  Dan 156 C3
City Of Edinburgh By-Pass The.
  Edin 154 B2
City Of Edinburgh By-Pass The.
  Kirkl 120 C2
City Of Edinburgh By-pass The.
  Rat 121 D1
City Of Edinburgh By-Pass The.
  White 126 A1
Clackmae Gr. Edin 154 C4
Clackmae Rd. Edin 154 C4
Clackmannan Rd. All 10 B3
Clare Ct. N Ber 54 B4
Clarebank Cres. Edin 94 A2
Claremont. All 9 F4
Claremont Bank. Edin 93 E2
Claremont Cres. Edin 93 E2
Claremont Ct. Edin 93 E2
Claremont Dr. B of A 2 B4
Claremont Gdns. Edin 94 B2
Claremont Gr. Edin 93 E2
Claremont Pk. Edin 94 A2
Claremont Rd. Edin 94 A2
Claremont St. Bon 57 F3
Clarence St. Edin 93 D1
Clarendon Cres. Edin 93 D1
Clarendon Cres. Lin 85 D3
Clarendon Pl. Stir 7 D3
Clarendon Rd. Lin 85 D3
Clarendon Rd. Stir 7 D3
Claret Rd. Gran 61 F3
Claret Rd. Gran 62 B4
Clarinda Ave. Falk 59 D3
Clarinda Gdns. Dalk 157 E2
Clarinda Terr. Edin 124 A1
Clark Ave. Edin 93 E3
Clark Bldgs. Orm 159 F4
Clark Pl. Edin 93 D3
Clark Pl. Kirk 17 D3
Clark Rd. Edin 93 D3
Clark Rd. Inver 47 D1
Clark St. Stir 7 D1
Claverhouse Dr. Edin 155 D4
Clayhills Gr. Bale 151 D1
Clayhills Pk. Bale 151 D1
Clayknowes Ave. Muss 126 A3
Clayknowes Cres. Muss 126 A3
Clayknowes Dr. Muss 125 F3
Clayknowes Pl. Muss 126 A3
Clayknowes Way. Muss 126 A3

Claymore Dr. Bann 7 E2
Clearburn Cres. Edin 124 A2
Clearburn Gdns. Edin 124 A2
Clearburn Rd. Edin 124 A2
Clearburn Rd. Gore 183 D1
Cleaves The. Tull 4 A1
Cleekim Dr. Edin 125 D2
Cleekim Rd. Edin 125 D2
Cleghorn Dr. Uph 117 D3
Cleikiminrig. Edin 125 D2
Cleish Gdns. Kirk 16 C3
Cleish Pl. Dunf 29 F1
Cleish Rd. Dunf 29 F1
Cleland St. Whit 170 A4
Clement Rise. Muri 148 A1
Clerics Hill. Kirkl 89 D1
Clerk Gr. Dunf 29 F1
Clerk Rd. Peni 203 E3
Clerk St. Edin 123 F3
Clerk St. Loan 181 E4
Clerkington Rd. Hadd 131 F4
Clerkington Wlk. Hadd 131 F4
Clermiston Ave. Edin 91 E1
Clermiston Cres. Edin 91 F1
Clermiston Dr. Edin 91 E1
Clermiston Gdns. Edin 91 E1
Clermiston Gn. Edin 91 E1
Clermiston Gr. Edin 91 E1
Clermiston Hill. Edin 91 F1
Clermiston Loan. Edin 91 E1
Clermiston Medway. Edin 91 E1
Clermiston Pk. Edin 91 E1
Clermiston Pl. Edin 91 E1
Clermiston Rd. Edin 121 F4
Clermiston Rd N. Edin 91 F1
Clermiston View. Edin 91 E1
Clerwood Bank. Edin 121 E4
Clerwood Gdns. Edin 121 E4
Clerwood Gr. Edin 121 E4
Clerwood Loan. Edin 121 E4
Clerwood Pk. Edin 121 E4
Clerwood Pl. Edin 121 E4
Clerwood Row. Edin 121 E4
Clerwood Terr. Edin 121 E4
Clerwood View. Edin 121 E4
Clerwood Way. Edin 121 E4
Cleuch Ave. Tull 4 A1
Cleuch Dr. Alva 4 A3
Cleuch Rd. N Mid 207 F1
Cleuchbrae. W Cal 172 B2
Cleveland Dr. Inver 47 D1
Clifford Rd. N Ber 54 B3
Clifford Rd. Stir 7 D3
Clifton Rd. Rat 118 C1
Clifton View. Brox 118 A3
Cliftonhall Rd. Kirkl 119 D3
Climpy Rd. For 214 B2
Clinkum Bank. Torr 26 B2
Clinton Rd. Edin 123 D2
Clive St. Shot 191 F3
Cloanden Pl. Kirk 17 D2
Clockhill La. Edin 94 A1
Clockluine Rd. D Bay 47 F3
Close The. Ros 46 B1
Clova Dr. Muri 173 F3
Clovenstone Dr. Edin 152 C4
Clovenstone Gdns. Edin 152 C4
Clovenstone Pk. Edin 152 C4
Clovenstone Rd. Edin 152 C4
Clover Pl. B' ness 63 F3
Cloverbank. Liv 147 F3
Cloves The. Men 4 A3
Cluanie Ave. Shot 191 F3
Cluflatt Brae. Que 67 F1
Cluflatt. Que 67 F1
Clune Rd. Oak 27 F4
Clunie Rd. Dunf 29 F2
Clunivar St. Dunf 28 B3
Cluny Ave. Edin 123 D1
Cluny Dr. Edin 123 D1
Cluny Dr. Sten 38 C2
Cluny Gdns. Edin 123 E1
Cluny Pl. Edin 123 E2
Cluny Terr. Edin 123 D1
Clyde Cres. Dunf 29 F1
Clyde Cres. Lar 38 A2
Clyde Dr. Liv 148 A2
Clyde Dr. Shot 192 A2
Clyde St. Edin 93 E1
Clyde St. Falk 59 F3
Clyde St. Gran 40 A1
Clydesdale St. B' ness 63 F3
Clydevale Pl. Pump 117 D3
Coal Neuk. Tran 128 B3
Coal Rd. Dunf 28 C2
Coal Wynd. Kirk 17 E2
Coalgate. All 10 A3
Coalgate Ave. Tran 128 C4
Coalgate Rd. Tran 128 C4
Coalhill. Edin 93 F3
Coalpots Way. Fish 5 F2
Coates Cotts. Ath 99 F2
Coates Cres. Edin 123 D4
Coates Gdns. Edin 122 C4
Coatfield La. Edin 94 A3
Cobblebrae Cres. Falk 39 D1
Cobden Cres. Edin 123 F2

Cobden Rd. Edin 123 F2
Cobden St. Alva 5 D3
Cobden St. Alva 5 D4
Coblecrook Gdns. Alva 4 C3
Coblecrook La. Alva 4 C3
Coblecrook Pl. Alva 4 C3
Coburg St. Edin 93 F3
Cochran Pl. Edin 93 E1
Cochrane Ave. Falk 60 A2
Cochrane Ave. Inver 47 E1
Cochrane Cres. Alva 4 C4
Cochrane Pl. Edin 94 A2
Cochrane Rd. Ros 46 A1
Cochrane Sq. Muri 173 E3
Cochrane St. Bath 145 D4
Cochrane St. Falk 60 A2
Cochrane Terr. Edin 93 E1
Cochrane Way. D Bay 48 A3
Cochrane Wlk. Dunf 29 F2
Cochranes The. Alva 5 D4
Cochrie Pl. Tull 4 B1
Cochrina Pl. Rose 181 E1
Cockburn Cres. Bale 177 D4
Cockburn Cres. Madd 84 A3
Cockburn Ct. Orm 159 F4
Cockburn Dr. Orm 159 E3
Cockburn Sq. Path 185 D3
Cockburn St. Edin 123 E4
Cockburn St. Falk 60 A2
Cockburnhill Rd. Bale 177 D4
Cocklaw St. Kel 12 B4
Cockles Brae. Giff 132 C2
Cockmilane Brae. Giff 132 B3
Cockmylane. Edin 153 F4
Cockpen Ave. Bonn 182 A3
Cockpen Cres. Bonn 182 A3
Cockpen Dr. Bonn 182 A3
Cockpen Pl. Bonn 182 A3
Cockpen Rd. Bonn 182 B3
Cockpen Terr. Bonn 182 A3
Cockpen View. Bonn 182 A3
Coilesdene Gr. Edin 125 E4
Coillesdene Ave. Edin 125 E4
Coillesdene Cres. Edin 125 E4
Coillesdene Dr. Edin 125 E4
Coillesdene Gdns. Edin 125 E4
Coillesdene Loan. Edin 125 E4
Coillesdene Terr. Edin 125 E4
Coire Loan. Shot 192 A2
Coldingham Pl. Dunf 29 E2
Colegate Rd. Path 208 B4
Coles Pl. Cross 31 D3
Colinshiel Ave. Bath 144 C4
Colinshiel St. Bath 144 C4
Colinshiel View. Arm 143 F4
Colinswell Rd. Burn 33 E1
Colinton Gr. Edin 122 B1
Colinton Gr W. Edin 122 B1
Colinton Mains Cres. Edin .. 153 F3
Colinton Mains Dr. Edin 153 E4
Colinton Mains Gdns. Edin . 153 E4
Colinton Mains Gn. Edin 153 E4
Colinton Mains Gr. Edin 153 F4
Colinton Mains Loan. Edin . 153 E4
Colinton Mains Pl. Edin 153 F4
Colinton Mains Rd. Edin 153 E3
Colinton Mains Terr. Edin .. 153 F4
Colinton Rd. Edin 122 C2
Coll Pl. Gran 61 E3
College Cres. Falk 60 B4
College Wynd. Edin 123 E4
Collingwood Ct. Falk 59 F3
Collins Pl. Edin 93 D1
Colliston Rd. Dunf 29 E3
Collyland Rd. N Sau 5 E2
Colmestone Gate. Edin 154 A3
Colonsay Ave. Pol 61 E1
Colonsay Terr. Falk 60 A1
Colquhoun St. Stir 7 E3
Colsnaur. Men 4 A3
Coltbridge Ave. Edin 122 B4
Coltbridge Gdns. Edin 122 C4
Coltbridge Terr. Edin 122 B4
Coltbridge Vale. Edin 122 C4
Coltness Ave. Alla 212 A4
Columba Ave. Edin 92 A1
Columba Rd. Edin 92 A1
Colvin St. Dunb 78 C1
Combfoot Cottages. E Cal .. 148 B2
Comely Bank Ave. Edin 93 D1
Comely Bank. Edin 92 C1
Comely Bank Gr. Edin 92 C1
Comely Bank Pl. Edin 93 D1
Comely Bank Place Mews.
    Edin 93 D1
Comely Bank Rd. Edin 93 D1
Comely Bank Row. Edin 93 D1
Comely Bank St. Edin 92 C1
Comely Bank Terr. Edin 93 D1
Comely Green Cres. Edin 94 A1
Comely Green Pl. Edin 94 A1
Comely Park La. Dunf 29 D2
Comely Park Terr. Falk 60 A2
Comely Pk. Dunf 29 D2
Comely Pk. Pol 82 C4
Comely Pl. Falk 60 A2
Comiston Dr. Edin 123 D1
Comiston Gdns. Edin 123 D1

Comiston Gr. Edin 154 A4
Comiston Pl. Edin 123 D1
Comiston Rd. Edin 154 A4
Comiston Rise. Edin 154 A4
Comiston Springs Ave.
    Edin 154 A4
Comiston Terr. Edin 123 D1
Comiston View. Edin 154 A4
Commercial Rd. Inver 47 E1
Commercial School La.
    Dunf 29 D2
Commercial St. Edin 93 F3
Commercial St. Kirk 17 E3
Commissioner St. B'ness 64 A4
Commodores Wlk. Ros 46 B1
Compressor House Rd.
    B'ness 62 B3
Compton Rd. Gran 61 E3
Comrie Terr. B' ness 63 F3
Comyn Dr. Pol 82 B4
Comyn Dr. Shi 82 A4
Concorde Way. Inver 47 E2
Coneyhill Rd. B of A 2 A4
Coneypark. Stir 6 C3
Conifer Rd. May 183 F4
Coningsby Pl. All 10 A3
Connaught Pl. Edin 93 E3
Conner Ave. Falk 60 A4
Considine Gdns. Edin 94 B1
Considine Terr. Edin 94 B1
Constable Rd. Stir 7 D3
Constitution Pl. Edin 94 A3
Constitution St. Edin 94 A3
Conway Ct. Falk 59 F2
Cook Cres. May 183 E3
Cook Pl. Kirk 18 A4
Cook Sq. Loch 14 A4
Cook St. Kirk 18 A4
Cooper's La. Kin 23 F2
Cooperage La. Falk 60 A3
Cope La. Cocke 97 E2
Copeland Cres. Cow 13 D1
Copland Pl. Alva 4 C4
Copper Beech Wynd.
    Crossf 27 E1
Corbett Pl. Dunf 29 F1
Corbiehall. B' ness 63 F4
Corbiehill Ave. Edin 92 A2
Corbiehill Cres. Edin 91 F2
Corbiehill Gdns. Edin 92 A2
Corbiehill Gr. Edin 92 A2
Corbiehill Pk. Edin 91 F2
Corbiehill Pl. Edin 91 F2
Corbiehill Rd. Edin 125 D3
Corbiehill Terr. Edin 91 F2
Corbieshot. Edin 125 D3
Corbiewood Dr. Bann 19 F4
Corentin Ct. Falk 60 B2
Cormailin Pl. H Val 26 A1
Corn Exchange Rd. Stir 7 D4
Cornhill Cres. Stir 7 D2
Cornhill Terr. Edin 94 A2
Cornton Cres. B of A 2 A3
Cornton Rd. B of A 2 A2
Cornton Rd. Stir 2 A2
Cornwall St. Edin 123 D4
Cornwallis Pl. Edin 93 E1
Coronation Pl. Gran 39 F2
Coronation Pl. May 183 E4
Corpach Dr. Dunf 28 C1
Corporation St. Falk 60 B2
Corrennie Dr. Edin 123 D1
Corrennie Gdns. Edin 123 D1
Corrie Ave. Sten 38 C2
Corrie Ct. Newt 183 D2
Corrie Pl. Falk 59 E2
Corruna Ct. Car 230 A1
Corslet Cres. Curr 152 A3
Corslet Pl. Curr 152 A3
Corslet Rd. Curr 152 A3
Corston Pk. Liv 148 A2
Corstorphine Bank Ave.
    Edin 121 E4
Corstorphine Bank Dr.
    Edin 121 E4
Corstorphine Bank Terr.
    Edin 121 E4
Corstorphine High St.
    Edin 121 E3
Corstorphine Hill Ave.
    Edin 121 F4
Corstorphine Hill Cres.
    Edin 121 F4
Corstorphine Hill Gdns.
    Edin 121 F4
Corstorphine Hill Rd.
    Edin 121 F4
Corstorphine House Ave.
    Edin 121 F3
Corstorphine Park Gdns.
    Edin 121 F3
Corstorphine Rd. Edin 122 A4
Cortachy Ave. Sten 39 D2
Cortleferry Dr. Dalk 156 C1
Cortleferry Gr. Dalk 156 C1
Cortleferry Pk. Dalk 156 C1
Cortleferry Terr. Dalk 156 C1
Corunna Pl. Edin 93 F3
Corunna Terr. Auch 204 A4

Cossars Wynd. Dunb 78 B1
Cotburn Cres. Burn 33 F1
Cotlands Ave. Long 98 B2
Cotlands Pk. Long 98 B2
Cotlands Rd. Long 98 B2
Cotlaws. Kirkl 89 D1
Cottage Gn. Edin 91 D2
Cottage Homes. Edin 153 D4
Cottage La. Muss 126 C3
Cottage Pk. Edin 92 A1
Cottage Pl. Gran 61 D2
Cotton La. Laur 61 D2
Cotts The. Winch 86 C2
Coulport Pl. Dunf 28 C1
Council Houses. Ath 101 F4
Council Houses. Giff 133 E3
Council Houses. Giff 162 C4
Council Houses. Gull 73 D2
Council Houses. Kir 97 F3
Countess Ave. Dunb 78 B1
Countess Cres. Dunb 78 B1
Countess Rd. Dunb 78 B1
County Houses. Cross 31 D3
County Rd. Pres 96 C1
County Sq. Pres 96 C1
Couper Ave. N Ber 54 B3
Couper Gr. Dunf 29 F1
Couper St. Edin 93 F3
Cousin's La. Dunf 28 C2
Cousland Cres. Black 146 A1
Cousland Interchange. Liv .. 147 F3
Cousland Rd. Liv 147 E2
Cousland Terr. Black 146 A1
Couston Dr. D Bay 48 A2
Couston Pl. D Bay 48 A2
Couston Rd. D Bay 48 A2
Couston St. Dunf 29 D2
Cove Cres. Shot 191 F3
Covenanter Rd. East 168 B2
Coville Pl. Edin 93 D1
Cow Wynd. Falk 60 A2
Cowan Rd. Edin 122 C2
Cowan St. Bog 145 F3
Cowan St. Bon 58 A3
Cowan Terr. Peni 203 F4
Cowan's Cl. Edin 123 F3
Cowane St. Stir 2 A1
Cowden Cres. Dalk 157 E2
Cowden Gr. Dalk 157 E2
Cowden La. Dalk 157 E2
Cowden Pk. Dalk 157 E2
Cowden Terr. Dalk 157 E2
Cowden View. Dalk 157 E2
Cowdenbeath Rd. Burn 33 F1
Cowdenhill Rd. B'ness 64 A4
Cowgate. Edin 123 E4
Cowgatehead. Edin 123 E4
Cowie Rd. Bann 20 A4
Cowiehall Rd. Cowie 20 B4
Cowpits Ford Rd. Muss 126 B2
Cowpits Rd. White 126 B1
Coxfield. Edin 122 B2
Coxithill Rd. Stir 7 D2
Craig Ave. Hadd 101 D1
Craig Ave. Whit 169 F3
Craig Cres. Stir 2 B2
Craig Ct. B of A 2 A3
Craig St. Blac 142 C2
Craig St. Ros 47 D2
Craigbank. Crossf 28 B1
Craigbank. N Sau 5 E1
Craigbank Rd. Avon 112 A3
Craigbeath Ct. Cow 13 D3
Craigburn Ct. Falk 59 F1
Craigcrook Ave. Edin 92 A1
Craigcrook Gdns. Edin 92 A1
Craigcrook Gr. Edin 92 A1
Craigcrook Pk. Edin 92 A1
Craigcrook Rd. Edin 92 A1
Craigcrook Sq. Edin 92 A1
Craigdimas Gr. D Bay 48 A1
Craigend Dr. Madd 83 D3
Craigend Pk. Edin 124 B1
Craigend Rd. Stir 7 D2
Craigentinny Ave. Edin 94 C1
Craigentinny Avenue N.
    Edin 94 B2
Craigentinny Cres. Edin 94 C1
Craigentinny Gr. Edin 94 C1
Craigentinny Pl. Edin 94 C1
Craigentinny Rd. Edin 94 B1
Craigford Dr. Bann 7 E1
Craigforth Cres. Stir 1 C1
Craighall Ave. Edin 93 E3
Craighall Bank. Edin 93 E3
Craighall Cres. Edin 93 E3
Craighall Gdns. Edin 93 E3
Craighall Rd. Edin 93 E3
Craighall Terr. Edin 93 E3
Craighall Terr. Muss 126 C3
Craighill Gdns. Edin 122 C1
Craighill View. Blac 142 C2
Craigholm La. Burn 33 F1
Craighorn Dr. Falk 59 F1
Craighorn. Men 4 A3
Craighorn Rd. Alva 4 C3

Craighouse Ave. Edin 122 C1
Craighouse Gdns. Edin 122 C1
Craighouse Pk. Edin 122 C1
Craighouse Rd. Edin 122 C1
Craighouse Terr. Edin 122 C1
Craigie Ct. Lar 38 A1
Craigiebield Cres. Peni 203 F2
Craigielaw Farm Cotts. Aber 71 D2
Craigievar Ave. Sten 39 D2
Craigievar Gdns. Kirk 16 C3
Craigievar Sq. Edin 121 D4
Craigievar Wynd. Edin 121 D4
Craiginn Terr. Blac 142 B2
Craigkennochie Terr. Burn .. 33 F1
Craiglaw. Dech 116 B1
Craiglea Dr. Edin 123 D1
Craiglea Pl. Edin 122 C1
Craigleith Ave. Falk 59 F1
Craigleith Ave. N Ber 54 B3
Craigleith Ave N. Edin 122 B4
Craigleith Ave S. Edin 122 B4
Craigleith Bank. Edin 92 B1
Craigleith Cres. Edin 92 B1
Craigleith Dr. Edin 92 B1
Craigleith. Fish 5 F1
Craigleith Gdns. Edin 92 B1
Craigleith Gr. Edin 92 B1
Craigleith Hill. Edin 92 B1
Craigleith Hill Ave. Edin 92 B1
Craigleith Hill Gdns. Edin 92 C1
Craigleith Hill Gn. Edin 92 B1
Craigleith Hill Gr. Edin 92 B1
Craigleith Hill Loan. Edin 92 B1
Craigleith Hill Pk. Edin 92 B1
Craigleith Hill Row. Edin 92 B1
Craigleith Ind Est. Edin 92 B1
Craigleith Rd. Edin 92 C1
Craigleith Rd. Gran 61 E3
Craigleith Rise. Edin 122 B4
Craigleith View. Edin 122 B4
Craigleith Hill Cres. Edin 92 B1
Craiglockhart Ave. Edin 122 B1
Craiglockhart Bank. Edin 122 B1
Craiglockhart Dell Rd. Edin 122 B1
Craiglockhart Dr N. Edin 122 B1
Craiglockhart Dr S. Edin 122 B1
Craiglockhart Gdns. Edin ... 122 B1
Craiglockhart Gr. Edin 153 E4
Craiglockhart Loan. Edin 122 B1
Craiglockhart Pk. Edin 122 B1
Craiglockhart Pl. Edin 122 B1
Craiglockhart Quadrant.
    Edin 122 B1
Craiglockhart Rd. Edin 122 B1
Craiglockhart Rd N. Edin 122 B1
Craiglockhart Terr. Edin 122 C2
Craiglockhart View. Edin 122 B1
Craigluscar Ct. Oak 28 A4
Craigluscar Rd. Oak 28 A4
Craigmillar Castle Ave.
    Edin 124 C2
Craigmillar Castle Gdns.
    Edin 124 B2
Craigmillar Castle Gr.
    Edin 124 B2
Craigmillar Castle Loan.
    Edin 124 C2
Craigmillar Castle Rd.
    Edin 124 B1
Craigmillar Castle Terr.
    Edin 124 B2
Craigmillar Pk. Edin 124 A2
Craigmillar Pl. Sten 38 C2
Craigmore. Torr 26 C1
Craigmount App. Edin 121 E4
Craigmount Ave. Edin 121 E4
Craigmount Ave N. Edin 91 D1
Craigmount Bank. Edin 91 D1
Craigmount Bank W. Edin ... 91 D1
Craigmount Brae. Edin 91 D1
Craigmount Cres. Edin 121 D4
Craigmount Ct. Edin 91 D1
Craigmount Dr. Edin 121 D4
Craigmount Gdns. Edin 121 D4
Craigmount Gr. Edin 121 D4
Craigmount Gr N. Edin 121 D4
Craigmount Hill. Edin 91 D1
Craigmount. Kirk 16 A4
Craigmount Loan. Edin 121 D4
Craigmount Pk. Edin 121 E4
Craigmount Pl. Edin 121 E4
Craigmount Terr. Edin 121 E4
Craigmount View. Edin 121 D4
Craigmount Way. Edin 91 E1
Craigmyle St. Dunf 29 E3
Craigmus Cres. Men 3 F3
Craigour Ave. Edin 155 E4
Craigour Cres. Edin 155 F4
Craigour Dr. Edin 155 F4
Craigour Gdns. Edin 155 F4
Craigour Gn. Edin 155 E4
Craigour Gr. Edin 155 F4
Craigour Loan. Edin 155 F4
Craigour Pl. Edin 155 F4
Craigour Terr. Edin 155 F4
Craigpark Ave. Rat 119 E1
Craigpark Cres. Rat 119 E1

Craigpark. Torp 113 F3
Craigridge Pl. D Bay 48 B3
Craigrie Terr. Clack 11 D2
Craigrigg Cotts. West 112 C2
Craigs Ave. Edin 121 E3
Craigs Bank. Edin 121 D4
Craigs Chalet Pk. Torp 84 A2
Craigs Cres. Edin 121 E4
Craigs Ct. Torp 113 F3
Craigs Dr. Edin 121 D4
Craigs Gdns. Edin 121 D4
Craigs Gr. Edin 121 E4
Craigs Loan. Edin 121 E4
Craigs Pk. Edin 121 D4
Craigs Rd. Edin 121 D4
Craigs Terr. Madd 82 C4
Craigseaton. Uph 117 D3
Craigshill E. Liv 148 A3
Craigshill Rd. Liv 148 A3
Craigshill St. Liv 148 A3
Craigton Dr. Dunf 29 E3
Craigswood. Liv 148 A3
Craigton Cres. Alva 4 C3
Craigton Pl. Cow 13 E1
Craigview. N Sau 5 E1
Craigward. All 10 A3
Craigwell Path. Lime 44 B4
Crame Terr. Dalk 156 C1
Cramond Ave. Edin 91 D3
Cramond Bank. Edin 91 D3
Cramond Brig Toll. Dal 90 C2
Cramond Cres. Edin 91 D3
Cramond Ct. Falk 60 A1
Cramond Gdns. Edin 91 D3
Cramond Gdns. Kirk 16 C4
Cramond Glebe Gdns. Edin 91 E3
Cramond Glebe Rd. Edin .. 91 D3
Cramond Glebe Terr. Edin .. 91 D3
Cramond Gn. Edin 91 D3
Cramond Gr. Edin 91 D3
Cramond Pk. Edin 91 D3
Cramond Pl. D Bay 48 B2
Cramond Pl. Edin 91 E3
Cramond Rd N. Edin 91 E3
Cramond Rd S. Edin 91 F2
Cramond Regis. Edin 91 D2
Cramond Terr. Edin 91 D3
Cramond Vale. Edin 91 D3
Cramond Village. Edin 91 D4
Cranshaws Dr. Laur 61 E1
Cranston Dr. Path 158 B3
Cranston St. Edin 123 F4
Cranston St. Peni 203 F3
Crarae Ave. Edin 122 B4
Crathes Ave. Sten 39 D2
Crathes Gdns. Muri 173 D2
Crathie Dr. Duni 36 B2
Craufurdland. Edin 91 D2
Crawfield Ave. B' ness 63 F3
Crawfield La. B' ness 63 F3
Crawfield Rd. B' ness 63 F2
Crawford Dr. Shi 82 A4
Crawford Pl. Dunf 29 E4
Crawford Sq. Air 22 B2
Crawfurd Rd. Edin 124 A2
Crawlees Cres. May 183 F3
Craws Knowe. For 215 D1
Creel Ct. N Ber 54 B4
Creran Dr. Bann 57 E3
Crescent The. Edin 123 D1
Crescent The. Gore 183 E2
Crescent The. Ros 46 A1
Creteil Pl. Gran 61 E4
Crewe Bank. Edin 92 C3
Crewe Cres. Edin 92 C3
Crewe Gr. Edin 92 C3
Crewe Loan. Edin 92 B3
Crewe Pl. Edin 92 B3
Crewe Rd N. Edin 92 B3
Crewe Rd S. Edin 92 C2
Crewe Rd W. Edin 92 B3
Crewe Road Gdns. Edin 92 B3
Crewe Terr. Edin 92 C3
Crewe Toll. Edin 92 B2
Crichton Ave. Path 185 D3
Crichton Dr. Gran 61 F4
Crichton Dr. Path 185 D3
Crichton Rd. Path 185 D3
Crichton St. Edin 123 E4
Crichton Terr. Path 185 D3
Crighton Pl. Edin 93 F2
Crimond Pl. Shi 81 F4
Cringate Gdns. Bann 7 F1
Crockett Gdns. Peni 203 E3
Croft An Righ. King 35 D2
Croft Pl. Liv 147 E3
Croft St. Dalk 157 D2
Croft St. Peni 203 F2
Croft's Rd. Tull 4 A2
Croft-An-Righ. Edin 93 F1
Crofters Way. Ston 170 C3
Croftfoot Dr. Fau 194 A3
Croftfoot Pl. Duni 36 B2
Crofthead Ct. Stir 2 A1
Crofthead Ct. Muri 173 E4
Crofthead Interchange.
   Muri 173 F4
Crofthead Rd. Stir 2 A1

Crofthead Rd. Ston 171 D1
Croftmalloch Rd. Whit 170 A3
Crofts Rd. Cock 140 C1
Crofts The. E Lin 104 C1
Croftsacre. Cock 140 C1
Croftshaw Rd. Alva 5 D4
Croftside Ct. Gran 61 F3
Cromarty Pl. Kirk 17 F4
Cromwell Dr. Falk 60 B2
Cromwell Pl. Edin 93 F3
Cromwell Rd. Burn 33 F1
Cromwell Rd. Falk 60 B2
Cromwell Rd N Ber 54 A4
Cromwell Rd. Ros 46 C3
Cromwell Rd W. Falk 60 B2
Crookston Rd. Muss 126 C2
Crophill. N Sau 5 E1
Cross Brae. Shi 81 E3
Cross Loan. Orm 159 F4
Cross Row. Lime 45 D2
Cross St. Falk 39 D1
Cross St. Kirk 18 A4
Cross The. Lin 85 D4
Cross Way. D Bay 48 B3
Cross Wynd. Dunf 29 D2
Crossen La. Car 230 A1
Crossgatehead Rd. Pol 82 B4
Crossgreen Dr. Uph 117 D3
Crossgreen Pl. Uph 117 D3
Crosshill Dr. B' ness 63 F3
Crosshill Rd. Bath 145 E3
Crossroads Pl. Ros 46 C2
Crosswood Ave. Bale 177 D4
Crosswood Cres. Bale 177 D4
Crosswood Terr. Auc 217 F2
Crowhill Rd. D Bay 48 B2
Crown Gdns. All 9 F4
Crown Pl. Edin 93 F3
Crown St. Edin 93 F2
Crownest Loan. Lar 38 C1
Cruachan Ave. Stir 2 A2
Cruachan Ct. Falk 60 B1
Cruachan Ct. Peni 204 A3
Cruachan Pl. Gran 61 F3
Cruickness Rd. Inver 68 B4
Cruickshank Dr. Shi 81 E3
Cruikshank's Ct. Den 36 C1
Crum Cres. Stir 7 E1
Crusader Dr. Rosl 180 C2
Crusader Rise. Muri 148 A1
Cuddy La. Edin 123 D2
Cuddyhouse Rd. Cow 12 B2
Cuddyhouse Rd. Hal 12 B2
Cuffabouts. B'ness 64 B4
Cuguen Pl. Bonn 156 A1
Cuiken Ave. Peni 203 E3
Cuiken Bank. Peni 203 E3
Cuiken Terr. Peni 203 E3
Cuikenburn. Peni 203 F4
Cuil Gr. Dunf 28 B3
Cuillin Ct. Falk 60 B1
Cuillin Pl. Gran 61 F3
Cullalo Cres. Abe 49 E4
Cullaloe Ct. D Bay 48 B2
Cullaloe View. Cow 13 E1
Cullen Cres. Kirk 16 C4
Culloch Rd. Slam 110 A3
Culmore Pl. Falk 60 C1
Cultenhove Cres. Gran 61 F3
Cultenhove Cres. Stir 6 C2
Cultenhove Pl. Stir 7 D2
Cultenhove Rd. Stir 7 D2
Cultins Rd. Edin 121 D1
Cultrig Dr. Whit 170 A3
Culvain Pl. Falk 60 B1
Culzean Cres. Kirk 16 B4
Culzean Pl. Sten 38 C2
Cumberland St. Edin 93 E1
Cumbernauld Rd. Bank 57 D2
Cumbrae Ct. Kirk 17 D4
Cumbrae Dr. Falk 59 E2
Cumbrae Terr. Kirk 17 D4
Cumin Pl. Edin 123 F2
Cumlodden Ave. Edin 122 B4
Cumnor Cres. Edin 124 A1
Cunnigar Gdns. E Cal 148 B2
Cunnigar Hill View. Liv 148 B2
Cunningham Ct. Long 98 B3
Cunningham Ct. N Ber 54 A3
Cunningham Dr. East 168 B3
Cunningham Gdns. Falk 60 C3
Cunningham Rd. Ros 46 B1
Cunningham Rd. Sten 39 D3
Cunningham Rd. Stir 7 E4
Cunningham St. Gran 61 E3
Curran Cres. Brox 117 F3
Currie Cres. Bann 7 F1
Curriehill Castle Dr. Curr .. 151 E2
Curriehill Rd. Curr 151 F3
Currieside Ave. Shot 191 F2
Currieside Pl. Shot 191 E2
Currievale Dr. Curr 151 E2
Currievale Park Gr. Curr .. 151 E2
Currievale Pl. Curr 151 E2
Cushenquarter Dr. Plea 20 B2
Custom House Sq. Dunb 78 C2
Custonhall Pl. Den 36 B1
Cuthbert Rd. Muri 148 A1
Cuthill Cres. Ston 171 E1
Cuthill Terr. Ston 171 E1

Cuttyfield Pl. Sten 39 E2
Cypress Gr. Dunf 46 B4
D'arcy Rd. May 183 F3
Daiches Braes. Edin 125 E3
Dairy Cotts. Dir 53 D1
Daisy Terr. Edin 122 C2
Dalachy Cotts. Abe 32 C1
Dalbeath Cres. Cow 13 D1
Dalbeath Gdns. Cow 12 C1
Dalcross Way. Dunf 29 F3
Dalderse Ave. Falk 60 A3
Dalgety Ave. Edin 94 A1
Dalgety Gdns. D Bay 48 B3
Dalgety House View. D Bay 48 B3
Dalgety Rd. Edin 94 A1
Dalgety St. Edin 94 A1
Dalgleish Ct. Stir 7 D4
Dalgrain Rd. Gran 40 A1
Dalhousie Ave. Bonn 182 A3
Dalhousie Ave W. Bonn 182 A3
Dalhousie Dr. Bonn 182 A3
Dalhousie Gdns. Bonn 182 A3
Dalhousie Rd. Dalk 156 C1
Dalhousie Rd E. Bonn 182 A3
Dalhousie Rd W. Bonn 182 A3
Dalhousie Terr. Edin 123 D1
Dalkeith Rd. Edin 123 F3
Dalkeith St. Edin 125 E4
Dallas Ave. Burn 33 F1
Dallas Dr. Kirk 16 C4
Dalling Rd. Bath 144 C3
Dalmahoy Cres. Bale 151 E2
Dalmahoy Rd. Rat 119 E1
Dalmeny Rd. Edin 93 E3
Dalmeny St. Edin 93 F2
Dalmeny View. D Bay 48 B3
Dalmore Dr. Alva 4 C3
Dalmorglen Pk. Stir 6 C3
Dalratho Rd. Gran 61 F3
Dalry Pl. Edin 123 D4
Dalry Rd. Edin 122 C4
Dalrymple Cres. Edin 123 F2
Dalrymple Cres. Muss 126 A3
Dalrymple Gdns. Path 158 B3
Dalrymple Loan. Muss 126 B3
Dalton Ct. May 183 D3
Dalum Ct. Loan 181 D4
Dalum Dr. Loan 181 D4
Dalum Gr. Loan 181 D4
Dalum Loan. Loan 181 D4
Dalziel Pl. Edin 94 A1
Damhead Holdings Scheme.
   Rosl 154 B1
Damside. Edin 123 D4
Danderhall Cres. Dan 156 A4
Daniel Pl. Ros 46 B3
Danube St. Edin 93 D1
Dargai Pl. Uph 117 D3
Darian La. B' ness 63 F4
Darnaway St. Edin 93 D1
Darnell Rd. Edin 93 D3
Darney Terr. King 34 C1
Darnley St. Stir 7 D4
Darrach Dr. Duni 36 A1
Darwin St. Liv 148 A3
Davaar Dr. Kirk 16 C4
Davarr Pl. Falk 59 E2
Davenport Pl. Ros 46 C2
David Millar Pl. Dunf 28 C3
David Scott Ave. May 183 F4
David St. Dunf 29 D3
David St. Kirk 17 D2
David St. Loch 14 A4
David The First St. King 34 C1
David's Loan. Falk 39 E1
Davidson Gdns. Edin 92 A2
Davidson La. Car 230 A1
Davidson Pk. Edin 92 C2
Davidson Rd. Edin 92 C2
Davidson St. Bann 7 E1
Davidson Terr. Hadd 100 C1
Davidson Way. Liv 147 F4
Davie St. Edin 123 F4
Daviot Rd. Dunf 29 F3
Dawson Ave. All 9 F4
Dawson Ave. Liv 147 F3
Dawson Pl. B' ness 63 F3
Dawson St. Falk 60 A4
De Quincey Path. Bonn 181 D3
De Quincey Rd. Bonn 181 D3
Deacons Ct. Lin 85 D3
Dean Bank La. Edin 93 D1
Dean Cres. Stir 2 B1
Dean Ct. Long 98 B2
Dean Dr. Crossf 28 A1
Dean Gr. Crossf 28 A1
Dean Park Cres. Edin 93 D1
Dean Park Mews. Edin 93 D1
Dean Path. Edin 92 C1
Dean Pk. Long 98 B2
Dean Pk. Newt 183 D3
Dean Pk. Oak 27 F4
Dean Pk St. Newt 183 D3
Dean Pl. Black 146 A1
Dean Pl. Peni 203 E3

Dean Rd. B' ness 63 F3
Dean Rd. Kirk 17 D2
Dean Rd. Long 98 B2
Dean Rd. Peni 203 E3
Dean Ridge. Oak 27 F4
Dean St. Edin 93 D1
Dean St. Whit 170 A4
Dean Terr. Edin 93 D1
Dean The. E Lin 75 F1
Deanburn. Peni 203 F4
Deanburn Pk. Lin 84 C3
Deanburn Rd. Lin 84 C3
Deanburn Wlk. B' ness 63 E3
Deanery Cl. Edin 94 B1
Deanfield Cres. B' ness 63 F4
Deanfield Dr. B' ness 63 F3
Deanfield Pl. B' ness 63 F3
Deanfield Rd. B' ness 63 F4
Deangate Gdns. B' ness 63 E3
Deanhaugh St. Edin 93 D1
Deanpark Ave. Bale 151 E1
Deanpark Bank. Bale 151 E1
Deanpark Brae. Bale 151 E1
Deanpark Cres. Bale 151 E1
Deanpark Ct. Bale 151 D1
Deanpark Gdns. Bale 151 E1
Deanpark Gr. Bale 151 E1
Deanpark Pl. Bale 151 E1
Deans N. Liv 146 C3
Deans Roundabout. Liv 146 B3
Deans S. Liv 146 C3
Deans Service Units. Liv .. 146 C3
Deanswood Pk. Liv 146 C3
Deantown Ave. White 157 F4
Deantown Dr. White 126 C1
Deantown Path. White 126 C1
Deas Rd. Inver 47 D1
Deas Rd. Shot 191 E3
Dechmont Rd. Edin 121 D3
Dedridge East Rd. Muri .. 148 A1
Dedridge North Rd. Muri .. 147 F1
Dedridge Nursery Units.
   Muri 148 A1
Dedridge West Rd. Muri .. 173 F4
Dee Dr. Liv 148 A3
Dee Pl. Dunf 29 F1
Dee St. Shot 191 E3
Deer Pk Rd. New 66 C1
Deerhill. Dech 116 B3
Deerpark. N Sau 5 F1
Deeside Dr. Car 230 A2
Delisle St. Dunb 78 B1
Dell Ave. Arm 143 F3
Dell Rd. Edin 153 D4
Delph Rd. Tull 4 B1
Delphwood Cres. Tull 4 B1
Delta Ave. Muss 127 D3
Delta Cres. Muss 127 D3
Delta Dr. Muss 127 D3
Delta Gdns. Muss 127 D3
Delta Pl. Muss 126 B2
Delta Rd. Muss 127 D3
Delta View. Muss 127 D3
Dempster Pl. Dunf 28 C3
Den La. Shot 191 F4
Den Rd. Kirk 17 E3
Denburn Pl. Kirk 17 E4
Denburn Rd. Kirk 17 E4
Denend Cres. Kirk 17 D3
Denham Green Ave. Edin .. 93 D3
Denham Green Pl. Edin 93 D3
Denham Green Terr. Edin .. 93 D3
Denholm Gr. Arm 143 F4
Denholm Rd. Muss 125 F3
Denholm Way. Muss 125 F3
Denny St. Bank 57 F3
Denny Rd. Lar 38 A1
Denovan Rd. Duni 36 C2
Denovan Rd. Tor 36 C2
Dequincey Wlk. Tran 128 B3
Derby St. Edin 93 E3
Deroran Pl. Stir 6 C3
Derwent Ave. Falk 59 F2
Devon Ct. Tull 4 A1
Devon Dr. Men 4 C2
Devon Pl. Camb 4 A1
Devon Pl. Edin 122 C4
Devon Rd. All 10 B3
Devon St. Gran 40 A1
Devon Terr. Dunf 29 F1
Devon Village. Fish 5 F2
Devonbank. Fish 5 F2
Devonway. Clack 11 D3
Dewar Ave. Kin 23 F2
Dewar Pl. Edin 123 D4
Dewar Place La. Edin 123 D4
Dewar Sq. Liv 146 B3
Dewar St. Dunf 28 C2
Dewar St. Loch 14 A4
Dewshill Cotts. Sals 167 D2
Dick Cres. Burn 33 F1
Dick Gdns. Whit 169 F3
Dick Pl. Edin 123 E2
Dick Pl. Ros 46 C3
Dick Pl. Ston 171 E1

Dick St. Dunf 29 E3
Dick Terr. Peni 203 F3
Dickburn Cres. Bon 57 F3
Dickies Wells. Alva 5 E4
Dickson Ct. Loch 14 A4
Dickson St. Dunf 29 D1
Dickson St. Edin 93 F2
Dickson St. W Cal 172 B3
Dicksons Gr. Bonn 182 A4
Dinmont Dr. Edin 124 A1
Dirleton Ave. N Ber 54 A4
Dirleton Gdns. All 9 F4
Dirleton La. All 9 F3
Dirleton Rd. Dir 53 D3
Dirleton Rd. N Ber 53 F3
Distillery La. Edin 122 C4
Diverswell. N Sau 5 E1
Dixon Terr. Whit 170 A3
Dobbie Ave. Lar 38 B1
Dobbie's Rd. Bonn 182 A4
Dobson's View. Hadd 131 F4
Dobson's Wlk. Hadd 131 F4
Dochart Cres. Pol 61 F1
Dochart Dr. Edin 91 E1
Dochart Path. Gran 61 E3
Dochart Pl. Falk 60 B1
Dock Pl. Edin 93 F3
Dock Rd. Gran 40 B1
Dock St. Edin 93 F3
Dock St. Sten 39 E1
Doctor's Row. Kirk 17 F4
Dog Well Wynd. Lin 85 D4
Dollar Ave. Falk 60 A4
Dollar Cres. Kirk 16 B4
Dollar Ct. Dunf 28 C3
Dollar Gdns. Falk 60 A4
Dollar Gr. Burn 33 F1
Dollar Rd. Burn 33 F2
Dolphin Ave. Curr 151 F2
Dolphin Gdns E. Curr 151 F2
Dolphin Gdns W. Curr 151 F2
Dolphin Rd. Curr 151 F2
Don Dr. Liv 148 A3
Don Rd. Dunf 29 F1
Don St. Gran 40 A1
Donald St. Dunf 29 E3
Donaldson Ct. Kin 23 F2
Donaldson Pl. Cam 6 B3
Donibristle Gdns. D Bay .. 48 A1
Doo'cot Brae. All 10 A4
Doocot Brae. B'ness 64 A4
Doon Ave. Dunb 78 B4
Doon Wlk. Liv 148 A2
Dornie Wynd. Shot 192 A2
Dorrator Rd. Falk 59 F3
Dorset Pl. Edin 123 D3
Double Dykes. Muss 126 B2
Double Hedges Pk. Edin .. 124 A1
Double Hedges Rd. Edin .. 124 A1
Double Row. Lime 45 D2
Dougall Ct. May 183 E3
Dougall Pl. May 183 E3
Dougall Rd. May 183 E3
Douglas Ave. Crossf 28 A1
Douglas Ave. Gran 61 F3
Douglas Ave. Lin 84 C3
Douglas Ave. Pol 82 B4
Douglas Cres. Bonn 182 A4
Douglas Cres. Edin 122 C4
Douglas Dr. B' ness 63 F3
Douglas Dr. Dunf 28 C3
Douglas Dr. Stir 7 E2
Douglas Gdns. Edin 122 C4
Douglas Gdns Mews. Edin 122 C4
Douglas Pk. Dunf 28 C3
Douglas Pl. B' ness 63 F3
Douglas Pl. Lin 84 C3
Douglas Pl. Sten 38 C2
Douglas Rd. B' ness 63 F3
Douglas Rd. Long 98 C3
Douglas Rd. Ros 46 B1
Douglas St. Bann 7 F1
Douglas St. Dunf 29 D2
Douglas St. Kirk 17 D2
Douglas St. Stir 2 A1
Douglas Terr. B' ness 63 F3
Douglas Terr. Stir 6 C3
Douglaswynd. Uph 117 D3
Doune Cres. Sten 39 D2
Doune Pk. D Bay 48 B2
Doune Terr. Edin 93 D1
Dovecot Brae. Tran 128 B4
Dovecot Gr. Edin 122 A1
Dovecot Loan. Edin 122 A1
Dovecot Pk. Abe 49 D3
Dovecot Pk. Edin 153 D4
Dovecot Pk. Lin 85 E4
Dovecot Pk. Pen 160 C3
Dovecot Pl. Tull 4 A2
Dovecot Rd. Edin 121 E3
Dovecot Rd. Laur 61 D1
Dovecot Rd. Tull 4 A2
Dovecot Way. Pen 160 C4
Dovecote Pl. Liv 147 E2
Dovehill. All 10 A4

Dowan Pl. Stir ... 6 C3
Dower Cres. B'ness ... 64 A4
Dowie's Mill La. Edin ... 90 C2
Downfield. Cow ... 13 E3
Downfield Pl. Edin ... 122 C3
Downie Gr. Edin ... 121 F3
Downie Pl. Muss ... 126 B3
Downing Point. D Bay ... 48 A4
Downs Cres. All ... 9 F3
Dreghorn Ave. Edin ... 153 F3
Dreghorn Dr. Edin ... 153 F3
Dreghorn Gdns. Edin ... 153 F3
Dreghorn Gr. Edin ... 153 F3
Dreghorn Junc. Edin ... 153 F3
Dreghorn Link. Edin ... 153 F3
Dreghorn Loan. Edin ... 153 D3
Dreghorn Pk. Edin ... 153 F3
Dreghorn Pl. Edin ... 153 F3
Drem Farm Cotts. Gull ... 73 D2
Drip Rd. Stir ... 1 C1
Dronachy Rd. Kirk ... 16 C2
Drossie Rd. Falk ... 60 A2
Drove Loan. Bon ... 57 F3
Drove Loan Cres. Bank ... 57 F4
Drove Loan. Den ... 57 F3
Drove Rd. Arm ... 143 F4
Droverhall Ave. Cross ... 31 D3
Droverhall Pl. Cross ... 31 D3
Drovers Rd. Brox ... 118 A3
Drum Ave. Edin ... 155 F3
Drum Brae Ave. Edin ... 121 E4
Drum Brae Cres. Edin ... 91 E1
Drum Brae Dr. Edin ... 91 E1
Drum Brae Gdns. Edin ... 121 E4
Drum Brae Gr. Edin ... 91 E1
Drum Brae N. Edin ... 91 D1
Drum Brae Neuk. Edin ... 91 E1
Drum Brae Park App. Edin ... 121 E4
Drum Brae Pk. Edin ... 121 E4
Drum Brae Pl. Edin ... 121 E4
Drum Brae S. Edin ... 121 E4
Drum Brae Terr. Edin ... 91 E1
Drum Brae Wlk. Edin ... 91 D1
Drum Cotts. Edin ... 155 F3
Drum Cres. Edin ... 155 F3
Drum Pl. Edin ... 155 F3
Drum Pl. Whit ... 170 C4
Drum Rd. Dunf ... 29 F1
Drum Rd. Muir ... 64 B3
Drum St. Edin ... 155 F3
Drum Terr. Edin ... 94 A1
Drum View Ave. Dan ... 156 A4
Drumacre Rd. B'ness ... 64 A3
Drumclair Ave. Slam ... 110 A3
Drumcross Rd. Bath ... 145 D4
Drumdryan St. Edin ... 123 D3
Drummohr Ave. Muss ... 127 D3
Drummohr Gdns. Muss ... 127 D3
Drummond La. Stir ... 7 D3
Drummond Pk. Gran ... 61 F3
Drummond Pl. Blac ... 142 B2
Drummond Pl. Bon ... 58 A4
Drummond Pl. Dunf ... 29 E3
Drummond Pl. Edin ... 93 E1
Drummond Pl. Gran ... 61 F4
Drummond Pl. Stir ... 7 D3
Drummond Sq. Muri ... 173 E3
Drummore Dr. Pres ... 127 F4
Drummormie Rd. Crossf ... 27 E1
Drumond Sq. Loch ... 14 A4
Drumpark Ave. B'ness ... 64 A3
Drumpark St. Stir ... 7 D2
Drumsheugh Gdns. Edin ... 123 D4
Drumshoreland Ave. Pump ... 148 A4
Drumshoreland Cres. Pump ... 148 A4
Drumshoreland Pl. Pump ... 148 A4
Drumshoreland Rd. Pump ... 148 A4
Drumside Terr. B'ness ... 64 B4
Dryburgh Ave. Den ... 36 B1
Dryburgh Way. Gran ... 61 F3
Dryden Ave. Loan ... 181 D4
Dryden Cres. Loan ... 181 D4
Dryden Gdns. Edin ... 93 F2
Dryden Glen. Loan ... 180 C4
Dryden Gr. Rosl ... 181 D2
Dryden Pl. Edin ... 123 F3
Dryden Rd. Loan ... 180 C4
Dryden St. Edin ... 93 F2
Dryden Terr. Edin ... 93 F2
Dryden Terr. Loan ... 181 D4
Dryden View. Loan ... 181 D4
Drylaw Ave. Edin ... 92 B1
Drylaw Cres. Edin ... 92 A1
Drylaw Gdns. E Lin ... 103 E4
Drylaw Gdns. Edin ... 92 A2
Drylaw Gn. Edin ... 92 A1
Drylaw Gr. Edin ... 92 A1
Drylaw House Gdn. Edin ... 92 A2
Drylaw House Paddock. Edin ... 92 A2
Drylaw Terr. E Lin ... 103 E4
Drylawhill. E Lin ... 75 E1
Drylie St. Cow ... 13 D2

Drysdale Ave. Whit ... 170 A4
Drysdale St. All ... 10 A3
Duart Cres. Edin ... 91 E1
Dublin Meuse. Edin ... 93 E1
Dublin St. Edin ... 93 E1
Dublin Street La N. Edin ... 93 E1
Dublin Street La S. Edin ... 93 E1
Duddingston Ave. Edin ... 124 C4
Duddingston Cres. New ... 88 A4
Duddingston Gdns S. Edin ... 124 C3
Duddingston Gr E. Edin ... 124 C4
Duddingston Gr W. Edin ... 124 C3
Duddingston Loan. Edin ... 124 C3
Duddingston Mills. Edin ... 124 C4
Duddingston Pk. Edin ... 125 D4
Duddingston Pk S. Edin ... 125 D3
Duddingston Rd. Edin ... 124 C4
Duddingston Rd W. Edin ... 124 B3
Duddingston Rise. Edin ... 124 C3
Duddingston Row. Edin ... 124 C3
Duddingston Sq E. Edin ... 124 C4
Duddingston Sq W. Edin ... 124 C3
Duddingston View. Edin ... 124 C3
Duddingston Yards. Edin ... 125 D3
Duddingstone Terr. New ... 88 A4
Duddington Gdns N. Edin ... 124 C4
Dudgeon Pl. Kirkl ... 89 D1
Dudley Ave. Edin ... 93 E3
Dudley Ave S. Edin ... 93 F3
Dudley Bank. Edin ... 93 E3
Dudley Cres. Edin ... 93 E3
Dudley Gdns. Edin ... 93 E3
Dudley Gr. Edin ... 93 E3
Dudley Terr. Edin ... 93 E3
Duff Cres. Stir ... 1 C1
Duff St. Edin ... 122 C3
Duff Street La. Edin ... 122 C3
Duffy Pl. Ros ... 46 C2
Dugald Stewart Ave. B'ness ... 64 A4
Duglas Rise. Muri ... 148 A1
Duke Pl. Edin ... 94 A2
Duke St. Alva ... 5 D4
Duke St. Bann ... 7 E1
Duke St. Clack ... 11 D2
Duke St. Dalk ... 157 D2
Duke St. Den ... 36 B1
Duke St. Dunb ... 77 F1
Duke St. Dunb ... 78 A1
Duke St. Edin ... 94 A2
Duke St. Gran ... 61 F4
Duke St. Rose ... 181 E1
Duke's Wlk. Edin ... 94 A1
Dumbarton Rd. Stir ... 6 C4
Dumbarton Rd. Stir ... 7 D4
Dumbiedykes Rd. Edin ... 123 F4
Dumbryden Dr. Edin ... 121 F1
Dumbryden Gdns. Edin ... 121 F1
Dumbryden Gr. Edin ... 121 F1
Dumbryden Rd. Edin ... 121 F1
Dumyat Ave. Tull ... 4 A1
Dumyat Dr. Falk ... 59 F2
Dumyat Rd. Alva ... 4 C3
Dumyat Rd. Men ... 3 F3
Dumyat Rd. Stir ... 2 B2
Dumyat St. All ... 4 C1
Dunard Gdn. Edin ... 123 E2
Dunbar Ave. Sten ... 38 C2
Dunbar Gate. Duni ... 36 C2
Dunbar Pl. Kirk ... 16 C3
Dunbar Rd. Hadd ... 101 D1
Dunbar Rd. N Ber ... 54 C3
Dunbar St. Edin ... 123 D3
Duncairn Ave. Bon ... 57 F3
Duncan Ave. Sten ... 39 D2
Duncan Cres. Dunf ... 29 F1
Duncan Ct. N Ber ... 54 A3
Duncan Gdns. Tran ... 128 B4
Duncan Gn. Liv ... 147 D4
Duncan Pl. Edin ... 94 A2
Duncan St. Bon ... 57 F3
Duncan St. Edin ... 123 F2
Duncan St. Kirk ... 17 D2
Duncanson Ave. All ... 10 A4
Duncanson Dr. Burn ... 34 A1
Duncarron Pl. Den ... 36 C1
Duncur Rd. Gull ... 52 B2
Dundaff Ct. Den ... 36 B1
Dundarroch St. Lar ... 38 A1
Dundas Ave. N Ber ... 54 B3
Dundas Ave. Que ... 89 E4
Dundas Cotts. Bon ... 57 D1
Dundas Cres. Clack ... 11 D2
Dundas Cres. Dalk ... 156 C1
Dundas Cres. Laur ... 61 D2
Dundas Gr. Dalk ... 156 C1
Dundas Pk. Bonn ... 182 B4
Dundas Pl. Kirkl ... 89 D1
Dundas Rd. Dalk ... 156 C1
Dundas Rd. Laur ... 61 D2
Dundas Rd. N Ber ... 54 B3
Dundas Rd. Ros ... 67 E4
Dundas St. Bath ... 2 A2
Dundas St. B'ness ... 63 F4
Dundas St. Bath ... 145 D4
Dundas St. Bonn ... 182 B4
Dundas St. Dunf ... 29 E4
Dundas St. Edin ... 93 E1

Dundas St. Gran ... 61 E4
Dundas St. Loch ... 14 A4
Dundee Pl. Falk ... 60 A4
Dundee Terr. Edin ... 122 C3
Dundonald Rd. Ros ... 46 B2
Dundonald St. Edin ... 93 E1
Dundrennan Cotts. Edin ... 124 B1
Dunearn Bank. Burn ... 33 E1
Dunearn Dr. Kirk ... 16 C3
Dunedin St. Edin ... 93 E2
Dunfermline Rd. Cross ... 30 C3
Dunfermline Rd. Lime ... 45 F2
Dunfermline Wynd. Inver ... 47 D1
Dunkeld Pl. Falk ... 39 E1
Dunlop Sq. Liv ... 146 B3
Dunlop Terr. Peni ... 204 A3
Dunmar Cres. All ... 4 C1
Dunmar Dr. All ... 4 C1
Dunn Cres. Dunf ... 29 F2
Dunn Pl. Winch ... 87 F1
Dunn St. Uph ... 117 D3
Dunn Terr. East ... 168 C3
Dunnet Way. Brox ... 118 A3
Dunnikier Rd. Kirk ... 17 E3
Dunnikier Way. Kirk ... 17 E4
Dunning Pl. Falk ... 39 E1
Dunnottar Dr. Sten ... 38 C2
Dunnottar Pl. Kirk ... 16 C2
Dunollie Ct. Edin ... 121 D4
Dunollie Gdns. Hadd ... 132 B4
Dunpender Pl. Hadd ... 100 C1
Dunpender Rd. E Lin ... 103 E4
Dunrobin Ave. Sten ... 38 C3
Dunrobin Pl. Edin ... 93 D1
Dunrobin Rd. Kirk ... 16 C2
Duns Rd. Giff ... 163 F3
Dunsire St. Kirk ... 17 F4
Dunsmuir Ct. Edin ... 121 E3
Dunster Rd. Stir ... 2 B2
Dunure Cres. Bon ... 58 A3
Dunure Pl. Kirk ... 16 C2
Dunure St. Bon ... 58 A3
Dunvegan Ave. Kirk ... 16 B3
Dunvegan Ave. Sten ... 38 C2
Dunvegan Ct. All ... 10 A3
Dunvegan Ct. Crossf ... 28 A1
Dunvegan Ct. Edin ... 91 D2
Dunvegan Dr. Falk ... 39 E1
Dunvegan Dr. Stir ... 2 A2
Dunvegan Gdns. Muri ... 173 F3
Dunvegan Pl. Bon ... 57 F3
Dunvegan Pl. Pol ... 62 A1
Dura Rd. Alla ... 212 B3
Durar Dr. Edin ... 91 E1
Durham Ave. Bath ... 144 C3
Durham Ave. Edin ... 124 C4
Durham Bank. Bonn ... 182 B3
Durham Dr. Bath ... 144 C3
Durham Dr. Edin ... 125 D3
Durham Gdns N. Edin ... 125 D4
Durham Gdns S. Edin ... 125 D3
Durham Gr. Bonn ... 182 B3
Durham Gr. Edin ... 125 D4
Durham Pl. Bonn ... 182 B3
Durham Pl E. Edin ... 125 D4
Durham Pl W. Edin ... 124 C4
Durham Place La. Edin ... 125 D4
Durham Rd. Edin ... 125 D4
Durham Rd S. Edin ... 125 D3
Durham Sq. Edin ... 125 D4
Durham Terr. Edin ... 124 C4
Durham Terr. Torr ... 26 B1
Durie Pk. Burn ... 50 B4
Durie Pl. Dunf ... 29 F2
Durie's Pk. Elph ... 128 A1
Durward Rise. Muri ... 148 A1
Durwood Gr. Edin ... 124 A1
Dyfrig St. Shot ... 191 F3
Dyke Brow. Hart ... 169 D3
Dyke Rd. Hart ... 169 D3
Dykeside Rd. Peni ... 203 F4
Dymond Gr. Dunf ... 46 C4
Dysart Rd. Kirk ... 17 F3

Eagle Brae. Liv ... 147 E2
Earl Grey St. Edin ... 123 D4
Earl Haig Gdns. Edin ... 93 D3
Earl Of Mar Ct. All ... 10 A3
Earl's Rd. Gran ... 61 D4
Earls Ct. All ... 10 A3
Earls Pl. Fau ... 193 F3
Earlsburn Ave. Stir ... 7 D2
Earlshill Dr. Bann ... 7 F1
Earlston Pl. Edin ... 94 A1
Earn Ct. All ... 10 B3
Earn Ct. Gran ... 61 E3
Earn Gr. Dunf ... 29 F2
Earn Pl. Bank ... 57 E3
Earn Rd. Kirk ... 17 E4
Earn Terr. Shot ... 191 F3
East Adam St. Edin ... 123 F4
East Ave. Bla ... 26 A4
East Ave. Dunf ... 46 C4
East Baldridge Dr. Dunf ... 28 C3
East Bankton Pl. Muri ... 173 F4

East Barnton Ave. Edin ... 91 F2
East Barnton Gdns. Edin ... 91 F2
East Bay. Inver ... 68 B3
East Boreland Pl. Den ... 36 C1
East Bridge St. Falk ... 60 B2
East Brighton Cres. Edin ... 125 D4
East Broomhill Rd. Burn ... 50 C4
East Caiystane Pl. Edin ... 154 A3
East Caiystane Rd. Edin ... 154 A3
East Campbell Ct. Long ... 98 B3
East Castle Rd. Edin ... 123 D3
East Castle St. All ... 10 A3
East Champanyie. Edin ... 123 F2
East Clapperfield. Edin ... 124 A1
East Claremont St. Edin ... 93 E2
East Comiston. Edin ... 154 A3
East Croft. Rat ... 119 F1
East Cromwell St. Edin ... 93 F3
East Crosscauseway. Edin ... 123 F3
East Ct. Edin ... 92 B1
East Ct. Edin ... 124 C2
East Dr. Lar ... 38 B1
East End. W Cal ... 172 B2
East Farm Of Gilmerton. Edin ... 155 F3
East Fenton Farm Cotts. Dir ... 73 E4
East Fergus Pl. Kirk ... 17 D2
East Fettes Ave. Edin ... 92 C2
East Fountainbridge. Edin ... 123 D4
East Garleton Cotts. Ath ... 100 C3
East Glen Ave. Liv ... 146 C3
East Harbour Rd. Lime ... 45 D2
East Hermitage Pl. Edin ... 94 A2
East Leven St. Burn ... 50 C4
East Lillypot. Edin ... 93 D3
East Link Rd. B of A ... 2 B3
East Links Rd. Dunb ... 78 C1
East Links Rd. Gull ... 52 A1
East Linton Station Ind Est. E Lin ... 103 F4
East Loan. Pres ... 97 D1
East London St. Edin ... 93 E1
East Lorimer Pl. Cocke ... 97 E2
East Main St. Arm ... 144 A3
East Main St. Black ... 171 E4
East Main St. Brox ... 117 F3
East Main St. East ... 168 C3
East Main St. Hart ... 168 C3
East Main St. Uph ... 117 D2
East Main St. Whit ... 170 A4
East Mains. Men ... 4 A3
East March St. Kirk ... 17 F4
East Market St. Edin ... 123 F4
East Mayfield. Edin ... 123 F2
East Montgomery Pl. Edin ... 93 F1
East Murrayfield. Bann ... 7 F1
East Newington Pl. Edin ... 123 F3
East Norton Pl. Edin ... 93 F1
East Park Gr. Uph ... 117 D3
East Parkside. Edin ... 123 F3
East Pier St. B' ness ... 63 F4
East Port Ave. Giff ... 132 A3
East Port. Dunf ... 29 D2
East Preston St. Edin ... 123 F3
East Preston Street La. Edin ... 123 F3
East Quality St. Kirk ... 18 A4
East Queensway. Peni ... 203 F3
East Rd. B'ness ... 62 B3
East Rd. N Ber ... 54 B4
East Restalrig Terr. Edin ... 94 A2
East Savile Rd. Edin ... 123 F2
East Sciennes St. Edin ... 123 F3
East Scotland Street La. Edin ... 93 E1
East Silvermills La. Edin ... 93 D1
East Stirling St. Alva ... 5 D4
East Suffolk Rd. Edin ... 124 A2
East Telferton. Edin ... 94 C1
East Terr. Que ... 68 B1
East Toll. Burn ... 33 F1
East Trinity Rd. Edin ... 93 E3
East Vennel. All ... 10 A3
East Way. D Bay ... 48 B3
Eastburn Dr. Falk ... 60 B2
Eastcroft Dr. Pol ... 62 A1
Easter Bankton. Muri ... 174 A4
Easter Belmont Rd. Edin ... 122 A4
Easter Cornton Rd. Stir ... 2 A2
Easter Currie Cres. Curr ... 152 A3
Easter Currie Ct. Curr ... 152 A3
Easter Currie Pl. Curr ... 152 A3
Easter Currie Terr. Curr ... 152 A2
Easter Drylaw Ave. Edin ... 92 B2
Easter Drylaw Bank. Edin ... 92 B2
Easter Drylaw Dr. Edin ... 92 B2
Easter Drylaw Gdns. Edin ... 92 B2
Easter Drylaw Gr. Edin ... 92 B2
Easter Drylaw Loan. Edin ... 92 B2
Easter Drylaw Pl. Edin ... 92 B2
Easter Drylaw View. Edin ... 92 B2
Easter Drylaw Way. Edin ... 92 B2
Easter Ferrygate Pk. N Ber ... 53 F4
Easter Haugh. Edin ... 153 F4
Easter Livilands. Stir ... 7 E2
Easter Park Dr. Edin ... 91 F2
Easter Rd. Brox ... 117 F3

Easter Rd. Edin ... 94 A2
Easter Rd. Shot ... 191 E3
Easter Warriston. Edin ... 93 E2
Easterfield Ct. Liv ... 147 E2
Eastern Ind Est. Edin ... 125 E2
Easterton Cres. Cowie ... 20 C4
Easterton Dr. Cowie ... 20 C4
Easterton Gr. Cowie ... 20 C4
Eastertoun Gdns. Arm ... 143 F3
Eastfield Dr. Peni ... 203 F3
Eastfield Farm Rd. Peni ... 203 F3
Eastfield Gdns. Edin ... 125 F4
Eastfield Park Rd. Peni ... 203 F3
Eastfield Pl. Edin ... 125 F4
Eastfield Rd. Car ... 230 A1
Eastfield Rd. Fau ... 193 F4
Eastfield Rd. Kirkl ... 120 A3
Eastfield Rd. N Ber ... 54 B3
Eastfield View. Fau ... 193 F4
Easthouses Ct. May ... 183 E4
Easthouses Ind Est. May ... 183 E4
Easthouses Pl. May ... 157 E1
Easthouses Rd. Dalk ... 157 E1
Easthouses Rd. May ... 183 E4
Easthouses Way. May ... 157 E1
Easton Ct. Stir ... 2 A1
Easton Dr. Shi ... 81 E4
Easton Rd. Bath ... 144 C4
Eastwood Pk. Liv ... 147 D4
Ebenezer Pl. Cali ... 81 F3
Ecclesmachan Rd. Uph ... 116 C3
Echline Ave. Que ... 89 D4
Echline Dr. Que ... 88 C4
Echline Farm Cotts. Que ... 88 C4
Echline Gdns. Que ... 67 F1
Echline Gn. Que ... 67 F1
Echline Pk. Que ... 88 C4
Echline Rigg. Que ... 68 A1
Echline Steadings. Que ... 88 C4
Echline Terr. Que ... 89 D4
Echline View. Que ... 89 D4
Echobank. Inver ... 47 D1
Eden Dr. Liv ... 148 A3
Eden La. Edin ... 123 D2
Eden Rd. All ... 9 F4
Eden Rd. Dunf ... 29 F1
Edenhall Bank. Muss ... 126 C3
Edenhall Cres. Muss ... 126 C3
Edenhall Rd. Muss ... 126 C3
Edgefield Ind Est. Loan ... 155 E1
Edgefield Pl. Loan ... 181 E4
Edgefield Rd. Loan ... 155 E1
Edgehead Rd. Path ... 184 B4
Edina Pl. Edin ... 94 A1
Edina St. Edin ... 93 F1
Edinburgh Rd. Auch ... 204 A4
Edinburgh Rd. Bog ... 145 E3
Edinburgh Rd. Cocke ... 97 D2
Edinburgh Rd. Dalk ... 157 D2
Edinburgh Rd. Dunb ... 77 F1
Edinburgh Rd. East ... 168 B3
Edinburgh Rd. Kirkl ... 119 D3
Edinburgh Rd. Lin ... 85 D4
Edinburgh Rd. Muss ... 126 A3
Edinburgh Rd. Tran ... 128 A3
Edinburgh Rd W. Lin ... 220 A1
Edinburgh Rd. Bath ... 145 D3
Edington Pl. Kirk ... 18 A4
Edmonton Ave. Dan ... 156 A4
Edmonstone Dr. Dan ... 156 A4
Edmonstone Rd. Dan ... 156 A4
Edmonstone Terr. Dan ... 156 A4
Edmonton Ave. Liv ... 147 F2
Edward Ave. Sten ... 38 C2
Edward Ave. Stir ... 2 B1
Edward Pl. Gran ... 39 F2
Edward Rd. Stir ... 2 A1
Edward St. Dunf ... 29 D3
Edward St. Kirk ... 17 D2
Eglington Pl. Inver ... 47 E1
Eglintoun Dr. Dunf ... 28 C2
Eglinton Cres. Edin ... 122 C4
Eighth St. Newt ... 183 D3
Eildon Dr. Edin ... 93 E2
Eildon Terr. Edin ... 93 E2
Eilean La. Torr ... 26 C1
Elam Terr. B' ness ... 63 F4
Elbe St. Edin ... 94 A3
Elcho Ct. Long ... 98 C3
Elcho Pl. Cocke ... 97 E2
Elcho Rd. Long ... 98 C3
Elcho Terr. Aber ... 71 E2
Elcho Terr. Edin ... 125 E4
Elcho Terr. Long ... 98 C3
Elder Pl. Ros ... 46 C3
Elder St. Dunb ... 78 A1
Elder St E. Edin ... 93 E1
Elder St. Edin ... 93 E1
Elder St. Tran ... 128 B4
Elderslie Dr. Shi ... 82 A4
Eldindean Pl. Bonn ... 182 A4
Eldindean Rd. Bonn ... 182 B4
Eldindean Terr. Bonn ... 182 B4
Eldrick Ave. Fau ... 193 F3
Eldrick Cres. Fau ... 193 E3
Electra Pl. Edin ... 95 D1
Elgin Ct. Dunf ... 29 D1

Elgin Dr. Stir 7 E2
Elgin Pl. Falk 60 B2
Elgin Rd. Cow 13 E2
Elgin St. Dunf 29 D1
Elgin St. Edin 93 F1
Elgin St. Kirk 17 D3
Elgin St N. Edin 93 F1
Elgin Terr. Edin 93 F1
Eliburn North Interchange. Liv 147 D3
Eliburn Rd. Liv 147 D2
Eliburn South Rd. Liv 147 E2
Elie Ave. Liv 146 C3
Elizabeth Ave. Gran 61 F4
Elizabeth Ave. Lar 38 B1
Elizabeth Cres. Falk 59 D3
Elizabeth Dr. Bog 145 F3
Elizabeth Gdns. Ston 171 D1
Elizabeth La. Bog 145 F3
Elizabeth St. Dunf 29 E1
Elizabeth St. Stir 7 D3
Elizafield. Edin 93 F2
Ellaleen Gr. Crossf 28 A1
Ellangowan Terr. Edin 124 B1
Ellen St. Whit 170 A4
Ellen's Glen Loan. Edin ... 155 E4
Ellen's Glen Rd. Edin 155 E4
Ellersly Rd. Edin 122 B4
Elliot Gdns. Edin 153 E4
Elliot Pk. Edin 153 E4
Elliot Pl. Edin 153 E4
Elliot Rd. Edin 153 E4
Elliot St. Dunf 29 D1
Elliot St. Edin 93 F1
Elliothill St. Dunf 29 D1
Ellis Pl. Uph 117 D3
Ellon Rd. Kirk 16 B4
Elm Dr. Laur 61 D1
Elm Dr. Shi 81 E3
Elm Gr. All 10 B3
Elm Gr. Black 171 F4
Elm Gr. Dunf 46 B4
Elm Gr. Lar 38 B1
Elm Gr. Liv 148 A3
Elm Pk. Black 171 F4
Elm Pl. Edin 94 A2
Elm Pl. Kirk 16 C3
Elm Pl. May 183 E3
Elm Rd. Bog 145 F3
Elm Row. Bonn 156 A1
Elm Row. Edin 93 F1
Elm Sq. Whit 170 B3
Elm St. Dunb 78 A1
Elm St. Stir 1 C1
Elmbank Cres. Bank 57 E3
Elmbank. Men 4 A3
Elmbank Rd. Stir 7 D2
Elmbank St. Gran 61 E3
Elmfield Ct. Dalk 157 D2
Elmfield Pk. Dalk 157 D2
Elmfield Rd. Dalk 157 D2
Elms The. Edin 153 F4
Elmwood Pk. Liv 146 C4
Elmwood Rd. Shot 192 A1
Elmwood Terr. Edin 94 A2
Elphinstone Cres. Air 22 C2
Elphinstone Rd. Tran 128 A3
Elphinstone St. Kin 23 F2
Elphinstone Wlk. Tran 128 B3
Eltringham Gdns. Edin 122 B2
Eltringham Gr. Edin 122 B2
Eltringham Terr. Edin 122 B2
Emily Ct. Gore 183 E1
Emily Pl. Gore 183 E1
Empire St. Whit 170 A4
Endrick Dr. Bank 57 F3
Endrick Pl. Stir 7 D2
Engelen Dr. All 10 A3
Engine La. Bath 145 D3
Engine Pl. Bath 145 D3
Engine Rd. Gore 183 D1
Engine Rd. Loan 181 E4
Ennis Pk. W Cal 172 C3
Eppiestane Rd. Whit 170 B3
Epworth Gdns. Shi 82 A4
Erbach Ave. Laur 61 D2
Ercall Rd. Pol 82 C4
Erica Gr. Dunf 46 C4
Ericht Pl. Shot 191 F3
Eriskay Ct. Falk 60 B1
Erngath Rd. B'ness 64 A4
Erskine Brae. Cul 25 E1
Erskine Hill. Pol 61 F1
Erskine Loan. Gull 52 A2
Erskine Pl. Clack 10 C3
Erskine Pl. Pump 148 B3
Erskine Rd. Brox 117 E3
Erskine Rd. Gull 52 A2
Erskine Sq. Dunf 29 E1
Erskine St. All 10 A4
Erskine St. Alva 5 D4
Erskine St. Loch 14 A3
Erskine Way. Liv 147 E4
Erskine Way. Shot 191 F2
Erskine Wynd. Oak 27 D4
Esk Dr. Liv 148 A2
Esk Glades. Dalk 157 D2

Esk Pl. Dalk 156 C2
Eskbank Rd. Bonn 182 B4
Eskbank Rd. Dalk 156 C1
Eskbank Road Roundabout.
  Dalk 156 B1
Eskbank Terr. Dalk 156 C1
Eskdaill Ct. Dalk 157 D2
Eskdaill St. Dalk 157 D2
Eskdale Ct. Bonn 182 A4
Eskdale Dr. Bonn 182 A4
Eskdale Mews. Muss 126 B3
Eskdale Terr. Bonn 182 A4
Eskgrove Dr. Rosl 180 C3
Eskhill. Peni 203 F3
Eskmill Rd. Peni 204 A3
Eskside E. Muss 126 B3
Eskside W. Muss 126 B3
Eskvale Cres. Peni 204 A3
Eskvale Dr. Peni 204 A3
Eskview Ave. Muss 126 A3
Eskview Cres. Muss 126 A3
Eskview Gr. Dalk 156 C2
Eskview Gr. Muss 126 A3
Eskview Rd. May 183 E3
Eskview Rd. Muss 126 A3
Eskview Terr. Muss 126 A3
Eskview Villas. Dalk 156 C1
Esmonde Ct. Ros 46 C1
Esplanade. Edin 123 E4
Esplanade. Kirk 17 E1
Esplanade Terr. Edin 125 E4
Essendean Pl. Edin 91 E1
Essendean Terr. Edin 91 E1
Essex Brae. Edin 91 D2
Essex Pk. Edin 91 D2
Essex Rd. Edin 91 D2
Esslemont Rd. Edin 124 A1
Estate Ave. Falk 60 B2
Ethel Terr. Edin 123 D1
Etive Pl. D Bay 48 A1
Etive Pl. Stir 2 A2
Etive Way. Pol 62 A1
Etive Way. Shot 192 A2
Etive Wlk. Liv 148 A2
Etna Rd. Falk 60 B4
Eton Terr. Edin 93 D1
Ettrick Cres. D Bay 48 A2
Ettrick Ct. Falk 60 B1
Ettrick Ct. Gran 61 F3
Ettrick Dr. Liv 148 A3
Ettrick Gr. Edin 123 D3
Ettrick Rd. Edin 122 C2
Ettrickdale Pl. Edin 93 D2
Eva Pl. Edin 123 F1
Evans Gdns. Bonn 182 B4
Evans St. Lar 38 B2
Evelyn Terr. Auch 180 B1
Everard Rise. Muri 148 A1
Evershed Ct. Dunf 29 F1
Evershed Dr. Dunf 29 F1
Ewart Ave. Arm 144 A3
Ewart Gr. B' ness 63 F3
Ewerland. Edin 91 D2
Ewing Ave. Falk 60 A4
Ewing Ct. Stir 7 E2
Ewing Dr. Falk 60 A4
Ewing Pl. Falk 60 A4
Ewing St. Auch 203 F4
Ewing St. Cow 13 D1
Ewing St. Loch 14 A3
Excise La. Kin 23 F2
Excise St. Kin 23 F2
Exmouth St. Liv 148 A3
Eyre Cres. Edin 93 E1
Eyre Pl. Edin 93 E1
Eyre Terr. Edin 93 E1

Fa'side Ave N. Muss 127 D2
Fa'side Ave S. Muss 127 D2
Fa'side Ave. Tran 128 B3
Fa'side Avenue Ct. Muss .. 127 D2
Fa'side Bldgs. Muss 127 D2
Fa'side Cres. Muss 127 D2
Fa'side Cres. Tran 128 B3
Fa'side Dr. Muss 127 D2
Fa'side Gdns. Muss 127 D2
Fa'side Rd. Tran 128 B3
Fa'side Terr. Muss 127 D2
Factory Rd. Bath 144 C2
Factory Rd. Cow 13 E2
Factory Rd. Kirk 17 E3
Fair Isle Rd. Kirk 16 C4
Fair Pl. Inver 47 D1
Fair-a-Far Cotts. Edin 91 D3
Fair-A-Far. Edin 91 D3
Fairbairn Rd. Liv 147 E2
Fairfax Ct. Burn 33 F1
Fairfield Ave. Bon 58 A3
Fairfield. N Sau 5 E1
Fairfield Pl. Falk 60 B3
Fairford Gdns. Edin 124 A1
Fairgreen Pl. Bann 19 F4
Fairhaven Terr. Shi 82 A4
Fairhill Rd. Stir 7 D1
Fairinsfell. Uph 117 D3
Fairley Ct. Crossf 27 E1
Fairlie Dr. Falk 59 E3
Fairlie Gdns. Falk 59 E3

Fairlie St. Falk 59 E3
Fairmile Ave. Edin 154 A3
Fairmont Pk. Whit 169 F3
Fairmount Dr. N Sau 5 D1
Fairspark Terr. B'ness ... 63 E3
Fairview Rd. Kirkl 119 F4
Fairview Terr. Shi 82 A4
Fairway. Hadd 131 F4
Fairway The. Kirk 17 F4
Fairways Ave. Madd 82 C3
Fairways Pl. Bon 58 A4
Fairways Pl. Bon 58 A4
Fairy Fa' Cres. Cross 30 C3
Fairyburn Rd. All 9 F4
Fairykirk Rd. Ros 47 D2
Falahill Cotts. Stow 228 A2
Falcon Ave. Edin 123 D2
Falcon Brae. Liv 147 D3
Falcon Ct. Edin 123 D2
Falcon Dr. Lar 38 A2
Falcon Gdns. Edin 123 D2
Falcon Rd. Edin 123 D2
Falcon Rd W. Edin 123 D2
Falconer Ct. Stir 7 E2
Falconer Rise. Muri 147 F1
Falcons The. Gull 52 A2
Falkirk Rd. Bann 19 E4
Falkirk Rd. Bon 58 B3
Falkirk Rd. Falk 60 A1
Falkirk Rd. Gran 61 D4
Falkirk Rd. Lar 38 A1
Falkirk Rd. Lar 38 A1
Falkirk Rd. Lin 84 C4
Falkland Gdns. Edin 91 F1
Falkland Pl. Sten 38 C2
Fallas Pl. Fau 193 E3
Fallodon Cres. Kirk 17 D2
Falside Cres. Bath 144 C3
Falside Dr. Bath 144 C3
Falside Terr. Bath 144 C3
Faraday Pl. Add 171 F1
Farm Ave. Bonn 181 F3
Farm Cotts. Muss 127 E3
Farm Cotts. Pen 160 B3
Farm Rd. Cow 13 D1
Farm Rd. Cowie 20 B4
Farm Rd. Fall 8 B3
Farm Rd. Lime 44 B3
Farm Rd. Rose 204 C3
Farm St. Falk 39 D1
Farmer's Bldgs. Path 185 D3
Farne Ct. Kirk 16 C4
Farquhar Sq. Blac 142 B2
Farquhar Terr. Que 68 A1
Farrer Gr. Edin 94 C1
Farrer Terr. Edin 94 C1
Fauldburn. Edin 91 D1
Fauldburn Pk. Edin 91 D1
Fauldhouse Rd. Fau 170 A1
Featherhall Ave. Edin 121 E3
Featherhall Cres. Edin ... 121 E3
Featherhall Cres N. Edin . 121 E3
Featherhall Cres S. Edin . 121 E3
Featherhall Gr. Edin 121 E3
Featherhall Pl. Edin 121 E3
Featherhall Rd. Edin 121 E3
Featherhall Terr. Edin ... 121 E3
Fell's Rd. W Cal 172 C3
Fells Rigg. Liv 147 D4
Fendoch Rd. Gran 61 F4
Fenton St. All 10 A4
Fentoun Gait. Gull 52 B1
Fere Gait. Kin 23 F2
Fergus Ave. Liv 147 F2
Fergus Pl. Dunf 29 E1
Fergus Wynd. Kirk 17 D1
Ferguson Ct. Muss 126 B2
Ferguson Dr. Den 36 B1
Ferguson Dr. Muss 126 A2
Ferguson Dr. Sten 39 D3
Ferguson Gdns. Muss 126 B2
Ferguson Gn. Muss 126 A2
Ferguson Pl. Bon 58 A3
Ferguson Pl. Burn 33 F1
Ferguson St. Stir 1 C1
Ferguson View. Muss 126 A2
Ferguson Way. Liv 147 E4
Ferguson Way. Newt 183 D2
Fergusson Rd. Brox 117 F3
Fern Lea Gr. Sten 39 E2
Fernbank. Liv 147 F3
Fernie Pl. Dunf 28 C3
Ferniehill Ave. Edin 155 F3
Ferniehill Dr. Edin 155 F3
Ferniehill Gdns. Edin 155 F4
Ferniehill Gr. Edin 155 F4
Ferniehill Pl. Edin 155 F4
Ferniehill Rd. Edin 155 F4
Ferniehill Sq. Edin 155 F4
Ferniehill St. Edin 155 F4
Ferniehill Terr. Edin 155 F4
Ferniehill Way. Edin 155 F4
Fernielaw Ave. Curr 152 C2
Fernielaw Ave. Edin 153 D3
Fernieside Ave. Edin 155 F4
Fernieside Cres. Edin 155 F4
Fernieside Dr. Edin 155 F4

Fernieside Gdns. Edin 155 F4
Fernieside Gr. Edin 155 F4
Fernlea. Uph 116 C3
Ferrard Rd. Kirk 17 D2
Ferrier Cres. Arm 144 A3
Ferris Way. D Bay 48 A2
Ferry La. Inver 68 A3
Ferry Muir Gait. Que 89 D4
Ferry Orch. Stir 2 B1
Ferry Rd. Air 9 F2
Ferry Rd. Edin 92 B2
Ferry Rd. Stir 2 B1
Ferry Road Ave. Edin 92 B2
Ferry Road Dr. Edin 92 B3
Ferry Road Gdns. Edin 92 B2
Ferry Road Gr. Edin 92 B2
Ferry Road Pl. Edin 92 B2
Ferry Toll Pl. Ros 46 C1
Ferry Toll Rd. Ros 46 C1
Ferrybarns Ct. Inver 68 A3
Ferryburn Gn. Que 89 E4
Ferryfield. Edin 93 D2
Ferrygate Cottages. Dir .. 53 E3
Ferryhill Rd. Inver 68 B4
Ferrymuir La. Que 89 D4
Fetteresk Cotts. Peni 203 F2
Fettes Ave. Edin 92 C1
Fettes Rise. Edin 92 C2
Fettes Row. Edin 93 E1
Fidra Ave. Dir 53 D3
Fidra Ct. N Ber 53 F4
Fidra Rd. N Ber 54 A4
Fife Pl. Ros 46 A1
Fifth St. Newt 183 D1
Figgate Bank. Edin 95 D1
Figgate La. Edin 95 D1
Figgate St. Edin 95 D1
Fillyside Ave. Edin 94 C1
Fillyside Rd. Edin 94 C2
Fillyside Terr. Edin 94 C2
Finches The. Gull 52 A2
Findhorn Pl. Edin 123 F2
Findhorn Pl. Falk 60 B1
Findhorn Pl. Kirk 16 C4
Findlay Ave. Edin 94 B2
Findlay Cotts. Edin 94 B2
Findlay Cres. Ros 46 C2
Findlay Gdns. Edin 94 B2
Findlay Gr. Edin 94 B2
Findlay Medway. Edin 94 B2
Findlay St. Ros 46 C2
Fingal Pl. Edin 123 E3
Fingzies Pl. Edin 94 A2
Finistere Ave. Falk 60 A2
Finlaggan Ct. Edin 121 D4
Finlarig Ct. Sten 38 C2
Finlay Ave. E Cal 148 C2
Finlay Pl. May 183 F3
Fintry Rd. Gran 61 F3
Fir Gr. Dunf 46 C4
Fir Gr. Laur 61 D1
Fir Gr. Liv 148 A3
Fir La. Lar 38 B1
Firbank Gr. E Cal 148 C2
Firpark Terr. Cam 6 B3
Firrhill Cres. Edin 153 F4
Firrhill Dr. Edin 153 F4
Firrhill Loan. Edin 153 F4
Firs Cres. Bann 7 E1
Firs Entry. Bann 7 E1
Firs Rd. Tull 4 B1
Firs St. Falk 60 B3
Firs The. Bann 7 E1
Firs The. D Bay 48 A1
First Gait. Rat 151 F4
First St. Newt 183 D2
Firth Cres. Auch 180 B1
Firth Rd. Liv 147 F4
Firth Rd. Rose 204 C3
Firwood Dr. B'ness 63 E3
Fishergate Rd. Cocke 97 F2
Fisherrow Ind Est. Muss . 126 A3
Fishers' Rd. B' ness 63 E4
Fishers Rd. Cocke 97 E2
Fishers Wynd. Muss 126 A3
Fishmarket Sq. Edin 93 E4
Fishwives' Cswy. Edin 94 C1
Fitzgerald Pl. Torp 113 F3
Fitzroy Sq. Kirk 18 A4
Fitzroy St. Kirk 18 A4
Five Gates. E Lin 76 A3
Flare Rd. B'ness 62 A3
Flax Mill Rd. East 168 C3
Fleets Gr. Tran 128 B2
Fleets Rd. Tran 128 B3
Fleets View. Tran 128 B3
Fleming Dr. Sten 39 D2
Fleming Gdns. Falk 59 F3
Fleming Pl. Blac 142 C2
Fleming Rd. Liv 146 C1
Fleming Way. Burn 33 F1
Flemington Gdns. Whit ... 169 F3
Flesh Wynd. Kirk 17 E3
Fletcher Gr. Auch 203 F4
Floors Pl. Kirk 16 B3
Floors Terr. Dunf 78 B1
Florabank Rd. Hadd 101 D1

Flower Pl. Kel 12 C4
Fod St. Hal 30 A3
Fodbank View. Dunf 29 F2
Foot Pl. Ros 46 C2
Foote St. Loch 14 A3
Forbes Cres. Lar 38 B1
Forbes Ct. Falk 60 C3
Forbes Rd. Edin 123 D3
Forbes Rd. Falk 60 B2
Forbes Rd. Ros 46 B1
Forbes St. All 9 F3
Forbes St. Edin 123 F3
Forbeslea Gdns. Oak 27 F4
Ford Rd. Bon 58 A3
Ford Rd. Hadd 132 B4
Ford View. Crossf 27 E1
Ford's Rd. Edin 122 A2
Fordell Bank. D Bay 48 B2
Fordell Way. Inver 47 E1
Forebraes. All 10 A4
Foredale Terr. B'ness 64 B4
Forest Kirk. Car 230 A1
Forest Pl. Dunf 29 E4
Forest Rd. Dunf 29 E4
Forest View. Pol 61 F1
Forestbank. Liv 147 F3
Forester Gr. All 4 C1
Forester's Lea Cres. Dunf ... 29 F2
Forester's View. Tran 128 B3
Forfar Pl. Pol 62 A1
Forgie Cres. Madd 83 D3
Forglen Cres. B of A 2 A3
Forglen Rd. B of A 2 A3
Forker Ave. Ros 46 B2
Forkneuk Rd. Uph 116 C2
Forman Gr. Dunf 29 F1
Forres Dr. Kirk 16 B4
Forres St. Edin 93 D1
Forrest Hill. Edin 123 E4
Forrest Pl. East 168 C3
Forrest Rd. Cald 141 D1
Forrest Rd. Edin 123 E4
Forrest Rd. Sals 167 D3
Forrest Rd. Stir 2 A1
Forrest St. Shot 191 F3
Forrest Wlk. Uph 116 C2
Forrester Ct. Loch 14 A4
Forrester Park Ave. Edin . 121 E2
Forrester Park Dr. Edin .. 121 E2
Forrester Park Gdns. Edin 121 E2
Forrester Park Gn. Edin .. 121 F2
Forrester Park Gr. Edin .. 121 E2
Forrester Park Loan. Edin . 121 E2
Forrester Park Rd. Edin .. 121 E2
Forrester Pl. Air 22 B2
Forrester Rd. Arm 143 F4
Forrester Rd. Edin 121 E3
Forrestfield Rd. Cald ... 141 D3
Fort House. Edin 93 F3
Forth Ave. Kirk 17 D3
Forth Ave. Lar 38 A2
Forth Cres. All 10 B3
Forth Cres. D Bay 48 A2
Forth Cres. H Val 26 A1
Forth Cres. Stir 7 E4
Forth Ct. Cocke 97 F2
Forth Ct. D Bay 48 A2
Forth Ct. Dunf 29 D1
Forth Ct. Stir 2 A1
Forth Dr. Liv 148 A3
Forth Gdns. Cocke 97 F2
Forth Gdns. Oak 26 C4
Forth Gr. Cocke 97 F2
Forth Park Dr. Kirk 17 D3
Forth Park Gdns. Kirk 17 D3
Forth Pk. B of A 2 A3
Forth Pl. Burn 50 C4
Forth Pl. Que 68 A1
Forth Rd. Ros 46 A1
Forth St. Camb 9 D4
Forth St. Dunf 29 D1
Forth St. Edin 93 E1
Forth St. Fall 8 B2
Forth St. Gran 61 E4
Forth St. Kin 23 E2
Forth St La. N Ber 54 B4
Forth St. Stir 2 A1
Forth Terr. Que 89 E4
Forth View Ave. Curr 151 F2
Forth View Cotts. H Val .. 26 A1
Forth View Cres. Curr ... 151 F2
Forth View Cres. Dan 156 A4
Forth View. Dunb 77 F1
Forth View. Inver 47 D1
Forth View. Kin 23 F2
Forth View. Kirk 149 F2
Forth View Rd. Curr 151 F2
Forth View. Stir 2 A1
Forth Wynd. Cocke 97 F2
Forthbank Pl. Cul 25 F1
Forthside Terr. Inver 68 B3
Forthvale. Men 4 A3
Forthview Ave. Muss 127 D2
Forthview. Bann 7 F1
Forthview Cres. B' ness .. 63 F3
Forthview Cres. Muss 127 D3
Forthview Ct. Falk 59 F1

Forthview Dr. Muss 127 D3
Forthview Gdns. Shi 82 B4
Forthview Rd. Edin 92 B1
Forthview Rd. Long 98 C3
Forthview Terr. Edin 92 A1
Forthview Terr. Muss 127 D2
Forthview Terr. Shi 82 A4
Forties Rd. B'ness 62 B3
Fortingall Cres. Pol 62 A1
Fortissat Ave. Shot 191 F4
Fortisset Rd. Sals 167 D1
Fortune Ave. Hadd 101 D1
Foulden Pl. Dunf 29 E2
Foulford Pl. Cow 13 D2
Foulford Rd. Cow 13 D2
Foulford St. Cow 13 E2
Foulis Cres. Curr 152 C3
Foulshiels Rd. Ston 171 E1
Foundry La. Loan 155 E1
Foundry Loan. Lar 38 A1
Foundry Rd. Bon 58 A3
Foundry Rd. Shot 191 F2
Foundry St. Dunf 29 D2
Foundry St. Falk 60 A4
Fountain Pl. Loan 181 E4
Fountain Rd. B of A 2 A4
Fountainbridge. Edin 123 D3
Fountainhall Rd. Edin 123 F2
Fountainhead Rd. Bath 145 D4
Fountainpark Cres. B'ness .. 64 B4
Fourth Gait. Rat 151 F4
Fourth St. Newt 183 D3
Fowler Cres. Loan 181 D4
Fowler Pl. Pol 61 F2
Fowler St. Tran 128 B4
Fowler Terr. Edin 122 C3
Fowlers Ct. Pres 96 C1
Fox Covert Ave. Edin 91 F1
Fox Covert Gr. Edin 91 F1
Fox Spring Cres. Edin 154 A4
Fox Spring Rise. Edin 154 A4
Fox St. Edin 94 A3
Foxknowe Pl. Liv 147 D2
Franchi Dr. Sten 38 C3
Francis Ct. Dunf 28 B3
Francis St. Loch 14 A4
Frankfield Cres. D Bay 48 B2
Frankfield Pl. D Bay 48 B2
Frankfield Rd. D Bay 48 B2
Fraser Ave. Edin 93 D3
Fraser Ave. Inver 47 E1
Fraser Cres. Edin 93 D3
Fraser Gdns. Edin 93 D3
Fraser Gr. Edin 93 D3
Fraser Pl. Gran 61 E3
Fraser Pl. Kirk 18 A4
Fraser Pl. Stir 2 A1
Fraser Rd. Liv 146 C1
Frederick Cres. Dunf 29 D1
Frederick St. Edin 123 E4
Freeland Ave. Uph 117 D3
Freelands Rd. Kirkl 120 A2
Freelands Rd. Rat 119 F2
Fremantle St. Liv 148 A3
Freskyn Pl. Brox 118 A3
Frew Ct. Dunf 29 E1
Friars Brae. Lin 85 D3
Friars Loan. Lin 85 D3
Friars St. Stir 7 D4
Friars Way. Lin 85 D3
Friarton Gdns. Peni 203 E3
Friendship Gdns. Sten 39 E2
Frobisher Ave. Falk 59 F2
Frogston Ave. Edin 154 A3
Frogston Brae. Edin 154 C2
Frogston Gdns. Edin 154 B3
Frogston Gr. Edin 154 B3
Frogston Rd E. Edin 154 C3
Frogston Rd W. Edin 154 B2
Frogston Terr. Edin 154 B3
Fullerton Dr. Pol 61 F2
Fulmar Brae. Liv 147 E3
Fulmar Way. D Bay 48 A2
Furnace La. B'ness 64 B4
Furnace Pl. Loch 13 F3
Furniss Ave. Ros 46 B3
Fyne La. Shot 191 F3

Gaberston Ave. All 10 B4
Gagarin Way. Loch 13 F3
Gair Cres. Car 230 A2
Gair Rd. Car 230 A3
Gair Wynd. Shot 192 A2
Gairdoch Dr. Sten 39 E2
Gairdoch St. Falk 60 A4
Gairloch Cres. Laur 61 E1
Gala Gn. Dunf 78 A1
Galabraes Cres. Bath 145 E4
Galachlawshot. Edin 154 B3
Galachlawside. Edin 154 B3
Galadale Cres. Newt 183 D3
Galadale Dr. Newt 183 D3
Galadale. Newt 183 D3
Gallacher Pl. Loch 13 F3
Gallamuir Dr. Plea 20 B2
Gallamuir Rd. Plea 20 B3
Gallolee The. Edin 153 E3

Galloway Cres. Brox 117 E3
Galloway St. Falk 60 A3
Gallows Loan. Cul 25 E1
Galmeilen. Uph 117 E3
Galt Ave. Muss 127 D3
Galt Cres. Muss 127 D3
Galt Dr. Muss 127 D3
Galt Rd. Muss 127 D3
Galt Terr. Muss 127 D3
Gamekeeper's Loan. Edin ... 91 D3
Gamekeeper's Pk. Edin 91 D3
Gamekeeper's Rd. Edin 91 D3
Garden City. Ston 171 D1
Garden Ct. Dunf 29 E4
Garden Pl. Clack 11 D2
Garden Pl. Crossf 27 E1
Garden Pl. Dunf 29 E4
Garden Pl. Liv 147 E2
Garden St. Falk 60 B3
Garden Terr. Edin 91 F2
Garden Terr. Falk 60 B3
Garden Terr. Laur 61 D1
Gardener Rd. Dunb 78 B1
Gardener St. Dunb 78 B2
Gardener's Wlk. Peni 203 E3
Gardeners Ct. Dunf 29 D2
Gardeners' St. Dunf 29 D2
Gardenhead. Pol 61 F1
Gardens The. Aber 71 E3
Gardens The. Dir 53 D3
Gardiner Cres. Pres 97 D1
Gardiner Gr. Edin 92 A1
Gardiner Pl. Cow 13 D1
Gardiner Pl. Newt 183 D3
Gardiner Rd. Cow 13 E1
Gardiner Rd. Edin 92 A1
Gardiner Rd. Pres 97 D1
Gardiner St. Loch 14 A4
Gardiner Terr. Edin 92 A1
Gardiner Terr. Pres 128 A4
Gardiner Terr. Whit 169 F3
Gardner Terr. Ston 171 D1
Gardner's Cres. Edin 123 D4
Gardners La. Bath 145 D3
Gardrum Gdns. Shi 81 E4
Gardrum Pl. Madd 82 C4
Gareloch Way. Whit 170 B4
Garleton Ct. Gull 52 A1
Garleton Dr. Hadd 100 C1
Garngrew Rd. Bank 57 D2
Garrison Pl. Falk 60 A3
Garry Pl. Falk 60 B1
Garry Pl. Gran 61 F3
Garry St. Loch 14 A4
Garry Way. Shot 191 F3
Garry Wlk. Liv 148 A2
Garscube Terr. Edin 122 B4
Gartclush Gdns. Bann 19 F4
Gartcows Ave. Falk 60 A2
Gartcows Cres. Falk 60 A2
Gartcows Dr. Falk 60 A2
Gartcows Gdns. Falk 59 F2
Gartcows Pl. Falk 60 A2
Gartcows Rd. Falk 60 A2
Garten Dr. Shot 192 A2
Garthill Gdns. Falk 60 A2
Garthill La. Falk 60 A2
Gartmorn Rd. N Sau 5 E1
Garvald La. Den 36 B1
Garvald Rd. Bank 57 E4
Garvally Cres. All 10 A4
Garvock Bank. Dunf 29 F2
Garvock Hill. Dunf 29 E2
Garvock Terr. Dunf 29 E2
Gas Wynd. Kirk 17 D1
Gasworks La. N Ber 53 F3
Gasworks La. Whit 170 A4
Gateshead Rd. Kirkl 88 C1
Gateside Ave. Bon 58 B3
Gateside Ave. Hadd 100 B1
Gateside Ct. Cow 13 D2
Gateside Rd. Hadd 131 E4
Gateside Rd. Kirkl 89 D1
Gateside Rd. Stir 7 D2
Gateside Rd. Whit 169 F3
Gauger's Bush. E Lin 76 A4
Gauze Pl. B'ness 64 A3
Gauze Rd. B'ness 64 A3
Gavin Pl. Liv 147 D3
Gavins Rd. All 4 C1
Gayfield Cl. Edin 93 F1
Gayfield Place La. Edin 93 F1
Gayfield Sq. Edin 93 F1
Gayfield St. Edin 93 F1
Gayfield Street La. Edin 93 E1
Gaynor Ave. Loan 181 D4
Gean Rd. All 9 F4
Gellatly Rd. Dunf 29 E1
Gelnorchy Terr. Edin 123 F2
George Ave. Loan 181 D4
George Cres. Loan 181 E4
George Cres. Orm 159 E4
George Dr. Loan 181 E4
George IV Bridge. Edin 123 E4
George Sq. Edin 123 E3
George Square La. Edin 123 E3
George St. Alva 5 D3

George St. Arm 143 F3
George St. B'ness 63 F3
George St. Bath 145 D4
George St. Cow 13 D2
George St. Dunf 29 D1
George St. Edin 123 E4
George St. Falk 60 A3
George St. Gran 61 F4
George St. Kin 23 F2
George St. Kirk 17 D2
George St. Lar 38 B2
George St. Laur 60 C2
George St. Orm 159 F4
George Terr. Loan 181 D4
Georgy Way. Tran 128 B3
George Wlk. Tran 128 B3
Gerald Terr. Sten 38 C2
Gib Gr. Dunf 29 F1
Gibbdun Pl. Bank 57 F4
Gibbs Entry. Edin 123 F4
Gibbshill Pl. East 168 B3
Gibraltar Ct. Dalk 157 D2
Gibraltar Gdns. Dalk 157 D2
Gibraltar Rd. Dalk 157 D2
Gibraltar Terr. Dalk 157 D2
Gibson Dr. Dalk 157 E2
Gibson St. Edin 93 F2
Gibson Terr. Edin 123 D3
Gibsongray St. Falk 60 A4
Gideon Ct. Bath 145 D4
Gideon St. Bath 145 D4
Gifford Pk. Edin 123 F3
Gifford Rd. Hadd 132 B4
Giffordgate. Hadd 132 A4
Gilbertoun. Edin 125 E3
Gilbertoun Pl. Edin 125 E3
Gilbert Ave. N Ber 54 B3
Gilburn Pl. B' ness 63 E3
Gilburn Pl. Shot 191 F2
Gilchrist Cres. Whit 170 A3
Gilchrist Pl. Falk 59 F2
Giles St. Edin 93 F3
Gilfillan Rd. Dunf 29 F2
Gill Pk. Den 36 C1
Gill Way. Ros 46 B3
Gillespie Cres. Edin 123 D3
Gillespie Gr. Bla 26 C4
Gillespie Pl. Bann 7 D1
Gillespie Pl. Edin 123 D3
Gillespie Rd. Edin 152 C3
Gillespie St. Edin 123 D3
Gillies Dr. Stir 7 E2
Gillies Hill. Cam 6 B3
Gillsland Rd. Edin 122 C2
Gilmerton Dykes Ave. Edin 155 E3
Gilmerton Dykes Cres.
    Edin 155 E3
Gilmerton Dykes Dr. Edin .. 155 E3
Gilmerton Dykes Gr. Edin .. 155 E3
Gilmerton Dykes Loan.
    Edin 155 E3
Gilmerton Dykes Pl. Edin .. 155 E3
Gilmerton Dykes Rd. Edin . 155 E3
Gilmerton Dykes St. Edin .. 155 E3
Gilmerton Dykes Terr.
    Edin 155 E3
Gilmerton Dykes View.
    Edin 155 E3
Gilmerton Pl. Edin 155 E3
Gilmerton Rd. Edin 124 A1
Gilmerton Rd. Edin 156 A2
Gilmerton Road Roundabout.
    Dalk 156 B2
Gilmerton Station Rd. Edin 155 F2
Gilmore Pk. Edin 123 D3
Gilmore Pl. Edin 123 D3
Gilmour Rd. Edin 123 F2
Gilmour St. Cow 13 E3
Gilmour St. Edin 123 F4
Gilsay Ct. Falk 60 B1
Gilston Cres. Pol 62 A1
Gladney Sq. Kirk 17 D1
Gladsmuir. For 215 D1
Gladstone Pl. Dunf 29 D3
Gladstone Pl. Edin 94 A3
Gladstone Pl. Stir 7 D3
Gladstone Rd. Sten 38 B2
Gladstone Terr. Edin 123 F3
Glaive Ave. Bann 7 E2
Glamis Gdns. D Bay 48 A2
Glamis Pl. D Bay 48 A2
Glamis Rd. King 34 C2
Glamis Rd. Kirk 16 B4
Glamis Terr. King 34 C2
Glasclune Ct. N Ber 54 B4
Glasclune Gdns. N Ber 54 B4
Glasgow Rd. Bank 57 E2
Glasgow Rd. Bann 19 E4
Glasgow Rd. Bath 144 C3
Glasgow Rd. Den 36 C1
Glasgow Rd. Edin 121 D3
Glasgow Rd. Falk 59 D3
Glasgow Rd. Kirkl 119 E3
Glasgow Rd. Kirkl 120 B3
Glasgow Rd. Stir 7 D1
Glaskhill Terr. Peni 203 F3
Glass Cres. Winch 87 F1

Glass Pl. Winch 87 F1
Glass Rd. Winch 87 F1
Glassel Pk Rd. Long 98 B2
Glasshouse Loan. All 10 A3
Glasswork St. Kirk 17 D2
Glebe Ave. Stir 7 D1
Glebe Ave. Uph 117 D2
Glebe Cres. Alva 5 D4
Glebe Cres. Ath 101 F4
Glebe Cres. Stir 7 D4
Glebe Gdns. Edin 121 E3
Glebe Gr. Edin 121 E3
Glebe Pk. Inver 47 D1
Glebe Pk. Kirk 17 E3
Glebe Pl. Bonn 155 F1
Glebe Pl. Burn 33 F1
Glebe Pl. King 34 C2
Glebe Rd. Bath 145 D4
Glebe Rd. Edin 121 E3
Glebe Rd. Kin 23 F3
Glebe Rd. Uph 117 D2
Glebe Rd. W Cal 172 A3
Glebe Rd. Whit 170 A3
Glebe St. Dalk 157 D2
Glebe St. Den 36 C1
Glebe St. Falk 60 A3
Glebe Terr. All 10 A3
Glebe Terr. Edin 121 E3
Glebe Terr. Hadd 101 D1
Glebe Terr. Inver 47 D1
Glebe Terr. Uph 117 D2
Glebe The. Abe 49 E4
Glebe The. Alva 5 D4
Glebe The. Clack 11 D2
Glebe The. E Lin 103 F4
Glebe The. Kirkl 89 D1
Glebe The. Kirkl 89 D1
Glebe The. Lin 85 D3
Glebe The. Pen 160 C4
Glebe The. Pen 161 F2
Glebe The. W Cal 172 B1
Glen Albyn Dr. Kirk 16 A4
Glen Artney Gr. Dunf 29 E1
Glen Avon Pl. Madd 82 C4
Glen Beasdale Ct. Dunf 29 E1
Glen Brae. Falk 60 A2
Glen Bridge. Dunf 28 C2
Glen Bruar Pl. Kirk 16 A4
Glen Clova Cres. Crossf 27 E1
Glen Cres. Falk 60 A1
Glen Cres. Liv 146 C3
Glen Ct. Liv 146 B3
Glen Fruin Gr. Dunf 29 E1
Glen Gdns. Falk 60 A2
Glen Isla Gr. Dunf 29 E1
Glen Isla Rd. Kirk 16 B4
Glen Lyon Ct. Pol 62 A1
Glen Moriston Dr. Crossf 27 E1
Glen Nevis Dr. Dunf 29 E1
Glen Ogle Ct. Pol 62 A1
Glen Pl. Peni 203 F3
Glen Rd. Arm 143 F3
Glen Rd. Bath 145 D4
Glen Rd. Liv 146 C3
Glen Rd. Plea 37 E4
Glen Rd. Shot 191 F2
Glen Rd. Tor 37 E4
Glen St. Edin 123 E3
Glen Terr. Den 36 B1
Glen Terr. Liv 146 C3
Glen View. B'ness 63 E2
Glen View. Dalk 57 E3
Glen View Cres. Gore 207 E4
Glen View Ct. Gore 207 E4
Glen View Rd. Gore 207 E4
Glen Way. Bath 145 D4
Glenafeoch Rd. Car 230 A1
Glenallan Dr. Edin 124 A1
Glenallan Loan. Edin 124 A1
Glenalmond Ct. Uph 117 D3
Glenalmond Ct. Whit 170 B3
Glenalmond Terr. Bath 145 D4
Glenalmond. Whit 170 B3
Glenavon Dr. Crossf 27 E1
Glenavon Terr. Bath 145 D4
Glenbank. Falk 60 A1
Glenbervie Ave. Lar 38 A2
Glenbervie Cres. Lar 38 A2
Glenbervie Dr. Lar 38 A2
Glenbervie Gr. Dunf 29 E1
Glenbervie Rd. Gran 61 F3
Glenbo Dr. Bank 57 F4
Glenbrae Ct. Falk 60 A2
Glenbridge Ct. Dunf 28 C2
Glenbrook. Bale 176 C4
Glenburn Gdns. Whit 170 B3
Glenburn Gr. Bla 26 C4
Glenburn Rd. Falk 60 B1
Glenburn Rd. N Ber 54 B3
Glencairn Cres. Edin 122 C4
Glencairn St. Falk 59 D3
Glencairn St. Stir 7 D2
Glencairn Terr. Bath 145 E4
Glencoe Rd. Car 230 A1
Glencoe Rd. Stir 2 A1
Glencorse Pk. Auch 204 B4

Glencoul Ave. D Bay 48 A2
Glencross Gdns. Peni 203 E3
Glendevon Ave. Edin 122 A3
Glendevon Dr. Stir 1 C1
Glendevon Gdns. Edin 122 A3
Glendevon Gr. Edin 122 A3
Glendevon Pk. Edin 122 A3
Glendevon Pk. Winch 87 F1
Glendevon Pl. Edin 122 A3
Glendevon Terr. Edin 122 A3
Glendinning Cres. Edin 155 D4
Gleneagles Ct. Whit 170 B3
Gleneagles Way. Liv 146 C3
Glenesk Cres. Dalk 156 C1
Glenfield Ave. Cow 13 E3
Glenfield Cres. Cow 13 E3
Glenfield Ct. Cow 13 E3
Glenfield Gdns. Cow 13 E3
Glenfield. Liv 147 D2
Glenfield. Oak 27 E3
Glenfield Rd. Cow 13 E3
Glenfinlas St. Edin 123 D4
Glenfuir Rd. Falk 59 F3
Glenfuir St. Falk 59 F3
Glengairn Wlk. Dunf 29 E1
Glengyle Terr. Edin 123 E3
Glenisla Gardens La. Edin .. 123 E2
Glenisla Gdns. Edin 123 E2
Glenlee Ave. Edin 124 B4
Glenlee Gdns. Edin 124 B4
Glenlockhart Bank. Edin 122 B1
Glenlockhart Rd. Edin 122 C1
Glenlockhart Valley. Edin .. 122 B1
Glenmavis Cres. Car 230 A1
Glenmavis Dr. Bath 145 D4
Glenmore Dr. Bon 57 F2
Glenmore. Whit 170 B3
Glennie Gdns. Tran 128 B3
Glenochil Pk. Men 4 C2
Glenochil Rd. Falk 60 A2
Glenochil Terr. Men 4 C2
Glenogle Ct. Edin 93 D1
Glenogle House. Edin 93 D1
Glenogle Pl. Edin 93 D1
Glenogle Rd. Edin 93 D1
Glenogle Terr. Edin 93 D2
Glenorchy Rd. N Ber 54 A3
Glensburgh Rd. Gran 61 D3
Glenshiel Gr. Dunf 29 E1
Glenside Ct. Arm 143 F3
Glenside Ct. Gran 61 F3
Glenside Gdns. Arm 143 F3
Glentye Gdns. Falk 59 F1
Glenure Loan. Edin 91 E1
Glenvarloch Cres. Edin 155 D4
Glenview Cres. Ston 171 D1
Glenview Dr. Falk 59 F1
Glenview. Duni 36 A2
Glenview. Men 4 A3
Glenview. Peni 203 F3
Glenview Rd. Ston 171 D1
Glenwinnel Rd. Alva 4 C1
Glenwood Dr. Arm 143 E3
Glenyards Rd. Bon 58 A1
Gloag Pl. W Cal 172 B2
Globe Rd. Ros 46 B1
Gloucester La. Edin 93 D1
Gloucester Pl. Edin 93 D1
Gloucester Sq. Edin 93 D1
Gloucester St. Edin 93 D1
Glover's Ct. King 35 D2
Glowrorum Dr. Bank 57 F4
Glynwed Ct. Falk 60 B4
Godfrey Ave. Den 36 B1
Godfrey Cres. Lar 38 B1
Goff Ave. Edin 94 C1
Gogar Loan. B of A 3 E3
Gogar Pl. Stir 7 E1
Gogar Station Rd. Edin 121 D1
Gogar Station Rd. Kirkl 120 C2
Gogar Station Rd. Rat 120 C2
Gogarbank Farm. Rat 120 B1
Gogarloch Haugh. Edin 121 D3
Gogarloch Muir. Edin 121 D3
Gogarloch Rd. Edin 121 D3
Gogarloch Syke. Edin 121 D3
Gogarstone Rd. Kirkl 120 A3
Goldenacre Terr. Edin 93 D2
Goldenstones Ave. Dunb 78 C1
Golf Course Rd. Bonn 182 A4
Golf Course Rd. Cow 13 E3
Golf Course Rd. Liv 147 D4
Golf Ct. Aber 71 E2
Golf Dr. Cocke 97 F2
Golf House Rd. Dunb 78 C1
Golfdrum St. Dunf 28 C2
Goodall Cres. Dech 116 B1
Goodall Pl. Hadd 132 B4
Goodall's Pl. Hadd 132 B4
Goodman Pl. Madd 82 C4
Goose Green Ave. Muss 126 B4
Goose Green Cres. Muss ... 126 B4
Goose Green Pl. Muss 126 B4
Goose Green Rd. Gull 52 A1
Goose Green Rd. Muss 126 B4
Goosecroft Rd. Stir 7 D4
Gordon Ave. Bath 145 D3

Gordon Ave. Bonn 181 F3
Gordon Cres. B of A 2 A4
Gordon Cres. Stir 1 C1
Gordon Dr. All 10 B4
Gordon Loan. Edin 121 F4
Gordon Pl. Falk 59 F3
Gordon Rd. Edin 121 F4
Gordon Rd. Ros 46 A1
Gordon St. Cow 13 E3
Gordon St. Edin 94 A2
Gordon St. Loch 14 A4
Gordon St. May 183 E4
Gordon Terr. Dunf 29 D1
Gordon Way. Liv 147 E4
Gore Ave. Gore 207 E4
Goremire Rd. Car 230 B1
Gorgie Rd. Edin 122 B2
Gorrie St. Den 36 B1
Gorrie St. Dunf 29 E1
Gorsebank. Liv 147 F3
Gort Pl. Gran 61 E3
Gorton Loan. Rose 181 E1
Gorton Pl. Rose 181 E1
Gorton Rd. Rose 181 E1
Goschen Pl. Uph 117 D3
Goschen Terr. Uph 117 D3
Gosford Pl. Edin 93 E3
Gosford Rd. Cocke 97 E2
Gosford Rd. Kirk 16 B4
Gosford Rd. Long 98 C3
Gote La. Que 68 A1
Gourlay Cotts. Rose 205 D4
Gourlay St. Kirk 17 D2
Gourlaybank. Hadd 101 D1
Gow Cres. Kirk 17 D2
Gowan Ave. Falk 60 A3
Gowan La. Falk 60 A3
Gowanbank. Liv 147 E3
Gowanbrae Dr. Dunf 29 E2
Gowanbrae. Fau 193 F4
Gowanbrae Pl. Dunf 29 E2
Gowanbrae Terr. Dunf 29 E2
Gowanhill Gdns. Stir 1 C1
Gowanlea Dr. Slam 110 A3
Grace St. Loch 14 B4
Gracefield Ct. Muss 126 A3
Gracemount Ave. Edin 155 D3
Gracemount Dr. Edin 155 D3
Gracemount Pl. Edin 155 D3
Gracemount Rd. Edin 155 D3
Gracemount Sq. Edin 155 D3
Gracie Cres. Fall 8 B2
Gracie's Wynd. Arm 144 A3
Gradlon Pl. Falk 60 A4
Graeme Pl. Falk 59 F1
Graham Ave. Lar 38 A2
Graham Ave. Stir 2 B2
Graham Ct. Black 171 F4
Graham Ct. B of A 2 A4
Graham St. Edin 93 F3
Graham Terr. Air 22 B2
Graham Way. Liv 147 E4
Graham's Rd. Auch 204 B4
Grahams Rd. Falk 60 A3
Grahamsdyke Ave. B'ness .. 64 A4
Grahamsdyke Cres. Bon 58 A2
Grahamsdyke La. B'ness 64 A4
Grahamsdyke Rd. B'ness 64 B3
Grahamsdyke Rd. Bon 58 A2
Grahamsdyke Rd. Muir 64 B3
Grahamsdyke St. Laur 61 D2
Grahamsdyke Terr. B'ness .. 64 A4
Graiglaw Pl. Dech 116 B1
Graigleith View. Tull 4 B2
Grainger St. Loch 14 A4
Grampian Cres. Gran 61 F3
Grampian Ct. Ros 46 C1
Grampian Gdns. Kirk 16 C3
Grampian House. Edin 93 F3
Grampian Pl. Ros 46 C1
Grampian Rd. Ros 46 C1
Grampian Rd. Stir 6 C3
Grampion Ct. Muri 147 F1
Granary Rd. Falk 60 A4
Granary Sq. Falk 60 A4
Granby Ave. Liv 147 F2
Granby Rd. Edin 123 F2
Grandfield. Edin 93 E3
Grandville. Edin 93 E3
Grange Ave. Falk 60 B3
Grange Cotts. King 34 C3
Grange Cres E. Pres 96 C1
Grange Cres. Edin 123 E2
Grange Cres W. Pres 127 F4
Grange Dr. Dunf 46 B4
Grange Dr. Falk 60 B3
Grange Gdns. B of A 2 B4
Grange Gr. Pres 96 C1
Grange La. Gran 40 B1
Grange Loan. B'ness 64 A4
Grange Loan. Edin 123 E2
Grange Loan Gdns. Edin .. 123 E2
Grange Pl. Laur 61 E1
Grange Pl. Gran 61 E4
Grange Rd. All 9 F3
Grange Rd. B of A 2 B3

Grange Rd. Brox 117 F2
Grange Rd. Burn 33 E1
Grange Rd. Dunf 46 B3
Grange Rd. Edin 123 E3
Grange Rd. Liv 148 A4
Grange Rd. N Ber 54 A3
Grange Rd. Pol 61 F2
Grange Rd. Pres 96 C1
Grange Rd. Ros 46 B3
Grange Terr. B'ness 64 A4
Grange Terr. Edin 123 E2
Grange The. Pol 82 C4
Grange View. Lin 85 E4
Grangeburn Rd. Gran 40 C1
Grangemouth Rd. Falk 60 C3
Grangepans. B'ness 64 A4
Grangeview. Lar 38 C1
Grant Ave. Edin 153 D3
Grant St. All 9 F3
Grant St. W Cal 172 B2
Granton Cres. Edin 92 C3
Granton Gdns. Edin 92 C3
Granton Gr. Edin 92 C3
Granton Mains Ave. Edin .. 92 B3
Granton Mains Brae. Edin .. 92 B3
Granton Mains Ct. Edin 92 B3
Granton Mains Gait. Edin .. 92 B3
Granton Mains Vale. Edin .. 92 B3
Granton Mains Wynd. Edin . 92 B3
Granton Medway. Edin 92 C3
Granton Park Ave. Edin 92 C4
Granton Pl. Edin 92 C3
Granton Rd. Edin 93 D3
Granton Sq. Edin 92 C4
Granton Terr. Edin 92 C3
Granton View. D Bay 47 F1
Granton View. Edin 92 C3
Grants Bank. Dunf 29 D2
Grantully Pl. Edin 123 F2
Granville Terr. Edin 123 D3
Granville Way. Ros 46 C2
Grassmarket. Edin 123 E4
Gray Pk. Cow 13 E3
Gray Pl. Inver 47 E4
Gray St. Shot 192 A2
Gray's Loan. Edin 122 C2
Graystale Rd. Stir 7 D2
Graystonelee Rd. Shot 191 E3
Great Cannon Bank. Edin ... 95 D1
Great Carleton Sq. Edin 125 D2
Great Junction St. Edin 93 F3
Great King St. Edin 93 E1
Great Michael Cl. Edin 93 E4
Great Michael Rd. Ros 46 A1
Great Michael Rise. Edin 93 E3
Great Michael Sq. Edin 93 E4
Great Stuart St. Edin 93 D1
Great Stuart St. Edin 123 D4
Green Apron Pk. N Ber 54 A3
Green La. Bonn 181 F4
Green St. Dunf 29 E4
Green St. Edin 93 E1
Green The. Alva 5 D4
Green The. Bath 145 E4
Green The. Edin 91 F2
Green The. Pen 160 C3
Green Tree La. B' ness 63 E3
Greenacre Ct. Bann 7 F1
Greenacre Pl. Bann 7 F1
Greenbank Ave. Edin 123 D1
Greenbank Dr. Edin 123 D1
Greenbank Cres. Edin 154 A4
Greenbank Dr. Cow 13 D1
Greenbank Gdns. Edin 153 F4
Greenbank Gr. Edin 153 F4
Greenbank La. Edin 122 C1
Greenbank Loan. Edin 122 C1
Greenbank Pk. Edin 153 F4
Greenbank Pl. Edin 123 D1
Greenbank Rd. Edin 122 C1
Greenbank Rd. Falk 59 E2
Greenbank Rise. Edin 153 F4
Greenbank Row. Edin 153 F4
Greenbank Terr. Edin 123 D1
Greenburn Rd. Fau 193 F3
Greencraig Ave. Shi 81 E3
Greendykes Ave. Edin 124 C2
Greendykes Dr. Edin 124 C2
Greendykes Gdns. Edin 124 C2
Greendykes Loan. Edin 124 C2
Greendykes Rd. Brox 117 F3
Greendykes Rd. Edin 124 C1
Greendykes Terr. Edin 124 C2
Greenend Dr. Edin 155 E4
Greenend Gdns. Edin 155 E4
Greenend Gr. Edin 155 E4
Greenfield Cres. Bale 177 E4
Greenfield Rd. Bale 177 E4
Greenfield St. All 10 A4
Greenfield St. Bon 58 A3
Greenhall Rd. Gore 183 E1
Greenhead. Alva 5 D3
Greenheads Rd. N Ber 54 B2
Greenhill Ct. Fau 193 F3
Greenhill Gdns. Edin 123 D2
Greenhill Pk. Edin 123 D2

Greenhill Pk. Peni 203 E3
Greenhill Pl. Edin 123 D2
Greenhill Rd. Blac 142 C2
Greenhill Rd. Bon 58 A2
Greenhill Terr. Edin 123 D3
Greenhithe Terr. Madd 82 C4
Greenhorn's Well Ave. Falk 59 F2
Greenhorn's Well Cres. Falk 59 F2
Greenhorn's Well Dr. Falk .. 59 F2
Greenlaw Dr. Auch 180 A1
Greenlaw Hedge. Edin 153 F4
Greenlaw Rig. Edin 153 F4
Greenloanings. Kirk 16 B4
Greenmantle Loan. Edin 124 A1
Greenmount. Cow 13 D1
Greenmount Dr. Burn 33 F1
Greenmount Dr. Shi 81 E3
Greenmount Rd N. Burn 33 F1
Greenmount Rd S. Burn 34 A1
Greenpark Dr. Pol 61 F1
Greenrigg Cotts. Hart 169 D3
Greenside La. Edin 93 F1
Greenside Pl. Edin 93 F1
Greenside Pl. Rose 181 E1
Greenside Row. Edin 93 F1
Greenside. Torp 113 F3
Greenvale Dr. Pol 82 C4
Greenville Ct. Falk 59 F2
Greenwell St. Fau 193 F3
Greenwell Terr. Madd 82 C4
Greenwells Dr. Madd 82 C4
Greenwood Ave. Stir 7 D4
Greenwood Pk. Liv 147 E3
Greenwood St. Shot 191 F4
Gregory Rd. Liv 147 D1
Gregory Rd. W Cal 173 D4
Greig Cres. Arm 144 A3
Greig Pl. Loch 14 A4
Greig Rd. Ros 46 A1
Grendon Ct. Stir 7 D3
Grendon Gdns. Stir 7 D3
Grey Craigs. Crossf 27 E1
Grey School Cnr. Pres 96 C1
Greyfriar's Wlk. Inver 47 E2
Greyfriars. Edin 123 E4
Greygoran. N Sau 5 E1
Grierson Ave. Edin 93 D3
Grierson Cres. Cam 6 C3
Grierson Cres. Edin 93 D3
Grierson Gdns. Edin 93 D3
Grierson Rd. Edin 92 C3
Grierson Sq. Edin 93 D3
Grierson Villas. Edin 93 D3
Grieve Ct. Auch 203 F4
Grieve St. Dunf 28 C2
Grieve St. Kirk 17 D3
Griffith Dr. Whit 170 A3
Griffiths St. Falk 60 A2
Grigor Ave. Edin 92 B2
Grigor Dr. Edin 92 B2
Grigor Gdns. Edin 92 C2
Grigor Terr. Edin 92 B2
Grindlay St. Edin 123 D4
Grindlay Street Ct. Edin 123 D4
Groathill Ave. Edin 92 B1
Groathill Gdns E. Edin 92 B1
Groathill Gdns W. Edin 92 B1
Groathill Rd N. Edin 92 B2
Groathill Rd S. Edin 92 B1
Grodwell Dr. Alva 4 C4
Grosvenor Gdns. Edin 122 C4
Grosvenor St. Edin 123 D4
Grove End. Bonn 182 A4
Grove St. Den 36 B1
Grove St. Edin 123 D4
Grove St. Muss 126 B3
Grove The. Muss 126 C3
Grundie's Well Rd. Edin 155 F3
Guardians Wood. Edin 122 B4
Guildhall St. Dunf 29 F2
Guildie Howes Rd. N Mid .. 207 F1
Guildiehaugh Roundabout.
  Bath 145 E2
Guildry Gr. Dunf 29 F2
Gullan's Cl. Edin 123 F4
Gunn Rd. Gran 61 E3
Gunner Rd. Gran 62 B4
Guthrie St. Edin 123 E4
Guttergates Rd. Hal 30 A3
Gyle Park Gdns. Edin 121 D3
Gylemuir Rd. Edin 121 E3
Gylers Rd. Dir 53 D2

Haddington Pl. Edin 93 F1
Haddington Rd. E Lin 103 E4
Haddington Rd. Muss 127 D3
Haddington Rd. N Ber 54 B3
Haddington Rd. Tran 128 C3
Haddington Station Ind Est.
  Hadd 131 F4
Haddon's Ct. Edin 123 F4
Haddow Gr. Burn 50 C4
Hadfast Rd. Path 158 B3
Hadrian Way. B'ness 64 A3
Haig Ave. Kirk 17 E4
Haig Ave. Stir 2 A1
Haig Cres. Bath 145 E3

Haig Cres. Dunf 29 E3
Haig St. Gran 61 E3
Hailes App. Edin 153 D4
Hailes Ave. Edin 153 D4
Hailes Bank. Edin 153 D4
Hailes Cres. Edin 153 D4
Hailes Gdns. Edin 153 D4
Hailes Gr. Edin 153 D4
Hailes Loan. E Lin 103 D2
Hailes Pk. Edin 152 C4
Hailes Pl. Dunf 29 E2
Hailes St. Edin 123 D3
Hailes Terr. Edin 153 D4
Hailesland Gdns. Edin 121 F1
Hailesland Gr. Edin 121 F1
Hailesland Pk. Edin 121 F1
Hailesland Pl. Edin 121 F1
Hailesland Rd. Edin 121 F1
Hailstonegreen. For 215 D1
Hailstones Cres. Arm 143 F3
Hainburn Pk. Edin 153 F3
Haining Pl. Gran 61 F4
Haining Rd. Madd 83 F3
Haining Terr. Madd 83 F3
Hakness Cres. Tran 128 B3
Halbeath Dr. Dunf 29 F3
Halbeath Pl. Dunf 29 F3
Halbeath Rd. Dunf 29 F3
Halbeath Rd. Hal 30 A3
Halberts Cres. Stir 7 D1
Haldane Ave. B of A 2 A3
Haldane Ave. Hadd 100 C1
Haldane Gr. Bla 26 B4
Haldane Sq. Muri 173 E3
Halketshall. Lime 45 E2
Halkett Cres. Dunf 29 E1
Hall Cres. Gull 52 A1
Hall La. Loch 14 A4
Hall Rd. Brox 117 F3
Hall Row. Lime 45 D2
Hall St. Cow 13 E2
Hall St. Loch 14 A4
Hallcroft Cl. Rat 119 E1
Hallcroft Cres. Rat 119 E1
Hallcroft Gdns. Rat 119 E1
Hallcroft Gn. Rat 119 E1
Hallcroft Neuk. Rat 119 E1
Hallcroft Pk. Rat 119 E1
Hallcroft Rise. Rat 119 E1
Hallglen Rd. Falk 60 A1
Hallglen Terr. Falk 60 A1
Hallhead Rd. Edin 123 F1
Hallhill. Dunb 106 B4
Halliburton Terr. Dir 53 D2
Hallows The. Kirk 17 F4
Hallpark. N Sau 10 B4
Hallyards Rd. Kirkl 119 D4
Hallyards Rd. Kirkl 119 E3
Halmyre St. Edin 94 A2
Halyard Terr. Aucht 15 D1
Hamburgh Pl. Edin 93 F3
Hamilton Ave. Lin 84 C3
Hamilton Ave. Sten 38 C2
Hamilton Cres. Gull 52 A1
Hamilton Cres. Madd 82 C3
Hamilton Cres. Newt 183 D3
Hamilton Dr. Edin 124 C4
Hamilton Dr. Falk 60 A2
Hamilton Dr. Stir 2 B2
Hamilton Dr W. Edin 124 C4
Hamilton Gdns. Edin 124 C4
Hamilton Gr. Edin 124 C4
Hamilton La. B' ness 63 F4
Hamilton La. Bath 144 C4
Hamilton Pk. Edin 124 C4
Hamilton Pk. Lin 84 C3
Hamilton Pl. Edin 93 D1
Hamilton Pl. Lin 84 C3
Hamilton Pl. Ros 46 C2
Hamilton Rd. Bath 144 C4
Hamilton Rd. Gran 61 F3
Hamilton Rd. Gull 52 A1
Hamilton Rd. N Ber 54 A4
Hamilton Rd. Sten 38 B3
Hamilton Sq. B' ness 63 E3
Hamilton St. Falk 59 E3
Hamilton St. Loch 14 A3
Hamilton Terr. Edin 125 D4
Hamilton Terr. H Val 26 A1
Hamilton Terr. Inver 47 E1
Hamilton Wynd. Edin 93 F3
Handax. For 215 D1
Haney's Way. B'ness 64 A4
Hanover Ct. Brox 117 F3
Hanover Ct. Liv 147 D2
Hanover Grange. Gran 61 E4
Hanover St. Edin 93 E1
Harbour Dr. D Bay 47 F2
Harbour Pl. Burn 50 C4
Harbour Pl. D Bay 47 F1
Harbour Pl. Edin 95 D1
Harbour Pl. Inver 47 E1
Harbour Rd. B'ness 64 A4
Harbour Rd. Edin 95 D1
Harbour Rd. King 35 D1
Harbour Rd. Muss 126 A3
Harburn Ave. Liv 146 C3
Harburn Ave W. Liv 146 C4

Harburn Dr. W Cal 172 C2
Harburn Gdns. W Cal 172 C2
Harburn La. W Cal 172 C2
Harburn Rd. W Cal 172 C2
Harcourt Rd. Kirk 17 D3
Harden Pl. Edin 122 C3
Hardengreen Ind Est. Dalk 156 C1
Hardengreen Junc. Dalk 182 C4
Hardgate. Hadd 101 D1
Hardhill Dr. Bath 144 C3
Hardhill Pl. Arm 144 A3
Hardhill Rd. Bath 144 C3
Hardhill Terr. Bath 144 C3
Hardie Cres. Fall 8 B2
Hardie Ct. Stir 7 E2
Hardie Rd. Bog 146 B4
Hardie Rd. Liv 146 C4
Hardie Terr. E Lin 103 E4
Hardwell Cl. Edin 123 F4
Hardy Gdns. Bog 145 F3
Hareburn Ave. Avon 112 A3
Harelaw Rd. Edin 153 D3
Hares Cl. Cocke 97 E2
Harestanes Rd. Arm 143 F2
Harewood Cres. Edin 124 C2
Harewood Dr. Edin 124 C2
Harewood Rd. Edin 124 C2
Harkenburn Garders. Peni 203 E3
Harlaw Gr. Peni 203 E3
Harlaw Hill. Pres 96 C1
Harlaw March. Bale 177 E4
Harlaw Rd. Bale 177 F4
Harlaw Rd. Curr 152 B2
Harlawhill Gdns. Pres 97 D1
Harley Ct. Falk 60 A4
Harley St. Ros 47 D2
Harlington Pl. Madd 82 C4
Harpenside Cres. Dir 53 E3
Harper's Brae. Auch 204 A3
Harperdean Terr. Hadd 100 C1
Harriebrae Pk. Dunf 28 C2
Harriet St. Kirk 17 F3
Harris Ct. All 10 A3
Harris Dr. Kirk 16 C4
Harris Pl. Dunf 29 E1
Harris Pl. Gran 61 E3
Harrison Gdns. Edin 122 C2
Harrison La. Edin 122 C3
Harrison Pl. Edin 122 C2
Harrison Pl. Falk 59 F3
Harrison Rd. Edin 122 C3
Harrysmuir Cres. Pump 148 A4
Harrysmuir N. Pump 148 A4
Harrysmuir Rd. Pump 148 A4
Harrysmuir S. Pump 148 A4
Harrysmuir Terr. Pump 148 A4
Hart St. Edin 93 E1
Hart Street La. Edin 93 E1
Hart Wynd. Bann 7 F1
Hartfield Terr. Alla 212 A4
Harthill Rd. Blac 142 C1
Harthill Rd. Fau 193 E3
Hartington Gdns. Edin 123 D3
Hartington Pl. Edin 123 D3
Hartley Pl. Gran 61 D3
Hartwood Gdns. Shot 191 D1
Hartwood Rd. Shot 191 D2
Hartwood Rd. W Cal 172 A2
Harvest Dr. Kirkl 119 D3
Harvest Rd. Kirkl 119 D3
Harvey Ave. Pol 61 F1
Harvey Wynd. Stir 2 A1
Harvieston Villas. Gore 207 E4
Hatfield Pl. Bath 145 D4
Hatton Pl. Edin 123 E3
Haugh Gdns. Falk 39 D1
Haugh Park. Edin 122 A1
Haugh Park. Edin 122 A1
Haugh Rd. Burn 50 B4
Haugh Rd. Stir 2 A1
Haugh St. Edin 93 D1
Haugh St. Falk 39 D1
Haven The. D Bay 47 F1
Haven's Edge. Lime 45 F2
Hawes Brae. Dal 68 B1
Hawk Brae. Liv 147 E3
Hawkcraig Rd. Abe 49 E4
Hawkhead Cres. Edin 155 D4
Hawkhead Gr. Edin 155 D4
Hawkhill Ave. Edin 94 A2
Hawkhill Rd. All 10 B3
Hawkhill Rd. Kin 23 E4
Hawkins Terr. Auch 204 A4
Hawkwood Terr. For 215 D1
Hawley Rd. Falk 60 B2
Hawthorn Bank. Oak 27 E3
Hawthorn Bank. Que 68 A1
Hawthorn Cres. Cow 12 C1
Hawthorn Cres. Fall 8 B2
Hawthorn Cres. May 183 E4
Hawthorn Cres. Stir 1 C1
Hawthorn Dr. Duni 36 B2
Hawthorn Dr. East 168 C3
Hawthorn Dr. Falk 59 F2
Hawthorn Dr. Fall 8 B2
Hawthorn Dr. Shot 192 B2
Hawthorn Gdns. Loan 155 D3
Hawthorn Pl. Alla 212 A4

Entry	Page	Grid
Hawthorn Pl. Edin	155	F3
Hawthorn Pl. Orm	159	E4
Hawthorn Pl. Uph	116	C2
Hawthorn Rd. Pres	97	D1
Hawthorn St. Gran	61	E3
Hawthorn Terr. Cocke	97	D2
Hawthornbank La. Edin	123	D4
Hawthornbank Pl. Edin	93	E3
Hawthornbank Rd. Hadd	100	C1
Hawthornbank Terr. Edin	93	F3
Hawthornden Ave. Bonn	182	A4
Hawthornden Gdns. Bonn	182	A4
Hawthorne Pl. Lar	38	B1
Hawthorns The. Gull	52	A2
Hawthornvale. Edin	93	E3
Hay Ave. Edin	124	C2
Hay Dr. Edin	125	D2
Hay Gr. Dunf	29	F1
Hay Pl. Edin	124	C2
Hay Rd. Edin	124	C2
Hay Terr. Edin	124	C2
Hayfield. Edin	121	D4
Hayfield. Falk	60	B4
Hayfield Rd. Kirk	17	E4
Hayfield Terr. Bank	57	F4
Haygate Ave. Pol	82	C4
Haymaker. Edin	123	D4
Haymarket Terr. Edin	122	C4
Haypark Rd. Bank	57	E3
Hayworth Ave. Laur	61	D2
Hazel Ave. Kirk	17	D3
Hazel Cres. Duni	36	B2
Hazel Ct. Dunb	78	A1
Hazel Dr. Bonn	182	A3
Hazel Gr. Dunf	46	C4
Hazel Gr. Falk	60	B4
Hazel Gr. Liv	148	A3
Hazel La. Loan	180	C4
Hazel Rd. Gran	61	E3
Hazelbank Gdns. Stir	2	A1
Hazelbank Terr. Edin	122	C2
Hazeldean Ave. B'ness	63	E3
Hazeldean Terr. Edin	124	A1
Hazelhurst. Pol	82	C4
Hazelwood Gr. Edin	124	B1
Headlesscross Rd. Shot	192	C1
Headrig Rd. New	67	E1
Headrigg Row. Edin	124	A1
Headwell Ave. Dunf	29	D3
Headwell Rd. Dunf	29	D3
Heaney Ave. Pump	148	A4
Heath Rd. Ros	46	C2
Heather Ave. Shi	81	E3
Heather Gr. Dunf	46	C4
Heather Gr. Madd	83	D3
Heather Pk. Black	146	A1
Heatherbank. Liv	147	E3
Heatherdale Gdns. Bank	57	F4
Heathervale Wlk. Arm	144	A3
Heatherwood Pk. Pump	148	A4
Hedge Row. Loan	180	C4
Hedges The. Falk	59	F3
Heggie's Wynd. Kirk	17	D1
Heights Rd. Blac	142	B2
Helen Pl. Inver	68	B3
Helmsdale Pk. Dunf	28	C1
Henderland Rd. Edin	122	B4
Henderson Ave. All	10	A4
Henderson Cres. Uph	117	D3
Henderson Ct. E Cal	148	C2
Henderson Gdns. Edin	93	F3
Henderson Gdns. Tran	128	B3
Henderson Pl. Alva	5	D4
Henderson Pl. Edin	93	E1
Henderson Pl. Uph	117	D3
Henderson Place La. Edin	93	D1
Henderson Row. Edin	93	D1
Henderson St. B of A	2	A4
Henderson St. Edin	93	F3
Henderson St. Hal	12	A1
Henderson St. Loch	14	A4
Henderson Terr. Edin	122	C3
Hendry Cres. Kirk	17	D3
Hendry Rd. Kirk	17	D3
Hendry St. Falk	60	A4
Hendry's Wynd. Kirk	17	D1
Hennings The. N Sau	5	E1
Henry Ross Pl. Que	68	A1
Henry St. Alva	5	D3
Henry St. B'ness	64	A3
Henry St. Gran	61	F4
Henryson Rd. Dunf	29	F2
Hens Nest Rd. Ston	170	C3
Hepburn Dr. Dalk	157	E1
Hepburn Rd. Hadd	101	D1
Herald Rise. Muri	147	F1
Herbertshire St. Den	36	C1
Hercus Loan. Muss	126	A3
Herd Gn. Liv	147	D4
Herd Terr. Loan	181	D4
Herdmanflatt. Hadd	101	D1
Herdshill Ave. Shi	81	E3
Heriot Bridge. Edin	123	E4
Heriot Gdns. Burn	33	F1
Heriot Hill Terr. Edin	93	E2
Heriot Pl. Edin	123	E4
Heriot Row. Edin	93	E1
Heriot St. Inver	47	E1
Heriot Way. Stow	228	B1
Heritage Dr. Sten	39	D2
Hermand Cres. Edin	122	C2
Hermand St. Edin	122	B2
Hermand Terr. Edin	122	B2
Hermiston House Rd. Rat	120	C1
Hermitage Dr. Edin	123	D1
Hermitage Gdns. Edin	123	D1
Hermitage Park Gr. Edin	94	A2
Hermitage Park S. Edin	94	A2
Hermitage Pk. Edin	94	A2
Hermitage Pl. Edin	94	A2
Hermitage Rd. B of A	2	C3
Hermitage Terr. Edin	123	D1
Heron Ind Comlex. Liv	146	B4
Hervey St. All	10	A4
Heugh Brae. N Ber	54	C3
Heugh Rd. N Ber	54	C3
Heugh St. Falk	60	A2
Heugh The. Tran	128	B4
Heyford Pl. Cam	6	B3
Higginson Loan. May	183	F3
High Academy Gr. Arm	143	F3
High Academy St. Arm	143	F3
High Beveridgewell. Dunf	28	C3
High Brae. Torp	113	F3
High Buckstone. Edin	154	B3
High Meadow. Car	230	B1
High Mill Rd. Car	230	A1
High Park Rise. Peni	203	F2
High Port. Lin	85	D4
High Rd. E Lin	106	B2
High Rd. Madd	83	D3
High Rd. Rose	204	C3
High Riggs. Edin	123	D4
High School Yards. Edin	123	F4
High St. Abe	49	D4
High St. Aber	71	E2
High St. Air	22	B2
High St. All	10	A3
High St. Bath	145	D4
High St. Bon	58	A3
High St. Bonn	156	A1
High St. Bonn	182	A4
High St. Burn	50	C4
High St. Clack	10	C2
High St. Cocke	97	E2
High St. Cow	13	E2
High St. Dalk	157	D2
High St. Dunb	78	A1
High St. Dunb	78	B1
High St. Dunf	29	D2
High St. E Lin	103	E4
High St. Edin	123	E4
High St. Falk	60	A2
High St. Giff	163	F2
High St. Hadd	132	A4
High St. Inver	47	D1
High St. Kin	23	F2
High St. King	34	C1
High St. Kirk	17	E2
High St. Kirk	18	A4
High St. Kirkl	89	D1
High St. Lin	85	D4
High St. Loan	181	E4
High St. Loch	14	A4
High St. Muss	126	B3
High St. N Ber	54	B4
High St. Orm	159	F4
High St. Peni	203	F2
High St. Pres	96	C1
High St. Que	68	B1
High St. Shot	191	F2
High St. Slam	110	A4
High St. Tran	128	B3
High Station Rd. Falk	60	A2
High View Gr. Shi	81	E3
Highfield Ave. Lin	84	C4
Highfield Cres. Lin	84	C4
Highfield. E Lin	54	A2
Highfield. Liv	147	D2
Highfield Rd. N Ber	54	A3
Highland Dr. Lar	38	B2
Highland Dykes Cres. Bon	58	A3
Highland Dykes Dr. Bon	58	A3
Highlea Circ. Bale	177	D4
Highlea Gr. Bale	177	D4
Hill Cres. Bath	145	D4
Hill Gr. Bla	26	B4
Hill House Rd. Bank	57	F4
Hill Pl. All	10	A4
Hill Pl. Edin	123	F4
Hill Pl. Kirk	17	E2
Hill Pl. May	183	F3
Hill Pl. Shot	191	F3
Hill Rd. East	168	B3
Hill Rd. Gull	51	F1
Hill Rd. Path	185	D3
Hill Sq. Edin	123	F4
Hill St. All	10	A4
Hill St. Cow	13	E2
Hill St. Dunf	29	D2
Hill St. Edin	93	E1
Hill St. Inver	47	D1
Hill St. Kirk	17	D2
Hill St. Kirk	18	A4
Hill St. Stir	7	D2
Hill Street La N. Edin	93	E1
Hill Street La S. Edin	93	E1
Hill View. Peni	204	A3
Hillary Rd. Lar	38	C1
Hillbank. Inver	47	D2
Hillcoat Loan. Edin	95	D1
Hillcoat Pl. Edin	95	D1
Hillcrest Ave. Kirk	16	C3
Hillcrest. B'ness	63	F3
Hillcrest. Cow	13	D2
Hillcrest Dr. All	10	B3
Hillcrest Pl. Bank	57	E4
Hillcrest Rd. Falk	59	F1
Hillend Rd. Inver	47	E2
Hillfield Rd. Inver	47	D1
Hillfoot Terr. Car	230	A1
Hillfoots Rd. B of A	2	C2
Hillhead Ave. Car	230	A1
Hillhead Dr. Falk	59	F1
Hillhouse Ave. Bath	144	C4
Hillhouse Cres. Kir	149	F2
Hillhouse Rd. Edin	92	A1
Hillhouse Terr. Kir	149	F2
Hillouseridge Rd. Shot	191	E3
Hillock Ave. Laur	61	E1
Hillpark Ave. Edin	91	F2
Hillpark Brae. Edin	91	F1
Hillpark Cres. Bann	7	E1
Hillpark Cres. Edin	91	F1
Hillpark Ct. Edin	91	F2
Hillpark Dr. Bann	7	E1
Hillpark Dr. Edin	91	F2
Hillpark Gdns. Edin	91	F1
Hillpark Gn. Edin	91	F1
Hillpark Gr. Edin	91	F1
Hillpark Loan. Edin	92	A1
Hillpark Rd. Edin	91	F1
Hillpark Terr. Edin	91	F1
Hillpark Way. Edin	92	A1
Hillpark Wood. Edin	92	A1
Hillside Ave. D Bay	48	A2
Hillside Camp Rd. Ros	46	C1
Hillside Cres. Edin	93	F1
Hillside Cres N. Gore	207	E4
Hillside Cres S. Gore	207	E4
Hillside Dr. Blac	142	B2
Hillside. N Sau	5	E1
Hillside Pl. Blac	142	B2
Hillside Pl. Fau	170	B1
Hillside Rd. Dal	90	B2
Hillside St. Edin	93	F1
Hillside Terr. All	10	A4
Hillside Terr. Dal	90	B3
Hillside Terr. Laur	61	D2
Hillview Ave. Brox	117	F3
Hillview Cotts. Rat	119	E1
Hillview. Cow	13	D2
Hillview Cres. Cross	30	C3
Hillview Cres. Edin	121	E4
Hillview Dr. B of A	2	A3
Hillview Dr. Edin	121	E4
Hillview. Edin	92	A1
Hillview. Fau	193	F3
Hillview. Oak	26	C4
Hillview Pl. Brox	117	F3
Hillview Pl. Cross	30	C3
Hillview Pl. Fall	8	B2
Hillview Rd. Bon	58	B2
Hillview Rd. Edin	121	E4
Hillview Rd. Lar	38	B2
Hillview Rd. Orm	159	F4
Hillview Rd. Pol	82	B4
Hillview Terr. All	10	B3
Hillview Terr. Edin	121	E4
Hillwood Ave. Kirkl	119	E3
Hillwood Cres. Kirkl	119	E3
Hillwood Gdns. Kirkl	119	E3
Hillwood Rd. Kirkl	119	E3
Hillwood Rise. Kirkl	119	E3
Hillwood Terr. Kirkl	119	E3
Hillwood Terr. Ros	47	D2
Hilton. Cowie	20	C4
Hilton Cres. All	10	B4
Hilton Ct. Hadd	132	A4
Hilton Rd. All	10	B4
Hilton Rd. Crossf	27	F1
Hilton Rd. Ros	46	B1
Hilton Terr. Fall	8	B2
Hilton View. Loch	13	F3
Hirst Cairns. Shot	191	E3
Hirst Rd. East	167	E2
Hirst Rd. Sals	167	E2
Hirstrigg Cotts. Sals	167	D2
Hoban Sq. Brox	117	F3
Hobart St. Liv	148	A3
Hodge St. Falk	60	A2
Hogarth Ave. Gore	183	E1
Hoggan Cres. Dunf	29	E1
Hoghill Ct. E Cal	148	C2
Hoghill Pl. E Cal	148	C2
Hoghill Rd. E Cal	148	C2
Holborn Pl. Ros	46	C3
Holbourne Pl. Men	4	A4
Holden Way. D Bay	48	A3
Holly Ave. Sten	38	C2
Holly Bank. May	183	F4
Holly Cres. Dunf	46	C4
Holly Pl. Kirk	17	E4
Holly Terr. Bonn	182	A3
Holly Wlk. Loan	180	C4
Hollybank Pl. E Cal	148	C1
Hollybank Terr. Edin	122	C2
Holmes Farm La. Uph	117	D3
Holmes Holdings. Brox	117	E2
Holmes Rd. Uph	117	D2
Holmlea Ave. Pol	82	B4
Holton Cres. N Sau	5	E1
Holton Sq. N Sau	5	E1
Holygate Pl. Brox	117	E3
Holyrood Park Rd. Edin	123	F3
Holyrood Pl. Dunf	29	D2
Holyrood Pl. Sten	38	C2
Holyrood Rd. Edin	123	F4
Home Farm Cotts. Den	57	F3
Home Pk. Abe	49	E4
Home St. Edin	123	D3
Homesteads The. Stir	6	B4
Honeybank Cres. Car	230	A2
Honeyman Ct. Arm	143	F4
Hookney Terr. Den	36	B1
Hope Cotts. Muir	64	B3
Hope La. Edin	125	D4
Hope Park Cres. Edin	123	F3
Hope Park Terr. Edin	123	F3
Hope Pk. Cres. Hadd	101	D1
Hope Pk Gdns. Bath	144	C3
Hope Pk. Hadd	101	D1
Hope Pl. Muss	126	C3
Hope St. B'ness	63	F4
Hope St. Car	230	A1
Hope St. Edin	123	D4
Hope St. Falk	60	A3
Hope St. Inver	47	D1
Hope St. Loch	13	F3
Hope St. Que	89	D4
Hope St. Stir	1	C1
Hope Street La. Edin	123	D4
Hope Terr. Edin	123	E2
Hopefield Dr. Black	171	E4
Hopefield Pk. Bonn	182	A3
Hopefield Pl. Black	171	E4
Hopefield Pl. Bonn	182	A3
Hopefield Rd. Black	171	E4
Hopefield Terr. Bonn	182	A3
Hopefield Terr. Edin	93	F3
Hopelands Rd. Peni	202	C3
Hopepark. Bath	144	C3
Hopepark Terr. Bon	57	F3
Hopetoun Cres. Edin	93	F1
Hopetoun Crescent La. Edin	93	F1
Hopetoun Dr. B of A	2	A1
Hopetoun La. Bath	145	D3
Hopetoun Mews. Hadd	101	D1
Hopetoun Pl. Kirk	16	B3
Hopetoun Rd. Que	68	A1
Hopetoun Rd. Ros	46	B1
Hopetoun St. Bath	145	D3
Hopetoun St. Edin	93	F2
Hopetoun Terr. Gull	52	A2
Hopetoun Terr. Orm	159	F4
Hopetoune View. D Bay	48	B2
Hopeward Ct. D Bay	48	B2
Hopeward Mews. D Bay	48	B1
Hoprig Pk. Cock	140	C1
Hoprig Rd. Cock	140	C1
Hornbeam Cres. Laur	61	D2
Horne Terr. Edin	123	D3
Horsburgh Bank. Bale	151	E2
Horsburgh Gdns. Bale	151	E2
Horsburgh Gr. Bale	151	E2
Horse Wynd. Edin	123	F4
Hoseason Gdns. Edin	91	E1
Hosie Rigg. Edin	125	D3
Hospital Hill. Dunf	29	D1
Hospital Interchange. Liv	147	E4
Hospital Rd. Hadd	100	C1
Hot Pot Wynd. Kirk	18	A3
Houldsworth Cotts. Alla	212	A4
Houldsworth St. Bla	26	A4
Houliston Ave. Inver	47	D2
House O' Muir Rd. Sals	167	D2
House O'Hill Ave. Edin	92	A2
House O'Hill Brae. Edin	92	A2
House O'Hill Cres. Edin	92	A2
House O'Hill Gdns. Edin	92	A2
House O'Hill Gn. Edin	92	A2
House O'Hill Gr. Edin	92	A2
House O'Hill Pl. Edin	92	A2
House O'Hill Rd. Edin	92	A2
House O'Hill Row. Edin	92	A2
House O'Hill Terr. Edin	92	A1
Houston Ct. Dunf	28	C2
Houston Rd. Pump	117	D1
Houstoun Gdns. Uph	116	C2
Houstoun Interchange. Liv	147	F4
Houstoun Rd. Liv	147	F3
Howard Cres. Dunf	29	E1
Howard Pl. Edin	93	E2
Howard Pl. Kirk	18	A4
Howard St. Edin	93	E2
Howard St. Falk	59	F2
Howburn Cres. East	168	C3
Howburn Rd. East	168	B3
Howden East Rd. Liv	147	F2
Howden Hall Cres. Edin	154	C3
Howden Hall Ct. Edin	154	C3
Howden Hall Dr. Edin	154	C3
Howden Hall Gdns. Edin	155	C3
Howden Hall Loan. Edin	154	C3
Howden Hall Pk. Edin	154	C3
Howden Hall Rd. Edin	155	D3
Howden Hall Way. Edin	155	D3
Howden South Rd. Liv	147	F2
Howden South Rd. Muri	147	F2
Howden St. Edin	123	F3
Howden West Rd. Liv	147	E2
Howe Pk. Edin	153	F3
Howe St. Edin	93	E1
Howetown. Fish	5	E2
Howie's Pl. Falk	59	D2
Howieson Ave. B'ness	63	F3
Howieson Gn. Uph	116	C2
Howlands Rd. Stir	7	D2
Howley Ave. Liv	147	F2
Hudson Rd. Ros	46	C2
Hugh Miller Pl. Edin	93	D1
Hugh Pl. Loch	14	A4
Hugh Russell Pl. Que	89	D4
Hughes Cres. May	183	F3
Humbie Rd. Kirkl	89	D1
Humbie Terr. Abe	49	E4
Hume Cres. B of A	2	A3
Hume Ct. B of A	2	A3
Hummel Rd. Gull	51	F1
Hungerage Sq. Tran	128	B3
Hunt Cl. Dalk	157	D2
Hunt Pl. Crossf	28	A1
Huntburn Ave. Lin	85	E4
Hunter Ave. Loan	181	E4
Hunter Ct. Loan	181	E4
Hunter Gdns. Brox	118	A3
Hunter Gdns. Den	36	B1
Hunter Gr. Bog	145	F3
Hunter Gr. Whit	169	F3
Hunter Pl. Dunf	28	C3
Hunter Pl. Kirk	17	D2
Hunter Pl. Shot	191	F3
Hunter Pl. Sten	39	D2
Hunter Rd. Liv	147	E1
Hunter Sq. Edin	123	E4
Hunter Sq. Gore	207	E4
Hunter St. Kirk	17	D2
Hunter St. Shot	191	E3
Hunter Terr. Bonn	182	A4
Hunter Terr. Loan	181	E4
Hunter's Cl. Edin	123	E4
Hunter's La. Whit	170	A3
Hunterfield Ct. Gore	207	E4
Hunterfield Pk. Gore	183	E1
Hunterfield Rd. Gore	207	E4
Hunterfield Terr. Gore	183	D1
Hunters Hill. Peni	203	E3
Huntlaw Rd. Pen	160	C3
Huntley Cres. Stir	1	C1
Huntly Ave. Liv	146	C3
Huntly Cres. Kirk	16	B4
Huntly St. Edin	93	E2
Huntly Terr. Shot	192	A2
Huron Ave. Liv	147	F2
Hursted Ave. May	183	E4
Hurworth St. Falk	59	F2
Husband Pl. Dunf	29	F1
Hutchison Ave. Edin	122	B2
Hutchison Cotts. Edin	122	B2
Hutchison Crossway. Edin	122	B2
Hutchison Gdns. Edin	122	B2
Hutchison Loan. Edin	122	B2
Hutchison Medway. Edin	122	B2
Hutchison Pk. Edin	122	B2
Hutchison Pl. Edin	122	B2
Hutchison Rd. Edin	122	B2
Hutchison Terr. Edin	122	B2
Hutchison View. Edin	122	B2
Hutton Pk. All	10	B4
Hutton Sq. Muri	173	E3
Hyndshaw Rd. Car	230	A2
Hyvot Ave. Edin	155	E3
Hyvot Bank Ave. Edin	155	E3
Hyvot Ct. Edin	155	E3
Hyvot Gdns. Edin	155	E3
Hyvot Gn. Edin	155	E3
Hyvot Gr. Edin	155	E3
Hyvot Loan. Edin	155	E3
Hyvot Pk. Edin	155	E3
Hyvot Terr. Edin	155	E3
Hyvot View. Edin	155	E3
Ibris Pl. N Ber	54	A4
Icehouse Brae. Laur	61	D2
Implement Rd. Dunb	77	F2
Imrie Pl. Peni	203	F3
Inch Ave. Abe	49	D3
Inch Cres. Bog	145	E3
Inch View. King	34	C1
Inchcolm Dr. Inver	68	A3
Inchcolm Rd. Dunf	29	F2
Inchcolm Terr. Que	89	D4
Inchcorse Pl. Black	145	E1
Inches The. D Bay	48	A1
Inchgarvie Cres. Dunf	29	F2

Inchgarvie Pk. Que 68 A1
Inchgarvie Rd. Kirk 16 C4
Inchkeith Ave. Que 89 E4
Inchkeith Dr. Dunf 29 F2
Inchkeith Pl. Falk 60 A1
Inchmickery Ave. D Bay 48 B3
Inchmickery Rd. D Bay 48 B3
Inchna. Men 4 A3
Inchview Cres. Muss 127 E3
Inchview Gdns. D Bay 48 A2
Inchview N. Pres 96 C1
Inchview. Pres 96 C1
Inchview Rd. Muss 127 E3
Inchview Terr. Edin 94 C1
Inchyra Rd. Gran 61 F3
India Pl. Edin 93 D1
India St. Edin 93 D1
Industrial Rd. Edin 94 A2
Industry La. Edin 93 F3
Infirmary St. Edin 123 F4
Ingleston Ave. Duni 36 B2
Inglewood. All 9 F4
Inglewood Pl. Edin 155 D4
Inglewood Rd. All 9 F4
Inglewood St. Liv 147 F3
Inglis Ave. Cocke 97 E2
Inglis Cres. King 34 C2
Inglis' Ct. Edin 123 E4
Inglis Gn Rd. Edin 122 A1
Inglis Pl. Pol 82 C4
Inglis St. Dunf 29 D2
Inkerman Ct. Auch 204 A4
Inn Pl. Liv 147 D1
Innerpeffray Dr. Sten 39 D2
Institution St. Kirk 17 F4
Inver Ct. Falk 39 E1
Inverallan Ct. B of A 1 C4
Inverallan Dr. B of A 1 C4
Inverallan Rd. B of A 1 C4
Inveralmond Dr. Edin 91 D3
Inveralmond Gdns. Edin 91 D3
Inveralmond Gr. Edin 91 D3
Inverary Dr. Sten 38 C3
Inveravon Rd. Loan 155 D1
Inveravon Roundabout.
    B'ness 62 B3
Inveravon Terr. Muss 126 B3
Inveresk Brae. Muss 126 B3
Inveresk Ind Est. Muss 126 B3
Inveresk Rd. Muss 126 B3
Inveresk Village Rd. Muss . 126 B2
Inverkeithing Rd. Abe 49 D4
Inverkeithing Rd. Cross 30 C3
Inverkip Dr. Shot 191 F3
Inverleith Ave. Edin 93 D2
Inverleith Ave S. Edin 93 D2
Inverleith Gr. Edin 92 C2
Inverleith Pl. Edin 93 D2
Inverleith Place La. Edin 93 D2
Inverleith Row. Edin 93 D2
Inverleith Terr. Edin 93 D2
Inverleith Terrace La. Edin .. 93 D2
Invertiel Rd. Kirk 35 D4
Invertiel Terr. Kirk 17 D1
Inzievar Terr. Oak 27 D3
Iona Pl. Falk 60 A1
Iona Rd. Dunf 29 F2
Iona St. Edin 93 F2
Ireland Ave. Whit 169 F3
Irene Terr. Avon 82 C1
Ironmills Rd. Dalk 156 C2
Irvine Cres. Bath 144 C3
Irvine Pl. Stir 7 D4
Irving Ct. Falk 59 F3
Islands Cres. Falk 60 A1
Islay Ct. Gran 61 E3
Islay Rd. Dunf 29 F1
Ivanhoe Cres. Edin 124 A1
Ivanhoe Pl. Stir 2 A1
Ivanhoe Rise. Muri 148 A1
Ivy Gr. Dunf 46 C4
Ivy La. Kirk 18 A4
Ivy Terr. Edin 122 C3
Izatt Ave. Dunf 29 D1
Izatt St. All 10 A4
Izatt Terr. Clack 11 D2

Jacklin Gn. Liv 147 D4
Jackson Ave. Gran 61 E4
Jackson Pl. Liv 147 E2
Jackson St. Peni 203 F3
Jacob Pl. Falk 60 A2
Jail Wynd. Stir 7 D4
Jamaica Mews. Edin 93 D1
Jamaica St. Edin 93 E1
Jamaica St W. Edin 93 D1
Jamaica Street North La.
    Edin 93 D1
Jamaica Street South La.
    Edin 93 D1
James Croft Dr. Falk 59 F1
James Ct. Cow 13 E1
James Gr. Kirk 17 D1
James Hog Cres. Oak 26 C3
James Lean Ave. Dalk 157 D2
James Leary Way. Bonn ... 182 B4
James' Park La. Burn 33 F1
James' Pk. Burn 33 F1

James St. Alva 5 D3
James St. Arm 143 F3
James St. Bank 57 D2
James St. Bann 7 E1
James St. Cow 13 E1
James St. Dunf 29 D2
James St. Edin 125 E4
James St. Falk 60 A3
James St. Lar 38 B1
James St. Laur 60 C2
James St. Muss 126 B3
James St. Stir 2 A1
James Street La. Edin 125 E4
James Watt Ave. B'ness 64 A4
James Wilson Dr. Madd 83 D3
Jameson Pl. Edin 93 F2
Jamieson Ave. B' ness 63 F3
Jamieson Gdns. Shot 191 F3
Jane St. Edin 93 F2
Janefield. Edin 155 D2
Jarnac Ct. Dalk 157 D2
Jarvey St. Bath 145 D4
Jarvie Pl. Falk 60 A4
Jasper Ave. Laur 61 D2
Jawbanes Rd. Kirk 35 D4
Jean Armour Dr. Dalk 157 E1
Jeffrey Ave. Edin 92 A1
Jeffrey Bank. B' ness 63 F4
Jeffrey St. Edin 123 F4
Jeffrey Terr. Pol 61 F1
Jellyholm Rd. N Sau 10 A1
Jennie Rennie's Rd. Dunf ... 29 D1
Jessfield Pl. B' ness 63 F4
Jessfield Terr. Edin 93 E3
Jewel The. Edin 125 D3
Jock's Hill Cres. Lin 84 C4
John Bernard Way. Gore ... 207 E3
John Brown Ct. Hadd 132 A4
John Cres. Tran 128 B3
John Davidson Dr. Duni 36 B2
John Humble St. May 183 F3
John Knox Rd. Long 98 C3
John Mason Ct. Que 89 E4
John Murray Dr. B of A 2 A4
John Row Pl. Oak 27 D4
John Rushforth Pl. Stir 1 C2
John St. Bank 57 D2
John St. Dunf 29 D1
John St. Edin 125 E4
John St. Falk 60 A4
John St. Kin 23 E2
John St. Kirk 17 D3
John St. Peni 203 F3
John St. Stir 7 D4
John Street La E. Edin 125 E4
John Street La. Edin 125 E4
John Street La. Peni 203 F3
John Street La W. Edin 125 E4
John Stuart Gait. Oak 26 C3
John's La. Edin 94 A3
John's Pl. Edin 94 A3
Johnnie Cope's Rd. Tran ... 128 A4
Johnsburn Gn. Bale 151 D1
Johnsburn Haugh. Bale 151 D1
Johnsburn Pk. Bale 177 D4
Johnsburn Rd. Bale 151 D1
Johnston Ave. Sten 38 C2
Johnston Ave. Stir 2 A1
Johnston Ave. Uph 116 C2
Johnston Cres. Dunf 29 D1
Johnston Cres. Loch 14 A4
Johnston Pk. Cow 13 E3
Johnston Pk. Inver 47 D1
Johnston Pl. Auch 203 F4
Johnston Pl. Den 36 B1
Johnston St. Bann 7 E1
Johnston Terr. Cocke 97 E2
Johnston Terr. Edin 123 E4
Johnstone La. Car 230 A1
Johnstone St. Alva 5 D3
Johnstone St. Men 3 F3
Jones Ave. Lar 59 E4
Jones Gn. Liv 147 D4
Joppa Gdns. Edin 125 E4
Joppa Gr. Edin 125 E4
Joppa Pk. Edin 125 E4
Joppa Rd. Edin 125 E4
Joppa Terr. Edin 125 E4
Jordan La. Edin 123 D2
Joseph Scott Gdns. Brox .. 117 F2
Jubilee Ave. Liv 146 C3
Jubilee Cres. Gore 183 E1
Jubilee Dr. Ros 46 A1
Jubilee Rd. Duni 36 C2
Jubilee Rd. Kirkl 119 F4
Jubilee Rd. Whit 170 A3
Junction Pl. Edin 93 F3
Junction Rd. Kirk 17 E4
Juner Pl. Gore 183 E1
Juniper Ave. Curr 152 B3
Juniper Gdns. Curr 152 B3
Juniper Gr. Curr 152 B3
Juniper Gr. Dunf 46 B4
Juniper Gr. Liv 148 A3
Juniper Park Rd. Curr 152 B3
Juniper Pl. Curr 152 B3
Juniper Terr. Curr 152 B3

Juniperlee. Curr 152 B3
Jura. Liv 146 C3
Jura Pl. Gran 61 E3
Justinhaugh Dr. Lin 84 B4

Kaemuir Ct. West 112 C3
Kaim Cres. Bog 145 E3
Kaimes Ave. Kir 149 F2
Kaimes Cres. Kir 149 F2
Kaimes Gdns. Kir 149 F2
Kaimes Gr. Kir 149 F2
Kaimes Pl. Kir 149 F2
Kaimes Rd. Edin 121 F4
Kaimes View. Dan 156 A3
Kames Pl. Dunf 29 E3
Kames Rd. Shot 191 F3
Katesmill Rd. Edin 153 D4
Katherine St. Kirk 17 D3
Katherine St. Liv 148 A3
Katrine Cres. Kirk 16 C4
Katrine Ct. All 10 B3
Katrine Dr. Crossf 28 A1
Katrine Pl. Bank 57 E3
Katrine Rd. Shot 191 F3
Katrine Rd. Whit 170 B4
Kay Gdns. Cocke 97 E2
Keavil Pl. Crossf 28 A1
Kedslie Pl. Edin 154 C4
Kedslie Rd. Edin 154 C4
Keilarsbrae. N Sau 5 E1
Keir Ave. Stir 2 A1
Keir Gdns. B of A 2 A4
Keir Hardie Ave. Laur 61 D2
Keir Hardie Dr. May 183 F3
Keir Hardie Rd. Alva 5 E4
Keir Hardie Terr. Dunf 29 D1
Keir St. B of A 2 A4
Keir St. Cow 13 D2
Keir St. Edin 123 E4
Keirsbeath Ct. Hal 12 A1
Keith Ave. Stir 7 E2
Keith Cres. Edin 92 A1
Keith Gdns. Brox 117 E3
Keith Pl. Dunf 29 E2
Keith Pl. Inver 47 E2
Keith Rd. Ros 46 B1
Keith Row. Edin 92 B1
Keith St. Kin 23 F2
Keith Terr. Edin 92 A1
Kekewich Ave. Edin 94 C1
Kellie Pl. All 10 A4
Kelliebank. All 9 F3
Kelly Dr. Den 36 C2
Kelly's La. Car 230 A1
Kellywood Cres. Kin 23 F2
Kelso Dr. Car 230 B1
Kelso Pl. Kirk 17 D3
Kelso St. Uph 117 D3
Kelty Ave. B'ness 64 A4
Kelvin Dr. Shot 192 A2
Kelvin Sq. Pump 148 A4
Kelvin St. Gran 40 A1
Kemp Pl. Edin 93 D1
Kemper Ave. Falk 60 B2
Kendieshill Ave. Madd 83 D3
Kenilworth Dr. Edin 155 D4
Kenilworth Dr. Laur 60 C2
Kenilworth La. Gran 61 E3
Kenilworth Rd. B of A 2 A4
Kenilworth Rise. Muri 147 F1
Kenilworth St. Gran 61 E3
Kenmore Ave. Liv 146 C3
Kenmore Ave. Pol 62 A1
Kenmore Terr. Kirk 16 C4
Kenmuir St. Falk 59 D3
Kenmure Ave. Edin 124 B4
Kenmure Pl. Dunf 29 E3
Kenmure Pl. Sten 38 C2
Kennard Rd. Pol 82 B4
Kennard St. Falk 60 B3
Kennard St. Loch 14 A4
Kennedie Pk. E Cal 148 B2
Kennedy Cres. Dunf 29 D3
Kennedy Cres. Kirk 17 D3
Kenningknowes Rd. Stir 6 C3
Kennington Ave. Loan 181 D4
Kennington Terr. Loan 181 D4
Kent Rd. All 9 F4
Kent Rd. Stir 7 D3
Kent St. Dunf 29 E3
Kentigern Mall. Peni 203 F3
Keppel Rd. N Ber 54 A3
Kepscaith Cres. Whit 170 A3
Kepscaith Gr. Whit 170 A3
Kepscaith Rd. Whit 170 A3
Kerr Ave. Dalk 156 C1
Kerr Cres. Bank 57 D2
Kerr Pl. Den 36 B1
Kerr Pl. Dunf 29 F1
Kerr Rd. Tran 128 B3
Kerr St. Edin 93 D1
Kerr's Wynd. Muss 126 B3
Kerrisk Dr. Dunf 29 F1
Kerse Gdns. Falk 60 C3
Kerse Gn Rd. Clack 10 C3
Kerse La. Falk 60 B3
Kerse Pl. Falk 60 B3
Kerse Rd. Fal 7 F3

Kerse Rd. Gran 61 E4
Kerse Rd. Stir 7 E3
Kersebonny Rd. Cam 6 B4
Kersie Rd. Fall 9 D2
Kersie Terr. Air 9 F2
Kersiebank Ave. Gran 61 F3
Kestrel Brae. Liv 147 E3
Kestrel Dr. Madd 82 C4
Kettil'stoun Gr. Lin 84 B3
Kettil'stoun Mains. Lin 84 B3
Kettilstoun Rd. Lin 84 B4
Keverkae. All 9 F3
Kevock Rd. Bonn 181 F4
Kidd St. Kirk 17 E4
Kilbagie St. Kin 23 E2
Kilbean Dr. Falk 59 F1
Kilbirnie Terr. Den 36 B2
Kilbrennan Dr. Falk 59 D2
Kilburn Rd. Crossf 28 A1
Kilchurn Ct. Edin 121 D4
Kilcruik Rd. King 34 C2
Kildonan Pk. Dunf 28 C1
Kildrummy Ave. Sten 38 C2
Kilfinan Rd. Shot 191 E3
Kilgour Ave. Kirk 17 E4
Kilgraston Rd. Edin 123 E2
Killin Ct. Dunf 28 C1
Killin Dr. Pol 62 A1
Killochan Way. Dunf 29 E3
Kilmartin Way. Dunf 29 E3
Kilmaurs Rd. Edin 124 A2
Kilmaurs Terr. Edin 124 A2
Kilmory Gdns. Car 230 A2
Kilmun Rd. Kirk 16 B4
Kilmundy Dr. Burn 33 E1
Kilncadzow Rd. Car 230 B1
Kilncraigs Ct. All 10 B3
Kilncraigs Rd. All 10 B3
Kilncroft Side. Edin 122 A1
Kilns Pl. Falk 59 F3
Kilns Rd. Falk 60 A3
Kilpair St. Hadd 132 A4
Kilpunt View. Brox 118 A3
Kilrie Cotts. Aucht 33 F4
Kilrymont. For 215 D1
Kilspindie Ct. Aber 71 E2
Kilsyth Rd. Bank 57 D2
Kilwinning Pl. Muss 126 B3
Kilwinning St. Muss 126 B3
Kilwinning Terr. Muss 126 B3
Kinacres Gr. B'ness 64 B4
Kincairne Ct. Kin 23 F2
Kincardine Rd. Sten 39 E2
Kincraig Pl. Dunf 28 C1
Kinellan Gdns. Edin 122 B4
Kinellan Rd. Edin 122 B4
King Cres. W Cal 172 B2
King Edwards Way. Kirkl 89 D1
King James IV Rd. Ros 46 B1
King O' Muirs Ave. Men 4 C2
King St. Arm 144 A3
King St. Bath 145 D3
King St. Cow 13 E2
King St. Edin 93 F3
King St. Falk 60 B3
King St. Fall 8 B2
King St. Inver 47 E1
King St. Kirk 17 D3
King St. Muss 126 B3
King St. Shot 191 F2
King St. Sten 38 B1
King St. Stir 7 D4
King's Ave. Long 98 B2
King's Court. Long 98 B2
King's Cramond. Edin 91 D2
King's Cres. Car 230 A1
King's Cres. Ros 46 C2
King's Dr. King 34 C2
King's Gr. Long 98 B2
King's Knoll Gdns. N Ber 54 B3
King's Park Dr. Stir 6 C3
King's Park Rd. Stir 7 D4
King's Pk. Long 98 B3
King's Pl. Ros 46 C2
King's Rd. Edin 95 D1
King's Rd. Long 98 B3
King's Rd. Ros 46 C3
King's Rd. Tran 128 B3
King's Rd. Whit 170 A3
King's Stables La. Edin 123 E4
King's Stables Rd. Edin 123 E4
King's Terr. Edin 94 C1
Kinghorn Pl. Burn 33 F1
Kinghorn Pl. Edin 93 E3
Kinghorn Rd. Burn 34 A1
Kinghorn Rd. Burn 50 C4
Kinghorn Rd. Kirk 35 D1
Kinglass Ave. B'ness 64 A4
Kings Ct. All 10 A4
Kings Gn. Edin 124 B2
Kings Haugh. Edin 124 B2
Kings Rd. Gran 61 F4
Kingsburgh Ct. E Lin 103 E4
Kingsburgh Gdns. E Lin 103 E4

Kingsburgh Rd. Edin 122 B4
Kingseat Ave. Gran 61 E3
Kingseat Pl. Falk 59 F2
Kingseat Rd. Dunf 29 E3
Kingsfield. Lin 85 E4
Kingshill Rd. Alla 212 A4
Kingsknowe Ave. Edin 122 A1
Kingsknowe Cres. Edin 122 A1
Kingsknowe Ct. Edin 121 F1
Kingsknowe Dr. Edin 122 A1
Kingsknowe Gdns. Edin 153 D4
Kingsknowe Gr. Edin 153 D4
Kingsknowe Pk. Edin 153 D4
Kingsknowe Pl. Edin 121 F1
Kingsknowe Rd N. Edin 122 A1
Kingsknowe Rd S. Edin 122 A1
Kingsknowe Terr. Edin 122 A1
Kingslaw Ct. Tran 128 B3
Kingslaw Farm Cotts. Tran 128 C3
Kingsley Ave. Sten 38 C2
Kingsport Ave. Liv 147 F2
Kingstables La. Stir 7 D4
Kingston Ave. Edin 124 B1
Kingston Cotts. E Lin 53 F1
Kingswell Pk. All 10 B4
Kininmonth St. Kirk 17 D1
Kinloch Pl. Gran 61 F3
Kinloss Ct. H Val 26 A1
Kinnaird Ave. Sten 39 D2
Kinnaird Dr. Sten 38 C2
Kinnaird Park. Edin 125 E2
Kinnaird Pl. Dunf 29 E3
Kinnear Rd. Edin 93 D2
Kinneil Dr. B' ness 63 E3
Kinneil Rd. B' ness 63 E4
Kinnell Rd. Inver 47 D1
Kinnis Ct. Dunf 29 F1
Kinnonmonth Ave. Burn 33 E1
Kintyre Pl. Falk 59 E2
Kippielaw Dr. Dalk 157 E1
Kippielaw Gdns. Dalk 157 E1
Kippielaw Medway. Dalk ... 157 E1
Kippielaw Pk. May 183 E4
Kippielaw Rd. Dalk 157 E1
Kippielaw Wlk. Dalk 157 E1
Kippithill. Hum 187 D1
Kirk Ave. Sten 38 C1
Kirk Brae. E Lin 108 A1
Kirk Brae. Edin 155 D4
Kirk Brae. Fau 170 B1
Kirk Brae. Kin 23 F3
Kirk Cramond. Edin 91 E3
Kirk La. Liv 147 D1
Kirk Loan. Edin 121 F3
Kirk Path. Alla 212 A4
Kirk Pk. Dunb 78 A4
Kirk Pk. Edin 155 D4
Kirk Ports. N Ber 54 B4
Kirk Rd. Aber 71 E3
Kirk Rd. Dath 145 E3
Kirk Rd. Shot 191 F2
Kirk St. Cul 25 E1
Kirk St. Edin 93 F2
Kirk St. Kin 23 F2
Kirk St. Pres 96 C1
Kirk View. Hadd 132 B4
Kirk Wynd. Clack 11 D3
Kirk Wynd. Falk 60 A4
Kirk Wynd. Kirk 17 E2
Kirk Wynd. Stir 7 D2
Kirkbank Rd. Burn 33 F1
Kirkbrae. Clack 10 C2
Kirkbride Terr. Plea 20 B3
Kirkburn. Slam 110 A4
Kirkcaldy Rd. Burn 33 F1
Kirkcaldy Rd. King 35 D2
Kirkfield E. Liv 147 E2
Kirkfield View. Liv 147 E2
Kirkfield W. Liv 147 D2
Kirkflat. Uph 117 D3
Kirkford Ct. Cow 13 D2
Kirkgate. All 10 A3
Kirkgate. Burn 50 C4
Kirkgate. Curr 152 A2
Kirkgate. Dunf 28 C2
Kirkgate. Edin 155 D4
Kirkgate. Inver 47 D1
Kirkgate. Lin 85 D4
Kirkgate. W Cal 172 B2
Kirkhall Pl. Den 36 C1
Kirkhill Ct. Fau 193 F3
Kirkhill Dr. Edin 124 A2
Kirkhill Gdns. Edin 124 A3
Kirkhill Gdns. Peni 203 F3
Kirkhill Pk. Brox 117 E3
Kirkhill Rd. Brox 117 E3
Kirkhill Rd. Edin 124 A2
Kirkhill Rd. Peni 203 F3
Kirkhill Terr. Brox 117 E3
Kirkhill Terr. Edin 124 A3
Kirkhill Terr. Gore 183 D1
Kirkland Dr. Duni 36 A1
Kirklands. Dunf 29 D1
Kirklands. Edin 121 E2
Kirklands. Peni 203 F3
Kirkliston Rd. Que 89 D4
Kirkslap. Den 36 C1
Kirkstyle Gdns. Kirkl 89 D1

Kirkton Ave. Bath 145 E3
Kirkton Bank. Peni 203 E3
Kirkton N. Liv 147 D2
Kirkton Pl. Cow 13 D3
Kirkton Pl. Sten 39 E2
Kirkton Rd. Burn 33 F1
Kirkton S Rd. Muri 147 E1
Kirkway. Air 22 B2
Kirkwood Ave. Laur 61 E1
Kirkwood Cres. Crossf 28 A1
Kisimul Ct. Edin 121 D4
Kitchener Cres. Long 98 C3
Kittle Yards. Edin 123 F2
Knights Way. Den 36 B1
Knightsbridge Rd. Dech 116 B1
Knightsbridge Rd. Liv 147 E4
Knightsiaw Pl. Peni 203 E3
Knightsridge Ct. Dech 116 B1
Knightsridge E. Liv 147 E4
Knightsridge Rd. Dech 116 B1
Knightsridge Roundabout.
  Liv 147 E4
Knightsridge W. Liv 147 D4
Knockenhair Rd. Dunb 78 A1
Knockhill Cl. Loch 14 A4
Knockhouse Gdns. Crossf .. 28 A1
Knockhouse Rd. Crossf 28 A1
Knoll Croft Rd. Shot 192 A2
Knowe Park Rd. Ston 171 D1
Knowe The. D Bay 48 B2
Knowe The. N Sau 5 E1
Knowefaulds Rd. Tull 4 A2
Knowehead Rd. Laur 61 E1
Knowes Rd. Hadd 131 F4
Knowetop. Muri 173 E4
Knowetop Pl. Rosl 180 C2
Knowhead Rd. Crossf 28 A1
Knox Pl. Hadd 132 A4
Komarom Pl. Dalk 157 E2
Kyle Ave. Cowie 20 C4
Kyle Pl. Edin 93 F1
Kyles The. Kirk 17 F3

La Porte Prec. Gran 61 E4
Labrador Ave. Liv 147 F2
Laburnum Dr. Kirk 17 E4
Laburnum Gr. Burn 33 F1
Laburnum Gr. Stir 6 C3
Laburnum Pl. May 183 F3
Laburnum Rd. Dunf 29 E1
Laburnum Rd. Whit 170 B3
Lade Braes. D Bay 48 A2
Lade Ct. Lin 84 C4
Lade Dr. Lar 59 E4
Lade Gn. D Bay 48 A2
Lade Rd. Bon 58 A3
Ladehead. Edin 93 E2
Ladeside Ave. Black 171 E4
Ladeside Cres. Lar 38 C1
Ladeside Dr. Black 171 E4
Ladeside Rd. Black 171 E4
Ladiemeadow. Edin 121 F3
Lady Anne Ct. Cross 30 C3
Lady Brae. Gore 207 F4
Lady Brae Pl. Gore 207 F4
Lady Helen Cottages. Card . 15 D4
Lady Helen St. Kirk 17 D1
Lady Jane Gdns. N Ber 54 B3
Lady Jane Rd. N Ber 54 B3
Lady Lawson St. Edin 123 E4
Lady Menzies Pl. Edin 94 A1
Lady Nairn Ave. Kirk 17 F3
Lady Nairne Cres. Edin 124 B4
Lady Nairne Gr. Edin 124 B4
Lady Nairne Loan. Edin 124 B4
Lady Nairne Pl. Edin 124 B4
Lady Nairne Rd. Dunf 28 C3
Lady Pl. Liv 147 D3
Lady Rd. Edin 124 A2
Lady Road Pl. Newt 183 D3
Lady Victoria Bsns Ctr.
  Newt 183 D2
Lady Wood Pl. Liv 147 D3
Lady Wynd. Edin 123 E4
Ladyburn Pl. King 35 D2
Ladycroft. Bale 151 E1
Ladysgate Ct. Sten 39 D2
Ladysmill. Falk 60 B3
Ladysmith Rd. Edin 123 F1
Ladysneuk Rd. Stir 2 B1
Ladywell Ave. Edin 121 E3
Ladywell Ct. Edin 121 E3
Ladywell Ct. Lar 38 A2
Ladywell Dr. Tull 4 A2
Ladywell E. Liv 147 E3
Ladywell East Rd. Liv 147 F3
Ladywell Gdns. Edin 121 E3
Ladywell Gr. Clack 11 D2
Ladywell. Muss 126 B3
Ladywell Pl. Tull 4 A2
Ladywell Rd. Edin 121 E3
Ladywell View. B' ness 63 E3
Ladywell Way. Muss 126 B3
Ladywell West Rd. Liv 147 E3
Ladywood. Clack 11 E2
Lagan Rd. Car 230 A1
Laggan Ave. Shot 192 A2
Laggan Path. Shot 191 F3

Laichfield. Edin 122 A2
Laichpark Pl. Edin 122 A2
Laichpark Rd. Edin 122 A2
Laing Gdns. Brox 117 E3
Laing Terr. Edin 125 E4
Laing Terr. Peni 203 F4
Laird Terr. Bonn 182 B3
Laird's Entry. Path 185 E2
Lakeside Rd. Kirk 16 C2
Lamb's Cl. Edin 123 F3
Lamb's Pend. Peni 203 F2
Lambert Dr. Dunf 29 E2
Lambert Terr. All 10 B4
Lamberton Ave. Stir 7 E2
Lamberton Ct. Pen 160 C3
Lambie St. Whit 170 A4
Lamer St. Dunb 78 C2
Lamington Rd. Glad 130 C4
Lammerlaws Rd. Burn 50 C4
Lammermoor Gdns. Tran .. 128 A3
Lammermoor Terr. Edin 124 B1
Lammermoor Terr. Tran 128 A3
Lammermuir Cres. Dunb 78 B1
Lammermuir Cres. Hadd ... 132 B4
Lammermuir Ct. Gull 52 A1
Lammermuir Pl. Kirk 16 C3
Lammerview. Glad 130 B4
Lammerview. Tran 128 B3
Lamond View. Lar 38 B1
Lamont Cres. Fall 8 B3
Lamont Way. Liv 147 E4
Lampacre Rd. Edin 121 F3
Lanark Ave. Liv 147 D3
Lanark Rd. Curr 152 C3
Lanark Rd. Edin 122 A1
Lanark Rd. Edin 152 C3
Landale Gdns. Burn 33 F1
Landale Pl. Burn 33 F1
Landale St. Loch 14 A4
Lane The. White 126 C1
Lang Loan. Edin 155 E2
Langfauld Gdns. Bath 144 C3
Langhill Pl. Den 36 B1
Langlaw Rd. May 183 E4
Langlees St. Falk 39 E1
Langriggs. Hadd 132 A4
Langside Cres. W Cal 173 D3
Langside Dr. Blac 142 A2
Langside. E Lin 103 E4
Langside Gdns. W Cal 173 D3
Langton Ave. E Cal 148 C2
Langton Gdns. E Cal 148 C2
Langton Rd. E Cal 148 C2
Langton Rd. Edin 123 F2
Langton Rd. Laur 61 D2
Langton View. E Cal 148 C2
Lanrigg Ave. Fau 193 F4
Lanrigg Rd. Fau 193 F4
Lansbury Ct. Dalk 157 D2
Lansbury St. Kirk 17 F4
Lansdowne Cres. Edin 123 D4
Lansdowne Cres. Kin 23 F2
Lansdowne Cres. Shot 192 A2
Lapicide Pl. Edin 93 F3
Larbert Ave. Liv 147 D4
Larbert Rd. Bon 58 A3
Larbourfield. Edin 121 E1
Larch Cres. May 183 F3
Larch Dr. Whit 170 B3
Larch Gr. Dunf 46 B4
Larch Gr. Sten 38 C2
Larch St. Gran 61 E3
Larchbank. Liv 147 F3
Larches The. All 10 A4
Larchfield. Bale 151 E1
Larchfield La. Shot 192 A1
Larchfield Neuk. Bale 151 E1
Largo Pl. Edin 93 F3
Larkfield Dr. Dalk 156 C1
Larkfield Rd. Dalk 156 C1
Lasswade Bank. Edin 155 E3
Lasswade Gr. Edin 155 E3
Lasswade Rd. Bonn 156 A1
Lasswade Rd. Dalk 156 C1
Lasswade Rd. Edin 155 E3
Lasswade Rd. Loan 155 F1
Lasswade Rd. Loan 181 E4
Latch Rd. Dunb 78 C1
Latch The. Crossf 27 E1
Lathallan Dr. Pol 61 F1
Lauder Gdns. Edin 123 F2
Lauder Lodge. Dalk 157 D2
Lauder Pl. E Lin 103 F4
Lauder Rd. Dalk 157 E1
Lauder Rd. Edin 123 E2
Lauder Rd. Kirk 17 E3
Lauder St. Dunf 29 E3
Lauderdale Cres. Dunb 78 B1
Lauderdale St. Edin 123 E3
Laurel Bank. Dalk 157 E1
Laurel Bank Pl. May 183 F3
Laurel Bank Rd. May 183 F3
Laurel Cres. Kirk 17 D4
Laurel Ct. Falk 59 E2
Laurel Gr. Bon 57 F2
Laurel Gr. Laur 61 D1
Laurel Pl. Bon 57 F2
Laurel Rd. Ros 46 B1

Laurel Terr. Edin 122 C3
Laurelbank Ave. Bon 58 A2
Laurelbank Ct. E Cal 148 C1
Laurelhill Gdns. Stir 6 C3
Laurelhill Pl. Stir 7 D3
Laurels The. Tull 4 A1
Laurencecroft Rd. Stir 2 A1
Laurie St. Edin 94 A2
Laurieston Rd. Gran 61 D3
Lauriston Dr. Dunf 29 E3
Lauriston Farm Rd. Edin 91 F2
Lauriston Gdns. Edin 123 E4
Lauriston Pk. Edin 123 E4
Lauriston Pl. Edin 123 E4
Lauriston St. Edin 123 E4
Lauriston Terr. Edin 123 E4
Laurmont Ct. Laur 61 D2
Laverock Dr. Peni 203 E3
Laverock Pk. Lin 85 D3
Laverockbank Ave. Edin 93 E3
Laverockbank Cres. Edin ... 93 E3
Laverockbank Gdns. Edin . 93 E3
Laverockbank Gr. Edin 93 E3
Laverockbank Rd. Edin 93 E3
Laverockbank Terr. Edin ... 93 E3
Laverockdale Cres. Edin ... 153 D3
Laverockdale Loan. Edin . 153 D3
Laverockdale Pk. Edin 153 D3
Law Pl. Edin 95 D1
Law Rd. Dunf 29 F2
Law Rd. N Ber 54 B4
Lawers Cres. Pol 62 A1
Lawers Pl. Gran 61 F3
Lawers Sq. Peni 204 A4
Lawfield Rd. May 183 E4
Lawhead Cotts. E Lin 75 F2
Lawhead Pl. Peni 203 E3
Lawnmarket. Edin 123 E4
Lawrence St. Hadd 131 F4
Lawrie Dr. Peni 203 F4
Lawson Cres. Que 89 E4
Lawson Gdns. Kirk 17 F4
Lawson Pl. Madd 83 D3
Lawson Pl. Dunb 78 B1
Lawson St. Kirk 17 F4
Lawswell. Fish 5 F2
Laxdale Dr. Bank 57 E4
Laxford Cres. D Bay 48 A2
Leadburn Ave. Dunf 29 D4
Leadervale Rd. Edin 154 C4
Leadervale Terr. Edin 154 C4
Leadside Cres. Dunf 29 D4
Leamington Pl. Edin 123 D3
Leamington Rd. Edin 123 D3
Leamington Terr. Edin 123 D3
Learmonth Ave. Edin 92 C1
Learmonth Cres. Edin 92 C1
Learmonth Ct. W Cal 172 B2
Learmonth Ct. Edin 92 C1
Learmonth Gardens Mews.
  Edin 93 D1
Learmonth Gdns. Edin 92 C1
Learmonth Gr. Edin 92 C1
Learmonth Pk. Edin 92 C1
Learmonth Pl. Edin 93 D1
Learmonth St. Falk 60 A2
Learmonth Terr. Edin 93 D1
Learmonth Terrace La. Edin 93 D1
Ledi Ave. Tull 4 A1
Ledi Terr. Peni 204 A4
Ledi View. Stir 2 A2
Ledmore Pl. Falk 60 C1
Lee Cres. Edin 125 D4
Leighton Cres. May 183 E4
Leighton St. H Val 26 A1
Leith Ave. Burn 33 F1
Leith Pl. Bank 57 E4
Leith St. Edin 93 E1
Leith Wlk. Edin 93 F2
Lempockwells Rd. Pen 160 C3
Lendrick Ave. Falk 59 F1
Lennel Ave. Edin 122 B4
Lenniemuir. Kirkl 90 A1
Lennox Ave. Stir 7 D2
Lennox Gdns. Lin 84 B4
Lennox Milne Ct. Hadd 132 A4
Lennox Rd. Hadd 132 B4
Lennox Row. Edin 93 D3
Lennox St. Edin 93 D1
Lennox Street La. Edin 93 D1
Lennox Terr. Gran 61 F3
Lennoxlove Acredales. Giff 132 A4
Leny Pl. Dunf 29 D3
Lenzie Ave. Liv 147 D3
Leopold Pl. Edin 93 F1
Leslie Pl. Edin 93 D1
Leslie Rd. Ros 46 C3
Leslie St. Kirk 35 D4
Lestrange Terr. Alva 5 D4
Letham Ave. Pump 148 A4
Letham Cotts. Air 39 E4
Letham Cres. Pump 148 A4
Letham Dr. Hadd 131 F4
Letham Gdns. Pump 148 A4
Letham Gr. Pump 148 A4
Letham Hill Ave. D Bay 47 F2
Letham Pk. Dunb 78 B1
Letham Pk. Pump 148 A4

Letham Pl. Dunb 78 B2
Letham Pl. Pump 148 A4
Letham Rd. Dunb 78 B1
Letham Rd. Liv 148 A4
Letham Rise. D Bay 47 F2
Letham Terr. Pump 148 A4
Letham Terrs. Air 22 B1
Letham Way. D Bay 47 F2
Leuchatsbeath Dr. Cow 13 D3
Leven Ct. All 10 B3
Leven Pl. Shot 191 F3
Leven St. Edin 123 D3
Leven St. Falk 60 A4
Leven Terr. Edin 123 E3
Leven Wlk. Liv 148 A2
Leving Pl. Liv 147 E2
Lewis Ct. All 10 A3
Lewis Ct. Falk 60 A1
Lewis Rd. Pol 61 F1
Lewisvale Ave. Muss 126 C3
Lewisvale Ct. Muss 126 C3
Leyden Pl. Bonn 182 A4
Leyden Pl. Bonn 182 A4
Leys Park Rd. Dunf 29 D2
Liberton Brae. Edin 155 D4
Liberton Dr. Edin 154 C4
Liberton Gdns. Edin 155 D4
Liberton Pl. Edin 155 D4
Liberton Rd. Edin 124 A1
Library La. Gran 40 B1
Liddesdale Pl. Edin 93 D1
Liddle Dr. B' ness 63 F3
Lidgate Shot. Rat 119 F1
Liggar's Pl. Dunf 28 C1
Liggat Pl. Brox 117 F3
Liggat Syke Pl. Brox 118 A3
Lighton Terr. Ston 171 D1
Lilac Ave. May 183 F3
Lilac Cres. Kirk 17 E4
Lilac Gr. Dunf 46 B4
Lillies La. Giff 163 F3
Lilly's La. Dunf 29 D1
Lily Terr. Edin 122 C2
Lilybank St. N Sau 5 E1
Lilyhill Terr. Edin 94 B1
Lime Ave. New 66 C1
Lime Gr. Dunf 29 F1
Lime Gr. Lar 38 B1
Lime Gr. May 183 F3
Lime Gr. N Ber 54 C3
Lime Gr. Pol 61 F1
Lime Pl. Bonn 182 A3
Lime Rd. Falk 59 D2
Lime St. Gran 61 E3
Limebank Pk. E Cal 148 C1
Limefield Ave. W Cal 173 D3
Limefield Cres. Bog 145 F3
Limefield Gdns. W Cal 173 D3
Limefield Pl. Bog 145 E3
Limefield Rd. Bath 145 E4
Limefield Rd. W Cal 173 D3
Limekilns. Pen 161 D3
Limekilns Gr. E Cal 149 D2
Limekilns Rd. Dunf 28 C1
Limes The. Edin 123 D2
Limetree Wlk. E Lin 76 B3
Limeylands Cres. Orm 159 E4
Limeylands Rd. Orm 159 E4
Lina St. Kirk 17 D3
Linburn Gr. Dunf 29 F2
Linburn Pk. E Cal 150 A3
Linburn Pl. Dunf 29 F2
Linburn Rd. Dunf 29 F2
Lindean Pl. Edin 94 A2
Lindean Terr. E Cal 149 F3
Linden Ave. Duni 36 B2
Linden Ave. Stir 7 E3
Linden Gr. Liv 148 A3
Linden Pl. Loan 181 E4
Lindores Dr. Kirk 16 C4
Lindores Dr. Tran 128 B3
Lindsay Dr. Stir 2 A2
Lindsay Pl. Edin 93 F3
Lindsay Rd. Edin 93 F3
Lindsay Sq. Liv 146 B3
Lindsay St. Edin 93 F3
Lindsay Way. Liv 147 E4
Lindsay's Wynd. Oak 26 C3
Lingerwood Farm Cotts.
  Newt 183 D2
Lingerwood Rd. Newt 183 D2
Lingerwood Wlk. Newt 183 D2
Linhouse Dr. E Cal 148 C2
Linhouse Rd. E Cal 148 C2
Linkfield Ct. Muss 126 C3
Linkfield Rd. Muss 126 C3
Links Ave. Muss 126 A4
Links Ct. Cocke 97 E2
Links Dr. Crossf 28 A1
Links Gardens La. Edin 94 A3
Links Gdns. Edin 94 A3
Links Gdns. Edin 94 A2
Links Gdns. Edin 94 A3
Links Pl. B'ness 64 A4
Links Pl. Burn 50 C4
Links Pl. Cocke 97 F2
Links Pl. Edin 94 A3
Links Rd. B'ness 64 A4

Links Rd. Cocke 97 F2
Links Rd. Long 98 C3
Links Rd. N Ber 54 A4
Links St. Kirk 17 D1
Links St. Muss 126 B3
Links View. Cocke 97 F2
Links View. Muss 126 B4
Links Wlk. Cocke 97 F2
Linlithgow Pl. Sten 38 C2
Linlithgow Rd. B' ness 63 F3
Linlithgow Terr. Orm 159 F4
Linmill Rd. Avon 112 A3
Linn Mill. Que 67 F1
Linn Pl. Brox 117 F2
Linsay Macdonald Ct. Dunf . 29 E2
Lint Riggs. Falk 60 A3
Linton La. Kirk 16 C3
Linton Pl. Ros 46 C2
Linty La. Peni 203 E3
Lion Well Wynd. Lin 84 C4
Lionthorn Rd. Falk 59 F1
Lipney. Men 4 A3
Lismore Ave. Edin 94 B1
Lismore Ave. Kirk 16 C4
Lismore Cres. Edin 94 B1
Lismore Ct. Falk 60 A1
Lismore Pl. Kirk 16 C4
Lister Ct. B of A 2 A3
Lister Rd. Liv 147 D1
Listloaning Pl. Lin 84 B4
Listloaning Rd. Lin 84 B4
Liston Dr. Kirkl 89 D1
Liston Pl. Kirkl 89 D1
Liston Rd. Kirkl 89 D1
Little Acre. May 183 E4
Little Carriden. Muir 64 B3
Little Cswy. Cul 42 B4
Little Denny Rd. Den 36 B1
Little France Mills. Edin ... 124 B1
Little King St. Edin 93 E1
Little Rd. Edin 155 D4
Livery St. Bath 145 D4
Livesay Rd. Ros 46 B1
Livesey Terr. Auch 204 A4
Livilands Ct. Stir 7 D3
Livilands Gate. Stir 7 D3
Livilands La. Stir 7 D3
Livingston Rd. Liv 147 F3
Livingstone Cres. Falk 60 C3
Livingstone Dr. B' ness 63 E3
Livingstone Dr. Burn 33 F1
Livingstone Dr. Laur 61 D1
Livingstone La. Abe 49 E4
Livingstone Pl. Edin 123 E3
Livingstone Quadrant. East 168 B2
Livingstone St. Add 171 F1
Livingstone Terr. Laur 61 D1
Lixmount Ave. Edin 93 E3
Lixmount Gdns. Edin 93 E3
Lizzie Brice's Interchange.
  E Cal 148 A1
Llynallan Rd. East 168 A3
Loan Pl. East 168 C3
Loan The. B' ness 63 E3
Loan The. Loan 181 D4
Loan The. Path 184 A4
Loan The. Que 68 A1
Loan The. Torp 113 F3
Loanburn Ave. Peni 203 F3
Loanburn. Peni 203 F3
Loanfoot Cres. Uph 117 D3
Loanfoot Gdns. Plea 20 D2
Loanfoot Rd. Uph 117 D2
Loanhead Ave. Bank 57 E3
Loanhead Ave. Gran 61 F3
Loanhead Pl. Kirk 17 D3
Loanhead Rd. Edin 155 D1
Loaning Cres. Edin 94 B1
Loaning Rd. Edin 94 B1
Loaninghill Pk. Uph 117 D2
Loaninghill Rd. Uph 117 D2
Loch Aww Way. Whit 170 B4
Loch Earn Way. Whit 170 B4
Loch Fyne Way. Whit 170 B4
Loch Linnhe Ct. Whit 170 B4
Loch Maree Way. Whit 170 B4
Loch Pl. Que 68 A1
Loch Rd. Edin 92 A1
Loch Rd. Que 68 A1
Loch Rd. Tran 128 B3
Loch Sq. Tran 128 B3
Loch St. Dunf 29 E4
Loch Trool Way. Whit 170 B4
Lochaber Cres. Shot 192 A2
Lochaber Dr. Sten 38 C2
Lochbank. Liv 147 F3
Lochbrae. N Sau 5 E1
Lochbridge Rd. N Ber 54 B3
Lochend Ave. Dunb 78 C1
Lochend Castle Barns. Edin 94 A1
Lochend Cl. Edin 123 F4
Lochend Cres. Dunb 78 B1
Lochend Cres. Edin 94 B1
Lochend Dr. Edin 94 B1
Lochend Gdns. Edin 94 A1
Lochend Gr. Edin 94 B1
Lochend Ind Est. Kirkl 119 D3

Lochend Pk. Edin
Marmion St. Falk

Lochend Pk. Edin .... 94　A2
Lochend Quadrant. Edin ...... 94　B1
Lochend Rd. Dunb .... 78　C1
Lochend Rd. Edin .... 94　A2
Lochend Rd. Kirkl .... 119　D4
Lochend Rd N. Muss .... 126　A3
Lochend Rd S. Muss .... 126　A3
Lochend Sq. Edin .... 94　A1
Lochgelly Rd. Cow .... 13　E3
Lochgreen Rd. Falk .... 59　F1
Lochhead Ave. Den .... 36　C1
Lochhill Cotts. Ath .... 99　F4
Lochies Rd. Burn .... 34　A1
Lochies Rd. Clack .... 11　D2
Lochinvar Pl. Bon .... 58　B2
Lochinvar Rd. Ros .... 46　B1
Lochlands Ind Est. Falk ...... 59　D4
Lochmaben Dr. Sten .... 38　C2
Lochpark Pl. Den .... 36　C1
Lochridge Pl. Den .... 36　B1
Lochrin Pl. Edin .... 123　D3
Lochside Cres. Laur .... 61　D1
Lochside Rd. Slam .... 110　B1
Lock Rd. Ros .... 67　D4
Lock Sixteen. Falk .... 59　E3
Lockerby Cotts. Edin .... 155　E3
Lockerby Cres. Edin .... 155　E3
Lockerby Gr. Edin .... 155　E3
Lockhart Terr. Rosl .... 180　C2
Lockharton Ave. Edin .... 122　C1
Lockharton Cres. Edin .... 122　C1
Lockharton Gdns. Edin .... 122　C2
Lodge Dr. Sten .... 38　C1
Lodge St. Hadd .... 132　A4
Logan St. Edin .... 93　E1
Logan Way. Liv .... 147　E4
Loganlea Ave. Edin .... 94　B1
Loganlea Cres. Add .... 171　E1
Loganlea Dr. Edin .... 94　B1
Loganlea Gdns. Edin .... 94　B1
Loganlea Loan. Edin .... 94　B1
Loganlea Pl. Edin .... 94　B1
Loganlea Rd. Add .... 171　E1
Loganlea Rd. Edin .... 94　B1
Loganlea Terr. Add .... 171　E1
Loganlea Terr. Edin .... 94　B1
Logie Dr. Lar .... 38　A2
Logie Green Gdns. Edin ...... 93　E2
Logie Green Loan. Edin ...... 93　E2
Logie Green Rd. Edin .... 93　E2
Logie La. B of A .... 2　B4
Logie Mill. Edin .... 93　E2
Logie Pl. Dunf .... 28　B3
Logie Rd. Stir .... 2　B2
Lomond Cres. Dunf .... 29　F1
Lomond Cres. Sten .... 38　C2
Lomond Cres. Stir .... 2　A2
Lomond Cres. Whit .... 170　A3
Lomond Ct. All .... 10　B3
Lomond Dr. Bann .... 7　F1
Lomond Dr. Falk .... 39　E1
Lomond Gdns. Kirk .... 16　C3
Lomond Rd. Edin .... 93　D3
Lomond Rd. Gran .... 61　F3
Lomond Rd. Shot .... 191　F3
Lomond St. All .... 4　C1
Lomond Vale. Peni .... 204　A4
Lomond View. West .... 112　C2
Lomond Way. Bank .... 57　E3
Lomond Wlk. Edin .... 155　D1
London Rd. Dalk .... 157　D2
London Rd. Edin .... 94　A1
London St. Edin .... 93　E1
Loney Cres. Den .... 57　F4
Long Byres. Brox .... 117　F3
Long Craigs. Cocke .... 97　F2
Long Craigs Terr. King ...... 35　D2
Long Cram. Hadd .... 131　F4
Long Crook. Que .... 89　D4
Long Dalmahoy Rd. Bale .... 150　B2
Long Dalmahoy Rd. Kir ..... 150　B2
Long Dalmahoy Rd. Rat ..... 150　B2
Long Row. Hal .... 30　A4
Long Row. Men .... 4　A4
Longannet Cotts. Kin .... 24　A1
Longbraes Gdns. Kirk .... 16　B3
Longcroft Gdns. Lin .... 84　C4
Longdales Ave. Falk .... 60　A4
Longdales Ct. Falk .... 60　A4
Longdales Pl. Falk .... 60　A4
Longdales Rd. Falk .... 60　A4
Longdyke Pl. Sten .... 39　E2
Longdykes Rd. Pres .... 97　D1
Longford. For .... 215　D1
Longformacus Rd. Edin ..... 155　D4
Longhill Gdns. D Bay .... 48　A2
Longridge Rd. Whit .... 170　A3
Longstone Ave. Edin .... 122　A1
Longstone Cres. Edin .... 122　A2
Longstone Gdns. Edin .... 121　F2
Longstone Gr. Edin .... 122　A1
Longstone Pk. Edin .... 122　A1
Longstone Rd. Edin .... 122　A1
Longstone St. Edin .... 122　A1
Longstone Terr. Edin .... 121　F2
Longstone View. Edin .... 121　F2
Lonsdale Cres. Burn .... 33　F1

Lonsdale Terr. Edin .... 123　E3
Lookaboutye Brae. Clack .... 11　D2
Loom Rd. Kirk .... 17　D3
Lord President Rd. N Ber .... 54　A4
Loretto Ct. Muss .... 126　A2
Lorimar Pl. Sten .... 39　D1
Lorne Gdns. Laur .... 60　C2
Lorne Gr. Edin .... 155　D1
Lorne Pl. Edin .... 93　F2
Lorne Rd. Lar .... 38　B1
Lorne Sq. Edin .... 93　F2
Lorne Sq. N Ber .... 54　B4
Lorne St. Edin .... 93　F2
Lorne St. Kirk .... 17　F4
Lornshill Cres. All .... 9　F4
Losshill. Men .... 4　A3
Lothian Bank. Dalk .... 156　C1
Lothian Cres. B'ness .... 64　A3
Lothian Cres. Stir .... 2　B2
Lothian Ct. Inver .... 47　E1
Lothian Dr. May .... 183　E4
Lothian Rd. Dalk .... 157　D2
Lothian Rd. Edin .... 123　D4
Lothian St. B'ness .... 64　A3
Lothian St. Bath .... 145　D4
Lothian St. Bonn .... 182　B4
Lothian St. Burn .... 50　C4
Lothian St. Dalk .... 157　D2
Lothian St. Rose .... 181　E1
Lothian Terr. Kirk .... 17　D4
Lothian Terr. Newt .... 183　D2
Lothians View. Ros .... 47　D1
Louburn. Blac .... 142　B2
Loudens Wlk. Duni .... 36　B3
Loughborough Rd. Kirk ...... 17　F4
Louisa Sq. Rose .... 181　E1
Louise St. Dunf .... 29　E1
Lovedale Ave. Bale .... 151　D1
Lovedale Cres. Bale .... 151　D1
Lovedale Gdns. Bale .... 151　D1
Lovedale Gr. Bale .... 151　D1
Lovedale Rd. Bale .... 151　D1
Lovells Glen. Lin .... 84　B4
Lovers La. Que .... 89　E4
Lovers Loan. Alva .... 5　D4
Lovers Loan. Dunf .... 28　C1
Lovers Wlk. Stir .... 2　A1
Low Brae. Torp .... 113　F3
Low Causewayside. Cul ..... 42　B4
Low Causewayside. Torr ..... 26　B1
Low Cswy. Cul .... 25　F1
Low Cswy. Torr .... 26　C1
Low Doors The. Kir .... 149　F1
Lower Alderston Rd. Hadd ... 100　C1
Lower Bathville. Arm .... 144　A3
Lower Bridge St. Bath ...... 145　D3
Lower Bridge St. Stir .... 2　A1
Lower Broomieknowe.
　Bonn .... 182　A4
Lower Castlehill. Stir .... 2　A1
Lower Gilmore Pl. Edin ..... 123　D3
Lower Glebe. Abe .... 49　E4
Lower Granton Rd. Edin ..... 93　D3
Lower Joppa. Edin .... 125　E4
Lower London Rd. Edin ..... 94　A1
Lower Wellheads. Lime ...... 45　E2
Lowrie Ave. Peni .... 203　E3
Lowry Pl. Ros .... 46　C2
Ludgate. All .... 10　A3
Luffness Ct. Aber .... 71　E2
Luffness Mains Cotts. Aber . 72　A2
Lugton Brae. Dalk .... 156　C2
Lumley Ct. Gran .... 61　E4
Lumley Pl. Gran .... 61　E4
Lumley St. Gran .... 61　E4
Lumphinnans Rd. Loch ...... 14　A4
Lumsdaine Dr. D Bay .... 48　A1
Lumsden Ct. Rat .... 119　E1
Lundin Rd. Crossf .... 28　A2
Lussielaw Rd. Edin .... 123　F2
Lutton Pl. Edin .... 123　F3
Lyall Cres. Pol .... 61　F1
Lyars Rd. Long .... 98　C3
Lyarthall. Uph .... 117　E3
Lychgate La. Brox .... 117　F3
Lychgate Rd. Tull .... 4　A1
Lydgait Gdns. Hadd .... 101　D1
Lydgait. Hadd .... 101　D1
Lygon Rd. Edin .... 123　F1
Lyle Gn. Liv .... 147　D4
Lyne Gr. Crossf .... 28　B1
Lyne St. Edin .... 94　A1
Lyne Terr. Peni .... 204　A4
Lyneburn Cres. Hal .... 30　A3
Lynedoch Pl. Edin .... 123　D4
Lynedoch Place La. Edin .... 123　D4
Lyness Ct. Pol .... 61　F1
Lynn Lea Ave. Hadd .... 132　B4
Lyon Cres. B of A .... 2　A3
Lyon Ct. B' ness .... 63　E3

Mac Cormick Terr. Auch ..... 203　F4
Macadam Place. Falk .... 59　E3
Macarthur Cres. Madd ...... 82　C3
Macbeth Moir Rd. Muss ..... 127　D3
Macbeth Rd. Dunf .... 29　E1
Macdonald Ave. Arm .... 143　F3
Macdonald Dr. Stir .... 7　D2

Macdonald Pl. Burn .... 34　A1
Macdonald Sq. Hal .... 30　A3
Macdowall Rd. Edin .... 123　F2
Macduff Cres. King .... 34　C1
Mace Ct. Bann .... 7　E2
Macfarlane Cres. Falk ...... 60　A3
Macfarlane Pl. Uph .... 116　C2
Machrie Ct. Falk .... 59　E2
Macindoe Cres. Kirk .... 17　E4
Macintosh Rd. Liv .... 146　C1
Mackenzie Cres. Loch ...... 14　B4
Mackenzie Pl. Edin .... 93　D1
Mackenzie Terr. Gran .... 61　E3
Mackie Pl. Dunf .... 29　F1
Maclachlan Ave. Den .... 36　B1
Maclardy Ct. Uph .... 116　C2
Maclaren Terr. Sten .... 39　D1
Maclean Cres. Alva .... 5　A4
Maclean Ct. Stir .... 7　E2
Maclean Terr. Blac .... 142　B2
Macmerry Ind Est. Glad .... 129　F3
Macmillan Rd. Muri .... 147　E1
Macnair Ave. N Ber .... 54　B3
Mactaggart Loan. Newt ..... 183　D2
Maddiston Rd. Pol .... 82　C4
Madeira Pl. Edin .... 93　F3
Madeira St. Edin .... 93　F3
Madill Pl. Sten .... 38　C2
Maesterton Pl. Newt .... 183　D2
Mag's Bank. Giff .... 133　D1
Magdala Cres. Edin .... 122　C4
Magdala Mews. Edin .... 122　C4
Magdalene Ave. Edin .... 125　D3
Magdalene Ct. Edin .... 125　D3
Magdalene Dr. Edin .... 125　D3
Magdalene Gdns. Edin ...... 125　D3
Magdalene Loan. Edin ...... 125　D3
Magdalene Medway. Edin . 125　D3
Magdalene Pl. Edin .... 125　D3

Main St. Oak .... 27　E4
Main St. Orm .... 159　F4
Main St. Path .... 184　B3
Main St. Path .... 185　D3
Main St. Pen .... 161　F2
Main St. Plea .... 20　B2
Main St. Pol .... 61　F1
Main St. Pol .... 82　B4
Main St. Rat .... 119　E1
Main St. Rosl .... 181　D2
Main St. Shi .... 81　E3
Main St. Shot .... 192　A2
Main St. Slam .... 110　A4
Main St. Sten .... 38　C1
Main St. Sten .... 39　E2
Main St. Ston .... 171　D1
Main St. Torr .... 26　B1
Main St. Tull .... 4　A1
Main St. W Cal .... 172　B2
Main St W. Men .... 3　F3
Main St. Whit .... 170　B4
Main St. Winch .... 87　F2
Mains Of Craigmillar. Edin 124　B1
Mains Rd. East .... 168　C3
Mains Rd. Lin .... 84　C3
Maitland Ave. Bann .... 7　E1
Maitland Ave. Muss .... 126　A3
Maitland Cres. Stir .... 7　D2
Maitland Hog La. Kirkl ..... 89　D1
Maitland Park Rd. Muss .... 126　A3
Maitland Rd. Kirkl .... 89　D1
Maitland Rd. Ros .... 67　D4
Maitland St. Dunf .... 28　C2
Maitland St. Muss .... 126　A3
Majors Loan. Falk .... 60　A2
Majors Pl. Falk .... 60　A2
Malcolm Ct. Bath .... 144　C3
Malcolm Dr. Sten .... 38　C2
Malcolm St. Dunf .... 29　D1
Mall Ave. Muss .... 126　B3
Mallens Brae. Torp .... 114　A3
Malleny Millgate. Bale ..... 177　D1
Malplaquet Ct. Car .... 230　A1
Malta Gn. Edin .... 93　D1
Malta Terr. Edin .... 93　D1
Maltings The. Aucht .... 15　D1
Maltings The. Lin .... 84　B3
Mamre Dr. Cali .... 81　F3
Man O' War Way. B'ness ... 64　A4
Mandela Ave. Falk .... 60　B4
Manderston St. Edin .... 93　F2
Mandora Ct. Car .... 230　A1
Manitoba Ave. Liv .... 147　F2
Mannan Dr. Clack .... 11　D2
Mannering Pl. Edin .... 155　D4
Mannfield Ave. Bon .... 57　F2
Manor Cres. Tull .... 4　A1
Manor Loan. B of A .... 3　D2
Manor Pl. Edin .... 123　D4
Manor Powis Cotts. B of A . 3　D2
Manor St. Falk .... 60　A2
Manor Wynd. Madd .... 83　D2
Manse Ave. Arm .... 143　F3
Manse Ave. Whit .... 170　A3
Manse Cres. Stir .... 7　D2
Manse Ct. E Cal .... 148　C2
Manse Gr. Ston .... 171　E1
Manse La. Burn .... 33　F1
Manse La. Cocke .... 97　E2
Manse La. Muss .... 126　B3
Manse Pk. Uph .... 116　C3
Manse Pl. Bann .... 7　F1
Manse Pl. Bog .... 145　F3
Manse Pl. Falk .... 60　A2
Manse Pl. Inver .... 47　D1
Manse Pl. Slam .... 110　A4
Manse Rd. Cross .... 30　C4
Manse Rd. Dir .... 53　D3
Manse Rd. Edin .... 121　E3
Manse Rd. For .... 215　D1
Manse Rd. Inver .... 47　D1
Manse Rd. Kin .... 23　F3
Manse Rd. King .... 34　C2
Manse Rd. Kirkl .... 89　D1
Manse Rd. Lin .... 85　D3
Manse Rd. Newt .... 206　B3
Manse Rd. Rosl .... 181　D2
Manse Rd. Shot .... 192　A2
Manse Rd. Torp .... 113　F2
Manse Rd. Whit .... 170　A3
Manse St. Abe .... 49　E4
Manse St. Edin .... 121　E3
Manse View. Arm .... 143　F3
Manse View. E Lin .... 107　F1
Mansfield Ct. Bath .... 145　D4
Mansfield Ct. Liv .... 147　E2
Mansfield. E Cal .... 148　B2
Mansfield Gr. Bath .... 145　D3
Mansfield St. Bath .... 145　D4
Mansewood Cres. Whit .... 170　A3
Mansfield Ave. Muss .... 126　B3
Mansfield Ave. N Sau ...... 5　E1
Mansfield Ave. Newt .... 183　D1
Mansfield Ct. Muss .... 126　B3
Mansfield Pl. Edin .... 93　E1
Mansfield Pl. Muss .... 126　B3
Mansfield Pl. Newt .... 183　D3

Mansfield Rd. Bale .... 177　E4
Mansfield Rd. Muss .... 126　B3
Mansfield Rd. Newt .... 183　D3
Mansionhouse Rd. Edin .... 123　E3
Mansionhouse Rd. Falk .... 59　E3
Manson Sq. Liv .... 146　B3
Manuel Terr. Madd .... 83　F3
Maple Ave. Sten .... 38　C2
Maple Ct. All .... 10　A3
Maple Gr. Liv .... 148　A3
Maple Pl. Duni .... 36　B2
Maple St. Kirk .... 17　D4
Mar Pl. All .... 10　A4
Mar Pl. N Sau .... 5　E1
Mar Pl. Stir .... 7　D4
Mar St. All .... 10　A3
Mar Terr. Clack .... 11　D2
Maranatha Cres. Pol .... 82　B4
March Gr. Edin .... 92　A1
March Pines. Edin .... 91　F1
March Rd. Edin .... 92　A1
Marchbank Dr. Bale .... 177　E4
Marchbank Gdns. Bale ..... 177　E4
Marchbank Gr. Bale .... 177　E4
Marchbank Pl. Bale .... 177　E4
Marchbank Way. Bale ...... 151　E1
Marchburn Dr. Peni .... 203　E3
Marches Dr. Arm .... 144　A3
Marches The. Arm .... 144　A3
Marchfield Gr. Edin .... 92　A2
Marchfield Park La. Edin ... 91　F2
Marchfield Pk. Edin .... 91　F2
Marchfield Terr. Edin ...... 92　A2
Marchglen. Fish .... 5　F3
Marchhall Cres. Edin .... 124　A3
Marchhall Pl. Edin .... 124　A3
Marchhall Rd. Edin .... 124　A3
Marchlands Ave. B'ness .... 64　A4
Marchlands La. B'ness ..... 64　A4
Marchmont Ave. Pol .... 61　F1
Marchmont Cres. Edin ..... 123　E3
Marchmont Ct. Pol .... 61　F1
Marchmont Rd. Edin .... 123　E3
Marchmont St. Edin .... 123　E3
Marchside Ct. N Sau ...... 5　E1
Marchwood Ave. Bath ...... 145　E3
Marchwood Cres. Bath ..... 145　E3
Mardale Cres. Edin .... 123　D2
Maree Ct. All .... 10　B3
Maree Pl. Crossf .... 28　A1
Maree Pl. Kirk .... 16　C4
Maree Wlk. Liv .... 148　A2
Margaret Ave. Bank .... 57　D2
Margaret Ave. Bog .... 145　F3
Margaret Ct. Den .... 36　C1
Margaret Dr. Bon .... 58　A3
Margaret Rd. Bann .... 7　E1
Margaret Terr. Sten .... 38　C2
Maria St. Kirk .... 17　E3
Marina Rd. Bog .... 145　F3
Marine Dr. Edin .... 92　A3
Marine Espl. Edin .... 94　B3
Marine Par. N Ber .... 54　B4
Marine Rd. Dunb .... 78　B2
Marine Rd. Gull .... 52　A2
Marine Terr. Gull .... 52　A2
Mariner Ave. Falk .... 59　D3
Mariner Dr. Falk .... 59　D3
Mariner Gdns. Falk .... 59　E3
Mariner Rd. Falk .... 59　D3
Mariner St. Falk .... 59　D3
Mariners St. Kirk .... 17　D3
Mariners Wlk. D Bay .... 47　F2
Marion St. Kirk .... 17　D1
Marionville Ave. Edin ...... 94　B1
Marionville Cres. Edin ..... 94　B1
Marionville Dr. Edin .... 94　B1
Marionville Gr. Edin .... 94　B1
Marionville Pk. Edin .... 94　A1
Marionville Rd. Edin .... 94　A1
Marischal Dr. Edin .... 124　C2
Maritime La. Edin .... 94　A3
Maritime St. Edin .... 94　A3
Marjoribanks St. Bath ..... 145　D3
Market Ct. Hadd .... 101　D1
Market La. Lin .... 85　D4
Market Pl. N Ber .... 54　B4
Market Pl. Whit .... 170　A4
Market St. B' ness .... 63　F4
Market St. Dunf .... 29　D2
Market St. E Cal .... 148　C2
Market St. Edin .... 123　E4
Market St. Hadd .... 132　A4
Market St. Muss .... 126　A3
Marketgate. Orm .... 159　F4
Markfield Rd. D Bay .... 48　B2
Markle Steading. E Lin .... 103　D4
Marlborough Dr. Stir .... 2　B2
Marlborough St. Edin ...... 125　D4
Marly Gn. N Ber .... 54　A3
Marly Rise. N Ber .... 54　A3
Marmion Ave. Rosl .... 180　C2
Marmion Cres. Edin .... 124　A1
Marmion Cres. N Ber ...... 54　A4
Marmion Rd. Bath .... 145　D4
Marmion Rd. Gran .... 61　E3
Marmion Rd. N Ber .... 54　A4
Marmion St. Falk .... 60　A2

Marquis Dr. Clack 11 D2
Marrfield Rd. Pump 117 D1
Marrfield Terr. Pump 117 D1
Marschal Ct. Bann 7 E2
Marshall Pl. Dunf 29 D1
Marshall Rd. Kirkl 89 D1
Marshall St. Cocke 97 D2
Marshall St. Cow 13 E2
Marshall St. Edin 123 E4
Marshall St. Gran 61 E4
Marshall's Ct. Edin 93 F1
Marshill. All 10 A3
Martin Brae. Liv 147 E3
Martin Gr. Bonn 182 B4
Martin Pl. Dalk 156 C1
Mary Pl. Clack 11 D3
Mary Pl. Dunf 29 D1
Mary Sq. Laur 61 D2
Mary St. Laur 60 C2
Mary Stevenson Dr. All 10 A4
Maryburn Rd. May 183 E4
Maryfield. Edin 93 F1
Maryfield. Edin 95 D1
Maryfield Pk. E Cal 148 B1
Maryfield Pl. Bonn 182 B4
Maryfield Pl. Edin 94 A1
Maryfield Pl. Falk 59 D2
Maryflats Pl. Gran 61 F4
Maryhall St. Kirk 17 E3
Marywell. Kirk 17 E3
Mason Pl. Bonn 181 F3
Masserene Rd. Kirk 16 C3
Masterton Rd. Dunf 47 D4
Mather Terr. Laur 60 C2
Mathers Ave. Whit 169 F3
Mathieson Pl. Dunf 29 F1
Matthew St. Kirk 17 D3
Maukeshill Ct. Liv 147 E1
Maulsford Ave. Dan 156 A4
Maurice Ave. Bann 7 E2
Maurice Pl. Edin 123 E1
Mauricewood Ave. Peni 203 F4
Mauricewood Bank. Peni ... 203 F4
Mauricewood Gr. Peni 203 F4
Mauricewood Pk. Peni 203 F4
Mauricewood Rd. Auch 203 F4
Mauricewood Rise. Peni ... 203 F4
Mavisbank Ave. Shi 81 E3
Mavisbank. Loan 181 E4
Mavisbank Pl. Bonn 181 F3
Maxton Cres. Alva 5 E4
Maxton Ct. Dalk 157 D2
Maxton Pl. Ros 46 C2
Maxwell Cres. Cow 13 D1
Maxwell Pl. Stir 7 D2
Maxwell Rd. Dir 53 D2
Maxwell Sq. Muri 173 E3
Maxwell St. Edin 123 D2
May Terr. N Ber 54 A4
Maybank Villas. Edin 121 E4
Mayburn Ave. Loan 155 D1
Mayburn Bank. Loan 181 D4
Mayburn Cres. Loan 155 D1
Mayburn Ct. Loan 181 D4
Mayburn Dr. Loan 155 D1
Mayburn Gr. Loan 181 D4
Mayburn Hill. Loan 181 D4
Mayburn Loan. Loan 155 D1
Mayburn Terr. Loan 155 D1
Mayburn Vale. Loan 181 D4
Mayburn Wlk. Loan 181 D4
Maybury Rd. Edin 121 D4
Mayfield Ave. Muss 126 A2
Mayfield Cres. Clack 11 D3
Mayfield Cres. Loan 181 E4
Mayfield Cres. Muss 126 A2
Mayfield Ct. Arm 143 F2
Mayfield Ct. Loan 181 E4
Mayfield Ct. Stir 7 D2
Mayfield Dr. Arm 143 F3
Mayfield Dr. Bank 57 D2
Mayfield Gardens La. Edin 123 F2
Mayfield Gdns. Edin 123 F2
Mayfield Ind Est. Newt 183 E3
Mayfield Mews. Falk 59 F2
Mayfield Pk. Muss 126 A2
Mayfield Pl. May 183 E3
Mayfield Pl. Muss 126 A2
Mayfield Rd. Edin 123 F2
Mayfield Rd. Laur 61 C1
Mayfield Rd. May 183 E4
Mayfield St. Stir 7 D2
Mayfield Terr. Edin 123 F2
Mayflower St. Dunf 29 E4
Maygate. Dunf 29 D2
Mayne Ave. B of A 2 A3
Mayshade Rd. Loan 155 D1
Mayville Bank. Muss 127 D3
Mayville Gdns E. Edin 93 E3
Mayville Gdns. Edin 93 E3
Mayville Pk. Dunb 78 B2
Mc Call Gdns. E Lin 103 E4
Mc Kinnon Dr. Fau 193 F4
Mc Leod St. Brox 117 F3
McAdam Sq. Muri 173 E3
McAlley Ct. B of A 1 C4
McAllister Ct. Bann 7 E1

McCallum Ct. Arm 143 F4
McCann Ave. Uph 117 D3
McCathie Dr. Newt 183 D3
McClelland Cres. Dunf 29 D1
McDiarmid Gr. Newt 183 D2
McDonald Pl. Edin 93 F2
McDonald Rd. Edin 93 F2
McDonald St. Edin 93 F2
McDouall Stuart Pl. Kirk 18 A4
McGregor Ave. Loch 14 A4
McGrigor Rd. Ros 46 B1
McGrigor St. Stir 7 D2
McIntosh Ct. Brox 117 E3
McKay Dr. Dunf 29 F1
McKenzie St. Kirk 17 F4
McKinlay Cres. All 10 B4
McKinlay Terr. Loan 181 D4
McKinnon Dr. May 183 F3
McLachlan Ave. Stir 7 D1
McLachlan St. Lar 38 B1
McLaren Ave. Madd 84 A3
McLaren Ct. Lar 38 B1
McLaren Rd. Edin 124 A2
McLaren Terr. Stir 7 D2
McLauchlan Rise. Abe 49 D4
McLean Pl. Bonn 181 F3
McLean Pl. Gore 207 E4
McLean Wlk. Newt 183 D2
McLeod Cres. Pres 96 C1
McLeod St. Edin 122 C3
McNeil Cres. Arm 144 A3
McNeil Path. Tran 128 B3
McNeil Way. Tran 128 B3
McNeil Wlk. Tran 128 B3
McNeil Ave. Loan 181 D4
McNeil Pl. Loan 181 D4
McNeil St. Edin 123 D3
McNeill Terr. Loan 181 D4
McPhail Sq. Tran 128 B3
McPherson Dr. Stir 2 A1
McQuade St. Bonn 182 B4
McRae Cres. Burn 33 F1
McVean Pl. Bank 57 D2
Meadow Cres. Fau 193 F3
Meadow Ct. Burn 33 F1
Meadow Ct. Car 230 B1
Meadow Dr. Ston 171 D1
Meadow Gn. N Sau 5 D1
Meadow La. Edin 123 F3
Meadow Pk. Alva 5 E3
Meadow Pl. Dunf 29 F2
Meadow Pl. Edin 123 E3
Meadow Pl. Rosl 180 C3
Meadow Pl. Stir 2 B1
Meadow Pl. Ston 171 D1
Meadow Place Rd. Edin .. 121 E3
Meadow Rd. Rat 151 F4
Meadow Rd. Ston 171 D1
Meadow St. Falk 60 B2
Meadowbank Ave. Edin 94 A1
Meadowbank Cres. Edin ... 94 A1
Meadowbank Cres. Orm .. 159 E4
Meadowbank. Edin 94 A1
Meadowbank. Liv 147 F3
Meadowbank. Pen 159 F3
Meadowbank Rd. Orm 159 F4
Meadowbank View. Ner .. 149 F2
Meadowend. Crossf 28 B1
Meadowfield Ave. Edin ... 124 C4
Meadowfield. Cow 13 E3
Meadowfield Ct. Edin 124 B4
Meadowfield. D Bay 48 A2
Meadowfield Dr. Edin 124 B4
Meadowfield Gdns. Edin .. 124 B3
Meadowfield Rd. Edin 120 C4
Meadowfield Terr. Edin ... 124 B4
Meadowforth Rd. Stir 7 E4
Meadowhead Ave. Add ... 171 F1
Meadowhead Cres. Add .. 171 F1
Meadowhead Gdns. Add .. 171 F1
Meadowhead Gr. Add 171 F1
Meadowhead Loan. Add .. 171 F1
Meadowhead Pl. Add 171 E1
Meadowhead Rd. Add 171 E1
Meadowhead Terr. Add ... 171 E1
Meadowhouse Rd. Edin .. 121 F3
Meadowland Rd. B of A 2 A3
Meadowpark. Hadd 132 A4
Meadowpark Rd. Bath 144 C3
Meadowside. Tran 128 C3
Meadowspot. Edin 122 C1
Meadowview. Crossf 28 A1
Mearenside. Edin 121 D4
Medwyn Pl. All 9 F3
Meeks Rd. Falk 60 A3
Meeting House Dr. Tran .. 128 B3
Meggat Pl. Peni 204 A4
Meggetland Terr. Edin 122 C2
Meikle Rd. Liv 147 E1
Melbourne Pl. N Ber 54 B4
Melbourne Rd. Brox 117 F3
Melbourne Rd. N Ber 54 B4
Melbourne St. Liv 148 A3
Melbourne Cres. Burn 33 E1
Meldrum Ct. Dunf 29 E1
Meldrum Rd. Kirk 17 D3
Melford Ave. Shot 192 A2

Melfort Dr. Stir 7 D2
Melgund Pl. Loch 14 A4
Melgund Terr. Edin 93 E1
Mellerstain Rd. Kirk 16 B3
Mellock Gdns. Falk 59 F1
Mellor Ct. Ros 46 C2
Melrose Cres. Kirk 17 E3
Melrose Dr. Gran 61 F3
Melrose Pl. Falk 60 A2
Melville Cotts. Dalk 156 B2
Melville Cres. Edin 123 D4
Melville Dr. Edin 123 E3
Melville Dykes Rd. Dalk .. 156 B1
Melville Gate. Dalk 156 B2
Melville Gate Rd. Dalk ... 156 C2
Melville Gdns. Burn 50 B4
Melville Pl. B of A 2 A4
Melville Pl. Kirk 16 B3
Melville Rd. Dalk 156 C1
Melville St. Edin 123 D4
Melville St. Falk 60 A3
Melville St. Loch 14 A4
Melville Street La. Edin .. 123 D4
Melville Terr. Dalk 156 C1
Melville Terr. Edin 123 F3
Melville Terr. Stir 7 D3
Melville View. Bonn 182 A4
Menstrie Pl. Men 4 A3
Mentone Ave. Edin 95 D1
Mentone Gdns. Edin 123 F2
Mentone Terr. Edin 123 F2
Menzies Cres. Kirk 16 C3
Menzies Dr. Stir 2 A1
Menzies Rd. Bath 145 D3
Mercat Pl. Clack 11 D2
Mercat The. Kirk 17 E2
Mercer Pl. Dunf 29 F2
Mercer St. Kin 23 F2
Merchant St. Edin 123 E4
Merchiston Ave. Edin 123 D3
Merchiston Ave. Falk 60 A4
Merchiston Bank Ave. Edin 123 D2
Merchiston Bank Gdns.
   Edin 123 D2
Merchiston Cres. Edin 123 D2
Merchiston Gdns. Edin ... 122 C2
Merchiston Gr. Edin 122 C2
Merchiston Mews. Edin .. 123 D3
Merchiston Pk. Edin 123 D3
Merchiston Pl. Edin 123 D3
Merchiston Rd. Falk 60 A3
Merchiston Terr. Edin 123 D3
Merchiston Terr. Falk 60 A4
Meredith Dr. Sten 38 C2
Merker Terr. Lin 84 C3
Merkland Cres. D Bay 48 A2
Merkland Dr. Falk 60 C1
Merlin Way. Peni 203 E4
Merlyon Way. Peni 203 E4
Merrick Rd. Gran 61 F3
Merrick Way. Gran 61 F3
Merryfield Ave. Glad 129 E3
Mertoun Pl. Edin 122 C3
Merville Cres. Cali 81 F3
Merville Terr. Cali 81 F3
Methven Dr. Dunf 29 D3
Methven Rd. Kirk 17 D1
Methven Terr. Bonn 181 F3
Meuse La. Edin 123 E4
Mid Beveridgewell. Dunf .. 28 C3
Mid Brae. Dunf 28 C3
Mid Cswy. Cul 42 B4
Mid Liberton. Edin 124 A1
Mid New Cultins. Edin 121 D1
Mid Rd. King 34 C2
Mid St. Bath 145 D3
Mid St. Kirk 17 E3
Mid St. Liv 146 C3
Mid St. Loch 14 A4
Middle St. La. Gran 61 B1
Middlebank St. Ros 46 C3
Middleby St. Edin 123 F2
Middlefield. Edin 93 F2
Middlefield Rd. Falk 60 B3
Middlemass Ct. Falk 60 A3
Middlemuir Rd. Stir 7 E3
Middleshot Rd. Gull 52 A2
Middleshot Sq. Pres 97 D1
Middleton Ave. Uph 117 D2
Middleton. Men 4 A3
Middleton Rd. Uph 117 D2
Middlewood Pk. Liv 146 C4
Midhope Pl. Winch 88 A1
Midmar Ave. Edin 123 E1
Midmar Dr. Edin 123 E1
Midmar Gdns. Edin 123 D1
Midthorn Cres. Falk 60 C3
Midtown. Men 3 F3
Milburn Cres. Arm 143 E3
Milburn Cres. Arm 143 E4
Milesmark Ct. Dunf 28 B3
Mill Farm Rd. Abe 49 D4
Mill Hill. Cam 6 B3
Mill La. Edin 93 F3

Mill Lade. Lin 84 C4
Mill Rd. All 10 A3
Mill Rd. Arm 143 F3
Mill Rd. Bath 145 D4
Mill Rd. Black 171 E4
Mill Rd. Cam 6 B3
Mill Rd. Clack 11 D3
Mill Rd. Dunf 29 D1
Mill Rd. E Lin 104 B1
Mill Rd. East 168 C3
Mill Rd. Lin 84 B4
Mill Rd. Sten 39 D2
Mill Road Ind Est. Lin 84 B4
Mill Roundabout. Liv 147 D2
Mill St. All 10 A3
Mill St. Dunf 28 C2
Mill St. Kirk 17 D1
Mill Wynd. E Lin 103 F4
Mill Wynd. Hadd 132 A4
Mill Wynd. Pres 96 C1
Millar Cres. Edin 123 E4
Millar Pl. Bon 58 A2
Millar Pl. Edin 123 D2
Millar Pl. Sten 39 D3
Millar Pl. Stir 2 B2
Millar Rd. Tran 128 B3
Millars Wynd. N Sau 5 E1
Millbank Pl. Uph 116 C2
Millbank Sq. Whit 170 A4
Millbank Terr. Madd 82 C4
Millbrae. Liv 148 B3
Millbrook Pl. Men 3 F3
Millburn Rd. Bath 144 C3
Millburn Rd. West 112 C3
Millburn St. Falk 60 B3
Milldean Gr. Dunf 29 E3
Miller Ave. Crossf 28 A1
Miller Cres. Muir 64 B3
Miller Pk. Pol 61 F1
Miller Pl. Air 22 C2
Miller Pl. East 168 C3
Miller Rd. B'ness 62 C3
Miller Rd. Dunf 28 C3
Miller Row. Edin 123 D4
Miller St. Car 230 A1
Miller St. East 168 C3
Miller St. Kirk 17 F4
Millerfield. Lin 84 B4
Millerfield Pl. Edin 123 E3
Millerhill Rd. Dan 125 D1
Millerhill Rd. Dan 156 C4
Millfield Dr. Pol 61 F1
Millfield. Hadd 132 A4
Millfield. Liv 147 D1
Millflats St. Falk 39 D1
Millgate. Winch 87 F1
Millhall Rd. Stir 7 E3
Millhaugh La. Bath 145 D4
Millhill La. Muss 126 B3
Millhill. Muss 126 B3
Millhill St. Dunf 29 D1
Millie St. Kirk 17 E3
Millway. Pen 161 D3
Miln-acre. Edin 93 E2
Milne Cres. Cow 13 E2
Milne Rd. Ros 46 C1
Milnepark Rd. Bann 19 F4
Milton Brae. Stir 7 D1
Milton Cl. Duni 36 B2
Milton Cres. Bann 7 E1
Milton Cres. Edin 125 D3
Milton Dr. Edin 125 E4
Milton Gdns. Bann 7 E1
Milton Gdns N. Edin 125 D3
Milton Gdns S. Edin 125 D3
Milton Glen. Edin 125 F4
Milton Gn. Dunf 28 C1
Milton Gn. Dunf 29 D1
Milton Gr. Edin 125 F4
Milton Link. Edin 125 E3
Milton Pl. Duni 36 B2
Milton Pl. Edin 125 D4
Milton Rd. Bann 7 E1
Milton Rd E. Edin 125 E4
Milton Rd. Edin 125 D3
Milton Rd. Kirk 17 D1
Milton Rd W. Edin 124 C3
Milton Row. Duni 36 C2
Milton St. Edin 94 A1
Milton Terr. Bann 7 D1
Milton Terr. Edin 125 E4
Minard Rd. Shot 191 E3
Mine Rd. B of A 2 A4
Miner's Terr. Muss 127 D3
Mingle Pl. B'ness 64 A3
Minstrel Ct. Rosl 181 D4
Minthill Pl. East 168 B3
Minto Ct. Alva 5 D3
Minto Gdns. Alva 5 D3
Minto Pl. Kirk 16 C3
Minto St. Edin 123 F2
Minto St. Loch 14 A4
Mission La. Falk 60 A2
Mitchell Cres. All 9 F4
Mitchell Cres. Cow 13 D1
Mitchell Pl. Falk 59 F1
Mitchell Pl. Kirk 17 E3
Mitchell Rd. Ros 46 B1
Mitchell St. Dalk 156 C2

Mitchell St. Edin 94 A3
Mitchell St. Kirk 17 E2
Mitchell Wlk. Ros 46 C2
Mitchellhall Brae. Giff 132 C3
Moat Dr. Edin 122 B2
Moat Pl. Edin 122 B2
Moat St. Edin 122 B2
Moat Terr. Edin 122 B2
Moat View. Rosl 180 C2
Mochrum Dr. Crossf 45 D4
Modan Rd. Stir 7 D2
Moffat Ave. Bonn 182 A3
Moffat Ave. Sten 39 E2
Moffat Cres. Loch 14 A4
Moffat Rd. Orm 159 E3
Moidart Rd. Whit 170 B4
Moir Ave. Muss 127 D3
Moir Cres. Muss 127 D3
Moir Ct. Kel 12 C4
Moir Dr. Muss 127 D3
Moir Pl. Muss 127 D3
Moir St. All 10 A4
Moir Terr. Muss 127 D3
Moira Pk. Edin 94 C1
Moira Terr. Edin 94 C1
Mollison Ave. East 168 C3
Monar Ct. D Bay 48 A2
Monastery St. Dunf 29 D2
Moncks Rd. Falk 60 B2
Moncrieff Terr. Edin 123 F3
Moncrieff Way. Liv 147 E4
Moncur St. Dunf 29 E4
Monkbarns Gdns. Edin ... 155 D4
Monkland Rd. Bath 144 C3
Monkmains Rd. Hadd 132 B4
Monkrigg Pl. Hadd 132 B4
Monksrig Rd. Peni 203 E3
Monkswood Rd. Newt 183 D2
Monktonhall Pl. Muss 126 A2
Monktonhall Terr. Muss .. 126 A2
Monkwood Ct. Edin 123 E2
Monmouth Terr. Edin 93 D2
Montagu Terr. Edin 93 D2
Montague St. Edin 123 F3
Montfort Pl. Falk 60 A2
Montgomery St. Edin 93 F1
Montgomery St. Falk 60 C3
Montgomery St. Gran 61 E3
Montgomery St. Kirk 17 D3
Montgomery Street La. Edin 93 F1
Montgomery Way. Stir 2 A2
Montpelier. Edin 123 D3
Montpelier Pk. Edin 123 D3
Montpelier Terr. Edin 123 D3
Montrose Rd. Pol 62 A1
Montrose Terr. Edin 93 F1
Moodie St. Dunf 29 D1
Moor Rd. Path 185 E2
Moor Rd. Path 210 B3
Moor Rd. Pen 186 A3
Mooreland Gdns. Add 171 E1
Moorelands. Add 171 E1
Moorfield Cotts. Dan 156 B4
Moorfoot Ct. Bonn 182 A3
Moorfoot Pl. Bonn 182 A3
Moorfoot Pl. Peni 203 F4
Moorfoot View. Bonn 182 A3
Moorfoot View. Rosl 180 C3
Moorside St. Car 230 A1
Morar Ct. Gran 61 E3
Morar Dr. Falk 39 E1
Morar Pl. Gran 61 E3
Morar Rd. Crossf 28 A1
Morar Way. Shot 192 A2
Moray Ct. Aucht 15 D1
Moray Ct. D Bay 48 A2
Moray Dr. Lin 84 C3
Moray Pk. D Bay 48 A2
Moray Pl. Edin 93 D1
Moray Pl. Gran 61 F4
Moray Pl. Lin 84 C3
Moray Way N. D Bay 48 B2
Moray Way S. D Bay 48 A1
Morayvale. Abe 49 E4
Moredun Dykes Rd. Edin 155 E4
Moredun Park Ct. Edin ... 155 E4
Moredun Park Dr. Edin ... 155 E4
Moredun Park Gdns. Edin . 155 E4
Moredun Park Gn. Edin .. 155 F4
Moredun Park Loan. Edin . 155 E4
Moredun Park Rd. Edin .. 155 E4
Moredun Park St. Edin ... 155 F4
Moredun Park View. Edin . 155 F4
Moredun Park Way. Edin .. 155 E4
Moredun Park Wlk. Edin .. 155 E4
Moredunvale Bank. Edin . 155 E4
Moredunvale Gn. Edin ... 155 E4
Moredunvale Gr. Edin 155 E4
Moredunvale Loan. Edin . 155 E4
Moredunvale Pl. Edin 155 E4
Moredunvale Rd. Edin ... 155 E4
Moredunvale View. Edin . 155 E4
Moredunvale Way. Edin .. 155 E4
Morgan Ct. Stir 7 E2

Morison Gdns. Que 68 A1
Moriston Ct. Gran 61 F2
Morley Cres. Stir 7 D2
Morlich Cres. D Bay 48 A1
Morlich Gr. D Bay 48 A1
Morlich Ct. D Bay 48 A1
Morlich Pk. D Bay 48 A1
Morlich Pl. D Bay 48 A1
Morlich Rd. D Bay 48 A1
Mornay Way. Shot 191 E3
Morningside Ct. Edin 123 D1
Morningside Dr. Edin 123 D1
Morningside Gdns. Edin 122 C1
Morningside Gr. Edin 122 C1
Morningside Pk. Edin 123 D2
Morningside Pl. Edin 123 D2
Morningside Rd. Edin 123 D2
Morningside Terr. Edin 123 D2
Morris Ct. Inver 47 E1
Morris Rd. Newt 183 E4
Morris Terr. Stir 7 D4
Morrison Ave. Bon 57 F3
Morrison Ave. Tran 128 C3
Morrison Dr. Bann 7 E1
Morrison Dr. Dunf 46 C4
Morrison St. Edin 123 D4
Morrison Street La. Edin ... 123 D4
Morrison Way. Liv 147 E4
Mortimer Ct. D Bay 48 A1
Morton St. Edin 125 E4
Mortonhall Gate. Edin 154 C3
Mortonhall Park Ave. Edin . 154 C3
Mortonhall Park Bank. Edin 155 D3
Mortonhall Park Cres. Edin 155 D3
Mortonhall Park Dr. Edin .. 155 D3
Mortonhall Park Gdns. Edin 154 C3
Mortonhall Park Gr. Edin .. 154 C3
Mortonhall Park Pl. Edin ... 155 D3
Mortonhall Park Terr. Edin 155 D3
Mortonhall Park Way. Edin 154 C3
Mortonhall Rd. Edin 123 E2
Morven Ct. Falk 60 B1
Morven Dr. Pol 61 E1
Morven Gr. Kirk 16 C4
Morven Pl. D Bay 48 A2
Morven St. Edin 91 E1
Moss Interchange. Liv 147 E3
Moss Rd. Fall 8 B2
Moss Rd. Liv 147 E4
Moss Way. D Bay 48 A3
Moss-side Rd. Cow 13 D2
Mossband La. Shot 191 F3
Mossbank. Cow 13 D1
Mossbank. Liv 147 F3
Mossbank. Ros 46 C3
Mossburn Ave. East 168 B3
Mosscastle Rd. Slam 110 A4
Mossend Terr. Cow 13 D1
Mossgiel Ave. Cowie 20 B4
Mossgiel Ave. Stir 2 A2
Mossgiel Cotts. Liv 146 B4
Mossgiel St. Falk 59 D3
Mossgiel Terr. Laur 61 D2
Mosshat Rd. Auc 216 C2
Mosside Dr. Black 145 E1
Mosside Rd. Black 171 E4
Mosside Terr. Black 145 E1
Moston Terr. Edin 123 F2
Motion St. Loch 14 A4
Moubray Gr. Que 89 E4
Moubray Rd. D Bay 48 B3
Moulin Way. Dunf 29 F3
Mound Pl. Edin 123 E4
Mound The. Edin 123 E4
Mount Grange. Edin 123 E2
Mount Hooly Cres. Inver ... 68 B3
Mount Hope. B of A 2 B4
Mount Lodge Pl. Edin 125 D4
Mount Oliphant. Cowie 20 B4
Mount Pleasant. Arm 143 F3
Mount Vernon Rd. Edin 155 D4
Mount William. N Sau 5 F1
Mountbatten Pl. Ros 46 C2
Mountbatten St. Gran 61 E2
Mountcastle Bank. Edin ... 124 C4
Mountcastle Cres. Edin 124 C4
Mountcastle Dr N. Edin 124 C4
Mountcastle Dr S. Edin 124 C4
Mountcastle Gdns. Edin ... 124 C4
Mountcastle Gn. Edin 94 C1
Mountcastle Gr. Edin 124 C4
Mountcastle Loan. Edin 124 C4
Mountcastle Pk. Edin 94 C1
Mountcastle Pl. Edin 94 C1
Mountcastle Terr. Edin 124 C4
Mountfair Pl. Glad 129 E3
Mounthooly Loan. Edin 154 B3
Mountjoy Terr. Muss 126 B4
Mowbray Ct. Bann 7 E2
Mowbray Gdns. Cross 30 C3
Mowbray Rise. Muri 147 F1
Moy Ct. Gran 61 E3
Muckle Hill Pk. Inver 47 D1
Mucklets Ave. Muss 126 A2
Mucklets Cres. Muss 126 A2
Mucklets Ct. Muss 126 A2
Mucklets Dr. Muss 126 A2
Mucklets Pl. Muss 126 A2

Mucklets Rd. Muss 125 F2
Mudale Ct. Falk 60 B1
Muir Ct. Cross 30 C3
Muir Rd. Bath 144 C4
Muir Rd. Dunf 29 E4
Muir Rd. Liv 148 A4
Muir St. Lar 38 B1
Muir Wood Cres. Curr 152 A3
Muir Wood Dr. Curr 152 A3
Muir Wood Gr. Curr 152 A3
Muir Wood Pl. Curr 152 A3
Muiralehouse Rd. Bann 19 F4
Muiredge And Jersy Rd.
        Shot 191 D4
Muirend Ave. Edin 152 C4
Muirend Ct. B'ness 64 A3
Muirend Rd. Stir 7 D3
Muirepark Ct. B'ness 64 A3
Muirfield Cres. Gull 52 A1
Muirfield Dr. Gull 52 A1
Muirfield Dr. Uph 116 C2
Muirfield Gdns. Loan 181 E4
Muirfield Pk. Gull 52 A2
Muirfield Rd. Lar 38 C1
Muirfield Steading. Gull 52 B2
Muirfield Terr. Gull 52 A1
Muirfield Way. Liv 146 C3
Muirhall Pl. Lar 38 B2
Muirhall Rd. Lar 38 B2
Muirhead Pl. Auch 203 F4
Muirhead Pl. East 168 B4
Muirhead Rd. Sten 38 C2
Muirhouse Ave. Edin 92 A2
Muirhouse Bank. Edin 92 A2
Muirhouse Cres. Edin 92 A3
Muirhouse Dr. Edin 92 A3
Muirhouse Gdns. Edin 92 A3
Muirhouse Gn. Edin 92 A2
Muirhouse Gr. Edin 92 A3
Muirhouse Loan. Edin 92 A3
Muirhouse Medway. Edin .. 92 A3
Muirhouse Parkway. Edin .. 92 A3
Muirhouse Pk. Edin 92 A2
Muirhouse Pl E. Edin 92 A2
Muirhouse Pl W. Edin 92 A2
Muirhouse Terr. Edin 92 A2
Muirhouse View. Edin 92 A3
Muirhouse Way. Edin 92 A2
Muirlaun. For 215 D1
Muirlee Rd. Car 230 A1
Muirpark Ct. Tran 128 C3
Muirpark. Dalk 156 C1
Muirpark Dr. Shi 81 E3
Muirpark Dr. Tran 128 C3
Muirpark Gdns. Men 4 C2
Muirpark Gdns. Tran 128 C3
Muirpark Gr. Tran 128 C3
Muirpark Pl. Tran 128 C3
Muirpark Rd. Tran 128 C3
Muirpark Terr. Tran 128 C3
Muirpark Wynd. Tran 128 C3
Muirside Dr. Tran 128 B3
Muirside Gr. Crossf 27 E1
Muirside La. Lime 44 B4
Muirside Rd. Tull 4 B2
Muirton Rd. Fal 7 F3
Muirton Way. D Bay 48 A3
Mulberry Dr. Dunf 29 F1
Mulberry Pl. Edin 93 E3
Muldron Terr. Shot 192 A1
Mull Ct. All 10 A3
Mull Ct. Gran 61 E3
Mungalend. Falk 60 A4
Mungalhead Rd. Falk 60 A4
Mungle St. W Cal 172 B2
Munro Ave. Stir 2 A2
Munro Dr. Edin 153 D3
Munro Gdns. Laur 60 C2
Munro Pl. All 9 F3
Munro Rd. Fal 7 F3
Munro St. Kirk 17 D1
Munro St. Sten 38 C2
Munro Way. Liv 147 E4
Murano Pl. Edin 93 F1
Murderdean Rd. Newt 183 D3
Murdoch Terr. Edin 123 D3
Murdock Rd. Liv 146 C2
Murdostoun Cres. East 168 C3
Murieston Cres. Edin 122 C3
Murieston Cres La. Edin ... 122 C3
Murieston Ct. Muri 174 A3
Murieston Dr. Muri 174 A3
Murieston E. Muri 174 A4
Murieston Gdns. Muri 174 A4
Murieston Gn. Muri 173 F3
Murieston Gr. Muri 174 A3
Murieston La. Edin 122 C3
Murieston Pk. Muri 173 F3
Murieston Pl. Edin 122 C3
Murieston Rd. Edin 122 C3
Murieston Rd. Muri 173 F2
Murieston Terr. Edin 122 C3
Murieston Vale. Muri 173 F2
Murieston Valley. Muri 173 F3
Murieston W. Muri 173 F4
Murieston Way. Muri 174 A4

Murieston Wlk. Muri 173 F2
Murieston Wood. Muri 173 F3
Murnin Ct. Stir 7 E2
Murnin Rd. Bon 58 A2
Murray Cotts. Edin 121 E3
Murray Cres. Madd 83 D3
Murray Pl. Cam 6 B3
Murray Pl. Stir 7 D4
Murray Rd. Ros 46 B1
Murray Wlk. Dunf 29 F2
Murrayburn App. Edin 121 E1
Murrayburn Dr. Edin 121 E1
Murrayburn Gate. Edin 152 B4
Murrayburn Gdns. Edin 121 F1
Murrayburn Gn. Edin 121 F1
Murrayburn Gr. Edin 121 F1
Murrayburn Pk. Edin 121 E1
Murrayburn Pl. Edin 121 E1
Murrayburn Rd. Edin 121 F1
Murrayfield Ave. Edin 122 B4
Murrayfield Dr. Black 171 E4
Murrayfield Dr. Edin 122 B4
Murrayfield Gdns. Edin 122 B4
Murrayfield Pl. Bann 7 E1
Murrayfield Pl. Edin 122 B4
Murrayfield Rd. Edin 122 B4
Murrayfield Terr. Bann 7 E1
Murrayfield Terr. Black 171 E4
Murrays Brae The. Edin 155 E2
Murrays Brae The. Edin 155 E3
Murrays The. Edin 155 E2
Murraysgate Cres. Whit ... 169 F3
Murraysgate Ind Est. Whit . 169 F3
Murrayshall Rd. Stir 7 D2
Murrel Rd. Abe 49 E4
Murrel Terr. Abe 49 E4
Music Hall La. Dunf 29 D2
Musselburgh Rd. Dalk 157 D2
Musselburgh Rd. Edin 125 F4
Myers Ct. Dunf 29 E3
Mylne Pl. Sten 39 D1
Mylneburn Gdns. Lime 45 E2
Myothill Rd. Bank 57 E4
Myre Cres. King 35 D2
Myre Dale. Bonn 182 B3
Myreside Ct. Edin 122 C1
Myreside Rd. Edin 122 C2
Myreton Dr. Bann 19 F4
Myreton Rd. Gran 61 E3
Myreton Way. Falk 59 F2
Myretoungate. Alva 4 A3
Myrtle Cres. Kirk 17 D4
Myrtle Cres. Rosl 180 C3
Myrtle Gr. May 183 E4
Myrtle Terr. Edin 122 C3

Nailer Rd. Falk 59 F3
Nailer Rd. Stir 7 D1
Nairn Ct. Falk 60 B1
Nairn Rd. Liv 146 C4
Nairn St. Kirk 17 E3
Naismith Ct. Liv 148 A3
Namayo Ave. Laur 61 D2
Namur Rd. Auch 204 A4
Nantwich Dr. Edin 94 C2
Napier Ave. Bath 145 E3
Napier Cres. Falk 60 A4
Napier Pl. Falk 60 A4
Napier Rd. Edin 123 D2
Napier Rd. Ros 46 B1
Napier Sq. Liv 148 A4
Napier St. Kirk 17 F4
Nasmyth Ct. Liv 148 A3
Nasmyth Rd. Ros 46 A1
Nasmyth Sq. Liv 148 A3
Natal Pl. Cow 13 E2
Navar Ct. Shot 192 A2
Nebit The. Alva 4 C3
Neidpath Ct. Edin 121 D4
Neidpath Ct. Long 98 C3
Neidpath Dr. Sten 38 C2
Neidpath Pl. Dunf 29 E3
Neilson Gr. Burn 33 F1
Neilson Park Rd. Hadd 132 A4
Neilson Sq. Liv 146 B3
Neilson St. Falk 60 A3
Nellburn. Liv 146 C3
Nellfield. Edin 155 D4
Nelson Ave. Liv 147 F2
Nelson Gdns. Gran 40 C1
Nelson Pl. Stir 7 E3
Nelson Rd. B'ness 62 C3
Nelson St. Edin 93 E1
Nelson St. Gran 61 F4
Nelson St. Kirk 17 D3
Nelson St. Ros 46 C3
Ness The. Torr 26 C1
Nether Craigour. Edin 124 B1
Nether Currie Cres. Curr .. 152 A3
Nether Currie Pl. Curr 152 A3
Nether Currie Rd. Curr 152 A3
Nether Dechmont Cotts.
        Liv 147 D4
Nether St. Kirk 17 E3
Nether St. Kirk 18 A4
Netherbank. Edin 154 C3
Netherbeath Rd. Cross 30 C4

Netherby Rd. Air 22 B2
Netherby Rd. Edin 93 D3
Netherfield Rd. Pol 61 E1
Nethergate. King 35 D1
Nethergate The. Alva 4 C3
Netherlaw. N Ber 54 A3
Nethermains Rd. Den 36 B1
Nethershot Rd. Pres 97 D1
Netherton Gr. Whit 170 A2
Netherton Pl. Whit 170 A2
Netherton St. East 168 B3
Netherwood Pk. Liv 147 D4
Nettlehill Dr. Pump 116 C1
Nettlehill Rd. Liv 147 F4
Nettlehill Rd. Pump 117 D1
Neucks The. Slam 111 D3
Nevis Ct. Kirk 10 A4
Nevis Pl. Falk 60 B1
Nevis Pl. Gran 61 F3
Nevis Pl. Shot 192 A2
New Arthur Pl. Edin 123 F4
New Broompark. Edin 92 C4
New Broughton. Edin 93 E1
New Hallglen Rd. Falk 60 B1
New Halls Rd. Que 68 B1
New Holygate. Brox 117 E3
New Houses. Ath 74 B2
New Huntorfield. Gore 183 D1
New John's Pl. Edin 123 F3
New La. Edin 93 E3
New Line Rd. Bann 19 D4
New Liston Rd. Kirk 89 D1
New Market Rd. Edin 122 B2
New Mart Rd. Edin 122 A2
New Meadowspott. Dalk ... 157 D1
New Orchardfield. Edin 93 F2
New Rd. Bann 7 E1
New Row. Ath 74 A2
New Row. Dunf 29 D2
New Row. Kin 24 A2
New Row. Tran 128 B3
New Skinners Cl. Edin 123 F4
New St. B of A 1 C4
New St. Cocke 97 E2
New St. Edin 123 F4
New St. Muss 126 A3
New St. Pres 96 C1
New St. Slam 110 A4
New St. Tran 128 B4
New Swanston. Edin 153 F3
New Tower Pl. Edin 95 D1
New Well Wynd. Lin 84 C3
Newbattle Abbey Cres.
        Dalk 182 C4
Newbattle Terr. Edin 123 D2
Newbiggin Cres. Tull 4 B1
Newbiggin Rd. Gran 61 F3
Newbigging. Aucht 15 E1
Newbigging. Muss 126 B3
Newbigging Terr. Aucht 15 E1
Newbridge Ind Est. Kirkl .. 119 D3
Newburn Pl. Dunf 29 E2
Newbyres Ave. Gore 183 E1
Newbyres Cres. Gore 207 E4
Newcraighall Rd. Edin 125 E2
Newcraighall Rd. Edin 125 D2
Newcraighall Rd. Edin 125 E1
Newhailes Ave. Muss 126 A3
Newhailes Cres. Muss 126 A3
Newhailes Rd. Muss 125 F3
Newhaven Pl. Edin 93 E4
Newhaven Rd. Edin 93 E3
Newhouse Ave. Dunb 78 C1
Newhouse Dr. Falk 59 F1
Newhouse Pl. Dunb 78 C1
Newhouse Rd. Gran 61 E4
Newhouse. Stir 7 D3
Newhouses Rd. Brox 118 A2
Newington Rd. Edin 123 F3
Newland Ave. Bath 145 E3
Newlands Pk. Dunf 29 D3
Newlands Pk. Edin 123 F2
Newlands Pl. Tull 4 B2
Newlands Rd. Bann 19 E4
Newlands Rd. Gran 61 E3
Newlands Rd. Pol 82 B4
Newliston Dr. Kirk 16 B4
Newmains Farm La. Kirkl .. 89 D1
Newmains Rd. Kirkl 89 D1
Newmarket. Bann 7 F1
Newmarket St. Falk 60 A3
Newmill And Canthill Rd.
        Shot 191 D1
Newmill-Canthill Rd. Shot . 191 D2
Newmills Ave. Curr 151 E2
Newmills Cres. Curr 151 E2
Newmills Gr. Curr 151 E2
Newmills Rd. Curr 151 E2
Newmills Rd. Dalk 157 D2
Newmills Rd. Rat 151 E2
Newmills Terr. Dalk 157 D2
Newmills. Tull 4 A2
Newpark Cres. Stir 7 D1
Newpark Rd. Muri 173 E3
Newpark Rd. Stir 7 D1
Newpark Roundabout.

        Muri 173 E4
Newtoft St. Edin 155 F3
Newton Ave. Gran 40 A2
Newton Church Rd. Dan ... 156 B4
Newton Cres. Ros 47 D2
Newton Pl. Ros 46 C2
Newton Port. Hadd 101 D1
Newton Rd. Gran 40 A1
Newton St. Edin 122 C3
Newton St. May 183 E4
Newtonshaw. N Sau 5 E1
Newtown. B' ness 63 F3
Newtown St. B' ness 63 F3
Newyearfield Roundabout.
        Liv 147 E3
Nicholson Way. Liv 147 E4
Nicklaus Gn. Liv 147 D4
Nicol St. Kirk 17 D2
Nicolson Sq. Edin 123 F4
Nicolson St. Edin 123 F4
Nicolton Ave. Madd 82 C4
Nicolton Rd. Pol 62 B1
Niddrie Farm Gr. Edin 124 C2
Niddrie House Ave. Edin .. 124 C2
Niddrie House Dr. Edin 125 D2
Niddrie House Gdns. Edin 124 C2
Niddrie House Pk. Edin 124 C2
Niddrie House Sq. Edin 124 C2
Niddrie Mains Ct. Edin 125 D2
Niddrie Mains Dr. Edin 124 C2
Niddrie Mains Rd. Edin 124 C2
Niddrie Mains Terr. Edin .. 124 C2
Niddrie Marischal Cres.
        Edin 124 C2
Niddrie Marischal Dr. Edin 124 C2
Niddrie Marischal Gdns.
        Edin 124 C2
Niddrie Marischal Gn. Edin 124 C2
Niddrie Marischal Loan.
        Edin 124 C2
Niddrie Marischal Pl. Edin 124 C2
Niddrie Marischal Rd. Edin 125 D2
Niddrie Marischal St. Edin 124 C2
Niddrie Mill Ave. Edin 125 D2
Niddrie Mill Cres. Edin 125 D3
Niddrie Mill Dr. Edin 125 D2
Niddrie Mill Gr. Edin 125 D2
Niddrie Mill Pl. Edin 125 D2
Niddrie Mill Terr. Edin 125 D2
Niddry Rd. Winch 87 F1
Niddry St. Edin 123 E4
Niddry Street S. Edin 123 F4
Niddry View. Winch 87 F1
Nidrie Cotts. Edin 125 E2
Nielson Ct. Black 171 D4
Nigel Loan. Edin 155 D4
Nigel Rise. Muri 147 F1
Nile Gr. Edin 123 D2
Nile St. Kirk 17 D3
Nimmo Ave. Pres 97 D1
Ninian Rd. B'ness 62 C3
Ninth St. Newt 183 E4
Nisbet Dr. Den 36 B1
Nisbet Rd. Gull 51 F1
Nith St. Dunf 29 F1
Nithsdale St. Shot 191 E3
Niven Rd. Inver 47 E2
Niven's Knowe Rd. Loan .. 180 C4
Nivenskowe Pk. Loan 180 C4
No 7 Pit Rd. Cow 13 E2
Nobel Pl. Rosl 180 C2
Nobel View. Shi 82 A4
Noble Pl. Edin 94 A2
Norman Rise. Muri 147 F1
Normand Brae. Kirk 18 A4
Normand Rd. Kirk 18 A4
North App Rd. Kin 23 F2
North Ave. Madd 83 D4
North Bank Rd. Pres 127 F4
North Bank St. Edin 123 E4
North Bridge. Edin 123 E4
North Bridge St. Bath 145 D3
North Bridge St. Gran 40 B1
North Bughtlin Bank. Edin . 91 D1
North Bughtlin Brae. Edin .. 91 D1
North Bughtlin Gate. Edin .. 91 D1
North Bughtlin Neuk. Edin . 91 D1
North Bughtlin Pl. Edin 91 D1
North Bughtlin Rd. Edin 91 D1
North Bughtlinfield. Edin 91 D1
North Bughtlinrig. Edin 91 D1
North Bughtlinside. Edin 91 D1
North Cairntow. Edin 124 B3
North Castle St. All 10 A3
North Charlotte St. Edin ... 123 D4
North Clyde Street La. Edin 93 E1
North Cres. Pres 97 D1
North East Circus Pl. Edin . 93 E1
North East Cumberland Street La.
        Edin 93 E1
North East Thistle Street La.
        Edin 93 E1
North Esk Rd. Ros 46 B1
North Fort St. Edin 93 E3
North Gate. Torp 113 F3
North Grange Ave. Pres 96 C1

North Grange Gr. Pres 96 C1
North Grange Rd. Pres 96 C1
North Greendykes Rd.
　Brox 117 F4
North Greens. Edin 125 D3
North Gyle Ave. Edin 121 D3
North Gyle Dr. Edin 121 D4
North Gyle Farm Ct. Edin .. 121 D3
North Gyle Farm La. Edin . 121 D3
North Gyle Gr. Edin 121 D3
North Gyle Loan. Edin 121 D4
North Gyle Pk. Edin 121 D4
North Gyle Rd. Edin 121 D4
North Gyle Terr. Edin 121 D3
North High St. Muss 126 A3
North Hillhousefield. Edin 93 F3
North Junction St. Edin 93 F3
North Leith Sands. Edin 93 F3
North Loanhead. Lime 45 F2
North Lorimer Pl. Cocke 97 D2
North Main St. Sten 39 E2
North Meggetland. Edin 122 C2
North Overgate. King 34 C2
North Park Terr. Edin 93 D1
North Peffer Pl. Edin 124 B2
North Rd. Dunb 78 B2
North Rd. Fau 193 F4
North Rd. Inver 47 E2
North Reeves Pl. Whit 170 A3
North Richmond St. Edin ... 123 F4
North Roundall. Lime 45 F2
North Row. Lime 45 D2
North Seton Pk. Cocke 97 E2
North Shore Rd. Gran 40 C1
North St. All 10 A4
North St Andrew La. Edin 93 E1
North St Andrew St. Edin 93 E1
North St. Arm 143 F3
North St. B' ness 63 F4
North St. Clack 11 D2
North St David St. Edin 93 E1
North St. Dunb 78 A1
North St. Falk 60 A4
North St. Loch 14 A4
North St. Rat 119 E1
North St. Stir 2 B1
North View. Burn 50 C4
North View. W Cal 172 B2
North Way. D Bay 48 B3
North Werber Pk. Edin 92 C2
North West Circus Pl. Edin .. 93 D1
North West Cumberland Street La.
　Edin 93 E1
North West Thistle Street La.
　Edin 93 E1
North Wood Rd. Tull 4 B1
North Wynd. Dalk 157 D2
Northbank Ct. B'ness 64 A3
Northbank Dr. B'ness 64 A3
Northbank Pk. B' ness 63 F3
Northbank Rd. Crossf 27 E1
Northend. Cam 6 B3
Northfield Ave. Edin 124 B4
Northfield Ave. Shot 192 A1
Northfield Broadway. Edin . 124 C4
Northfield Cir. Edin 124 B4
Northfield Cotts. W Cal 172 B2
Northfield. Cow 13 E3
Northfield Cres. Edin 124 C4
Northfield Cres. Fau 170 B1
Northfield Ct. Pres 127 F4
Northfield Dr. Edin 124 C4
Northfield E. Tran 128 C3
Northfield Farm Ave. Edin . 124 C4
Northfield Farm Rd. Edin ... 124 C4
Northfield Gdns. Clack 11 D2
Northfield Gdns. Edin 124 C4
Northfield Gdns. Pres 127 F4
Northfield Gr. Edin 124 C4
Northfield Meadows. Fau ... 170 B1
Northfield Park Gr. Edin ... 124 C4
Northfield Pk. Edin 124 C4
Northfield Rd. Duni 36 B2
Northfield Rd. Edin 124 B4
Northfield Sq. Edin 124 C4
Northfield Terr. Edin 124 B4
Northfield Terr. Fau 170 B1
Northfield. Tran 128 C3
Northlawn Ct. Edin 91 F2
Northlawn Terr. Edin 91 F2
Northrig Cotts. Giff 133 D4
Northumberland Place La.
　Edin 93 E1
Northumberland St. Edin 93 E1
Northumberland Street North East
La.
　Edin 93 E1
Northumberland Street North West
La.
　Edin 93 E1
Northumberland Street South East
La.
　Edin 93 E1
Northumberland Street South West
La.
　Edin 93 E1
Northwood Pk. Liv 146 C4
Norton Pk. Edin 94 A1

Norton Pl. Dunf 29 F1
Norton St. Alva 5 D4
Norval Pl. Ros 46 C2
Norwood Ave. All 9 F4
Norwood Ave. Bon 58 A4
Norwood Ave. Whit 170 A3
Norwood Cres. All 9 F4
Norwood Ct. Whit 170 A3
Norwood Gr. All 9 F4
Norwood Pl. Bon 58 A4
Nottingham Pl. Edin 93 F1
Novar Cres. Kirk 17 D1
Nungate Rd. N Ber 54 A4
Nursery Rd. Falk 59 F2

Oak Ave. Loan 180 C4
Oak Bank. Laur 61 D1
Oak Cres. May 183 F3
Oak Cres. Plea 20 B2
Oak Dr. Fall 8 B2
Oak Dr. Lar 38 B1
Oak Gr. Dunf 46 C4
Oak Gr. Liv 148 A3
Oak Hill View. Madd 83 D3
Oak La. Edin 91 F1
Oak Pl. May 183 F3
Oak St. Stir 1 C1
Oakbank Ave. E Cal 148 C1
Oakbank Cotts. Ston 172 B3
Oakbank Pl. Winch 88 A1
Oakbank Rd. E Cal 148 C1
Oakfield Pl. Edin 123 F4
Oakfield St. Kel 12 C4
Oaktree Ct. Kirk 17 E4
Oaktree Sq. Kirk 17 E4
Oakville Terr. Edin 94 A2
Oatlands Pk. Lin 85 D3
Oberon. All 9 F4
Observatory Gn. Edin 123 F1
Observatory Rd. Edin 123 F1
Ochil Ave. Kirk 16 C3
Ochil Cres. Stir 2 A1
Ochil Ct. Que 89 E4
Ochil Ct. Tull 4 B2
Ochil Dr. Madd 83 D3
Ochil Dr. Sten 38 C2
Ochil La. Whit 169 F3
Ochil Rd. Alva 5 D4
Ochil Rd. Men 4 A3
Ochil Rd. Stir 2 B2
Ochil St. All 10 A4
Ochil St. Fall 8 B2
Ochil St. Gran 61 E4
Ochil St. Tull 4 A2
Ochil Terr. Dunf 29 F1
Ochil View. Den 57 E4
Ochil View. Kin 23 E2
Ochil View. Shi 81 E4
Ochilmount. Bann 7 F1
Ochiltree Cres. E Cal 148 A1
Ochiltree Ct. E Cal 148 A1
Ochiltree Dr. E Cal 148 A1
Ochiltree Gdns. Edin 124 B1
Ochiltree Terr. Falk 59 D3
Ochilview. Alva 5 D4
Ochilview. Cowie 20 C3
Ochilview Dr. H Val 26 A1
Ochilview. Loch 13 F3
Ochilview Pl. B' ness 63 F3
Ochilview Terr. B' ness 63 F3
Ochville Terr. Fish 5 E2
Octavia St. Kirk 17 D3
Ogilface Cres. Blac 142 B1
Ogilvie Pl. B of A 2 A1
Ogilvie Rd. Stir 7 D3
Ogilvie Terr. Edin 122 C2
Ogilvie Way. Liv 147 E4
Ogilvy Cres. Fau 193 F3
Old Abbey Rd. N Ber 54 A4
Old Bellsdyke Rd. Lar 38 A2
Old Bridge St. All 10 A3
Old Broughton. Edin 93 E1
Old Burdiehouse Rd. Edin . 155 D2
Old Church La. Edin 124 B3
Old Craighall Junc. White .. 126 A1
Old Craighall Rd. Dan 156 C4
Old Dalkeith Rd. Edin 156 B3
Old Dean Rd. Long 98 B3
Old Denny Rd. Lar 38 A2
Old Drove Rd. Carn 6 B3
Old Drove Rd. W Lin 219 D2
Old Eastfield St. East 168 B3
Old Edinburgh Rd. Dalk 156 C2
Old Farm Ave. Edin 153 E4
Old Farm Pl. Edin 153 D4
Old Fishmarket Cl. Edin 123 E4
Old Forge Gr. Bla 26 C4
Old Hillview Pl. Cross 30 C3
Old Kirk Pl. Dunf 29 E2
Old Kirk Rd. Dunf 29 E2
Old Kirk Rd. Edin 121 F4
Old Kirk Rd. Inver 68 B3
Old Linbun Rd. Dunf 29 F2
Old Liston Rd. Kirkl 119 D3
Old Mill Courtyard The.
　Dunf 29 D1
Old Mill Ct. Whit 170 C4

Old Mill Gr. Whit 170 C4
Old Mill La. Edin 124 A1
Old Mill La. Oak 26 C3
Old Mill Rd. Alla 191 D1
Old Mill Rd. Brox 117 F3
Old Newmills Rd. Curr 151 E2
Old Orch The. Lime 45 E2
Old Perth Rd. Cow 13 D2
Old Redding Rd. Laur 60 C2
Old Refinery Rd. Gran 62 A4
Old School Ct. Tull 4 A1
Old Tolbooth Wynd. Edin .. 123 F4
Old Town. Bann 7 E1
Old Town. Brox 117 F3
Oldwalls Pl. Gran 61 F4
Oldwalls Rd. Gran 62 B4
Oldwood Pl. Liv 147 D2
Olive Bank Rd. Muss 126 A3
Oliver Rd. Falk 60 B2
Olympia Arc. Kirk 17 D2
Onich Pl. Shot 192 A2
Onslow St. Liv 148 A3
Orchard Bank. Edin 92 C1
Orchard Brae. Edin 92 C1
Orchard Brae Ave. Edin 92 C1
Orchard Brae Gdns. Edin ... 92 C1
Orchard Brae Gdns W. Edin 92 C1
Orchard Brae W. Edin 92 C1
Orchard Cres. Edin 92 B1
Orchard Cres. Pres 96 C1
Orchard Ct. E Lin 103 F4
Orchard Ct. King 35 D2
Orchard Ct. Long 98 B2
Orchard Dr. Edin 92 B1
Orchard Gr. Edin 92 C1
Orchard Gr. Hadd 101 D1
Orchard Gr. Kin 23 F2
Orchard Gr. Pol 61 F1
Orchard La. Dunf 29 E1
Orchard La. Kirk 18 A4
Orchard Pl. Edin 92 C1
Orchard Pl. Kirk 18 A4
Orchard Pl. Liv 147 D3
Orchard Rd. B of A 2 A3
Orchard Rd. Edin 92 C1
Orchard Rd. Gran 62 B4
Orchard Rd. King 34 C2
Orchard Rd S. Edin 92 B1
Orchard Sq. Lime 45 E2
Orchard St. Falk 60 A3
Orchard St. Gran 61 E4
Orchard Terr. Clack 11 E1
Orchard Terr. Edin 92 C1
Orchard Terr. Torr 26 C1
Orchard The. Crossf 28 A1
Orchard The. Orm 159 F4
Orchard The. Pol 82 B4
Orchard The. Tran 128 B4
Orchard The. Tull 4 A1
Orchard Toll. Edin 92 C1
Orchard View. Dalk 156 C1
Orchardcroft. Stir 7 D4
Orchardfield Ave. Edin 121 E3
Orchardfield. E Lin 103 E4
Orchardfield Terr. E Cal 150 A3
Orchardhead Loan. Edin ... 155 D4
Orchardhead Rd. Edin 155 D4
Ordnance Rd. Lime 44 B4
Oriel Cres. Kirk 17 D2
Oriel Rd. Kirk 16 C3
Orkney Ct. All 10 A3
Orkney Pl. Falk 60 A1
Orkney Pl. Kirk 17 F4
Orlit Cotts. Ath 74 B2
Ormelie Terr. Edin 125 E4
Ormiston Ave. Tran 128 C3
Ormiston Cres E. Tran 128 C3
Ormiston Cres W. Tran 128 C3
Ormiston Dr. All 4 C1
Ormiston Dr. E Cal 149 D2
Ormiston Pk. Dunf 29 E3
Ormiston Pl. Pres 96 C1
Ormiston Rd. Tran 128 B3
Orr Terr. East 168 B2
Orrin Gr. D Bay 48 A2
Orrock Dr. Burn 33 F1
Orrok Pk. Edin 124 A1
Orwell Pl. Dunf 29 E2
Orwell Pl. Edin 122 C3
Orwell Terr. Edin 122 C3
Osborne Ct. Cocke 97 E2
Osborne Dr. Kin 23 F2
Osborne Gdns. Falk 59 F2
Osborne St. Falk 59 F2
Osborne Terr. Cocke 97 E2
Osborne Terr. Edin 122 C4
Oswald Ave. Gran 61 F4
Oswald Ct. Edin 123 E2
Oswald Rd. Edin 123 E2
Oswald St. Falk 60 A2
Oswald Terr. Edin 121 E3
Oswalds Wynd. Kirk 17 E2
Otterburn Pk. Edin 153 D4
Otterston Dr. D Bay 48 A2
Otterston Pl. Edin 16 C4
Oudenarde Ct. Car 230 A1
Overhaven. Lime 45 F2

Overton Cres. Den 36 B1
Overton Cres. E Cal 149 D2
Overton Cres. Laur 61 D1
Overton Mains. Kirk 17 F4
Overton Rd. Gran 61 F3
Overton Rd. Gran 62 A4
Overton Rd. Kirk 17 E4
Owen sq. Muri 147 F1
Oxcars Dr. D Bay 48 A2
Oxcraig St. Edin 92 C4
Oxenfoord Ave. Path 185 D3
Oxenfoord Dr. Path 185 D3
Oxford St. Edin 123 F3
Oxford Terr. Edin 93 D1
Oxgang Rd. Gran 61 F4
Oxgangs Ave. Edin 153 F4
Oxgangs Bank. Edin 153 F3
Oxgangs Brae. Edin 153 F3
Oxgangs Broadway. Edin ... 153 F3
Oxgangs Cres. Edin 153 F4
Oxgangs Dr. Edin 153 F4
Oxgangs Farm Ave. Edin ... 153 F3
Oxgangs Farm Dr. Edin 153 F3
Oxgangs Farm Gdns. Edin 153 F3
Oxgangs Farm Gr. Edin 153 F3
Oxgangs Farm Loan. Edin 153 F3
Oxgangs Farm Terr. Edin ... 153 F3
Oxgangs Gdns. Edin 153 F3
Oxgangs Gn. Edin 153 F4
Oxgangs Gr. Edin 153 F4
Oxgangs Hill. Edin 153 F4
Oxgangs House. Edin 153 F4
Oxgangs Loan. Edin 153 F4
Oxgangs Medway. Edin 153 F3
Oxgangs Path. Edin 153 F3
Oxgangs Pk. Edin 153 F3
Oxgangs Pl. Edin 153 F4
Oxgangs Rd. Edin 154 A3
Oxgangs Rd N. Edin 153 F4
Oxgangs Rise. Edin 153 F4
Oxgangs Row. Edin 153 F3
Oxgangs St. Edin 153 F3
Oxgangs Terr. Edin 153 F3
Oxgangs View. Edin 153 F3

Paddock The. Gull 52 A1
Paddock The. Muss 126 B4
Paddockholm The. Edin 121 F3
Page St. Loch 14 A4
Paisley Ave. Edin 124 B4
Paisley Cres. Edin 124 B4
Paisley Dr. Edin 124 B4
Paisley Gdns. Edin 124 B4
Paisley Gr. Edin 124 B4
Paisley Terr. Edin 124 B4
Palmer Cres. Curr 151 F2
Palmer Rd. Curr 151 F2
Palmer Rise. Muri 147 F1
Palmerston Pl. Edin 123 D4
Palmerston Place La. Edin 123 D4
Palmerston Rd. Edin 123 E3
Pan Ha'. Kirk 18 A3
Panbrae Rd. B' ness 63 F4
Pankhurst Loan. Dalk 157 E2
Panmure Pl. Edin 123 E3
Pannie Rd. Kirk 17 E4
Panstead St. Gran 61 F4
Panton Gn. Liv 147 D4
Papana Cotts. Giff 134 B1
Papple Farm Cotts. E Lin .. 134 B3
Paradise La. Kin 23 F2
Paradykes Ave. Loan 181 D4
Pardovan Cres. Brid 86 B4
Pardovan Pl. Falk 59 F3
Pariothall. Edin 93 D1
Paris Ave. Den 36 C1
Paris St. Gran 61 F4
Park Ave. Bank 57 F3
Park Ave. Cow 13 E2
Park Ave. Dunb 78 B1
Park Ave. Dunf 29 D2
Park Ave. Edin 125 D4
Park Ave. Gore 183 E1
Park Ave. Lar 38 B1
Park Ave. Laur 60 C2
Park Ave. Loan 181 D4
Park Ave. Muss 126 C3
Park Ave. Pol 82 B4
Park Ave. Rosl 180 B3
Park Ave. Stir 7 D3
Park Cres. Bann 7 E1
Park Cres. Bonn 182 A4
Park Cres. Edin 155 D4
Park Cres. Giff 163 F3
Park Cres. Laur 61 D2
Park Cres. Loan 181 D4
Park Cres. May 183 F3
Park Cres. N Sau 5 E1
Park Cres. Sten 39 D1
Park Ct. Muss 126 C3
Park Dr. Bann 7 E1
Park Dr. Lar 38 B1
Park Dr. Pol 82 B4
Park Dr. W Cal 173 D3
Park Gdns. Bann 7 E1
Park Gdns. Edin 155 D4
Park Gr. Edin 155 D4
Park Gr. Uph 117 D3

Park Grove Pl. Muss 126 C3
Park Grove Terr. Muss 126 C3
Park Hill. Gore 183 D1
Park La. Abe 49 D4
Park La. B'ness 64 A4
Park La. Edin 125 D4
Park La. Hadd 131 F4
Park La. Muss 126 C3
Park La. Stir 7 D4
Park Lea. Ros 47 D3
Park Par. Fau 193 F3
Park Pl. All 10 B4
Park Pl. Clack 11 D2
Park Pl. Dunf 29 D2
Park Pl. Edin 93 E3
Park Pl. King 34 C1
Park Pl. Kirk 17 D2
Park Pl. Liv 147 D3
Park Pl. Stir 6 C3
Park Rd. Blac 142 C2
Park Rd. Bonn 182 A4
Park Rd. Brox 117 F3
Park Rd. Cocke 97 E2
Park Rd. Cow 13 D2
Park Rd. Dalk 156 C1
Park Rd. Edin 93 E3
Park Rd. Falk 39 D1
Park Rd. Giff 163 F2
Park Rd. Gore 183 E1
Park Rd. Gran 61 E4
Park Rd. Hart 169 D3
Park Rd. Kirk 17 F4
Park Rd. Men 4 A3
Park Rd. Newt 183 D3
Park Rd. Orm 159 E3
Park Rd. Ros 46 C3
Park Rd. Shot 191 E3
Park Rd W. Ros 46 B3
Park St. Alva 5 D4
Park St. Bon 58 B2
Park St. Cow 13 E2
Park St. Cowie 20 C4
Park St. Falk 60 A4
Park St. Loch 14 A4
Park Terr. Edin 125 D4
Park Terr. Kir 149 F1
Park Terr. Pol 82 B4
Park Terr. Stir 7 D3
Park Terr. Tull 4 A1
Park Terr. Uph 117 D3
Park View E. Cocke 97 E2
Park View. Fau 193 F4
Park View. Kirk 16 C3
Park View. Loan 181 D4
Park View. Muss 126 C3
Park View. Pen 160 C4
Park View. Pol 82 C4
Park View. Pres 97 D1
Park View. Ston 171 E3
Park View Terr. Inver 47 D1
Park View. Uph 117 D3
Park View W. Cocke 97 E2
Park View. West 112 C2
Park View. Whit 170 A3
Parkandarroch Cres. Car ... 230 A1
Parkdyke. Stir 6 C3
Parker Ave. Edin 94 C1
Parker Rd. Edin 94 C1
Parker Terr. Edin 94 C1
Parkfoot Ct. Falk 60 A2
Parkgate. Alva 4 C3
Parkgate. Ros 46 C2
Parkgrove Ave. Edin 91 E1
Parkgrove Bank. Edin 91 E1
Parkgrove Cres. Edin 91 E1
Parkgrove Dr. Edin 91 E1
Parkgrove Gdns. Edin 91 E1
Parkgrove Gn. Edin 91 E1
Parkgrove Loan. Edin 91 E1
Parkgrove Neuk. Edin 91 E1
Parkgrove Path. Edin 91 E1
Parkgrove Pl. Edin 91 E1
Parkgrove Rd. Edin 91 E1
Parkgrove Row. Edin 91 E1
Parkgrove St. Edin 91 E1
Parkgrove Terr. Edin 91 E1
Parkgrove View. Edin 91 E1
Parkhall Dr. Madd 83 D3
Parkhead Ave. Edin 121 F1
Parkhead Cotts. W Cal 172 C1
Parkhead Cres. Edin 121 F1
Parkhead Cres. W Cal 121 F1
Parkhead Ct. N Sau 10 B4
Parkhead Dr. Edin 121 F1
Parkhead Gdns. Edin 121 F1
Parkhead Gdns. W Cal 172 C2
Parkhead Gr. Edin 121 F1
Parkhead Loan. Edin 121 F1
Parkhead Pk. May 183 E4
Parkhead Pl. Edin 121 F1
Parkhead Pl. May 183 E4
Parkhead Rd. Falk 60 A1
Parkhead Rd. Lin 84 C4
Parkhead Rd. N Sau 10 B4
Parkhead St. Edin 121 F1
Parkhead Terr. Edin 121 F1

Parkhead View. Edin 121 F1
Parkland Gr. Bla 26 B4
Parkland Gr. Ston 170 C1
Parklands. Brox 117 E2
Parkneuk Rd. Dunf 28 B3
Parkside Ct. Plea 20 B2
Parkside. Kirkl 119 D3
Parkside Pl. Dalk 157 D2
Parkside Rd. Shot 191 E2
Parkside Sq. Ros 47 D2
Parkside St. Edin 123 F3
Parkside St. Ros 46 C2
Parkside Terr. Edin 123 F3
Parkvale Pl. Edin 94 A2
Parkview Ave. Falk 59 F1
Parkway. All 10 A4
Parkwood Cres. Brox 117 E2
Parkwood Gdns. Brox 117 E3
Parliament Sq. Edin 123 E4
Parliament St. Edin 93 F3
Parrotshot. Edin 125 D3
Parsonage The. Muss 126 B3
Parsons Green Terr. Edin 94 B1
Parsonspool. Bonn 182 B3
Parsonspool. Dunb 78 B1
Paterson Dr. Shi 81 E3
Paterson Pl. B of A 2 A3
Paterson Pl. Bon 58 B3
Paterson Way. Dunf 29 D1
Paterson's Ct. Brox 117 F3
Path Brae. Kirkl 89 D1
Path The. Bann 7 E1
Path The. Kirk 17 E3
Pathfoot Ave. B of A 2 B4
Pathfoot Dr. B of A 2 B4
Pathfoot Rd. B of A 2 B3
Patie's Rd. Edin 153 E4
Paton St. All 10 A4
Paton St. Dunf 29 E3
Patrick Dr. Shi 81 F4
Patterson La. Cow 13 E2
Patterson Pl. Kirk 17 D3
Patterson St. Kirk 17 D3
Pattison St. Edin 94 A3
Pattle Ct. N Ber 54 A4
Paul Dr. Air 22 C2
Paul Pl. Cow 13 E2
Paul St. Loch 14 A3
Pavilion View. All 9 F4
Paxstone Cres. East 168 C3
Paxstone Dr. East 168 C3
Paxton Cres. Loch 14 A4
Peachdales. Hadd 131 F4
Peacock Ct. Edin 93 E4
Peacocktail Cl. Edin 125 D2
Pearce Ave. Edin 121 E4
Pearce Gr. Edin 121 E4
Pearce Rd. Edin 121 E4
Pearson Pl. Bank 57 E3
Peathill Rd. Bon 58 A3
Peatville Gdns. Edin 122 A1
Peatville Terr. Edin 122 A1
Peddie Pl. Gran 61 F4
Peden St. East 168 B3
Peebles Rd. Peni 203 F2
Peebles St. Kirk 35 D4
Peel Roundabout. Liv 147 E2
Peel Terr. Edin 123 F2
Peffer Bank. Edin 124 B2
Peffer Pl. Edin 124 B2
Peffer St. Edin 124 B2
Peffer's Pl. Hadd 132 A4
Peffermill Ind Est. Edin 124 B2
Peffermill Rd. Edin 124 B2
Peggy's Mill Rd. Edin 91 D2
Peirson Rd. Dunf 29 F2
Pelstream Ave. Stir 7 D2
Pembroke Pl. Edin 122 C4
Pembroke St. Lar 38 B2
Pencraig Brae. E Lin 103 E3
Penders La. Edin 60 A3
Pendreich Ave. Bonn 182 B4
Pendreich Dr. Bonn 182 B4
Pendreich Gr. Bonn 182 B4
Pendreich Terr. Bonn 182 B4
Pendreich Way. Bonn 182 B4
Pendreich Way. Stir 2 A2
Penicuik Rd. Rosl 180 C2
Pennelton Pl. B' ness 63 F3
Pennyschool Pl. Clack 11 D2
Pennywell Ct. Edin 92 A3
Pennywell Gdns. Edin 92 A3
Pennywell gt. Edin 92 A3
Pennywell Medway. Edin 92 A3
Pennywell Pl. Edin 92 A3
Pennywell Rd. Edin 92 A3
Pennywell Villas. Edin 92 A3
Pentland Ave. Bog 145 F3
Pentland Ave. Curr 151 F2
Pentland Ave. Edin 153 D4
Pentland Ave. Gore 183 D2
Pentland Ave. Peni 203 F3
Pentland Cres. Edin 154 A4
Pentland Cres. Rose 181 E2
Pentland Ct. D Bay 48 B2
Pentland Ct. Rosl 180 C3
Pentland Dr. Edin 153 F3
Pentland Dr. Whit 170 B3

Pentland Gr. Edin 154 A4
Pentland Ind Est. Loan 181 D4
Pentland Pk. Liv 148 A2
Pentland Pk. Loan 180 C4
Pentland Pl. Curr 151 F2
Pentland Pl. Kirk 16 C3
Pentland Rd. Bonn 182 A4
Pentland Rd. Edin 153 D4
Pentland Rd. Rosl 154 B1
Pentland Rise. D Bay 48 B3
Pentland Terr. Dunf 29 F1
Pentland Terr. Edin 154 A4
Pentland Terr. H Val 26 A1
Pentland Terr. Peni 203 F3
Pentland View Cres. Rosl . 180 C2
Pentland View Ct. Liv 147 D3
Pentland View. Curr 151 F2
Pentland View. Dalk 157 E1
Pentland View. Edin 154 A3
Pentland View Pl. Rosl 180 C2
Pentland View Rd. Kirkl 89 D1
Pentland View Rd. Rosl 180 C2
Pentland View Terr. Rosl 180 C2
Pentland View. Uph 117 D3
Pentland Way. Gran 61 F3
Pentland Wlk. Whit 170 B3
Pentlands Gdns. Edin 154 A4
Percival St. Kirk 17 D3
Perdieuc Mount. Dunf 29 D1
Perdrixknowe. Edin 122 B1
Perth Rd. Cow 13 E3
Perth St. Edin 93 D1
Petershill Gdns. Bath 145 E4
Pettigrew's Cl. Dalk 157 D2
Pettycur Bay. King 34 C1
Pettycur Rd. King 34 C1
Peveril Rise. Muri 173 F4
Peveril Terr. Edin 155 D4
Phantassie Sq. E Lin 103 F4
Philip Ave. Bog 145 F3
Philip Ave. Lin 84 C4
Philip Dr. Lar 38 B1
Philip Pl. Peni 203 F4
Philip St. Falk 60 A4
Philpingstone La. B'ness 64 B4
Philpingstone Rd. B'ness 64 B4
Phoenix La. Dunf 28 C2
Picardy Pl. Edin 93 E1
Pier Pl. Edin 93 E4
Pier Rd. B'ness 64 B4
Pierhead Bldgs. Inver 68 B3
Piersfield Gr. Edin 94 B1
Piersfield Pl. Edin 94 B1
Piersfield Terr. Edin 94 B1
Piershill La. Edin 94 B1
Piershill Pl. Edin 94 B1
Piershill Sq E. Edin 94 B1
Piershill Square W. Edin 94 B1
Piershill Terr. Edin 94 B1
Pilgrims Hill. Lin 85 E4
Pilkham Ct. Cow 13 E2
Pilmuir St. Dunf 29 D3
Pilrig Gdns. Edin 93 F2
Pilrig House Cl. Edin 93 F2
Pilrig St. Edin 93 F2
Pilton Ave. Edin 92 C3
Pilton Cres. Edin 92 C3
Pilton Dr. Edin 92 C3
Pilton Dr N. Edin 92 C3
Pilton Gdns. Edin 92 C3
Pilton Loan. Edin 92 C3
Pilton Pk. Edin 92 C3
Pilton Pl. Edin 92 C3
Pine Av. B' ness 63 E2
Pine Gr. All 10 B3
Pine Gr. Dunf 46 C4
Pine Gr. Laur 61 D1
Pine Gr. Liv 148 A3
Pine St. Dunb 78 A1
Pine Wlk. Lar 38 B1
Pinebank. Liv 147 F3
Pines The. Gull 52 A2
Pinewood Dr. D Bay 48 A2
Pinewood Pk. Liv 146 C4
Pinewood Pl. May 183 F3
Pinewood Rd. May 183 F3
Pinewood View. May 183 F3
Pinkerton Pl. Ros 46 C3
Pinkhill. Edin 121 F3
Pinkie Ave. Muss 126 C3
Pinkie Dr. Muss 126 C3
Pinkie Hill Cres. Muss 126 C3
Pinkie Pl. Muss 126 C3
Pinkie Rd. Muss 126 C3
Pinkie Terr. Muss 126 C3
Pinkie Wlk. Tran 128 B3
Pinnel Pl. D Bay 48 B2
Pipe La. Edin 95 D1
Pipe St. Edin 95 D1
Piper Cres. Burn 33 E1
Pirig Cotts. Edin 93 F2
Pirleyhill Dr. Shi 81 E3
Pirleyhill Gdns. Falk 60 A1
Pirnhall Rd. Bann 19 E4
Pirniefield Bank. Edin 94 B2
Pirniefield Gdns. Edin 94 B2
Pirniefield Gr. Edin 94 B2
Pirniefield Pl. Edin 94 B2

Pirniefield Terr. Edin 94 B2
Pirrie St. Edin 93 F2
Pitbauchlie Bank. Dunf 29 E1
Pitcairn St. Dunf 29 E1
Pitcorthie Dr. Dunf 46 C4
Pitcorthie Rd. Dunf 29 E1
Pitdinnie Pl. Crossf 27 E1
Pitdinnie Rd. Crossf 27 E1
Pitfairn Rd. Fish 5 F2
Pitfirane Pk. Crossf 28 A1
Pitfour Pl. Kirk 16 B4
Pitlochry Pl. Edin 94 A1
Pitsligo Rd. Edin 123 D2
Pitt St. Edin 93 F3
Pitt Terr. Stir 7 D3
Pittencrieff Ct. Muss 126 C3
Pittencrieff St. Dunf 28 C2
Pittville St. Edin 125 E4
Pittville Street La. Edin 125 D4
Place Charente. Dalk 157 E1
Plane Gr. Dunf 46 C4
Plane St. Dunb 78 A1
Plantation St. Loch 14 A4
Player Gn. Liv 147 D4
Pleasance Brae. Crossf 27 F1
Pleasance Ct. Falk 60 A2
Pleasance Ct. Hal 30 A4
Pleasance. Edin 123 F4
Pleasance. Falk 60 A2
Pleasance Gdns. Falk 60 A2
Pleasance Rd. Falk 60 A2
Pleasance Rd. Hal 30 A3
Pleasance Row. For 215 D2
Pleasance Sq. Falk 60 A2
Pleasance The. Aber 71 E2
Plewlandcroft. Que 68 A1
Plewlands Ave. Edin 122 C1
Plewlands Gdns. Edin 122 C1
Plewlands Pl. Que 89 D3
Plewlands Terr. Edin 122 C1
Pleydell Pl. Edin 155 D4
Poachers Gn. Clack 11 D3
Pointgarry Rd. N Ber 54 A4
Polbeth Ave. W Cal 172 C3
Polbeth Cres. W Cal 172 C3
Polbeth Gdns. W Cal 172 C3
Polbeth Pl. W Cal 172 C3
Polbeth Rd. W Cal 172 C3
Poldrate. Hadd 132 A4
Polkemmet Dr. Hart 169 D3
Polkemmet La. Hart 168 C3
Polkemmet Rd. Hart 168 C3
Polkemmet Rd. Whit 169 F3
Pollock Wlk. Dunf 28 C3
Polmaise Cres. Stir 7 D2
Polmaise Cres. Fall 8 B3
Polmaise Ct. Stir 7 D2
Polmaise Rd. Cam 6 C2
Polmaise Rd. Stir 6 C3
Polmont House Gdns. Pol 61 F1
Polmont Pk. Pol 61 F2
Polmont Rd. Laur 61 D2
Polson Gdns. Tran 128 A3
Polton Avenue Rd. Bonn 182 A3
Polton Bank. Bonn 181 F3
Polton Bank. Rose 181 F3
Polton Bank Terr. Bonn 181 F3
Polton Cotts. Rose 181 E3
Polton Ct. Bonn 182 A4
Polton Gdns. Bonn 182 A4
Polton La. Bonn 181 E4
Polton Rd. Loan 181 F3
Polton Rd W. Bonn 181 F3
Polton St. Bonn 182 A3
Polton Terr. Bonn 182 A4
Polwarth Ave. Pol 82 B4
Polwarth Cres. Edin 123 D3
Polwarth Cres. Pres 97 D1
Polwarth Gdns. Edin 122 C3
Polwarth Gr. Edin 122 C3
Polwarth Pk. Edin 122 C3
Polwarth Pl. Edin 122 C3
Polwarth Terr. Edin 122 C2
Polwarth Terr. Edin 122 C3
Polwarth Terr. Pres 97 D1
Polworth Pl. Cow 13 E2
Pomathorn Bank. Peni 203 F2
Pomathorn Rd. How 203 F2
Pompee Rd. N Sau 5 D1
Ponton St. Edin 123 D3
Poolewe Dr. Laur 61 E1
Poplar Cres. Kirk 17 D4
Poplar Gr. Dunf 46 C4
Poplar Gr. Liv 148 A3
Poplar La. Edin 94 A3
Poplar St. Dunb 78 A1
Poplar St. Gran 61 E4
Poplar St. May 183 F3
Poplar Terr. Bonn 182 A3
Poplars The. Tull 4 A1
Port Buchan. Brox 117 E3
Port St. Clack 11 D2
Port St. Inver 47 E1
Port Str. Stir 7 D4
Portal Rd. Gran 61 E3
Portdownie. Falk 59 E3
Porterfield. Bla 26 C4
Porterfield Rd. Edin 92 C2

Portgower Pl. Edin 93 D1
Portland Pl. Edin 93 F3
Portland Pl. Fau 193 E3
Portland St. Edin 93 F3
Portobello Rd. Edin 94 C1
Portree Cres. Pol 62 A1
Post Office La. Inver 68 B3
Posthill. N Sau 5 E1
Potter Pl. Gran 39 F2
Potterrow. Edin 123 E4
Pottery St. Kirk 17 F4
Pottery The. Edin 95 D1
Pottery The. Pres 96 C1
Pottis Rd. Bann 7 E2
Pottishaw Pl. Black 145 E1
Povert Rd. Gore 182 C1
Powdermill Brae. Gore 207 E3
Powdrake Rd. Gran 61 F4
Pratt St. Kirk 17 D1
President Kennedy Dr. Plea 20 B2
Preston Ave. Lin 84 C3
Preston Ave. Pres 97 D1
Preston Cres. Inver 47 E1
Preston Cres. Lin 84 C3
Preston Cres. Pres 97 D1
Preston Cross Cotts. Pres 97 D1
Preston Ct. Lin 84 C3
Preston Ct. Pres 127 F4
Preston Pk. Lin 84 C3
Preston Pl. Path 185 D2
Preston Rd. E Lin 103 F4
Preston Rd. Lin 84 C3
Preston Rd. Pres 97 D1
Preston St. H Val 26 A1
Preston St. Rose 181 E1
Preston Terr. Inver 47 E1
Preston Terr. Lin 84 C3
Preston Terr. Pres 97 D1
Preston Tower. Pres 97 D1
Prestonfield Ave. Edin 124 A2
Prestonfield Bank. Edin 124 A2
Prestonfield Cres. Edin 124 A2
Prestonfield Gdns. Edin 124 A2
Prestonfield Rd. Edin 124 A2
Prestonfield Terr. Edin 124 A2
Prestongrange Rd. Pres 127 F4
Prestongrange Terr. Pres 96 C1
Prestonhall Cres. Rose 181 E1
Prestonhall Rd. Rose 181 E1
Pretoria Pl. Cow 13 D2
Pretoria Pl. Pol 61 F1
Pretoria Pl. Lar 38 A1
Priest Bank. Giff 134 B1
Priestfield Ave. Edin 124 A3
Priestfield Cres. Edin 124 A2
Priestfield Gdns. Edin 124 A2
Priestfield Gr. Edin 124 A3
Priestfield Rd. Edin 124 A3
Priestfield Rd N. Edin 124 A3
Prime Gilt Box St. Kirk 17 D0
Primmer Pl. Cow 13 E2
Primrose Ave. Gran 61 D3
Primrose Ave. Ros 46 B3
Primrose Bank Rd. Edin 93 D3
Primrose Cres. Dalk 157 E1
Primrose Ct. Brox 117 F3
Primrose Ct. Ros 46 B3
Primrose Dr. Dal 90 B2
Primrose Gdns. Newt 206 B3
Primrose Gdns. Que 89 E4
Primrose La. Cow 13 E3
Primrose La. Kin 23 F2
Primrose La. Ros 46 B3
Primrose Pl. All 10 A3
Primrose Pl. Liv 147 D3
Primrose Rd. Lime 46 A3
Primrose St. Bon 58 A3
Primrose St. Edin 94 A2
Primrose Terr. Dalk 157 E1
Primrose Terr. Edin 122 C3
Prince Regent St. Edin 93 F3
Princes St. Cali 81 F3
Princes St. Edin 123 E4
Princes St. Falk 60 A3
Princes St. Gran 61 F4
Princes St. Stir 7 D4
Princess Mary Pl. Hadd 101 D1
Princess Mary Rd. Hadd 101 D1
Princess St. Bon 58 A3
Priors Grange. Torp 113 F3
Priorscroft. Torp 113 F3
Priory Gr. Que 89 D4
Priory La. Dunf 29 D2
Priory Rd. Lin 84 C3
Priory Rd. Madd 83 F3
Priory Sq. Kin 23 F2
Priory Wlk. Hadd 132 B4
Promenade. Edin 95 D2
Promenade. Lime 45 E2
Promenade. Muss 126 A4
Prora Cotts. Ath 73 E2
Prospect Bank Cres. Edin 94 B2
Prospect Bank Gdns. Edin . 94 A2
Prospect Bank Pl. Edin 94 B2
Prospect Bank Rd. Edin 94 B2
Prospect Bank Terr. Edin 94 B2

Prospect St. Cow 13 D2
Prospect St. Falk 59 F3
Prospecthill Rd. Falk 60 A1
Providence Brae. B' ness 63 F4
Provost Hunter Ave. Alva 5 E4
Provost Milne Gr. Que 89 E4
Provost Rd. B' ness 63 E4
Provost Rd. Lin 85 D4
Pryde Ave. Bonn 182 A4
Pryde Terr. Bonn 182 A4
Puir Wife's Brae. Bog 145 E3
Pullar Ave. B of A 2 A3
Pullar Ct. B of A 2 A3
Pumpherston Rd. E Cal 148 B3
Pumpherston Rd. Pump 148 B3
Pyothall Rd. Brox 117 E3
Pypers Wynd. Pres 96 C1

Quadrant La. N Ber 54 B4
Quadrant. N Ber 54 B4
Quadrant The. Peni 203 F3
Quakerfield. Bann 7 F1
Quality St. Edin 91 F2
Quality St. Kirk 18 A4
Quality St. N Ber 54 B4
Quality Street La. Edin 91 F2
Quaraywood Ct. Liv 147 E2
Quarrolhall Cres. Sten 39 D2
Quarry Brae. Kirk 17 F4
Quarry Brae. Pol 82 C4
Quarry Cl. Edin 123 F3
Quarry Cotts. Edin 125 D2
Quarry Ct. Cow 13 D2
Quarry Howe. Bale 151 E1
Quarry Knowe. Bann 19 F4
Quarry Pl. N Sau 10 B4
Quarry Pl. Shot 191 E3
Quarry Rd. Cam 6 B3
Quarry Rd. Fau 193 F3
Quarry Rd. Shot 191 E3
Quarry St. Shot 191 E3
Quarryfoot Gdns. Bonn 182 B4
Quarryfoot Gn. Bonn 182 B4
Quarryfoot Pl. Bonn 182 A4
Quarryford Farm Cotts.
    Giff 190 C4
Quarryknowes The. B' ness .. 63 F3
Quarryside Ct. Dunf 28 B3
Quayside St. Edin 93 F3
Quebec Ave. Liv 147 F2
Queen Anne Dr. Kirkl 119 D3
Queen Anne Pk. Kirkl 119 D3
Queen Anne St. Dunf 29 D2
Queen Charlotte La. Edin 94 A3
Queen Charlotte St. Edin 94 A3
Queen Margaret Cl. Edin 154 B3
Queen Margaret Dr. Que 89 E4
Queen Margaret St. King 34 C1
Queen Margaret's Pl. Inver .. 68 B3
Queen St. All 10 A4
Queen St. Alva 5 D4
Queen St. Bann 7 E1
Queen St. Edin 93 E1
Queen St. Falk 60 B3
Queen St. Fall 8 B2
Queen St. Gran 61 F4
Queen St. Inver 47 D1
Queen St. Stir 7 D4
Queen Street Gdns W. Edin 93 E1
Queen's Ave. B of A 2 A3
Queen's Ave. Edin 92 A1
Queen's Ave S. Edin 92 B1
Queen's Bay Cres. Edin 125 E4
Queen's Bldgs. Ros 46 C3
Queen's Cres. Car 230 A1
Queen's Cres. Edin 123 F2
Queen's Cres. Falk 59 F3
Queen's Ct. B of A 1 C4
Queen's Dr. Edin 124 B3
Queen's Dr. Lar 38 B3
Queen's Dr. Pen 160 C3
Queen's Gdns. Edin 92 B1
Queen's La. B of A 2 A4
Queen's Park Ave. Edin 94 A1
Queen's Park Ct. Edin 124 B4
Queen's Pl. Dunb 78 C1
Queen's Rd. Brox 117 F2
Queen's Rd. Dunb 78 C1
Queen's Rd. Edin 92 B1
Queen's Rd. Stir 6 C4
Queen's St. Cali 81 F3
Queen's Wlk. Edin 124 C2
Queens Ave. Brox 117 F2
Queens Ave. Hadd 100 C1
Queens Cres. King 34 C1
Queens Dr. Duni 36 C2
Queens Dr. Falk 59 F3
Queens Gdns. E Cal 148 C2
Queens Terr. E Cal 148 C2
Queens Way. Ros 46 A1
Queensferry Rd. Dunf 46 B4
Queensferry Rd. Edin 91 D2
Queensferry Rd. Edin 92 B1
Queensferry Rd. Kirkl 89 D1
Queensferry Rd. Ros 46 B3
Queensferry St. Edin 123 D4
Queensferry Street La.
    Edin 123 D4

Queensferry Terr. Edin 92 C1
Queenshaugh Dr. Stir 2 B1
Queensway. Peni 203 F4
Quench Rd. B'ness 62 A3
Quentin Rise. Muri 147 F1
Quidenham Ct. N Ber 54 A3
Quilts The. Edin 93 F3
Quilts Wynd. Edin 93 F3

Race Rd. Bath 144 C4
Rae St. Cow 13 E1
Rae St. Sten 38 B2
Raeburn Cres. Kirk 17 D2
Raeburn Cres. Whit 170 A3
Raeburn Mews. Edin 93 D1
Raeburn Pl. Edin 93 D1
Raeburn Rigg. Liv 147 D3
Raeburn St. Edin 93 D1
Raes Gdns. Bonn 182 B4
Rainhill Ave. Madd 82 C3
Raith Ave. Cow 13 E2
Raith Cres. Kirk 17 D2
Raith Dr. Kirk 17 D2
Raith Gdns. Kirk 16 C2
Raleigh Ct. Falk 59 F3
Ramage Rd. Car 230 A1
Ramillies Ct. Auch 204 A4
Ramillies Ct. Car 230 A1
Ramsay Ave. Laur 61 D2
Ramsay Cotts. Newt 182 C2
Ramsay Cres. Bath 145 E3
Ramsay Cres. Burn 34 A1
Ramsay Cres. May 183 F3
Ramsay Ct. Liv 148 B3
Ramsay La. Kin 23 F2
Ramsay La. Lime 45 E2
Ramsay Pl. Edin 95 D1
Ramsay Pl. Stir 2 A1
Ramsay Rd. Kirk 17 D1
Ramsay Terr. Bonn 181 F3
Ramsay Wlk. May 183 F3
Ramsey Ct. Kin 23 F2
Ramsey Gdn. Edin 123 E4
Ramsey La. Edin 123 E4
Ramsey Pl. Peni 203 E3
Ramsey Pl. Ros 46 C2
Ramsay Tullis Ave. Tull 4 B1
Ramsay Tullis Dr. Tull 4 B1
Randolph Cres. Bann 7 E1
Randolph Cres. Edin 123 D4
Randolph Cres. Pol 82 B4
Randolph Ct. Stir 7 D3
Randolph Gdns. Den 36 B1
Randolph La. Edin 123 D4
Randolph Pl. Bann 7 E1
Randolph Pl. Edin 123 D4
Randolph Pl. Kirk 18 A4
Randolph Rd. Stir 7 D3
Randolph St. Cow 13 E2
Randolph St. Dunf 29 D2
Randolph Terr. Stir 7 D2
Randyford Rd. Falk 60 B3
Randyford St. Falk 60 C3
Range Rd. Gran 62 B4
Rankeillor St. Edin 123 F3
Rankin Ave. Edin 123 F1
Rankin Dr. Edin 123 F1
Rankin Rd. Edin 123 F2
Rannoch Ct. All 10 B3
Rannoch Dr. Crossf 28 A1
Rannoch Dr. Whit 170 B4
Rannoch Gr. Edin 91 E1
Rannoch Pl. Edin 91 E1
Rannoch Pl. Shi 81 F4
Rannoch Pl. Shot 191 F3
Rannoch Pl. Sten 38 C2
Rannoch Rd. Edin 91 E1
Rannoch Rd. Gran 61 E2
Rannoch Rd. Kirk 16 C4
Rannoch Rd. Ros 46 C1
Rannoch Rd. Whit 170 B4
Rannoch Terr. Edin 91 E1
Rannoch Wlk. Liv 148 A2
Rannoch Wlk. Whit 170 B4
Ransome Gdns. Edin 91 E1
Raploch Rd. Stir 1 C1
Rashiehill Cres. Add 194 C3
Rashiehill Rd. Slam 110 A3
Rashiehill Terr. Add 194 C3
Rashienhill. For 215 D1
Rashierig. Uph 117 D3
Ratcliffe Terr. Edin 123 F2
Rathbone Pl. Edin 95 D1
Ratho Park Rd. Rat 119 F1
Ratho Pl. Dunf 29 E2
Rattray Gdns. Black 171 F4
Rattray St. B'ness 64 A4
Rattray Terr. Loch 14 A4
Ravelrig Hill. Bale 151 D1
Ravelrig Pk. Bale 151 D1
Ravelrig Rd. Bale 151 D2
Ravelston Dykes. Edin 122 B4
Ravelston Dykes La. Edin ... 122 A4
Ravelston Dykes Rd. Edin ... 122 A4
Ravelston Gdn. Edin 122 B4
Ravelston Heights. Edin 92 B1
Ravelston House Gr. Edin ... 92 B1
Ravelston House Loan. Edin 92 B1

Ravelston House Pk. Edin .. 92 B1
Ravelston House Rd. Edin .. 92 B1
Ravelston Pk. Edin 122 C4
Ravelston Rise. Edin 122 B4
Ravelston Terr. Edin 92 C1
Ravelsykes Rd. Peni 203 E3
Ravendean Gdns. Peni 203 E3
Ravens Craig. Kirk 17 E3
Ravenscraig St. Kirk 17 E3
Ravenscroft Gdns. Edin 155 F3
Ravenscroft Pl. Edin 155 F3
Ravenscroft St. Edin 155 F3
Ravenshaugh Cres. Muss . 127 D3
Ravenshaugh Rd. Muss ... 127 D4
Ravenswood Ave. Edin ... 124 B1
Ravenswood Rise. Muri ... 173 F4
Rectory La. Kirk 18 A4
Red Craigs. Kirk 16 B4
Red Fox Cres. Auch 180 A1
Red Row. Lime 45 E2
Redbrae Ave. B'ness 64 A3
Redbraes Gr. Edin 93 E2
Redbraes Pl. Edin 93 E2
Redburn Rd. Blac 142 A1
Redburn Rd N. Pres 96 C1
Redburn Rd. Pres 96 C1
Redburn Wynd. Kirk 17 E2
Redcraig Rd. E Cal 148 C1
Redcroft Pl. Ston 171 D1
Redcroft St. Dan 156 A4
Redcroft Terr. Ston 171 D1
Redding Rd. Laur 61 D1
Redding Rd. Pol 82 B4
Reddingmuirhead Rd. Shi ... 61 D1
Reddoch Rd. Gran 62 A3
Reddoch Rd. Pol 62 A2
Redford Ave. Edin 153 E3
Redford Bank. Edin 153 E3
Redford Cres. Edin 153 E3
Redford Dr. Edin 153 D3
Redford Gdns. Edin 153 E3
Redford Gr. Edin 153 E3
Redford Loan. Edin 153 E3
Redford Neuk. Edin 153 E3
Redford Pl. Edin 153 E3
Redford Rd. Edin 153 E3
Redford Terr. Edin 153 E3
Redford Wlk. Edin 153 E3
Redgauntlet Terr. Edin ... 124 B1
Redhall Ave. Edin 122 A1
Redhall Bank Rd. Edin ... 122 A1
Redhall Cres. Edin 122 A1
Redhall Dr. Edin 122 A1
Redhall Gdns. Edin 122 A1
Redhall Gr. Edin 122 A1
Redhall House Dr. Edin ... 122 A1
Redhall Pl. Edin 122 A1
Redhall Rd. Edin 122 A1
Redhall View. Edin 122 A1
Redhaws Rd. Shot 192 A2
Redheugh Loan. Gore 183 E1
Redheughs Ave. Edin 121 D2
Redheughs Rigg. Edin 121 D2
Redholm Pk. N Ber 54 C3
Redhouse Cotts. Winch 86 C2
Redhouse Ct. Black 171 F4
Redhouse Pl. Black 145 E1
Redhouse Rd. Black 172 A4
Redlands Ct. Whit 170 C4
Redlands Rd. Tull 4 A2
Redmill Cotts. Whit 170 C4
Redmill Ct. Whit 170 C4
Redmill View. Whit 170 C4
Redmire Cres. Alla 212 A4
Redpath Dr. Sten 39 D2
Redwell Pl. All 9 F4
Reed Dr. Newt 183 D4
Reedlands Dr. Den 57 E4
Regent Pl. Edin 94 A1
Regent Rd. Edin 93 F1
Regent Sq. Lin 85 D4
Regent St. Edin 125 D4
Regent St. Kin 23 F2
Regent Street La. Edin ... 125 D4
Regent Terr. Edin 93 F1
Regent Terrace Mews. Edin 93 F1
Regents Way. D Bay 48 A2
Regis Ct. Edin 91 D2
Register Pl. Edin 93 E1
Register St. B' ness 63 F4
Reid Ave. Cross 30 C3
Reid St. Dunf 29 D2
Reid St. Loch 14 A4
Reid Terr. Edin 93 D1
Reid's Cl. Edin 123 F4
Reilly Rd. Bon 58 A2
Relugas Gdns. Edin 123 F2
Relugas Pl. Edin 123 F2
Relugas Rd. Edin 123 F2
Rendall Gdns. Brox 117 F3
Rennie Pl. E Lin 103 E4
Rennie Sq. Muri 173 E3
Rennie St. Falk 60 A2
Research Ave 1. Rat 151 F4
Research Ave 2. Rat 151 F4
Research Ave N. Rat 120 C1
Research Park Rd. Rat ... 151 F4
Restalrig Ave. Edin 94 B1

Restalrig Cir. Edin 94 B2
Restalrig Cres. Edin 94 B2
Restalrig Dr. Edin 94 B1
Restalrig Gdns. Edin 94 B1
Restalrig Pk. Edin 94 A2
Restalrig Rd. Edin 94 B1
Restalrig Rd S. Edin 94 B1
Restalrig Sq. Edin 94 B2
Restalrig Terr. Edin 94 A2
Reveston La. Whit 170 A3
Reynard Gdns. Madd 84 A3
Rhodders Gr. Alva 5 D4
Rhodes St. Dunf 29 D1
Riccarton Ave. Curr 152 A3
Riccarton Cres. Curr 152 A2
Riccarton Dr. Curr 152 A3
Riccarton Gr. Curr 152 A3
Riccarton Mains Rd. Curr .. 152 A2
Riccarton Mains Rd. Rat ... 152 A3
Riccarton Rd. Lin 84 C3
Richmond Dr. Pol 82 B4
Richmond La. Edin 123 F4
Richmond Pl. Edin 123 F4
Richmond Pl. Loch 14 A4
Richmond Terr. B' ness 63 F4
Richmond Terr. Edin 123 D4
Riddochhill Cres. Black 171 E4
Riddochhill Dr. Black 171 E4
Riddochhill Rd. Black 171 E4
Riddochhill View. Black 171 D4
Ridge Way. D Bay 48 A3
Riding Pk. Edin 91 D2
Ridley Dr. Ros 46 C2
Rifle Rd. Gran 62 B4
Rig Pl. Aber 71 E2
Rig St. Aber 71 E2
Rigg Pk. Dunb 78 B1
Riggs View. Crossf 27 E1
Rigley Terr. Pres 127 F4
Rillbank Cres. Edin 123 E3
Rillbank Terr. Edin 123 E3
Rimmon Cres. Shot 191 F3
Ring Rd. All 10 A4
Ringwood Pl. Edin 155 D4
Rintoul Ave. Bla 26 A4
Rintoul Pl. Bla 26 A4
Rintoul Pl. Edin 93 D1
Riselaw Cres. Edin 154 A4
Riselaw Pl. Edin 154 A4
Riselaw Rd. Edin 154 A4
Riselaw Terr. Edin 154 A4
Ritchie Pl. B'ness 64 A3
Ritchie Pl. Edin 122 C3
Ritchie Pl. Gran 61 E3
Rivaldsgreen Cres. Lin 85 D3
River St. Falk 39 D1
River View. D Bay 48 A1
River Wlk. D Bay 48 A1
Riverbank View. Stir 7 E4
Riverdale Cres. Edin 122 B4
Riverdale Rd. Edin 122 B4
Riverside Ct. Liv 147 E2
Riverside Dr. Hadd 101 E1
Riverside. Dr. Stir 2 B1
Riverside. Edin 91 E4
Riverside Gdns. Muss 126 A3
Riverside. Kirkl 118 C3
Riverside Pl. Hadd 101 E1
Riverside Rd. B'ness 62 A3
Riverside Rd. Dal 90 C2
Riverside Terr. Kin 23 F2
Riverside View. All 10 A2
Road 10. Gran 62 B3
Road 11. Gran 62 B3
Road 13. Gran 62 B3
Road 15. Gran 62 B3
Road 24. Gran 62 A3
Road 25. Gran 62 A3
Road 27. Gran 62 A3
Road 28. Gran 62 A3
Road 29. Gran 62 A3
Road 30a. Gran 62 A3
Road 30c. Gran 62 A3
Road 31. Gran 62 A3
Road 32. Gran 62 A3
Road 33. B'ness 62 A3
Road 4. Gran 62 B3
Road 4a. Gran 62 B3
Road 4b. Gran 62 B3
Road 6. Gran 62 B3
Road 7. Gran 62 B3
Road 9. Gran 62 B3
Roanhead Terr. Kin 23 F2
Roanhead Rd. May 183 E4
Robb's Loan. Edin 122 B2
Robb's Loan Gr. Edin 122 B2
Robert Bruce Ct. Lar 38 A1
Robert Burns Dr. Edin 124 A1
Robert Burns Mews. Dalk . 157 E2
Robert Dick Ct. Tull 4 B1
Robert Kinmond Ave. Tull ... 4 B1
Robert Knox Ave. Tull 4 B1
Robert Smilie Ave. May ... 183 F3
Robert Smith Ct. Loch 13 F3
Robert St. Shot 191 F2
Roberts Ave. Pol 61 E1

Roberts St. Kirk 17 F4
Robertson Ave. Bath 144 C3
Robertson Ave. Bon 58 A3
Robertson Ave. Edin 122 B3
Robertson Ave. Pres 97 D1
Robertson Ave. Tran 128 B3
Robertson Bank. Gore 207 E3
Robertson Dr. Tran 128 B4
Robertson Pl. Stir 7 D2
Robertson Rd. Dunf 29 E3
Robertson St. Alva 5 D4
Robertson Way. Liv 147 E4
Robertson's Cl. Dalk 157 D2
Robertson's Cl. Edin 123 F4
Robertsons Bank. Gore 207 E4
Robins Neuk. Glad 129 E3
Rocheid Pk. Edin 92 C2
Rochester Terr. Edin 123 D2
Rocks Rd. Lime 45 D2
Rockville Gr. Lin 85 D3
Rockville Terr. Bonn 182 A4
Roddinglaw Rd. Kirkl 120 B2
Rodel Dr. Pol 61 F1
Rodney Pl. Edin 93 E1
Rodney St. Edin 93 E1
Roebuck Pl. B' ness 63 E3
Rolland St. Dunf 29 D2
Roman Camp Cotts. Pump 117 E1
Roman Camp. Path 185 D2
Roman Camp Way. Path ... 185 D2
Roman Dr. Falk 59 E3
Roman Rd. Bon 58 A2
Roman Rd. Inver 47 D1
Roman Way. B' ness 63 E3
Romero Pl. Edin 123 F3
Romyn Rd. Ros 46 B1
Ronades Rd. Falk 60 A4
Ronald Cres. Lar 38 A1
Ronald Pl. Stir 7 D4
Ronaldshay Cres. Gran 61 F4
Ronaldson Gr. Dunf 29 E3
Ronaldson's Wharf. Edin ... 93 F3
Rood Well Cotts. E Lin ... 104 C1
Roods Cres. Inver 47 D2
Roods Rd. Inver 47 D1
Roods Sq. Inver 47 E2
Roomlin Gdns. Kirk 17 F4
Roosevelt Rd. Kir 149 F2
Rope Wlk. Pres 96 C1
Ropeway. Ros 46 A1
Rosabelle Rd. Rosl 180 C2
Rosabelle St. Kirk 17 F4
Rose Cres. Dunf 29 D2
Rose Ct. Edin 91 F2
Rose Gdns. Crossf 27 E1
Rose La. Loch 14 A4
Rose La. Que 68 A1
Rose La. Torr 26 C1
Rose Pk. Edin 93 D3
Hose St. All 4 C1
Rose St. Bon 58 A3
Rose St. Burn 50 C4
Rose St. Cow 13 E2
Rose St. Dunf 29 D2
Rose St. Edin 123 E4
Rose Street North La. Edin 123 E4
Rose Street South La. Edin 123 E4
Rose Terr. Den 36 B1
Rose Terr. Sten 38 C2
Rosebank Ave. Falk 59 F3
Rosebank Cotts. Edin 123 D4
Rosebank. Cow 13 F2
Rosebank. Dunf 29 E1
Rosebank Gdns. Dunf 28 B3
Rosebank Gdns. Edin 93 D3
Rosebank Gdns. Kin 23 F2
Rosebank Gr. Edin 93 D3
Rosebank. N Sau 5 E1
Rosebank Pl. Falk 59 F3
Rosebank Rd. Edin 93 D3
Rosebank Roundabout.
  W Cal 173 D4
Rosebery Ct. Que 89 E4
Roseberry Pl. Liv 147 D3
Rosebery Ave. Que 89 E4
Rosebery Cres. Bath 145 D3
Rosebery Cres. Edin 122 C4
Rosebery Cres. Gore 207 E4
Rosebery Crescent La.
  Edin 122 C4
Rosebery Ct. D Bay 47 F1
Rosebery Ct. Kirk 17 F1
Rosebery Gr. D Bay 47 F1
Rosebery Pl. D Bay 47 F1
Rosebery Pl. Stir 2 A1
Rosebery Terr. Kirk 17 D3
Rosebery View. D Bay 47 F1
Roseburn Ave. Edin 122 B4
Roseburn Cliff. Edin 122 B4
Roseburn Cres. Edin 122 B4
Roseburn Dr. Edin 122 B4
Roseburn Gdns. Edin 122 B4
Roseburn Pl. Edin 122 B4
Roseburn St. Edin 122 B3
Rosebush Cres. Dunf 29 E2
Rosefield Ave. Edin 125 D4
Rosefield Avenue La. Edin 125 D4

Rosefield La. Edin 125 D4
Rosefield Pl. Edin 125 D4
Rosefield St. Edin 125 D4
Rosehall. Hadd 131 F4
Rosehall Pl. Hadd 131 F4
Rosehall Rd. Shot 191 E2
Rosehall Terr. Falk 60 A2
Rosehill Cres. Cow 13 D2
Rosehill Terr. Dal 89 E4
Roselea Dr. Pol 82 C4
Rosemead Terr. Cali 81 F3
Rosemill Ct. Torr 26 B1
Rosemount Ave. Kirk 17 D4
Rosemount Bldgs. Edin 123 D4
Rosemount Ct. Bath 145 D3
Rosemount Dr. Uph 116 C2
Roseneath Pl. Edin 123 E3
Roseneath Terr. Edin 123 E3
Rosevale Pl. Edin 94 A2
Rosevale Terr. Edin 94 A2
Roseville Gdns. Edin 93 E3
Rosewell Rd. Bonn 181 F2
Ross Ave. D Bay 48 A1
Ross Cres. Falk 59 E3
Ross Cres. Tran 128 B3
Ross Ct. Stir 7 D2
Ross Gdns. Edin 123 F2
Ross Gdns. Kirk 17 F4
Ross La. Dunf 28 C2
Ross Pl. Edin 123 F2
Ross Pl. King 34 C1
Ross Pl. Newt 183 D3
Ross Rd. Edin 123 F1
Ross St. Dunf 29 D3
Rossend Terr. Burn 50 B4
Rossie Pl. Edin 94 A1
Rossland Pl. King 34 C1
Rosslyn Cres. Edin 93 F2
Rosslyn St. Kirk 17 F4
Rosslyn Terr. Edin 93 F2
Rossness Dr. King 34 C1
Rothesay Mews. Edin 122 C4
Rothesay Pl. Edin 123 D4
Rothesay Pl. Muss 126 B3
Rothesay Terr. Edin 123 D4
Roughburn Rd. B of A 2 A3
Roughlands Cres. Sten 39 D2
Roughlands Dr. Sten 39 D2
Roull Gr. Edin 121 E3
Roull Pl. Edin 121 F3
Roull Rd. Edin 121 E3
Round The. Dunf 29 E2
Roundel The. Falk 60 B4
Roundelwood. N Sau 5 D1
Rowallan Ct. Edin 121 D4
Rowallen Dr. Bann 19 F4
Rowan Cres. Falk 59 D2
Rowan Ct. Bann 7 F1
Rowan Dr. Black 145 E1
Rowan Gdns. Bonn 182 A3
Rowan Gr. Dunf 29 E1
Rowan Gr. Liv 148 A3
Rowan La. Black 145 E1
Rowan St. Black 145 E1
Rowan St. Dunb 78 A1
Rowan Terr. Black 171 E4
Rowan Terr. Cow 13 E2
Rowan Tree Ave. Curr 151 F2
Rowan Tree Gr. Curr 151 F2
Rowans The. Gull 52 A2
Rowans The. N Sau 5 E1
Rowantree Rd. May 183 F4
Roxburgh Pl. Edin 123 F4
Roxburgh Pl. Sten 38 C2
Roxburgh St. Edin 123 F4
Roxburgh St. Gran 61 F4
Roxburghe Pk. Dunb 78 C1
Roxburghe Terr. Dunb 78 C1
Royal Cir. Edin 93 D1
Royal Cres. Edin 93 E1
Royal Ct. Peni 203 E4
Royal Gdns. Stir 7 D4
Royal Park Terr. Edin 94 A1
Royal Scot Way. Dunf 29 D3
Royal Terr. Edin 93 F1
Royal Terr. Lin 84 C3
Royston Mains Ave. Edin ... 92 C3
Royston Mains Cl. Edin ... 92 C3
Royston Mains Cres. Edin .. 92 C3
Royston Mains Gdns. Edin .. 92 C3
Royston Mains Gn. Edin ... 92 C3
Royston Mains Pl. Edin ... 92 B3
Royston Mains Rd. Edin ... 92 B3
Royston Mains St. Edin ... 92 C3
Royston Rd. Liv 146 C4
Royston Terr. Edin 93 D2
Rulley View. Duni 36 B2
Rullion Green Ave. Peni ... 203 E4
Rullion Green Cres. Peni ... 203 E4
Rullion Green Gr. Peni ... 203 E4
Rullion Rd. Peni 203 E3
Rumblingwell. Dunf 28 B3
Rumlie The. Slam 110 A3
Run The. B'ness 64 B4
Rushbank. Liv 147 F3
Ruskie Rd. Stir 2 A1
Ruskin Pl. May 183 F3
Russel Ct. Loch 14 A4

Russel Pl. Edin 93 D3
Russel St. Falk 60 A3
Russell Ave. Arm 143 F4
Russell Ct. Dunf 29 F1
Russell Gr. Burn 33 F1
Russell Pl. Kirk 17 E3
Russell Pl. Oak 26 C4
Russell Rd. Edin 122 C3
Russell St. Cow 13 D2
Russell St. Loch 14 A4
Rutherford Ct. B of A 2 A4
Rutherford Ct. Kirk 17 F4
Rutherford Dr. Edin 124 A1
Rutherford Sq. Muri 173 E3
Ruthven Rd. Dir 53 D2
Rutland Court La. Edin 123 D4
Rutland Sq. Edin 123 D4
Rutland St. Edin 123 D4
Ryebank. Liv 147 F3
Ryehill Ave. Edin 94 A2
Ryehill Gdns. Edin 94 A2
Ryehill Gr. Edin 94 A2
Ryehill Pl. Edin 94 A2
Ryehill Terr. Edin 94 A2

Saddletree Loan. Edin 124 B1
Sailors' Wlk. Burn 50 B4
Sainford Cres. Falk 39 D1
St Alban's Rd. Edin 123 F2
St Andrew Pl. Edin 94 A2
St Andrew Sq. Edin 93 E1
St Andrew St. Dalk 157 D2
St Andrew St. Dunf 29 E1
St Andrew St. N Ber 54 B4
St Andrew's Ct. Lar 38 A2
St Andrew's Dr. Air 22 A4
St Andrew's Dr. Arm 143 F4
St Andrew's Dr. Uph 116 C2
St Andrew's Way. Liv 146 C3
St Andrews Pl. Falk 60 A2
St Ann's Ave. Bonn 181 F3
St Ann's Path. Bonn 181 F3
St Anne's Cres. Bann 7 F1
St Anne's Ct. Newt 183 D3
St Anthony La. Edin 93 F3
St Anthony Pl. Edin 93 F3
St Anthony St. Edin 93 F3
St Baldred's Cres. N Ber 54 B4
St Baldred's Rd. N Ber 54 B3
St Bernard's Cres. Edin 93 D1
St Bernard's Row. Edin 93 D1
St Bridgets Brae. D Bay 48 B2
St Brycedale Ave. Kirk 17 D2
St Brycedale Rd. Kirk 17 D2
St Catherine. Madd 82 C4
St Catherine's Gdns. Edin . 122 A3
St Catherine's Pl. Edin 123 F3
St Catherine's Wynd. Dunf ... 28 C2
St Catherines Cres. Shot .. 191 F3
St Clair Ave. Edin 94 A2
St Clair Cres. Rosl 181 D2
St Clair Pl. Edin 94 A2
St Clair Rd. Edin 94 A2
St Clair St. Edin 94 A2
St Clair St. Kirk 17 F4
St Clair Terr. Edin 122 C1
St Clement's Cres. Muss .. 127 D2
St Clement's Gdns N.
    Muss 127 D2
St Clement's Gdns S.
    Muss 127 D2
St Clement's Terr. Muss 127 D2
St Colme Ave. Abe 49 D3
St Colme Cres. Abe 49 D4
St Colme Dr. D Bay 48 B3
St Colme Rd. D Bay 48 B2
St Colme St. Edin 93 D1
St Crispin's Pl. Falk 60 A2
St David's Ct. D Bay 48 A2
St David's Ct. Lar 38 A1
St David's Pl. Edin 123 D4
St David's Terr. Edin 123 D4
St Davids. Newt 183 D3
St Fillan's Terr. Edin 123 D1
St Fillans Cres. Abe 49 E4
St Fillans Gr. Abe 49 E4
St Fillans Pl. Kirk 16 B4
St Fillans Rd. Kirk 16 B4
St George's Ct. Lar 38 A1
St Germains Terr. Glad 129 E3
St Giles Sq. Falk 59 D3
St Giles St. Edin 123 E4
St Giles Way. Falk 59 D3
St James' Orch. Stir 2 B1
St James' Pl. Edin 93 E1
St James Pl. King 35 D1
St James Sq. Edin 93 E1
St James's Gdns. Peni 203 F2
St James's View. Peni 203 F2
St John St. E Lin 106 B2
St John St. Edin 123 F4
St John's Ave. Edin 121 F3
St John's Ave. Falk 60 B3
St John's Ave. Lin 84 C3
St John's Cres. Edin 121 F3
St John's Ct. Inver 47 E2
St John's Dr. Dunf 29 E2

St John's Gate. Den 36 B1
St John's Gdns. Den 36 B1
St John's Gdns. Edin 121 F3
St John's Gr. Den 36 B1
St John's Hill. Edin 123 F4
St John's Pl. Dunf 29 E2
St John's Pl. Torp 113 F3
St John's Rd. Brox 117 F2
St John's Rd. Edin 121 E3
St John's Terr. Edin 121 F3
St John's Way. B'ness 63 F3
St Joseph's Cotts. Tran 128 B4
St Katharine's Cres. Edin .. 155 D3
St Katharine's Loan. Edin . 155 D3
St Katherine's Brae. Edin .. 155 D3
St Kentigern Rd. Peni 203 E3
St Kilda Cres. Kirk 16 C4
St Lawrence St. Dunf 29 E1
St Laurence Cres. Slam ... 110 A3
St Leonard's Bank. Edin ... 123 F3
St Leonard's Ct. King 35 D2
St Leonard's. Edin 123 F3
St Leonard's Hill. Edin 123 F3
St Leonard's La. Edin 123 F3
St Leonard's Pl. Dunf 29 D1
St Leonard's Pl. King 34 C2
St Leonard's St. Dunf 29 D1
St Leonard's St. Edin 123 F3
St Magdalene's. Lin 85 D4
St Margaret St. Dunf 29 D2
St Margaret's Cres. Pol 61 F1
St Margaret's Dr. Arm 143 F3
St Margaret's Rd. Edin 123 D2
St Margaret's Rd. N Ber ... 54 B4
St Margarets Ct. N Ber 54 B4
St Margarets Dr. Dunf 29 D2
St Mark's La. Edin 125 D4
St Mark's La. Edin 125 D4
St Mark's Pl. Edin 125 D4
St Martin's Ct. Hadd 132 B4
St Martin's Gate. Hadd 132 A4
St Martin's Pl. Hadd 132 B4
St Mary's Pl. Edin 125 D4
St Mary's Pl. Kirk 17 E3
St Mary's Place La. Edin .. 125 E4
St Mary's Rd. Kirk 17 E3
St Mary's St. Edin 123 F4
St Mary's Wynd. Stir 7 D4
St Marys Pl. Gran 61 F4
St Michael's Ave. Muss 126 B3
St Michael's Wynd. Lin 85 D4
St Modans Ct. Falk 60 A2
St Mungo's View. Peni 203 F3
St Ninian's Ave. Lin 84 C4
St Ninian's Dr. Edin 121 E4
St Ninian's Rd. Edin 121 E4
St Ninian's Rd. Lin 84 C4
St Ninian's Row. Edin 93 E1
St Ninian's Terr. Edin 122 C1
St Ninian's Way. Lin 84 C4
St Ninians Rd. Stir 6 C3
St Ninians Rd. Stir 7 D4
St Ninians Way. Muir 65 F2
St Patrick Sq. Edin 123 F3
St Patrick St. Edin 123 F3
St Paul's Dr. Arm 144 A3
St Peter's Ct. Inver 47 E2
St Ronan's Terr. Edin 123 D1
St Serf's Pl. Tull 4 A2
St Serf's Rd. Tull 4 A2
St Serf's Wlk. Alva 4 C3
St Serfs Gr. Clack 11 D2
St Stephen Pl. Edin 93 D1
St Stephen St. Edin 93 D1
St Teresa Pl. Edin 122 C2
St Thomas Rd. Edin 123 F2
St Thomas's Pl. Stir 6 C3
St Thomas's Well. Stir 6 B4
St Valery Dr. Stir 7 D2
St Vincent St. Edin 93 D1
Sainthill St. N Ber 54 A4
Salamanca Cres. Auch 204 A4
Salamander Pl. Edin 94 A3
Salamander St. Edin 94 A3
Salen Loan. Shot 192 A2
Salisbury Pl. Edin 123 F3
Salisbury Rd. Edin 123 F3
Salisbury St. Kirk 17 D3
Salisbury View. May 183 D3
Salmon Dr. Falk 59 F1
Salmon Inn Rd. Laur 61 E1
Salmon Inn Rd. Pol 61 E1
Salmond Pl. Edin 94 A1
Salt Preston Pl. Pres 96 C1
Saltcoats Dr. Gran 61 F4
Saltcoats Rd. Gran 62 A4
Saltcoats Rd. Gull 52 A1
Salter's Rd. Dalk 157 E3
Salter's Rd. Muss 127 D2
Salter's Rd. Path 186 A1
Salter's Rd. White 127 E3
Salters' Gr. Dalk 157 E2
Salters' Rd. Dalk 157 E2
Salters' Rd. Path 185 F1
Salters' Terr. Dalk 157 E2
Saltire Gdns. Ath 101 F4
Saltpans. Lime 45 D2
Salvage Rd. Ros 46 B1

Salvesen Cres. Edin 92 A3
Salvesen Gdns. Edin 92 A3
Salvesen Gr. Edin 92 A3
Salvesen Terr. Edin 92 A3
Samoa Terr. Auch 204 A4
Sand Port. Edin 94 A3
Sandeman Ct. Kin 23 F2
Sanderson Terr. Aucht 15 D1
Sanderson's Gr. Tran 128 B4
Sandersons Wynd. Tran ... 128 B4
Sandford Gdns. Edin 125 D4
Sandiland Dr. E Cal 148 A1
Sandilands. Lime 45 E2
Sandport Pl. Edin 93 F3
Sandport St. Edin 93 F3
Sands The. Hadd 132 A4
Sandy Loan. Gull 52 A1
Sandy Loan. Laur 61 D2
Sandy Rd. Abe 32 B3
Sandyford Ave. Madd 84 A3
Sandyhill Ave. Shot 192 A2
Sandyloan Cres. Laur 61 D2
Sandyvale Pl. Shot 192 A2
Sang Pl. Kirk 17 D2
Sang Rd. Kirk 17 D2
Sarazen Gn. Liv 147 D4
Sauchenbush Rd. Kirk 16 C3
Sauchie Ct. Bann 7 F1
Sauchiebank. Edin 122 C3
Saughbank. Uph 117 D3
Saughs The. Newt 183 D2
Saughton Ave. Edin 122 B2
Saughton Cres. Edin 122 A3
Saughton Gdns. Edin 122 A3
Saughton Gr. Edin 122 A3
Saughton Loan. Edin 122 A3
Saughton Mains Ave. Edin 121 F2
Saughton Mains Bank.
    Edin 122 A2
Saughton Mains Dr. Edin .. 121 F2
Saughton Mains Gdns.
    Edin 121 F2
Saughton Mains Gr. Edin .. 122 A2
Saughton Mains Loan.
    Edin 121 F2
Saughton Mains Pk. Edin .. 121 F2
Saughton Mains Pl. Edin .. 121 F2
Saughton Mains St. Edin .. 121 F2
Saughton Mains Terr. Edin 121 F2
Saughton Pk. Edin 122 A3
Saughton Rd. Edin 121 F2
Saughton Rd N. Edin 121 F3
Saughtonhall Ave. Edin 122 B3
Saughtonhall Ave W. Edin 122 A3
Saughtonhall Cir. Edin 122 B3
Saughtonhall Cres. Edin ... 122 A3
Saughtonhall Dr. Edin 122 A3
Saughtonhall Gdns. Edin .. 122 B3
Saughtonhall Gr. Edin 122 B3
Saughtonhall Pl. Edin 122 B3
Saughtonhall Terr. Edin ... 122 B3
Saunders Pl. Edin 93 D1
Saunders St. Kirk 17 D1
Savile Pl. Edin 123 F2
Savile Terr. Edin 123 F2
Sawers Ave. Den 36 B1
Saxe Coburg Pl. Edin 93 D1
Saxe Coburg St. Edin 93 D1
Schaw Ct. N Sau 5 E1
Schaw Rd. Pres 97 D1
Schawpark Ave. N Sau 5 E1
Schiltron Way. Bann 7 E2
Scholars' Brae. Burn 50 C4
School Brae. B'ness 63 F4
School Brae. Bonn 156 A1
School Brae. Dunb 105 F4
School Brae. Edin 91 D3
School Brae. Kirk 18 A4
School Gn. Bonn 156 A1
School Gn. Long 98 C3
School La. Alla 212 A4
School La. Bath 145 D3
School La. Cocke 97 E2
School La. E Cal 148 B2
School La. Men 4 A4
School Pl. Uph 116 C2
School Rd. Aber 71 E2
School Rd. E Lin 103 F4
School Rd. Fau 170 B1
School Rd. Laur 61 D1
School Rd. Laur 61 D2
School Rd. N Ber 54 B4
School Rd. Tull 4 A1
School Row. Dunf 28 B3
School St. Cow 13 E2
School St. Shot 191 F2
School Wlk. Sten 38 B2
School Wynd. Kirk 17 D1
Sciennes. Edin 123 F3
Sciennes Gdns. Edin 123 F3
Sciennes Hill Pl. Edin 123 F3
Sciennes House Pl. Edin .. 123 F3
Sciennes Pl. Edin 123 F3
Sciennes Rd. Edin 123 E3
Sclanderston Rd. Den 57 E4
Scobie Pl. Dunf 29 E2
Scollon Ave. Bonn 182 B4
Scone Gdns. Edin 94 B1

Scotia Pl. Falk 60 B3
Scotland Dr. Dunf 29 F2
Scotland St. Edin 93 E1
Scotlands Cl. B'ness 63 F4
Scotmill Way. Inver 47 E2
Scotstoun Ave. Que 89 E4
Scotstoun Gn. Que 89 D4
Scotstoun Pk. Que 89 E4
Scotstoun Rd. Cowie 20 C4
Scott Ave. Pol 61 F1
Scott Cres. All 10 A3
Scott Ct. Liv 148 B3
Scott Pl. Fau 193 F3
Scott Rd. Peni 203 F4
Scott St. Dunf 28 C3
Scott St. Gran 61 E3
Scott St. Kirk 17 D1
Scott St. Stir 2 A1
Scott Terr. Bath 145 E3
Seabegs Cres. Bon 58 A2
Seabegs Pl. Bon 57 F2
Seabegs Rd. Bon 57 F2
Seacliff. E Lin 56 A3
Seacot. Edin 94 B2
Seafield Ave. Edin 94 B2
Seafield Cres. Dunb 78 A1
Seafield Ct. Edin 59 F1
Seafield Moor Rd. Rosl 180 B3
Seafield Pl. D Bay 48 A1
Seafield Pl. Edin 94 B2
Seafield Rd. Black 171 F4
Seafield Rd. Edin 94 B2
Seafield Rd. Kirk 35 D4
Seafield Rd. Rosl 180 C3
Seafield Road E. Edin 94 C2
Seafield Rows. Black 146 A1
Seafield St. Edin 94 B2
Seafield View. King 35 D2
Seafield View. Kirk 35 D4
Seafield Way. Edin 94 C2
Seaforth Dr. Edin 92 B1
Seaforth Pl. Burn 50 C4
Seaforth Pl. Kirk 17 F4
Seaforth Pl. Stir 7 D4
Seaforth Rd. Falk 39 E1
Seaforth Terr. Bonn 181 F3
Sealcar St. Edin 92 C4
Sealock Ct. Gran 61 E3
Sealstrand. D Bay 48 B2
Seaport St. Edin 94 A3
Seaside Pl. Abe 49 E4
Seaton Pl. Falk 60 B2
Seaview Cres. Edin 125 F4
Seaview Pl. B'ness 63 F4
Seaview Terr. Edin 125 F4
Seco Pl. Cow 13 E2
Second Gait. Rat 151 F4
Second St. Newt 183 D2
Sedgebank. Liv 147 F3
Seggarsdean Ct. Hadd 132 B4
Seggarsdean Pk. Hadd 132 B4
Seggarsdean Terr. Hadd .. 132 B4
Selkirk Ave. Cow 13 E1
Selkirk Rd. Ros 67 D4
Selm Pk. Liv 148 A2
Selvage Pl. Ros 47 D2
Selvage St. Ros 47 D2
Semple St. Edin 123 D4
Seton Ct. Cocke 97 F2
Seton Terr. Tran 128 B3
Seton Dr. Stir 7 E2
Seton Mains. Cocke 98 A2
Seton Pl. Cocke 97 F2
Seton Pl. D Bay 48 B3
Seton Pl. Edin 123 F3
Seton Pl. Kirk 16 B4
Seton Rd. Long 98 C3
Seton Terr. B'ness 64 A4
Seton View. Cocke 97 F2
Seton Wynd. Cocke 97 F2
Seventh St. Newt 183 D3
Shadepark Cres. Dalk 157 D2
Shadepark Dr. Dalk 157 D2
Shadepark Gdns. Dalk 157 D2
Shaftesbury Pk. Edin 122 C2
Shaftesbury St. All 10 A4
Shafto Pl. B'ness 63 F3
Shamrock Pl. Cow 13 D2
Shamrock St. Dunf 29 D3
Shandon Cres. Edin 122 C2
Shandon Pl. Edin 122 C2
Shandon Rd. Edin 122 C2
Shandon St. Edin 122 C2
Shandon Terr. Edin 122 C2
Shandwick Pl. Edin 123 D4
Shanks Ave. Den 57 F4
Shanks Rd. Whit 170 A4
Shannon Dr. Falk 59 F2
Sharp Terr. Gran 61 E3
Sharpdale Loan. Edin 124 A2
Shaw Ave. Arm 143 F3
Shaw Cres. Loch 14 A4
Shaw Pl. Arm 143 F3
Shaw Pl. Gran 61 E3
Shaw Pl. May 183 E4
Shaw St. Dunf 29 E1
Shaw's Pl. Edin 93 F2
Shaw's Sq. Edin 93 F1

Shaw's St. Edin 93 F2
Shaw's Terr. Edin 93 F2
Shaws Ct. Auch 180 A1
Sheephousehill. Fau 193 F3
Sheperdlands Gr. Bla 26 B4
Shepherd Cres. Burn 50 B4
Sherbrooke Rd. Ros 46 B2
Sheriff Bank. Edin 93 F3
Sheriff Brae. Edin 93 F3
Sheriff Pk. Edin 93 F3
Sheriffhall Junction. Dan ... 156 B3
Sheriffmuir Rd. B of A 2 B4
Sheriffmuirlands. Stir 2 B2
Sheriffs Pk. Lin 85 F4
Sherriff Hall Cotts. E Lin ... 74 C4
Sherriff La. Sten 38 C2
Sherwood Ave. Bonn 182 B3
Sherwood Cres. Bonn 182 B3
Sherwood Dr. Bonn 182 B3
Sherwood Gr. Bonn 182 B3
Sherwood Ind Est. Bonn ... 182 B4
Sherwood Loan. Bonn 182 B3
Sherwood Pk. Bonn 182 B3
Sherwood Pl. Bonn 182 B3
Sherwood Terr. Bonn 182 B3
Sherwood View. Bonn 182 B3
Sherwood Way. Bonn 182 B3
Sherwood Wlk. Bonn 182 B3
Shetland Ct. All 10 A3
Shetland Pl. Kirk 17 F4
Shiel Ct. Gran 61 E2
Shiel Gdns. Falk 39 E1
Shiel Gdns. Shot 192 A2
Shiel Wlk. Liv 148 A3
Shields Rd. Dunf 29 F2
Shieling The. Crossf 27 F1
Shillinghill. All 10 A3
Shinwell Pl. Ros 46 C2
Shiphaugh Pl. Stir 2 B1
Shire Way. All 9 F3
Shirra's Brae Rd. Stir 7 E2
Shoestanes Rd. Stow 228 B1
Shoestanes Terr. Stow 228 B1
Shore. Edin 94 A3
Shore Pl. Edin 94 A3
Shore Rd. Abe 49 E4
Shore Rd. Air 22 B2
Shore Rd. Kirk 18 A3
Shore Rd. Que 68 A1
Shore Rd. Stir 7 D4
Shore St. Dunb 78 C2
Shore The. All 10 A4
Shorthope St. Muss 126 B3
Shotts Rd. Fau 193 E2
Shotts Rd. Sals 167 F1
Shottsburn Rd. Sals 167 D2
Shottskirk Rd. Shot 191 E3
Shrub Mount. Edin 95 D1
Shrub Place La. Edin 93 F1
Sibbald Pl. Liv 147 D3
Sibbalds Brae. Bath 144 B3
Sidegate. Hadd 132 A4
Sidehead Rd. East 168 C3
Sidlaw Pl. Gran 61 F3
Sidlaw St. Kirk 16 C4
Sienna Gdns. Edin 123 F3
Sighthill Ave. Edin 121 F1
Sighthill Bank. Edin 121 E1
Sighthill Cres. Edin 121 E1
Sighthill Ct. Edin 121 E1
Sighthill Dr. Edin 121 E1
Sighthill Gdns. Edin 121 E1
Sighthill Gn. Edin 121 E1
Sighthill Gr. Edin 121 F1
Sighthill Ind Est. Edin 121 D2
Sighthill Loan. Edin 121 E1
Sighthill Neuk. Edin 121 E1
Sighthill Pk. Edin 121 E1
Sighthill Pl. Edin 121 E1
Sighthill Rd. Edin 121 E1
Sighthill Rise. Edin 121 E1
Sighthill St. Edin 121 E1
Sighthill Terr. Edin 121 E1
Sighthill View. Edin 121 E1
Sighthill Wynd. Edin 121 E1
Silver St. Dunb 78 B1
Silver St. Kin 23 F2
Silverbarton Terr. Burn 33 E1
Silverburn Dr. Peni 203 E3
Silverdale Rd. Pol 82 C4
Silverknowes Ave. Edin 91 F2
Silverknowes Bank. Edin ... 91 F2
Silverknowes Brae. Edin ... 92 A2
Silverknowes Cres. Edin ... 91 F2
Silverknowes Ct. Edin 91 F2
Silverknowes Dell. Edin 91 F2
Silverknowes Dr. Edin 91 F2
Silverknowes Eastway. Edin 91 F2
Silverknowes Gdns. Edin ... 92 A2
Silverknowes Gn. Edin 92 A2
Silverknowes Gr. Edin 91 F2
Silverknowes Hill. Edin 91 F2
Silverknowes Loan. Edin ... 91 F2
Silverknowes Midway. Edin 91 F2
Silverknowes Neuk. Edin ... 92 A2
Silverknowes Parkway. Edin 91 F3
Silverknowes Pl. Edin 91 F3

Silverknowes Rd E. Edin 92 A2
Silverknowes Rd. Edin 91 F3
Silverknowes Rd S. Edin 91 F2
Silverknowes Southway.
  Edin 92 A2
Silverknowes Terr. Edin 91 F2
Silverknowes View. Edin 92 A2
Simon Sq. Edin 123 F4
Simpson Cres. Bath 145 E3
Simpson Dr. Madd 83 D3
Simpson Parkway. Liv 147 D1
Simpson Parkway. W Cal 173 D4
Simpson Rd. Brox 118 A3
Simpson St. Falk 59 F3
Simpson Wlk. Dunf 29 F1
Sinclair Cres. Den 36 B1
Sinclair Ct. Aber 71 E2
Sinclair Ct. Bann 7 F1
Sinclair Dr. Cow 13 D1
Sinclair Dr. Fall 8 B2
Sinclair Way. Liv 147 E3
Sir George Bruce Rd. Oak .. 26 C4
Sir Harry Lauder Rd. Edin . 125 D4
Sir James Black Gait. Loch . 14 A4
Sir Walter Scott Pend. Pres 96 C1
Sir William Fraser Homes.
  Edin 153 D4
Sixth St. Newt 183 D3
Skaithmuir Ave. Sten 39 D2
Skaithmuir Cres. Sten 39 D2
Skelmorlie Pl. Sten 38 C2
Skeltie Muir Ave. Bonn 182 A3
Skeltiemuir Ct. Bonn 182 A3
Skeltiemuir Gr. Bonn 182 A3
Skene St. Bon 58 A3
Skibo Ct. Dunf 29 D2
Skibo Pl. Kirk 16 B3
Skye Ct. Gran 61 E3
Skye Dr. Pol 61 F1
Skye Rd. Dunf 29 F1
Skylaw Terr. For 215 D1
Skythorn Way. Falk 59 F1
Slaeside. Bale 151 E1
Slamannan Rd. Avon 112 A3
Slamannan Rd. Falk 60 A1
Slamannan Rd. Slam 110 A1
Slateford Rd. Edin 122 B2
Sleigh Dr. Edin 94 B1
Sleigh Gdns. Edin 94 B1
Sligo St. Edin 93 F2
Sloan St. Edin 93 F2
Small St. Loch 14 A3
Smallburn Pl. Gran 61 F3
Smeaton Gdns. Kirk 17 E3
Smeaton Gr. Muss 126 B3
Smeaton Rd. Kirk 17 E3
Smith Ave. Cow 13 D2
Smith Pl. Den 36 B1
Smith St. Falk 60 A4
Smith's Pl. Edin 93 F2
Smith's Terr Kirk 17 E3
Smithfield Loan. All 9 F3
Smithfield St. Edin 122 B3
Smithy Brae. Kir 149 F1
Smithy Gn Ave. Dan 156 A4
Smithy Row. Ath 74 A2
Snab Brae. B' ness 63 E3
Snab La. B' ness 63 E4
Snowdon Pl. Stir 7 D3
Snowdon Place La. Stir 7 D3
Society La. W Cal 172 B2
Society Pl. W Cal 172 B2
Society Rd. Que 67 F1
Solway Dr Rank 57 C4
Somerset Pl. Edin 94 A2
Somerville Rd. Ros 46 B1
Somerville Sq. Burn 50 C4
Somerville St. Burn 50 C4
Sommers Pk. E Cal 148 B1
Sommerville Gdns. Que 89 E4
Somnerfield Ave. Hadd 131 F4
Somnerfield Cres. Hadd 131 F4
Somnerfield Ct. Hadd 131 F4
Somnerfield Gr. Hadd 131 F4
Somnerfield Pk. Hadd 131 F4
Souillac Dr. Den 36 B1
South Approach Rd. Air 23 D1
South Ave. Bla 26 A4
South Ave. Madd 83 D4
South Bantaskine Rd. Falk .. 60 A2
South Barnton Ave. Edin 91 F2
South Beechwood. Edin 122 A3
South Brae. Madd 83 D3
South Bridge. Edin 123 E4
South Bridge St. Bath 145 D3
South Bridge St. Gran 40 B1
South Broomage Ave. Lar ... 38 B1
South Charlotte St. Edin 123 D4
South Clerk St. Edin 123 F3
South College St. Edin 123 E4
South Craigs Rd. Madd 82 C4
South Cres. Pres 97 D1
South Dewar St. Dunf 28 C2
South Doors. Cocke 97 E2
South Dr. Dunf 46 C3
South Drummond St. Edin . 123 F4
South East Circus Pl. Edin .. 93 D1
South East Cumberland Street La.
  Edin 93 E1
South East Thistle Street La.
  Edin 93 E1
South Ettrick Rd. Edin 122 C2
South Fergus Pl. Kirk 17 D2
South Fort St. Edin 93 F3
South Gayfield La. Edin 93 F1
South Gillsland Rd. Edin 122 C2
South Grange Ave. Pres 127 F4
South Gray St. Edin 123 F4
South Gray's Cl. Edin 123 F4
South Green Dr. Air 22 C2
South Groathill Ave. Edin 92 B1
South Gyle Access. Edin .. 121 E2
South Gyle Broadway.
  Edin 121 D2
South Gyle Broadway.
  Kirkl 120 C3
South Gyle Cres. Edin 121 D2
South Gyle Cres La. Edin .. 121 D2
South Gyle Gdns. Edin 121 D3
South Gyle Loan. Edin 121 D3
South Gyle Mains. Edin 121 D3
South Gyle Pk. Edin 121 D3
South Gyle Rd. Edin 121 D3
South Gyle Wynd. Edin 121 E2
South Hill St. Burn 50 C4
South Hirst Rd. Sals 167 E2
South Lauder Rd. Edin 123 F2
South Laverockbank Ave.
  Edin 93 E3
South Learmonth Ave. Edin . 92 C1
South Loanhead. Lime 45 F2
South Loch Pk. Bath 145 D3
South Lodge Ave. E Cal 148 B1
South Lorimer Pl. Cocke 97 E2
South Lorne Pl. Edin 93 F2
South Lumley St. Gran 61 E4
South Marshall St. Gran 61 E4
South Maybury. Edin 121 D3
South Mellis Pk. Edin 124 C4
South Melville La. Falk 60 A3
South Mid St. Bath 145 D3
South Morton St. Edin 125 E4
South Oswald Rd. Edin 123 E2
South Overgate. King 35 D2
South Oxford St. Edin 123 F3
South Park. Arm 143 F2
South Philpingstone La.
  B'ness 64 B4
South Pilmuir Rd. Clack 11 D2
South Pk. Edin 93 E3
South Pleasance Ave. Falk . 60 A2
South Rd. B'ness 62 A3
South Rd. Fau 193 F4
South Riggs Acres. Crossf .. 27 E1
South Roundall. Lime 45 F2
South Row. Kirk 17 F4
South Row. Lime 45 D2
South Scotstoun. Que 89 E4
South Seton Pk. Cocke 97 E2
South Shore Rd. Gran 41 D1
South Sloan St. Edin 93 F2
South St Andrew St. Edin 93 E1
South St. Arm 143 F3
South St. B' ness 63 F4
South St. Camb 9 D4
South St. Cow 13 E1
South St. Dalk 157 D2
South St. Dunb 78 A1
South St. Loch 14 A3
South St. Muss 126 A3
South St. Stir 2 B1
South Trinity Rd. Edin 93 D3
South View. Burn 50 C4
South View. Lar 38 B1
South Village. Pump 148 B3
South West Cumberland Street La.
  Edin 93 E1
South West Thistle Street La.
  Edin 93 E1
Southbank Ct. Edin 91 F2
Southcroft. Alva 4 C3
Southerton Cres. Kirk 16 C2
Southerton Gdns. Kirk 16 C2
Southerton Rd. Kirk 16 C2
Southfield Ave. Shot 192 A2
Southfield Bank. Edin 124 C3
Southfield. Cow 13 E3
Southfield Cres. Shot 192 A2
Southfield Cres. Stir 7 D3
Southfield Dr. Slam 110 A3
Southfield Farm Gr. Edin .. 124 C4
Southfield Gdns E. Edin 124 C3
Southfield Gdns W. Edin 124 C3
Southfield Loan. Edin 124 C3
Southfield Pl. Edin 125 D4
Southfield Rd E. Edin 124 C3
Southfield Rd. Path 158 B3
Southfield Rd. Shot 192 A2
Southfield Rd W. Edin 124 C3
Southfield Sq. Edin 124 C3
Southhouse Ave. Edin 155 D3
Southhouse Broadway.
  Edin 155 D2
Southhouse Cres. Edin 155 E2
Southhouse Gdns. Edin 155 D2
Southhouse Gr. Edin 155 D2
Southhouse Loan. Edin 155 D2
Southhouse Medway. Edin 155 D3
Southhouse Rd. Edin 155 D2
Southhouse Sq. Edin 155 D2
Southhouse Terr. Edin 155 D3
Southlawn Ct. Edin 91 F2
Spa Pl. Edin 95 D1
Spalding Cres. Dalk 157 D2
Speedwell Ave. Dan 156 A4
Spence Ave. Burn 33 F1
Spence St. Bon 58 A3
Spence St. Edin 123 F3
Spencer Pl. Edin 93 D3
Spencer Pl. Kirk 17 F4
Spencerfield Rd. Inver 47 E1
Spencerfield Steadings.
  Inver 47 F2
Spens La. Ros 46 B1
Spey Ct. Gran 61 E3
Spey Ct. Stir 7 E3
Spey Dr. Liv 148 A2
Spey St. Edin 93 F2
Spey Street La. Edin 93 F2
Spey Terr. Edin 93 F2
Spier's Pl. Edin 93 F3
Spinkhill. Laur 60 C1
Spinner's Ct. Crossf 27 E1
Spinney The. Edin 155 E3
Spinneys The. D Bay 48 B2
Spittal Hill. B of A 2 B2
Spittal St. Edin 123 D4
Spittal St. Stir 7 D4
Spittalfield Cres. Inver 47 E1
Spittalfield Rd. Inver 47 E1
Spott Ave. E Lin 106 B2
Spott Loan. E Lin 106 B2
Spott Rd. Dunb 78 C1
Spottiswoode Gdns. E Cal 148 B1
Spottiswoode Rd. Edin 123 E3
Spottiswoode St. Edin 123 E3
Sprig Way. East 168 C3
Spring Gdns. Edin 94 A1
Springbank Gdns. Falk 60 B3
Springbank Rd. Shot 191 E3
Springbank Rd. Stir 7 D2
Springbank Terr. Dunf 29 D3
Springfield Cres. N Ber 54 A4
Springfield Cres. Que 67 F1
Springfield Ct. Lin 85 E4
Springfield Dr. Falk 59 F3
Springfield. Dunb 105 F4
Springfield. Edin 93 F2
Springfield Gdns. N Ber 54 A4
Springfield Lea. Que 67 F1
Springfield Pl. Gore 207 E4
Springfield Pl. Que 67 F1
Springfield Pl. Rosl 181 D2
Springfield Rd. All 10 B4
Springfield Rd. Den 36 C1
Springfield Rd. How 222 C1
Springfield Rd. Lin 85 E4
Springfield Rd. Que 67 F1
Springfield Rd. Stir 7 E3
Springfield St. Edin 93 F2
Springfield Terr. Dunb 77 F1
Springfield Terr. Que 67 F1
Springfield View. Que 68 A1
Springhead Rd. Alla 212 A4
Springhill And Leadloch Rd.
  Shot 102 C1
Springhill Brae. Cross 30 C3
Springhill Rd. Shot 192 A2
Springkerse Rd. Stir 7 E3
Springvalley Gdns. Edin 123 D2
Springvalley Terr. Edin 123 D2
Springwell Pl. Edin 122 C3
Springwood Ave. Stir 6 C3
Springwood Pk. Edin 155 D4
Sprinty Ave. Orm 159 E4
Sprinty Dr. Orm 159 E4
Sprotwell Terr. N Sau 5 E1
Spruce Dr. Whit 170 B3
Spruce Gr. Dunf 46 B4
Spruce Gr. Liv 148 A3
Spylaw Ave. Edin 152 C4
Spylaw Bank Rd. Edin 153 D4
Spylaw Pk. Edin 152 C4
Spylaw Rd. Edin 122 C2
Spylaw St. Edin 153 D4
Square The. Cock 140 C2
Square The. Dan 156 A4
Square The. E Lin 103 F4
Square The. E Lin 106 B2
Square The. Fall 8 B2
Square The. Giff 163 F3
Square The. Kirkl 89 D1
Square The. Newt 183 D3
Square The. Peni 203 F2
Square The. Torp 113 F3
Stable La. Edin 123 D2
Stable Rd. Shot 192 A3
Stables Rd. Ros 46 B1
Staffa. Liv 146 C3
Staffa Pl. Falk 60 A1
Stafford St. Edin 123 D4
Stair Pk. Edin 122 B4
Stair Pk. Tran 128 A4
Standalane. Kin 23 F2
Standing Stone Wlk. Dunf ... 29 F1
Standingstone Rd. Dal 89 F3
Standingstone Rd. Que 89 F3
Standrigg Rd. Cali 82 A3
Standrigg Rd. Shi 82 A3
Stane Rd. Shot 192 A1
Stanedykehead. Edin 154 C3
Stanhope Pl. Edin 122 C4
Stanhope St. Edin 122 C4
Stanistone Rd. Car 230 A1
Stankards Rd. Uph 116 C2
Stanley Ave. Rosl 180 C3
Stanley Dr. B of A 2 A4
Stanley Dr. Hart 169 D3
Stanley Pl. Edin 94 A1
Stanley Rd. Edin 93 E3
Stanley Rd. Hart 169 D3
Stanley St. Edin 125 D4
Stanley Terr. Oak 27 D3
Stanton Ave. All 9 F3
Stanwell St. Edin 93 F2
Stapeley Ave. Edin 94 C1
Starbank Rd. Edin 93 E3
Stark Ave. Falk 59 E3
Stark's Brae. B'ness 64 A4
Starlaw Ave. Bog 145 F3
Starlaw Cres. Bog 145 F3
Starlaw Gdns. Bog 145 F3
Starlaw Rd. Black 146 B2
Starlaw Rd. Liv 146 C2
Starlaw Terr. Bog 145 F3
Starlaw West Roundabout.
  Black 146 A2
Starlaw Walk. Bog 145 F3
Starryshaw Rd. Shot 191 F3
Station Ave. Hadd 131 F4
Station Brae. Edin 125 D4
Station Brae. King 34 C1
Station Ct. Hadd 131 F4
Station Ct. N Ber 54 A4
Station Hill. N Ber 54 A4
Station Loan. Bale 151 E2
Station Rd. Add 171 F1
Station Rd. Arm 143 F2
Station Rd. B of A 1 C4
Station Rd. Bann 7 F1
Station Rd. Blac 142 B1
Station Rd. Brox 116 C2
Station Rd. Brox 117 F3
Station Rd. Camb 4 A1
Station Rd. Cow 13 E2
Station Rd. Cowie 20 B3
Station Rd. Dal 89 E4
Station Rd. Dalk 156 C1
Station Rd. Dir 53 E3
Station Rd. Dunb 78 C1
Station Rd. E Lin 53 E2
Station Rd. E Lin 103 F4
Station Rd. Edin 121 F3
Station Rd. Giff 163 F3
Station Rd. Gore 207 E4
Station Rd. Gran 40 B1
Station Rd. Gull 52 A1
Station Rd. Kin 23 E2
Station Rd. Kir 149 E2
Station Rd. Kirk 17 D2
Station Rd. Kirk 18 A4
Station Rd. Kirkl 89 D1
Station Rd. Kirkl 119 E3
Station Rd. Lin 85 D4
Station Rd. Loan 181 E4
Station Rd. Loch 14 A4
Station Rd. Madd 83 F3
Station Rd. Muss 126 B3
Station Rd. N Ber 54 A4
Station Rd. Newt 183 D3
Station Rd. Oak 26 C3
Station Rd. Pol 61 F1
Station Rd. Pol 82 C4
Station Rd. Pres 128 A4
Station Rd. Pump 117 D1
Station Rd. Que 68 B1
Station Rd. Rosl 181 D2
Station Rd. Shot 191 F2
Station Rd. Slam 110 A3
Station Rd. Stir 7 D4
Station Rd. Tull 4 A1
Station Row. Slam 110 A3
Station Terr. Kirkl 89 D1
Staunton Rise. Muri 173 E4
Stead's Pl. Edin 93 F2
Steading The. Glad 98 B1
Steadings The. Pol 84 A4
Steel Gr. Bla 26 B4
Steel's Pl. Edin 123 D2
Steele Ave. May 183 F3
Steelyard The. Bath 145 D3
Steeple Cres. D Bay 48 A2
Steil Gr. Tran 128 B3
Steils The. Edin 122 C1
Stein Sq. Bann 7 F1
Stein's Pl. Cow 13 E2
Stenhouse Ave. Edin 122 A2
Stenhouse Ave W. Edin 122 A2
Stenhouse Cotts. Edin 122 A2
Stenhouse Cres. Edin 122 A2
Stenhouse Cross. Edin 122 A2
Stenhouse Dr. Burn 33 E1
Stenhouse Dr. Edin 122 A2
Stenhouse Gdns. Edin 122 A2
Stenhouse Gdns N. Edin .. 122 A2
Stenhouse Gr. Edin 122 A2
Stenhouse Mill Cres. Edin . 122 A2
Stenhouse Mill La. Edin 122 A2
Stenhouse Mill Wynd. Edin 122 A2
Stenhouse Pl E. Edin 122 A2
Stenhouse Pl W. Edin 122 A2
Stenhouse Rd. Edin 122 A2
Stenhouse St. Sten 38 C1
Stenhouse St. Cow 13 D2
Stenhouse St E. Edin 122 A2
Stenhouse St W. Edin 121 F2
Stenhouse Terr. Edin 122 A2
Stennis Gdns. Edin 155 E4
Stenton Loan. E Lin 104 C1
Stenton Loan. E Lin 135 F4
Stenton Rd. Dunb 105 F4
Stephen Pl. Loch 14 A4
Stephen's Dr. Inver 47 E2
Steps St. Sten 38 C2
Steuart Rd. B of A 1 C4
Stevenlaw's Cl. Edin 123 E4
Stevenson Ave. Edin 122 B3
Stevenson Ct. B of A 2 A3
Stevenson Ct. Liv 148 B3
Stevenson Ct. Long 98 B2
Stevenson Dr. Edin 122 A2
Stevenson Gr. Edin 122 B3
Stevenson La. Newt 183 D2
Stevenson Pk. Long 98 B2
Stevenson Pl. Rose 181 E3
Stevenson Rd. Auch 204 A4
Stevenson Rd. Edin 122 B3
Stevenson St. Gran 61 E3
Stevenson Terr. Bath 145 E3
Stevenson Terr. Edin 122 B3
Stevenson Way. Long 98 B2
Stewart Ave. B' ness 63 F4
Stewart Ave. Curr 151 F2
Stewart Ave. Lin 84 C3
Stewart Clark Ave. Que 89 E4
Stewart Cres. Curr 151 F2
Stewart Cres. Loch 14 A4
Stewart Dr. Whit 169 F4
Stewart Gdns. Curr 151 F2
Stewart Gr. East 168 C3
Stewart Pk. Path 158 B3
Stewart Pl. Curr 151 F2
Stewart Pl. Kirkl 89 D1
Stewart Rd. Curr 151 F2
Stewart Rd. Falk 60 B3
Stewart Sq. Stir 2 A1
Stewart St. Bon 57 F3
Stewart St. Cam 6 B3
Stewart St. Dunf 29 E4
Stewart St. Kirk 18 A4
Stewart St. W Cal 172 B1
Stewart Terr. Edin 122 C3
Stewart Terr. Que 68 A1
Stewart Way. Liv 147 E3
Stewartfield Cres. Brox 117 F3
Stewartfield. Edin 93 E2
Stewartfield Rd. Brox 117 F3
Stirling Rd. All 9 F4
Stirling Rd. Alva 4 C4
Stirling Rd. Edin 93 D3
Stirling Rd. Falk 59 E4
Stirling Rd. Fall 8 B2
Stirling Rd. Lar 38 A1
Stirling Rd. Tor 37 F3
Stirling Rd. Tull 4 A2
Stirling St. Alva 5 D4
Stirling St. Den 36 C1
Stirling St. Duni 36 B2
Stobhill Rd. Gore 183 D2
Stobhill Rd. Newt 183 D2
Stobie Pl. Oak 26 C4
Stone Ave. May 183 E3
Stone Pl. May 183 E3
Stonebank. Liv 147 F3
Stonedyke Cres. Car 230 A2
Stonedyke Rd. Car 230 A2
Stonelaws Cotts. E Lin 75 D3
Stoneybank Ave. Muss 126 A2
Stoneybank Cres. Muss 126 A2
Stoneybank Ct. Muss 126 A3
Stoneybank Dr. Muss 126 A3
Stoneybank Gdns. Muss 126 A3
Stoneybank Gdns N. Muss 126 A3
Stoneybank Gdns S. Muss 126 A3
Stoneybank Gr. Muss 126 A3
Stoneybank Pl. Muss 126 A3
Stoneybank Rd. Muss 126 A2
Stoneybank Terr. Muss 126 A2
Stoneyflatts Cres. Que 89 D4
Stoneyflatts. Que 89 D4
Stoneyhill Ave. Muss 126 A3
Stoneyhill Cres. Muss 126 A3
Stoneyhill Ct. Muss 126 A3
Stoneyhill Dr. Muss 126 A3

Stoneyhill Farm Rd. Muss . 126 A3
Stoneyhill Gr. Muss 126 A3
Stoneyhill Pl. Muss 126 A3
Stoneyhill Rd. Muss 126 A3
Stoneyhill Rise. Muss 126 A3
Stoneyhill Steadings. Muss 126 A3
Stoneyhill Terr. Muss 126 A3
Stoneyhill Wynd. Muss 126 A3
Stoneywood Pk. Duni 36 A1
Stony Brae. Kin 24 B1
Stony Croft Rd. Que 68 B1
Stories Pk. E Lin 103 F4
Strachan Gdns. Edin 92 A1
Strachan Rd. Edin 92 A1
Strachan St. Falk 59 F2
Straehouse Wynd. Car 230 A1
Straiton Mains. Edin 155 D1
Straiton Pl. Edin 125 D4
Straiton Rd. Edin 155 D1
Straiton Rd. Loan 180 C4
Strang's Pl. Cali 81 F3
Strathallan Ct. B of A 2 A3
Strathallan Dr. Kirk 16 C3
Strathallan Rd. B of A 2 A3
Strathalmond Ct. Edin 90 C2
Strathalmond Gn. Edin 90 C2
Strathalmond Pk. Edin 90 C2
Strathalmond Rd. Edin 90 C2
Strathavon Terr. West 112 C3
Strathbeg Dr. D Bay 47 F2
Strathbrock Pl. Brox 117 F3
Strathbrock Pl. Uph 116 C2
Strathearn Pl. Edin 123 D2
Strathearn Rd. Edin 123 E2
Strathearn Rd. Kirk 17 F4
Strathearn Rd. N Ber 53 F4
Strathesk Gr. Peni 204 A3
Strathesk Pl. Peni 204 A3
Strathfillan Rd. Edin 123 E2
Strathkinnes Rd. Kirk 17 D2
Strathlachlan Ave. Car 230 A1
Strathlogie. West 112 C3
Strathmiglo Pl. Sten 38 C2
Strathmore Cres. Stir 2 A2
Strathmore Dr. Dunf 29 E3
Strathmore Dr. Stir 2 A2
Strathmore St. King 34 C2
Strathyre Dr. Ston 171 E1
Strawberry Bank. Dalk 156 C1
Strawberry Bank. Lin 85 D3
Streets Pl. Dunf 29 E4
Stripehead. All 10 A3
Striven Dr. Falk 39 E1
Striven Pl. Kirk 16 C4
Strowan Rd. Gran 61 F4
Strowan Sq. Gran 61 F4
Struan Dr. Inver 47 D2
Struan Pl. Inver 47 D2
Strude Howe. Alva 5 D4
Strude Mill. Alva 5 D4
Strude St. Alva 5 D4
Stuart Cres. Edin 121 D4
Stuart Ct. Edin 121 D4
Stuart Gn. Edin 121 D4
Stuart Pk. Edin 121 D4
Stuart Pl. Cow 13 E3
Stuart Rd. Ros 46 B1
Stuart Sq. Edin 121 D4
Stuart Terr. Bath 145 D3
Stuart Wynd. Edin 121 D4
Succoth Ave. Edin 122 B4
Succoth Ct. Edin 122 B4
Succoth Gdns. Edin 122 B4
Succoth Pk. Edin 122 B4
Succoth Pl. Edin 122 B4
Suffolk Rd. Edin 123 F2
Suilven Hts. Laur 61 D2
Summer Bank. Edin 93 E1
Summer Pl. Edin 93 E2
Summerfield Gdns. Edin 94 A2
Summerfield Pk. Dunb 78 A1
Summerfield Pl. Edin 94 A2
Summerfield Rd. Dunb 78 B1
Summerford. Falk 59 E2
Summerford Gdns. Falk 59 E2
Summerford Rd. Falk 59 E2
Summerhall. Edin 123 F3
Summerhall Pl. Edin 123 F3
Summerhall Sq. Edin 123 F3
Summerlee. Pres 96 C1
Summerside Pl. Edin 93 E3
Summerside St. Edin 93 E3
Summertrees Ct. Edin 124 A1
Summerville Ct. Pump 148 A4
Suna Path. Shot 192 A2
Sunart Pl. Gran 61 E3
Sunbury Mews. Edin 122 C4
Sunbury Pl. Edin 122 C4
Sunningdale La. Dunf 28 B3
Sunnybank Pl. Edin 94 A1
Sunnybank Rd. Stir 7 D2
Sunnybrae. Pur 215 D1
Sunnydale Dr. Blac 142 C2
Sunnydale Rd. Blac 142 C2
Sunnylaw Pl. Falk 59 F2
Sunnylaw Rd. B of A 2 A4
Sunnyside Ave. Bath 145 E4
Sunnyside Pl. All 10 A4

Sunnyside Pl. Loch 14 A3
Sunnyside Rd. All 10 A4
Sunnyside Rd. Falk 59 F3
Sunnyside Rd. Pol 82 B4
Sunnyside St. Falk 59 F3
Sunnyside. Stir 7 D2
Sunnyside. Ston 171 D1
Sutherland Ave. All 10 B4
Sutherland Ave. Stir 2 B1
Sutherland Cres. Bath 145 D3
Sutherland Dr. Den 57 E4
Sutherland Pl. Kirk 17 F4
Sutherland St. Edin 122 C4
Sutherland Way. Liv 147 E3
Suttieslea Cres. Newt 183 E3
Suttieslea Dr. Newt 183 E3
Suttieslea Pl. Newt 183 E3
Suttieslea Rd. Newt 183 E3
Suttieslea Wlk. Newt 183 E3
Sutton Pk Cres. Sten 38 C2
Sutton Pl. Falk 60 B3
Swallow Craig. D Bay 48 A1
Swallowdrum Rd. Dunf 28 B3
Swan Cres. Gore 207 E4
Swan Pl. Gran 61 E3
Swan Rd. Kirk 17 D2
Swan Rd. Tran 128 B3
Swan Spring Ave. Edin 154 A4
Swanfield. Edin 93 F3
Swanston Ave. Edin 154 A3
Swanston Cres. Edin 154 A3
Swanston Dr. Edin 154 A2
Swanston Gdns. Edin 154 A3
Swanston Gn. Edin 154 A3
Swanston Gr. Edin 154 A2
Swanston Loan. Edin 154 A3
Swanston Muir. Edin 153 F3
Swanston Pk. Edin 154 A3
Swanston Pl. Edin 154 A3
Swanston Rd. Edin 154 A2
Swanston Row. Edin 154 A3
Swanston Terr. Edin 154 A3
Swanston View. Edin 154 A3
Swanston Way. Edin 154 A3
Swintons Pl. Cow 12 C1
Sword's Way. Falk 39 D1
Sycamore Ave. B' ness 63 E3
Sycamore Ave. Kirk 17 E4
Sycamore Cres. Loch 13 E3
Sycamore Dr. Whit 170 B3
Sycamore Gdns. Edin 121 F3
Sycamore Gr. Dunf 46 B4
Sycamore Gr. Winch 87 F1
Sycamore Pl. Stir 6 C3
Sycamore Rd. May 183 F3
Sycamore Wlk. Black 171 E4
Sycamores The. Tull 4 A1
Sydney Pk. Edin 94 C1
Sydney Pl. Edin 94 C1
Sydney St. Liv 148 A3
Sydney Terr. Edin 94 C1
Sylvan Gr. B' ness 63 E3
Sylvan Pl. Edin 123 E3
Sylvan Way. Bath 144 C3
Syme Pl. Ros 46 B3
Symington Pl. Sten 39 D2

Ta-Verne La. Dunf 29 E1
Tailend Roundabout. Liv ... 146 B2
Tait Dr. Lar 59 E4
Tait Dr. Peni 203 F3
Tait St. Dalk 157 D2
Talbot St. Gran 61 E4
Talisman Pl. Edin 124 A1
Talman Gdns. Pol 61 F2
Tam O'Shanter Dr. Cowie .. 20 B4
Tamfourhill Ave. Falk 59 E2
Tamfourhill Rd. Falk 59 E2
Tanhouse Brae. Cul 42 B4
Tanners Rd. Falk 60 A2
Tannery La. Stir 2 A1
Tantallon Dr. Sten 39 D2
Tantallon Pl. Edin 123 E3
Tantallon Rd. N Ber 54 C3
Tantallon Terr. N Ber 54 C4
Tantera Ct. Falk 60 A1
Tapitlaw Gr. Bla 26 B4
Tappoch Pl. Lar 38 A2
Taransay Dr. Pol 61 F1
Tarbert Pl. Pol 61 F1
Tarbert Terr. Kin 23 F2
Tarbet Pl. Car 230 A1
Tarbrax Path. Shot 192 A2
Tarbrax Rd. Auc 217 F1
Tarduff Dr. Madd 83 D3
Tarduff Pl. Duni 36 A1
Targate Rd. Dunf 28 B3
Target Rd. Gran 62 B4
Tartraven Pl. Brox 118 A3
Tarvit St. Edin 123 E3
Tashieburn Rd. For 215 F1
Tavern Ct. Cow 31 D4
Taxi Way. D Bay 48 B3
Tay Ct. All 10 B3
Tay Pl. Shot 191 F3
Tay St. Edin 122 C3
Tay St. Falk 39 E1
Tay St. Gran 40 A1

Tay Terr. Dunf 29 F1
Tay Wlk. Liv 148 A2
Taylor Ave. Cow 13 E2
Taylor Gdns. Edin 93 F3
Taylor Pl. Dalk 157 E1
Taylor Rd. Whit 169 F3
Taylor's Rd. Lar 38 B1
Taymouth Rd. Pol 62 A1
Tedder St. Gran 61 E3
Telferton. Edin 94 C1
Telford Ct. Bann 7 E1
Telford Dr. Edin 92 B2
Telford Gdns. Edin 92 B2
Telford Pl. Edin 92 B2
Telford Pl. Lin 84 B4
Telford Rd. Edin 92 B2
Telford Sq. Falk 59 F3
Telford St. Liv 147 F4
Telford View. Lin 84 B3
Telny Pl. Abe 49 E4
Templar La. Gull 52 A1
Templar Pl. Gull 52 A1
Templar Rise. Muri 173 E4
Templars Cres. King 34 C2
Temple Ave. Arm 144 A3
Temple Denny Rd. Den 36 B1
Temple Pk Cres. Edin 122 C3
Temple Pk. Newt 206 B1
Templedean Pk. Hadd 101 D1
Templehall Ave. Kirk 16 C4
Templeland Gr. Edin 121 E4
Templeland Rd. Edin 121 E4
Ten Acres. N Sau 5 D1
Tenacres Pl. Gran 61 F3
Tenacres Rd. Gran 62 A4
Tenant's March. W Cal 172 B2
Tennant St. Edin 93 F2
Tennent Pk. E Cal 148 B1
Tenth St. Newt 183 D3
Tern Brae. Liv 147 E3
Terrace St. Kirk 18 A4
Terragles. Peni 203 E3
Terris St. Cow 13 E2
Teviot Gr. Peni 203 F4
Teviot Pl. Edin 123 E4
Teviot Pl. Falk 59 F2
Teviotdale Pl. Edin 93 D1
Thane Pl. Dunf 29 F1
Thimblehall Dr. Dunf 29 E2
Thimblehall Pl. Dunf 29 E2
Thimblehall Rd. Dunf 29 F2
Third Gait. Rat 151 F4
Third St. Newt 183 D3
Thirlestane. B'ness 64 A4
Thirlestane La. Edin 123 E3
Thirlestane Pl. B'ness 64 A4
Thirlestane Rd. Edin 123 E3
Thistle Ave. Duni 36 B2
Thistle Ave. Gran 61 D3
Thistle Pl. Edin 123 D3
Thistle St. All 10 B3
Thistle St. Burn 50 C4
Thistle St. Cow 13 E2
Thistle St. Dunf 29 D3
Thistle St. Edin 93 E1
Thistle St. Falk 60 B3
Thistle St. Kirk 17 E2
Thompson Pl. Slam 110 A2
Thomson Cres. Cocke 97 E3
Thomson Cres. Curr 152 A3
Thomson Ct. Uph 116 C2
Thomson Dr. Curr 152 B3
Thomson Gn. Liv 147 D4
Thomson Gr. Curr 152 A3
Thomson Gr. Uph 116 C2
Thomson Pl. Cam 6 B3
Thomson Pl. Ros 46 C2
Thomson Rd. Curr 152 A3
Thomson Terr. Shot 191 E3
Thorburn Gr. Edin 153 E3
Thorburn Rd. Edin 153 D3
Thorn Gr. Dunf 46 C4
Thorn Tree Pl. Oak 26 C3
Thornbridge Gdns. Falk 60 C2
Thornbridge Rd. Falk 60 C3
Thornbridge Sq. Falk 60 C3
Thorndale Gdns. Bon 57 D1
Thorndene Ct. Falk 59 F1
Thorne Ct. N Ber 54 A4
Thorne Rd. All 4 C1
Thornhill Dr. Kirk 17 D3
Thornhill Rd. Falk 60 B3
Thornhill Rd. Kirk 17 E3
Thornton Ave. Bon 58 A3
Thornton Pl. Fau 193 E3
Thornton Rd. Rose 181 E1
Thorntree Cres. Pres 97 D1
Thorntree St. Edin 94 A2
Thorntreeside. Edin 94 A2
Thornville Terr. Edin 94 A2
Thorny Bank. Dalk 157 E2
Thornybauk. Edin 123 D3
Threipmuir Ave. Bale 177 E4
Threipmuir Gdns. Bale 177 E4
Threipmuir Pl. Bale 177 E4
Thrums The. Laur 61 D2
Thurston Pl. Liv 147 E3

Timber Bush. Edin 94 A3
Timmeryetts. Uph 117 E3
Timmons Pk. Loch 14 A4
Timmons Pl. Den 36 B1
Tinian Cres. Torr 26 B1
Tinto Dr. Gran 61 F3
Tinto Pl. Dunf 29 F1
Tinto Pl. Edin 93 F2
Tipperlin Rd. Edin 123 D2
Tippet Knowes Ct. Winch .. 87 F2
Tippet Knowes Pk. Winch .. 87 F2
Tippet Knowes Rd. Winch .. 87 F1
Tiree Cres. Pol 61 E1
Tiree Pl. Falk 60 A1
Tiree Pl. Kirk 16 C4
Titania. All 10 A4
Todd Sq. Liv 116 C1
Toddshill Rd. Kirkl 89 D1
Tolbooth St. Falk 60 A2
Tolbooth St. Kirk 17 E2
Tolbooth Wynd. Edin 94 A3
Toll Rd. Kin 23 F2
Toll Roundabout. Liv 146 C2
Toll View. Cock 140 C2
Tollgate. Dunf 29 D1
Tolmount Dr. Dunf 29 E2
Tolsta Cres. Pol 61 F1
Tophill Entry. Falk 59 F3
Toravon Dr. Madd 83 D3
Torbain. Kirk 16 B4
Torbain Rd. Kirk 16 A3
Torbane Ave. Whit 170 C4
Torbane Dr. Whit 170 C4
Torbeith Gdns. Cow 12 C1
Torbothie Rd. Shot 192 A2
Torbrex Farm Rd. Stir 7 D2
Torbrex La. Stir 7 D3
Torbrex Rd. Stir 6 C2
Torburn Ave. Plea 20 B2
Torduff Rd. Edin 153 D2
Toronto Ave. Liv 147 F2
Torosay Ave. Madd 82 C3
Torphichen Ave. E Cal 148 A1
Torphichen Pl. Edin 123 D4
Torphichen Rd. Bath 145 D4
Torphichen St. Bath 145 D4
Torphichen St. Edin 123 D4
Torphin Rd. Edin 152 C3
Torrance Pk. Edin 91 E1
Torridon Ave. Falk 39 E1
Torridon Ct. All 10 B3
Torridon Dr. Ros 46 C1
Torridon La. Ros 46 C1
Torridon Pl. Kirk 16 C4
Torridon Pl. Ros 46 C1
Torridon Rd. Whit 170 B4
Torridon Wlk. Liv 148 A2
Torrin Loan. Shot 192 A2
Torry Dr. Alva 4 C4
Torsonce Rd. Dalk 156 C1
Torvean Pl. Dunf 29 E1
Torwood Ave. Gran 61 F3
Torwood Ave. Lar 38 A1
Torwood Pl. Dunf 29 E2
Touch Rd. Cam 6 A3
Touch Wards. Dunf 29 F2
Touchhill Cres. Plea 20 B2
Tovey Rd. Ros 46 B1
Toward Ct. Edin 121 D4
Tower Gdns. B'ness 64 B4
Tower Pl. Clack 10 C3
Tower Pl. Edin 94 A3
Tower St. All 10 A4
Tower St. Edin 94 A3
Tower Street La. Edin 94 A3
Tower Terr. Kirk 17 F4
Tower View. N Sau 5 F1
Towers Ct. Falk 60 A3
Towers Pl. Stir 2 B2
Town House St. Den 36 C1
Townhall St. Inver 47 E1
Townhead Gdns. Whit 170 B3
Townhead. King 34 C2
Townhead. Kirk 18 A4
Townhill Rd. Dunf 29 D3
Townsend Cres. Kirk 17 E2
Townsend Pl. Kirk 17 E2
Trafalgar La. Edin 93 F3
Trafalgar St. Edin 93 F3
Train Terr. Ros 46 B3
Tranent Rd. Elph 128 A1
Transy Gr. Dunf 29 E2
Transy Pl. Dunf 29 E2
Traprain Cres. Bath 144 C4
Traprain Terr. Hadd 101 D1
Traprain Terr. Loan 181 E4
Traquair Pk E. Edin 121 F3
Traquair Pk W. Edin 121 F3
Trelawney Terr. Auch 204 A4
Tremayne Pl. Dunf 28 C3
Trench Knowe. Edin 154 A3
Trenchard Pl. Dunf 28 C3
Tressilian Gdns. Edin 124 A1
Trevelyan Cres. Pen 160 C3
Trevelyan Pl. Pen 160 C3
Trinity Cres. Edin 93 D3
Trinity Ct. Edin 93 D3
Trinity Gr. Edin 93 D3

Trinity Rd. Edin 93 D3
Tron Ct. Tull 4 A1
Trondheim Parkway. Dunf .. 29 F1
Trondheim Pl. Dunf 29 F1
Trongate. King 35 D2
Troup Ct. Gran 61 E4
Tryst Pk. Edin 153 F3
Tryst Rd. Sten 38 B2
Tryst Way. Sten 38 B1
Tudor Ct. Laur 61 E1
Tuke St. Dunf 29 D3
Tulliallan Pl. Sten 39 D2
Tulliallan Terr. Kin 23 F3
Tullibody Rd. All 9 F4
Tullibody Rd. Tull 4 C1
Tulligarth Pk. All 10 A4
Tulloch Ct. Cow 13 E3
Tulloch Rd. Shot 192 A2
Tummel Dr. Kirk 16 B4
Tummel Pl. Gran 61 F2
Tummel Pl. Sten 38 C2
Turnbull Gr. Dunf 29 F1
Turner Ave. Bale 151 E2
Turner Pk. Bale 151 E2
Turner St. Bath 145 D4
Turnhigh Rd. Whit 170 A2
Turnhouse Farm Rd. Kirkl .. 90 B1
Turnhouse Rd. Edin 120 B4
Turnhouse Rd. Kirkl 120 B4
Turret Ct. All 10 B3
Turret Dr. Pol 62 A1
Turret Gdns. Pres 127 D4
Turret Rd. Gran 61 E3
Turriff Pl. Kirk 16 C4
Twain Ave. Sten 39 D2
Tweed Dr. Liv 148 A3
Tweed St. Dunf 29 F1
Tweed St. Gran 40 A1
Tweedale Cres. Giff 163 F3
Tweeddale Ave. Giff 163 F3
Tweeddale Dr. Dunf 29 F1
Tweeddale Gr. Giff 163 F2
Tyhmebank. Liv 147 F3
Tyler's Acre Ave. Edin 121 F3
Tyler's Acre Gdns. Edin ... 121 F3
Tyler's Acre Rd. Edin 121 F3
Tyndrum Pl. Kirk 16 C4
Tyne Cl. E Lin 103 F4
Tyne Cl. Hadd 132 A4
Tynebank Rd. Hadd 132 A4
Tynecastle La. Edin 122 C4
Tynecastle Terr. Edin 122 C3
Tynemount Ave. Orm 159 F3
Tynemount Rd. Orm 159 F3
Tyneview. Pen 159 F4
Tyrwhitt Pl. Ros 46 C2

Ugston Cotts. Hadd 100 B1
Ulg Way. Shot 192 A2
Ulster Cres. Edin 124 B4
Ulster Dr. Edin 124 B4
Ulster Gdns. Edin 124 B4
Ulster Gr. Edin 124 B4
Ulster Terr. Edin 124 B4
Underwood Cotts. Cam 6 B3
Underwood Rd. Cam 6 B3
Union Ct. Whit 170 A3
Union Pk. Bonn 182 A3
Union Pl. Edin 93 F1
Union Pl. Lar 38 A1
Union Rd. Bath 145 D3
Union Rd. Brox 117 E3
Union Rd. Falk 59 E3
Union Rd. Gran 40 B1
Union Rd. Lin 84 C3
Union Rd. Whit 170 A3
Union St. All 10 A3
Union St. B of A 2 A4
Union St. B'ness 64 A4
Union St. Burn 50 C4
Union St. Cow 13 E2
Union St. Edin 93 F1
Union St. Falk 60 A4
Union St. Kirk 17 F4
Union St. Loch 14 A4
Union St. Shot 191 E3
Union St. Sten 38 C2
Union St. Stir 2 A1
Unity Pk. Shot 191 E2
Universal Rd. Gran 60 C4
University Rd W. B of A 2 B3
Uphall Station Rd. Pump ... 148 A4
Upper Bathville. Arm 143 F2
Upper Bow. Edin 123 E4
Upper Bridge St. Stir 2 A1
Upper Broomieknowe.
   Bonn 182 A4
Upper Castlehill. Stir 7 D4
Upper Coltbridge Terr.
   Edin 122 C4
Upper Craigour. Edin 155 F4
Upper Craigour Way. Edin 124 B1
Upper Craigs. Stir 7 D4
Upper Cramond Ct. Edin .. 91 D2
Upper Dean Terr. Edin 93 D1
Upper Gilmore Pl. Edin 123 D3
Upper Gilmore Terr. Edin .. 123 D3
Upper Gray St. Edin 123 F3

Upper Grove Pl. Edin ... 123 D3
Upper Millhill St. Dunf ... 29 D2
Upper Newmarket St. Falk .. 60 A3
Upper Wellheads. Lime 45 F2
Ure Cres. Bon ... 58 A3
Ure Ct. Gran ... 61 E4
Urquhart Cres. Dunf ... 28 C2
Urquhart Cut. Dunf ... 28 C2
Urquhart Farm Cotts.
  Crossf ... 28 B1
Vale Pl. Duni ... 36 C2
Valeview. Lar ... 38 B1
Valley Field View. Peni ... 203 F2
Valley Gdns. Kirk ... 16 C3
Valley Gdns S. Kirk ... 16 C3
Valley View. Kirk ... 16 C3
Valleyfield Ave. H Val ... 26 A1
Valleyfield Pl. Cow ... 13 E3
Valleyfield Pl. Stir ... 7 E3
Valleyfield Rd. Peni ... 203 F2
Valleyfield St. Edin ... 123 E3
Valleyview Dr. Falk ... 60 A4
Vancouver Ave. Liv ... 147 F2
Vandeleur Ave. Edin ... 94 C1
Vandeleur Gr. Edin ... 94 C1
Vandeleur Pl. Edin ... 94 C1
Vardon Rd. Gull ... 52 A2
Vaucluse Pl. Peni ... 203 F2
Veere Pk. Cul ... 25 F1
Veitch's Sq. Edin ... 93 D1
Vellore Rd. Madd ... 83 D3
Venachar St. Shot ... 191 F3
Vennel The. Den ... 36 C1
Vennel The. Dunb ... 78 C1
Vennel The. Lin ... 85 D4
Ventnor Pl. Edin ... 124 A2
Ventnor Terr. Edin ... 123 F2
Venturefair Ave. Dunf ... 29 D3
Veronica Cres. Kirk ... 17 E4
Vetch Pk. Hadd ... 101 D1
Vexhim Pk. Edin ... 125 D3
Vicar St. Falk ... 60 A3
Viceroy St. Kirk ... 17 D3
Victor Park Terr. Edin ... 121 E4
Victoria Gdns. Kirk ... 17 D2
Victoria Gdns. Newt ... 182 C3
Victoria Gdns. Fau ... 193 F4
Victoria Pk. Hadd ... 101 D1
Victoria Pl. B'ness ... 64 A4
Victoria Pl. Dunb ... 78 B2
Victoria Pl. Pol ... 61 E1
Victoria Pl. Stir ... 7 D4
Victoria Rd. East ... 168 C3
Victoria Rd. Falk ... 60 B3
Victoria Rd. Fau ... 193 F4
Victoria Rd. Gran ... 61 F4
Victoria Rd. Hadd ... 132 A4
Victoria Rd. Kirk ... 17 E3
Victoria Rd. Lar ... 38 A1
Victoria Rd. N Ber ... 54 B4
Victoria Rd. Newt ... 182 C3
Victoria Rd. Stir ... 7 D4
Victoria Sq. Stir ... 7 D4
Victoria St. All ... 10 A4
Victoria St. Dunb ... 78 B2
Victoria St. Dunf ... 29 D3
Victoria St. East ... 168 C3
Victoria St. Edin ... 123 E4
Victoria St. Gore ... 183 D1
Victoria St. Kirk ... 18 A4
Victoria St. Liv ... 148 A2
Victoria St. Rooo ... 181 E1
Victoria Terr. Dunf ... 29 D3
Victoria Terr. Hadd ... 132 A4
Victoria Terr. Men ... 4 A4
Victoria Terr. Muss ... 126 C3
Viewbank Dr. Bonn ... 182 B4
Viewbank Rd. Bonn ... 182 A4
Viewbank View. Bonn ... 182 B4
Viewcraig Gdns. Edin ... 123 F4
Viewcraig St. Edin ... 123 F4
Viewfield Ave. Bonn ... 182 B4
Viewfield. Bonn ... 182 B4
Viewfield Dr. Alva ... 4 C3
Viewfield Rd. Auc ... 217 F2
Viewfield Rd. Edin ... 152 C4
Viewfield St. East ... 168 C3
Viewfield St. Stir ... 7 D4
Viewfield Terr. Dunf ... 29 D2
Viewfield Terr. Loch ... 13 F3
Viewforth. Kirk ... 17 F4
Viewforth. B'ness ... 64 A4
Viewforth. Cocke ... 97 E2
Viewforth Dr. Laur ... 61 D2
Viewforth. Dunb ... 78 B2
Viewforth. Edin ... 123 D3
Viewforth Gdns. Edin ... 123 D3
Viewforth Gdns. Kirk ... 17 F4
Viewforth Gdns. Tran ... 128 B3
Viewforth. N Ber ... 54 B4
Viewforth Pl. Que ... 89 D4
Viewforth Sq. Edin ... 123 D3
Viewforth St. Kirk ... 17 F4
Viewforth Terr. Edin ... 123 D3
Viewforth Terr. Kirk ... 17 F4

Viewforth Terr. Tran ... 128 B3
Viewpark Gdns. Bonn ... 182 A4
Villa Bank. Den ... 36 C1
Villa Rd. Que ... 68 A1
Village La. Liv ... 147 D2
Vinefields. Pen ... 160 C3
Violet Terr. Edin ... 122 C3
Vivian Terr. Edin ... 92 A2
Vogrie Cres S. Gore ... 207 E4
Vogrie Pl. Gore ... 207 E4
Vogrie Rd. Gore ... 207 E4
Voil Rd. Stir ... 2 A2
Volunteer's Gn. Kirk ... 17 E2
Vorlich Cres. Peni ... 204 A4
Vorlich Dr. Shi ... 81 F4
Vorlich Pl. Stir ... 2 A2
Waddell St. Sten ... 39 E1
Wadingburn La. Bonn ... 155 F1
Wadingburn Rd. Bonn ... 181 F4
Waggon Rd. B'ness ... 63 F4
Waggon Rd. Crossf ... 28 A1
Waggon Rd. Falk ... 60 A4
Waggon Rd. Inver ... 47 E1
Waggon Rd. Lime ... 45 E4
Waggon Rd. Shi ... 82 B4
Wakefield Ave. Edin ... 94 C1
Walden Dr. Giff ... 163 F3
Walden Pl. Giff ... 163 F2
Walden Terr. Giff ... 163 F2
Walk The. All ... 10 A3
Walk The. Kirk ... 18 A4
Walker Cres. Dalk ... 156 C1
Walker Dr. Que ... 68 A1
Walker Pl. Bonn ... 181 F3
Walker Pl. Dunf ... 29 F1
Walker Rd. Fau ... 193 E3
Walker St. Cow ... 13 D2
Walker St. Edin ... 123 D4
Walker St. Kin ... 23 F2
Walker St. Kirk ... 17 D3
Walker St. Loch ... 14 A4
Walker Terr. E Lin ... 103 E4
Walkers Ct. Edin ... 121 F1
Walkers Rig. Edin ... 121 F1
Walkers Wynd. Edin ... 121 F1
Wall Gdns. Falk ... 59 E3
Wall St. Falk ... 59 E3
Wallace Cres. Den ... 36 B1
Wallace Cres. Plea ... 20 B2
Wallace Cres. Pol ... 82 B4
Wallace Cres. Rosl ... 181 D2
Wallace Ct. Gran ... 61 E4
Wallace Ct. Stir ... 2 A1
Wallace Gdns. Stir ... 2 B2
Wallace Mill Gdns. E Cal ... 148 B2
Wallace Pl. Cam ... 6 B3
Wallace Pl. Falk ... 60 B3
Wallace Pl. Fall ... 8 B2
Wallace Pl. Tran ... 128 B4
Wallace Rd. Bath ... 145 E3
Wallace St. All ... 10 B4
Wallace St. Bann ... 7 F1
Wallace St. Cow ... 13 E2
Wallace St. Dunf ... 29 E1
Wallace St. Falk ... 60 B3
Wallace St. Gran ... 61 E4
Wallace St. Stir ... 2 A1
Wallace View. B'ness ... 63 E3
Wallace View. Shi ... 81 E4
Wallace View. Tull ... 4 B2
Wallace Wlk. Ston ... 171 D1
Wallacelea. Pol ... 82 C4
Wallacestone Brae. Shi ... 82 A4
Walls Pl. Dunf ... 29 F1
Wallsend St. Dunf ... 28 B3
Wallstale Rd. Stir ... 7 D2
Walmer Dr. Dunf ... 29 D2
Walnut Gr. Dunf ... 46 B4
Walter Hay Ct. Ros ... 46 C2
Walter Scott Ave. Edin ... 124 A1
Ward St. All ... 10 A3
Warden's Cl. Edin ... 123 E4
Wardie Ave. Edin ... 93 D3
Wardie Cres. Edin ... 93 D3
Wardie Dell. Edin ... 93 D3
Wardie Gr. Edin ... 92 C3
Wardie House La. Edin ... 93 D3
Wardie Pk. Edin ... 93 D3
Wardie Rd. Edin ... 93 D3
Wardie Sq. Edin ... 93 D3
Wardieburn Dr. Edin ... 92 C3
Wardieburn Pl E. Edin ... 92 C3
Wardieburn Pl N. Edin ... 92 C3
Wardieburn Pl S. Edin ... 92 C3
Wardieburn Pl W. Edin ... 92 C3
Wardieburn Rd. Edin ... 92 C3
Wardieburn St E. Edin ... 92 C3
Wardieburn St W. Edin ... 92 C3
Wardieburn Terr. Edin ... 92 C3
Wardiefield. Edin ... 93 D3
Wardlaw Cres. Dunf ... 29 E1
Wardlaw Cres. Oak ... 26 C4
Wardlaw Pl. Edin ... 122 C3
Wardlaw St. Cow ... 13 E2
Wardlaw St. Edin ... 122 C3

Wardlaw Terr. Edin ... 122 C3
Wardlaw Way. Oak ... 26 C4
Wardrop Cres. Arm ... 143 F3
Ware Rd. Dir ... 53 E3
Ware Rd. N Ber ... 54 A4
Warrender Cres. Dunb ... 78 C1
Warrender Park Cres. Edin 123 E3
Warrender Park Rd. Edin . 123 E3
Warrender Park Terr. Edin 123 E3
Warriston Ave. Edin ... 93 E2
Warriston Cres. Edin ... 93 E2
Warriston Dr. Edin ... 93 E2
Warriston Gdns. Edin ... 93 E2
Warriston Gr. Edin ... 93 D2
Warriston Rd. Edin ... 93 D2
Warriston Terr. Edin ... 93 D2
Washington La. Edin ... 122 C3
Water St. Edin ... 94 A3
Water Yett. Lin ... 84 C4
Waterfall Wlk. Dalk ... 157 D1
Waterlands Gdns. Car ... 230 A2
Waterloo Pl. Edin ... 93 E1
Waterloo Pl. Elph ... 128 A1
Waters' Cl. Edin ... 94 A3
Waterside. Hadd ... 132 A4
Watertoun Rd. Edin ... 123 F2
Watling Ave. Falk ... 59 E3
Watling Dr. Falk ... 59 E3
Watling Gdns. Falk ... 59 E3
Watling St. Falk ... 59 E3
Watson Cres. Edin ... 122 C3
Watson Pl. Arm ... 144 A3
Watson Pl. Bank ... 57 E2
Watson Pl. Dunf ... 29 D3
Watson St. Cow ... 13 E2
Watson St. Falk ... 60 A3
Watson St. Peni ... 203 F3
Watt Ave. Arm ... 144 A3
Watt Gdns. Falk ... 59 F3
Watt Gr. May ... 183 F3
Watt Pk. Newt ... 183 D2
Watt Rd. Ros ... 46 A1
Watt St. Kirk ... 18 A4
Watt's Cl. Muss ... 126 A3
Watters Cres. Loch ... 14 A3
Wauchope Ave. Edin ... 124 C2
Wauchope Cres. Edin ... 124 C2
Wauchope Pl. Edin ... 124 C2
Wauchope Rd. Edin ... 124 C2
Wauchope Sq. Edin ... 124 C2
Wauchope Terr. Edin ... 124 C2
Waugh Path. Bonn ... 182 B4
Waughton Cotts. E Lin ... 74 C3
Waulkmill Dr. Peni ... 204 A3
Waulkmill Loan. Curr ... 151 F2
Waulkmill Rd. Peni ... 204 A3
Waulkmill View. Peni ... 203 F3
Wavell St. Gran ... 61 E3
Waverley Bridge. Edin ... 123 E4
Waverley Cres. Bon ... 58 A2
Waverley Cres. Bonn ... 182 B4
Waverley Cres. Gran ... 61 E3
Waverley Cres. Stir ... 2 B1
Waverley Dr. Bonn ... 182 B4
Waverley Park Terr. Edin ... 94 A1
Waverley Pk. Bonn ... 182 B4
Waverley Pk. Laur ... 61 D1
Waverley Pk. May ... 183 E3
Waverley Rd. Bonn ... 182 B4
Waverley Rd. Dalk ... 156 C1
Waverley Rd. Lar ... 38 B1
Waverley St. Bath ... 145 D4
Waverley St Ind Units.
  Bath ... 145 D4
Waverley St. May ... 183 D4
Waverley Terr. Bonn ... 182 B4
Waverley Terr. Lar ... 38 B1
Waverley Terr. May ... 183 E3
Weaver Pl. Bath ... 145 D4
Weaver Row. Stir ... 7 D2
Weaver's Knowe Cres.
  Curr ... 151 F3
Weavers Cres. Kirk ... 17 D3
Weavers La. Whit ... 170 A3
Weavers Wlk. Dunf ... 29 D1
Webster Ave. Sten ... 39 D2
Webster Ct. Brox ... 117 F3
Webster Pl. Ros ... 46 B3
Wedderburn Cres. Dunf ... 29 F1
Wedderburn Pl. Dunf ... 29 E1
Wedderburn Rd. Kirk ... 16 B4
Wedderburn St. Dunf ... 29 E1
Wedderburn Terr. Muss ... 126 B2
Wee Brae. Bonn ... 156 A1
Wee Row. Falk ... 60 A3
Weir Ave. Cow ... 13 D1
Weir Cres. Dalk ... 156 C1
Weir Dr. Fall ... 8 B2
Weir St. Falk ... 60 A3
Weir St. Stir ... 1 C1
Well Rd. B of A ... 2 A4
Well Rd. Loch ... 14 A4

Well Wynd. Tran ... 128 B3
Wellflats Rd. Kirkl ... 89 D1
Wellgate Dr. B of A ... 2 B4
Wellgreen. Stir ... 7 D3
Wellington Pl. Edin ... 94 A3
Wellington St. Edin ... 93 F1
Wellmyre. Clack ... 11 D2
Wellpark. Brid ... 116 C4
Wellpark Cres. Stir ... 6 C2
Wellpark Terr. Bon ... 58 A3
Wellside. Hadd ... 131 F4
Wellside Pl. Falk ... 60 A3
Welsh Gdns. B of A ... 2 A4
Welsh Rd. Whit ... 169 F3
Wemyss Gdns. Muss ... 127 E3
Wemyss Pl. Cocke ... 97 E2
Wemyss Pl. Edin ... 93 D1
Wemyss Place Mews. Edin . 93 D1
Wemyss St. Long ... 98 C3
Wemyss St. Cow ... 13 E2
Wemyss St. Ros ... 46 C3
Wemyss Terr. Long ... 98 C3
Wemyssfield. Kirk ... 17 D2
Wesley Pl. Shi ... 82 A4
West Adam St. Edin ... 123 F4
West Albert Rd. Kirk ... 17 D2
West Annandale St. Edin .. 93 E2
West Approach Rd. Edin ... 123 D4
West Baldridge Rd. Dunf ... 28 C3
West Bankton. Muri ... 173 F4
West Bay Rd. N Ber ... 54 A4
West Benhar Rd. East ... 168 A2
West Boreland Rd. Den ... 36 B1
West Bow. Edin ... 123 E4
West Bowling Green St.
  Edin ... 93 F3
West Bridge St. Falk ... 60 A3
West Brighton Cres. Edin .. 125 D4
West Broomhill Rd. Burn ... 50 C4
West Bryson Rd. Edin ... 122 C3
West Burnside. Brox ... 117 F3
West Cairn Cres. Peni ... 203 F3
West Caiystane Rd. Edin .. 154 A3
West Carmuirs Loan. Bon ... 58 C3
West Carnethy Ave. Edin ... 153 D3
West Castle Rd. Edin ... 123 D3
West Catherine Pl. Edin ... 122 C4
West Church Dr. Gran ... 40 A1
West Clifton Farm Cotts.
  Rat ... 149 E4
West Coates. Edin ... 122 C4
West College St. Edin ... 123 E4
West Craigs Ave. Edin ... 120 C3
West Craigs Cres. Edin ... 120 C4
West Cres. Pen ... 161 F2
West Croft. Rat ... 119 F1
West Cromwell St. Edin ... 93 F3
West Crosscauseway.
  Edin ... 123 F3
West Ct. Edin ... 92 B1
West Ct. Edin ... 124 C2
West Dr. Dunf ... 29 D2
West Dr. Lar ... 38 B1
West End Gdns. All ... 10 A3
West End Pl. Edin ... 122 C3
West End. W Cal ... 172 B1
West Fenton Cotts. Gull ... 72 C4
West Fergus Pl. Kirk ... 17 D2
West Ferryfield. Edin ... 92 C2
West Fountain Pl. Edin ... 122 C3
West Gate Rd. Gran ... 62 A4
West Glen Ave. Liv ... 146 C3
West Gorgie Pk. Edin ... 122 B2
West Gorgie Pl. Edin ... 122 B2
West Grange Gdns. Edin .. 123 E2
West Granton Cres. Edin ... 92 A3
West Granton Dr. Edin ... 92 B3
West Granton Gn. Edin ... 92 A3
West Granton Pl. Edin ... 92 A3
West Granton Rd. Edin ... 92 B3
West Granton Row. Edin ... 92 B3
West Granton Terr. Edin ... 92 B3
West Granton View. Edin ... 92 B3
West Harbour Rd. Cocke ... 97 D2
West Harbour Rd. Edin ... 92 C4
West Harbour Rd. Lime ... 45 D2
West Holmes Gdns. Muss . 126 A3
West James St. Alva ... 5 D3
West Johnstone St. Alva ... 5 D3
West La. Cow ... 13 D1
West Leven St. Burn ... 50 C4
West Link Rd. B of A ... 2 B3
West Links Rd. Gull ... 51 F1
West Loan Ct. Pres ... 127 F4
West Loan. Pres ... 96 C1
West Lodge Gdns. All ... 9 F4
West Lorimer Pl. Cocke ... 97 D2
West Main St. Arm ... 143 F3
West Main St. Black ... 171 E4
West Main St. East ... 168 C3
West Main St. Uph ... 116 C2
West Main St. Uph ... 117 E3
West Main St. Whit ... 169 F3
West Mains Rd. Edin ... 123 F1

West Mains Rd. Gran ... 60 C4
West Mains St. Aber ... 71 E2
West Maitland St. Edin ... 123 D4
West March St. Kirk ... 17 E4
West Mayfield. Edin ... 123 F2
West Mill La. Edin ... 123 D4
West Mill Rd. Edin ... 152 C3
West Montgomery Pl. Edin . 93 F1
West Muir Rd. W Cal ... 172 B1
West Murrayfield. Bann ... 7 E1
West Nethertown St. Dunf ... 29 D1
West Newington Pl. Edin ... 123 F3
West Nicolson St. Edin ... 123 F4
West Norton Pl. Edin ... 93 F1
West Park Gr. Uph ... 117 D3
West Park Pl. Edin ... 122 C3
West Pilton Ave. Edin ... 92 B2
West Pilton Bank. Edin ... 92 B3
West Pilton Cres. Edin ... 92 A3
West Pilton Crossway. Edin 92 B3
West Pilton Dr. Edin ... 92 B3
West Pilton Gdns. Edin ... 92 B3
West Pilton Gn. Edin ... 92 B3
West Pilton Gr. Edin ... 92 B3
West Pilton Lea. Edin ... 92 B3
West Pilton Loan. Edin ... 92 B3
West Pilton Pk. Edin ... 92 B3
West Pilton Pl. Edin ... 92 B3
West Pilton Rise. Edin ... 92 B3
West Pilton St. Edin ... 92 B3
West Pilton Terr. Edin ... 92 B3
West Pilton View. Edin ... 92 B2
West Pk. Loch ... 14 A4
West Pk. Oak ... 27 E3
West Port. Dunb ... 78 B1
West Port. Edin ... 123 E4
West Port. Kirk ... 18 A4
West Port. Lin ... 84 C4
West Powburn. Edin ... 123 F2
West Preston St. Edin ... 123 F3
West Quality St. Kirk ... 18 A4
West.Rd. Hadd ... 131 F4
West.Rd. Lime ... 45 D2
West Register St. Edin ... 93 E1
West Register Street La.
  Edin ... 93 E1
West Relugas Rd. Edin ... 123 E2
West Richmond St. Edin ... 123 F4
West Savile Rd. Edin ... 123 F2
West Savile Terr. Edin ... 123 F2
West Scotland Street La.
  Edin ... 93 E1
West Seaside. Pres ... 96 C1
West Shore Rd. Edin ... 92 B4
West Silvermills La. Edin ... 93 D1
West Sq. Dunf ... 46 C3
West St. Peni ... 203 F2
West Stirling St. Alva ... 4 C4
West Telferton. Edin ... 94 C1
West Tollcross. Edin ... 123 D3
West Torbain. Kirk ... 16 B4
West Vennel. All ... 10 A3
West Way. D Bay ... 48 A3
West Werberside. Edin ... 92 C2
West Windygoul. Tran ... 128 A3
West Winnelstrae. Edin ... 92 C2
West Woods. Edin ... 92 C2
West Wynd. Kirk ... 17 E3
Westbank Ct. Glad ... 129 E3
Westbank Gdns. Glad ... 129 E3
Westbank Loan. Edin ... 95 D1
Westbank Pl. Edin ... 95 D1
Westbank Rd. Glad ... 129 E3
Westbank St. Edin ... 95 D1
Westbank Terr. Glad ... 129 E3
Westburn Ave. Cow ... 13 D1
Westburn Ave. Edin ... 152 B4
Westburn Ave. Falk ... 59 F2
Westburn Gdns. Edin ... 152 B4
Westburn Gr. Edin ... 152 B4
Westburn Middlefield. Edin 152 B4
Westburn Pk. Curr ... 152 B4
Westcliffe Ct. Gran ... 61 F3
Westcraigs Pk. Blac ... 142 B2
Westcraigs Rd. Blac ... 142 B2
Westcraigs Rd. East ... 168 C3
Westend Pl. N Ber ... 54 A4
Wester Bankton. Muri ... 174 A4
Wester Bogie Rd. Kirk ... 16 A4
Wester Broom Ave. Edin ... 121 E3
Wester Broom Dr. Edin ... 121 E3
Wester Broom Gdns. Edin 121 E3
Wester Broom Pl. Edin ... 121 E3
Wester Broom Terr. Edin ... 121 E3
Wester Coates Ave. Edin .. 122 C4
Wester Coates Gdns. Edin 122 C4
Wester Coates Pl. Edin ... 122 C4
Wester Coates Rd. Edin ... 122 C4
Wester Coates Terr. Edin .. 122 C4
Wester Drylaw Ave. Edin ... 92 A2
Wester Drylaw Dr. Edin ... 92 A2
Wester Drylaw Pk. Edin ... 92 B2
Wester Drylaw Pl. Edin ... 92 A2
Wester Drylaw Row. Edin ... 92 B2
Wester Hailes Dr. Edin ... 152 B4
Wester Hailes Pk. Edin ... 152 C4

Wester Hailes Rd. Edin 152 B4
Wester Row. Rat 120 C1
Wester Steil. Edin 122 C1
Westerdunes Pk. N Ber 53 E4
Westerglen Rd. Falk 60 A1
Westerlands Dr. Stir 7 D3
Westerlea Ct. B of A 2 A3
Westerlea Dr. B of A 2 A3
Westermains. Arm 143 F3
Western Ave. Crossf 28 A1
Western Ave. Falk 60 A3
Western Gdns. Edin 122 B4
Western Pl. Edin 122 B4
Western Terr. Edin 122 B4
Westerton. Cowie 20 B4
Westerton Dr. B of A 2 A4
Westerton Rd. Brox 118 A3
Westerton Rd. Gran 61 F4
Westerton Terr. Sten 39 E2
Westfield Ave. Edin 122 B3
Westfield Ct. Dalk 156 C1
Westfield Dr. Dalk 156 C1
Westfield Gr. Cross 30 C3
Westfield Gr. Dalk 156 C1
Westfield. Kin 24 A2
Westfield Pk. Dalk 156 C1
Westfield Pl. Den 36 C1
Westfield Rd. Edin 122 B3
Westfield St. Edin 122 B3
Westfield St. Falk 60 C3
Westgarth Ave. Edin 153 D3
Westgate. Dunb 78 B2
Westgate. E Cal 148 A2
Westgate. N Ber 54 A4
Westhall Cres. Crossf 27 E1
Westhall Gdns. Edin 123 D3
Westhall Gdns. Uph 117 D2
Westhall Rd. Brox 117 F2
Westhouse Ave. May 183 F3
Westhouse Dr. May 183 F3
Westhouse St. May 183 F3
Westhouses Rd. May 183 F3
Westmill Rd. Bonn 182 A4
Westmill Wynd. Bonn 182 A4
Westminster Pl. Sten 38 C2
Westpoint. Dunb 78 B1
Westquarter Ave. Laur 61 D1
Westray Terr. Falk 60 B1
Westview Cres. Tull 4 B1
Westview. Lin 84 B4
Westwater St. Loch 14 A4
Westwood Ave. Kirk 17 F4
Westwood Pk. Liv 146 C4
Westwood Pl. Dunf 29 F2
Westwood View. W Cal 172 B2
Wharry Rd. Alva 4 C4
Wheatfield Pl. Edin 122 B3
Wheatfield Rd. Edin 122 B3
Wheatfield St. Edin 122 C3
Wheatfield Terr. Edin 122 B3
Wheatlands Ave. Bon 58 A3
Wheatsheaf La. Dalk 157 D2
Whim Rd. Gull 51 F1
Whin Park Ind Est. Cocke ... 97 D2
Whin Pk. Cocke 97 D2
Whinbank. Liv 147 F3
Whinhill. Dunf 29 E2
Whinneyknowe. Inver 68 B3
Whinniehill Terr. Oak 27 E3
Whinny Hill Cres. Inver 47 D1
Whinnyburn Pl. Ros 46 B3
Whinrig. Uph 117 E3
Whins Pl. Edin 95 D1
Whins Rd. All 10 B4
Whins Rd. Stir 7 D1
Whinwell Rd. Stir 2 A1
Whirlbut Cres. Dunf 29 D1
Whirlbut St. Dunf 29 D1
Whitburn Rd. Bath 144 C2
Whitburn Rd. Liv 147 E2
White Hart St. Dalk 157 D2
White St. Whit 170 A3
White's Cl. Dalk 157 D2
Whitecraig Ave. White 126 C1
Whitecraig Cres. White 126 C1
Whitecraig Gdns E. White . 126 C1
Whitecraig Gdns. White 126 C1
Whitecraig Rd. White 126 C1
Whitedalehead Rd. Whit ... 170 B3
Whitedales. Edin 154 B3
Whitefield Rd. Dunf 29 F3
Whitegates Pl. Falk 59 E2
Whitehead Gr. Que 89 E4
Whitehill Ave. Muss 126 A2
Whitehill Dr. Black 171 E4
Whitehill Dr. Dalk 157 E1
Whitehill Farm Rd. Muss ... 126 A2
Whitehill Gdns. Muss 126 A2
Whitehill Gr. Dalk 157 E1
Whitehill Ind Est. Black 145 E1
Whitehill Pl. Rose 181 E1
Whitehill Pl. Stir 7 D3
Whitehill Rd. Black 145 E1
Whitehill Rd. Dan 125 E2
Whitehill Rd. Dalk 125 E2
Whitehill St. Edin 125 F2
Whitehill View. Black 171 E4
Whitehouse Loan. Edin 123 E3

Whitehouse Rd. Edin 91 D2
Whitehouse Rd. Stir 7 E4
Whitelaw Cres. Dunf 29 E1
Whitelaw Dr. Bog 145 F3
Whitelaw Pl. Dunf 29 E1
Whitelaw Rd. Dunf 29 E1
Whitelaw St. Blac 142 B1
Whitelea Cres. Bale 177 E4
Whitelea Rd. Bale 177 E4
Whiteloch Rd. Glad 129 E3
Whitemoss Rd. Kir 149 F1
Whitemyre Ct. Dunf 28 B3
Whites Quay. D Bay 47 F1
Whiteside. Bath 144 C3
Whiteside Ind Est. Bath 144 C2
Whitesideloan. Pol 82 C4
Whitestone Pl. Black 145 E1
Whitingford. Edin 93 E3
Whitson Cres. Edin 122 A3
Whitson Gr. Edin 122 A3
Whitson Pl E. Edin 122 A3
Whitson Pl W. Edin 122 A3
Whitson Rd. Edin 122 A3
Whitson Terr. Edin 122 A3
Whitson Way. Edin 122 A3
Whitson Wlk. Edin 122 A3
Whitten La. Lin 84 C4
Whittingehame Dr. Hadd ... 132 A4
Whittinghame Dr. Hadd 132 B4
Wholeflats Rd. B'ness 62 A2
Wholeflats Rd. Gran 61 F2
Wholequarter Ave. Laur 61 E1
Whyte Pl. Edin 94 A1
Whyte St. East 168 C3
Whyte St. Loch 14 A4
Whyte Wlk. Dunf 29 F2
Whytehouse Ave. Kirk 17 D2
Whyteman's Brae. Kirk 17 E4
Whytescauseway. Kirk 17 D2
Wilderness The. Air 22 B2
Wildridge Way. Loch 14 A4
Wilfred Terr. Edin 94 B1
Wilkieston Rd. Rat 119 E1
William Black Pl. Que 89 E4
William Booth Pl. Stir 7 D2
William Jameson Pl. Edin ... 95 D1
William St. Dunf 28 C2
William St. Edin 123 D4
William St. Kirk 17 D1
William Street La NE. Edin 123 D4
William Street La NW. Edin 123 D4
William Street La SE. Edin 123 D4
William Street La SW. Edin 123 D4
Williamfield Ave. Stir 7 D2
Williamfield Sq. Edin 125 D4
Williamson Ave. Falk 39 D1
Williamson Pl. Falk 60 B4
Williamson St. Falk 60 A2
Williamston Interchange.
    Muri 148 A1
Willow Ave. Bonn 182 A3
Willow Brae. Fau 193 F3
Willow Dell. B' ness 63 E3
Willow Dr. Kirk 17 D4
Willow Gr. Dunf 46 C4
Willow Gr. Liv 148 A3
Willow Pk. Fau 193 F3
Willow Rd. May 183 F3
Willowbank. Liv 147 F3
Willowbank Row. Edin 93 E3
Willowbrae Ave. Edin 124 B4
Willowbrae Gdns. Edin 124 B4
Willowbrae. Pol 82 B4
Willowbrae Rd. Edin 124 B4
Willowdean. Brid 86 B2
Willows The. Tull 4 A1
Wilson Ave. Dalk 157 E2
Wilson Ave. Den 36 B1
Wilson Ave. Falk 59 E3
Wilson Ave. Kirk 17 D3
Wilson Ave. Pol 61 F1
Wilson Ave. Pres 96 C1
Wilson Dr. Bann 7 E1
Wilson Dr. Falk 59 E3
Wilson Gdns. Falk 59 E3
Wilson Pl. Bon 58 B2
Wilson Rd. Alla 212 A4
Wilson Rd. Falk 59 E3
Wilson Rd. Gore 183 E1
Wilson Rd. Liv 146 C2
Wilson St. Bla 26 A4
Wilson St. Cow 13 E2
Wilson St. Dunf 29 E4
Wilson St. Gran 61 E3
Wilson St. Peni 203 F3
Wilson Terr. Ston 171 D1
Wilson Terr. Uph 117 D3
Wilson Wlk. Tran 128 B3
Wilson's Cl. Dunf 29 D2
Wilson's Pk. Edin 95 D1
Wilsontown Rd. For 215 E1
Wilton Rd. Car 230 A1
Wilton Rd. Edin 123 F2
Winchburgh Cotts. Winch ... 87 F1
Winchester Ave. Den 36 C2
Windlebrook. Dunf 47 D4
Windmill Gn. Kirk 17 F4
Windmill Knowe. Cross 30 C3

Windmill La. Edin 123 F3
Windmill Pl. Kirk 18 A4
Windmill Rd. Kirk 17 F4
Windsor Ave. Falk 59 F2
Windsor Cres. Falk 59 F2
Windsor Cres. Madd 83 D3
Windsor Cres. Peni 204 A3
Windsor Dr. Duni 36 B2
Windsor Dr. Falk 59 F2
Windsor Dr. Peni 204 A3
Windsor Gdns. All 9 F4
Windsor Gdns. Falk 59 F2
Windsor Gdns. Muss 126 C3
Windsor Park Dr. Muss 126 C3
Windsor Park Pl. Muss 126 C3
Windsor Park Terr. Muss ... 126 C3
Windsor Pk. Muss 126 C3
Windsor Pl. Edin 125 D4
Windsor Pl. Shot 191 F3
Windsor Pl. Stir 7 D4
Windsor Rd. Falk 59 F2
Windsor Rd. Peni 204 A3
Windsor Sq. Peni 204 A3
Windsor St. Edin 93 F1
Windsor St. Men 3 F4
Windsor St. Shot 191 F3
Windsor Street La. Edin 93 F1
Windsor Terr. Peni 204 A3
Windygate. Kirk 16 C1
Windygates Rd. N Ber 54 A3
Windygoul Cres. Tran 128 C3
Windyhill Ave. Kin 23 E3
Windyknowe Cres. Bath 144 C3
Windyknowe Pk. Bath 144 C3
Wingate Cres. Dunb 78 B1
Winifred Cres. Kirk 17 D3
Winifred St. Kirk 17 D3
Winton Cl. Tran 128 C2
Winton Ct. Orm 129 D2
Winton Dr. Tran 128 C2
Winton Dr. Edin 154 B2
Winton Gdns. Edin 154 B2
Winton Gr. Edin 154 A3
Winton Gr. Tran 128 C2
Winton Loan. Edin 154 B2
Winton Loan. Glad 129 D3
Winton Pk. Cocke 97 E2
Winton Pk. Edin 154 A2
Winton Pl. Tran 128 C2
Winton Terr. Edin 154 A3
Winton Terr. Orm 129 D2
Winton Way. Tran 128 B2
Wishart Ave. Bonn 182 B4
Wishart Ave. N Ber 54 B3
Wishart Dr. Stir 7 E2
Wishart Pl. Dalk 156 C1
Wishart Pl. Kirk 17 F3
Wishaw Terr. Edin 94 A1
Wisp Gn. Edin 125 D2
Wisp The. Dan 125 D1
Wisp The. Edin 125 D2
Witchbrae. Dunf 29 D2
Wolfe Rd. Falk 60 B4
Wolrige Rd. Edin 155 D4
Wolseley Cres. Edin 94 B1
Wolseley Pl. Edin 94 B1
Wolsey Ave. Bonn 182 B3
Wood Avens. Tull 4 B1
Wood Dr. Whit 169 F3
Wood Lea. Kin 23 F3
Wood Pl. Liv 147 E2
Wood Pl. Ros 46 C3
Wood Rd. Ros 46 B1
Wood St. Gran 61 E4
Wood's Ct. Bonn 182 A4
Woodbank. Cow 13 D1
Woodbank Gr. Bla 26 B4
Woodbine Terr. Edin 94 A2
Woodburn Ave. Dalk 157 E1
Woodburn Ave. Laur 61 D1
Woodburn Bank. Dalk 157 E2
Woodburn Cres. Bon 57 F2
Woodburn Cres. Laur 61 D1
Woodburn Cres. Oak 26 C4
Woodburn Dr. All 4 C1
Woodburn Dr. Dalk 157 D2
Woodburn Gdns. Dalk 157 E2
Woodburn Gdns. Falk 60 C3
Woodburn Gr. Dalk 157 E1
Woodburn Loan. Dalk 157 E2
Woodburn Medway. Dalk .. 157 E2
Woodburn Pk. Dalk 157 E2
Woodburn Pl. Dalk 157 E2
Woodburn Rd. Dalk 157 E2
Woodburn Rd. Falk 60 B3
Woodburn St. Dalk 157 E2
Woodburn St. Falk 60 C3
Woodburn Terr. Dalk 157 E1
Woodburn Terr. Edin 123 D2
Woodburn View. Dalk 157 E2
Woodburn Way. Alva 5 D3
Woodbush Brae. Dunb 78 C1
Woodbush Ct. Dunb 78 C1
Woodbush. Dunb 78 C1
Woodend Pl. Cow 13 D1
Woodend Rd. Car 230 A1
Woodend Wlk. Arm 143 F3

Woodfield Ave. Edin 152 C3
Woodfield Pk. Edin 152 C3
Woodfield Pk. Edin 153 D3
Woodfield Pk. Rosl 180 B3
Woodhall Ave. Curr 152 B3
Woodhall Bank. Edin 152 C3
Woodhall Dr. Curr 152 B3
Woodhall Gr. Edin 152 C3
Woodhall Millbrae. Edin 152 C3
Woodhall Pl. Pen 160 C3
Woodhall Rd. Pen 160 B3
Woodhall Terr. Curr 152 B3
Woodhead Farm Rd. Cul 25 F1
Woodhead Pl. Bath 144 C3
Woodhead St. H Val 26 A1
Woodhill Ct. Gran 61 E3
Woodhill Gr. Crossf 28 A1
Woodhill Rd. Blac 142 A2
Woodland Way. Den 57 E4
Woodlands Bank. D Bay 48 A2
Woodlands Cotts. Arm 144 A3
Woodlands Cres. Falk 60 A2
Woodlands Dr. B' ness 63 E3
Woodlands Dr. Crossf 28 A1
Woodlands Dr. Pol 82 C4
Woodlands Gr. Arm 144 A3
Woodlands Gr. Dunf 29 E4
Woodlands Gr. Edin 124 C3
Woodlands. N Sau 5 F1
Woodlands Pk. Liv 146 C4
Woodlands Rd. Kirk 16 B3
Woodlands Terr. Bla 26 A4
Woodlands The. Ros 46 C3
Woodlea Pk. N Sau 10 A4
Woodmill Cres. Dunf 29 E2
Woodmill Pl. Dunf 29 F2
Woodmill Rd. Dunf 29 E2
Woodmill St. Dunf 29 D2
Woodmill Terr. Dunf 29 D2
Woodmuir Pl. Add 194 C3
Woodmuir Rd. Add 194 C3
Woodmuir Rd. Whit 170 B3
Woodrow. Gore 183 E1
Woodside Ave. Ros 46 C3
Woodside. Cow 13 E2
Woodside Ct. Cam 6 B3
Woodside Dr. Peni 203 F3
Woodside Gdns. Muss 126 C3
Woodside Gdns. Pol 82 C4
Woodside Pl. Brid 86 B2
Woodside Pl. Fall 8 B2
Woodside Rd. All 4 C1
Woodside Rd. Cald 141 D2
Woodside Rd. Stir 2 A2
Woodside Rd. Tull 4 A1
Woodside St. Ros 46 C3
Woodside Terr. Auc 217 F2
Woodside Terr. Brid 86 B2
Woodside Terr. Clack 10 C2
Woodside Terr. Edin 125 E4
Woodside Terr. Falk 60 A2
Woodstock Pl. Edin 124 A1
Woodville Terr. Edin 94 A2
Wooer St. Falk 60 A2
Woolfords Cotts. Auc 217 D4
Woolmet Cres. Dan 156 A4
Wotherspoon Cres. Arm 143 F3
Wotherspoon Dr. B' ness 63 E3
Wright Pl. Kirk 17 E4
Wright St. Falk 60 A3
Writers Ct. Dunb 78 B2
Wynd The. Aber 71 E3
Wynd The. Alva 5 D4
Wynd The. D Bay 48 B2
Wynd The. Giff 163 F3
Wynd The. Orm 159 F4
Wyndford Ave. Uph 117 D3
Wyndford Pl. Uph 117 D3
Wyvern Pk. Edin 123 E2
Wyvis Pk. Peni 204 A4
Wyvis Pl. Shot 192 A2

Yardheads. Edin 93 F3
Yardley Pl. Falk 39 D1
Yarrow Ct. Peni 204 A4
Yarrow Pl. Gran 61 F3
Yeaman La. Edin 122 C3
Yeaman Pl. Edin 122 C3
Yester Pl. Hadd 100 C1
Yetholm Pk. Dunf 28 C1
Yetts The. Cam 6 B3
Yew Gr. Liv 148 A3
Yew Terr. Laur 61 D1
Yewlands Cres. Edin 155 D4
Yewlands Gdns. Edin 155 D4
Yieldshields Rd. Car 231 E2
York Arc. Gran 40 B1
York Dr. Falk 60 B3
York La. Edin 93 E1
York La. Gran 40 B1
York Pl. Dunf 29 E3
York Pl. Edin 93 E1
York Pl. Kirk 17 F4
York Rd. Edin 93 E3
York Rd. N Ber 54 A4
York Sq. Gran 40 B1
York St. Falk 60 B3

Young Ave. Tran 128 B3

Young Cres. Bath 144 C3
Young Ct. Cow 13 E2
Young Sq. Muri 173 E3
Young Sq. W Cal 173 D3
Young St. Edin 123 D4
Young St. W Cal 172 B1
Young Street La N. Edin ... 123 D4
Young Street La S. Edin ... 123 D4
Young Terr. Cow 13 D2
Young's Terr. Kirk 17 E3
Youngs Rd. Brox 118 A3
Yule Pl. Black 145 E1
Yule Terr. Black 171 E4

Zealandia Rd. Ros 46 A1
Zetland Dr. Laur 61 D2
Zetland Pl. Edin 93 D3
Zetland Pl. Gran 39 F2
Zetland Pl. Loch 14 A4
Zetland St. Clack 11 D2
Zetland Terr. Pol 61 F1

ORDNANCE SURVEY
STREET ATLASES

The Ordnance Survey / Philip's Street Atlases provide unique and definitive mapping of entire counties

Street Atlases available

- Berkshire
- Bristol and Avon
- Buckinghamshire
- Cardiff
- Cheshire
- Derbyshire
- Edinburgh
- East Essex
- West Essex
- Glasgow
- North Hampshire
- South Hampshire
- Hertfordshire
- East Kent
- West Kent
- Nottinghamshire
- Oxfordshire
- Staffordshire
- Surrey
- East Sussex
- West Sussex
- Warwickshire

The Street Atlases are revised and updated on a regular basis and new titles are added to the series. Many counties are now available in full-size hardback and softback editions as well as handy pocket-size versions. All contain Ordnance Survey mapping except Surrey which is by Philip's

The series is available from all good bookshops or by mail order direct from the publisher. However, the order form opposite may not reflect the complete range of titles available so it is advisable to check by telephone before placing your order. Payment can be made by credit card or cheque / postal order in the following ways:

By phone
Phone your order through on our special Credit Card Hotline on **01933 414000**. Speak to our customer service team during office hours (9am to 5pm) or leave a message on the answering machine, quoting T511N99CO1, your full credit card number plus expiry date and your full name and address

By post
Simply fill out the order form opposite (you may photocopy it) and send it to: **Cash Sales Department, Reed Book Services, PO Box 5, Rushden, Northants, NN10 6YX**

OS STREET ATLASES ORDER FORM

T511N99CO1

	Hardback QUANTITY TOTAL	Softback QUANTITY TOTAL	Pocket QUANTITY TOTAL	
	£12.99	£8.99	£4.99	
Berkshire	ISBN 0-540-05992-7	ISBN 0-540-05993-5	ISBN 0-540-05994-3	➤
Buckinghamshire	ISBN 0-540-05989-7	ISBN 0-540-05990-0	ISBN 0-540-05991-9	➤
East Essex	ISBN 0-540-05848-3	ISBN 0-540-05866-1	ISBN 0-540-05850-5	➤
West Essex	ISBN 0-540-05849-1	ISBN 0-540-05867-X	ISBN 0-540-05851-3	➤
North Hampshire	ISBN 0-540-05852-1	ISBN 0-540-05853-X	ISBN 0-540-05854-8	➤
South Hampshire	ISBN 0-540-05855-6	ISBN 0-540-05856-4	ISBN 0-540-05857-2	➤
Hertfordshire	ISBN 0-540-05995-1	ISBN 0-540-05996-X	ISBN 0-540-05997-8	➤
East Kent	ISBN 0-540-06026-7	ISBN 0-540-06027-5	ISBN 0-540-06028-3	➤
West Kent	ISBN 0-540-06029-1	ISBN 0-540-06031-3	ISBN 0-540-06030-5	➤
Nottinghamshire	ISBN 0-540-05858-0	ISBN 0-540-05859-9	ISBN 0-540-05860-2	➤
Oxfordshire	ISBN 0-540-05986-2	ISBN 0-540-05987-0	ISBN 0-540-05988-9	➤
East Sussex	ISBN 0-540-05875-0	ISBN 0-540-05874-2	ISBN 0-540-05873-4	➤
West Sussex	ISBN 0-540-05876-9	ISBN 0-540-05877-7	ISBN 0-540-05878-5	➤
	£12.99	£9.99	£4.99	
Bristol and Avon	ISBN 0-540-06140-9	ISBN 0-540-06141-7	ISBN 0-540-06142-5	➤
Cardiff	ISBN 0-540-06186-7	ISBN 0-540-06187-5	ISBN 0-540-06207-3	➤
Cheshire	ISBN 0-540-06143-3	ISBN 0-540-06144-1	ISBN 0-540-06145-X	➤
Derbyshire	ISBN 0-540-06137-9	ISBN 0-540-06138-7	ISBN 0-540-06139-5	➤
Edinburgh	ISBN 0-540-06180-8	ISBN 0-540-06181-6	ISBN 0-540-06182-4	➤
Glasgow	ISBN 0-540-06183-2	ISBN 0-540-06184-0	ISBN 0-540-06185-9	➤
Staffordshire	ISBN 0-540-06134-4	ISBN 0-540-06135-2	ISBN 0-540-06136-0	➤
	£10.99	£8.99	£4.99	
Surrey	ISBN 0-540-05983-8	ISBN 0-540-05984-6	ISBN 0-540-05985-4	➤
Warwickshire	ISBN 0-540-05642-1			➤ ▼

Name _____

Address _____

_____

_____ Postcode

◆ *Free postage and packing* ◆ *All available titles will normally be dispatched within 5 working days of receipt of order but please allow up to 28 days for delivery*
☐ *Please tick this box if you do not wish your name to be used by other carefully selected organisations that may wish to send you information about other products and services*

I enclose a cheque / postal order, for a **total** *of* ▢

made payable to **Reed Book Services**, *or please debit my*

☐ *Access* ☐ *American Express* ☐ *Visa*

account by ▢

Account no ▢▢▢▢ ▢▢▢▢ ▢▢▢▢ ▢▢▢▢

Expiry date ▢▢ ▢▢

Signature _____

Registered office: Michelin House, 81 Fulham Road, London SW3 6RB. Registered in England No 1974080